D1740615

Introduction to Management Science

Mastering Quantitative Analysis

Michael E. Hanna

UNIVERSITY OF HOUSTON–CLEAR LAKE

SOUTH-WESTERN College Publishing

An International Thomson Publishing Company

To: Susan, Mickey, and Katie

Sponsoring Editor: DeVilla Williams/Randy G. Haubner
Development Editors: Laura Ellingson/Abby Reip/Jeanne Busemeyer
Production Editor: Sandy Cence/Nancy Lamm/Holly Terry
Compositor: Pre-Press Company, Inc.
Cover and Internal Design: Rebecca Lemna
Marketing Manager: Stephen E. Momper

International Thomson Publishing
South-Western College Publishing is an ITP company. The trademark ITP is used under license.

Library of Congress Cataloging-in-Publication Data:

Hanna, Michael.
Introduction to management science : mastering quantitative analysis / Michael Hanna.
p. cm.
Includes bibliographical references and index.
ISBN 0-87709-603-1
1. Management science--Mathematical models. 2. Decision-making--Mathematical models. I. Title.
T56.M225 1995
658'.001'5118--dc20 95-35105
CIP

1 2 3 4 5 KI 0 9 8 7 6
Printed in the United States of America

ISBN 0-87709-603-1 Student Edition

Preface

Introduction to Management Science is about the use of quantitative models to aid in managerial decision making. This text is intended for the introductory management science course that is taught in most business schools. As most students taking such a course will not become experts in management science, the book focuses on the managerial use of the management science models instead of the mathematical computations. An emphasis is placed on understanding the management science models and utilizing the results of these models in a way that is meaningful to a decision maker.

While the very nature of management science requires the use of mathematical models and tools, this book is written to ease the apprehension felt by many students who do not look forward to taking courses dealing with quantitative material. Students who have had a course in college algebra and who have been introduced to probability and statistics should find this book to be very clearly written and easy to understand. The mathematical details are clearly and carefully illustrated in each of the examples. This is intended to refresh the memory of any student who is several semesters or quarters removed from the last mathematics course. However, students will be challenged to thoroughly understand the concepts associated with management science and to apply these concepts to managerial problems.

Near the beginning of each chapter, a problem faced by a decision maker is presented to provide motivation to the student. From this problem, students realize management science models and techniques were developed in response to problems faced by managers. The methods involved in developing and solving the management science model then are demonstrated using this example.

The first example in each chapter tends to be relatively simple. I have found that the use of simple examples allows students to focus on the concepts being presented instead of the mathematical computations required. Other, more complex problems are seen in later examples or end-of-chapter problems. These demonstrate that the techniques are applicable to problems that more closely resemble real-world applications. Computer software is provided for use with the larger problems. Students will be asked to use software to solve these problems and to interpret the results in a meaningful way.

To further illustrate the widespread use of management science models, summaries of applications both on the national and the global arenas will be provided in boxes throughout the book. References are provided so additional details may be investigated.

TO THE INSTRUCTOR

The method of presentation used throughout this book emphasizes the recognition of a managerial problem, the development of an appropriate model, the computer solution, and the interpretation of the results. With the widespread availability of computer software, I believe this is very appropriate for most introductory management science courses. Emphasis is placed on understanding the basic concepts (sometimes from an intuitive perspective) rather than on understanding complex mathematical calculations.

In most chapters, a brief explanation of the solution technique is sufficient. However, in Chapters 5 (The Simplex Method and Sensitivity Analysis) and 6 (Transportation and Assignment Problems), more time is spent on the algorithms. These chapters may be omitted should the instructor so choose without losing continuity. The transportation and assignment problems (instead of the algorithms) also are presented in the chapter on applications of linear programming where they are viewed from a linear programming perspective. Thus, it is not necessary to cover Chapter 6 in order to present the transportation and assignment problems.

The chapters are written so an instructor may cover the material in a modified order with a few obvious exceptions. Chapter 2, which introduces linear programming, should be covered before any of the other linear programming chapters (Chapters 3, 4, and 5), before the transportation and assignment chapter (Chapter 6), and before the integer programming and goal programming chapter (Chapter 7). Also, Chapter 12, which is the first chapter on decision models, should be covered before Chapter 13, which is a continuation of decision models. Aside from these restrictions, the instructor should have no difficulty presenting the material in a modified order.

PEDAGOGICAL FEATURES

To enhance the effectiveness of this textbook, several features have been implemented.

- A modular design allows the instructor to modify the order in which the material is covered.
- A chapter outline is presented at the beginning of each chapter.
- A Best Practices box is provided in each chapter to illustrate the real-world application of the technique.
- A Global Perspectives box in each chapter highlights the global nature of business and the applicability of the technique throughout the world.
- A glossary of key terms is provided at the end of the chapter.
- The key equations are summarized at the end of appropriate chapters.
- Solved problems are used to reinforce the methods presented in the chapter and to provide additional examples.
- Questions of a conceptual nature are presented to require the students to think about the concepts discussed in the chapter.
- Problems that require the student to apply the techniques presented in the chapter are provided. In many cases these are

phrased to require the student to supply an answer to the managerial problem instead of simply supplying an answer to the mathematical statement of the problem.
- End of chapter cases provide students with the opportunity to apply the concepts to larger problems. These cases ask for brief executive summary reports, forcing the student to put the information in the form that would be most appropriate for managerial use.
- Readings and references are provided to guide students who wish to further explore the concepts.
- Video cases at key points in the book bring to life the real applications of the concepts presented in the text.

INSTRUCTIONAL SUPPLEMENTS

Several supplements are available to the instructor. These include:

- An Annotated Instructor's edition that provides tips and suggestions for presenting the material.
- An Instructor's Manual that provides additional instructional aids and notes on using the videos.
- A Solutions Manual that provides complete solutions to all of the end of chapter problems.
- A Test Bank in printed form providing multiple choice, true/false, and short discussion questions.
- A computerized test generator, MicroExam 4.0, containing all the questions from the printed Test Bank, with a pull-down menu that allows instructors to edit, add, delete, or randomly mix questions for customized tests.
- Videos based on CNBC business network clips related to the material in several parts of the text.
- A Study Guide for students with additional solved problems and examples.
- Software may be packaged with the text. Available software includes: *LINDO, Decision Support Software (DSS),* and What's*Best!*.

ACKNOWLEDGEMENTS

I would like to thank numerous people for their contributions to this project. Special thanks goes to DeVilla Williams who was responsible for putting together a wonderful team at boyd & fraser publishing to work on this project. DeVilla had the vision to make this a truly unique textbook. Laura Ellingson, the developmental editor, deserves a great deal of credit for coordinating the many aspects of this work. Abby Reip performed several tasks related to this book for which I am truly grateful. I have enjoyed working with Nancy Lamm during the final stages of this process. Her efforts throughout the copy editing and production stages of this process truly have been extraordinary.

I would like to acknowledge the support of many people at the University of Houston-Clear Lake who helped in this project. These begin with my dean, Bill Staples, and my faculty chair, Grady Perdue, who relieved me of service commitments to allow time to work on this project. My secretary, Noel Turner, was most helpful in providing immediate response with whatever I asked her to do. My graduate assistant, Raquel Jumonville, was extremely helpful in preparing figures and performing other tasks related to this book.

I would like to thank my wife, Susan, for providing encouragement throughout this process. Thanks to my children Mickey and Katie who understood when I did not have the usual time available to devote to them.

The creative talents of many individuals helped to make this a complete product. Jen Robinson did a wonderful job in preparing the Global Perspectives and Best Practices boxes for this book. The Study Guide was prepared by Shad Dowlatshahi of the University of Texas-El Paso; the Test Bank was prepared by Kenneth Lawrence of the New Jersey Institute of Technology; the Instructor's Manual was prepared by Faizul Huq of the University of Texas-Arlington; and the Solutions Manual was prepared by Vincent Calluzzo of Iona College. My heartfelt thanks goes to all of these.

I would like to thank all of the reviewers for their helpful comments as well as those individuals who participated in the Focus Group for Management Science in Washington, D.C. These people include:

Thomas M. Box
Pittsburgh State University

Stuart B. Boxerman
Washington University–St. Louis

James R. Buffington
Indiana State University

Arnold H. Buss
Washington University–St. Louis

Cecilia Carrera
Northeastern University

Maria Carrera
Northeastern University

Sharad Chitgopekar
Illinois State University

Shad Dowlatshahi
University of Texas–El Paso

Peter M. Ellis
Utah State University

Yiannis Glegles
Suffolk University

Damodar Golhar
Western Michigan University

Faizul Huq
University of Texas–Arlington

Vaidyanathan Jayaraman
University of Southern Mississippi–Gulf Coast

Lawrence Jones
St. Louis University

Ching-Chung Kuo
The Pennsylvania State University–Harrisburg

Darlene R. Lanier
Louisiana State University

Kenneth Lawrence
New Jersey Institute of Technology

Jooh Lee
Rowan College of New Jersey

Jerrold H. May
University of Pittsburgh

Jaideep Motwani
Grand Valley State University

Harvey N. Nye
University of Central Oklahoma

David Olson
Texas A & M University

Cliff T. Ragsdale
Virginia Polytechnic Institute and State University

B. Madhu Rao
Bowling Green State University

Don R. Robinson
Illinois State University

Asim Roy
Arizona State University

John Seydel
The University of Mississippi

Toni M. Somers
Wayne State University

Giri Kumar Tayi
State University of New York–Albany

James W. Vigen
California State University–Bakersfield

Rakesh Vohra
The Ohio State University

Mustafa R. Yilmaz
Northeastern University

Focus Group for Management Science

Timothy W. Butler
Wayne State University

William Cosgrove
California Polytechnic University

Ching-Chung Kuo
The Pennsylvania State University–Harrisburg

John Seydel
University of Mississippi

Suresh Tadisina
Southern Illinois University

MICHAEL E. HANNA — BIOGRAPHICAL SKETCH

Michael E. Hanna is an Associate Professor of Decision Sciences at the University of Houston–Clear Lake. Dr. Hanna has a B.A. in Economics, M.S. in Mathematics, and Ph.D. in Operations Research from Texas Tech University.

For over twenty years, Dr. Hanna has been teaching courses in statistics, management science, forecasting, and other quantitative methods. He has received numerous teaching awards and has published several articles related to math anxiety in business students. He has been actively involved in the development of innovative educational methods.

The current research interests of Dr. Hanna include: cost estimation methods, goal programming, and least absolute value regression methods. He has published articles in *The Journal of the Operational Research Society, Computers and Operations Research, Naval Research Logistics Quarterly,* among others. He currently is serving on the editorial board of *Computers and Operations Research.*

Dr. Hanna is very active in the *Decision Sciences Institute,* serving on several national committees. In the *Southwest Region of the Decision Sciences Institute,* he has held numerous offices including President. His administrative duties at the University of Houston–Clear Lake have included Program Coordinator of Decision Sciences and Chair of the Economics, Finance, Marketing, and Decision Sciences unit.

Brief Contents

Contents

CHAPTER ONE

Introduction to Management Science

LEARNING OBJECTIVES

Upon completing Chapter 1, you should be able to:

- Recognize what management science is and how it fits into the general field of management.
- Understand the concept of a model.
- Understand and be able to apply the management science approach to problem solving.
- Be aware of some of the management science models that will be seen later in the book.

CHAPTER OUTLINE

1.1

INTRODUCTION

Management science
An approach to problem solving based on the scientific method. Also, an approach to management based on the use of mathematical models.

Managers constantly are faced with problems and must make decisions to affect solutions. **Management science** is an approach to problem solving based upon the scientific method that may be used to aid in the decision-making process. Mathematical models are an important part of this field. Many of these models also might be studied in the fields of operations research, quantitative analysis, quantitative methods, and decision sciences.

In this chapter we will see how the management science approach to problem solving fits into the general field of management. We also will identify the steps used in this approach to problem solving. Later in this book we will be introduced to some of the mathematical models and tools that are available to help managers make better decisions. As a future manager, you should possess as many tools as possible to help you make decisions.

This book and course will not make you an expert in management science. However, upon completion you should have a good introduction to many of the management science tools available to a manager. A good manager must recognize when these tools are or are not appropriate. A good manager must be able to communicate with the experts in management science and implement the results from the model used. A good manager must understand how decisions based on these techniques might change if economic and other conditions change.

1.2

THEORIES OF MANAGEMENT

Classical approach to management
A view of management emphasizing the structure and output of an organization.

Scientific method
A systematic approach to problem solving.

Behavioral school of management
A view of management in which favorable treatment of the employees is emphasized.

Quantitative methods approach to management
An approach to management based on the use of mathematical models.

In a management principles course, you probably learned that management is the process of planning, organizing, leading, and controlling the personnel and resources of an organization to move toward a specific goal. Over the years, theories have been developed about what this process should be. Early **classical and scientific approaches to management** focused on the structure and administration of an organization, with the output of the organization as the primary concern. Little regard was given to the workers. This led to the labor movement, and the attention drawn to the plight of the workers resulted in the **behavioral school of management** emphasizing the human element of an organization. Favorable treatment of the employees was seen as a way of having satisfied workers, and a satisfied worker should be a productive worker.

During World War II, diverse groups of mathematicians, physicists, military tacticians, and other scientists were formed to study military operations. Thus, the field of operations research was developed. As these individuals returned to civilian life, they brought what they had learned to their companies and the **management science or quantitative methods approach to management** became formalized. One emphasis of this approach is the use of mathematical models to help managers make better

Advances in computer technology have contributed greatly to the widespread use of mathematical models. SOURCE: Photo courtesy of Arvin Industries, Inc.

decisions. The tremendous advances in computer technology have contributed greatly to the proliferation of these techniques.

One of the modern approaches to management is the **systems approach** in which parts of an organization are viewed as interrelated parts of a whole. The organization itself is viewed as a part of a national or international economic system.

Systems approach
A view of management in which parts of an organization are viewed as parts of an entire system instead of as isolated units.

The **contingency approach to management** is emerging, and the basic premise of this school of thought is that the best managerial approach or style to use in a particular situation depends upon that particular situation. Very few concepts or principles of management are universal without regard to the specific situation involved.

Contingency approach to management
A view of management in which different approaches are viewed as best in different situations.

Both the systems and contingency approaches indicate that all facets of a decision need to be considered. Even proponents of the behavioral and management science approaches recognize that a good manager benefits from considering aspects of all schools of thought about management.

Both the quantitative and the qualitative factors should be important to a manager. The **quantitative factors** are measurable ingredients such as cost or profit. This quantitative side of management tends to be the focus of the management science models that we will be studying. The qualitative factors are ingredients that are difficult, and at times impossible, to measure. These might include employee job satisfaction, employee motivation, and the company's public image. All of these should be important to a manager, and yet they are all difficult to measure. These qualitative aspects of management are typically discussed in other management courses. The focus of this book is the quantitative side of management, and management science as an integral part.

Quantitative analysis
An approach to problem solving based on the scientific method and the use of mathematical models. (Related terms include management science, decision science, decision analysis, and operations research.)

1.3

HISTORY OF MANAGEMENT SCIENCE

Many of the management science techniques used today had their beginnings in the 1800s or early 1900s. Frederick W. Taylor is credited with developing the principles of scientific management in the late 1800s. He placed emphasis on the most efficient way to do a job in the manufacturing area. Shortly thereafter, Henry L. Gantt extended the work of Taylor and developed a method of using charts to schedule jobs, which resulted in considerable improvement over the existing techniques. Also building on the work of Frederick Taylor, Frank and Lillian Gilbreth developed the basic principles of time and motion studies in the early 1900s.

Early work in inventory modeling was performed by George D. Babcock. In 1912 he established formulas to determine the optimal production quantity. This work was extended in 1915 by F. W. Harris who is credited with the development of the economic order quantity model. About this same time, World War I began, and further developments in operations research were seen as F. W. Lanchester used a quantitative approach to forecasting the outcome of military battles in 1914.

In 1917, A. K. Erlang studied the pattern of telephone calls and developed formulas to describe the operations of queuing models. This became the basis for the queuing theory used today. In 1924, Walter Shewart used probability and statistics to establish control charts that are the basis for quality control. Applications of probability and statistics continued as H. F. Dodge and H. G. Romig in 1928 developed statistical sampling charts commonly used in quality control.

In the 1930s, Horace C. Levinson used mathematical models to represent the responses of consumers to certain marketing conditions such as changing prices and advertising. Also during this time, Wassily Leontief developed an input-output model to represent the U.S. economy. This was in the form of a linear programming model. Linear programs were later used to determine the optimal way to allocate scarce resources discussed in the next chapter.

While numerous mathematical models were used prior to World War II, the concept of operations research (or operational research as it is called in England) as an interdisciplinary team approach to problem solving was developed as a result of this war. To aid in military operations, diverse groups of individuals were put together as teams in support of the war effort. One such group, called Blackett's Circus, was headed by the physicist P. M. S. Blackett. This group consisted of an Army officer, a surveyor, three physiologists, an astrophysicist, a general physicist, two mathematicians, and two mathematical physicists. Groups like this studied such things as radar, submarine patterns, and the logistics of providing weapons and supplies to the troops. An operations group working with the U.S. Army's 8th Air Force was responsible for increasing the accuracy of visual and radar bombing missions. In 1942, only 15 percent of all bombs hit within 1,000 feet of the intended target. Two years later, this accuracy rate was over 60 percent as a result of improvements in target sighting based on the operations analysis group's recommendations.

After the war, many of the individuals from these teams were eager to apply their concepts to peacetime industries. While greeted with some skepticism, these scientists from England and the United States continued to pursue their interests. In 1947, George Dantzig developed the simplex method for solving linear programming problems, which is widely used today. With developments in computer technology in the 1950s and 1960s, the use of linear programming became more widespread.

More focus to the field of management science was observed as professional organizations began to be developed. The Operational Research Society was started in England in 1950. In 1952 and 1953 respectively, the Operations Research Society and the Institute of Management Sciences were started in the United States. In 1995 these two organizations joined to become the Institute for Operations Research and Management Sciences (INFORMS). In 1969, another major professional organization, the Decision Sciences Institute, was formed.

Academic degree programs began to appear at universities in the 1960s. Continued advances in computer technology and computer software have stimulated a rapid growth in the applications of management science techniques. Many of these techniques and applications will be presented in later chapters.

1.4 MODELS

An important part of management science is the use of models. A **model** is a representation of a real situation or object. The management science models that we will be using are **mathematical models**. Frequently mathematical models are used in the development of computer models as will be seen later in this chapter.

Model
A representation of a real situation, process, or object.

Mathematical model
A model based on mathematical expressions.

A mathematical model may be very complex or as simple as an equation to indicate the cost of building a house based on the size of the house. If we let the variable x represent the square footage of the house, a mathematical model of the cost might be:

$$\text{cost} = 20{,}000 + 50x$$

This would tell us that if a 3,000-square-foot house ($x = 3{,}000$) is to be built, the estimated cost would be:

$$\text{cost} = 20{,}000 + 50(3{,}000) = \$170{,}000$$

This model would be helpful in developing a budget for the next year when the company plans to build 30 new homes.

Another type of model is a **physical or iconic model,** such as a replica of an airplane or automobile, which is intended to appear similar to the actual object. Models such as these allow engineers to analyze the impact of a change in the design on wind resistance without actually building the airplane or automobile.

Iconic model
A physical model similar in appearance to the object it represents.

A third type of model is an **analog model** that is physical in nature but is not intended to appear the same as the original object. A thermometer is

Analog model
A physical model with a different appearance than the object it represents.

A company considering building a new facility may use mathematical models to determine the best location. SOURCE: Photo courtesy of Raychem Corporation

an analog model because the needle pointing to a number represents the temperature.

A mathematical or management science model allows a manager to determine the impact of changes in decisions without actually making the decision. For example, a company considering building a new manufacturing facility in one of two possible locations may wish to use mathematical models to determine how each of these locations would affect overall costs. A mathematical model may be used to determine how the overall distribution system would be modified if each of the possible locations were selected. The total cost associated with each of these two could then be compared without actually having to build either plant. This model also could be used to see how costs would change if future transportation or production costs were to increase. We will see that mathematical models are an integral part of solving problems with the management science approach.

1.5 THE MANAGEMENT SCIENCE APPROACH TO PROBLEM SOLVING

An important part of management science is the basic approach used to solve problems. The approach has its roots in the scientific method, which is an approach to problem solving that has been used by scientists for centuries. Now, this basic philosophy is becoming widely accepted in other areas as well. The steps used in this management science process are illustrated in Figure 1.1. Each of these will be discussed and illustrated with the example that follows on page 8.

BEST PRACTICES

Management Science Brews Success

San Miguel Corporation (SMC) is the most diversified company in the Philippines today. Its operations span the entire archipelago, employing more than 30,000 people. The company's three major businesses are beverages (beer, soft drinks, wines, and spirits), packaging (for internal and external customers), and foods and livestock (chicken and cattle, ice cream, and coconut oil). The company manages this variety of businesses with the help of its Operations Research (OR) department.

The OR department at SMC was established in 1971, and has been growing ever since. SMC uses management science techniques for facilities planning (including warehouse siting), job and machine scheduling, product mix formulation, and inventory modeling. At any given time the OR group is busy with two warehouse siting projects for the beer businesses alone. Product mix formulation applications (a classical linear programming problem) have been used for everything from various animal feeds to ice cream base mixes. The group also has used simulation for doing what-if analyses on facility expansions, selection of wastewater treatment equipment, and brewery design and costing.

In 1992 the group was awarded the Operations Research Society of America (ORSA) prize for effective integration of OR into corporate decision-making processes. In part, the group's impact on the bottom line of SMC was responsible for its success in the competition. The impact ranged "from $66,000 for a capacity expansion study to $15 million for an ice cream plant siting study." Another factor was the way SMC has "OR-type people throughout the organization." The president of SMC, Francisco Eizmendi Jr., said in his acceptance speech for the prize, "San Miguel's senior management appreciates the vital role of operations research in attaining our corporate goals."

"Coca-Cola" is a registered trademark of The Coca-Cola Company

SOURCE: Rosario, E. A., del, October 1994. "OR Brew Success for San Miguel." *OR/MS Today*: 24-30.

FIGURE 1.1

The Management Science Approach to Problem Solving

Identify the problem
↓
Develop the model and collect data
↓
Apply the model and generate a solution
↓
Assess the solution
↓
Implement the results
↓
Monitor the results

An Example

Bayou City Builders manufactures approximately 30 new homes each year. For planning purposes, the company needs to estimate the cost of construction of a 3,000-square-foot house. Other homes built by the company range in size from 1,800 square feet to 3,500 square feet. The company would like to develop a simple method for estimating the cost of construction of this and other houses. Based on experience, the company believes the size of the house is the primary factor in determining the cost.

This example will be used throughout the discussion of the steps in the management science approach to problem solving. While this is a very simple example and most problems are more complex, this illustrates the basic concepts involved in this process.

Identify the Problem

The first step in the management science process is to identify and define the problem. To do this, a manager must clearly understand the organization and situation in which the problems are occurring. The factors that affect this situation should be observed to see how they specifically impact the situation.

While this step may seem obvious, it is critical that sufficient time and care be taken in defining the problem. The environment surrounding the problem should be observed to ensure that the decision maker totally understands the situation. If a problem is not properly defined, the real problem will go unresolved while efforts are made to resolve the improperly defined problem.

The potential benefits of a problem also should be considered at this stage. If the cost of resolving the problem outweighs the potential benefits, then perhaps the problem is not important enough to warrant the time and money required for a thorough resolution.

In the Bayou City Builders example, the immediate problem is to estimate the construction cost of a 3,000-square-foot house. However, the company also wishes to develop a simple method of estimating the cost of construction that may be applied to other houses in the future. Management should clearly understand the factors that would be most important in determining the cost of the house.

Develop the Model and Collect Data

Once the problem is understood, a manager should determine which model is appropriate for the particular situation. In this book, we will consider several management science models that are commonly used in business today.

A part of the model-development process is the collection of the necessary data to use the model. We may find that a particular model would be very appropriate in a particular circumstance, but the data required for using the model is not available or is too expensive to obtain.

In the Bayou City Builders example, management wishes to estimate the construction cost of a house. Because management believes the cost is primarily influenced by the size of the house, a mathematical model might have the form:

$$C = a + bx$$

where

C = cost of construction
a = constant (fixed cost)
b = variable cost
x = square footage of the house

Data should be collected on the costs and sizes of houses previously built by this company. From this, we might use regression analysis (discussed in a later chapter) to obtain the values of a and b resulting in the model:

$$C = 20{,}000 + 50x$$

This model then could be used to estimate the cost of the house.

Apply the Model and Generate a Solution

The next step in the management science process is the actual use of the model with the data that pertains to the current problem. Output from the model is generated and this output is used by the manager to develop a possible solution to the problem. In some cases, more than one possible solution might be developed.

In the Bayou City Builders example, the model is:

$$C = 20{,}000 + 50x$$

and we wish to determine the cost of a 3,000-square-foot house ($x = 3{,}000$). Thus, we would get:

$$C = 20{,}000 + 50(3{,}000) = \$170{,}000$$

and we estimate the cost of the house to be $170,000.

Assess the Solution

Once a solution has been generated, it is the manager's responsibility to assess and evaluate this to determine if it is a good solution to the problem. It is possible that the input data was not valid or complete. This would mean the model that was developed is not correct.

If the data used is correct, the solution that is found will be an appropriate solution to the management science model being used. However, this may not be the appropriate solution to the identified managerial problem. Perhaps the model was not a complete reflection of the real-world situation, or perhaps there are other important factors in the problem that cannot be included in a management science model. The manager must use judgment to determine if the solution found is actually the appropriate solution to the problem. At times the model would be modified based on this evaluation, and another solution could be found based on the modified model. At other times the manager might decide that, due to factors not included in the model, the solution to the model must be modified before a valid solution to the real-world problem can be obtained. The solution to the mathematical model may provide important information for the manager even if the solution to the model is not implemented.

In the Bayou City Builders example, an estimate of $170,000 was obtained as the cost of construction of the 3,000-square-foot house. Management of this firm could use experience to determine if this is a reasonable estimate or not. Knowledge about current situations also might indicate if adjustments should be made. Perhaps labor costs have recently increased, or this particular home may have unique features that would cause the cost to be abnormally high. In assessing the accuracy of this model, management may look at how well it would have worked on houses built in the past. This would provide an indication of how close the cost estimate may be to the actual construction cost in a specific instance.

Implement the Results

Once the solution has been found, it must be implemented. If this implementation causes people to change the way they do their jobs, the solution may be quite difficult to implement. The manager must understand the impact of the decisions on the people and the organization. Behavioral aspects of management may be very important in implementing the results.

In the Bayou City Builders example, there is little implementation associated with this decision. An estimated cost was obtained, and now this value would simply be used in planning the house's construction. The model developed should be saved so it may be used with cost estimates for future houses to be built. This would eliminate the need for repeating the data collection and model-building process in the future. If management had been using another technique to estimate cost in the past, the person who had that responsibility might not have confidence in this new technique. Efforts to convince this individual of the model's validity might be required.

Monitor the Results

While some decisions based on management science are one time decisions to fit a particular situation, there are many decisions which affect the day-to-day operations of an organization. With these, a good manager will monitor the results of the decisions to see if conditions do change. Other solutions might become more desirable due to changing economic conditions. This book considers how changes in input data might impact the optimal solution to a mathematical model of a managerial problem.

In monitoring the model built in the Bayou City Builders example, management should periodically check to see if the model is still appropriate. Inflation and changes in building materials and procedures may cause this model to lose accuracy. If management finds that this model is not performing adequately, it may become necessary to collect new data and update this model.

1.6 MANAGEMENT SCIENCE IN YOUR CAREER

There are many career opportunities in the area of management science, and there are numerous other careers in which the use of management science techniques will at times play an integral part. If the word "analyst" is in a job title, it is likely that management science models could be used to aid in decision making in that occupation.

Many large corporations hire quantitative analysts or operations researchers who work in special departments as a resource for others in the organization. American Airlines, USAir, and other airlines have Operations Research departments that are constantly recruiting. The success they have experienced in crew scheduling, yield management, schedule planning, and marketing have lead other companies in the transportation industry to hire operations researchers to help with similar problems.

Management consulting divisions exist in many large accounting firms. These groups hire individuals who are skilled in technical analysis, computer usage, and communications. Courses in management science or operations research would help to provide the training in technical analysis that is essential for individuals in these positions. In addition to large accounting firms, employment opportunities exist with independent business consulting firms who specialize in similar types of functions.

Careers as financial analysts, production planners, marketing researchers, and inventory control analysts are available for persons with analytical skills as well as expertise in the appropriate area. In recent years, new career opportunities have been found in areas of environmental and health management. Cost/benefit analysis is extensively used in these areas, and management science techniques may be helpful in identifying minimum cost or maximum benefit solutions.

1.7 MANAGEMENT SCIENCE AND COMPUTER SYSTEMS

Many of the management science models that will be presented in this book are integrated into computer-based systems used to aid in decision making. A system that is used to store, organize, and process data to provide useful information to the management of a firm is referred to as a **management information system** (**MIS**). Managers use these systems for routine things such as report generation and transaction processing. The systems also are used to provide needed information to aid in decision making. A forecast of future demand would require information on past sales figures readily available in an MIS. Better production schedules can be made when information about the availability of materials and other resources is provided. In situations such as these, an MIS may include management science models that automatically set production schedules or provide demand forecasts. This is possible in very structured situations where standard operating procedures and decision rules are included as a part of the management information system.

Management information system (MIS)
A system used to store, organize, and process data to provide useful information to the management of a firm.

Decision Support Systems

In recent years computer-based **decision support systems** (DSS) have become prevalent. While there is not total agreement on what a decision support system actually is, a DSS is sometimes defined as a set of people, procedures, databases, and devices that are used to aid in decision making.

Decision support system (DSS)
A set of people, procedures, databases, and devices used to aid in decision making.

Management Science in the Timber Industry

The timber industry plays a major role in Chile's economy, with about $1.4 billion per year in global sales. In the last five years, management science techniques have begun to be important in timber management decisions. One reason credited for the growth of management science techniques is that "the globalization of markets created an industry increasingly dependent on exports. To be competitive in world markets, the Chilean timber industry was compelled to reduce operational costs and improve production, sales and investment decisions."

Fundacion Chile, a nonprofit foundation, provided a link between the timber industry and academia, and helped to articulate to researchers the industry's needs. This partnership resulted in development of a truck scheduling system called ASICAM. ASICAM centralized transportation decisions, and generated schedules using a simulation model. Because transportation comprises about 40 percent of the industry's operational costs, the new system has led to total annual savings of about $7 million across the industry.

Researchers also developed a linear programming model for short-range timber harvesting. The goal of the model was to match supply of timber with demand for exports, sawmills, and pulp plants, without waste. The linear programming model used an inventory simulator to predict changing demand patterns, and then showed companies where they could save money by avoiding unnecessary transfers of timber. This has led to a saving of $50,000 per month for one of the companies involved.

Linear programming and integer programming models also have been set up to solve higher-level strategic decisions about overall industry resources. Over a horizon of about 45 years, the models help make decisions involving long-range optimal levels of production, investment in forest lands, construction of new plants, and financial strategies for the global marketplace. Overall, management science techniques have helped Chile to save money today, and to plan for the future.

SOURCE:
Weintraub, A., R. Epstein, R. Morales, and J. Seron, October 1994. "Chopping Management Problems Down to Size: OR/MS Boosts Productivity in Chile's Timber Industry." *OR/MS Today:* 40-42.

The decision maker is an integral part of this system, as are the computer, software, and databases. The decision maker uses the computer interactively to obtain information about a particular decision.

Figure 1.2 provides one possible conceptual model of a decision support system. This indicates that a DSS generator is the core of the system. Information may be obtained both from an internal database and external sources. With the recent growth in information sources such as the Internet, these external sources may become increasingly important in future decision making. Management science models are often a part of the model base that is used to process data.

Decision support systems are typically used for problems that are semistructured. They are not so structured that decision making could be done by the computer alone. Some managerial judgment is required, but the problem has enough structure so the manager may use the computer as a tool to provide quick answers to "what-if" questions or to recommend possible solutions for evaluation.

Expert Systems

Expert system
A computerized information system which imitates the thinking of an expert.

A step beyond a decision support system is an **expert system** in which the analysis and thinking of an expert is imitated by a computer. An

FIGURE 1.2

Components of a Decision Support System

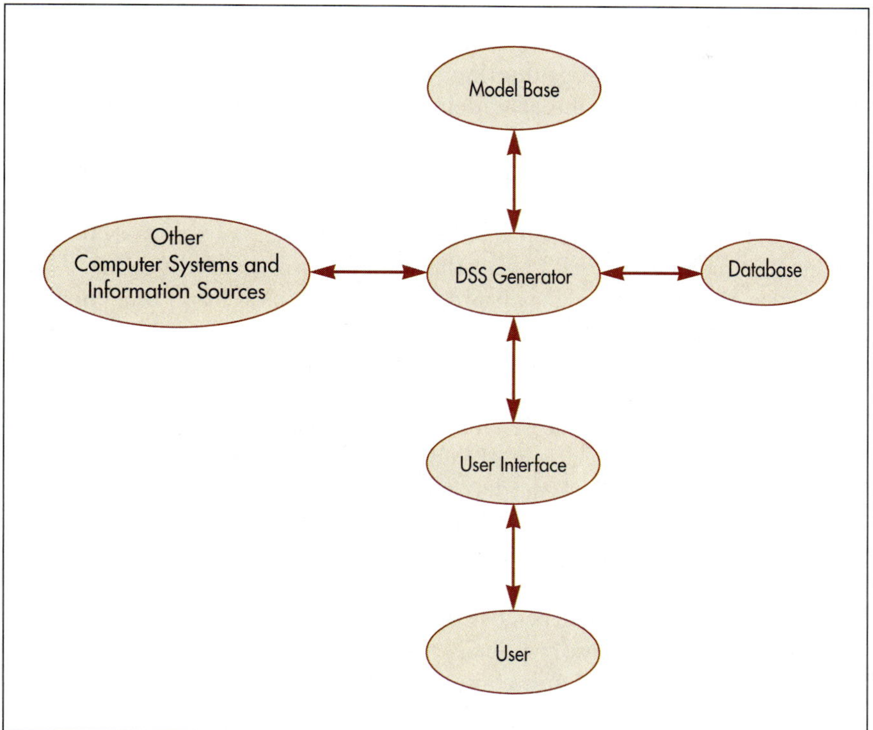

expert system might be viewed as a decision support system in which an expert's knowledge in a particular area is included in a knowledge base. The term artificial intelligence is used to describe computers which try to duplicate the processes of the human brain, which is the basis for expert systems.

In the development of an expert system, a knowledge engineer captures the knowledge of an expert and puts this into a computerized system. Once the expert system has been developed, this expertise becomes available to any user of the system. In using an expert system, the user is often queried by the computer regarding the specific situation. Based on the responses, the computer system may then ask other relevant questions. Once all the necessary information has been provided, the expert system provides a recommendation in the specific decision-making situation. The user may ask the computer to explain the reasoning behind the recommendation. By providing this reasoning, the expert system provides training for the user of the system. Applications of expert systems have been reported in the diagnosis of medical problems, automobile repair, insurance rate determination, planning computer systems, and maintenance of telephone networks.

1.8

OVERVIEW OF THE BOOK

In this book we will be studying several different mathematical techniques used in businesses today. These techniques include linear programming and certain variations of linear programming such as transportation and assignment models, integer programming, and goal programming. Linear programming is one of the most widely used quantitative tools in business today. For example, it has been used by the Burger King Corporation to reduce the cost of meat purchases and distribution while maintaining quality, resulting in savings of over two million dollars annually.

We also will study project management using the program evaluation and review technique (PERT) and the critical path method (CPM). These techniques aid in managing such projects as the construction of a chemical plant, the development of the Polaris missile, and preparing for the launch of the space shuttle. With these techniques, the project manager is able to determine when to schedule the start of particular activities and which activities should be monitored most closely to keep the project on schedule. They also provide help in the development of budget and resource allocation schedules.

We will study network models which have been used to plan pipeline and computer cable layouts to minimize the cost. In recent years network models have been used in planning satellite orbits to help provide worldwide coverage of telecommunications systems. We will look at inventory models used to determine the cost of inventory and to aid in the development of lower cost inventory policies. We will see that queuing theory may be used to plan telephone and computer systems. By using queuing models

Linear programming has been used by Burger King Corporation to increase profitability. SOURCE: Courtesy of Burger King Corporation

Decision theory, forecasting, and simulation are techniques that have applications in such areas as plant operations. SOURCE: Photo — Sam Clemmons/Ball Corporation

to evaluate the performance of various sized systems with varying levels of demand, a company is better able to determine which system would be appropriate.

Decision theory, forecasting, and simulation also will be presented. These techniques have important applications in such areas as portfolio selection, budgeting, and plant operations.

In addition to presenting these techniques, this book will demonstrate how computer software may be used to perform the sometimes tedious computations to obtain a solution to the model being used. With computer software, we may simply input some numbers into a computer, and the outputs or solutions will be provided. Thus, it is important that a decision maker understand the inputs and outputs of a model. However, a good manager also must have a general understanding of the model upon which the computer software is based. Without a basic understanding of the model, it will be difficult if not impossible, to determine how closely the model represents reality. Therefore, without a basic understanding of the model, it will be difficult to evaluate the model's solution to determine whether or not it is a good solution to the managerial problem being studied.

1.9 USING COMPUTER SOFTWARE

While the management science models presented in this book will be illustrated with examples that may be worked manually, the computations for larger problems will require the use of computer software. Many special-purpose packages are available to perform the computations associated with management science models.

In this book, we will illustrate the use of a widely used linear and integer programming software package called LINDO. Some example problems will be solved using LINDO, and output will be provided.

We also will rely on a special-purpose management science software program called Decision Support Software (DSS). This is a menu driven system which is very easy to use. The main menu for this is shown in Figure 1.3. Throughout later chapters in this book, illustrations of sample input and output will be provided.

FIGURE 1.3

Main Menu for Decision Support Software (DSS)

DSS - Decision Support Software

Use the Right, Left, Up and Down Arrow keys to highlight processing choice and press ENTER or press the highlighted character.

Selections

Linear Programming	Queues
Integer Programming	Markov Chains
Assignment Model	Simulation
Transportation Model	OnLine Manual
Network Models	Browse Solutions
Forecasting Models	Color Options
Inventory & Production	Help
Dynamic Programming	
Decision Analysis	Quit

Spreadsheets also may be used for computational purposes, and some special add-in software programs such as What's*Best!* have been specifically developed to make it easier to perform certain types of calculations inside of a spreadsheet. Illustrations of this also will be shown in selected chapters.

GLOSSARY

Analog model A physical model with a different appearance than the object it represents. *p. 5*

Behavioral school of management A view of management in which favorable treatment of the employees is emphasized. *p. 2*

Classical approach to management A view of management emphasizing the structure and output of an organization. *p. 2*

Contingency approach to management A view of management in which different approaches are viewed as best in different situations. *p. 3*

Decision support system (DSS) A set of people, procedures, databases, and devices used to aid in decision making. *p. 11*

Expert system A computerized information system which imitates the thinking of an expert. *p. 12*

Iconic model A physical model similar in appearance to the object it represents. *p. 5*

Management information system (MIS) A system used to store, organize, and process data to provide useful information to the management of a firm. *p. 11*

Management science An approach to problem solving based on the scientific method. Also, an approach to management based on the use of mathematical models. *p. 2*

Mathematical model A model based on mathematical expressions. *p. 5*

Model A representation of a real situation, process, or object. *p. 5*

Quantitative analysis An approach to problem solving based on the scientific method and the use of mathematical models. (Related terms include management science, decision science, decision analysis, and operations research.) *p. 3*

Quantitative methods approach to management An approach to management based on the use of mathematical models. *p. 2*

Scientific method A systematic approach to problem solving. *p. 2*

Systems approach A view of management in which parts of an organization are viewed as parts of an entire system instead of as isolated units. *p. 3*

QUESTIONS AND PROBLEMS

1. In addition to a quantitative view of management, what other views exist?
2. Other than management science, there are several fields of study that use mathematical models to aid in decision making. Name some of these.
3. What is a model? What are some different types of models?
4. Identify the steps involved in solving a problem using the management science process.
5. What difficulties might arise when using a mathematical model to represent a real-world situation?
6. Why is it necessary for a manager to assess and evaluate the solution to a management science model before implementing the results?
7. What is a decision support system (DSS)?
8. What is an expert system?

9. A salesperson sold five computer systems during the past week, and the person was paid $1,500 for the week. Based on this information alone, the following model was developed to represent the before tax income for this employee:

$$I = \$300X$$

where

$$I = \text{income}$$
$$X = \text{number of computer systems sold}$$

a) If this model is an accurate reflection of the weekly income for this individual, what would the income be if seven computer systems were sold in one week?
b) Do you think that this model is an accurate reflection of the income for this individual? Explain.
c) Suppose additional information has been obtained, and it is now known that the salesperson receives a weekly salary of $500 in addition to a commission on each computer system sold. This $500 salary was a part of the $1,500 weekly income noted above when five systems were sold. Develop a new model to reflect the weekly income for this employee. Use this model to find the income if seven computer systems were sold in one week.
d) Do you think that the model in part (c) is an accurate reflection of the income for this individual? Explain.
e) Using the answer to parts (a) and (c) above, explain why it is important for a manager to understand the model as well as the real-world situation that it represents.

10. A company produces a product that costs $15 to manufacture, and this product sells for $25.
a) Develop a mathematical model to represent the contribution to profit generated by this product. Let P represent profit contribution and x represent the number of units sold.
b) Suppose an overhead cost of $3 per unit is allocated to each unit that is sold. Develop a mathematical model that would represent the contribution to profit for this situation.

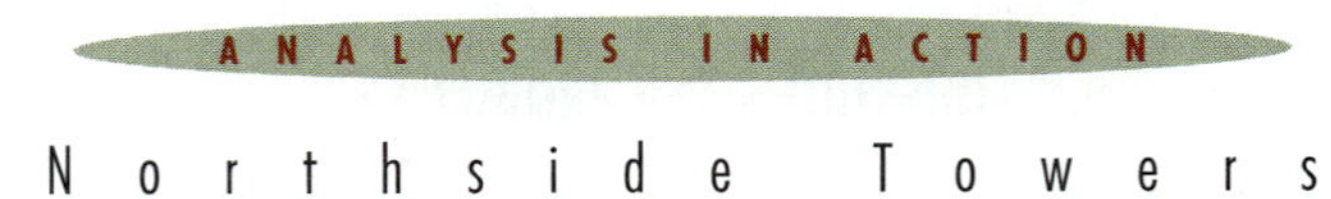

Northside Towers

The manager of Northside Towers, a new office building, had been receiving complaints from the tenants that the elevators were too slow. The company that installed the elevators had been out to investigate this situation. Adjustments were made and it was determined the elevators were operating at the maximum possible speed. However, it was suggested the elevators might be programmed so that one elevator might serve the lower floors and the other elevator would serve the upper floors. Another suggestion was that idle elevators should always return to the middle floor. Still another suggestion was that one idle elevator should wait near the top while the other elevator would wait near the bottom.

After trying all of these suggestions, the manager of Northside Towers was disappointed to find that the complaints from the tenants had not subsided. In fact, complaints seemed to increase as the tenants became very impatient about this situation. The manager knew that something must be done, but the cost of adding additional elevators or replacing these elevators with faster ones made these solutions impossible.

A consultant was hired to look at this situation. It was hoped that the consultant would find some way to make the elevators operate more efficiently. Upon analyzing the situation, the consultant found that the elevators were already programmed in the best possible way, and they could not be improved. However, the consultant recognized the true problem and informed the manager that the situation could be improved at a very low cost. Upon receiving the approval of the building manager who was skeptical but willing to do anything to make the tenants quit complaining, the consultant installed full-length mirrors on each floor by the elevators. Miraculously the complaints diminished. Now, instead of looking at their watches to see how long they had to wait for the elevator, people would look in the mirror and fix their hair or adjust their clothes. Time seemed to pass more quickly for the people waiting. The manager was happy because the tenants were no longer complaining about the elevators, and thus, the problem was solved.

1. Explain how the manager of Northside Towers defined his problem. What solutions were considered to address the problem defined in this way?
2. Explain how the consultant defined the problem. What are some possible solutions that might help to solve the problem defined in this way?

CHAPTER TWO

Introduction to Linear Programming

LEARNING OBJECTIVES

Upon completing Chapter 2, you should be able to:

- Understand what a linear program is.
- Know the steps taken in formulating a linear program.
- Solve a linear program graphically.
- Explain the concepts of feasible solutions, optimal solutions, infeasibility, alternate optimal solutions, and unboundedness.
- Know how to use slack and surplus variables to transform a linear program to standard form.
- List and explain the assumptions made when using linear programming.
- Find a basic solution to a linear program.

CHAPTER OUTLINE

2.1 INTRODUCTION

Linear programming (LP) is one of the most widely used of all the quantitative techniques in business today. Applications are seen in production, distribution, marketing, finance, scheduling, and other areas. Some examples include:

1. A manufacturing firm wants to decide how to get the maximum profit from the production of several products given a limited amount of resources.
2. A pension fund manager must decide how much money to invest in stocks, bonds, and other investment alternatives to get the highest expected return while not exceeding certain levels of risk.
3. A manufacturing firm has several plants with limited capacities and several distribution centers with certain demand requirements. The distribution manager of the firm must set up a distribution plan that will minimize the cost of sending these products from the factories to the regional distribution centers while meeting the capacity limits and the demand requirements.
4. The marketing manager of a firm must set up an advertising plan given a limited budget that will reach the largest number of people in the target market.

Linear programming may be used in these and numerous other situations, as will be seen in Chapter 4, to help managers make better decisions.

Several chapters in this book will be devoted to linear programming and its variations. In this chapter you will learn what a linear programming problem is, how to formulate a small problem, and how to solve a problem graphically. In Chapter 3 we will determine how sensitive the optimal solution is to changes in the problem's original numbers. In addition to this sensitivity analysis, we also will look at computer solutions to linear programming problems. In Chapter 4 you will see some very common larger applications of linear programming. The simplex algorithm, which is the basis for most of the computer software used to solve linear programming problems, will be presented in Chapter 5.

2.2 A MAXIMIZATION PROBLEM

The B & B Electronics Company produces two products—cellular phones and pagers. Weekly decisions are made regarding how many of these to produce. At the present time, all that can be manufactured are sold to a distributor. The cellular phones generate a profit of $15 each while the pagers generate a profit of $20 each. The production of both products involves an assembly process where the products are put together, and an inspection

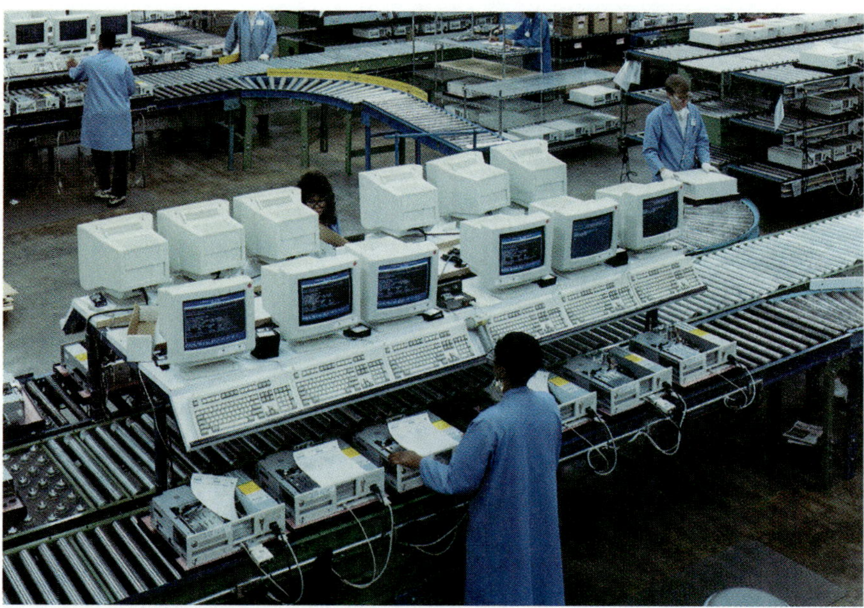

Managers can use linear programming to determine the number of machines to produce. SOURCE: Courtesy of SCI Systems, Inc.

and testing process where they are checked before being sent to the distributor. The cellular phones require four hours of assembly time and one hour of inspection time while the pagers require two hours of assembly time and two hours of inspection time. There are currently 36 hours of assembly time and 24 hours of inspection time available each week. The manager would like to determine how many units of each product to produce each week to generate the greatest profit.

Because this is a small problem, a manager might be able to look at this situation and determine what a good production schedule would be. However, for larger problems involving many products with numerous factors besides assembly time and inspection time to consider, it would be very difficult if not impossible to find the best production schedule using either judgment or trial and error. Fortunately, a linear programming model may be developed for this type of situation, and the best solution will be found very quickly.

2.3 FORMULATING A LINEAR PROGRAM

A **linear program** is a mathematical model or representation of a situation consisting of a single **objective function**, which is to be maximized or minimized, and one or more **constraints**, which limit what can be done. For example, a company may wish to maximize profit or total sales, which would be represented by the objective function. However, there are constraints such as production capacity or limited demand that prevent this

Linear programming
A mathematical technique that may help managers to allocate resources.

Objective function
The mathematical expression that is to be maximized or minimized in a linear programming problem.

Constraint
A restriction in the form of an equation or inequality, which limits the solutions in a linear programming problem.

from being an infinite amount. Minimizing cost also is a common objective. It will be impossible to have a zero total cost if there are constraints that require a minimum amount to be produced in order to meet demand.

The objective function and the constraints must all be linear functions. A linear function is a function in which each variable appears as a separate term and is raised to the first power. These may be represented by straight lines (if there are only two variables), planes (if there are three variables), or analogous figures in higher dimensions (if there are more than three variables). An example of a linear inequality would be:

$$4X_1 + 2X_2 - 0.5X_3 \leq 36$$

Notice the exponent for each of these variables is 1. Inclusion of any of the following terms, as well as numerous others, would have caused this to be nonlinear: X_1^2, X_1X_2, $X_1^{.5}$, and $\log(X_3)$.

In order to formulate a linear program, you must completely understand the managerial problem with which you are faced. The objective and any constraints must be clearly understood. Once these are understood, the following steps are used to formulate the linear programming problem:

1. Identify in words the objective function and the constraints.
2. Carefully define the decision variables. These represent the decisions that are made by the manager.
3. Use the decision variables in Step 2 to transform the verbal statements of the objective function and the constraints into mathematical expressions.

After the decision variables are defined, you should consider if it is possible for these variables to ever be negative. In most situations, variables are restricted to be nonnegative, and software used for solving linear programming problems often require this. We will return to the B & B Electronics problem to illustrate how to formulate a linear program.

2.4 A MAXIMIZATION PROBLEM REVISITED

The management of B & B Electronics would like to determine how many cellular phones and pagers to produce each week to yield the greatest profit. However, limited amounts of assembly time and inspection time will place restrictions on the production schedule. The information about this situation is summarized in Table 2.1. We will develop a linear programming model to represent this situation.

Identifying the Problem

Because there is a single objective with constraints, linear programming should be considered as a means to help the manager make production decisions. If the formulation results in an objective function and constraints which are linear, then linear programming will certainly be helpful.

TABLE 2.1

Information for B & B Electronics Problem

Product	Profit per Unit	Assembly Hours Used	Inspection Hours Used
Cellular Phone	\$15	4	1
Pager	\$20	2	2
36 assembly hours available			
24 inspection hours available			

To begin, the manager must clearly identify the objective and the constraints. From the situation stated above it is clear the objective is to *maximize profit.*

Because there are only 36 assembly hours and 24 hours of inspection time available per week, there will be limits to the amount of profit that can be achieved. Thus, we have the following two constraints in the problem:

1. The number of assembly hours used cannot exceed 36.
2. The number of inspection hours used cannot exceed 24.

We also cannot produce a negative number of units of either product, so we will have two additional constraints which restrict the number of units to be nonnegative.

Defining Decision Variables

Once the problem has been verbally stated in this form, the next step is to define the decision variables, which represent the actual decisions the manager must make. The manager must decide how many cellular phones and how many pagers to produce each week. Our variables are defined as:

X_1 = number of cellular phones produced each week

X_2 = number of pagers produced each week

Once values for both of these are found, the manager will know what the production schedule is.

Formulating Mathematical Expressions

The next step in the formulation process is to write mathematical expressions for the objective function and all of the constraints in the problem. The profit is \$15 for each cellular phone and \$20 for each pager. The profit generated by cellular phones would be:

$$(\$15 \text{ per cellular phone})(\text{number of cellular phones}) = 15X_1$$

Similarly, the profit generated by pagers would be:

$$(\$20 \text{ per pager})(\text{number of pagers}) = 20X_2$$

Thus, the objective function becomes:

$$\text{profit} = 15X_1 + 20X_2$$

The first constraint involves the number of assembly hours used. Each cellular phone requires four hours of assembly time while each pager requires two hours of assembly time. Thus, the assembly time used for cellular phones is:

$$(\text{4 hours per cellular phone})(\text{number of cellular phones}) = 4X_1$$

Similarly, the number of assembly hours used for pagers is:

$$(\text{2 hours per pager})(\text{number of pagers}) = 2X_2$$

Thus, the first constraint that was

the number of assembly hours used cannot exceed 36

is transformed into

$$4X_1 + 2X_2 \leq 36 \text{ assembly hours}$$

The second constraint that was

the number of inspection hours used cannot exceed 24

is converted to a mathematical expression in a similar fashion and becomes

$$X_1 + 2X_2 \leq 24 \text{ inspection hours}$$

It is important to remember what the left-hand sides of these inequalities represent, as they are very important in the interpretation of the final solution. In the first constraint, $4X_1 + 2X_2$ is the number of assembly hours actually used. In the second constraint, $X_1 + 2X_2$ is the number of inspection hours actually used. The maximum numbers of hours available for use in the production of cellular phones and pagers are given by the right-hand sides of these inequalities.

Because the number of cellular phones and pagers produced cannot be negative numbers, we also must include the constraints to:

$$X_1 \geq 0$$

and

$$X_2 \geq 0$$

Nonnegativity constraints
Constraints in a linear programming problem that restrict the values of the decision variables to be greater than or equal to zero.

These are called **nonnegativity constraints** and are normally written as:

$$X_1, X_2 \geq 0$$

Now the entire linear programming problem is:

$$\begin{aligned} &\text{Maximize profit} = 15X_1 + 20X_2 \\ &\text{Subject to: } 4X_1 + 2X_2 \leq 36 \quad \text{assembly hours} \\ &\qquad X_1 + 2X_2 \leq 24 \quad \text{inspection hours} \\ &\qquad X_1, X_2 \geq 0 \quad \text{nonnegativity constraints} \end{aligned}$$

GLOBAL PERSPECTIVES

Linear Programming in a Chinese Chemical Plant

Before 1983 the Chinese government completely controlled all products produced by chemical dye plants. Since then, however, global pressures have influenced economic reforms in China. The economy has become progressively more decentralized. As a result, plant managers are for the first time responsible for determining their own production. It is a particularly difficult problem because the economy is changing so rapidly that predicting what products will be needed is difficult, even in the immediate future.

The Dalian Dyestuff Plant is one of the largest chemical dye plants in China. The company has 11 workshops that produce about 100 different kinds of dyes and other products. These products are sold in domestic and foreign markets. Dalian Dyestuff worked with the Dalian University of Technology to develop an integrated decision support system (DSS) that, among other features, uses a linear programming model to do annual production planning.

The objective of the LP model is to maximize the company's profits for one year. Along with quantitative inputs, the model uses qualitative information, such as upper and lower bounds on market demand. This flexibility has helped make system implementation successful, because the rapid economic reforms in China have made it difficult to use traditional forecasting methods. Overall, the DSS has helped Dalian Dyestuff to increase profits by one million U.S. dollars per year.

SOURCE:
Yang, D-L, and W. Mou, 1993. "An Integrated Decision Support System in a Chinese Chemical Plant." *Interfaces* 23(6): 93–100.

This is a linear programming model that represents the production situation faced by B & B Electronics. When this problem is solved (i.e., optimal values for X_1 and X_2 are found), we will know how many cellular phones and pagers to produce each week.

2.5 SOLVING LINEAR PROGRAMS

The most common method for solving linear programs is the simplex algorithm, which will be discussed in Chapter 5. Another, more recently developed technique is Karmarkar's algorithm, which also is briefly described in Chapter 5. For problems with only two decision variables, a graphical approach may be used to solve the linear program. This graphical method is used for learning purposes. Most linear programs are solved using computer software as will be seen in the next chapter.

Solving Linear Programs Graphically

Because there are only two decision variables (X_1 and X_2) in the B & B Electronics problem, we may use the graphical approach. With the graphical approach, we wish to first identify the set of solutions (values for combinations of X_1 and X_2) that meet or satisfy all of the constraints. A

Feasible solution
A solution that satisfies all of the constraints in a linear programming problem.

Feasible region
The set of all feasible solutions.

solution that satisfies all of the constraints is called a **feasible solution.** The set of feasible solutions is called the **feasible region.** From this set of feasible solutions, an optimal solution will be found—in some cases there may be more than one optimal solution.

We begin by labeling the X_1 and X_2 axes on graph paper. Traditionally X_1 is the horizontal axis while X_2 is the vertical axis as illustrated in Figure 2.1. While the axes represent number lines that theoretically go from a negative to a positive infinity, we will only be concerned with the area in the first quadrant because of the nonnegativity constraints. Using this coordinate system, we will graph all of the constraints.

The first constraint is:

$$4X_1 + 2X_2 \leq 36$$

To graph any inequality, the first step is to graph the equality (=) portion. After this is done, the inequality (<) portion will be considered. Thus, we will first graph

$$4X_1 + 2X_2 = 36$$

which is a straight line. To graph any straight line we only have to find two points that are on the line. We may arbitrarily select any value for X_1 and solve the equation for X_2, or we may select any value for X_2 and solve the equation for X_1. We will choose

$$X_1 = 0$$

so

$$\begin{aligned} 4(0) + 2X_2 &= 36 \\ 2X_2 &= 36 \\ X_2 &= 36/2 \\ X_2 &= 18 \end{aligned}$$

FIGURE 2.1

Two-Dimensional Coordinate System

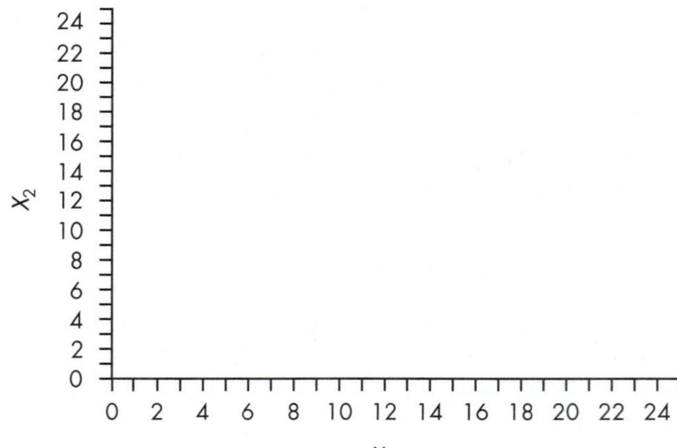

Now we have one point that lies on the line: (0,18). To find another point on the line, we will choose

$$X_2 = 0$$

so

$$\begin{aligned} 4X_1 + 2(0) &= 36 \\ 4X_1 &= 36 \\ X_1 &= 36/4 \\ X_1 &= 9 \end{aligned}$$

This gives us the second point on the line: (9,0). Putting these points on the graph and connecting them gives us the line segment in Figure 2.2. Note that if the constraint had been an equality constraint, points that satisfy the constraint would simply be the points on this line segment. However, this is an inequality, so other points also will satisfy this constraint.

The < portion of the inequality means that all the points on one side of the line or the other also will satisfy this constraint. To decide which side of the line will do this, we simply choose any point on either side of the line and see if it provides a value of $4X_1 + 2X_2$ that is less than 36. We will choose the point (5,5); so $X_1 = 5$ cellular phones and $X_2 = 5$ pagers are to be produced. This gives

$$4(5) + 2(5) = 30$$

which is less than 36. Thus, this point is feasible because we only would use 30 hours of assembly time and there are 36 hours available. Consequently, every other point on the same side of the line also is feasible. Figure 2.3 (on the next page) illustrates this. While we selected the point (5,5), we could

FIGURE 2.2

Graph of Assembly Hours Equation

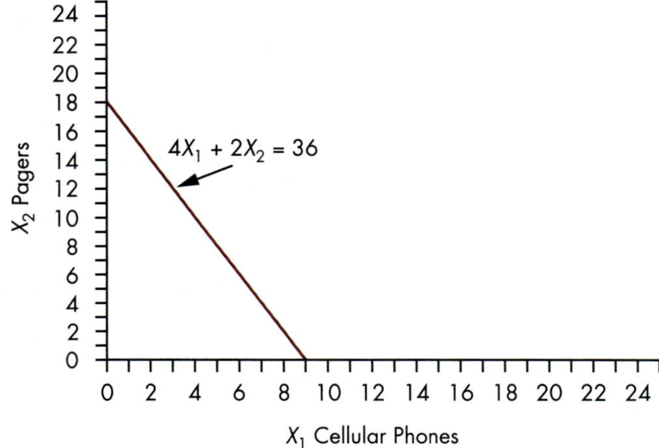

FIGURE 2.3

Feasible Side of Line for Assembly Hours Constraint

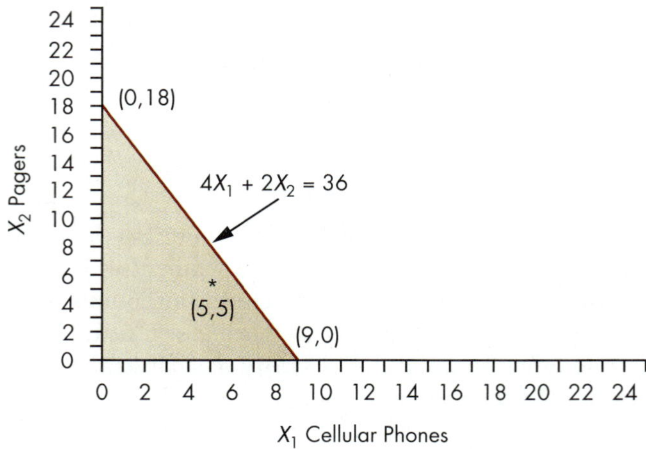

select any point to do this. Often the point (0,0) is selected for ease of use. Using this point, we find that

$$4(0) + 2(0) < 36$$

confirming that this side of the line is feasible. If you select a point on the other side of the line such as (10,10), you see that it is not feasible because

$$4(10) + 2(10) = 60$$

which means that 60 hours of assembly time would be required to produce 10 cellular phones and 10 pagers. Because there are only 36 hours available, this solution is not feasible.

Repeating this process, we will graph the second constraint which is:

$$X_1 + 2X_2 \leq 24$$

We will choose

$$X_1 = 0$$

so

$$\begin{aligned} 0 + 2X_2 &= 24 \\ 2X_2 &= 24 \\ X_2 &= 24/2 \\ X_2 &= 12 \end{aligned}$$

This gives us one point that is on the line, (0,12). To find another point we select

$$X_2 = 0$$

so

FIGURE 2.4

Feasible Points for Inspection Hours Constraint

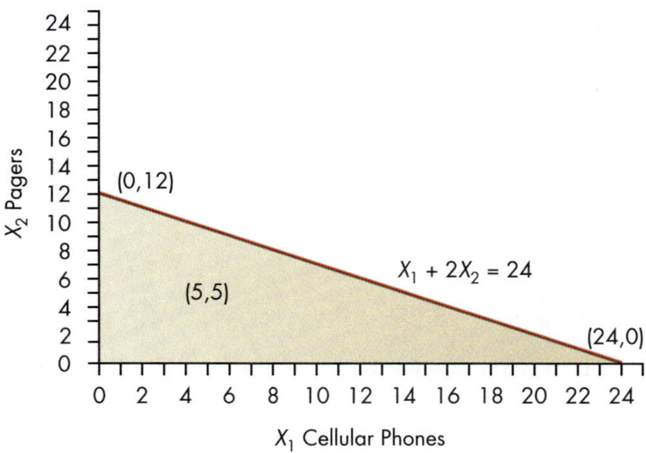

$$X_1 + 2(0) = 24$$
$$X_1 = 24$$

This second point is (24,0), which represents 24 cellular phones and 0 pagers. These points and this second line are shown in Figure 2.4 above. To see which side of the line satisfies the < portion of the constraint, we will arbitrarily select the point (5,5). This gives

$$5 + 2(5) = 15$$

which means that only 15 hours of inspection time are required to produce 5 cellular phones ($X_1 = 5$) and 5 pagers ($X_2 = 5$). Because this point is feasible, every other point on the same side of the line also is feasible. The set of points that are feasible relative to both constraints is where these two areas intersect, as shown in Figure 2.5 on the next page. This set of points is the feasible region. Each point in this region represents a combination of cellular phones and pagers that could be produced by B & B Electronics given the current level of resources (assembly hours and inspection hours). Any point not in the feasible region would represent an infeasible point or a combination of cellular phones and pagers that could not be produced by B & B Electronics without requiring more assembly hours, more inspection hours, or both. Thus, in looking for the solution that maximizes profit, we need only consider points in this feasible region.

Finding the Optimal Solution: The Iso-Profit Method

Iso-profit method
A graphical method for solving linear programming problems.

Corner-point method
A graphical method for solving linear programming problems, which have only two decision variables.

Once the feasible region is found, we must find the point in this feasible region that represents the optimal solution. In this problem, B & B Electronics would like to maximize profit, so the optimal solution is the one with the highest profit. We will consider two ways to find this optimal point. The first of these methods is the **iso-profit method** and the second is the **corner-point method.**

FIGURE 2.5

Feasible Region for B & B Electronics Problem

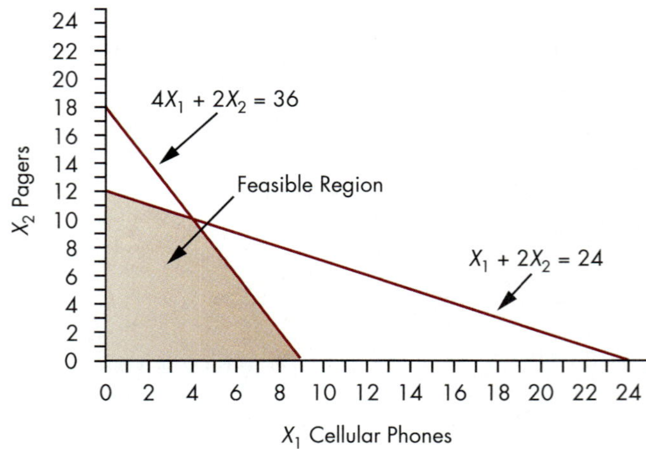

Start with the iso-profit method. Recall that we wish to maximize the objective function (profit) which is:

$$\text{profit} = 15X_1 + 20X_2$$

Notice this function is linear, as are all of the constraints. Arbitrarily select a point and determine the profit that would be generated at that point, although you could arbitrarily select a value for profit without selecting the point first. The profit line for this then would be drawn. Select a point in the feasible region such as (4,0), which says $X_1 = 4$ cellular phones and $X_2 = 0$ pagers, and use the profit from this to graph the objective function. For this combination (4,0), the profit would be:

$$15(4) + 20(0) = \$60$$

If profit is $60, the objective function would be:

$$15X_1 + 20X_2 = 60$$

and any point on this line would generate a profit of $60. We will graph this line and illustrate this in Figure 2.6. To graph this, we need any two points that satisfy this equation. One point is (4,0). To get another point, select any value for X_1 and solve the equation for X_2. If we let

$$X_1 = 0$$

then

$$15(0) + 20X_2 = 60$$
$$20X_2 = 60$$
$$X_2 = 60/20$$
$$X_2 = 3$$

FIGURE 2.6

Iso-Profit Line for $60 Profit

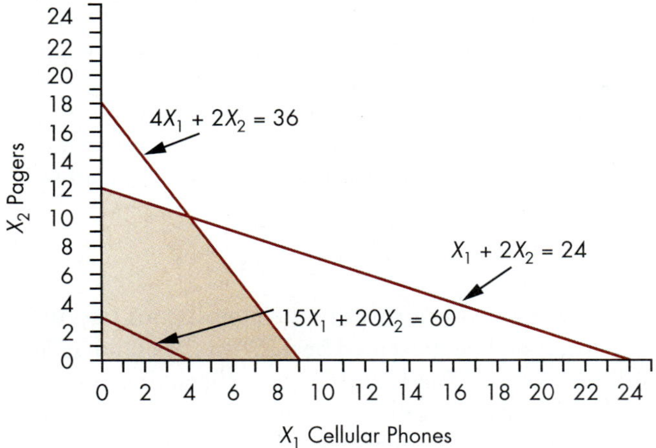

Thus, the points (4,0) and (0,3) may be used to graph the line as shown in Figure 2.6. Any point on this line will generate a profit of $60.

If we change the right-hand side of this equation to 120 instead of 60, we would be considering a profit of $120. A graph of this line may be drawn by selecting $X_1 = 0$ and solving for X_2; and we then select $X_2 = 0$ and solve for X_1. Thus, the line would pass through the points (8,0) and (0,6). Figure 2.7 illustrates this. Note that as the profit is increasing from 60 to 120, the objective function line is shifting parallel to the original line and moving further away from the origin (0,0). If we continue to move this line

FIGURE 2.7

Iso-Profit Lines for $60 and $120 Profits

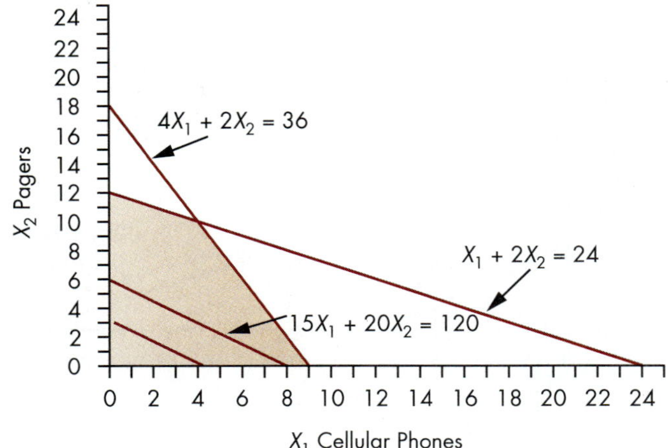

away from the origin, the profit would continue to increase. Therefore, in using the iso-profit method we will move the objective function line as far away from the origin as possible without leaving the feasible region. The last point in the feasible region that is touched by this line would be the feasible point that maximizes profit and would thus be the optimal solution. In Figure 2.8 this is shown as the corner point where the two constraint lines intersect. Once the exact values of X_1 and X_2 at this intersection are found, we will have the optimal solution to this problem.

To find where the two constraints intersect, we must solve two equations with two unknowns simultaneously. Thus we must solve:

$$4X_1 + 2X_2 = 36$$
$$X_1 + 2X_2 = 24$$

While there are many ways to solve two equations for two unknowns, the elimination method will be presented here. With the elimination method we want to eliminate one of the variables by subtracting one equation or a multiple of that equation from the other equation. In this example, the coefficient of X_2 is 2 in both equations. Thus, we may eliminate X_2 by subtracting the second equation from the first.

$$\begin{array}{r} 4X_1 + 2X_2 = 36 \\ -(X_1 + 2X_2 = 24) \\ \hline 3X_1 = 12 \\ X_1 = 12/3 \\ X_1 = 4 \end{array}$$

Putting this value of X_1 into either equation will enable us to find the value for X_2. If we select the first equation we have

FIGURE 2.8

Optimal Solution Found Using Iso-Profit Lines

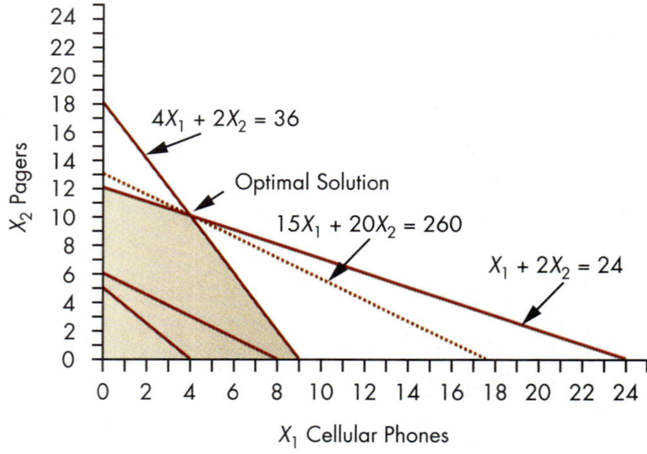

$$4(4) + 2X_2 = 36$$
$$16 + 2X_2 = 36$$
$$2X_2 = 20$$
$$X_2 = 20/2$$
$$X_2 = 10$$

Thus, the point where $X_1 = 4$ cellular phones and $X_2 = 10$ pagers represents the point where the two lines intersect. Because this is the last point where the iso-profit line intersects the feasible region, this point is the optimal solution to the problem and

$$\text{profit} = 15X_1 + 20X_2 = 15(4) + 20(10) = \$260$$

If we produce four cellular phones and 10 pagers, we will generate a profit of $260. To do this will require the use of

$$4X_1 + 2X_2 = 4(4) + 2(10) = 36 \quad \text{assembly hours}$$
$$X_1 + 2X_2 = 4 + 2(10) = 24 \quad \text{inspection hours}$$

Thus, in this problem all of the resources are used to maximize profit. In some problems, however, this is not true, and you should not assume that all resources must be used to maximize profit.

Evaluating the Solution

In Chapter 1, we learned that once a solution has been obtained, a manager must assess whether it is the appropriate solution to the managerial problem. While this solution certainly is the optimal solution to the linear programming problem, this linear program is a model of the real-world situation. The manager of B & B Electronics should look at this and determine if this solution is a good one or if perhaps the model did not clearly reflect the true situation. Perhaps the manager knows that more than four cellular phones need to be produced this week, and this was not explicitly included in the model. If this were to happen, the manager should modify the original linear program by adding a constraint that states the number of cellular phones produced must be at least a particular number. If there were any additional considerations, the model should be modified to include these as well.

Finding the Optimal Solution: The Corner-Point Method

Another graphical technique for finding the optimal (maximum-profit) solution to this problem is the corner-point method. Understanding both the iso-profit method and the corner-point method will provide useful insights when sensitivity analysis is presented later.

A careful analysis of the iso-profit method will indicate that an optimal solution to the linear programming problem must exist at one of the corner points of the feasible region. Therefore, we could find the optimal solution to the linear programming problem by only considering the corner points of the feasible region. We will find the value of the objective function, which is profit in this problem, for each of these and simply select the best one.

Again using the B & B Electronics example, we will first list the corner points of the feasible region. Most of these points may be found by an inspection of the graph of the feasible region. The last point (4,10) is found at the intersection of the two constraints. The two equations are solved simultaneously to find the values of X_1 and X_2 that satisfy both constraints as equality constraints. This was illustrated in the iso-profit section. The objective function (profit) for each of these points is calculated to determine which point yields the highest profit.

Feasible Corner Points	Profit
(X_1,X_2)	$15X_1 + 20X_2$
(0,0)	15(0) + 20(0) = 0
(0,12)	15(0) + 20(12) = 240
(9,0)	15(9) + 20(0) = 135
(4,10)	15(4) + 20(10) = 260

The point where profit is $260 represents the optimal solution to this problem because it generates more profit than all the other feasible corner points.

A manager is certainly interested in the solution that maximizes profits, but that manager also wants to know how many hours are being utilized to achieve this profit. As is seen in the iso-profit section, all 36 hours of assembly time and all 24 hours of inspection time will be used in the production of four cellular phones and 10 pagers. Table 2.2 provides a summary of the resource utilization as well as the profit for each of these feasible corner points.

Summary of Iso-Profit and Corner-Point Methods

Two graphical methods for solving linear programming problems have been presented in this chapter. Each of these helps to provide insights into linear programming, particularly when sensitivity analysis is discussed in the next chapter. Thus, it is important to understand both of these methods even though computers are normally used for solving linear programming problems. The steps in the iso-profit method and the corner-point method are summarized in Summary Table 2.1. Notice some slight modifications of

TABLE 2.2

Resource Utilization for B & B Electronics Problem

Feasible Corner Points (X_1,X_2)	Assembly Hours $4X_1 + 2X_2$	Inspection Hours $X_1 + 2X_2$	Profit $15X_1 + 20X_2$
(0,0)	0	0	0
(0,12)	24	24	240
(9,0)	36	9	135
(4,10)	36	24	260

SUMMARY TABLE 2.1

Summary of Graphical Methods

Iso-Profit (Iso-Cost) Method

1. Graph all constraints and find the feasible region.
2. Select a point and find the objective function value for that point. Graph the objective function for this given value.
3. Move the objective function line parallel to itself as far as possible in the direction of increasing profit (or decreasing cost for minimization) while still touching the feasible region.
4. The optimal solution will be the last point in the feasible region intersected by the objective function line. Find the coordinates and the objective function value of this point.

Corner-Point Method

1. Graph all constraints and find the feasible region.
2. Find the corner points of the feasible region.
3. Evaluate the objective function at each of the feasible corner points.
4. Select the corner point that yields the best value (highest for maximization, lowest for minimization) for the objective function. This is the optimal solution.

these steps are necessary if the objective function is to be minimized instead of maximized. These will be illustrated in the next example.

2.6 A MINIMIZATION EXAMPLE

The Two-Grains Cereal Company is in the process of developing a new cereal. Two grains, wheat and rice, will be combined to produce this new cereal. The company wishes to minimize the cereal's production cost, but there are certain nutritional requirements for two vitamins that must be met. Information concerning this is provided in Table 2.3. The manufacturer

TABLE 2.3

Information for Two-Grains Cereal Company Example

	Wheat	Rice
Cost per Ounce	$0.04	$0.03
Units of Vitamin #1 per Ounce	2	1
Units of Vitamin #2 per Ounce	2	3
Minimum Requirements per Box:		
20 Units of Vitamin #1		
24 Units of Vitamin #2		

A gift shop retailer may use a linear program to allocate space for each product. SOURCE: Courtesy of American Greetings Corporation

must decide how much wheat and how much rice to use in the production of this cereal.

Formulating the Problem

It is clear that the objective for Two-Grains is to **minimize cost.**

The constraints in this problem are:

1. The amount of Vitamin #1 in each box must be at least 20 units.
2. The amount of Vitamin #2 in each box must be at least 24 units.

The management of Two-Grains must decide how much of each grain to use in making the cereal. Thus, the decision variables may be defined as:

X_1 = number of ounces of wheat used in each box of cereal

X_2 = number of ounces of rice used in each box of cereal

Transforming the objective function and the constraints into the appropriate mathematical expressions, we have:

$$\begin{array}{lrl} \text{Minimize cost} = 0.04X_1 + 0.03X_2 & & \\ \text{Subject to:} & 2X_1 + X_2 \geq 20 & \text{Vitamin \#1} \\ & 2X_1 + 3X_2 \geq 24 & \text{Vitamin \#2} \\ & X_1, X_2 \geq 0 & \text{nonnegativity} \end{array}$$

Finding the Feasible Region

To solve this graphically, the first step is to graph the constraints. To graph the first constraint, we must find any two points that satisfy the equation

$$2X_1 + X_2 = 20$$

If we select $X_1 = 0$ and solve for X_2 we get $X_2 = 20$. Then selecting $X_2 = 0$ and solving for X_1 we get $X_1 = 10$. Thus, the two points (0,20) and (10,0) are on the line, as shown in Figure 2.9. To see which side of the line is feasible, we select any point on either side of the line and see if it is feasible. If we select (0,0) we get 2(0) + 0 = 0, which is not greater than 20. Therefore, the points which satisfy this inequality are on the other side of this line.

To graph the second constraint we must find two points on the line

$$2X_1 + 3X_2 = 24$$

If we let $X_1 = 0$ and solve for X_2, we get the point (0,8). Then if we let $X_2 = 0$ we find the point (12,0). To see which side of the line represents the > portion of the constraint, we select the point (0,0) and find it is not feasible because 2(0) + 3(0) = 0, which is not greater than 24. Thus, the points that are feasible relative to this constraint are shown in Figure 2.10 on the next page. Putting both of these two constraints on one graph we find the points that satisfy both constraints, and this is the feasible region in Figure 2.11 on the next page.

Finding the Optimal Solution Using the Iso-Cost Method

Because we wish to minimize cost in this problem, we will call the following procedure of determining the optimal solution the iso-cost method instead of the iso-profit method. The term "iso" means the same or similar.

FIGURE 2.9

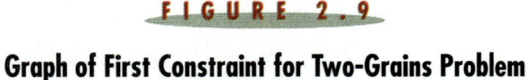

Graph of First Constraint for Two-Grains Problem

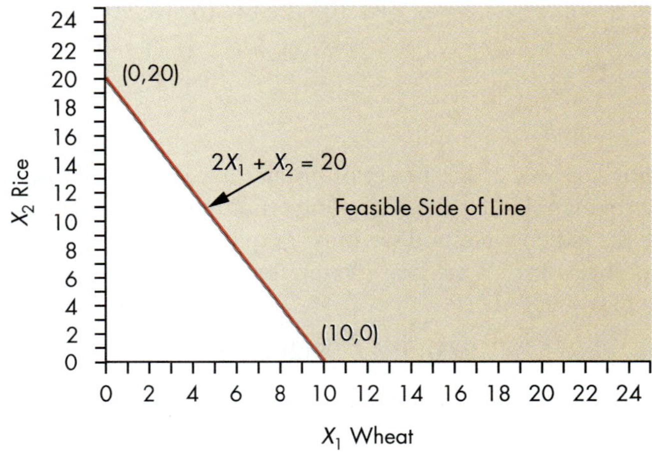

FIGURE 2.10

Graph of Second Constraint for Two-Grains Problem

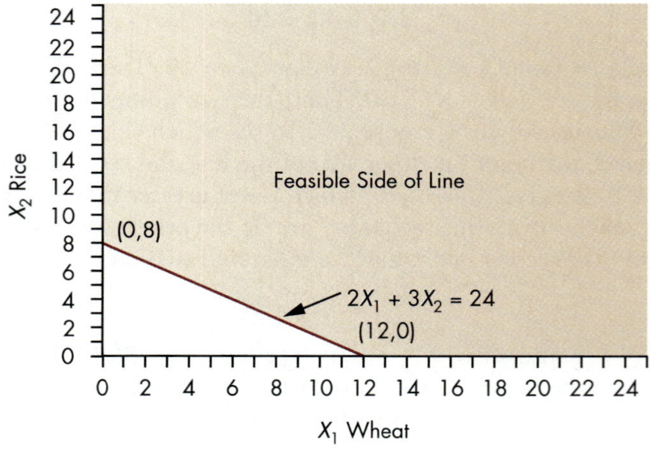

FIGURE 2.11

Feasible Region for Two-Grains Problem

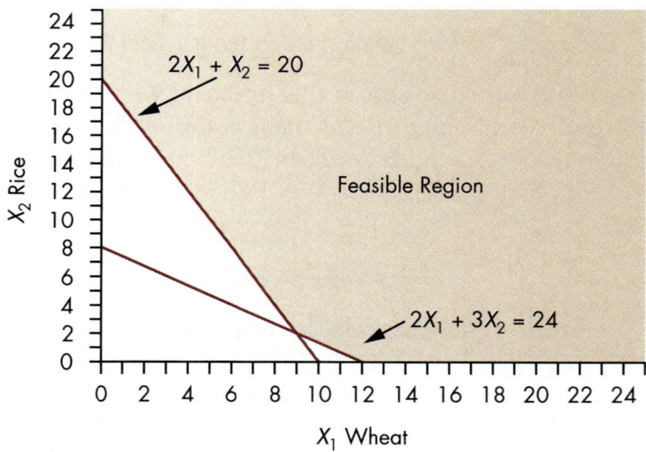

An iso-profit line would be the set of points that have the same profit, and an iso-cost line would be the set of points that have the same cost.

To use the iso-cost method we must graph the objective function for an arbitrary point or for an arbitrary value for the cost. If we select the point (0,20), the cost would be:

$$0.04(0) + 0.03(20) = 0.60$$

Therefore, we will graph the line:

$$0.04X_1 + 0.03X_2 = 0.60$$

FIGURE 2.12

Iso-Cost Lines for Two-Grains Problem

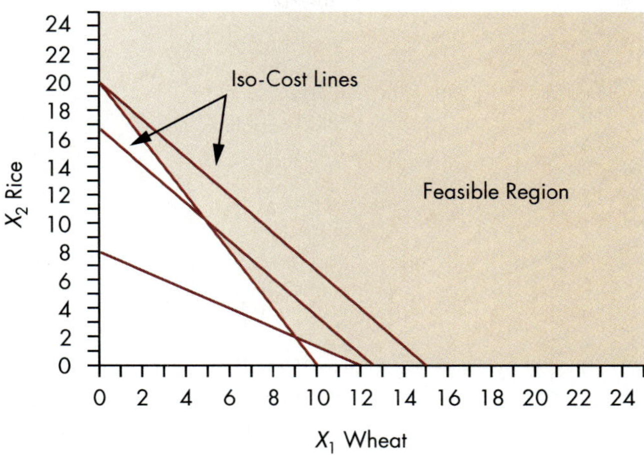

One point on this line is (0,20). By selecting $X_2 = 0$ and solving this equation we find another point to be (15,0). Thus, two points on the line $0.04X_1 + 0.03X_2 = 0.60$ are (0,20) and (15,0), as seen in Figure 2.12 above. The right-hand side of this equation represents the cost. As this value is decreased, the line would move parallel to itself and would get closer to the origin. Thus, with the iso-cost method we will move this line parallel to itself toward the origin. We will continue moving this until the last feasible point is touched. This will represent the optimal solution to this problem. We then must find the values for X_1 and X_2 at that point. As is shown in Figure 2.13 on the next page, this point is where the two constraints intersect. Solving the two equations

$$2X_1 + X_2 = 20$$
$$2X_1 + 3X_2 = 24$$

simultaneously yields $X_1 = 9$ and $X_2 = 2$. Thus, nine ounces of wheat and two ounces of rice would be used in producing a box of the cereal. The cost is:

$$0.04(9) + 0.03(2) = 0.42$$

From the first constraint, we see this would yield

$$2(9) + 2 = 20$$

units of Vitamin #1. From the second constraint, we see this would yield

$$2(9) + 3(2) = 24$$

units of Vitamin #2.

Finding the Optimal Solution Using the Corner-Point Method

If the corner-point method were used to solve this problem, we would list the feasible corner points and evaluate the objective function at each of

FIGURE 2.13

Optimal Solution for Two-Grains Problem

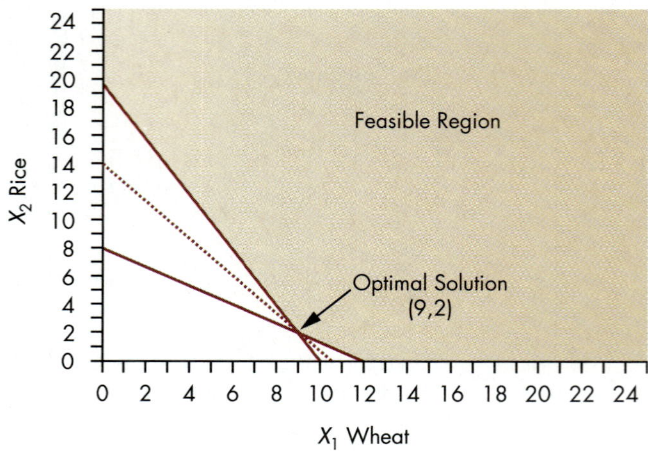

these points. The feasible corner points and the objective function values would be:

Feasible Corner Points	Cost
(X_1,X_2)	$0.04X_1 + 0.03X_2$
(0,20)	0.04(0) + 0.03(20) = 0.60
(12,0)	0.04(12) + 0.03(0) = 0.48
(9,2)	0.04(9) + 0.03(2) = 0.42

Once again we see that the optimal solution is to use nine ounces of wheat and two ounces of rice.

Evaluating the Solution

The manager of Two-Grains must look at this solution to determine if the solution to the model is the correct solution to the managerial problem. In this situation, we see that the total weight of the box of cereal is 11 ounces (nine ounces of wheat and two ounces of rice). If the box of cereal is intended to be 13 ounces, then this solution cannot be used. The evaluation of this solution might cause the manager to modify the original problem to include a constraint that requires the total weight of a box of cereal be equal to 13 ounces. This then could be solved and the problem's solution then could be evaluated.

Modifying the Graphical Techniques for Minimization Problems

To solve minimization problems graphically, there are only minor modifications required in the two graphical methods. For the iso-cost method, the objective function line is moved in the direction of decreasing cost. For the

BEST PRACTICES

A Linear Programming Model for Fuel Management

Fuel expenditures are a major cost for airlines, and indirectly, a major cost for consumers. McDonnell Douglas Corporation developed a fuel model to estimate the profit potential of various aircraft types under optimal fuel management policies. They also provide the model as a service to their airline customers. The model assesses fuel requirements by station for future aircraft schedules. It helps to reduce fuel costs or fuel consumption through efficient fueling policies, and can be used to give information to suppliers.

The fuel model is formulated as a linear program. However, if only a single aircraft is involved, the program may be converted to a pure network problem (significantly simplifying computations). When no constraints exist on how much fuel may be purchased at a single station, the systemwide solution for an airline can be found by solving a single network problem for each aircraft. Input data for the model include the aircraft schedule, fuel consumption by flight leg as a function of the landing fuel, and fuel prices and availability by station and vendor. Maximum fuel weight limits for takeoff, maximum fuel weights, and minimum fuel reserves also are required.

Courtesy McDonnell Douglas Corporation

The Brazilian airline VASP (Viação Aérea São Paulo) requested assistance from McDonnell Douglas in solving a fuel tankering problem. Using a week of data on Boeing 727 and 737 flights, the minimum cost solution was found to save 5.94 percent, nearly $13,000. Savings on individual flights ranged from 2.57 percent to 10.69 percent. McDonnell Douglas has used the linear programming model to help other customers, and has found cost savings of 5 to 6 percent to be common.

SOURCE:

Stroup, J. S., and R. D. Wollmer, 1992. "A Fuel Management Model for the Airline Industry." *Operations Research* 40 (2): 229–237.

corner-point method, the optimal point is selected as the one with the lowest objective function value instead of the one with the highest objective function value.

2.7 ANOTHER MAXIMIZATION EXAMPLE

Roadrider Bicycles produces a racing bike and a recreational bike at a manufacturing facility in Dayton, Ohio. Both of these are 21-speed bicycles that are in great demand. The bikes' profits and labor-hour requirements are given in Table 2.4 on the next page. The company wishes to develop a daily production schedule. A linear programming model will be developed to help with this. The objective is to maximize profit. In addition to the labor-hour limits, there are other restrictions set by management. The constraints are:

1. At least 50 but no more than 150 recreational bikes must be produced due to anticipated demand.
2. The number of racing bikes cannot exceed the number of recreational bikes.

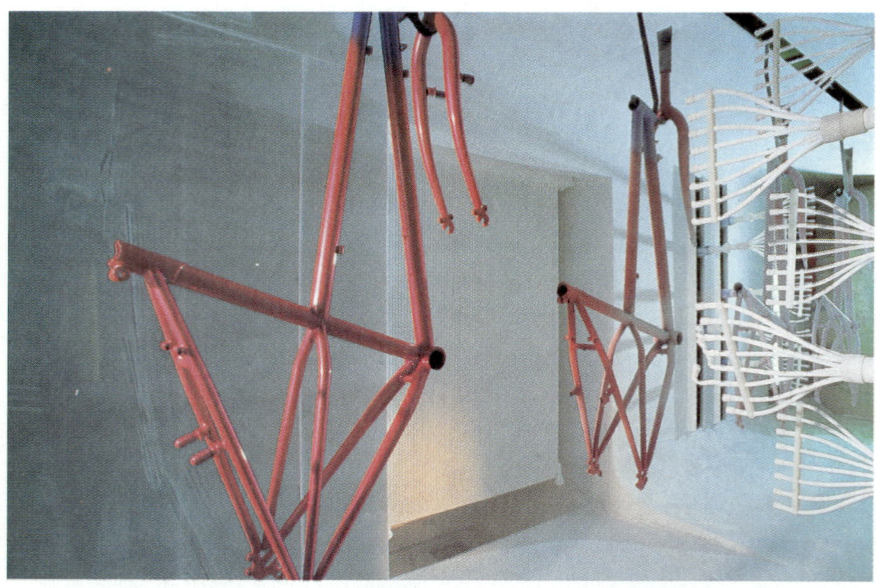

The production manager for Roadrider Bicycles must develop a linear programming model that will maximize profit while adhering to management's many restrictions, such as limited hours for painting and detailing. SOURCE: Courtesy Hoechst AG

3. The number of assembly hours used cannot exceed 360 per week.
4. The number of painting and detailing hours used cannot exceed 400 hours per week.

Formulating the Problem

We begin by defining the decision variables. These are:

X_1 = number of racing bikes produced per week

X_2 = number of recreational bikes produced per week

The objective function is:

$$\text{Maximize profit} = 80X_1 + 70X_2$$

TABLE 2.4

Information for Roadrider Bicycles Example

	Racing Bike	Recreational Bike
Profit	$80	$70
Assembly Time (Hrs.)	2	3
Painting Time (Hrs.)	4	2

The restriction that the number of recreational bikes must be between 50 and 150 results in two constraints:

$$X_2 \geq 50$$
$$X_2 \leq 150$$

The restriction that the number of racing bikes cannot exceed the number of recreational bikes is written as:

$$X_1 \leq X_2$$

or

$$X_1 - X_2 \leq 0$$

The number of assembly hours used cannot exceed 360 per week is written as:

$$2X_1 + 3X_2 \leq 360$$

The number of painting and detailing hours used cannot exceed 400 hours per week is written as:

$$4X_1 + 2X_2 \leq 400$$

The linear program that represents this situation is:

$$\begin{aligned} \text{Maximize profit} = 80X_1 + 70X_2 \\ X_2 \geq 50 \\ X_2 \leq 150 \\ X_1 - X_2 \leq 0 \\ 2X_1 + 3X_2 \leq 360 \\ 4X_1 + 2X_2 \leq 400 \\ X_1, X_2 \geq 0 \end{aligned}$$

We have five constraints plus the nonnegativity constraints.

Finding the Feasible Region

To solve this, we must first graph all of the constraints in order to find the feasible region. Graphing the equality portion of each constraint by finding any two points on each of the lines may give us the following:

For constraint 1:	$X_2 = 50$	(0,50) and (100,50)
For constraint 2:	$X_2 = 150$	(0,150) and (100,150)
For constraint 3:	$X_1 - X_2 = 0$	(0,0) and (50,50)
For constraint 4:	$2X_1 + 3X_2 = 360$	(0,120) and (180,0)
For constraint 5:	$4X_1 + 2X_2 = 400$	(0,200) and (100,0)

Note that in constraint 1, if we pick X_1 to be 0, X_2 will equal 50. We cannot pick X_2 to be zero because it must equal 50. However, we may pick any value (such as 100) for X_1, and X_2 will be 50. Also note that in constraint 3, selecting $X_1 = 0$ results in $X_2 = 0$. If we then select $X_2 = 0$, we get the same point. Thus, we select another value for X_1 (such as 50) and solve for X_2. This results in the point (50,50).

Plotting these points yields the lines shown in Figure 2.14a. The line numbers correspond to the constraint numbers. Selecting a point and determining which side of each line is feasible results in the feasible region shown in Figure 2.14b.

Finding the Optimal Solution Using the Iso-Profit Method

Using the iso-profit method and graphing the objective function, we find that corner point C is the optimal solution, as shown in Figure 2.14b. This

FIGURE 2.14A

Graph of Roadrider Bicycles Example

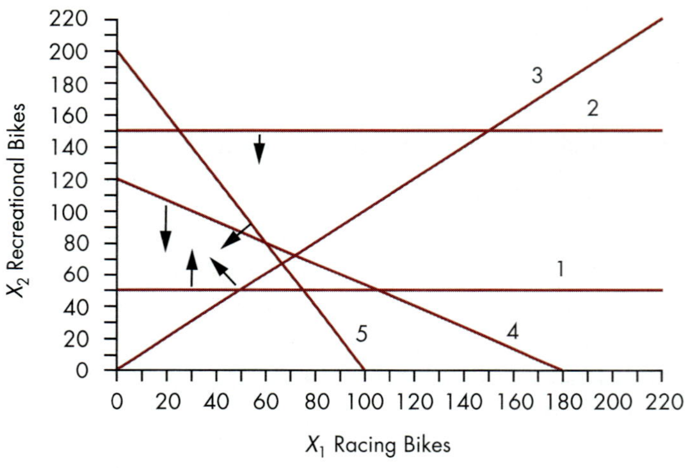

FIGURE 2.14B

Graph of Roadrider Bicycles Example

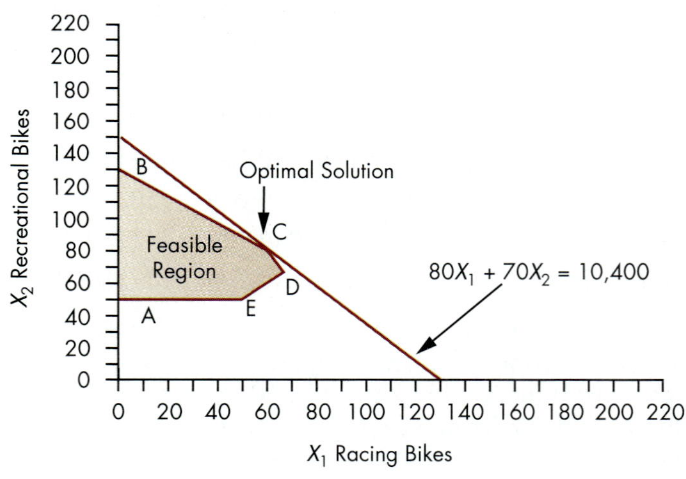

is where constraint line 4 intersects constraint line 5. We must solve these two simultaneously to find this point:

$$\begin{aligned} -2(2X_1 + 3X_2 &= 360) \\ 4X_1 + 2X_2 &= 400 \\ \hline 0 - 4X_2 &= -320 \\ X_2 &= 80 \end{aligned}$$

To find X_1, choose the second equation, which results in:

$$\begin{aligned} 4X_1 + 2(80) &= 400 \\ X_1 &= 60 \end{aligned}$$

Thus, to maximize profit, 60 racing bikes and 80 recreational bikes should be produced each week. The profit would be:

$$80X_1 + 70X_2 = 80(60) + 70(80) = \$10{,}400$$

In doing this, all 360 hours of assembly time and all 400 hours of painting time would be used each week.

2.8

EQUALITY CONSTRAINTS

There are times when a constraint has the form of an equation instead of an inequality. For example, a company making computers might require that the number of monitors produced equals the number of keyboards produced because every computer needs one of each. Perhaps a company wishes to have no idle time for workers in a particular department. A constraint requiring the number of labor hours used to equal the number of labor hours available would be an equality constraint.

In finding the feasible region when there is an equality constraint, we see that the points must be on the line. Any points on either side of the line are not feasible. Therefore, the feasible region will be a line segment, and the optimal solution will be a corner point of this line segment.

2.9

SLACK AND SURPLUS

Slack
The amount by which the right-hand side of a less-than or equal-to constraint exceeds the left-hand side. Typically this represents an unused resource.

Surplus
The amount by which the right-hand side of a greater-than or equal-to constraint is exceeded by the left-hand side of the constraint.

Important to managers in the analysis of the results from a linear programming problem is the utilization of the resources available and the degree to which constraints are met or exceeded. Many ≤ constraints represent resource restrictions, and the term **slack** is used to represent any unused excess amount of the resource. There are many other types of ≤ constraints as well, and the term slack refers to the amount by which the right-hand side of the constraint exceeds the left-hand side for a specific solution. Similarly, the term **surplus** is used to represent the amount by which the right-hand side of a ≥ constraint is exceeded for a specific solution. Slack variables and surplus variables are often used to represent these values. We will illustrate these using the problems previously presented.

Slack Variables

In the B & B Electronics problem, there were two less-than or equal-to constraints. The first of these was:

$$4X_1 + 2X_2 \leq 36 \text{ assembly hours available}$$

Any unused assembly hours would be called slack, and we will let S_1 represent this. Adding S_1 to this constraint we have:

$$\text{(hours used)} + \text{(slack)} = \text{(hours available)}$$
$$(4X_1 + 2X_2) + S_1 = 36$$

Thus, by definition,

$$\text{assembly hours slack} = \text{(amount available)} - \text{(amount used)}$$

or in this example,

$$S_1 = 36 - (4X_1 + 2X_2)$$

Consider the feasible corner point (0,12). At this point, the number of assembly hours unused would be:

$$\begin{aligned} \text{assembly hours slack} &= 36 - (4X_1 + 2X_2) \\ S_1 &= 36 - [4(0) + 2(12)] \\ &= 36 - (24) \\ &= 12 \end{aligned}$$

Thus, there are 12 hours of slack for the assembly constraint at the point (0,12). We would calculate the slack for any other point in a similar fashion.

The second constraint was:

$$X_1 + 2X_2 \leq 24$$

Letting S_2 represent the slack for this constraint, we have:

$$X_1 + 2X_2 + S_2 = 24$$

For the point (0,12), the slack would be zero.

Surplus Variables

To illustrate the concept of surplus, we will return to the Two-Grains problem. The first constraint was:

$$2X_1 + X_2 \geq 20 \text{ units of Vitamin \#1}$$

A surplus would exist if the amount of Vitamin #1 provided is greater than 20. If we let S_1 represent the surplus for Vitamin #1, we have:

$$\text{(units of Vitamin \#1 provided)} - \text{(surplus)} = \text{(units needed)}$$
$$(2X_1 + X_2) - S_1 = 20$$

Rearranging these terms we have

$$\text{surplus} = (\text{units of Vitamin \#1 provided}) - (\text{units needed})$$
$$S_1 = (2X_1 + X_2) - 20$$

Consider the feasible corner point (12,0) representing 12 ounces of wheat and zero ounces of rice. For this particular nonoptimal solution,

$$\text{Vitamin \#1 surplus} = [2(12) + 0] - 20$$
$$S_1 = 24 - 20$$
$$= 4$$

Thus, there are four more units of Vitamin #1 provided than are required by this constraint.

The surplus for the Vitamin #2 constraint would be found in a similar fashion. If we let S_2 represent the surplus for this vitamin, we have:

$$(2X_1 + 3X_2) - S_2 = 24$$

At the corner point (12,0) we have zero surplus for this constraint as the number of units of Vitamin #2 provided by this solution exactly equals 24.

2.10

STANDARD FORM OF A LINEAR PROGRAM

If a linear program is written such that all constraints are equations with nonnegative right-hand side values and all variables are restricted to be nonnegative, then the linear program is said to be in **standard form.** Slack variables are added to ≤ constraints while surplus variables are subtracted from ≥ constraints to convert a linear program into the standard form.

Standard form

A linear program is in the standard form if all constraints are equations and all variables are restricted to be nonnegative.

Examples

Consider the B & B Electronics problem. This was written as:

$$\text{Maximize profit} = 15X_1 + 20X_2$$
$$\text{Subject to: } 4X_1 + 2X_2 \le 36$$
$$X_1 + 2X_2 \le 24$$
$$X_1, X_2 \ge 0$$

Using slack variables this may be written in the standard form as:

$$\text{Maximize profit} = 15X_1 + 20X_2$$
$$\text{Subject to: } 4X_1 + 2X_2 + S_1 = 36$$
$$X_1 + 2X_2 + S_2 = 24$$
$$X_1, X_2, S_1, S_2 \ge 0$$

Notice all the variables are restricted to be nonnegative.

To illustrate the use of surplus variables, consider the Two-Grains cereal problem. This was written as:

$$\begin{aligned} &\text{Minimize cost} = 0.04X_1 + 0.03X_2 \\ &\text{Subject to: } 2X_1 + X_2 \geq 20 \\ &\qquad 2X_1 + 3X_2 \geq 24 \\ &\qquad X_1, X_2 \geq 0 \end{aligned}$$

Using surplus variables with each ≥ constraint, we convert this into standard form as:

$$\begin{aligned} &\text{Minimize cost} = 0.04X_1 + 0.03X_2 \\ &\text{Subject to: } 2X_1 + X_2 - S_1 = 20 \\ &\qquad 2X_1 + 3X_2 - S_2 = 24 \\ &\qquad X_1, X_2, S_1, S_2 \geq 0 \end{aligned}$$

All the constraints are equations and all the variables are restricted to be nonnegative.

2.11 BASIC SOLUTIONS

We have seen that an optimal solution to a linear program with two decision variables will be at a corner point of the feasible region. For problems with three decision variables, we might visualize the feasible region as a cube or other three-dimensional figure. An optimal solution would occur at a corner point of this figure. With more than three decision variables, the concept of a corner-point solution is difficult to visualize. For this reason it is helpful to introduce the concept of a basic solution. All corner-point solutions are basic solutions.

Consider a linear program written in the standard form with n variables (decision variables, slack variables, and surplus variables) and m constraints where $n \geq m$. A **basic solution** is found by setting $n - m$ equal to zero and solving for the remaining m variables. Variables that are set equal to zero are called **nonbasic variables** while the other variables are referred to as **basic variables.**

Basic solution

A solution to a linear program with n variables and m constraints, which is found by setting $n - m$ equal to zero and solving for the remaining m variables. All corner points are basic solutions.

Nonbasic variable

A variable that is set equal to zero in a basic solution to a linear programming problem.

Basic variable

A variable in a linear programming problem that is not set equal to zero in a basic solution.

Basic Solutions for B & B Electronics Example

Consider the B & B Electronics problem written in standard form:

$$\begin{aligned} &\text{Maximize profit} = 15X_1 + 20X_2 \\ &\text{Subject to: } 4X_1 + 2X_2 + S_1 = 36 \\ &\qquad X_1 + 2X_2 + S_2 = 24 \\ &\qquad X_1, X_2, S_1, S_2 \geq 0 \end{aligned}$$

In this problem, $n = 4$ and $m = 2$. We find a basic solution by setting $n - m = 4 - 2 = 2$ of these equal to zero. Suppose we set $X_1 = 0$ and $X_2 = 0$ and solve for S_1 and S_2. We have:

$$4(0) + 2(0) + S_1 = 36$$
$$S_1 = 36$$

and

$$(0) + 2(0) + S_2 = 24$$
$$S_2 = 24$$

So one basic solution is $X_1 = 0$, $X_2 = 0$, $S_1 = 36$, and $S_2 = 24$. Note that this is a corner-point solution. The nonbasic variables are X_1 and X_2. The basic variables are S_1 and S_2.

In finding another basic solution, suppose we set $X_1 = 0$ and $S_1 = 0$. Putting these values in the two equations gives us:

$$4(0) + 2X_2 + 0 = 36$$
$$0 + 2X_2 + S_2 = 24$$

This leaves us with two equations with two unknowns, and we must solve these simultaneously. In doing so, we get $X_2 = 18$ and $S_2 = -12$. Notice while this is a basic solution, it is not a feasible solution.

2.12

LINEAR PROGRAMMING ASSUMPTIONS

We have seen how a problem may be formulated as a linear programming problem and how graphical techniques may be used to find solutions when there are only two decision variables. Implicit in what we have done are four basic assumptions: certainty, divisibility, proportionality, and additivity.

Certainty means all of the numbers used in the problem (i.e., profit per unit and resource availability) are known with certainty. If there is not absolute certainty but some degree of certainty does exist, then linear programming might be used and sensitivity analysis could be performed. This will be discussed in the next chapter.

Divisibility means all variables may be divided into fractional values and need not be integer valued. If integer values are required, then we must use integer programming which will be seen in a later chapter. In many cases, this divisibility assumption is not as restrictive as it may first appear. For example, if X_1 is defined as the number of units of a product produced per week, a value of 6.75 units does have meaning to us. The fractional portion of this would mean that one unit is started this week and will be finished next week. There are many production examples that are of this type.

Proportionality means profit generation and resource utilization are proportional to the number of units produced. For example, if the production of one unit requires four hours, the production of five units would take 20 hours.

Additivity means each variable is independent of the other variables with regard to profit contribution and resource utilization. There are no interactions among the variables. We may find the total resource utilization by simply determining how much is used for each variable and adding these together.

2.13 SPECIAL SITUATIONS

There are several special conditions that may arise in linear programming problems. These are infeasibility, alternate optimal solutions, unboundedness, and redundant constraints. Each of these has implications that are important to a manager.

Infeasibility

In formulating a linear programming problem, there may be conflicting constraints. In the B & B Electronics example, there are only 36 assembly hours available. The marketing manager may wish to have at least eight cellular phones and eight pagers manufactured to meet the demand for some anticipated orders. If the constraints $X_1 \geq 8$ and $X_2 \geq 8$ are added to the problem, we find there is no feasible solution to the problem because it would require $4(8) + 2(8) = 48$ assembly hours and there are only 36 hours available. This is illustrated in Figure 2.15, which shows there is no feasible region. A linear programming problem in which this occurs is referred to as an infeasible problem. When a manager encounters this situation and is evaluating this solution (or lack thereof), it should be noted there are too many constraints on the problem or some of these are too restrictive. An attempt should be made to determine which constraints are causing this problem and these constraints should be relaxed if possible.

FIGURE 2.15

Graph of Problem with No Feasible Solution

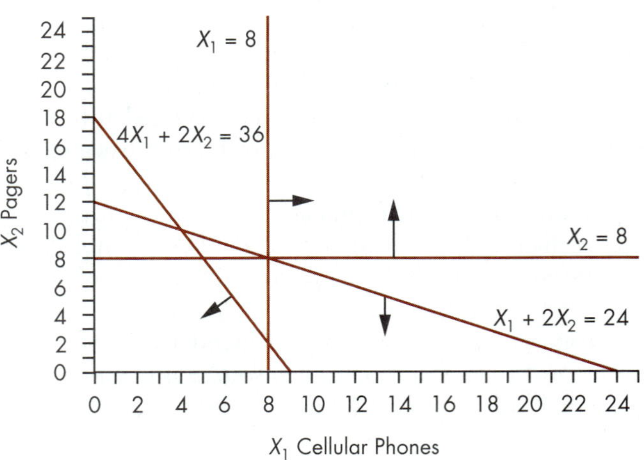

Alternate Optimal Solutions

A linear programming problem may have more than one optimal solution. This would be observed if two corner points both had the same optimal objective function value. When this occurs, we say there are alternate optimal solutions or multiple optimal solutions. If this situation occurs, the objective function line is parallel to one of the constraint lines in the problem. If there are alternate optimal solutions, then any point on the line segment joining those two corner points also will provide an optimal value to the objective function. Upon evaluating this solution, the manager should note that this situation provides a great deal of flexibility. Other criteria may be considered without sacrificing the original criteria. For example, if there are multiple solutions that maximize profit in a production problem, a manager may select from these solutions based on idle time in different departments or total units produced.

Unboundedness

If a maximization linear programming problem has no upper limit to the value of the objective function, then the problem is referred to as being **unbounded.** Generally this would mean that a constraint has been omitted from the problem.

Unbounded
A condition in which the objective function value in a linear programming problem may be made infinitely large for a maximization problem or infinitely small for a minimization problem.

Consider the following example.

$$\begin{aligned} \text{Maximize profit} &= 10X_1 + 20X_2 \\ \text{Subject to: } X_1 + X_2 &\geq 3 \\ X_1 &\leq 4 \\ X_1, X_2 &\geq 0 \end{aligned}$$

A graph of this is shown in Figure 2.16 on the next page. Notice the feasible region has no limit and X_2 may increase with no upper bound. Thus, the isoprofit line always will touch a feasible point no matter how far it is moved away from the origin and the problem is unbounded. Upon evaluating this solution, a manager should try to determine which constraint has been omitted from the problem, and the model should be modified to include this.

Redundant Constraints

A constraint which does not affect the feasible region is called a **redundant constraint**. The conditions that resulted in this type of constraint are automatically met if the other constraints in the problem are met.

Redundant constraint
A constraint which may be removed from a linear programming problem without affecting the feasible region.

For example, suppose a company is producing two products and the following linear program has been formulated for this:

X_1 = number of units of Product #1 produced each week
X_2 = number of units of Product #2 produced each week

$$\begin{aligned} \text{Maximize profit} &= 6X_1 + 2X_2 \\ \text{Subject to: } 2X_1 + X_2 &\leq 40 && \text{labor hours} \\ X_1 &\leq 10 && \text{demand for Product \#1} \\ X_2 &\leq 10 && \text{demand for Product \#2} \\ X_1, X_2 &\geq 0 && \text{nonnegativity constraints} \end{aligned}$$

FIGURE 2.16

Graph of Problem with Unbounded Solution

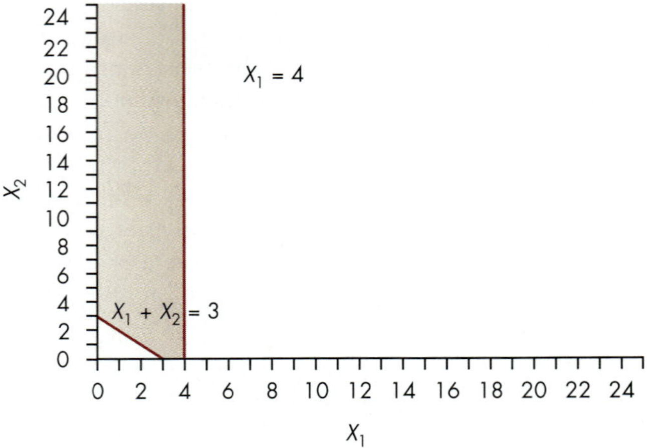

A graph of the feasible region is shown in Figure 2.17. Notice the labor-hours constraint does not touch the feasible region.

If a constraint is redundant, it could be omitted from the problem and the optimal solution would not change. Eliminating this constraint would make the problem smaller, and there may be benefits to this. However, eliminating a redundant constraint creates the possibility that it inadvertently might be omitted in the future if conditions change. In this example, if the future demand increases to 25 units for each product, the labor-hours constraint would no longer be redundant. Forgetting to put this constraint back into the problem would result in an incorrect model.

FIGURE 2.17

Graph of the Redundant Constraint

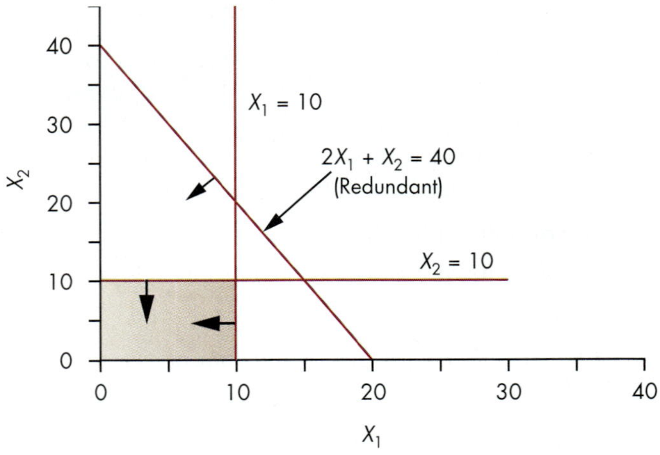

2.14 SUMMARY

This chapter has provided an introduction to linear programming. Many problems exist in which a manager must decide how to allocate scarce resources to achieve the best possible solution. Linear programming may provide very valuable information about the best way to do this. In addition to the allocation of scarce resources, linear programming has numerous other applications, as will be shown in Chapter 4.

We have seen that a linear programming problem consists of a single objective function and one or more constraints. The term linear implies certainty, additivity, divisibility, and proportionality. An optimal solution must be feasible and will occur at one of the corner points. When there are only two decision variables, the optimal solution may be found graphically using either the iso-profit (or iso-cost) method or the corner-point method. In the next chapter we will see how understanding the graphical methods aids in the understanding of the results found using computers and of the impact of changes in the problem.

GLOSSARY

Basic solution A solution to a linear program with n variables and m constraints, which is found by setting $n - m$ equal to zero and solving for the remaining m variables. All corner points are basic solutions. *p. 50*

Basic variable A variable in a linear programming problem that is not set equal to zero in a basic solution. *p. 50*

Constraint A restriction in the form of an equation or inequality, which limits the solutions in a linear programming problem. *p. 23*

Corner-point method A graphical method for solving linear programming problems, which have only two decision variables. *p. 31*

Feasible solution A solution that satisfies all of the constraints in a linear programming problem. *p. 28*

Feasible region The set of all feasible solutions. *p. 28*

Iso-profit method A graphical method for solving linear programming problems. *p. 31*

Linear programming A mathematical technique that may help managers to allocate resources. *p. 23*

Nonbasic variable A variable that is set equal to zero in a basic solution to a linear programming problem. *p. 50*

Nonnegativity constraints Constraints in a linear programming problem that restrict the values of the decision variables to be greater than or equal to zero. *p. 26*

Objective function The mathematical expression that is to be maximized or minimized in a linear programming problem. *p. 23*

Redundant constraint A constraint which may be removed from a linear programming problem without affecting the feasible region. *p. 53*

Slack The amount by which the right-hand side of a less-than or equal-to constraint exceeds the left-hand side. Typically this represents an unused resource. *p. 47*

Standard form A linear program is in the standard form if all constraints are equations and all variables are restricted to be nonnegative. *p. 49*

Surplus The amount by which the right-hand

side of a greater-than or equal-to constraint is exceeded by the left-hand side of the constraint. *p. 47*

Unbounded A condition in which the objective function value in a linear programming problem may be made infinitely large for a maximization problem or infinitely small for a minimization problem. *p. 53*

SOLVED PROBLEMS

SOLVED PROBLEM 2-1

A linear program has been formulated to determine how many units of each of two products to produce. Each product requires processing time in each of two departments. The total number of units produced each week must be at least 10 to satisfy existing orders.

$$\text{Maximize profit} = 60X_1 + 20X_2$$

Subject to:	$4X_1 + 5X_2 \leq 90$	hours in Department Y
	$2X_1 + X_2 \leq 30$	hours in Department Z
	$X_1 + X_2 \geq 10$	minimum number produced
	$X_1, X_2 \geq 0$	nonnegativity constraints

where

X_1 = number of units of Product #1 produced each week

X_2 = number of units of Product #2 produced each week

a) Solve this graphically. What is the maximum possible profit? How many units of Product #1 and Product #2 should be produced each week? Comment on this solution.

b) In maximizing profit, is there any slack in Department Y and Department Z? What implications might these have for management?

c) In maximizing profit, is there any surplus for the third constraint?

SOLUTION

Graph of Solved Problem 2-1

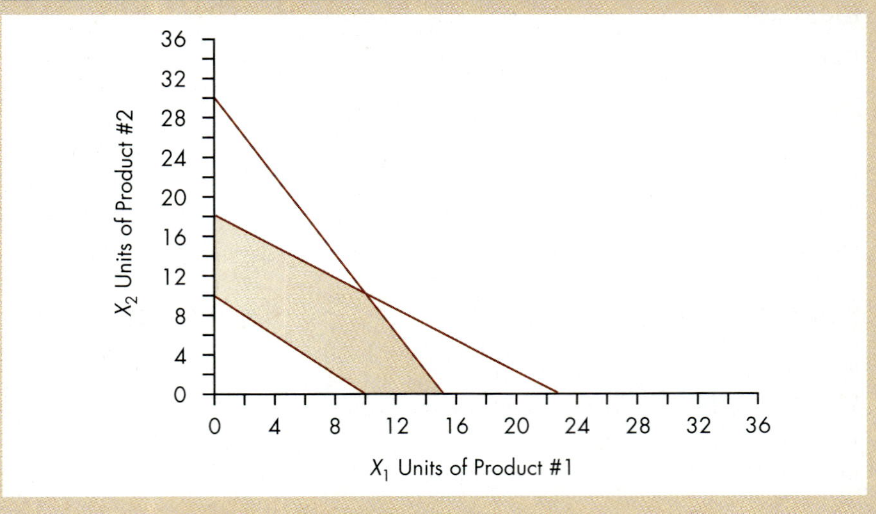

a) The feasible region is shown in the graph. Using the corner-point method, the feasible corner points and the profit for each of these are given in the table below. Corner point C (10,10) is at the intersection of the first two constraint lines. It is found by simultaneously solving the equations:

$$4X_1 + 5X_2 = 90$$

and

$$2X_1 + X_2 = 30$$

Feasible Corner Points	Profit = $80X_1 + 20X_2$
A (0,10)	200
B (0,18)	360
C (10,10)	1,000
D (10,0)	800
E (15,0)	1,200 * Optimal solution

To maximize profit, 15 units of Product #1 should be produced, and zero units of Product #2 should be produced. The profit would be $1,200.

Because no units of Product #2 would be produced, management may be concerned about this solution. If a minimum number of units of each are needed, we may wish to add additional constraints to the problem.

b) The time used in Department Y would be:

$$4(15) + 5(0) = 60 \text{ hours}$$

Because there are 90 hours available:

$$\text{slack for Department Y} = 90 - 60 = 30$$

The time used in Department Z would be:

$$2(15) + 0 = 30 \text{ hours}$$

Because there are 30 hours available:

$$\text{slack for Department Z} = 30 - 30 = 0$$

Because there are 30 hours in Department Y that are not being used with this optimal solution, management may try to find other uses for the extra 30 hours or perhaps reduce the hours available in the future to 60. However, while there may be excess hours in the short run, conditions may change (resulting in new constraints) in the next production period, and these hours may be needed then.

c) The third constraint requires:

$$X_1 + X_2 \geq 10$$

For the optimal solution, this is:

$$15 + 0 = 15$$

Therefore, the surplus is:

$$15 - 10 = 5$$

SOLVED PROBLEM 2-2

Consider the following linear program that was seen in the Solved Problem 2-1.

$$\begin{aligned} \text{Maximize profit} &= 60X_1 + 20X_2 \\ \text{Subject to: } 4X_1 + 5X_2 &\leq 90 \\ 2X_1 + X_2 &\leq 30 \\ X_1 + X_2 &\geq 10 \\ X_1, X_2 &\geq 0 \end{aligned}$$

a) Write this in the standard form.

b) For each of the feasible corner points (basic solutions), give the values for the slack and surplus variables.

c) Find the basic solution with both decision variables equal to zero. Is this solution feasible?

d) In finding each basic feasible solution (feasible corner point), which two variables would be set equal to zero?

SOLUTION

a)

$$\begin{aligned} \text{Maximize profit} &= 60X_1 + 20X_2 \\ \text{Subject to: } 4X_1 + 5X_2 + S_1 &= 90 \\ 2X_1 + X_2 + S_2 &= 30 \\ X_1 + X_2 - S_3 &= 10 \\ X_1, X_2, S_1, S_2, S_3 &\geq 0 \end{aligned}$$

b) Identifying the corner points as they were in the solution to the previous problem we have:

Point	X_1	X_2	S_1	S_2	S_3
A	0	10	40	20	0
B	0	18	0	12	8
C	10	10	0	0	10
D	10	0	50	10	0
E	15	0	30	0	5

c) $X_1 = 0, X_2 = 0, S_1 = 90, S_2 = 30, S_3 = -10$

This is not feasible because one of the variables is negative.

d)

Point	Variables Set to Zero	
A	X_1	S_3
B	X_1	S_1
C	S_1	S_2
D	X_2	S_3
E	X_2	S_2

QUESTIONS

1. Discuss the steps involved in formulating a linear programming problem.
2. Discuss the similarities and differences between the iso-profit method and the corner-point method.
3. Why is the feasible region important in linear programming and how is this determined in a problem with two decision variables?
4. Describe the basic shape of the feasible region if there is an equality constraint in a linear programming problem. What is the maximum number of feasible corner points that could exist in this situation?
5. How could you determine if a particular solution is feasible without looking at a graph of the feasible region?
6. Consider the feasible region defined by $X_1 \geq 4$ and $X_2 \geq 4$. This feasible region itself would be considered unbounded. If the objective function were to maximize profit, would the solution be unbounded? If the objective function were to minimize cost, would the solution be unbounded?
7. It has been said that if there are two optimal solutions to a linear programming problem, there must be an infinite number of optimal solutions. Explain.
8. A manager has used linear programming to determine how to get the greatest profit for his company. In obtaining the solution to the linear programming problem, the manager finds that the solution is unbounded. What should the manager do?
9. A manager has used linear programming to determine how to get the greatest profit for his company. In obtaining the solution to the linear programming problem, the manager finds there is no feasible solution. What should the manager do?
10. Give two examples of constraints that would not be linear.
11. What is the standard form of a linear program?
12. What is a basic solution to a linear program?

PROBLEMS

13. Consider the following linear programming problem:

$$\text{Maximize Profit} = 8X_1 + 5X_2$$
$$\text{Subject to: } 3X_1 + 4X_2 \leq 36$$
$$3X_1 + 2X_2 \leq 24$$
$$X_1, X_2 \geq 0$$

    a) Solve this using the corner-point method.
    b) Solve this using the iso-profit method.
    c) Is the point $X_1 = 5$, $X_2 = 5$ a feasible point? If it is not, which constraint is violated?
    d) Is the point $X_1 = 3$, $X_2 = 7$ a feasible point? If it is not, which constraint is violated?
14. Write the previous problem in standard form. Give the values for all variables at the feasible corner points. Each of these feasible corner points is a basic feasible solution. Which variables are set equal to zero in finding each of these basic solutions?

15. Consider the following linear programming problem:

$$\text{Maximize Profit} = 5X_1 + 2X_2$$
$$\text{Subject to: } 2X_1 + X_2 \leq 8$$
$$2X_1 + 3X_2 = 12$$
$$X_1, X_2 \geq 0$$

a) By simply looking at the constraints, describe the shape of the feasible region.
b) Solve this using the corner-point method.

16. Consider the following linear programming problem:

$$\text{Maximize profit} = 4X_1 + 10X_2$$
$$\text{Subject to: } X_1 + X_2 \leq 10$$
$$2X_1 + 4X_2 \leq 24$$
$$3X_1 + X_2 \leq 27$$
$$X_1, X_2 \geq 0$$

a) Solve this graphically.
b) What is the maximum possible profit for this situation?
c) How much slack is there for each constraint at the optimal solution?

17. Write the previous problem in standard form. Give the values for all variables at the feasible corner points (basic feasible solutions). Which variables are set equal to zero in finding each of these basic solutions?

18. Consider the following linear programming problem:

$$\text{Maximize profit} = 5X_1 + 4X_2$$
$$\text{Subject to: } 2X_1 + X_2 = 8$$
$$3X_1 + 4X_2 \leq 24$$
$$3X_1 + 4X_2 \geq 2$$
$$X_1, X_2 \geq 0$$

a) Solve this graphically.
b) What is the maximum possible profit for this situation?
c) In the optimal solution, how much slack is there in the second constraint?
d) In the optimal solution, how much surplus is there in the third constraint?

19.

$$\text{Minimize cost} = 10X_1 + 15X_2$$
$$\text{Subject to: } 4X_1 + 2X_2 \geq 12$$
$$2X_1 + 4X_2 \geq 16$$
$$X_1 \geq 2$$
$$X_1, X_2 \geq 0$$

a) Find the optimal solution.
b) How much surplus is there for each constraint?

20. Solve the following linear program graphically.

$$\text{Minimize cost} = 4X_1 + 5X_2$$
$$\text{Subject to: } X_1 + X_2 = 20$$
$$X_2 \geq 6$$

$$X_1 \geq 5$$
$$X_1, X_2 \geq 0$$

21. Solve the following linear program graphically.

$$\text{Minimize cost} = 12X_1 + 10X_2$$
$$\text{Subject to: } X_1 + X_2 \geq 8$$
$$3X_1 + X_2 \geq 12$$
$$4X_1 - 2X_2 \leq 24$$
$$X_1, X_2 \geq 0$$

22. What special condition exists for the following problem?

$$\text{Maximize profit} = 2X_1 + 5X_2$$
$$\text{Subject to: } 2X_1 + X_2 \geq 8$$
$$X_1 \geq 4$$
$$X_1, X_2 \geq 0$$

23. What special condition exists for the following problem?

$$\text{Maximize profit} = 10X_1 + 8X_2$$
$$\text{Subject to: } 3X_1 + 9X_2 \geq 36$$
$$X_1 \leq 8$$
$$X_1, X_2 \geq 0$$

24. Consider the following linear programming problem:

$$\text{Maximize profit} = X_1 + 2X_2$$
$$\text{Subject to: } X_1 + X_2 \leq 6$$
$$3X_1 + 6X_2 \leq 24$$
$$X_1, X_2 \geq 0$$

Solve this graphically. What special condition exists for this problem?

25. Solve the following problem graphically. What special condition exists?

$$\text{Maximize profit} = 12X_1 + 5X_2$$
$$\text{Subject to: } 5X_1 + 3X_2 \geq 30$$
$$2X_1 + 4X_2 \geq 20$$
$$X_1 \geq 4$$
$$X_1, X_2 \geq 0$$

26. Solve the following problem graphically. What special condition exists?

$$\text{Maximize profit} = 10X_1 + 8X_2$$
$$\text{Subject to: } 3X_1 + 3X_2 \geq 45$$
$$2X_1 + 4X_2 \leq 20$$
$$X_1 \leq 4$$
$$X_1, X_2 \geq 0$$

27. Consider the following linear programming problem:

$$\text{Maximize profit} = 4X_1 + 8X_2$$
$$\text{Subject to: } X_1 + X_2 \le 10$$
$$2X_1 + 4X_2 \le 24$$
$$X_1, X_2 \ge 0$$

a) What special condition exists for this problem?
b) What is the maximum possible profit?
c) Is the point (2,5) feasible? What is the profit at this point?
d) Is the point (12,0) feasible? Why or why not?

28. Consider the following linear programming problem:

$$\text{Maximize profit} = 8X_1 + 6X_2$$
$$\text{Subject to: } X_1 + 2X_2 \le 120$$
$$4X_1 + 3X_2 \le 240$$
$$X_1, X_2 \ge 0$$

a) What special condition exists for this problem?
b) What is the maximum possible profit?
c) Suppose a manager wishes to maximize profit, but if there are several possible ways to do this, the manager would like to maximize the total number of units produced. What solution would be selected by the manager in this situation?

29. Summer Fun Products produces wooden swing sets and picnic tables. The swing sets use 50 feet of wood and require four hours of labor. The picnic tables use 60 feet of wood and require three hours of labor. Currently the company has 3,000 feet of wood and 120 hours of labor available each week. The swing sets generate a profit of $40 each and the picnic tables generate a profit of $60 each. Due to a contract, the company must produce at least 15 swing sets each week. How many swing sets and picnic tables should be produced each week to maximize profit? What would the profit be for this? How much slack would exist for wood and labor hours?

30. Alpha Electronics produces video monitors in Montreal and Toronto. These are all sent to a computer manufacturer in the United States who sells them as part of a total computer system. Due to varying production and shipping costs, the cost of the monitors made in Montreal is $80 each while the cost of the monitors from Toronto is $90 each. The production capacity in Montreal is 20 units per week, while in Toronto it is 40 units per week. The current contract requires delivery of 50 units per week, and the company wishes to maintain a minimum production level of 75 percent of capacity at each location (15 at Montreal and 30 at Toronto). How many monitors should be produced at each of the two locations? What is the total cost?

31. A farmer grows wheat and corn on his land, and he would like to generate as much revenue as possible. Past experience shows that each acre of wheat will yield revenue of $800 and each acre of corn will yield revenue of $600. Each acre of wheat requires three labor hours while each acre of corn requires two labor hours. There are a total of 400 acres available for planting, and there are 900 labor hours available. Due to concerns for the soil and his history of

crop rotation, he has decided to plant no more than 240 acres in wheat this year.

How many acres should be planted in each crop? What is the total revenue? How many labor hours will be used?

32. Woofer Pet Foods produces a low calorie dog food for overweight dogs. This product is made from beef products and grain. Each pound of beef costs \$0.90 while each pound of grain costs \$0.80. A pound of the dog food must contain at least eight units of Vitamin #1 and 10 units of Vitamin #2. A pound of beef contains 10 units of Vitamin #1 and 12 units of Vitamin #2. A pound of grain contains six units of Vitamin #1 and nine units of Vitamin #2. Formulate this as a linear programming problem to minimize the cost of the dog food. How many pounds of beef and grain should be included in each pound of dog food? What is the cost and vitamin content of the final product?

33. A winner of the Texas Lotto has decided to invest \$50,000 per year in the stock market. Under consideration are stocks for a petrochemical firm and a public utility. While a long-range goal is to get the highest possible return, some consideration is given to the risk involved with the stocks. A risk index on a scale of 1–10 (with 10 being the most risky) is assigned to each of the two stocks. The total risk of the portfolio is found by multiplying the risk of each stock by the dollars invested in that stock.

The table below provides a summary of the return and risk.

Stock	Estimated Return Percentage	Risk Index
Petrochemical	12	9
Utility	6	3

The investor would like to maximize the return on the investment, but the average risk index of the investment should not be higher than six. How much should be invested in each stock? What is the average risk for this investment? What is the estimated return for this investment?

34. Referring to the situation in the previous problem, suppose the investor has changed his attitude about the investment and wishes to give greater emphasis to the risk of the investment. Now the investor wishes to minimize the risk of the investment as long as a return of at least eight percent is generated. Formulate this as a linear programming problem and find the optimal solution. How much should be invested in each stock? What is the average risk for this investment? What is the estimated return for this investment?

35. A candidate for mayor in a small town has allocated \$10,000 for last minute advertising in the days preceding the election. Two types of ads will be used—radio and television. Each radio ad costs \$200 and reaches an estimated 3,000 people. Each television ad costs \$500 and reaches an estimated 7,000 people. In planning the advertising campaign, the campaign manager would like to reach as many people as possible, but she has stipulated that at least 10 ads of each type must be used. Also, the number of radio ads must be at least as great as the number of television ads. How many ads of each type should be used? How many people will be reached?

36. The Modest Oil Company produces a premium gasoline for use with high performance engines. This gasoline is blended from two types of crude oil—

WT23 and AR15. Each of these contain two ingredients important to the performance of the gasoline as well as other inert ingredients. The costs and ingredients for these two crudes are given below:

Crude	Cost per Barrel	Percentage Ingredient A	Percentage Ingredient B
WT23	\$16	40	45
AR15	\$20	60	30

The premium gasoline must be at least 52 percent Ingredient A. In addition to this, the amount of AR15 used in the gasoline cannot be more than twice the amount of WT23. The company would like to minimize the cost of production of this gasoline.

Formulate this as a linear programming problem to determine how to mix these crudes to produce premium gasoline and solve. What will the cost of one barrel of gasoline be? If the gasoline were blended according to this mix, how much of Ingredients A and B would be in each barrel of gasoline?

37. The Modest Oil Company in the previous problem also produces a regular gasoline that must be at least 45 percent of Ingredient A. The amount of WT23 used in this gasoline must be at least as great as the amount of AR15. Formulate this as a linear programming problem and solve. What will the cost of one barrel of gasoline be? If the gasoline were blended according to this mix, how much of Ingredients A and B would be in each barrel of gasoline?
38. Referring to the previous two problems, suppose the Modest Oil Company must produce at least 2,000 barrels of the premium gasoline and at least 1,500 barrels of the regular gasoline. Currently the company only has 2,100 barrels of WT23 and 1,700 barrels of AR15 available. The company wishes to minimize the cost of production. Formulate this as a linear programming problem. Do not attempt to solve the resulting problem. (*Hint:* Use two variables for the amounts of the crudes used for premium gasoline and two other variables for the amounts of the crudes used in regular gasoline.)
39. A sporting goods manufacturer is developing a production schedule for two types of racquetball racquets. An order has been received for 180 of the regular model and 90 of the professional model. These are to be delivered at the end of this month. Another order has been received for 200 of the regular model and 120 of the professional model, but these are not to be delivered until the end of next month. Production in each of the two months may be in regular time or overtime. In the current month, a regular racquet may be produced at a cost of \$40 on regular time, while a professional model may be produced at a cost of \$60 on regular time. Overtime raises the price of these to \$50 and \$70. Due to a new labor contract for next month, all costs will increase by 10 percent at the end of this month.

    The total number of racquets that may be produced in a month on regular time is 230; an additional 80 racquets may be produced using overtime each month. Given the large order for delivery at the end of next month, the company is considering producing some extra racquets this month and keeping them in storage until the end of next month. The cost for keeping these in inventory for one month is estimated to be \$2 per racquet.

Formulate this as a linear programming problem. Why is it impossible to solve this linear programming problem graphically?

ANALYSIS IN ACTION

Mulrooney and Sons

Mulrooney and Sons is a small business consulting firm that specializes in the development of computerized accounting systems. During the income tax season, the company tries to generate additional revenues by offering tax preparation services to the general public. Based on past experience, Mulrooney has decided to advertise in two ways—on the radio and in newspapers. As the busy tax season is approaching, he wishes to determine the best mix of advertising based on his previous experience. During the same period last year the company used seven radio ads and 10 newspaper ads each month.

This tax season, a monthly advertising budget of $4,000 per month for each of the next three months has been established. Each radio ad costs $200 and reaches 12,000 people. Each newspaper ad costs $250 and reaches 15,000 people. Mulrooney has decided that the total number of radio ads should be no more than the number of newspaper ads. He also would like to place at least five ads of each type.

Your job is to help Mulrooney and Sons develop an advertising plan for this year. Formulate this as a linear programming problem to maximize the audience reached, and solve this problem. Prepare a one-page summary report of your recommendations. This should be in a nontechnical form that is easily understood by a manager. This report should indicate the number of ads of each type to place each month, the monthly cost, and the number of people reached each month. Your report also should indicate how this optimal solution compares with the advertising policy of last year.

Linear Programming, Graphical Spreadsheet Example

Solve the following linear programming problem using the graphical method.

$$
\begin{aligned}
\text{Max} \quad & 4x + 5y \\
\text{st} \quad & 3x + 4y \leq 36 \\
& 4x + 3y \leq 36 \\
& x \geq 0 \\
& y \geq 0
\end{aligned}
$$

To solve this linear program graphically using Excel:

1. To graph the lines:
   Enter range of X values (cells A11 to A23 shown in spreadsheet).
   Put each line in the slope intercept form:

   $$3x + 4y = 36 \text{ becomes } y = (36 - 3x)/4$$
   $$4x + 3y = 36 \text{ becomes } y = (36 - 4x)/3$$

   Write equations for constraints and copy these (B11 to C23).
   Highlight the range of values for x and y (A11:C23).
   Select Chart Wizard.
   Specify XY chart.
   Select the chart for lines.
   Indicate the X range is in the first column in the range.
2. To find the point of intersection:
   Enter coefficients for the constraints (A27 to B28) and right-hand side values for the constraints (C27, C28).

Find the inverse of the matrix using the formulas shown in A31 to B32 or using the **Minverse** command. To use the Minverse command, highlight range for output of inverse matrix (A31 to B32), type =MINVERSE(A27:B28), and press Ctrl-Shift-Enter.

Multiply inverse matrix (A31 to B32) by the right-hand side values (C27, C28) to get solution (C31, C32) using the **Mmult** (matrix multiplication) command. To use this command, highlight cells for output of solution (C31:C32), type =MMULT(A31:B32,C27:C28), and press Ctrl-Shift-Enter.

3. Find objective function value for each corner point (C36 to C39). Select the best one.

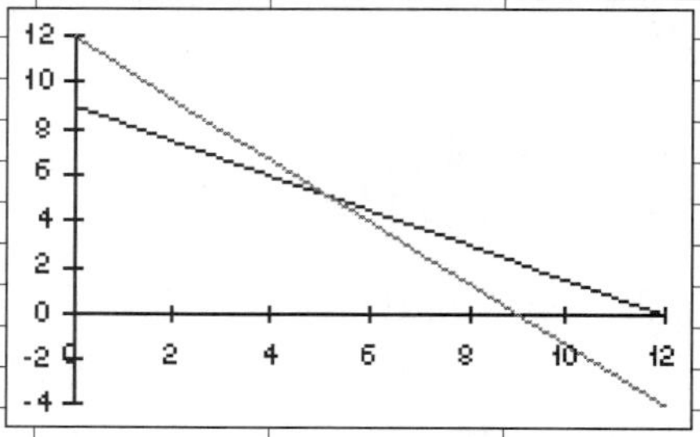

	A	B	C	D	E	F
1	Linear Programming , Graphical Example					
2						
3	Max 4x + 5y					
4	st 3x+4y<=36					
5	4x+3y<=36					
6	x>=0					
7	y>=0					
8						
9						
10	x	y1	y2			
11	0	9	12			
12	1	8.25	10.6666666			
13	2	7.5	9.33333333			
14	3	6.75	8			
15	4	6	6.66666666			
16	5	5.25	5.33333333			
17	6	4.5	4			
18	7	3.75	2.66666666			
19	8	3	1.33333333			
20	9	2.25	0			
21	10	1.5	-1.33333333			
22	11	0.75	-2.66666667			
23	12	0	-4			
24						
25	To find point of intersection using the matrix inverse method					
26	matrix		right side			
27	3	4	36			
28	4	3	36			
29						
30	matrix inverse		solution			
31	-0.4285714	0.5714285	5.14285714			
32	0.57142857	-0.4285714	5.14285714			
33						
34	corner points					
35	x	y	objective function value			
36	0	0	0			
37	0	9	45			
38	9	0	36			
39	5.14285714	5.1428571	46.2857142			

	A	B	C
1	Linear Programming , Graphical Example		
2			
3	Max 4x + 5y		
4	st 3x+4y<=36		
5	4x+3y<=36		
6	x>=0		
7	y>=0		
8			
9			
10	x	y1	y2
11	0	=(36-3*A11)/4	=(36-4*A11)/3
12	=A11+1	=(36-3*A12)/4	=(36-4*A12)/3
13	=A12+1	=(36-3*A13)/4	=(36-4*A13)/3
14	=A13+1	=(36-3*A14)/4	=(36-4*A14)/3
15	=A14+1	=(36-3*A15)/4	=(36-4*A15)/3
16	=A15+1	=(36-3*A16)/4	=(36-4*A16)/3
17	=A16+1	=(36-3*A17)/4	=(36-4*A17)/3
18	=A17+1	=(36-3*A18)/4	=(36-4*A18)/3
19	=A18+1	=(36-3*A19)/4	=(36-4*A19)/3
20	=A19+1	=(36-3*A20)/4	=(36-4*A20)/3
21	=A20+1	=(36-3*A21)/4	=(36-4*A21)/3
22	=A21+1	=(36-3*A22)/4	=(36-4*A22)/3
23	=A22+1	=(36-3*A23)/4	=(36-4*A23)/3
24			
25	To find point of intersection using the matrix inverse method		
26	matrix		right side
27	3	4	36
28	4	3	36
29			
30	matrix inverse		solution
31	=B28/(A27*B28-B27*A28)	=A28/(B27*A28-A27*B28)	=MMULT(A31:B32,C27:C28)
32	=B27/(B27*A28-A27*B28)	=A27/(A27*B28-B27*A28)	=MMULT(A31:B32,C27:C28)
33			
34	corner points		
35	x	y	objective function value
36	0	0	=4*A36+5*B36
37	0	9	=4*A37+5*B37
38	9	0	=4*A38+5*B38
39	=C31	=C32	=4*A39+5*B39
40			

CHAPTER THREE

Graphical Sensitivity Analysis and Computer Solutions

LEARNING OBJECTIVES

Upon completing Chapter 3, you should be able to:

- Know what sensitivity analysis is.
- Perform sensitivity analysis graphically.
- Interpret computer output.
- Explain how a change in the input of a linear program impacts the feasible region.
- Explain how a change in the feasible region impacts the optimal solution.
- Understand the terms redundant, binding, reduced cost, dual price, shadow price, and improvement index.
- Apply the 100% rule to changes in objective function coefficients and to changes in right-hand side values.

CHAPTER OUTLINE

3.1 INTRODUCTION

The world economy is constantly changing. New markets open while others close. Some suppliers are forced to shut their doors or abandon particular products just as other companies are entering the market. Prices may fluctuate for both raw materials and final products. Changing conditions may impose additional constraints on a problem or may eliminate constraints that are no longer necessary. Thus, a manager who has used linear programming to model a problem and has estimated many of the coefficients (or inputs to the model) may be hesitant to implement the optimal solution without additional analysis. The coefficients in a linear programming problem may represent such things as profit, cost, demand, and resource availability which may have been estimated and may not be completely accurate. Even if the estimates were accurate when first made,

Changing conditions, such as the availability of raw materials, may have a dramatic impact on the values in a linear programming model. SOURCE: Photo provided by Freeport-McMoRan Copper & Gold Company, Inc.

changing conditions may indicate the current values of these are not the same as the original values.

It is possible small changes in the data used in a linear programming problem may have a dramatic impact on the values of the decision variables and consequently on the decisions that are optimal. On the other hand, it is possible very large changes in some of the data may have no impact on the optimal solution. Also, there may be the potential for achieving a much better solution if additional resources could be obtained. Therefore, a manager may want to determine how sensitive the solution is to changes in the numbers used in the problem. A study of this type is referred to as **sensitivity analysis** or **postoptimality analysis**.

Most linear programming problems have more than two variables, and usually are solved with the aid of a computer. In this chapter we will provide a discussion of computer solutions as well as sensitivity analysis based on computer solutions. We will relate the computer output to the results obtained using graphical sensitivity analysis to aid in the understanding of the computer output.

Sensitivity analysis
A study of how the optimal solution of a linear program would change if some of the numbers used in the formulation of the problem were to change.

Postoptimality analysis
A study of how the optimal solution of a linear program would change if some of the numbers used in the formulation of the problem were to change.

3.2 B & B ELECTRONICS EXAMPLE REVISITED

Let us return to the example from Chapter 2 in which linear programming was used to determine that B & B Electronics should produce four cellular phones and 10 pagers each week. Upon evaluation, management decided this was an appropriate solution to the problem. However, new information has caused additional restrictions on the production schedule. The distributor who buys these products from B & B Electronics will purchase no more than 11 pagers each week and 20 items in total each week from B & B Electronics. There is also concern the costs associated with producing cellular phones were overestimated and the profit on these might be more than the $15 originally estimated. This has raised concern about the profit on pagers as well. Management wants to know if higher profits could be generated from a different production mix if the profits for phones and pagers vary from the original estimates. Also, the employees who provide assembly time and inspection time have expressed an interest in working overtime to obtain additional money. However, management does not know if the additional cost of overtime would cause total profits to decrease. Fortunately, sensitivity analysis may provide important information to help management in these situations, and we may rely on computers to perform most of the calculations associated with this sensitivity analysis.

3.3 SENSITIVITY ANALYSIS

We will investigate the impact of changing the objective function coefficients, changing the right-hand side values of the constraints, and adding or deleting a constraint. We will see how these types of changes impact not only the optimal value of the objective function, but also the values for the decision variables and the slack or surplus involved in the particular situation.

Binding
A constraint is considered binding when the optimal values of the decision variables cause the left-hand side of the constraint to equal the right-hand side. There is zero slack or surplus.

Nonbinding
A constraint is considered nonbinding when there is positive slack or surplus when the optimal values of the decision variables are put into the constraint.

Before beginning our discussion of sensitivity analysis, it is helpful to define some terms related to constraints. Recall from Chapter 2, a constraint that does not affect the feasible region is a redundant constraint. A redundant constraint may be added to, or removed from, a linear programming problem and the feasible region does not change. A constraint is said to be **binding** if, for the optimal values of the decision variables, the left-hand side of the constraint is equal to the right-hand side of the constraint. This means there is zero slack or surplus at the optimal solution. A constraint that does have positive slack or surplus for the optimal values of the decision variables is called a **nonbinding** constraint.

Key Concepts in Sensitivity Analysis

To understand sensitivity analysis, there are some key concepts to consider. These are:

1. An optimal solution to a linear programming problem will occur at a corner point of the feasible region and is a basic solution.
2. Changing an objective function coefficient has no effect on the feasible region or the feasible corner points. This may only impact which basic solution is optimal.
3. The only thing that may cause a change in the feasible region and, consequently, the basic feasible solutions, is a change in a constraint.

We will use these basic concepts with a modified example of the B & B Electronics example to illustrate different aspects of sensitivity analysis.

3.4

INTERPRETING COMPUTER OUTPUT

Consider the B & B Electronics example with two new restrictions placed on the situation due to demand considerations. Suppose the distributor who buys these products from B & B Electronics will purchase no more than 11 pagers each week and 20 items in total each week. Thus, the constraints

$$X_1 \leq 11$$

and

$$X_1 + X_2 \leq 20$$

would be added and we have the following problem:

$$\begin{aligned} &\text{Maximize profit} = 15X_1 + 20X_2 \\ &\text{Subject to: } 4X_1 + 2X_2 \leq 36 \quad \text{assembly hours} \\ &X_1 + 2X_2 \leq 24 \quad \text{inspection hours} \\ &X_2 \leq 11 \quad \text{demand for pagers} \\ &X_1 + X_2 \leq 20 \quad \text{total demand} \\ &X_1, X_2 \geq 0 \quad \text{nonnegativity constraints} \end{aligned}$$

A graph of this problem is seen in Figure 3.1. An iso-profit line shows the optimal solution is at the point (4,10). Notice the total demand constraint is redundant because it does not touch the feasible region. The demand for pagers constraint is a nonbinding constraint because there is some slack (the constraint line is not touching the optimal corner point), but it is not redundant because it does help define the feasible region. If it were eliminated, the feasible region would change.

Because there are still only two decision variables in this problem, it may be solved graphically or with the aid of a computer. Because we will be using information from computer output to help with further sensitivity analysis, we will present the output from the LINDO software package in Output 3.1.

To facilitate the discussion of sensitivity analysis, we will write this problem in standard form:

$$\begin{aligned} &\text{Maximize profit} = 15X_1 + 20X_2 \\ &\text{Subject to: } 4X_1 + 2X_2 + S_1 = 36 \\ &X_1 + 2X_2 + S_2 = 24 \\ &X_2 + S_3 = 11 \\ &X_1 + X_2 + S_4 = 20 \\ &X_1, X_2, S_1, S_2, S_3, S_4 \geq 0 \end{aligned}$$

FIGURE 3.1

B & B Electronics with Four Constraints

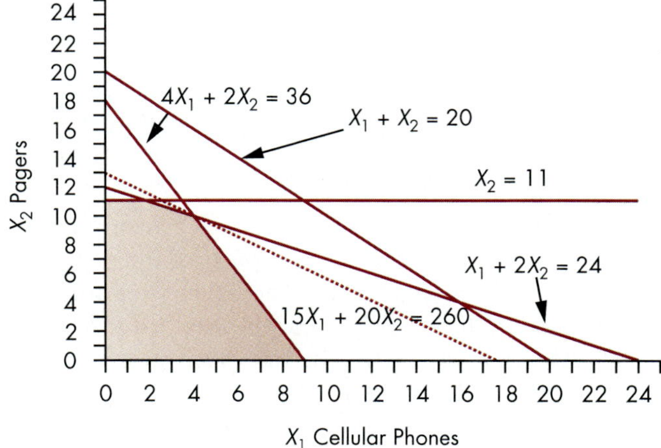

OUTPUT 3.1

LINDO Output for Expanded B & B Electronics Example

```
MAX      15 X1 + 20 X2
SUBJECT TO
       2)    4 X1 + 2 X2 <=   36
       3)    X1 + 2 X2 <=   24
       4)    X2 <=   11
       5)    X1 + X2 <=   20
END

      OBJECTIVE FUNCTION VALUE

      1)     260.00000

VARIABLE         VALUE          REDUCED COST
      X1          4.000000           .000000
      X2         10.000000           .000000

     ROW   SLACK OR SURPLUS     DUAL PRICES
      2)          .000000        1.666667
      3)          .000000        8.333333
      4)         1.000000         .000000
      5)         6.000000         .000000

 RANGES IN WHICH THE BASIS IS UNCHANGED:

                         OBJ COEFFICIENT RANGES
VARIABLE        CURRENT        ALLOWABLE        ALLOWABLE
                  COEF          INCREASE         DECREASE
     X1       15.000000        25.000000         5.000000
     X2       20.000000         9.999999        12.500000

                         RIGHTHAND SIDE RANGES
     ROW        CURRENT        ALLOWABLE        ALLOWABLE
                   RHS          INCREASE         DECREASE
       2      36.000000        36.000000         6.000000
       3      24.000000         1.500000        15.000000
       4      11.000000         INFINITY         1.000000
       5      20.000000         INFINITY         6.000000
```

The optimal corner point (4,10) is the basic solution with $S_1 = 0$ and $S_2 = 0$ because it occurs at the intersection of the first two constraints.

The LINDO output in Output 3.1 is typical of the output from many linear programming software packages. The linear programming problem is restated in the output. The decision variables are listed with their values and a reduced cost value. We see that the values for X_1 and X_2 are 4 and 10 respectively. The objective function value (profit) is \$260.

Reduced cost
The amount by which the objective function coefficient for a decision variable would have to improve before the optimal solution would include that variable with a positive value.

The reduced cost is zero for both decision variables. For a decision variable with a value of zero, the **reduced cost** tells how much the objective function coefficient would have to improve before the optimal solution could include that variable with a positive value. For example, if the optimal solution had called for making no pagers, the reduced cost would tell us by how much the unit profit on pagers would need to increase to allow us to make some of these and still maximize profit. In this example, however, both decision variables had positive values, and the reduced cost always will be zero for variables with positive values.

There were four constraints in the problem, and LINDO identifies these by row numbers 2 through 5. The objective function was identified as row number 1. The slack or surplus is given for each constraint. There is no slack in each of the first two constraints, but there is one unit of slack in the third constraint ($X_2 \leq 11$) because $X_2 = 10$ in this solution. There are also six units of slack in the last constraint because $X_1 + X_2 = 4 + 10 = 14$, which is six units less than 20. Also given for each constraint is a dual price. The **dual price** tells how much the objective function value would change if the right-hand side of the constraint were changed by one unit. Dual prices will be discussed in detail in a later section. The dual price for the first constraint is 1.666667 and for the second constraint is 8.333333. The dual price for each of the last two constraints is .000000.

Dual price
The improvement in the objective function value that results from a one unit increase in the right-hand side of a constraint.

The last portion of the output contains additional information about changes in the problem's original numbers. These ranges are a part of the sensitivity analysis performed by the computer.

Output 3.2 provides the output for the DSS software. Notice the values for all nonzero variables are provided. Any variable not listed has a value of zero. The improvement index instead of dual price is provided, and this has an interpretation similar to that of the dual price. Further discussion of this is provided later in this chapter.

Graphical methods, both the iso-profit method and the corner point method, provide some very valuable insights into sensitivity analysis. Consequently, we will consider the graphical methods to help us more fully understand the computer output.

3.5 CHANGES IN OBJECTIVE FUNCTION COEFFICIENTS

It is very important to remember that the feasible region is defined by the constraints in the problem. Therefore, *any change in the objective function will have absolutely no effect on the feasible region*, and consequently there is no change in the basic feasible solutions. The optimal solution must occur at one of these basic feasible solutions, which are the corner points of the feasible region.

Management of B & B Electronics originally estimated the profit on cellular phones to be \$15 each. However, it might be \$16, \$20, or some other value. Would changes in the profit on cellular phones result in a change in the manufacturing decisions? For the sake of illustration, we will consider profits of \$16, \$20, \$40, and \$41. Will the optimal solution change if the profit on X_1 is \$10? Will it change if the profit on X_1 is \$41? While we will see that these questions may be answered from the computer output, we will begin by using a graphical method of illustrating these changes.

OUTPUT 3.2

Decision Support Software (DSS) Output for Expanded B & B Electronics Example

```
Linear Programming

Z         X1        X2        Rel Op    R H S
MAX       15        20
Cons1     4         2         <=        36
Cons2     1         2         <=        24
Cons3     0         1         <=        11
Cons4     1         1         <=        20

SOLUTION:
Variable       Value
--------       --------
X1              4
X2              10
Slack 3         1
Slack 4         6

MAX       Z         =  260

SENSITIVITY ANALYSIS (Cj's):

Basis Variables
~~~~~~~~~~~~~~~

Variable   Value      Low        Current    High
--------   --------   --------   --------   --------
X1          4          10        15          40
X2          10         7.50000   20          30

Nonbasis Variables
~~~~~~~~~~~~~~~~~~

Variable   Value      Low        Current    High       Impr  Indx
--------   --------   --------   --------   --------   --------

SENSITIVITY ANALYSIS (Bi's):

Binding Constraints
~~~~~~~~~~~~~~~~~~~

Constraint Value      Low        Current    High       Impr Indx
---------- --------   --------   --------   --------   --------
Cons1       0          30        36          72        -1.666667
Cons2       0          9         24          25.5      -8.333333

Nonbinding Constraints
~~~~~~~~~~~~~~~~~~~~~~

Constraint Value      Low        Current    High
---------- --------   --------   --------   --------
Cons3       1          10        11         +INF
Cons4       6          14        20         +INF

Note: A '%' indicates rounding occurred to fit display space
```

TABLE 3.1

Changes in Objective Function Coefficients

Feasible Corner Points	Profit for Different Objective Functions				
(X_1, X_2)	$15X_1 + 20X_2$	$16X_1 + 20X_2$	$20X_1 + 20X_2$	$40X_1 + 20X_2$	$41X_1 + 20X_2$
(0,0)	0	0	0	0	0
(0,11)	220	220	220	220	220
(9,0)	135	144	180	360*	369*
(4,10)	260*	264*	280*	360*	364
(2,11)	250	252	260	300	302

*Indicates optimal solution

Graphical Analysis

Using the corner point method, we recognize that the feasible corner points are the same regardless of the objective function. To find the optimal corner point, we simply evaluate the objective function at each of these points. One of these points must be optimal. Table 3.1 provides a summary of the objective function values for profits of \$15, \$16, \$20, \$40, and \$41 on cellular phones.

Consider a change from \$15 to \$16 on the profit for X_1. Notice in Table 3.1 that the maximum profit still is generated at the point (4,10); it is simply \$4 more than it was before the change. This \$4 increase in total profit may be intuitive because we are producing four units of X_1 and we have increased the profit for X_1 by \$1 per unit. If we increase the profit by \$5 (from \$15 to \$20), the total profit will increase by

$$(\$5 \text{ per unit})(4 \text{ units}) = \$20$$

This \$4 increase in total profit will continue for each dollar increase in profit on X_1 as long as this remains the optimal corner point. At some point the profit on X_1 will be so high that a new corner point will be optimal. This may be seen graphically or by looking at information provided in the computer printout.

Figure 3.2 provides iso-profit lines for each of these objective functions. Notice that changing the objective function coefficient for X_1 changes the slope of the profit line. As a result, the profit line rotates. As the profit line is rotated, the same corner point is optimal until the objective function line is parallel to one of the constraint lines (when profit on X_1 is \$40), which happens when the two lines have the same slope. If we rotate beyond that point, another corner point is optimal so other production decisions must be made. If we do exceed this allowable increase and raise profit to \$41, we see in Table 3.1 that we would maximize profit by producing nine cellular phones ($X_1 = 9$) and no pagers ($X_2 = 0$).

FIGURE 3.2

Changing Profit Lines for B & B Electronics Example

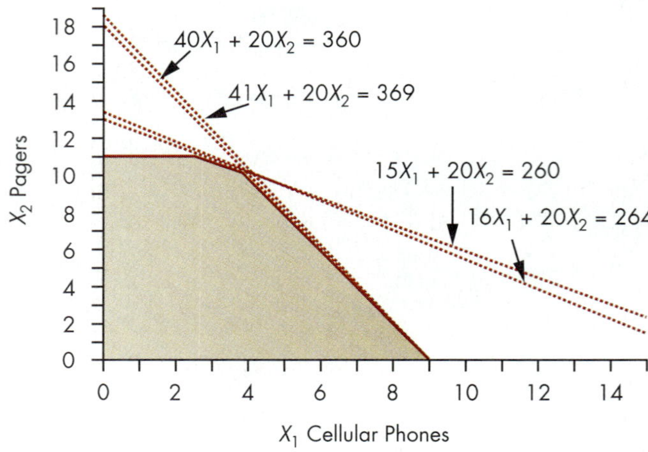

Computer Output

While the graphical method helps to illustrate what happens when objective function coefficients change, we will normally rely on the use of a computer to obtain this information. Looking at the OBJ COEFFICIENT RANGES column in Output 3.1 above, we see that the profit on X_1 is currently \$15 with an allowable increase of \$25 and an allowable decrease of \$5. The current solution is optimal as long as any change in the profit on X_1 is within these allowable amounts. Thus, the profit on cellular phones (X_1) may be increased by up to \$25 (to \$40) or decreased by up to \$5 (to \$10) before the optimal corner point changes. In Table 3.1 above we saw that when the profit on X_1 exceeded \$40, the optimal corner point did change. As long as the changes are within the appropriate ranges, the same basic solution remains optimal. Thus, the values for all decision variables and the amounts of slack and surplus do not change. The only thing that may change is the value of the objective function. It should be noted that if the change in an objective function coefficient exactly equals the allowable change, there will be multiple optimal solutions. Thus, the current solution remains optimal, but there also is another basic solution that is optimal.

Summary Table 3.1 summarizes what may happen if an objective function coefficient is changed. If a change is made in the objective function coefficient for one decision variable between the upper and lower limits, the values for all of the decision variables as well as the slack and surplus will not change. This occurs because the optimal corner point does not change. The objective function value will change by the amount of the change times the number of units of that decision variable in the optimal solution. This is clearly seen by referring to Table 3.1. If there are zero units being produced, then the objective function value will not change.

If the change puts the coefficient below the lower limit or above the upper limit, the objective function value and the values for some of the variables will

SUMMARY TABLE 3.1

Effect of Changes in Objective Function Coefficients

If change is within allowable limits, current basic solution remains optimal.
1. Values of all decision variables do not change.
2. Amounts of slack and surplus do not change.
3. Objective function value may change.

If change is equal to allowable limit, there are multiple optimal solutions.

If change is outside allowable limits, new basic solution becomes optimal.
1. Values of decision variables may change.
2. Amounts of slack and surplus may change.
3. Objective function value may change.

change because the optimal solution will be at a different corner point. The new problem may be solved on the computer to find these values. These rules may be used to evaluate the effect of a change in one of the coefficients in the objective function while all other coefficients remain constant.

While it is helpful to see how decisions would change if one of the objective function coefficients changed, managers at B & B Electronics may wish to know how decisions would change if the profits on both products

A management decision to use overtime in assembly hours is a change to the right-hand side of a constraint in a linear program. SOURCE: Courtesy of Newell Company

were modified simultaneously. Suppose the profit on cellular phones is only \$12 while the profit on pagers is \$28. To determine what would happen to production decisions if these coefficients are changed simultaneously, we may not use the rules given above because they relate to the impact of a change in one single coefficient while holding all other values constant. However, we may use the *100% rule* to examine the impact of simultaneous changes.

100% Rule for Simultaneous Changes in Objective Function Coefficients

100% rule for objective function coefficients

If each change in an objective function coefficient is expressed as a percentage of the allowable change, and if all the percentage changes do not add up to more than 100 percent, then the values for the decision variables in the optimal solution to a linear programming problem will not change although the objective function value itself may change.

As was seen in the previous section, a single coefficient either may increase or decrease by up to 100 percent of a specified allowable amount and the optimal solution (corner point) will not change. If several objective function coefficients are changed simultaneously, the current solution will remain optimal if the total of the changes expressed as percentages of the allowable changes is not more than 100 percent. This is referred to as the **100% rule for objective function coefficients.** If the total change is over 100 percent, we should solve the problem after the changes have been made as the optimal solution may be the current solution or it may be a different one.

Consider the B & B Electronics example. What would happen if the profit on cellular phones (X_1) is only \$12 and the profit on pagers (X_2) is \$28? Because the profit of \$12 represents a decrease of \$3 from the current value and the allowable decrease is \$5, this decrease is (3/5)100% = 60% of the allowable amount of decrease. Also, the increase in profit on X_2 to \$28 represents an \$8 increase. Because the allowable increase is \$10, this increase is (8/10)100% = 80% of the allowable amount. The total percentage change is 60% + 80% = 140%. Because this total percentage change is greater than 100 percent, the solution (corner point) that was previously optimal may no longer be optimal. You may verify to yourself that the optimal solution in this particular problem has changed by calculating the profit of $12X_1 + 28X_2$ for each of the feasible corner points. These results are shown in Table 3.2.

TABLE 3.2

Illustration of 100% Rule for Objective Function Coefficients

Feasible Corner Points	Profit for Different Objective Functions		
(X_1, X_2)	Original $15X_1 + 20X_2$	140% Change $12X_1 + 28X_2$	200% Change $40X_1 + 30X_2$
(0,0)	0	0	0
(0,11)	220	308	330
(9,0)	135	108	360
(4,10)	260*	328	460*
(2,11)	250	332*	410

* Indicates optimal solution

Linear Programming to Help a Plant Closure

The United States Department of Energy (DOE) requires microchips meet a high radiation tolerance level. In the early 1980s, no private sector companies could produce chips to meet this specification. Therefore, the DOE opened the Albuquerque Microelectronics Organization (AMO), and hired AlliedSignal Aerospace Company Inc. to manage and operate the facility. By 1989, however, commercial semiconductor companies had refined their processes enough to be able to manufacture suitable radiation-hardened chips. Because DOE policy calls for contracting with private suppliers whenever possible, the government decided to phase out the AMO, and purchase the chips from commercial suppliers.

At the time of the decision, some custom-designed products manufactured at the AMO already were available from commercial suppliers. Others were still in the planning phase. Phasing out production at the AMO gradually was necessary, while the private companies were bringing up production. This was a difficult task to manage, particularly because once the DOE announced the decision to close the facility, many AMO technical personnel sought other employment. Also, there was some uncertainty about when the chips would be available from the commercial suppliers. Eventually, they decided to close the plant in one year, and to produce a set amount of chips within that time.

The production planning and control department was asked to develop monthly production schedules for the different kinds of chips during the closure period. They did this manually. They based their schedules on the existing work in the system, the desire to decrease the number of different products in production (by completing those products with small volumes as soon as possible), and the capacity limitations for each product. The ad hoc nature of this schedule generation, however, left the department feeling uncomfortable with the plan. They decided to use linear programming to develop a more systematic production plan.

SOURCE:
Clements, D. W., and R. A. Reid, March-April 1994. "Analytical MS/OR Tools Applied to a Plant Closure." *Interfaces* 24(2): 1-12.

They formulated an LP model to maximize the number of chips scheduled for manufacture during the 12-month period, subject to upper and lower bounds on each product. This maximization was equivalent to minimizing future DOE costs, because the more the AMO could produce itself, the less it would have to purchase later from suppliers. The LP model ultimately produced results similar to those derived with the manual approach. This increased the confidence of both the customers and members of the production team. The LP model later was used to do a sensitivity analysis to assess customers' requests for changes in order quantities and product mix. The model showed, for example, the AMO could meet a request by a customer for more product, midway through the closure period. Without this information, they would have refused the request.

The LP model, used with a forecasting model, directly contributed to the closure of the facility three months ahead of schedule. The models helped by providing more accurate production lot scheduling, and also by planning and scheduling other phase-out activities. By closing three months early, the AMO avoided $1.2 million in expenditures.

To emphasize the fact that the optimal solution may sometimes not change even if the total percent change in objective function coefficients is more than 100 percent, consider the following situation. Suppose the unit profit on cellular phones increased by $25 (to $40), which is 100 percent of the allowable increase, while the profit on pagers increased by $10 (to $30), which also is 100 percent of the allowable increase. While the total percentage change is 200 percent, the optimal solution has not changed. This may be verified by evaluating the corner points once again, as shown in Table 3.3.

The 100% rule may be helpful to a manager who has estimated the profit for each of the products and recognizes that these estimates are not exact, but has some degree of confidence in the range of one of these. For example, the profit on the cellular phones (X_1) was originally estimated to be \$15, but perhaps the manager is absolutely certain that the profit is no less than \$12. As was calculated above, this would represent a decrease of 60 percent of the allowable amount. Thus, we know that the current solution is guaranteed to be optimal as long as the profit on pagers (X_2) is no further away from \$20 than 40 percent of the allowable increase or decrease. Suppose we are concerned that profit on X_2 may be higher than \$20. Because the allowable increase is \$10, if the true profit on X_2 is no more than 40%(\$10) = \$4 higher than \$20, the current solution must remain optimal. Thus, if the manager feels confident the profit on X_1 is at least \$12 and the profit on X_2 is no more than \$24, the manager should be confident about the production decisions based on the optimal solution to this linear programming model.

3.6

CHANGES IN CONSTRAINTS—RIGHT-HAND SIDE VALUES

There were four constraints in the B & B Electronics problem—assembly hours, inspection hours, demand for pagers, and total demand. Management may wish to evaluate the possibility of using overtime in assembly or inspection. Management also may wish to evaluate possible changes in demand to determine how production decisions would be affected. All of these types of changes relate to changing the right-hand sides of the constraints.

Because the feasible region is defined by the constraints in the problem, a change in the right-hand side of one of the constraints will have an impact on the feasible region unless that constraint is redundant. This change in the feasible region may or may not impact the optimal solution. If the problem is solved with available computer software, part of the output will provide information concerning the impact of such a change on the optimal solution, although there are numerous terms used for this.

Dual Price, Shadow Price, and Improvement Index

Shadow price
The change in the objective function value that results from a one unit change in the right-hand side of a constraint.

The change in the value of the objective function as a result of a change in the right-hand side of a constraint is called a dual price, shadow price, or improvement index. While some authors define dual prices and shadow prices exactly the same, other authors define a dual price as the *improvement* in an objective function value for a one unit increase in the right-hand side of a constraint and a **shadow price** as the *increase* in an objective function value. For maximization problems an improvement and an increase are the same, but for minimization problems an improvement would be a decrease in the objective function value. It is not uncommon in solving a problem using two different software packages to find a dual price or shadow price reported as positive in the output of one and negative in the output of the other. We will use the most common definition of dual price and say it is the improvement in the objective function value due to a one unit increase in the right-hand side of a constraint.

However, to eliminate confusion in the interpretation of dual prices, shadow prices, and improvement indices in computer output, it is best to simply ignore the sign of the dual price, shadow price or improvement index and logically think about the change in the feasible region and the resulting change in the objective function value. Thus, *a dual price, shadow price, or improvement index gives the change in the objective function value that results from a one unit change in the right-hand side of a constraint. If the constraint is relaxed, the objective function value will improve; if the constraint is tightened, the objective function value will worsen.* A change in the right-hand side of a constraint is a relaxation if it causes the feasible region to get larger. Thus, increasing the right-hand side of a ≤ constraint or decreasing the right-hand side of a ≥ constraint would be a relaxation. Both of these changes make a constraint less restrictive and add points to the feasible region. These will be illustrated in the examples that follow. A relaxation of an equality constraint is not as clear because any change in the right-hand side eliminates all the points that were previously feasible and adds an entirely new set of points to the feasible region.

In evaluating the change in the right-hand side of a constraint, it is helpful to consider two distinct situations. The first involves nonbinding constraints while the second involves binding constraints.

Changes in Right-Hand Sides of Nonbinding Constraints

The optimal solution to the revised B & B Electronics problem is at the corner point (4,10). Looking at the objective function and the four constraints for this, we have

$$\text{Profit} = 15X_1 + 20X_2 = 260$$
$$\text{Assembly hours used} = 4X_1 + 2X_2 = 36 \text{ (36 available, } S_1 = 0)$$
$$\text{Inspection hours used} = X_1 + 2X_2 = 24 \text{ (24 available, } S_2 = 0)$$
$$\text{Number of pagers} = X_2 = 10 \text{ (11 limit, } S_3 = 1)$$
$$\text{Total number produced} = X_1 + X_2 = 14 \text{ (20 limit, } S_4 = 6)$$

Notice the third and fourth constraints each have slack in the optimal solution, as seen in the LINDO output in Output 3.1 above. The dual price for each of these is zero. The maximum number of pagers allowed is 11, but we only wish to produce 10 of these to maximize profit. Thus, there is a slack of 11 – 10 = 1 unit for the third constraint.

Consider the demand for pagers constraint ($X_2 \leq 11$), which has one unit of slack. Management may be considering an attempt to increase the demand for this product by using another distributor. To see how an increase in demand would impact profits and production, we may evaluate a change in the right-hand side of this constraint. Because the dual price for this constraint is zero, profits would not change if the demand increased. To see why this occurs, consider the graph in Figure 3.3. An increase in the right-hand side of this constraint to 12 (i.e., the constraint is relaxed) will increase the size of the feasible region, but the optimal objective function value (profit) will remain the same. Using the iso-profit method we see that the optimal corner point has not changed although the feasible region has gotten larger. There will simply be more slack for this third constraint because the value of X_2 is still 10 while the right-hand side (demand) has increased. If this right-hand side is increased again, there will simply be more

FIGURE 3.3

Change in Right-Hand Side of Constraint 3

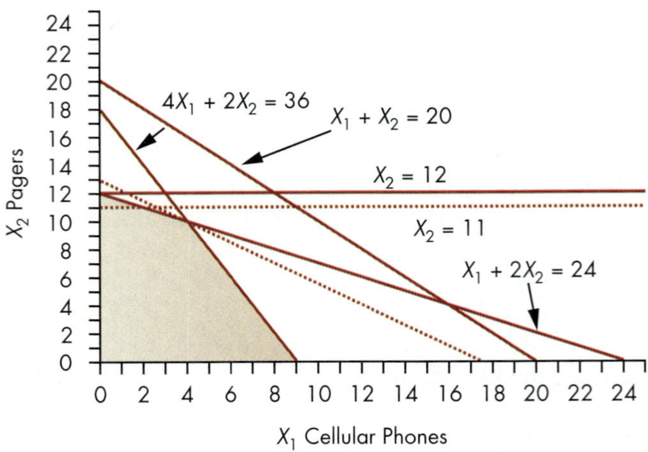

slack. The right-hand side of this constraint can be increased without limit and this will only impact the slack for this constraint. This could have been seen by looking at the LINDO output in Output 3.1 above, which indicated the allowable increase for the right-hand side of this constraint was infinity.

If the right-hand side of this constraint is decreased from 11 to 10 (i.e., the constraint is tightened), then the size of the feasible region will decrease. However, the optimal corner point (4,10) remains feasible so it remains optimal and only the amount of slack for this constraint changes. The right-hand side of this constraint may be reduced by the amount of the slack without impacting the optimal solution. Thus, if the right-hand side is changed to 10, the point (4,10) is still feasible and optimal, but there will be no slack for this constraint. If the right-hand side is decreased to nine units, then the point (4,10) will no longer be feasible and the optimal solution must change. The allowable decrease for this right-hand side amount from the LINDO output in Output 3.1 above was one unit.

From this example we see that *for a nonbinding ≤ constraint, the right-hand side of the constraint may be increased by any amount or decreased by the amount of the slack and the value of the objective function, and all of the decision variables do not change because the same basic solution is still optimal.* For nonbinding ≥ constraints, the right-hand side may be decreased by any amount or increased by the amount of the surplus and the same basic solution will remain optimal.

Changes in Right-Hand Sides of Binding Constraints

If a constraint representing a limited resource is binding and thus has no slack, then all of that resource is being utilized. Obtaining additional units of that resource will usually mean a better solution can be achieved. Management may wish to consider using overtime to obtain additional hours if the resource is time. If the resource is a raw material, perhaps paying a premium of some type will allow additional units to be obtained. Output from computer software will provide valuable information that may help management decide whether or not to use additional resources.

A change in the amount of a scarce resource in a linear programming model is the equivalent of a change in the right-hand side value for a constraint that has no slack. In the B & B Electronics problem, there are 36 hours of assembly time available originally, and these are all being utilized in the optimal solution ($S_1 = 0$). If through overtime or other means the assembly time is increased by one unit so there are 37 hours available, then the feasible region gets larger as shown in Figure 3.4. The point (4,10) is no longer a corner point and so it is no longer a basic solution. The point where the assembly constraint line and the inspection constraint line intersect is now (4.33,9.83). Thus, the basic solution where $S_1 = 0$ and $S_2 = 0$ is still the optimal solution although the values for the decision variables have changed from (4,10) to (4.33,9.83).

Notice the number of units of X_1 is increasing while the number of units of X_2 is decreasing. This frees up some inspection time to be used with the additional assembly time. The profit at this new corner point is \$261.67, which is \$1.67 higher than the original profit. If the right-hand side is increased by one more unit to 38, profits again increase by \$1.67. Thus, \$1.67 is the dual price for assembly hours because profits increase by this amount for each additional hour of assembly time. This increase is due to a change in the values of X_1 and X_2 (the number of cellular phones and pagers) in the optimal basic solution.

Right-Hand Side Ranges

This change in profit due to a change in assembly hours will continue to be \$1.67 per hour until an upper limit or lower limit for assembly time (right-hand side value) is reached. The computer output in Output 3.1 above

FIGURE 3.4

Assembly Hours Increased to 37

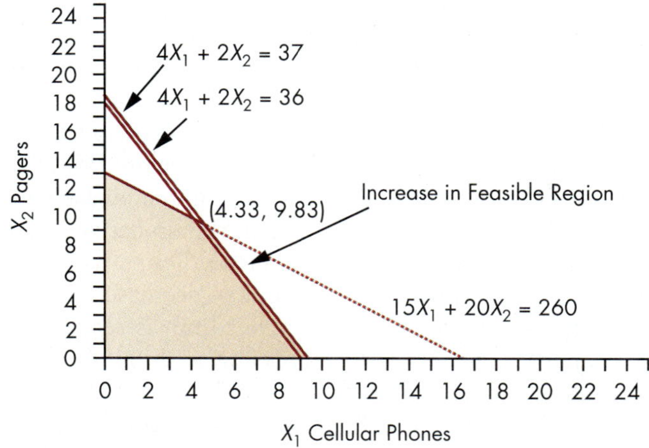

FIGURE 3.5

Assembly Hours Increased to 72

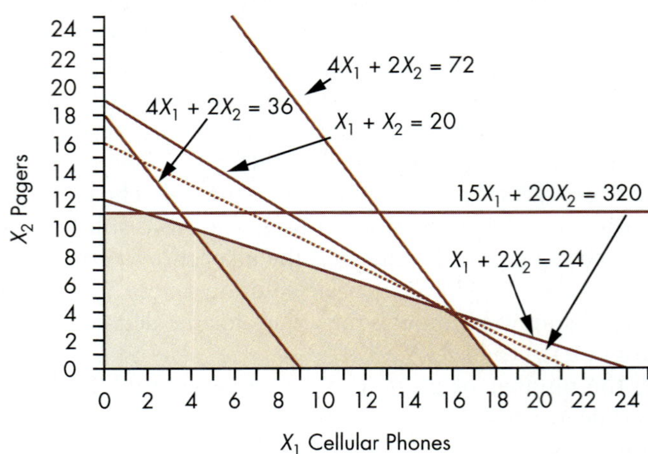

shows that the allowable increase in assembly time (row 2) is 36. Thus, profit will increase \$1.67 (the amount of the dual price) for each additional hour of assembly time up to a maximum of 36 additional hours. Figure 3.5 illustrates graphically what occurs when this limit is reached. If there are a total of 72 hours available, three constraint lines will intersect at the point (16,4). The constraints with the slack variables added are:

$$4X_1 + 2X_2 + S_1 = 72$$
$$X_1 + 2X_2 + S_2 = 24$$
$$X_1 + X_2 + S_4 = 20$$

Notice the total demand constraint ($X_1 + X_2 \leq 20$) has positive slack ($S_4 > 0$) until the assembly hours are increased to 72. If assembly hours are increased beyond 72 hours, the total demand constraint becomes a binding constraint, and additional assembly hours will no longer increase profits by \$1.67 per additional hour. Thus, the dual price for assembly hours will no longer be relevant. Figure 3.6 shows the feasible region if the assembly hours are increased to 80 hours. An inspection of the feasible region and the slope of the objective function will indicate that the optimal corner point occurs at (16,4).

While this discussion has concentrated on increasing the amount of a resource (relaxing the constraint), the dual price provides information about a decrease in the amount of a resource (tightening the constraint) as well. If the assembly constraint is tightened, the objective function value will get worse. Thus, a decrease of one assembly hour will cause the profit to decrease by \$1.67, and profit will continue to decrease by \$1.67 for each hour decrease in assembly time until a lower limit is reached. Of importance to the manager is the fact that increasing or decreasing the assembly hours will increase or decrease profit by \$1.67 (the dual price) per assembly hour as long as the increase or decrease is within a particular range.

FIGURE 3.6

Assembly Hours Increased to 80

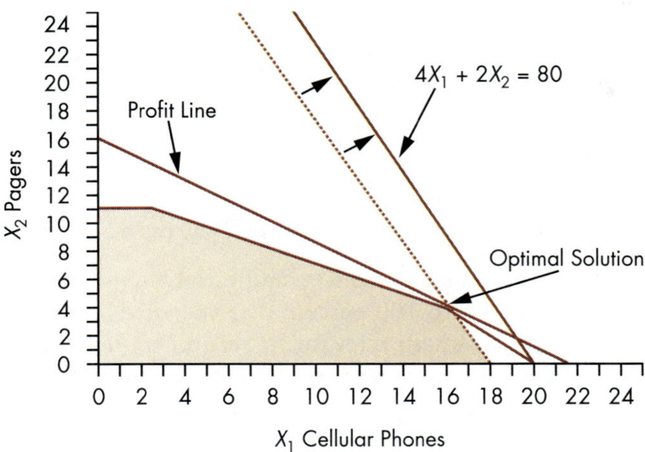

This would help a manager decide whether it would be profitable to use overtime or other means to gain additional assembly hours.

Summary of Changes in Right-Hand Sides

We have presented the graphical explanation of sensitivity analysis to provide a basis for understanding what is happening as right-hand side values are changed in a linear programming problem, and we have seen the computer output that presents this same information. A summary is given in Summary Table 3.2.

SUMMARY TABLE 3.2

Impact of Changes in Right-Hand Side Values

If change is within allowable limits

For nonbinding constraints (positive slack or surplus)

1. No change for values of decision variables.
2. Amount of slack and/or surplus changes for that constraint only.
3. Objective function value does not change (dual price is zero).

For binding constraint (zero slack or surplus)

1. Values of decision variables may change.
2. Amounts of slack and/or surplus may change for many constraints.
3. Objective function value changes described by dual price.

If change is outside allowable limits

All constraints

1. Values of decision variables may change (new basic solution is optimal).
2. Amounts of slack and/or surplus may change for many constraints.
3. Objective function value changes, but dual price is not relevant.

The explanations that have been provided regarding changes in the right-hand side of a constraint relate to the change in one single constraint. Management may be interested in obtaining additional resources of several types. For example, B & B Electronics may be considering increasing both the assembly hours and the inspection hours available. This would involve simultaneous changes in the right-hand sides of several constraints. The dual prices could be used to evaluate changes in these right-hand sides individually, but we must use the 100% rule to evaluate simultaneous changes in several of the right-hand side values.

100% Rule for Simultaneous Changes in Right-Hand Side Values

As was seen in the previous section, a single right-hand side value may increase or decrease by up to 100 percent of a specified allowable amount and the dual prices will remain relevant. *If several right-hand side values are changed simultaneously, the dual prices may be used to determine the change in the value of the objective function if the total of the percentage changes for these is not more than 100 percent.* This is referred to as the **100% rule for right-hand side values.** If the total change is over 100 percent, we should solve the problem with the changes as the dual prices may no longer be relevant.

100% rule for right-hand side values

If each change to the right-hand side value of a constraint is expressed as a percentage of the allowable change, and if all the percentage changes do not add up to more than 100 percent, then the dual prices may be used to determine the change in the objective function value.

Suppose that B & B Electronics is considering increasing the number of assembly hours by 12 hours per week and increasing the inspection hours by one hour. From Output 3.1 above we see the allowable increase for assembly hours is 36, so an increase of 12 hours is 33.3 percent of the allowable increase. Similarly, a one hour increase in inspection hours represents a 66.7 percent increase because the allowable increase is 1.5. Therefore, the total increase is 33.3% + 66.7% = 100%, and consequently the dual prices are relevant for these changes. Thus, total profit would increase by

(1.67 per hour)(12 hours) + (8.33 per hour)(1 hour) = $28.37

The basic solution where $S_1 = 0$ and $S_2 = 0$ remains the optimal basic solution, but the values of X_1 and X_2 at this point have changed due to the change in the right-hand side value. Thus, by changing the values for the decision variables (numbers of cellular phones and pagers made), an increase in profit is achieved. If the increase in either resource had been more than the given amount, the total percentage increase would have exceeded 100 percent, and the problem would have to be solved again after making the changes.

3.7 A LARGER EXAMPLE

Conrich Audio produces compact disk (CD) players in Louisville, Kentucky. A portable CD player has been added to the line to complement the regular model and the deluxe model. Each of these must be assembled, inspected, and packaged before shipping. The number of minutes required for each of these is given in Table 3.3.

Limited resources restrict the number of CD players that may be produced. There are 250 hours (15,000 minutes) available each week in the assembly process, 50 hours (3,000 minutes) available in the inspection process, and 40 hours (2,400 minutes) available in the packaging process. In addition to limits on these resources, the company is constrained by contracts to provide at least 10 portable CD players and a total of at least 50 of the other two types. To help the company develop weekly production

TABLE 3.3

Minutes Required in Conrich Audio Example

	Type of CD		
Department	**Portable**	**Regular**	**Deluxe**
Assembly	120	130	150
Inspection	20	35	30
Packaging	15	15	20

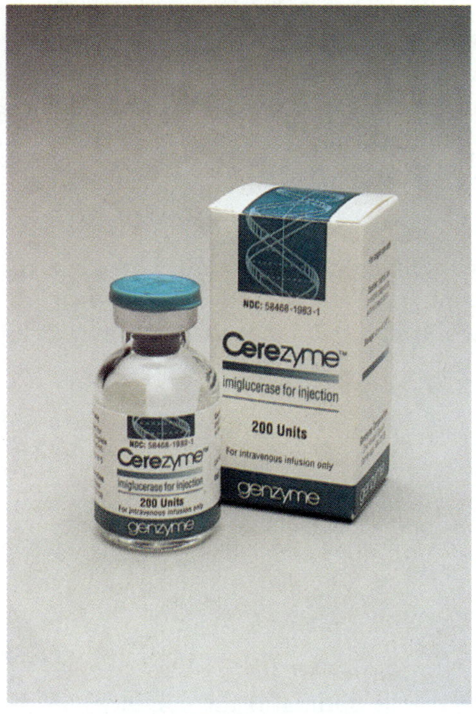

Awaiting U.S. regulatory review of new products, such as herbicides, may affect a linear program used by a production manager. SOURCE: Courtesy of Genzyme Corporation

plans that will maximize profits, the company has formulated the following linear programming problem:

X_1 = number of portable CD players produced each week
X_2 = number of regular CD players produced each week
X_3 = number of deluxe CD players produced each week

$$
\begin{array}{lll}
\text{Maximize profit} = 25X_1 + 30X_2 + 35X_3 & & \\
\text{Subject to: } 120X_1 + 130X_2 + 150X_3 \le 15{,}000 & & \text{assembly minutes} \\
20X_1 + 35X_2 + 30X_3 \le 3{,}000 & & \text{inspection minutes} \\
15X_1 + 15X_2 + 20X_3 \le 2{,}400 & & \text{packaging minutes} \\
X_1 \ge 10 & & \text{contract for portables} \\
X_2 + X_3 \ge 50 & & \text{contract for others} \\
X_1, X_2, X_3 \ge 0 & & \text{nonnegativity constraints}
\end{array}
$$

This problem was solved using LINDO, and the output is provided in Output 3.3. We see that a profit of \$3,470 per week may be generated by producing 10 of the portable CDs ($X_1 = 10$), none of the regular CDs ($X_2 = 0$), and 92 of the deluxe CDs ($X_3 = 92$). With this production plan, there is no slack in the first constraint (row 2) so all 15,000 minutes of assembly time are utilized. There are 40 minutes of slack in the second constraint (row 3) so only 2,960 minutes (3,000 – 40) of the available 3,000 inspection minutes are being used. There are 410 minutes of slack in the third constraint (row 4), so only 1,990 minutes (2,400 – 410) of the available 2,400 minutes of packaging time are being used. The computer output indicates there is zero surplus for the fourth constraint (row 5), and because $X_1 = 10$, we see that the minimum number is being produced. In the last constraint (row 6), we see that the number of the regular and deluxe CD players produced is

$$X_2 + X_3 = 0 + 92 = 92$$

which exceeds the minimum number of 50. Therefore, there is a surplus of 42 for this constraint.

Putting this problem in the standard form we have:

$$
\begin{array}{lll}
\text{Maximize profit} = 25X_1 + 30X_2 + 35X_3 & & \\
\text{Subject to: } 120X_1 + 130X_2 + 150X_3 + S_1 = 15{,}000 & & \text{assembly minutes} \\
20X_1 + 35X_2 + 30X_3 + S_2 = 3{,}000 & & \text{inspection minutes} \\
15X_1 + 15X_2 + 20X_3 + S_3 = 2{,}400 & & \text{packaging minutes} \\
X_1 - S_4 = 10 & & \text{contract for portables} \\
X_2 + X_3 - S_5 = 50 & & \text{contract for others} \\
X_1, X_2, X_3, S_1, S_2, S_3, S_4 \ge 0 & & \text{nonnegativity constraints}
\end{array}
$$

The basic solution that is optimal is the one in which $X_2 = 0$, $S_1 = 0$, and $S_4 = 0$. As long as changes are within the allowable ranges, the optimal solution will remain the basic solution in which these three variables are equal to zero.

OUTPUT 3.3

LINDO Output for Conrich Audio Example

```
 MAX     25 X1 + 30 X2 + 35 X3
 SUBJECT TO
        2)    120 X1 + 130 X2 + 150 X3 <=   15000
        3)    20 X1 + 35 X2 + 30 X3 <=   3000
        4)    15 X1 + 15 X2 + 20 X3 <=   2400
        5)    X1 >=   10
        6)    X2 + X3 >=   50
 END

LP OPTIMUM FOUND AT STEP       4

       OBJECTIVE FUNCTION VALUE

       1)      3470.0000

 VARIABLE        VALUE          REDUCED COST
       X1       10.000000           .000000
       X2         .000000           .333334
       X3       92.000000           .000000


      ROW   SLACK OR SURPLUS     DUAL PRICES
       2)         .000000           .233333
       3)       40.000000           .000000
       4)      410.000000           .000000
       5)         .000000         -3.000000
       6)       42.000000           .000000

 NO. ITERATIONS=        4

 RANGES IN WHICH THE BASIS IS UNCHANGED:

                             OBJ COEFFICIENT RANGES
VARIABLE          CURRENT        ALLOWABLE         ALLOWABLE
                    COEF          INCREASE          DECREASE
     X1         25.000000        3.000000          INFINITY
     X2         30.000000         .333334          INFINITY
     X3         35.000000        INFINITY           .384616

                             RIGHTHAND SIDE RANGES
     ROW          CURRENT        ALLOWABLE         ALLOWABLE
                    RHS           INCREASE          DECREASE
       2      15000.000000      200.000000       6300.000000
       3       3000.000000        INFINITY         40.000000
       4       2400.000000        INFINITY        410.000000
       5         10.000000       52.500000         10.000000
       6         50.000000       42.000000          INFINITY
```

Changes in Objective Function Coefficients

Management may be concerned that if the optimal solution were implemented, there would be no regular CDs produced. To understand this, the sensitivity analysis portion of the output is helpful. We see the reduced cost for regular CDs (X_2) is .333334. This means if we were to produce one of the regular CD players, total profit would decrease by .333334. This is due to the fact that some of the assembly hours currently being used to produce the other products would have to be used to produce regular CD players, thus reducing the numbers of the other CD players that could be produced. The allowable increase in the OBJ COEFFICIENT RANGES column is this same value of .333334. This says a new basic solution would become the optimal solution if the unit profit on X_2 were increased by more than .333334 because it would then be profitable to produce X_2. Thus, it would no longer be optimal to allow X_2 to remain equal to zero. If the unit profit on X_2 were increased by exactly .333334, the current solution would still be optimal, but there also would be another optimal solution. The infinite allowable decrease on the profit for X_2 indicates that any decrease in profit will not change the optimal solution.

If the profit on portable CD players (X_1) were to change by $1 per unit, the total profit would change by $10 because there are 10 units of X_1 being produced. The optimal solution will remain at the same corner point and total profit will continue to change in this same fashion as long as the change in profit on X_1 does not exceed the allowable increase or decrease limit. Thus, if the profit on X_1 increased by $3, total profit would increase by $30. If the profit increased by $4, which exceeds the allowable increase limit, another corner point would be optimal and we would have to solve this problem again. However, we can say that if profit increased by $4 per unit, total profit would increase by at least $30 because the allowable increase is $3 and there are 10 units being produced. Notice that the allowable decrease is infinity, which means this solution remains optimal for any decrease in the profit on X_1. This is because the fourth constraint (row 5) requires at least 10 portable CD players to be produced, and the optimal solution calls for exactly this minimum number of 10.

If the profit on deluxe CD players (X_3) were increased, this same basic solution will remain optimal because the allowable increase is infinity. Total profit would simply increase by $92 for each $1 increase in profit on X_3 because this solution calls for the production of 92 deluxe CD players ($X_3 = 92$). If the profit were to decrease by more than .384616 (the allowable decrease on X_3), the problem would have to be solved again as another basic solution would be optimal.

As long as the changes in the objective function coefficients are within the ranges indicated, the same basic solution will be optimal, which means the values for all decision variables and the amount of slack and surplus for all constraints will remain exactly the same as they are in this solution.

Changes in Constraints

If management wishes to evaluate the impact of adding more time for assembly, inspection, or packaging, the dual prices and right-hand side ranges (RHS) will help. The dual prices and RHS ranges also will tell us how the contracted minimums for portable CD players and other CD players would impact total profit.

All 15,000 minutes of assembly time are being used because there is no slack for this constraint. The dual price for this is .233333, which means that profits will increase by .233333 for each additional minute (within limits) of assembly time that we obtain. The RHS range for this constraint shows an allowable increase of 200 minutes and an allowable decrease of 6,300 minutes. Profits will continue to change by .233333 per minute change in assembly time within this range. The values for X_1 and X_3 will be changing to generate the change in total profit, while the number of units of X_2 will remain at zero. The amounts of slack and surplus for the constraints also would be changing, although any constraint with zero slack or surplus (the first and fourth constraints) would continue to have zero slack or surplus as long as the change in assembly minutes is within the indicated ranges. This is because the basic solution found as the basic solution where these are set equal to zero remains optimal.

The surplus for the fourth constraint is zero, and the dual price for this is –3. This means if we increase the right-hand side of this constraint by one unit the total profit will decrease by \$3. Notice this constraint is a ≥ constraint, and increasing the right-hand side from 10 to 11 would actually reduce the size of the feasible region. Thus, the objective function value would get worse (decrease). A decrease in this right-hand side from 10 to 9 would result in an increase of \$3 in total profit. The change in total profit would result from changing the number of units of portable CD players (X_1) and deluxe CD players (X_3) that are being produced. The number of units of regular CD players (X_2) would remain at zero. This will be true as long as the change in the minimum number of units of portable CD players (RHS of the third constraint) is not more than a 10-unit decrease or more than a 52.5-unit increase.

Management would notice there is slack for both the inspection minutes and packaging minutes. The dual price for both of these is zero, meaning that some changes in the number of minutes available would have no impact on total profits. We could decrease the inspection minutes by up to 40 minutes per week, and this same solution would remain optimal. Notice the allowable decrease is simply the amount of slack. Similarly, we could decrease the packaging hours by up to 410 minutes per week and the current solution would remain optimal. Increasing either of these would simply increase the amount of slack and would not change profits or the value for any of the decision variables.

The surplus for the last constraint is 42 units. We could increase the RHS of this constraint by up to 42 units and the current solution would remain optimal. The profits would continue to be \$3,470 and we would continue to produce 10 portable CD players and 92 deluxe CD players. The only thing that would change would be the amount of surplus for this last constraint.

The computer output obtained using DSS with the Conrich Audio problem is given in Output 3.4. An interpretation based on this output would be similar to the previous discussion of the LINDO output with improvement indices taking the place of the dual prices.

OUTPUT 3.4

DSS Output for Conrich Audio Example

```
Linear Programming

Z         X1        X2        X3        Rel Op    R H S
MAX       25        30        35
Cons1     120       130       150       <=        15000
Cons2     20        35        30        <=        3000
Cons3     15        15        20        <=        2400
Cons4     1         0         0         >=        10
Cons5     0         1         1         >=        50

SOLUTION:

Variable       Value
--------       --------
X1              10
X3              92
Slack 2         40
Slack 3         410
Slack 5         42

MAX       Z          =  3470

SENSITIVITY ANALYSIS (Cj's):

Basis Variables
~~~~~~~~~~~~~~~

Variable    Value        Low          Current      High
--------    --------     --------     --------     --------
X1           10          -INF         25            25
X3           92           34.6153     35           +INF

Nonbasis Variables
~~~~~~~~~~~~~~~~~~

Variable    Value        Low          Current      High         Impr Indx
--------    --------     --------     --------     --------     --------
X2           0           -INF         30            30.3333     -.333334

SENSITIVITY ANALYSIS (Bi's):

Binding Constraints
~~~~~~~~~~~~~~~~~~~

Constraint Value         Low          Current      High         Impr Indx
---------- --------      --------     --------     --------     --------
Cons1        0            8700        15000         15200       -.2333333
Cons4        0            9.53674     10            62.5        -3

Nonbinding Constraints
~~~~~~~~~~~~~~~~~~~~~~

Constraint Value         Low          Current      High
---------- --------      --------     --------     --------
Cons2        40           2960        3000         +INF
Cons3        410          1990        2400         +INF
Cons5        42          0 (-INF)     50            92

Note: A '%' indicates rounding occurred to fit display space
```

BEST PRACTICES

FINA Optimizes Raw Material Purchases and Product Distribution

SOURCE: FINA Annual Report, 1993.

FINA, Inc. is involved with crude oil and natural gas exploration and production, natural gas marketing, petroleum products refining, and chemicals manufacturing. In 1992, the company faced historically low profit margin levels and low demands. The circumstances were a response to weak economic growth in many parts of the world. Anticipating this difficult business environment, FINA spent 1993 trying to strengthen its balance sheet and position itself for future growth.

A key component in FINA's strategic plan was to control operating expenses. The Supply and Transportation Division helped by using optimization to minimize both raw material purchases and the cost of product distribution. By also improving coordination between the supply and marketing functions, the company could maintain supplies consistently, with no shortages. This in turn strengthened FINA's marketing position within the industry.

FINA's Research and Technology Center also contributed to the company's drive to reduce costs and increase sales. Researchers at the center employed optimization to select

Courtesy FINA, Inc.

catalysts at the styrene monomer plant. They also optimized process changes in the asphalt blending process. Both optimization models contributed to cost savings and profitability improvements.

Overall, and with the help of optimization models, FINA could characterize 1993 as a "year of improvement." The company reduced debt, improved operational results, and increased earnings, compared with the previous year.

3.8 ADDITION OR DELETION OF CONSTRAINTS

Upon examining the optimal solution to a linear programming problem, it is not uncommon for a manager to find that one or more constraints were inadvertently omitted when the problem was formulated. Perhaps a minimum number of units for each of several products was assumed but not explicitly stated; or limited warehouse space may have been overlooked. New government regulations may place additional restrictions on a particular decision making problem. These situations could cause additional constraints to be added to the linear programming problem. It also is possible some restrictions in a problem may become unnecessary due to government deregulation or other changes in the economy. This would result in the deletion of one or more constraints.

Because the feasible region is defined by the constraints in the problem, adding a new constraint or deleting one of the existing constraints will potentially have an impact on the feasible region. Consequently, the value of the objective function, as well as the values for the decision variables in the optimal solution, may be impacted by changes of this type.

B & B Electronics Example

Consider the B & B Electronics example previously presented. If we consider the problem with only the assembly-hour constraint and the inspection-hour constraint, we have the following:

$$\begin{aligned} \text{Maximize profit} &= 15X_1 + 20X_2 \\ \text{Subject to: } 4X_1 + 2X_2 &\le 36 \quad \text{assembly hours} \\ X_1 + 2X_2 &\le 24 \quad \text{inspection hours} \\ X_1, X_2 &\ge 0 \quad \text{nonnegativity constraints} \end{aligned}$$

A graph of this and the optimal profit line are seen in the first graph in Figure 3.7. The optimal solution has a profit of \$260. This is obtained by producing four cellular phones ($X_1 = 4$) and 10 pagers ($X_2 = 10$).

Adding Constraints

Suppose in addition to the constraints previously given, the demand for pagers (X_2) dictates that no more than 11 of these be produced. Thus, the constraint

$$X_1 \le 11$$

would be added and we have the following problem:

$$\begin{aligned} \text{Maximize profit} &= 15X_1 + 20X_2 \\ \text{Subject to: } 4X_1 + 2X_2 &\le 36 \quad \text{assembly hours} \\ X_1 + 2X_2 &\le 24 \quad \text{inspection hours} \\ X_2 &\le 11 \quad \text{demand for pagers} \\ X_1, X_2 &\ge 0 \quad \text{nonnegativity constraints} \end{aligned}$$

A graph of this revised problem is seen in the second graph in Figure 3.7 above. Notice that adding this new constraint reduces the size of the feasible region. However, the optimal solution to the original problem is still feasible, and consequently it will still be the optimal solution. *If the optimal solution satisfies a new constraint, then it must remain the optimal solution because no new points have been added to the feasible region.* If this new constraint were $X_2 \le 6$, then the previous solution would no longer be feasible (because $X_2 = 10$ in the original solution), and the new corner points would have to be evaluated to find the new optimal solution.

If it is determined that total production should not exceed 20 units due to limited demand, then the constraint $X_1 + X_2 \le 20$ would be added to the previous three constraints in the problem. This new constraint would not change the feasible region as seen in the third graph in Figure 3.7, and we also see this is a redundant constraint. A redundant constraint may be added to or removed from a linear programming problem and the feasible region does not change.

Thus, it is impossible to get a better solution by adding a constraint because no new points are added to the feasible region; but it is possible for the objective function value to get worse because some points may be eliminated from the feasible region.

FIGURE 3.7

Two Constraints Added to B & B Electronics Problem

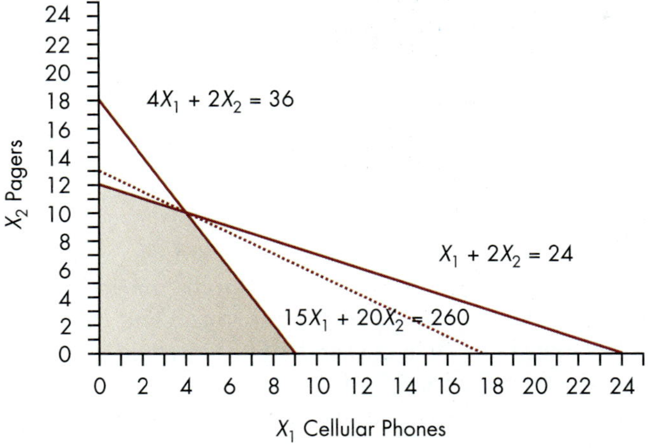

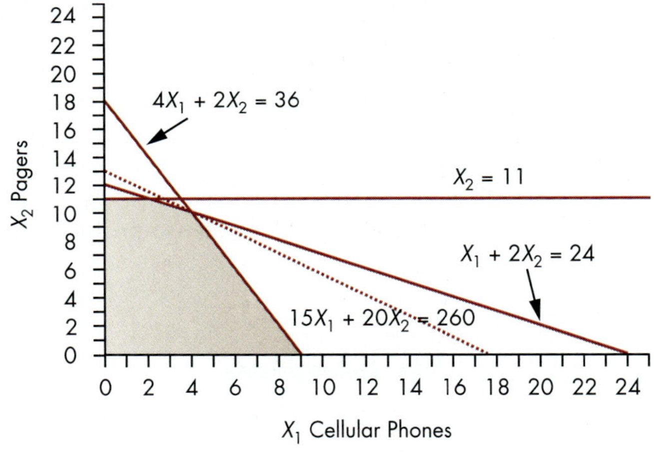

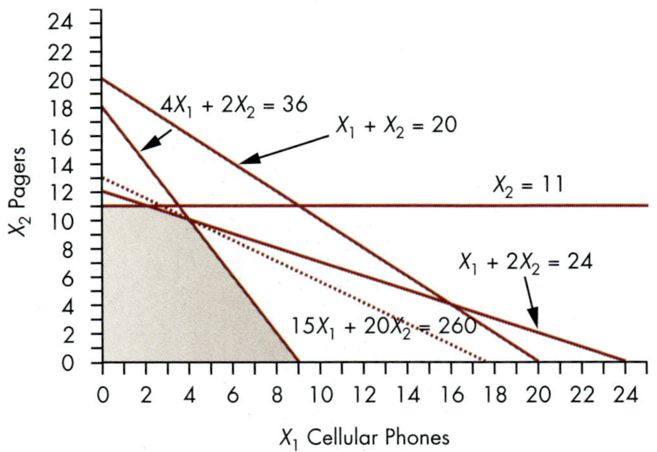

Deleting Constraints

On the other hand, if a constraint is removed from a linear programming problem, the feasible region will either get larger or stay the same. If the constraint that is removed is not redundant, the feasible region gets larger and more points are available for consideration. Thus, the optimal solution must be at least as good as the previous optimal solution. If a redundant constraint is removed from a linear programming problem, the feasible region stays the same, and thus the optimal solution cannot change.

By considering the B & B Electronics example with the constraints $X_2 \leq 11$ and $X_1 + X_2 \leq 20$ as seen in the third graph in Figure 3.7, we can see what happens when constraints are removed. If expanding markets caused the redundant constraint $X_1 + X_2 \leq 20$ to be unnecessary and consequently this constraint was removed from the problem, the feasible region would not be changed and thus the same solution would be optimal as seen in the second graph in Figure 3.7. If the constraint $X_2 \leq 11$ were similarly rendered unnecessary and was removed from the problem as shown in the first graph in Figure 3.7, the feasible region would get larger, but the optimal solution would be at the same corner point so the optimal solution would not change. Note that both of these constraints have slack in the optimal solution and are nonbinding.

If a binding constraint similar to the inspection-hours constraint were removed, the previous optimal solution would usually no longer be a basic solution, and thus a new optimal solution would exist. Figure 3.8 shows the feasible region for the B & B Electronics problem with the assembly-hours constraint removed but with the other three constraints remaining in the problem. The optimal solution found using the iso-profit method would

FIGURE 3.8

Feasible Region with One Constraint Deleted

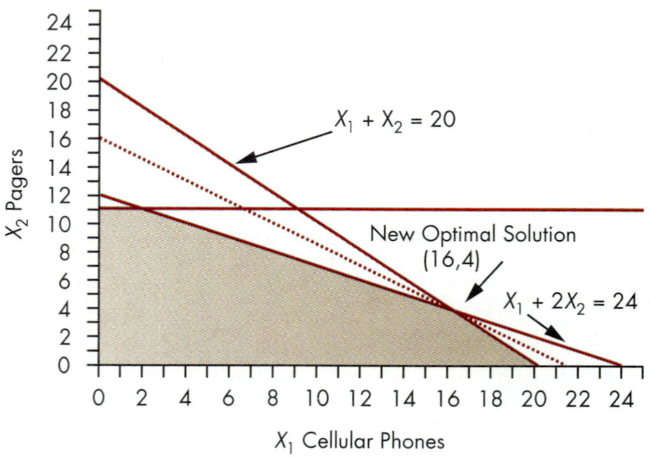

SUMMARY TABLE 3.3

Addition or Deletion of a Constraint

Addition of a constraint
1. Feasible region gets smaller or stays the same.
2. Objective function value gets worse if previous solution violates the new constraint, or it stays the same if previous solution satisfies the new constraint.

Deletion of a constraint
1. Feasible region gets larger or stays the same.
2. Objective function value gets better or stays the same.

be $X_1 = 16$ and $X_2 = 4$. Note that the redundant constraint $X_1 + X_2 \leq 20$ is no longer redundant when the assembly constraint is removed.

Thus, *when a constraint is removed from a linear programming problem, the objective function value for the optimal solution will either improve or stay the same because new points may be added to the feasible region.* It will improve if one of the new points added to the feasible region has a better objective function value than the previous optimal solution. The results from adding or deleting a constraint are summarized in Summary Table 3.3.

The managerial implications of adding or deleting a constraint are clear. If a constraint is added to a linear programming problem, a manager may simply check to see if the optimal solution satisfies the new constraint. If it does satisfy the constraint, it is still optimal. If it does not satisfy the constraint, the problem should be solved again with the new constraint included. If a constraint is removed from a linear programming problem, the current solution will remain optimal if there was slack for the constraint that is removed. If there was no slack for the constraint that is removed, the linear programming model without this constraint should be solved to obtain the new solution.

3.9

CHANGES IN CONSTRAINT COEFFICIENTS

We have considered what happens if changes are made in the objective function coefficients and the right-hand side values for constraints. In addition to these, the only other numbers seen in a linear programming problem are the coefficients for the decision variables in these constraints. We will call these the constraint coefficients. In the B & B Electronics example, some of the constraint coefficients represented the assembly hours required per cellular phone or per pager. Improvements in technology may cause these values to change. Changing one of these in a constraint changes the slope of the constraint, and consequently may change the shape of the feasible region. If such a change has occurred and you wish to determine the impact of this on the optimal solution, you should simply solve the problem again after making the change.

3.10

SUMMARY

In this chapter we looked at how a manager may view the final solution to a linear programming problem. We saw that adding a constraint may cause the objective function value to get worse, while deleting a constraint may cause the objective function value to get better.

Changing an objective function coefficient will either change the value of the objective function while leaving all variables unchanged, or it will cause a new corner point to become optimal. The objective function coefficient ranges provided by linear programming software indicate how large the change must be to cause a new solution to be optimal.

Obtaining additional resources or relaxing certain constraints may result in increased profits. The amount of change in the objective function value for each additional unit of a resource is given by the dual price or the shadow price. If the incremental cost of an additional unit of a resource is less than the gain seen from the dual price, then obtaining that additional unit would have a positive impact on total profit.

The right-hand side ranges provided in computer output indicate to what extent the dual price is relevant. As long as the increase or decrease in the amount of the resource is not more than the allowable increase or decrease, the objective function value will change by the amount of the dual price for each unit change in the right-hand side value.

The only numbers found in a linear programming problem for which no sensitivity information is available are the constraint coefficients. If changes are made in these, the revised problem should simply be solved on the computer.

This aspect of analyzing linear programming solutions is perhaps the most important to a manager, as this should give some measure of confidence to a manager who is estimating much of the data used in the linear program. If minor changes in the data result in major changes in the decisions, then perhaps additional work should be devoted to obtaining more accurate or more current estimates for these numbers. If major changes have little or no impact on the optimal solution, then a manager should be comfortable with the solution obtained through linear programming.

GLOSSARY

100% rule for objective function coefficients If each change in an objective function coefficient is expressed as a percentage of the allowable change, and if all the percentage changes do not add up to more than 100 percent, then the values for the decision variables in the optimal solution to a linear programming problem will not change although the objective function value itself may change. *p. 82*

100% rule for right-hand side values If each change to the right-hand side value of a constraint is expressed as a percentage of the allowable change, and if all the percentage changes do not add up to more than 100 percent, then the dual prices may be used to determine the change in the objective function value. *p. 90*

Binding A constraint is considered binding when

the optimal values of the decision variables cause the left-hand side of the constraint to equal the right-hand side. There is zero slack or surplus. *p. 74*

Dual price The improvement in the objective function value that results from a one unit increase in the right-hand side of a constraint. *p. 77*

Nonbinding A constraint is considered nonbinding when there is positive slack or surplus when the optimal values of the decision variables are put into the constraint. *p. 74*

Postoptimality analysis A study of how the optimal solution of a linear program would change if some of the numbers used in the formulation of the problem were to change. *p. 73*

Reduced cost The amount by which the objective function coefficient for a decision variable would have to improve before the optimal solution would include that variable with a positive value. *p. 76*

Sensitivity analysis A study of how the optimal solution of a linear program would change if some of the numbers used in the formulation of the problem were to change. *p. 73*

Shadow price The change in the objective function value that results from a one unit change in the right-hand side of a constraint. *p. 84*

SOLVED PROBLEMS

SOLVED PROBLEM 3-1

A company produces three models of desk chairs—superior, economy, and standard. Management wishes to maximize the profit given that certain resource limitations and demand limitations exist. The following linear program was developed to help with this decision:

X_1 = number of superior chairs to produce
X_2 = number of economy chairs to produce
X_3 = number of standard chairs to produce

$$\text{Maximize profit} = 40X_1 + 25X_2 + 30X_3$$

Subject to: $X_1 + X_2 + X_3 \leq 60$	materials
$4X_1 + 2X_2 + 3X_3 \leq 150$	labor hours
$X_1 \leq 25$	demand for superior
$X_2 + X_3 \geq 20$	contract requirement
$X_1, X_2, X_3 \geq 0$	nonnegativity constraints

This was solved using LINDO, and the printout is provided, as shown in Output 3.5. Use this to help answer the following questions.

a) How many of each model of chair will be produced? How much profit is generated?

b) How many labor hours are utilized if the optimal solution is used?

c) What would happen to profit if any standard chairs were produced instead of using the production schedule in part (a)?

d) How much would profits increase if one additional labor hour could be obtained?

e) What would happen to profits if 25 more labor hours could be obtained?

f) Using the original resources and solution, suppose the profit on a superior chair were increased to $45. What would the new total maximum profit be? Would any of the values of the decision variables or slack variables change?

g) Suppose the contracted number of economy and standard chairs in the last constraint were increased from 20 to 24. What would change in the optimal solution?

OUTPUT 3.5

LINDO Output

```
MAX      40 X1 + 25 X2 + 30 X3
SUBJECT TO
        2)    X1 + X2 + X3 <=    60
        3)    4 X1 + 2 X2 + 3 X3 <=    150
        4)    X1 <=    25
        5)    X2 + X3 >=    20
END

LP OPTIMUM FOUND AT STEP        5

       OBJECTIVE FUNCTION VALUE

       1)       1725.0000

VARIABLE          VALUE           REDUCED COST
      X1          15.000000            .000000
      X2          45.000000            .000000
      X3            .000000           2.500000


     ROW    SLACK OR SURPLUS       DUAL PRICES
      2)            .000000         10.000000
      3)            .000000          7.500000
      4)          10.000000           .000000
      5)          25.000000           .000000

NO. ITERATIONS=        5

RANGES IN WHICH THE BASIS IS UNCHANGED:

                             OBJ COEFFICIENT RANGES
VARIABLE          CURRENT          ALLOWABLE          ALLOWABLE
                   COEF            INCREASE           DECREASE
     X1          40.000000         10.000000           5.000000
     X2          25.000000         15.000000           5.000000
     X3          30.000000          2.500000           INFINITY

                             RIGHTHAND SIDE RANGES
     ROW          CURRENT          ALLOWABLE          ALLOWABLE
                   RHS             INCREASE           DECREASE
       2         60.000000         15.000000          10.000000
       3        150.000000         20.000000          30.000000
       4         25.000000          INFINITY          10.000000
       5         20.000000         25.000000           INFINITY
```

SOLUTION

a) X_1 = 15 superior chairs
X_2 = 45 economy chairs
X_3 = 0 standard chairs
Profit = \$1,725

b) The left-hand side of the second constraint represents hours used, and we have 4(15)+ 2(45) + 3(0) = 150. This also could be found by looking at the slack of zero, which means all 150 hours available have been used.
c) Profit would decrease by \$2.50 (reduced cost for X_3) for each standard chair produced.
d) Because this change represents a relaxation of the constraint, profits would increase by the dual price of \$7.50. Note that this change is within the allowable limit.
e) The allowable increase is 20, so profits would increase by the dual price of \$7.50 per hour for the first 20 hours (or \$150), but then a new basic solution would be optimal and this must be solved again to determine the new solution. We know that profits must increase by at least \$150.
f) This is an increase in profit of \$5, and is within the allowable limit. Therefore, the same basic solution would be optimal. The profit would increase by \$5(15) = \$75. The new profit would be \$1,800. The values for all decision variables, slack variables, and surplus variables would remain unchanged.
g) This is a tightening of the last constraint, but the dual price is zero and there is an allowable increase of 25 units. Therefore, the same basic solution is optimal, and the only thing that changes is the amount of surplus for this constraint. The surplus now would be 21 instead of 25.

SOLVED PROBLEM 3-2

A gardener is preparing his garden for planting. Fertilizer is needed, and the gardener would like to minimize the cost of this fertilizer. Three types of fertilizer are available, each having the necessary ingredients (Ingredients A and B) in different proportions. The gardener may mix these together before applying the fertilizer. A linear program has been formulated to help with this. This has been solved and the computer output is provided, as shown in Output 3.6.

The variables are defined as:

X_1 = number of bags of Fertilizer 1
X_2 = number of bags of Fertilizer 2
X_3 = number of bags of Fertilizer 3

$$\begin{aligned}
&\text{Minimize cost} = 12X_1 + 15X_2 + 14X_3 \\
&\text{Subject to: } X_1 + X_2 + X_3 \geq 30 && \text{total bags needed} \\
&3X_1 + 5X_2 + 5X_3 \geq 180 && \text{ounces of Ingredient A} \\
&2X_1 + 3X_2 + X_3 \geq 42 && \text{ounces of Ingredient B} \\
&X_1 + X_3 \leq 20 && \text{availability constraint} \\
&X_1, X_2, X_3, \geq 0 && \text{nonnegativity constraints}
\end{aligned}$$

a) How many bags of each type should be purchased? What will this cost?
b) How many ounces of Ingredient A will this provide?

c) Despite being the least cost, Fertilizer 1 is not used. How much would the price of this have to decrease before it would be included in the optimal solution?
d) If the last constraint were relaxed so that the right-hand side is 25 instead of 20, what would happen to the total cost of the optimal solution?
e) If the third constraint (Ingredient B) were relaxed so that the right-hand side is 40 instead of 42, what would happen to the total cost of the optimal solution?

OUTPUT 3.6

LINDO Output

```
 MIN      12 X1 + 15 X2 + 14 X3
 SUBJECT TO
        2)    X1 + X2 + X3 >=   30
        3)    3 X1 + 5 X2 + 5 X3 >=   180
        4)    2 X1 + 3 X2 + X3 >=   42
        5)    X1 + X3 <=   20
 END

LP OPTIMUM FOUND AT STEP       2

      OBJECTIVE FUNCTION VALUE

      1)      520.00000

 VARIABLE         VALUE          REDUCED COST
       X1          .000000          4.000000
       X2        16.000000           .000000
       X3        20.000000           .000000


      ROW   SLACK OR SURPLUS      DUAL PRICES
       2)         6.000000           .000000
       3)          .000000         -3.000000
       4)        26.000000           .000000
       5)          .000000          1.000000

NO. ITERATIONS=        2

RANGES IN WHICH THE BASIS IS UNCHANGED:

                           OBJ COEFFICIENT RANGES
VARIABLE          CURRENT        ALLOWABLE         ALLOWABLE
                    COEF         INCREASE          DECREASE
      X1        12.000000        INFINITY          4.000000
      X2        15.000000        INFINITY          1.000000
      X3        14.000000        1.000000          INFINITY

                           RIGHTHAND SIDE RANGES
     ROW          CURRENT        ALLOWABLE         ALLOWABLE
                    RHS          INCREASE          DECREASE
       2        30.000000        6.000000          INFINITY
       3       180.000000        INFINITY         30.000000
       4        42.000000       26.000000          INFINITY
       5        20.000000       13.000000         20.000000
```

SOLUTION

a) X_1 = 0 bags of Fertilizer 1
X_2 = 16 bags of Fertilizer 2
X_3 = 20 bags of Fertilizer 3
cost = 520

b) Surplus for Ingredient A (in the second constraint) is zero. Therefore, 180 ounces (the right-hand side value of the second constraint) are provided.
c) The price would have to decrease by four (the amount of the reduced cost). At this price, there would be multiple optimal solutions and X_1 could become positive.
d) By relaxing this constraint, the total cost would improve or decrease by one (the amount of the dual price) per unit. Because the increase in the right-hand side is five units, the total cost would decrease by 1(5) = 5 and would become 515.
e) Nothing would happen to the total cost. The dual price is zero and this change is within the allowable limits. There is a surplus of 26 for this constraint. Therefore, reducing the right-hand side of this constraint would simply increase the surplus.

QUESTIONS

1. If a coefficient in the objective function is changed, will the feasible region change? Will the basic feasible solutions (corner points) change?
2. Discuss how a change in an objective function coefficient could impact the optimal solution to a linear programming problem.
3. If the right-hand side of a ≤ constraint is increased, what would happen to the feasible region? What would happen if this were decreased?
4. If the right-hand side of a ≥ constraint is increased, what would happen to the feasible region? What would happen if this were decreased?
5. Explain what the terms "relaxation" and "tightening" mean relative to ≤ and ≥ constraints.
6. What could happen to the feasible region if a new constraint is added to a linear programming problem? How would this affect the value of the objective function for the optimal solution?
7. What could happen to the feasible region if a constraint is removed from a linear programming problem? How would this affect the value of the objective function for the optimal solution?
8. If the feasible region were to get larger, what could happen to the value of the objective function?
9. If the feasible region were to get smaller, would it be possible for the optimal objective function value to improve?
10. Suppose a change is made in an objective function coefficient, and this change is within the allowable limits. Would the optimal values for any decision variables change? Would the amount of slack or surplus change? Would the objective function value change?
11. What is a binding constraint? What is a nonbinding constraint?
12. Suppose a change is made in a right-hand side value of a binding constraint, and this change is within the allowable limits. Would the optimal values for any decision variables change? Would the amount of slack or surplus change? Would the objective function value change?
13. Suppose a change is made in a right-hand side value of a nonbinding constraint, and this change is within the allowable limits. Would the values for

any decision variables change? Would the amount of slack or surplus for any variable change? Would the objective function value change?

14. What is the dual price for a nonbinding constraint?

PROBLEMS

15. Consider the following linear programming problem:

$$\text{Maximize profit} = 8X_1 + 5X_2$$
$$\text{Subject to: } 3X_1 + 4X_2 \leq 36$$
$$3X_1 + 2X_2 \leq 24$$
$$X_1, X_2 \geq 0$$

a) Solve this using a graphical method.
b) Is the point (5,5) a feasible point?
c) If the objective function were changed to $8X_1 + 3X_2$, what would be the optimal solution?
d) If the objective function were changed to $8X_1 + 2X_2$, what would be the optimal solution?
e) What would happen to the feasible region if the constraint $X_1 \leq 7$ were added to this problem?

16. Consider the following linear programming problem:

$$\text{Maximize profit} = 4X_1 + 10X_2$$
$$\text{Subject to: } X_1 + X_2 \leq 10$$
$$2X_1 + 4X_2 \leq 24$$
$$3X_1 + X_2 \leq 27$$
$$X_1, X_2 \geq 0$$

a) Solve this graphically.
b) What is the maximum possible profit for this situation?
c) How much slack is there for each constraint at the optimal solution?
d) Add the constraint $X_1 \leq 11$ to this problem. What happens to the feasible region? Is this constraint redundant?

17. Solve Problem 16 using a computer. Compare your graphical results with the results in the computer output.

18. The Sysmon Corporation makes two types of personal computer monitors—a 15-inch model and a 17-inch model. Each of these is made in the same factory. The 15-inch monitor requires two hours of assembly time and one hour of inspection time. The 17-inch monitor requires three hours of assembly time and two hours of inspection time. There are 240 hours per week available of assembly time and 120 hours per week available of inspection time. Due to limited demand, the company has decided that it should produce no more than a total of 100 monitors per week. Each 15-inch monitor generates a profit of $50 while each 17-inch monitor generates a profit of $80. The company would like to maximize profit.

a) Solve this graphically to determine how many 15-inch and 17-inch monitors the company should produce to maximize profit?
b) How many assembly hours and inspection hours are used when profit is maximized?

c) Is it possible to produce 45 monitors of each type (i.e., would the point on the graph representing this be in the feasible region)?
d) The price of the 17-inch monitor might have to be decreased due to some actions by a competitor. If the profit on the 17-inch monitor were reduced to $60 per unit, would the current optimal production decisions change?
e) Returning to the original data in the problem, consider the following change. Due to increased competition, the company has decided no more than a total of 90 monitors per week should be produced. How will this affect production decisions and profit?
f) Returning to the original data in the problem, consider the following change. If the number of inspection hours available per week were increased by one hour and production decisions were modified to maximize profit with this additional hour, what would be the maximum possible profit? How many monitors of each type would be produced? What is the dual price for inspection hours?

19. Solve Problem 18 using a computer, and answer the previous questions again by using the information provided in the computer output.
20. A company produces two types of clock radios—a regular model and a deluxe stereo model. Each of these must be assembled and inspected, and there is a limited number of hours available per week. The company wishes to maximize profit. The following linear programming formulation represents this situation.

X_1 = number of regular radios
X_2 = number of deluxe radios

Maximize profit = $25X_1 + 20X_2$

Subject to:	$2X_1 + X_2 \leq 120$	assembly hours each week
	$X_1 + X_2 \leq 70$	inspection hours each week
	$X_1, X_2 \geq 0$	nonnegativity constraints

a) Solve this graphically. Give the optimal value of the objective function and give the slack for each of the constraints.
b) Change the right-hand side of the second constraint (inspection hours each week) from 70 to 71 and solve the problem again graphically. How much does the objective function value increase (this is the dual price) for this one unit increase in the right-hand side? Note that it is possible to generate more profit with this extra hour even though the assembly hours were being totally utilized.
c) Returning to the original data in the problem, consider the following change. Change the right-hand side of the second constraint (inspection hours each week) to 120 and solve the problem again. The total increase in the right-hand side from 70 to 120 is an increase of 50 units. How much does the objective function value increase with each unit increase in the right-hand side?
d) Returning to the original data in the problem, consider the following change. Change the right-hand side of the second constraint (inspection hours each week) to 121 and solve the problem again. Note that the objective function value no longer increases by the amount of the dual price because the upper limit of 120 is exceeded.
e) Returning to the original data in the problem, consider the following change. Change the right-hand side of the second constraint to 60 and solve

the problem again. Note that a decrease from 70 to 60 should result in a decrease in the objective function value of 10 times the dual price.

f) Returning to the original data in the problem, consider the following change. Change the right-hand side of the second constraint to 59 and solve the problem again. Note that the objective function value no longer decreases by the amount of the dual price because the lower limit has been reached.

21. Solve Problem 20 using a computer, and answer the previous questions again by using the information provided in the computer output.
22. Consider the following linear programming problem:

$$\begin{aligned} &\text{Maximize profit} = 5X_1 + 4X_2 \\ &\text{Subject to: } 2X_1 + X_2 = 8 \\ &\qquad 3X_1 + 4X_2 \leq 24 \\ &\qquad 3X_1 + 4X_2 \geq 2 \\ &\qquad X_1, X_2 \geq 0 \end{aligned}$$

a) Solve this graphically.

b) What is the maximum possible profit?

c) In the optimal solution, how much slack is there in the second constraint?

d) In the optimal solution, how much surplus is there in the third constraint?

e) Suppose the right-hand side of the second constraint is changed from 24 to 20. What is the new optimal solution? How much did profit decrease from the previous optimal solution. What is the dual price?

23. Solve Problem 22 again using a computer. Using the computer output, answer the questions again.
24. Consider the following linear programming problem.

$$\begin{aligned} &\text{Minimize cost} = 10X_1 + 15X_2 \\ &\text{Subject to: } 5X_1 + 3X_2 \geq 30 \\ &\qquad 2X_1 + 4X_2 \geq 20 \\ &\qquad X_1 \geq 2 \\ &\qquad X_1, X_2 \geq 0 \end{aligned}$$

a) Find the optimal solution.

b) How much surplus is there for each constraint?

c) Would the optimal solution change if the objective function coefficient for X_1 were changed from 10 to 12?

25. (Refer to Problem 31 in Chapter 2.) A farmer grows wheat and corn on his land, and he would like to generate as much profit as possible. Past experience shows each acre of wheat will yield a profit of \$800 and each acre of corn will yield a profit of \$600. Each acre of wheat requires three labor hours while each acre of corn requires two labor hours. There are a total of 400 acres available for planting, and there are 900 labor hours available. Due to the farmer's concerns for the soil and his history of crop rotation, he has decided to plant no more than 240 acres of wheat this year.

a) How many acres should be planted for each crop? What is the total profit? How many labor hours will be used?

b) Additional labor may be obtained at a cost of \$12 per hour. Should the farmer consider hiring someone to help? If so, how many additional hours could be used? (*Hint:* Look at the graph and shift the labor-hours constraint line.)

c) Using a computer, determine how much profit would increase if additional land or labor hours were available.

26. (Refer to Problem 31 in Chapter 2 and the previous problem.) If the profit on wheat increased to $900 for the yield from each acre, what would be the optimal solution?

27. (Refer to Problem 32 in Chapter 2.) Woofer Pet Foods produces a low calorie dog food for overweight dogs. This product is made from beef products and grain. Each pound of beef costs $0.90 while each pound of grain costs $0.80. A pound of the dog food must contain at least eight units of Vitamin #1 and 10 units of Vitamin #2. A pound of beef contains 10 units of Vitamin #1 and 12 units of Vitamin #2. A pound of grain contains six units of Vitamin #1 and nine units of Vitamin #2.
a) Identify the feasible corner points and the optimal solution.
b) If the requirement for Vitamin #1 were increased from eight units to nine units, how would the feasible region change? What would be the new optimal solution?

28. Referring to the original Woofer Pet Foods situation in Problem 32 of Chapter 2, suppose the cost for a pound of beef increased from $0.90 to $1.00. How would the feasible region change? What would be the optimal solution?

29. (Refer to the Modest Oil Company in Problem 36 of Chapter 2.) Solve the Modest Oil Company problem using any available computer software. How many barrels of WT23 and AR15 should be used to make premium gasoline? How much would the cost of WT23 have to change before the production mix would change?

30. The Air Modelers Manufacturing Company produces three types of model airplanes—the P51 Mustang, the B17 Bomber, and the Japanese Zero. In the production of each of these, three machines are used. The time (in minutes) required on each machine as well as the total time available are provided in the table below.

	P51	B17	Zero	Minutes Available
Machine A	4	6	7	720
Machine B	3	5	3	480
Machine C	8	7	8	960

The selling price for the P51 is $32, for the B17 is $36, and for the Zero is $26. The costs for each of these (including both materials costs and labor costs) are $20 for the P51, $25 for the B17, and $18 for the Zero.
a) Use linear programming and any available software to determine how many of each should be produced to maximize profit.
b) If additional time could be made available on one of the machines, which machine has the potential for generating the greatest increase in profit? How many minutes should be added to this machine?

31. Consider the Air Modelers Manufacturing Company situation in Problem 30. The company is considering raising the price on the Zero. How much would this have to increase before the production decisions would change? How much would the profit on each of the others have to increase before the production decisions would change?

32. Consider the Air Modelers Manufacturing Company situation in Problem 30. Suppose a reduction in costs has caused the profit on the P51 to increase by \$0.50, the profit on the B17 to increase by \$4, and the profit on the Zero to increase by \$2. Use the 100% rule to determine if these changes would cause a new solution to be optimal.
33. Consider the Air Modelers Manufacturing Company situation in Problem 30. Suppose a modification of the machinery has caused the time available on Machines A and C to decrease by 80 minutes each while the time on Machine B has increased by 200 minutes. Use the 100% rule to determine if this may cause a new basic solution to be optimal.
34. Finer Furniture produces three types of furniture—tables, chairs, and bookcases. The production of each of these involves both a carpentry process and a finishing process. The time required in each of these as well as lumber requirements are given in the table below.

	Table	Chair	Bookcase	Amount Available
Lumber	6 ft.	2 ft.	8 ft.	200 ft.
Carpentry	3 hrs.	2 hrs.	3 hrs.	80 hrs.
Finishing	2 hrs.	1 hr.	1 hr.	40 hrs.

The profit generated by each table is \$40, by each chair is \$20, and by each bookcase is \$35.

a) How many of each of these should be produced to maximize profit?

b) If one additional carpentry hour were available, how much would profits increase?

c) If additional finishing time could be obtained, how much would it increase profit?

d) If carpentry time could be obtained at an additional cost of \$8 per hour, should the company use this extra time? How many hours should be obtained at this price?

35. Consider the Finer Furniture situation in Problem 34. Explain what would happen if an additional 100 feet of lumber were available.
36. Consider the Finer Furniture situation in Problem 34. The optimal solution calls for no chairs to be made. What would happen to profit if one chair were made? What would happen to total profit if the profit on chairs was raised to \$25 instead of \$20?

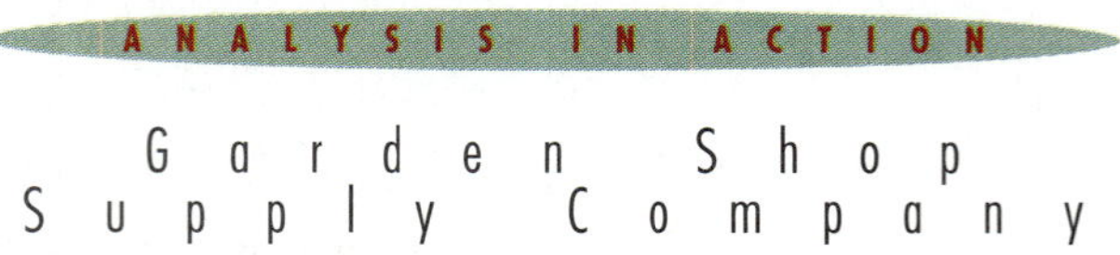

The Garden Shop Supply Company is a wholesale supplier of fertilizers, seeds, and other garden goods. In recent years, contracts for fertilizers have caused this particular area of business to be exceedingly lucrative. However, due to limited storage facilities, Garden Shop has begun to carefully evaluate the fertilizer production operations.

When an order is received for a particular type of fertilizer, the materials needed are ordered from a supplier, mixed together in appropriate proportions, bagged according to the particular order, and delivered to the customer. An order has been received from a chain of hardware stores for 5,000 40-pound bags of 8-10-12 fertilizer. This means that the fertilizer must be 8 percent nitrogen, 10 percent phosphorous, and 12 percent potash. While these are the minimum amounts this fertilizer must contain, it has been stipulated the fertilizer should not exceed any of these minimums by more than 3 percent (i.e., not more than 11 percent nitrogen, 13 percent phosphorous, and 15 percent potash). The delivery date on this order means production must begin almost immediately.

In producing fertilizer, three bulk fertilizers are mixed together to obtain the required percentages. The bulk fertilizers are purchased from a chemical company, and a phone call to this company reveals there are limited amounts currently available. Information regarding these bulk fertilizers is described in the table below.

Bulk	Cost per Pound	Availability in Pounds
6-8-6	$0.05	60,000
8-10-12	$0.07	80,000
16-16-16	$0.12	120,000

If additional quantities are needed immediately, the supplier is willing to prepare a special production run, although if other special orders are being processed, this might be delayed a few days. Also, the cost for the special order for amounts exceeding the availability given in the table above is an additional $0.02 per pound.

Prepare a brief managerial report indicating your recommendations. Be sure to provide information regarding the specific characteristics of the fertilizer as well as the cost. Use sensitivity analysis information to determine whether or not to order more than the available amounts.

Linear Programming Example Using Solver

Solve the following linear programming problem using Excel's Solver function.

$$\begin{aligned} \text{Max}\quad & 2x + 3y \\ \text{st}\quad & 4x + 5y \le 8 \\ & 2x + 7y \le 10 \\ & x \ge 0 \\ & y \ge 0 \end{aligned}$$

To solve a linear program using Excel's **Solver**:

1. Determine which cells will contain the values for the decision variables (cells B15 and B16 in this example).
2. Write formula for objective function (B12).
3. Write formulas for constraints (D12, D13, D15, D16). Note that nonnegativity constraints must explicitly be included.
4. Enter right-hand side values for constraints (F12, F13, F15, F16).
5. Run **Solver**:

   From main menu select **Tools** (or **Formula** in earlier versions of Excel), then select **Solver**. (This is an Add-in program. If it does not appear in the Tools menu, select **Add-in** and select it to be included in the menu.)

   Specify parameters for **Solver**:

      Objective function cell (B12) is entered in **Set Cell.**

      Select **Max** or **Min** for maximization or minimization.

      Enter decision variables cells (B15, B16) in **By Changing Cells.**

      Enter constraints giving cells for left-hand side and right-hand side of each constraint (F12, F13, H12, H13).

      Enter <=, =, or >= for each constraint.

   Select **Solve** to find the solution. Once the problem is solved, the solution is shown in the spreadsheet. You may select to have a **Solution** report or a **Limit** report prepared.

	A	B	C	D	E	F
1	Linear Programming Example					
2	Using Solver					
3						
4	Max 2x+3y					
5	st 4x+5y<=8					
6	2x+7y<=10					
7	x>=0					
8	y>=0					
9						
10						
11	objective function			constraints		
12	z	4.666666		7.999999	<=	8
13				10	<=	10
14	decision variables					
15	x	0.333333		0.333333	>=	0
16	y	1.333333		1.333333	>=	0

	A	B	C	D	E	F
1	Linear Programming Example					
2	Using Solver					
3						
4	Max 2x+3y					
5	st 4x+5y<=8					
6	2x+7y<=10					
7	x>=0					
8	y>=0					
9						
10						
11	objective function			constraints		
12	z	=2*B15+3*B16		=4*B15+5*B16	<=	8
13				=2*B15+7*B16	<=	10
14	decision variables					
15	x	0.333333086084		=+B15	>=	0
16	y	1.333333403975		=+B16	>=	0

CHAPTER FOUR

Linear Programming Applications

LEARNING OBJECTIVES

Upon completing Chapter 4, you should be able to:

- Formulate more complex linear programs.
- Recognize applications of linear programming in marketing and finance.
- Recognize situations that may be modeled using linear programming in the areas of production scheduling and employee scheduling.
- Understand how the transshipment, transportation, and assignment problems are modeled as linear programs.
- Explain the similarities between the assignment problem, the transportation problem, and the transshipment problem.

CHAPTER OUTLINE

4.1 INTRODUCTION

Linear programming has been used in a wide variety of business situations. Examples will be presented in this chapter to illustrate applications in marketing, finance, employee scheduling, production planning, and other areas. While these examples are simplified versions of real problems, they demonstrate the basic approaches to formulating common linear programs.

4.2 MEDIA SELECTION

Linear programming has been used in marketing to plan distribution systems, to sample individuals for market research studies, and to help companies get the greatest benefit from advertising expenditures. In this section we will see how a company may use linear programming to help in the selection of advertising outlets.

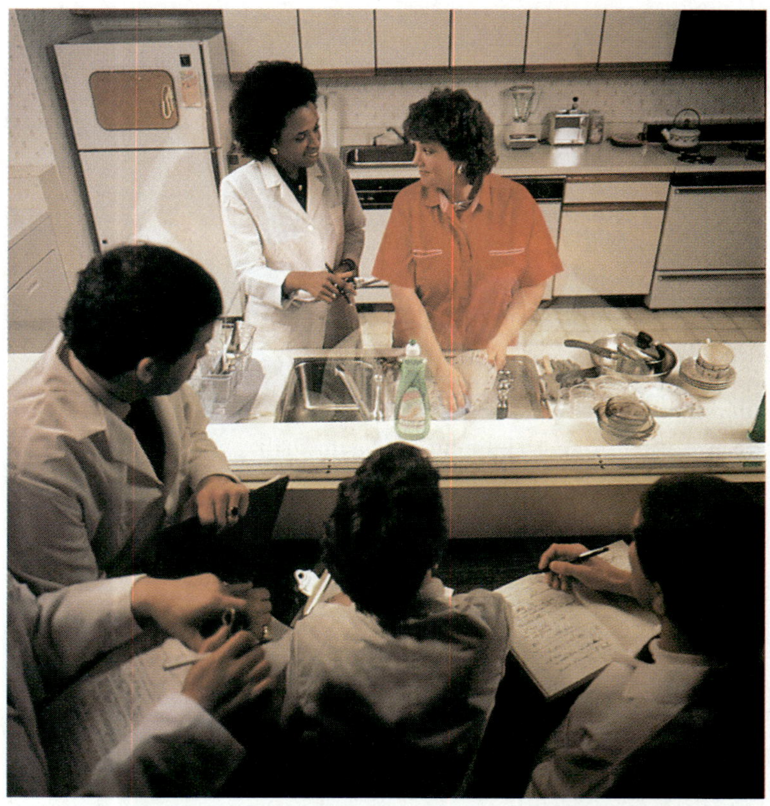

Linear programming has been used in marketing to sample individuals for market research studies. SOURCE: John S. Abbott, photographer; courtesy of Colgate-Palmolive Company

C. Moore Electronics Example

Charles Moore is the owner of C. Moore Electronics, a chain of audio and video stores specializing in stereos and televisions. Charles has begun evaluating his advertising procedures and is wondering if he is getting the maximum benefit from his advertising dollars. There are four types of media used to reach the target market: television, radio, newspapers, and weekly magazines. Calls to the advertising sales representatives for these four types of media have provided information regarding cost and target audience. Charles has budgeted $12,000 per week for advertising, and would like to reach as many people as possible while not exceeding his budget. He also has set a limit on the number of ads for each medium. This information is summarized in Table 4.1.

Charles also has determined that the total number of newspaper and magazine ads must be at least 20. Linear programming may be used to help Charles determine the best advertising plan.

To formulate this as a linear programming problem, we must identify the objective function and each constraint. The objective is to maximize the audience reached.

The constraints are:

1. The number of TV ads cannot exceed the limit (12).
2. The number of radio ads cannot exceed the limit (15).
3. The number of newspaper ads cannot exceed the limit (25).
4. The number of magazines ads cannot exceed the limit (10).
5. The total amount spent must not exceed $12,000.
6. The total number of newspaper and magazines ads should be at least 20.

Because the objective is to maximize the audience reached, and we have information about how many people are reached per ad, the decision variables will be:

X_1 = number of TV ads to be used

X_2 = number of radio ads to be used

X_3 = number of newspaper ads to be used

X_4 = number of magazine ads to be used

TABLE 4.1

Advertising Costs and Target Audience for Four Media Types

Type of Ad	Cost	Audience Reached	Maximum Number
Television	$900	10,000	12
Radio	200	2,600	15
Newspaper	700	5,500	25
Magazine	400	4,200	10

From this we get the following linear programming problem:

Maximize audience = $10{,}000X_1 + 2{,}600X_2 + 5{,}500X_3 + 4{,}200X_4$		
Subject to:	$X_1 \le 12$	TV ads
	$X_2 \le 15$	radio ads
	$X_3 \le 25$	newspaper ads
	$X_4 \le 10$	magazine ads
	$900X_1 + 200X_2 + 700X_3 + 400X_4 \le 12{,}000$	budget
	$X_3 + X_4 \ge 20$	total newspaper and magazine ads
	$X_1, X_2, X_3, X_4 \ge 0$	nonnegativity constraints

The solution to this problem found using LINDO is given in Output 4.1. This solution is to have zero TV ads ($X_1 = 0$), five radio ads ($X_2 = 5$), 10 newspaper ads ($X_3 = 10$), and 10 magazine ads ($X_4 = 10$), which results in an audience of 110,000 (the objective function value). The information about the constraints shows the entire budget of $12,000 is spent because the slack for constraint 5 is zero.

Looking at the sensitivity analysis from the LINDO output provides additional information about this situation. The reduced cost for variable X_1 (TV ads) is 1,700. This means the audience reached with TV ads would have to be 1,700 greater than it currently is before we would use any TV ads and still maximize the audience reached. If we decided to have one TV ad with the current level of the TV audience, the total number of people reached would be 1,700 less than the optimal value of 110,000. The dual price (shadow price) for constraint 4 (maximum number of magazine ads) is 2,600. This means if the right-hand side of that constraint were increased by one unit, the total audience reached would increase by 2,600 people. The right-hand side range for this has an allowable increase of 6.666667 and an allowable decrease of 3.333333. The dual price is relevant in this range, so the total audience will increase (or decrease) by 2,600 people for each one unit change in the right-hand side of constraint 4. Thus, if Charles is willing to change the maximum number of magazine ads from 10 to 11, the audience will increase by 2,600. Similar interpretations can be made for the other ranges and dual prices. The budget constraint was constraint 5, which has a shadow price of 13. If the budget increased by $1, the total audience reached would increase by 13 people. The negative dual (shadow) price for constraint 6 says if the right-hand side of this constraint is reduced by one unit (changed from 20 to 19), the total audience reached will increase by 3,600 people. Thus, it may be helpful for Charles to consider whether or not he truly desires to have at least 20 newspaper and magazine ads.

4.3

FINANCIAL APPLICATIONS

Some very common applications of linear programming and variations of linear programming are seen in the area of finance. A manager may evaluate capital budgeting decisions using a variation of linear programming

OUTPUT 4.1

LINDO Output for C. Moore Electronics Media Selection Problem

```
     OBJECTIVE FUNCTION VALUE

     1)      110000.000

 VARIABLE          VALUE           REDUCED COST
       X1          .000000         1700.000000
       X2         5.000000             .000000
       X3        10.000000             .000000
       X4        10.000000             .000000

      ROW    SLACK OR SURPLUS      DUAL PRICES
       2)        12.000000             .000000
       3)        10.000000             .000000
       4)        15.000000             .000000
       5)          .000000         2600.000000
       6)          .000000           13.000000
       7)          .000000        -3600.000000


RANGES IN WHICH THE BASIS IS UNCHANGED:

                           OBJ COEFFICIENT RANGES
VARIABLE         CURRENT        ALLOWABLE         ALLOWABLE
                  COEF          INCREASE          DECREASE
      X1    10000.000000      1700.000000          INFINITY
      X2     2600.000000         INFINITY        377.777800
      X3     5500.000000      2600.000000          INFINITY
      X4     4200.000000         INFINITY       2600.000000

                           RIGHTHAND SIDE RANGES
     ROW         CURRENT        ALLOWABLE         ALLOWABLE
                  RHS           INCREASE          DECREASE
       2       12.000000         INFINITY         12.000000
       3       15.000000         INFINITY         10.000000
       4       25.000000         INFINITY         15.000000
       5       10.000000         6.666667          3.333333
       6    12000.000000      2000.000000       1000.000000
       7       20.000000         1.428571          2.857143
```

with integer restrictions on the variables. This will be seen in a later chapter on integer programming. Pension fund managers often use linear programming to help decide where to invest funds. The objective function may be to maximize the expected return subject to risk and budget constraints, or it may be to minimize risk subject to a minimum rate of return and other constraints related to funds availability. An example of this last situation will be presented.

Capels and Associates Example

Consider the case of the investment firm Capels and Associates, which manages investments for a wide variety of clients. One particular client has sold a piece of real estate and has up to $200,000 to invest. Capels and Associates has been given instructions to invest this money in government securities, oil stocks, computer stocks, or utilities. The expected rate of return as well as maximum amounts for these are given in Table 4.2.

The client wishes to further control risk by setting limits on the amounts invested in oil and computers. The amount invested in oil stocks must be no more than the amount invested in government securities. Also, the total amount invested in oil and computers must be no more than 60 percent of the amount invested in government securities and utilities. Given these restrictions, Capels and Associates wishes to maximize the expected return.

The objective in this situation is to maximize the expected return while the constraints are:

1. The amount invested in government securities is no more than $130,000.
2. The amount invested in oil is no more than $100,000.
3. The amount invested in computers is no more than $100,000.
4. The amount invested in utilities is no more than $120,000.
5. The amount invested in oil is less than or equal to the amount in government securities.
6. The amount invested in oil and computers is less than or equal to 60 percent of the total of government securities and utilities.
7. The total amount invested is no more than $200,000.

Because we wish to determine how much to invest in each of the different alternatives, the decision variables will be defined as:

X_1 = dollars invested in government securities
X_2 = dollars invested in oil
X_3 = dollars invested in computers
X_4 = dollars invested in utilities

TABLE 4.2

Expected Returns and Limits for Capels and Associates Investment Problem

Type of Investment	Return	Maximum Investment
Government Securities	0.045	$130,000
Oil Stocks	0.060	100,000
Computer Stocks	0.080	100,000
Utilities	0.055	120,000

Converting the objective function and constraints into the mathematical expressions we have:

$$\text{Maximize return} = 0.045X_1 + 0.060X_2 + 0.080X_3 + 0.055X_4$$

$$\text{Subject to: } X_1 \leq 130{,}000$$
$$X_2 \leq 100{,}000$$
$$X_3 \leq 100{,}000$$
$$X_4 \leq 120{,}000$$
$$X_2 \leq X_1$$
$$X_2 + X_3 \leq 0.6\ (X_1 + X_4)$$
$$X_1 + X_2 + X_3 + X_4 \leq 200{,}000$$
$$X_1, X_2, X_3, X_4 \geq 0$$

Note that two of these constraints must be changed so the decision variables are on the left-hand side of the equation before these may be entered into a computer for solution. The constraint

$$X_2 \leq X_1$$

would be converted to

$$-X_1 + X_2 \leq 0$$

and the constraint

$$X_2 + X_3 \leq 0.6(X_1 + X_4)$$

would be changed to

$$-0.6X_1 + X_2 + X_3 - 0.6X_4 \leq 0$$

The constraint limiting the investment to \$200,000 is based on the assumption that up to \$200,000 may be invested, but it is possible some of it might not be invested. If this entire amount must be invested, this constraint would be an equality constraint instead of a less-than or equal-to constraint.

The computer solution found with LINDO is seen in Output 4.2. From this we see the amount invested in each of the areas would be:

X_1 = 5,000 dollars invested in government securities
X_2 = 0 dollars invested in oil
X_3 = 75,000 dollars invested in computers
X_4 = 120,000 dollars invested in utilities

The total return is \$12,825.

The sensitivity analysis shows the reduced cost for X_2 (dollars invested in oil) is 0.02. This means we would not invest in oil unless the expected return is 0.02 higher than it is currently. If the return on oil is decreased, or if it is increased by less than 0.02, there would be no change in the values for any of the decision variables or in the profit.

The allowable changes for the other decision variables indicate the same values for the decision variables will be optimal as long as the expected

OUTPUT 4.2

LINDO Output for Capels and Associates Investment Problem

```
        OBJECTIVE FUNCTION VALUE

        1)     12825.0000

  VARIABLE        VALUE           REDUCED COST
        X1     5000.000000            .000000
        X2         .000000            .020000
        X3    75000.000000            .000000
        X4   120000.000000            .000000


       ROW   SLACK OR SURPLUS     DUAL PRICES
        2)   125000.000000            .000000
        3)   100000.000000            .000000
        4)    25000.000000            .000000
        5)         .000000            .010000
        6)     5000.000000            .000000
        7)         .000000            .021875
        8)         .000000            .058125


 RANGES IN WHICH THE BASIS IS UNCHANGED:

                           OBJ COEFFICIENT RANGES
 VARIABLE        CURRENT        ALLOWABLE         ALLOWABLE
                  COEF          INCREASE          DECREASE
       X1       .045000         .010000           .093000
       X2       .060000         .020000          INFINITY
       X3       .080000        INFINITY           .020000
       X4       .055000        INFINITY           .010000

                           RIGHTHAND SIDE RANGES
      ROW        CURRENT        ALLOWABLE         ALLOWABLE
                  RHS           INCREASE          DECREASE
        2   130000.000000      INFINITY       125000.000000
        3   100000.000000      INFINITY       100000.000000
        4   100000.000000      INFINITY        25000.000000
        5   120000.000000    4999.998000     120000.000000
        6        .000000       INFINITY         4999.998000
        7        .000000     7999.997000     120000.000000
        8   200000.000000   66666.660000        7999.997000
```

return is not increased or decreased by more than the indicated amount. For example, if the return on X_1 (government securities) is increased by 0.01, the same dollar amount would be invested in each of the areas, although the return would increase because \$5,000 are currently invested in government securities ($X_1 = 5{,}000$). If the return on computers or utilities is increased by any amount, the only thing that would happen is the total return would increase. We would still invest the same amount in each of the four areas.

The dual (shadow) prices for the constraints show that if the right-hand side of the total investment constraint (the last constraint) is increased by one unit, the value for the objective function (return) will increase by 0.058125. Thus, if we had more money to invest, the return on that additional money would be approximately 5.8 percent.

4.4

MULTIPERIOD PRODUCTION SCHEDULING

In earlier chapters, several examples and end of chapter exercises involved problems typically classified as product mix problems. The decisions were related to the number of units of each product to produce in a single time period. A very common extension of this involves the use of linear programming for the development of a production schedule for several production periods. For example, a company may have orders for delivery of several products during the next few months. Assuming there is sufficient capacity, the company simply could produce enough units each month to satisfy that month's demand. However, this could lead to wide fluctuations in the number of units produced each month, and to wide fluctuations in the labor utilization resulting in hiring, training, and layoff costs. Also, the production of some extra units in months when demand is low may eliminate the need for overtime in future months. While this could keep production costs low because overtime would be avoided, the cost of storing the items from one month to the next must be considered.

While the initial development of the production scheduling model for a large problem is no trivial task, once the model has been developed, it can easily be modified each month to be used again with new demand information.

McGlassan Manufacturing Example

Consider the McGlassan Manufacturing firm that produces two types of gear assemblies used in the production of photocopying machines. A three-month demand schedule for Model AV7 and Model AV9 is shown in Table 4.3.

As the plant capacity is sufficient to produce a total of 2,200 units each month, the firm could meet the demand in March and April by producing the units in the month they are to be used. However, the demand in May exceeds the capacity, so some units must be produced in earlier months and stored until May.

TABLE 4.3

Three-Month Demand Schedule for McGlassan Manufacturing

	March	April	May	Total
Model AV7	800	1,000	1,200	3,000
Model AV9	900	1,000	1,400	3,300
Total	1,700	2,000	2,600	

The cost of producing one unit of AV7 is $30 while each unit of AV9 costs $35. McGlassan management has determined the storage cost is one percent of the cost of the unit per month of storage. Thus, the AV7 assembly has a storage cost of $0.30 per unit per month, while the AV9 assembly has a storage cost of $0.35 per unit per month.

A high employee turnover rate in the past has been blamed on excessive fluctuations in labor hours used each month. Consequently, the company has decided to maintain a production rate of at least 1,900 units per month in an attempt to smooth out the labor utilization rate.

The linear programming formulation for this situation begins with the identification of the objective function and the constraints. The company wishes to minimize the total production and storage cost.

The constraints are:

1. The number of units available of each product in each month must meet the demand.
2. The total number of units produced in each month cannot exceed 2,200.
3. The total number of units produced in each month must be at least 1,900.

The next step is to identify the decision variables. The objective function includes two types of costs, and decisions must be made regarding the number of units to produce each month and the number of units placed in storage each month. Consequently, we will define the following variables:

X_{ij} = the number of units of product i produced in month j

I_{ij} = inventory of product i left at end of month j

where i = 1 for Model AV7
= 2 for Model AV9

and j = 1 for March
= 2 for April
= 3 for May

Thus, our objective is to

$$\text{Minimize cost} = 30X_{11} + 30X_{12} + 30X_{13} + 35X_{21} + 35X_{22} + 35X_{23} + 0.3I_{11} + 0.3I_{12} + 0.3I_{13} + 0.35I_{21} + 0.35I_{22} + 0.35I_{23}$$

In formulating the constraints, we must remember the number of units available each month may be those produced that month or those left at the end of the previous month. If this total is greater than the demand for that month, the excess will be held in inventory for possible use in the next month. Thus, we have the following relationship:

inventory from previous month + current production =
current demand + inventory at end of current month

or

$$I_{ij-1} + X_{ij} = D_{ij} + I_{ij}$$

where D_{ij} = demand for product i in month j

If we assume there are no units in inventory at the beginning of March, we have the following constraints:

$X_{11} = 800 + I_{11}$	demand for AV7 in March
$X_{21} = 900 + I_{21}$	demand for AV9 in March
$I_{11} + X_{12} = 1{,}000 + I_{12}$	demand for AV7 in April
$I_{21} + X_{22} = 1{,}000 + I_{22}$	demand for AV9 in April
$I_{12} + X_{13} = 1{,}200 + I_{13}$	demand for AV7 in May
$I_{22} + X_{23} = 1{,}400 + I_{23}$	demand for AV9 in May

Because the decision variables must be on the left-hand side of the inequality to input these into the computer, we will rearrange these to obtain:

$X_{11} - I_{11} = 800$	demand for AV7 in March
$X_{21} - I_{21} = 900$	demand for AV9 in March
$I_{11} + X_{12} - I_{12} = 1{,}000$	demand for AV7 in April
$I_{21} + X_{22} - I_{22} = 1{,}000$	demand for AV9 in April
$I_{12} + X_{13} - I_{13} = 1{,}200$	demand for AV7 in May
$I_{22} + X_{23} - I_{23} = 1{,}400$	demand for AV9 in May

The maximum and minimum constraints become:

$X_{11} + X_{21} \leq 2{,}200$	maximum production for March
$X_{12} + X_{22} \leq 2{,}200$	maximum production for April
$X_{13} + X_{23} \leq 2{,}200$	maximum production for May
$X_{11} + X_{21} \geq 1{,}900$	minimum production for March
$X_{12} + X_{22} \geq 1{,}900$	minimum production for April
$X_{13} + X_{23} \geq 1{,}900$	minimum production for May

Adding the nonnegativity constraints, which require the variables to be greater than or equal to zero, finishes the linear programming formulation of this problem. The complete linear program is:

$$\text{Minimize cost} = 30X_{11} + 30X_{12} + 30X_{13} + 35X_{21} + 35X_{22} + 35X_{23} + 0.3I_{11} + 0.3I_{12} + 0.3I_{13} + 0.35I_{21} + 0.35I_{22} + 0.35I_{23}$$

Subject to:	$X_{11} - I_{11} = 800$	demand for AV7 in March
	$X_{21} - I_{21} = 900$	demand for AV9 in March
	$I_{11} + X_{12} - I_{12} = 1{,}000$	demand for AV7 in April
	$I_{21} + X_{22} - I_{22} = 1{,}000$	demand for AV9 in April
	$I_{12} + X_{13} - I_{13} = 1{,}200$	demand for AV7 in May
	$I_{22} + X_{23} - I_{23} = 1{,}400$	demand for AV9 in May
	$X_{11} + X_{21} \leq 2{,}200$	maximum production for March
	$X_{12} + X_{22} \leq 2{,}200$	maximum production for April
	$X_{13} + X_{23} \leq 2{,}200$	maximum production for May
	$X_{11} + X_{21} \geq 1{,}900$	minimum production for March
	$X_{12} + X_{22} \geq 1{,}900$	minimum production for April
	$X_{13} + X_{23} \geq 1{,}900$	minimum production for May
$X_{11}, X_{12}, \ldots, X_{23}, I_{11}, I_{12}, \ldots, I_{23} \geq 0$		nonnegativity constraints

The solution to this is found using DSS as shown in Output 4.3. The production schedule based on this is seen in Table 4.4.

There are numerous variations of this type of problem. If we wished to allow the possibility of existing units in inventory, we would have had two more inventory variables (one for each product) in this model, and we would have added a constraint for each one giving the current level. For example, if there were 100 units of AV7 and 150 units of AV9 in the warehouse, we would have the following two constraints added:

$$I_{10} = 100$$
$$I_{20} = 150$$

OUTPUT 4.3

DSS Output for McGlassan Manufacturing Multiperiod Production Scheduling Problem

Linear Programming Problem: MCGLASSAN

Z	X11	X12	X13	X21	X22	X23	I11	I12	I13	I21	I22	I23	Rel Op	R H S
MIN	30	30	30	35	35	35	.3	.3	.3	.35	.35	.35		
Cons1	1	0	0	0	0	0	−1	0	0	0	0	0	=	800
Cons2	0	0	0	1	0	0	0	0	0	−1	0	0	=	900
Cons3	0	1	0	0	0	0	1	−1	0	0	0	0	=	1000
Cons4	0	0	0	0	1	0	0	0	0	1	−1	0	=	1000
Cons5	0	0	1	0	0	0	0	1	−1	0	0	0	=	1200
Cons6	0	0	0	0	0	1	0	0	0	0	1	−1	=	1400
Cons7	1	0	0	1	0	0	0	0	0	0	0	0	<=	2200
Cons8	0	1	0	0	1	0	0	0	0	0	0	0	<=	2200
Cons9	0	0	1	0	0	1	0	0	0	0	0	0	<=	2200
Cons10	1	0	0	1	0	0	0	0	0	0	0	0	>=	1900
Cons11	0	1	0	0	1	0	0	0	0	0	0	0	>=	1900
Cons12	0	0	1	0	0	1	0	0	0	0	0	0	>=	1900

SOLUTION:

Variable	Value
X11	1000
X12	1200
X13	800
X21	900
X22	1000
X23	1400
I11	200
I12	400
Slack 7	300
Slack 8	0
Slack 11	300
Slack 12	300

MIN Z = 205680

TABLE 4.4

Three-Month Production Schedule for McGlassan Manufacturing

	March	April	May	Total
Model AV7	1,000	1,200	800	3,000
Model AV9	900	1,000	1,400	3,300
Total	1,900	2,200	2,200	

Airlines have used linear programming to schedule reservationists, baggage handlers, and other ground crews.
SOURCE: Courtesy of American Airlines

We also would change the first two constraints in the problem to:

$$I_{10} + X_{11} - I_{11} = 800 \quad \text{demand for AV7 in March}$$
$$I_{20} + X_{21} - I_{21} = 900 \quad \text{demand for AV9 in March}$$

Another variation involves labor balancing constraints (maximum and minimum productions). Implicit in the formulation above is the assumption that workforce utilization is stable if the number of units produced is stable. This would be true if the labor hours required for each of the two products is the same. If the labor hours vary for the two products, we may wish to change the maximum and minimum constraints so they represent the labor hours instead of the units produced.

Still another variation of this would allow an explicit cost to be assigned to fluctuations in the workforce. Thus, trade-offs may be made between fluctuations and costs. This may include the possibility of overtime costs if more than the normal maximum number of hours are used.

Optimal Lease Structuring at GE Capital

GE Capital is a $70 billion subsidiary of GE's financial services business. The company is one of the largest financial services firms in the U.S. GE Capital arranges and structures lease products in domestic and international markets for many segments of the leasing market. Markets supplied by the company include telecommunications, data processing, construction, production machinery, corporate aircraft, and fleets of cars, trucks, and commercial aircraft.

A leveraged lease is a financing agreement among the owner of an asset (the lessor), the user of the asset (the lessee), and a lender who provides a loan of 50 to 80 percent of the purchase price of the asset. GE Capital typically acts as the lessor in these transactions, claiming ownership and income tax benefits. Each leveraged lease must be tailored to lessee requirements, must be economically competitive, and must maintain profitability requirements. These factors complicate the process of structuring a leveraged lease. GE Capital uses lease analysis software to help analysts quickly structure complicated leases.

GE Capital's software uses linear programming to optimize leveraged lease structures. Typically, analysts minimize the net present value of the lessee's rental payments subject to a target profit. The target profit is expressed as the rate of growth of lessor after-tax cash flows. Other constraints are added to insure compliance with IRS guidelines, and to meet any other lessee or lessor guidelines. Alternatively, the analysts can elect to maximize the lessor's profit subject to a target lessee cost.

GE Capital's analysts perform sensitivity analyses to evaluate the effect of profit increases on lessee cost. They also use sensitivity analysis to evaluate the effect of potential changes in tax rates and regulations on lease structures. Overall, financial analysts can use sensitivity information to predict the impact of changes in the global marketplace on the fortunes of their customers.

SOURCE:
Litty, C. J., May-June 1994. "Optimal Lease Structuring at GE Capital." *Interfaces* 24 (3): 34-45.

4.5 EMPLOYEE SCHEDULING

Applications of linear programming abound in the area of employee scheduling. Airlines have used linear programming to assign flight crews to different flights. Some airlines also have used linear programming to schedule reservationists, baggage handlers and other ground crews. Large hotel chains have used linear programming to schedule reservation clerks to answer phones and take reservations. The assignment of individuals to various jobs can be modeled with linear programming, and this assignment problem will be considered in a later example and chapter. We will begin by presenting a typical employee scheduling problem.

Hometown Inns Example

Hometown Inns is a chain of hotels throughout the southern part of the United States. Customers may make reservations at any of these hotels by dialing a toll free telephone number at any time of the day and on any day of the week. Operators are standing by to take calls as they arrive. If the phone is busy, customers are put on hold and music is played. Management would like to schedule enough operators so the calls will be answered very quickly. However, because labor costs also are of concern to management, the number of operators should be as low as possible while still providing enough people to answer the calls in a timely fashion.

The number of operators needed at different times of the day is shown in Table 4.5. Each operator works an eight-hour shift, and shifts start at 8:00 A.M., 12:00 P.M., 4:00 P.M., 8:00 P.M., 12:00 A.M., and 4:00 A.M. as illustrated in Table 4.6. Management of Hometown Inns would like to determine the least cost schedule that will meet the demands. To minimize cost, the company will minimize the number of operators working while meeting the requirements shown in the table.

Formulating this as a linear programming problem, we identify the objective function and the constraints as:

Minimize number of operators

Subject to:

1. The number of operators working 8:00 A.M.–12:00 P.M. is at least 23.
2. The number of operators working 12:00 P.M.–4:00 P.M. is at least 18.

TABLE 4.5

Reservations Requirements for Hometown Inns

Time	Minimum Number of Operators
8:00 A.M.–12:00 P.M.	23
12:00 P.M. – 4:00 P.M.	18
4:00 P.M. – 8:00 P.M.	32
8:00 P.M.–12:00 A.M.	16
12:00 A.M. – 4:00 A.M.	8
4:00 A.M. – 8:00 A.M.	10

TABLE 4.6

Shift Times for Hometown Inns

Shift	Start Time	Ending Time
1	8:00 A.M.	4:00 P.M.
2	12:00 P.M.	8:00 P.M.
3	4:00 P.M.	12:00 A.M.
4	8:00 P.M.	4:00 A.M.
5	12:00 A.M.	8:00 A.M.
6	4:00 A.M.	12:00 P.M.

3. The number of operators working 4:00 P.M.–8:00 P.M. is at least 32.
4. The number of operators working 8:00 P.M.–12:00 A.M. is at least 16.
5. The number of operators working 12:00 A.M.–4:00 A.M. is at least 8.
6. The number of operators working 4:00 A.M.–8:00 A.M. is at least 10.

Decisions must be made regarding the number of workers assigned to each shift. We will define the decision variables as:

A fragrance manufacturer may use linear programming to determine how to blend the many ingredients in a product.
SOURCE: Courtesy of International Flavors & Fragrances, Inc./John Olson

X_1 = the number of operators working on Shift 1
X_2 = the number of operators working on Shift 2
X_3 = the number of operators working on Shift 3
X_4 = the number of operators working on Shift 4
X_5 = the number of operators working on Shift 5
X_6 = the number of operators working on Shift 6

It may appear that one of the assumptions of linear programming is violated. Fractional values for these variables would not be possible because we may not have 15.5 operators reporting at a specific time. However, due to the special structure of this problem, the values for the decision variables in the final solution will always be integers if the demands are expressed as integers. Were this not the case, we would have to use integer programming, which will be discussed in a later chapter.

Note that each shift overlaps two of these time periods, and thus each variable will appear in two constraints. The linear programming formulation for this is:

$$\text{Minimize operators} = X_1 + X_2 + X_3 + X_4 + X_5 + X_6$$

$$\begin{aligned} \text{Subject to:} \quad & X_1 + X_6 \geq 23 \\ & X_1 + X_2 \geq 18 \\ & X_2 + X_3 \geq 32 \\ & X_3 + X_4 \geq 16 \\ & X_4 + X_5 \geq 8 \\ & X_5 + X_6 \geq 10 \end{aligned}$$

$$X_1, X_2, X_3, X_4, X_5, X_6 \geq 0$$

Solving this with LINDO results in the computer output as shown in Output 4.4. From this output we see that we would have 18 operators report at 8:00 A.M. for Shift 1 ($X_1 = 18$), none at 12:00 P.M. for Shift 2 ($X_2 = 0$), 32 at 4:00 P.M. for Shift 3 ($X_3 = 32$), 3 at 8:00 P.M. for Shift 4 ($X_4 = 3$), 5 at midnight for Shift 5 ($X_5 = 5$), and 5 at 4:00 A.M. for Shift 6 ($X_6 = 5$). The total number of employees required would be 63 (the value of the objective function). Additional information from the output indicates there is no surplus for any constraint except for row 5 (time period 8:00 P.M.–12:00 A.M.), which has a surplus of 19 people.

Notice this solution would have no one working Shift 2. However, the reduced cost for this variable is zero. This means there is another solution where X_2 is positive that would have the same objective function value. Thus, there is another optimal solution. In this type of problem, it is common to find more than one optimal solution. Management may use this information to try to develop another solution where the surplus (extra operators) is more evenly distributed over the time periods. Notice if some workers were assigned to Shift 2, the number reporting for Shift 3 would be lower, and this would decrease the surplus in the 8:00 P.M.–12:00 A.M. time period.

OUTPUT 4.4

LINDO Output for Hometown Inns Employee Scheduling Problem

```
MIN      X1 + X2 + X3 + X4 + X5 + X6
SUBJECT TO
        2)    X1 + X6 >=   23
        3)    X1 + X2 >=   18
        4)    X2 + X3 >=   32
        5)    X3 + X4 >=   16
        6)    X4 + X5 >=   8
        7)    X5 + X6 >=   10
END

       OBJECTIVE FUNCTION VALUE

       1)      63.000000

VARIABLE          VALUE            REDUCED COST
      X1        18.000000              .000000
      X2          .000000              .000000
      X3        32.000000              .000000
      X4         3.000000              .000000
      X5         5.000000              .000000
      X6         5.000000              .000000


     ROW    SLACK OR SURPLUS        DUAL PRICES
      2)          .000000           -1.000000
      3)          .000000             .000000
      4)          .000000           -1.000000
      5)        19.000000             .000000
      6)          .000000           -1.000000
      7)          .000000             .000000
```

4.6 INGREDIENT MIX (BLENDING) PROBLEMS

Ingredient mix or blending problems Problems in which ingredients are mixed or blended to produce a final product.

Many types of cereals, pet foods, fertilizers, gasolines, and chemicals are produced by combining several ingredients which have specific characteristics. Linear programming may be used to determine how to mix these ingredients in a way that will meet the requirements while minimizing cost. Problems of this type are called **ingredient mix** or **blending problems**. The following blending problem will illustrate this.

Raptor Fuels Example

Raptor Fuels produces three types of gasoline—Regular, Premium, and Super. All of these are produced by blending two types of crude oil—Crude A and Crude B. The two types of crude contain specific ingredients, two of which determine the octane rating of the gasoline. The important ingredients contained in the two crudes are given in Table 4.7.

Crude A costs \$0.42 per gallon, and Crude B costs \$0.47 per gallon. In order to achieve desired octane ratings, at least 41 percent of the Regular gasoline must be Ingredient #1, at least 44 percent of the Premium gasoline must be Ingredient #1, and at least 48 percent of the Super gasoline must be Ingredient #1.

Due to current demand, the company must produce at least 20,000 gallons of Regular, at least 15,000 gallons of Premium, and at least 10,000 gallons of Super. Raptor Fuels would like to determine the least cost method for blending the crudes to produce the three types of gasoline with the desired ingredients.

In formulating this as a linear programming problem, we see the objective is to minimize cost.

The constraints are:

1. The amount of Ingredient #1 in Regular is at least 41 percent of the total.
2. The amount of Ingredient #1 in Premium is at least 44 percent of the total.
3. The amount of Ingredient #1 in Super is at least 48 percent of the total.
4. The number of gallons of Regular is at least 20,000.
5. The number of gallons of Premium is at least 15,000.
6. The number of gallons of Super is at least 10,000.

Because decisions must be made indicating how many gallons of each crude are used in the production of the three different types of gasolines, the decision variables must reflect this. In defining the variables, double subscripts will be used. The first subscript indicates the crude being used, and the second subscript indicates the gasoline being produced. The variables are:

X_{11} = number of gallons of Crude A used in Regular
X_{12} = number of gallons of Crude A used in Premium
X_{13} = number of gallons of Crude A used in Super
X_{21} = number of gallons of Crude B used in Regular
X_{22} = number of gallons of Crude B used in Premium
X_{23} = number of gallons of Crude B used in Super

TABLE 4.7

Ingredient Contents of Two Crudes

	Ingredient #1	Ingredient #2
Crude A	40%	55%
Crude B	52%	38%

Using these variables, we develop the mathematical statement of this problem. The objective function is:

$$\text{Minimize cost} = 0.42X_{11} + 0.42X_{12} + 0.42X_{13} + 0.47X_{21} + 0.47X_{22} + 0.47X_{23}$$

Because Crude A is 40 percent Ingredient #1 and Crude B is 52 percent Ingredient #1, the amount of Ingredient #1 in the final blend of Regular is:

0.40(amount of Crude A in Regular) +
0.52(amount of Crude B in Regular)

This must be at least 41 percent of the total amount of Regular. Because the total amount of Regular is $X_{11} + X_{21}$, the first constraint is:

$$0.40X_{11} + 0.52X_{21} \geq 0.41(X_{11} + X_{21})$$

Using the same formulation procedure with the other constraints we have:

$0.40X_{11} + 0.52X_{21} \geq 0.41(X_{11} + X_{21})$	Ingredient #1 in Regular
$0.40X_{12} + 0.52X_{22} \geq 0.44(X_{12} + X_{22})$	Ingredient #1 in Premium
$0.40X_{13} + 0.52X_{23} \geq 0.48(X_{13} + X_{23})$	Ingredient #1 in Super

The demand constraints are:

$X_{11} + X_{21} \geq 20{,}000$	demand for Regular
$X_{12} + X_{22} \geq 15{,}000$	demand for Premium
$X_{13} + X_{23} \geq 10{,}000$	demand for Super

Before this may be solved on a computer, it must be simplified by moving all of the decision variables to the left-hand side of the inequality and leaving a constant on the right-hand side. With the first constraint we have:

$$0.40X_{11} + 0.52X_{21} - 0.41(X_{11} + X_{21}) \geq 0$$
$$0.40X_{11} + 0.52X_{21} - 0.41X_{11} - 0.41X_{21} \geq 0$$
$$-0.01X_{11} + 0.11X_{21} \geq 0$$

Doing the same thing with constraints 2 and 3 results in the following linear program:

$$\text{Minimize cost} = 0.42X_{11} + 0.42X_{12} + 0.42X_{13} + 0.47X_{21} + 0.47X_{22} + 0.47X_{23}$$

$$\begin{aligned}
\text{Subject to: } -0.01X_{11} + 0.11X_{21} &\geq 0\\
-0.04X_{12} + 0.08X_{22} &\geq 0\\
-0.08X_{13} + 0.04X_{23} &\geq 0\\
X_{11} + X_{21} &\geq 20{,}000\\
X_{12} + X_{22} &\geq 15{,}000\\
X_{13} + X_{23} &\geq 10{,}000\\
X_{11}, X_{12}, X_{13}, X_{21}, X_{22}, X_{23} &\geq 0
\end{aligned}$$

Solving this using DSS gives the solution shown in Output 4.5. From this we determine that 18,333.33 gallons of Crude A and 1,666.668 gallons of Crude B would be used to produce 20,000 gallons of Regular. We would

OUTPUT 4.5

DSS Output for Raptor Fuels Blending Problem

```
Linear Programming                          Problem: RAPTOR

Z         X11    X12    X13    X21    X22    X23    Rel Op    R H S
MIN       .42    .42    .42    .47    .47    .47
Cons1     -.01   0      0      .11    0      0      >=        0
Cons2     0      -.04   0      0      .08    0      >=        0
Cons3     0      0      -.08   0      0      .04    >=        0
Cons4     1      0      0      1      0      0      >=        20000
Cons5     0      1      0      0      1      0      >=        15000
Cons6     0      0      1      0      0      1      >=        10000

SOLUTION:

Variable   Value
-          -
X11        18333.33
X12        10000
X13        3333.333
X21        1666.668
X22        5000
X23        6666.667

MIN   Z     =   19566.67
```

use 10,000 gallons of Crude A and 5,000 gallons of Crude B to produce 15,000 gallons of Premium. We would use 3,333.333 gallons of Crude A and 6,666.667 gallons of Crude B in producing 10,000 gallons of Super.

4.7 TRANSPORTATION PROBLEMS

The basic **transportation problem** involves trying to find the minimum cost way to transport items from a set of sources to a set of destinations. The sources may be factories or regional warehouses, each having a specific capacity or number of units available. Thus, there are some supply constraints on the problem. The destinations may be warehouses or retail outlets, each of these would have a specific demand and would result in demand constraints in the linear programming problem. Thus, a linear programming formulation would have an objective of minimizing cost, while there would be demand and supply constraints. These will be illustrated in the following example.

Transportation problem A linear programming problem in which the objective is to minimize transportation cost while meeting demand and supply constraints.

Capitol Electric Example

Capitol Electric produces electric motors in each of its three factories. These are located in Lubbock, Texas, Mobile, Alabama, and Lake Charles, Louisiana. The motors produced at these plants are identical, but the Lubbock plant can only produce 100 of these each week while the Mobile plant can produce 150 units per week and the Lake Charles plant can produce 180 per week. Each motor is shipped to one of three regional distribution centers that Capital Electric owns. These centers are in Miami, Florida, Dallas, Texas, and Atlanta, Georgia. Based on a forecast of demand, we must ship 210 motors to Miami, 120 motors to Dallas, and 100 motors to Atlanta. Figure 4.1 provides a network representation of this situation.

An analysis of the shipping cost from each source to each destination has resulted in the information in Table 4.8. While there are many ways for Capitol Electric to meet the demands at the different warehouses, management would like to minimize the shipping cost.

To formulate a linear program from this, we must first identify the objective function and the constraints. The objective is to minimize cost while the constraints are related to the supply from each source and demand at each destination. There will be three supply constraints and three demand constraints as follows:

1. The number of units shipped from Lubbock cannot exceed 100.
2. The number of units shipped from Mobile cannot exceed 150.

FIGURE 4.1

Network Representation of Capitol Electric Transportation Problem

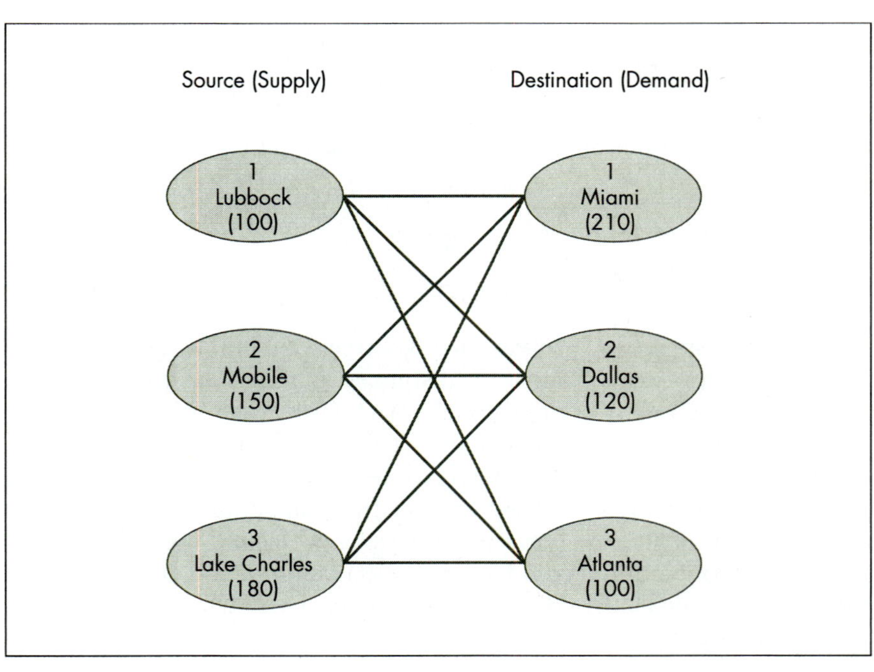

3. The number of units shipped from Lake Charles cannot exceed 180.
4. The number of units shipped to Miami must equal 210.
5. The number of units shipped to Dallas must equal 120.
6. The number of units shipped to Atlanta must equal 100.

TABLE 4.8

Shipping Costs for Capitol Electric Transportation Problem

	Destination		
Source	Miami	Dallas	Atlanta
Lubbock	\$6	2	5
Mobile	3	8	4
Lake Charles	7	6	7

A manager must decide how many units to ship from each source to each destination, and thus the decision variables must provide this information. Double subscripts will be used in defining the variables. The first subscript indicates the source and the second subscript indicates the destination. The decision variables are defined as:

X_{11} = the number of units shipped from Lubbock to Miami
X_{12} = the number of units shipped from Lubbock to Dallas
X_{13} = the number of units shipped from Lubbock to Atlanta
X_{21} = the number of units shipped from Mobile to Miami
X_{22} = the number of units shipped from Mobile to Dallas
X_{23} = the number of units shipped from Mobile to Atlanta
X_{31} = the number of units shipped from Lake Charles to Miami
X_{32} = the number of units shipped from Lake Charles to Dallas
X_{33} = the number of units shipped from Lake Charles to Atlanta

Using these variables, the linear program becomes:

$$\text{Minimize cost} = 6X_{11} + 2X_{12} + 5X_{13} + 3X_{21} + 8X_{22} + 4X_{23} + 7X_{31} + 6X_{32} + 7X_{33}$$

Subject to:

$$X_{11} + X_{12} + X_{13} \leq 100$$
$$X_{21} + X_{22} + X_{23} \leq 150$$
$$X_{31} + X_{32} + X_{33} \leq 180$$
$$X_{11} + X_{21} + X_{31} = 210$$
$$X_{12} + X_{22} + X_{32} = 120$$
$$X_{13} + X_{23} + X_{33} = 100$$

$$X_{11}, X_{12}, X_{13}, X_{21}, X_{22}, X_{23}, X_{31}, X_{32}, X_{33} \geq 0$$

The solution found using LINDO is shown in Output 4.6. Thus, to minimize cost we should ship 100 units from source 1 to destination 2 (Lubbock to Dallas) because $X_{12} = 100$. We ship 150 units from source 2 to destination 1 (Mobile to Miami) because $X_{21} = 150$. We ship 60 units from source 3 to destination 1 (Lake Charles to Miami) because $X_{31} = 60$. We send 20 units from source 3 to destination 2 (Lake Charles to Dallas) because $X_{32} = 20$ and we send 100 units from source 3 to destination 3 (Lake Charles to Atlanta) because $X_{33} = 100$. The total cost is $1,890.

OUTPUT 4.6

LINDO Output for the Capitol Electric Transportation Problem

```
  MIN     6 X11 + 2 X12 + 5 X13 + 3 X21 + 8 X22 + 4 X23 +
7 X31 + 6 X32  + 7 X33
  SUBJECT TO
         2)   X11 + X12 + X13 <=   100
         3)   X21 + X22 + X23 <=   150
         4)   X31 + X32 + X33 <=   180
         5)   X11 + X21 + X31 =    210
         6)   X12 + X22 + X32 =    120
         7)   X13 + X23 + X33 =    100
  END

        OBJECTIVE FUNCTION VALUE
        1)     1890.0000

  VARIABLE        VALUE          REDUCED COST
       X11           .000000         3.000000
       X12        100.000000          .000000
       X13           .000000         2.000000
       X21        150.000000          .000000
       X22           .000000         6.000000
       X23           .000000         1.000000
       X31         60.000000          .000000
       X32         20.000000          .000000
       X33        100.000000          .000000


       ROW   SLACK OR SURPLUS     DUAL PRICES
        2)           .000000         4.000000
        3)           .000000         4.000000
        4)           .000000          .000000
        5)           .000000        -7.000000
        6)           .000000        -6.000000
        7)           .000000        -7.000000
```

BEST PRACTICES

Linear Programming Cuts Pupil Transportation Costs

Costs are rising. Budgets are falling. Buses wear out and have to be replaced. Through it all, children have to get to school. In 1990, nearly 700,000 North Carolina students traveled to school by bus each day. The cost to the state was over $147 million. Faced with increasing costs, and decreasing budgets, the state developed a system for allocating funds that rewards local districts for operating efficiently.

In each of the 100 local districts, the number of buses run and the total operating expenditures are known inputs. The output of each district is the average number of pupils transported per day. Local site characteristics such as pupil and roadway density, number of schools, and local wage rates also are measured. These factors influence the number of pupils transported, but are beyond the control of local administrators.

A linear programming-based method called Data Envelopment Analysis (DEA) computes relative efficiency scores for each district based on the input and output variables. In order to take into account the variations across sites, a regression model adjusts the efficiency ratings. The resulting efficiency scores are used to determine funding allocations. Detailed analyses of the scores also help local districts to understand where to focus their efforts to increase their funding allocations.

Blue Bird Coach Lines, Inc.

The system has forced local governments to find more efficient solutions to the pupil transportation problem. (The threat of lost funding is a remarkable stimulus to creativity.) So far, the DEA method has inspired changes in bus routes and schedules, reductions in the number of buses on the roads, and improvements in maintenance policies. These have in turn led to reductions in capital expenditures of $25.2 million and savings in operational expenditures of $27.9 million over a three-year period. More savings are projected for the future.

SOURCE:

Sexton, T. R., S. Sleeper, and R. E. Taggart, Jr., January-February 1994. "Improving Pupil Transportation in North Carolina," *Interfaces* 24 (1): 87-103.

4.8 TRANSSHIPMENT PROBLEMS

The transportation problem is actually a special case of the transshipment problem. If items are being transported from the source through an intermediate point (called a transshipment point) before reaching a final destination, then the problem is referred to as a **transshipment problem**. For example, a company may be producing a product at several factories to be shipped to a set of regional distribution centers. From these centers the items are shipped to retail outlets, which are the final destinations. An example will be presented.

Transshipment problem
A transportation problem in which the items are shipped to an intermediate point (called a transshipment point) before reaching the final destination.

Frosty Machines Example

Frosty Machines manufactures snowblowers in factories located in Toronto, Canada and Detroit, Michigan. These are shipped to regional distribution centers in Chicago, Illinois and Buffalo, New York where they are delivered to the supply houses in New York City, New York, Philadelphia, Pennsylvania, and St. Louis, Missouri. The shipping costs vary as shown in Table 4.9. Forecasted demands for New York City, Philadelphia, and St. Louis also are seen in Table 4.9, as are the available supplies of snowblowers at the two factories. Figure 4.2 illustrates the basic network representation of this situation. Frosty would like to minimize the transportation costs associated with shipping sufficient snowblowers to meet the demands at the three destinations while not exceeding the supply of each factory. Thus, we have supply and demand constraints similar to the transportation problem. However, because there are no units being produced in Chicago or Buffalo, and anything shipped from these transshipment points must have arrived from either Toronto or Detroit, we must have a set of constraints indicating this. The verbal statement of this problem would be minimize cost such that:

1. The number of units shipped from Toronto is not more than 600.
2. The number of units shipped from Detroit is not more than 500.
3. The number of units shipped to New York City is 450.
4. The number of units shipped to Philadelphia is 350.
5. The number of units shipped to St. Louis is 300.
6. The number of units shipped out of Chicago is equal to the number of units shipped into Chicago.
7. The number of units shipped out of Buffalo is equal to the number of units shipped into Buffalo.

The decision variables should represent the number of units shipped from each source to each transshipment point and the number of units shipped

TABLE 4.9

Shipping Costs, Supplies, and Demands for Frosty Machines Transshipment Problem

	To		
From	**Chicago**	**Buffalo**	**Supply**
Toronto	$4	7	600
Detroit	5	7	500

	To		
From	**New York City**	**Philadelphia**	**St. Louis**
Chicago	$3	2	2
Buffalo	1	3	4
Demand	450	350	300

FIGURE 4.2

Network Representation of Frosty Machines Transshipment Problem

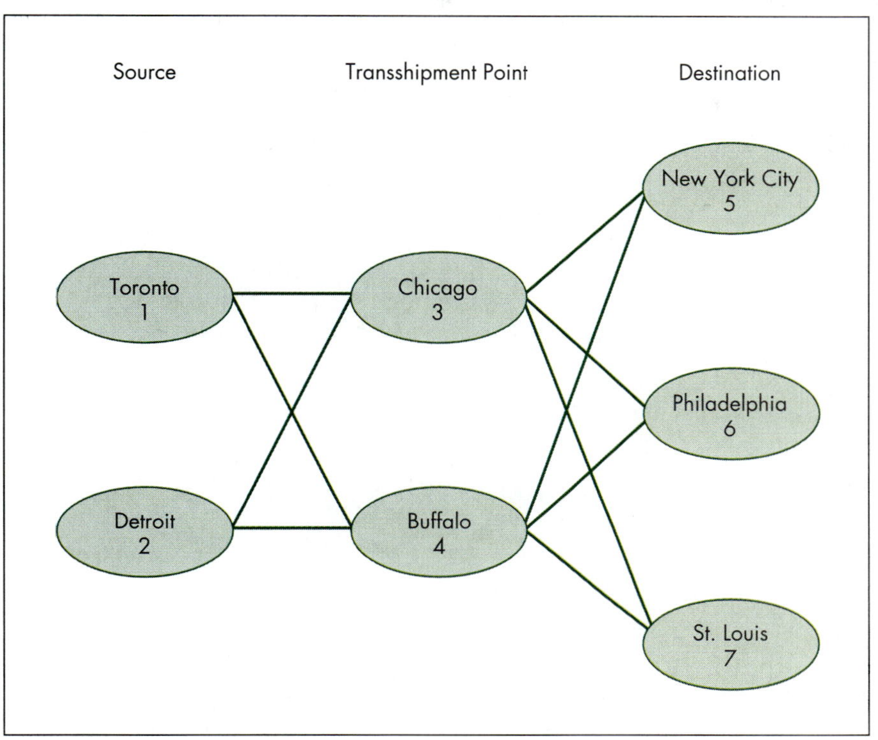

from each transshipment point to each final destination, as these are the decisions management must make. In defining the decision variables, double subscripts will be used with the first subscript indicating the source and the second subscript indicating the destination. The decision variables are:

X_{13} = the number of units shipped from Toronto to Chicago
X_{14} = the number of units shipped from Toronto to Buffalo
X_{23} = the number of units shipped from Detroit to Chicago
X_{24} = the number of units shipped from Detroit to Buffalo
X_{35} = the number of units shipped from Chicago to New York City
X_{36} = the number of units shipped from Chicago to Philadelphia
X_{37} = the number of units shipped from Chicago to St. Louis
X_{45} = the number of units shipped from Buffalo to New York City
X_{46} = the number of units shipped from Buffalo to Philadelphia
X_{47} = the number of units shipped from Buffalo to St. Louis

The linear program is:

Minimize cost = $4X_{13} + 7X_{14} + 5X_{23} + 7X_{24} + 3X_{35} + 2X_{36} + 2X_{37} + X_{45} + 3X_{46} + 4X_{47}$

Subject to:		
	$X_{13} + X_{14} \leq 600$	supply at Toronto
	$X_{23} + X_{24} \leq 500$	supply at Detroit
	$X_{35} + X_{45} = 450$	demand at New York
	$X_{36} + X_{46} = 350$	demand at Philadelphia
	$X_{37} + X_{47} = 300$	demand at St. Louis
	$X_{13} + X_{23} = X_{35} + X_{36} + X_{37}$	shipping through Chicago
	$X_{14} + X_{24} = X_{45} + X_{46} + X_{47}$	shipping through Buffalo
$X_{13}, X_{14}, X_{23}, X_{24}, X_{35}, X_{36}, X_{37}, X_{45}, X_{46}, X_{47} \geq 0$		nonnegativity constraints

To solve this on the computer, we must move all the decision variables in the last two constraints to the respective left-hand sides of the inequalities. Thus,

$$X_{13} + X_{23} = X_{35} + X_{36} + X_{37}$$

becomes

$$X_{13} + X_{23} - X_{35} - X_{36} - X_{37} = 0$$

and

$$X_{14} + X_{24} = X_{45} + X_{46} + X_{47}$$

becomes

$$X_{14} + X_{24} - X_{45} - X_{46} - X_{47} = 0$$

Solving this with LINDO yields the output in Output 4.7. From this we see that we should ship 600 units from Toronto to Chicago, 50 units from Detroit to Chicago, and 450 units from Detroit to Buffalo. A total of 350 units will be shipped from Chicago to Philadelphia, 300 from Chicago to St. Louis, and 450 from Buffalo to New York City. The total cost will be \$7,550.

4.9 ASSIGNMENT PROBLEMS

Assignment problem
A problem in which a specific set of people or items are assigned to specific tasks or jobs.

The basic **assignment problem** involves determining the best way to assign a set of people or items (such as machinery) to a set of jobs or tasks. Generally the objective is to minimize the cost or time of completing all of the jobs. Sometimes this problem is viewed as a special type of transportation problem. However, because each person may be assigned to one and only one job, and each job needs only one person, all the demands and all the supplies in the transportation model would be equal to one. Instead of shipping units from sources to destinations, we are assigning individuals (sources) to jobs (destinations). Technically, this is an integer programming problem in which

OUTPUT 4.7

LINDO Output for Frosty Machines Transshipment Problem

```
  MIN      4 X13 + 7 X14 + 5 X23 + 7 X24 + 3 X35 + 2 X36 +
2 X37 + X45  + 3 X46 + 4 X47

  SUBJECT TO
         2)    X13 + X14 <=   600
         3)    X23 + X24 <=   500
         4)    X35 + X45 =    450
         5)    X36 + X46 =    350
         6)    X37 + X47 =    300
         7)    X13 + X23 - X35 - X36 - X37 =     0
         8)    X14 + X24 - X45 - X46 - X47 =     0
  END

        OBJECTIVE FUNCTION VALUE
        1)      7550.0000

  VARIABLE          VALUE          REDUCED COST
       X13        600.000000           .000000
       X14           .000000          1.000000
       X23         50.000000           .000000
       X24        450.000000           .000000
       X35           .000000           .000000
       X36        350.000000           .000000
       X37        300.000000           .000000
       X45        450.000000           .000000
       X46           .000000          3.000000
       X47           .000000          4.000000


       ROW   SLACK OR SURPLUS        DUAL PRICES
        2)           .000000          1.000000
        3)           .000000           .000000
        4)           .000000         -8.000000
        5)           .000000         -7.000000
        6)           .000000         -7.000000
        7)           .000000         -5.000000
        8)           .000000         -7.000000
```

the decision variables are restricted to be either 0 or 1, and this will be discussed further in a later chapter. However, the special structure of this type of problem allows us to solve it using standard linear programming procedures. We will demonstrate this using the following example.

Erinburgh Construction Company Example

The Erinburgh Construction Company has three pieces of earth moving equipment. These have been purchased over time, and each type of equipment is versatile yet best-suited for a particular type of job. Erinburgh

Construction has three jobs that will be started next week. Each of these three jobs requires the use of an earth moving machine. Nick Piccolo, the manager of Erinburgh Construction, must decide the piece of equipment to assign to each of the three jobs. He has estimated the number of days required for each job using each of the three pieces of equipment, and this is given in Table 4.10. From this table we see if Equipment A is used on Job #1, it will take 10 days to complete this job. If Equipment B is used on Job #1, it will take only 8 days to complete the job. Equipment C could be used to complete the job in only 7 days. From the table we see Equipment C could complete any of the three jobs in the least amount of time, but we may only assign this piece of equipment to one job.

The verbal statement of the linear programming problem is minimize total time subject to the following constraints:

1. Equipment A must be assigned to no more than 1 job.
2. Equipment B must be assigned to no more than 1 job.
3. Equipment C must be assigned to no more than 1 job.
4. Job #1 must have a machine assigned to it.
5. Job #2 must have a machine assigned to it.
6. Job #3 must have a machine assigned to it.

Notice the objective function is to minimize total time, and we have information regarding the time required for each job with each machine. Thus, we should define decision variables which tell us if a machine is assigned to a particular job. The decision variables will be defined as:

X_{11} = 1 if Equipment A is assigned to Job #1
= 0 if Equipment A is not assigned to Job #1
X_{12} = 1 if Equipment A is assigned to Job #2
= 0 if Equipment A is not assigned to Job #2
X_{13} = 1 if Equipment A is assigned to Job #3
= 0 if Equipment A is not assigned to Job #3

TABLE 4.10

Days Required in Erinburgh Construction Problem

	Job		
Equipment	**#1**	**#2**	**#3**
A	10	14	9
B	8	16	5
C	7	14	4

X_{21} = 1 if Equipment B is assigned to Job #1
= 0 if Equipment B is not assigned to Job #1
X_{22} = 1 if Equipment B is assigned to Job #2
= 0 if Equipment B is not assigned to Job #2
X_{23} = 1 if Equipment B is assigned to Job #3
= 0 if Equipment B is not assigned to Job #3
X_{31} = 1 if Equipment C is assigned to Job #1
= 0 if Equipment C is not assigned to Job #1
X_{32} = 1 if Equipment C is assigned to Job #2
= 0 if Equipment C is not assigned to Job #2
X_{33} = 1 if Equipment C is assigned to Job #3
= 0 if Equipment C is not assigned to Job #3

This gives us the following linear program, which is the same as a transportation problem in which the right-hand side of each constraint is 1.

$$\text{Minimize time} = 10X_{11} + 14X_{12} + 9X_{13} + 8X_{21} + 16X_{22} + 5X_{23} + 7X_{31} + 14X_{32} + 4X_{33}$$

$$\begin{aligned} \text{Subject to: } & X_{11} + X_{12} + X_{13} \le 1 \\ & X_{21} + X_{22} + X_{23} \le 1 \\ & X_{31} + X_{32} + X_{33} \le 1 \\ & X_{11} + X_{21} + X_{31} = 1 \\ & X_{12} + X_{22} + X_{32} = 1 \\ & X_{13} + X_{23} + X_{33} = 1 \\ & X_{11}, X_{12}, \ldots, X_{33} \ge 0 \end{aligned}$$

Notice the first three constraints are written as less-than or equal-to constraints instead of equality constraints. This says a machine may be assigned to at most one job, but it leaves the possibility for the machine to be idle if we were to have more machines than jobs. In this particular example, these constraints could have been written as equality constraints and the same solution would be found. If the constraints are written as equality constraints and there were more machines than jobs, the computer would report there is no feasible solution to the problem.

The LINDO output for this is given in Output 4.8. From this we see that $X_{12} = 1$, $X_{21} = 1$, and $X_{33} = 1$, which means that Equipment A is assigned to Job #2, Equipment B is assigned to Job #1, and Equipment C is assigned to Job #3. All other variables are equal to zero. Because the objective function value is 26, the total time required to complete these jobs using these assignments is 26 days.

The linear programming formulations for the transportation, transshipment, and assignment problems have a very special structure. As a result of this structure, if all of the constraints have right-hand side values that are integer valued, then the optimal solution also will be integer valued. Thus, even though the values must be integer valued and this violates an assumption of linear programming, it is not a problem here because the optimal solution will have integer values for all the decision variables.

OUTPUT 4.8

LINDO Output for Erinburgh Construction Assignment Problem

```
  MIN     10 X11 + 14 X12 + 9 X13 + 8 X21 + 16 X22 + 5 X23 +
7 X31 + 14 X32 + 4 X33

  SUBJECT TO
          2)    X11 + X12 + X13 <=   1
          3)    X21 + X22 + X23 <=   1
          4)    X31 + X32 + X33 <=   1
          5)    X11 + X21 + X31 =    1
          6)    X12 + X22 + X32 =    1
          7)    X13 + X23 + X33 =    1
  END

        OBJECTIVE FUNCTION VALUE

        1)      26.000000

  VARIABLE          VALUE            REDUCED COST
       X11          .000000            2.000000
       X12         1.000000             .000000
       X13          .000000            4.000000
       X21         1.000000             .000000
       X22          .000000            2.000000
       X23          .000000             .000000
       X31          .000000             .000000
       X32          .000000            1.000000
       X33         1.000000             .000000


       ROW   SLACK OR SURPLUS      DUAL PRICES
        2)          .000000            .000000
        3)          .000000            .000000
        4)          .000000           1.000000
        5)          .000000          -8.000000
        6)          .000000         -14.000000
        7)          .000000          -5.000000
```

4.10 SUMMARY

In this chapter we saw common applications of linear programming. While these are small problems, they do illustrate the basic formulation of problems that may be much larger.

Some of these examples may require the values for the decision variables to be integer valued. However, due to the special structure of these problems, the solutions will be integer valued when they are solved as linear programming problems. For problems that require integer solutions and for which linear programming solutions are not necessarily integer value, we may use integer programming, which will be discussed in a later chapter.

A CLOSER LOOK

Data Envelopment Analysis (DEA)

An emerging application of linear programming is in the area of **data envelopment analysis (DEA)**. This is sometimes used to measure the efficiency of several similar operating units, such as hospitals, schools, fast-food chain restaurants, and a group of branch banks within a banking system.

In using DEA, the inputs and outputs for each of the units in the system being evaluated are compared to see if some units are operating less efficiently than others. A unit would be operating less efficiently if another unit in the system could obtain the same outputs with fewer inputs or could obtain greater outputs with equal inputs.

The inputs may be the size of the staff, capital equipment available, size of the individual unit (i.e., number of beds in a hospital or number of workstations for tellers in a bank), and operating expenses. The outputs may be market share, profits, number of operations performed, and number of customers served. Multiple inputs and outputs may be incorporated into one DEA model.

If, in using DEA, an operating unit is identified as inefficient relative to others in the study, management may use information provided in this analysis to investigate areas of inefficiencies. If the causes for the inefficiencies may be corrected, management should take appropriate measures. However, some apparent inefficiencies may actually be attributed to other factors not included in the model, such as the economic conditions surrounding a particular fast-food restaurant or the types of patients admitted to a particular hospital. If a hospital specializes in care for cancer patients, the inputs required for this treatment may be significantly higher than inputs required in a small, general hospital. Highlighting these types of differences may help management to see the expectations for certain units should be adjusted according to their specific circumstances.

SOURCES: Callen, J., 1991. "Data Envelopment Analysis: Practical Survey and Managerial Accounting Applications." *Journal of Management Accounting Research*, 3: 35-57. Also, Winston, W. L., 1994. *Operations Research: Applications and Algorithms*. 3rd ed. Belmont: Duxbury Press.

The transportation problem, transshipment problem, and assignment problem may be solved using standard linear programming software. Some special-purpose algorithms have been developed to solve these problems, and these other techniques will be presented in a later chapter. They require much less computer time than standard linear programming software, which is very beneficial for extremely large problems. However, most small- to medium-sized problems are solved so quickly with standard linear programming software that many users find little reason to use special-purpose algorithms.

Data envelopment analysis (DEA)
An application of linear programming that may be used to identify inefficient operating units.

GLOSSARY

Assignment problem A problem in which a specific set of people or items are assigned to specific tasks or jobs. *p. 144*

Data envelopment analysis (DEA) An application of linear programming that may be used to identify inefficient operating units. *p. 149*

Ingredient mix or blending problems Problems in which ingredients are mixed or blended to produce a final product. *p. 134*

Transportation problem A linear programming problem in which the objective is to minimize transportation cost while meeting demand and supply constraints. *p. 137*

Transshipment problem A transportation problem in which the items are shipped to an intermediate point (called a transshipment point) before reaching the final destination. *p. 141*

QUESTIONS

1. How is the assignment problem a special type of transportation problem?
2. The transportation problem is a special type of transshipment problem. How are these two problems similar and how are they different?
3. In some instances, all of the constraints in an assignment problem may be written as equality constraints. What problems could doing this create if the number of jobs does not equal the number of workers?
4. If a standard transportation problem with three sources and five destinations is formulated as a linear programming problem, how many decision variables and how many constraints would be needed?
5. If a standard assignment problem with four individuals and four jobs is formulated as a linear programming problem, how many decision variables and how many constraints would be needed?

PROBLEMS

6. In the C. Moore Electronics media selection problem, suppose a new restriction has been added to the advertising plan. Management has decided the total number of TV and radio ads should be at least 40 percent of the total number of ads placed. Formulate a constraint that would guarantee this.
7. For the Capels and Associates investment problem presented in this chapter, formulate a constraint that will insure that at least 20 percent of the funds invested will be in government securities.
8. In the McGlassan Manufacturing multiperiod production scheduling example, management has decided 200 units of the AV7 and 250 units of the AV9 should be on-hand at the end of May to protect against an anticipated future increase in demand. Formulate constraints that would do this.
9. Consider the Hometown Inns employee scheduling problem presented in this chapter.

   a) Suppose management has decided there is no need to have the telephones answered between the hours of 12:00 A.M. and 8:00 A.M. Consequently, Shift 1 will arrive at 8:00 A.M. and Shift 3 will leave at 12:00 A.M. each day. Assuming the minimum number of operators required from 8:00 A.M. to 12:00 A.M. has not changed, formulate this as a linear programming problem.

   b) Suppose in the original Hometown Inns example, upon reviewing the solution, management has decided the surplus employees in any time period should be no more than 50 percent of the minimum required. Modify the formulation so this new condition will be met.
10. In the Raptor Fuels ingredient blending problem, suppose a changing world situation has caused a shortage of Crude B. The maximum amount of Crude B is 25,000 gallons. Develop a constraint for this and solve using any available software. How does this shortage affect the total cost of production?
11. In the Frosty Machines transshipment problem presented in this chapter, suppose it has become possible to ship directly from the Detroit factory to St. Louis without going through any transshipment point at a cost of $6 per unit. All of the previous routes are still available. What changes would have to be made to the formulation of this problem? Solve using any available software.

12. Consider the Erinburgh Construction Company assignment example presented in this chapter. Suppose a fourth machine has been purchased by the company and may be used in addition to the three machines currently used. There still are only three construction jobs to be performed, and only one piece of machinery is needed on any one job. Thus, one of the machines will be idle. The times required for the jobs with the new piece of equipment are 7 days for Job #1, 12 days for Job #2, and 7 days for Job #3. Make the necessary changes to the linear programming formulation and solve using any available software. How does this affect the total time required for completing the jobs? Which machines will be assigned to the three jobs and which machine will be idle?
13. Robert Neely is the campaign manager for a politician who is running for reelection to a political office. In planning the campaign, Neely has selected four ways to advertise and promote his client—television ads, radio ads, billboards, and newspaper ads. The costs of these are $800 for each TV ad, $400 for each radio ad, $500 for a billboard for one month, and $100 for each newspaper ad. The audience reached by each type of advertising has been estimated to be 30,000 for each TV ad, 22,000 for each radio ad, 24,000 for each billboard, and 8,000 for each newspaper ad. To reach a good number of the registered voters, Neely has decided that no more than 10 of any one type of advertising be used, but at least 6 must be either TV ads or radio ads. The total monthly advertising budget is $15,000, and the total amount spent on billboards and newspapers must not exceed the amount spent on TV ads. Neely would like to reach as many people as possible with the advertising. Formulate this as a linear programming problem. Solve using any available software. How many ads of each type should be used? How much should be spent on each type of ad? How many people will be reached each month by the ads? Comment on the impact of increasing the advertising budget.
14. Bamm Mining Company is currently extracting ore from two mines. Once ore is taken from the ground and loaded on a truck, it is sent to one of two plants for processing. The cost of transportation, the supply available at each mine, and the processing capacity of each plant are given in the following table.

Cost per Ton for Shipping

	Processing plant		
Mine	**#1**	**#2**	**Daily Supply**
A	$6	8	300 tons
B	7	10	450 tons
Processing Capacity (per Day)	500	500	

Formulate a linear program that could be used to determine how many tons should be taken from each mine and shipped to each processing plant to minimize the cost of transportation. Assume the entire daily supply must be taken from the mines each day.

15. Referring to the Bamm Mining Company situation in Problem 14, suppose once the ore is processed, it is shipped to one of three builders' supply stores. The cost for shipping from each processing plant to each supply house is given in the table below.

	Cost per Ton for Shipping to:		
Plant	**Builders' Home**	**Homeowners' Headquarters**	**Hardware City**
#1	$13	17	20
#2	19	22	21
Daily Demand	200	240	330

a) Formulate a transshipment linear program that can be used to determine the minimum cost way to meet the demands of the three supply houses. Solve using any available computer software.
b) Suppose the cost of processing the ore is $22 per ton at Plant #1 and $18 per ton at Plant #2. Formulate this as a linear program to minimize to the total processing and transportation cost. Solve using any available computer software.

16. Mickey Lawson is the United States distribution manager for Lumbro, a world leader in the manufacture of soccer balls. The soccer balls are manufactured overseas and delivered to two major distribution centers—New York City, New York and Los Angeles, California. From these two cities, they are sent to regional warehouses in Chicago, Illinois, Atlanta, Georgia, Dallas, Texas, and Phoenix, Arizona. Currently, there are 20,000 balls in Los Angeles and 25,000 in New York City. Demand at each of the regional warehouses has been estimated to be 9,000 in Chicago, 11,000 in Atlanta, 15,000 in Dallas, and 10,000 in Phoenix. The shipping costs are given in the following table.

	To			
	Chicago	**Atlanta**	**Dallas**	**Phoenix**
From NYC	$3	$4	$4	$5
LA	$5	$6	$4	$3

Mickey would like to minimize the cost of shipping the soccer balls. Formulate this as a linear programming problem. Solve with the aid of a computer. How many soccer balls should be shipped from NYC and LA to each of the cities? What is the total cost of doing this? If additional soccer balls were received in NYC before the soccer balls are shipped to the regional centers, would it be possible to develop a lower cost solution? Explain using information on sensitivity analysis.

17. May K. Mooney is a Certified Financial Planner (CFP) who has been asked by a client to invest $100,000. This money may be placed in stocks, bonds, or a mutual fund in real estate. The expected return on investment is 12 percent for stocks, 10 percent for bonds, and 14 percent for real estate. However, due to risk considerations, at least 30 percent of the money must be put in bonds and

the amount invested in real estate cannot exceed 50 percent of the total amount invested in stocks and bonds. No more than $50,000 may be invested in any one of these three alternatives. Formulate this as a linear programming problem. How much money should be invested in each of the three areas? What is the expected return?

18. The Phone Shopping Center sells products by displaying products on television and taking orders by telephone. The hours of operation are 8:00 A.M. to 5:00 P.M. The number of operators needed at different times of the day has been determined, as shown in the table below.

8:00 A.M. – 9:00 A.M.	13
9:00 A.M. – 10:00 A.M.	15
10:00 A.M. – 11:00 A.M.	17
11:00 A.M. – 12:00 P.M.	14
12:00 P.M. – 1:00 P.M.	15
1:00 P.M. – 2:00 P.M.	17
2:00 P.M. – 3:00 P.M.	19
3:00 P.M. – 4:00 P.M.	18
4:00 P.M. – 5:00 P.M.	16

The center may be staffed by full-time employees who start at 8:00 A.M. and leave at 5:00 P.M., and by part-time employees who work four consecutive hours. Half of the full-time employees have a lunch break from 11:00 A.M. to 12:00 P.M., while the other half have a lunch break from 12:00 P.M. to 1:00 P.M. The cost for a full-time employee is $72 per day (including salary and benefits), while a part-time employee only costs $5 per hour or $20 for four hours. The number of full-time employees cannot exceed 14. The company wishes to minimize cost. Formulate this as a linear programming problem. How many full-time employees should be used? How many part-time employees should be reporting for work at each of the different hours during the day? What is the total cost for this solution?

19. Major Foods, Inc., is developing two new breakfast cereals. The two products will both be made using wheat, rice, and oats. The first new product (Product A) will appeal to the health food market, and must contain at least 25 units of a particular vitamin (Vitamin #1) and at least 18 units of another vitamin (Vitamin #2) in each 12-ounce box. The second product (Product B) must contain at least 12 units of Vitamin #1 and 6 units of Vitamin #2 in each 12-ounce box.

The cost of one ounce of each ingredient as well as the vitamin content in units per ounce is given in the table below.

	Wheat	Rice	Oats
Cost	0.02	0.03	0.04
Vitamin #1	3	4	3
Vitamin #2	2	2	1

Formulate this as a linear program. Solve using any available computer software. How much will a 12-ounce box of each cereal cost to manufacture? What is the vitamin content of each type of cereal?

20. Elliot and Elliot is a public accounting firm with four persons working in the auditing department—Smith, Jones, Davis, and Nguyen. Each of these individuals is uniquely qualified with experience in specific industries. The manager of this department has just received four jobs that must be assigned to these individuals, and only one job may be assigned to each. The estimated number of days required to complete each of these jobs by the four individuals is given in the table below.

	Job #1	Job #2	Job #3	Job #4
Smith	4	10	8	9
Jones	5	14	8	10
Davis	4	13	9	12
Nguyen	5	11	7	11

The manager would like to minimize the number of days required for the completion of these jobs. Formulate this as a linear programming problem. Solve using any available computer software. How many work days will be required to complete these jobs? Who will be assigned to each job?

21. Ginny Rait is the general manager for N.R.G., Inc., a company producing two types of electric generators—the BR54 and the BR49. Orders have been received, and a production schedule is to be set up for the next three months. Generators may be produced in one month and stored until the next month. However, the cost of holding these in inventory is one percent of the cost per month. The BR54 costs $80 each and the BR49 costs $95 each. The company can produce a total of 1,100 units each month. Currently, there are 50 units of each type in the warehouse, and at the end of October, the company would like to have 100 units of the BR54 and 150 units of the BR49 in stock. The demand for each product in each month is given in the table below.

	BR54	BR49
August	320	450
September	740	420
October	500	480

Formulate this as a linear programming problem to minimize cost. How many units of each type should be produced each month? What is the total cost of this solution?

22. Coast-to-Coast Airlines is investigating the possibility of reducing the cost of fuel purchases by taking advantage of lower fuel costs in certain cities. Because fuel purchases represent a substantial portion of operating expenses for an airline, it is important these costs be carefully monitored. However, fuel adds weight to an airplane, and consequently, excess fuel raises the cost of getting from one city to another. In evaluating one particular flight rotation, a plane begins in Atlanta, flies from Atlanta to Los Angeles, from Los Angeles to Houston, from Houston to New Orleans, and from New Orleans to Atlanta. When the plane arrives in Atlanta, the flight rotation is said to have been completed, and then it starts again. Thus, the fuel onboard when the flight arrived in Atlanta must be taken into consideration when the flight begins. Along each leg of this route, there is a minimum and maximum amount of fuel that may be carried. This and additional information is provided in the table below.

Leg	Minimum Fuel Required	Maximum Fuel Allowed	Regular Fuel Consumption	Price per Gallon
Atlanta-Los Angeles	24	36	12	$1.15
Los Angeles-Houston	15	23	7	$1.25
Houston-New Orleans	9	17	3	$1.10
New Orleans-Atlanta	11	20	5	$1.18

The regular fuel consumption is based on the plane carrying the minimum amount of fuel. If more than this is carried, the amount of fuel consumed is five percent higher than normal for each 1,000 gallons of fuel above the minimum. For example, if 25,000 gallons of fuel were onboard when the plane takes off from Atlanta, the fuel consumed on this route would be $12 + 0.05(12) = 12.6$ thousand gallons. If 26,000 gallons were onboard, the fuel consumed would be increased by another 0.6 thousand so the total would be 13.2 thousand gallons.

Formulate this as a linear programming problem to minimize the cost. How many gallons should be purchased in each city? What is the total cost?

23. Sundown Rent-a-Car, a large automobile rental agency operating in the Midwest, is preparing a leasing strategy for the next six months. Sundown leases cars from an automobile manufacturer and then rents them to the public on a daily basis. A forecast for the demand for Sundown's cars in the next six months is given in the table below.

March	April	May	June	July	August
420	400	430	460	470	440

Cars may be leased from the manufacturer for either three, four, or five months. These are leased on the first day of the month and are returned on the last day of the month. Every six months the automobile manufacturer is notified by Sundown about the number of cars needed during the next six months. The automobile manufacturer has stipulated that at least 50 percent of the cars rented during a six-month period must be on the five-month lease. The cost per month on each of the three types of leases are $420 for the three-month lease, $400 for the four-month lease and $370 for the five-month lease.

Currently, Sundown has 390 cars. The lease on 120 expires at the end of March. The lease on another 140 expires at the end of April, and the lease on the rest of these expires at the end of May.

a) Use linear programming to determine how many cars should be leased in each month on each type of lease to minimize the cost of leasing over the six-month period. How many cars are left at the end of August?

b) Use linear programming to determine how many cars should be leased in each month on each type of lease to minimize the cost of leasing over the entire life of these leases.

24. Daniel Grady is the financial advisor for a number of professional athletes. An analysis of the long-term goals for many of these athletes has resulted in a recommendation to purchase stocks with some of their income that is set aside for investments. Five stocks have been identified as having very favorable expectations for future performance. While the expected return is important in these investments, the risk as measured by the *beta* of the stock also is

important. (A high value of beta indicates that the stock has a relatively high risk.) The expected return and the betas for five stocks are given in the table below.

Stock	1	2	3	4	5
Expected Return (%)	11.0	9.0	6.5	15.0	13.0
Beta	1.20	0.85	0.55	1.40	1.25

Daniel would like to minimize the beta of the stock portfolio (calculated using a weighted average of the amounts put into the different stocks), while maintaining an expected return of at least 11 percent. Because future conditions may change, Daniel has decided that no more than 35 percent of the portfolio should be invested in any one stock.

Formulate this as a linear program. (*Hint*: Define the variables to be the proportion of the total investment that would be put in each stock. Include a constraint that restricts the sum of these variables to be 1.) Solve using any available software. What is the beta for this portfolio? What is the expected return for this portfolio?

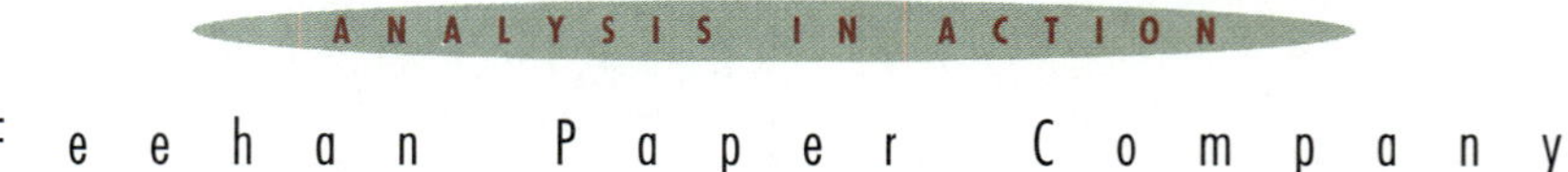

Feehan Paper Company

The Feehan Paper Company serves customers in the southeastern part of the United States. Various types of commercial and retail paper products are made in the manufacturing facility and sold to dealers. Each month a forecast is made of the demand for the products, and a production schedule is developed.

The company makes rolls of paper for use in cash registers, adding machines, calculators, and similar devices. The production process involves the use of 200-foot long rolls that are 10-inches wide. These are cut using machinery that may be set to produce cuts of certain widths. Particular combinations or patterns of these cuts are used to produce rolls that are 1.5-inches, 2-inches, and 2.5-inches wide. Waste is generated with some of the patterns, and while the waste is recycled, it represents a cost to the company. The specific cutting patterns used are given in the table below.

	Number of Rolls			
Cutting Pattern	1.5" Wide	2" Wide	2.5" Wide	Waste (in Inches)
1	0	0	4	0
2	0	5	0	0
3	6	0	0	1
4	2	1	2	0
5	4	2	0	0
6	2	2	1	0.5
7	0	2	2	1

For example, in cutting a 10-inch roll on Cutting Pattern 6, we would get two of the 1.5-inch rolls, two of the 2-inch rolls, and one of the 2.5-inch rolls. This leaves 0.5 inches of waste from each 10-inch roll that is cut using this pattern.

Forecasted demand for next month has resulted in a need to produce 2,300 of the 1.5-inch rolls, 800 of the 2-inch rolls, and 2,000 of the 2.5-inch rolls. The production manager of Feehan Paper Company always has tried to minimize the waste generated in meeting this demand. However, when this has been done, the number of smaller rolls produced sometimes has exceeded the demand. These have been stored and used in later months, while the cost of storage has been ignored. Now, however, concern about this storage cost has been expressed by the general manager. Data currently is being collected regarding the costs for storing excess rolls. However, before this data is available, management would like to know how many 10-inch rolls to cut on each pattern to meet the demand while minimizing waste and how many rolls to cut on each pattern to minimize the number of 10-inch rolls used.

Prepare a managerial report indicating what the waste would be and how many 10-inch rolls would be used for each of these criteria. Also, give your recommendation for what the appropriate criterion should be.

CASE ONE

Linear Programming at AT&T's Network Operation Center

AT&T's World-Wide Intelligent Network handles more than 175 million calls on the average business day. These calls are routed over a complex series of transmission and switching devices located all around the world. In addition, the Network provides data and multimedia services to its business and residential customers. These service offerings equate to an annual revenue of more than forty billion dollars for AT&T.

Keeping the Network maintained, not to mention making improvements, is a complex problem, one that is highly dependent on the workforce of AT&T's Network Services Division (NSD). Every minute of every day, NSD employees are busy monitoring the performance of the Network, planning new service and feature offerings, and developing new capacity and capabilities.

John Zuk is the district manager of NSD's Production Planning and Control (PP & C) group. His team helps local offices — the ones that house AT&T's Network equipment — decide what work to do when, to support the Network. AT&T has hundreds of local offices around the world. All of the offices have equipment and also technicians.

Technicians work to provide additional capacity, maintain existing equipment, and prepare for future work. For example, as the number of residential and business customers in a given geographic area grows, it becomes necessary to add more capacity to the local telephone switch. This switch routes calls into and out of the Network. Technicians install additional capacity based on existing demand and forecasted growth, as indicated in marketing forecasts. Technicians also are called on to perform routine maintenance and upgrades to the equipment in their local offices. Finally, they may be asked to prepare for imminent upgrades or modifications to existing Network equipment modules. Work associated with these tasks is of varying duration and different skill sets are necessary to do different jobs. Requests to perform the tasks come from marketing, research and development, planning, maintenance, and provisioning organizations within NSD.

Often the "to do" list of tasks for a given office can exceed the resources available in an office location. Resource levels are constantly changing due to personnel schedules (i.e., sickness, vacation, etc.). Priorities associated with tasks also are always being changed. Unexpected events, such as natural disasters, can alter schedules and reset priorities at any given moment. Every day, John Zuk and his PP & C team help decide which offices should do what work when, to minimize overall cost. They also help at a higher level, deciding what annual staffing levels should be used at the different regions. These levels are based on demand forecasts and pending work. Finally, they make assignments of technicians on daily, weekly, and monthly levels to appropriate sites to minimize overall cost. This is achieved by balancing the "rolling" costs (accrued cost on a month-to-month basis) with the annual budget.

John Zuk and his team use linear programming to help with the high level problem of setting annual staffing levels. To use LP, they need to first identify the variables, constraints, and objective function of the problem. The variables are the number of workers of each skill type to be assigned to each region in each period, where monthly time buckets are used. At this level, the constraints are related primarily to the demand. The pending and forecast work of each type specify the minimum numbers of worker hours by skill set required in each region. Other constraints establish the maximum number of hours a worker can be expected to work, including allowances for training, vacation and sick time. Additional variables can be added to allow for the temporary assignment of workers from one region to another. Costs are associated with the total number of workers of each skill level (i.e., salary and benefits), and also with the number of workers temporarily assigned (i.e., per diem allotments, etc.).

AT&T might then formulate a time-staged linear program for a particular region. An example of the problem formulation is described below. The initial formulation assumes that the following are known:

$P_{t,i}$ days of work required in period t by workers of skill level i

n_t number of working days in period t

$c_{t,i}$ cost of paying a worker of type i for period t

$b_{t,i}$ additional cost of hiring a worker of type i from the pool in period t

N_i number of workers of type i assigned to the region

$M_{t,i}$ maximum number of workers of type i that may be borrowed from other regions in period t

$S_{t,i}$ maximum number of workers of type i that may be sent to the pool in period t

The following values are selected as decision variables:

$O_{t,i}$ number of workers of skill level i borrowed from other regions in period t

$R_{t,i}$ number of workers of skill level i released to pool during the period

The primary problem constraint is that enough workers be used in period i to complete the tasks required. This constraint takes the form:

$$P_{t,i} \leq (N_i = O_{t,i} - R_{t,i})^{*}\ n_t \quad \text{for} \quad 1 \leq t \leq T$$

Other constraints restrict the number of workers sent to and received from other regions, as shown below:

$$O_{t,i} \leq M_{t,i} \quad \text{for } 1 \leq t \leq T$$
$$R_{t,i} \leq S_{t,i} \quad \text{for } 1 \leq t \leq T$$

Every minute of every day, AT&T's Network Services Division employees are busy monitoring the performance of the Network, planning new services and feature offerings, and deploying new capacity and capabilities. CREDIT: AT&T Network Operations Center

Naturally, the linear programming formulation also requires that all variables be nonnegative. The objective of this problem is to minimize the cost due to the workers, and appears as:

$$\min \sum\sum (N_i + O_{t,i} - R_{t,i})^* c_{t,i} + O_{t,i}{}^* b_{t,i}$$

The linear program described here would yield the optimal number of workers to be sent to or received from a common pool by period for a given region. An aggregate problem would be used first to set the N_i, the base number of workers of each skill type for each region. Alternatively, N_i could be allowed to vary by period. Additional variables would need to be added to account for variations in the workforce in each period for each region. The only changes required in the above formulation would be the replacement of N_i with $N_{t,i}$ everywhere it appears, and the addition of the conservation of workforce constraint as follows:

$$N_{t,i} = N_{t,i-1} + H_{t,i} - F_{t,i} \quad \text{for } 1 \leq t \leq T$$

where H represents the number of workers hired, and F the number of workers fired or leaving the company. Constraints also could be added to limit the number of allowable hirings and firings per period. A cost of hiring and a cost for firing also could be added to the objective function if wanted.

The formulation defined above assumes that all tasks required for a given period must be completed. Another extension of the model would be to allow incomplete work to be completed in the next period, subject to an additional cost. Defining the costs to include and setting limits on the work allowed to be carried over would be highly situation-specific decisions. However, linear programming certainly could handle them.

PROBLEM 1:

Suppose AT&T wants to plan for two periods for a single skill level of workers.

Let:

P_{11} = 200 days
P_{21} = 250 days
n_1 = 20 days
n_2 = 22 days
c_{11} = \$250 per day
c_{21} = \$270 per day
b_{11} = \$400 per worker
b_{21} = \$450 per worker
N_{11} = 6 workers
N_{21} = 15 workers
M_{11} = 50 workers
M_{21} = 30 workers
s_{11} = 6 workers
s_{21} = 5 workers

(*NOTE:* The number of workers of type 1 assigned to the region varies over the two time periods.)

The linear programming is:

$$\min\ (6 + O_{11} - R_{11})250 + (15 + O_{21} - R_{21})270 + O_{11}(400) + O_{21}(450)$$

$$\begin{aligned}
\text{st}\ \ & 200 \le (6 + O_{11} - R_{11})20 \\
& 250 \le (15 + O_{21} - R_{21})22 \\
& O_{11} \le 50 \\
& O_{21} \le 30 \\
& R_{11} \le 6 \\
& R_{21} \le 5 \\
& O_{11} \ge 0 \\
& O_{21} \ge 0 \\
& R_{11} \ge 0 \\
& R_{21} \ge 0
\end{aligned}$$

Rewriting the LP problem in standard form:

$$\begin{aligned}
\min\ & 5550 + 650O_{11} + 720O_{21} - 250R_{11} - 270R_{21} \\
\text{st}\ & 20O_{11} - 20R_{11} \ge 80 \\
& -22O_{21} + 22R_{21} \ge 80 \\
& O_{11} \le 50 \\
& O_{21} \le 30 \\
& R_{11} \le 6 \\
& R_{21} \le 5 \\
& O_{11} \ge 0 \\
& O_{21} \ge 0 \\
& R_{11} \ge 0 \\
& R_{21} \ge 0
\end{aligned}$$

The problem and the solution found using LINDO are:

```
MIN     650 011 + 720 021 - 250 R11 - 270 R21
SUBJECT TO
       2)   20 011 - 20 R11 >=   80
       3) - 22 021 + 22 R21 <=   80
       4)   011 <=   50
       5)   021 <=   30
       6)   R11 <=   6
       7)   R21 <=   5
END

LP OPTIMUM FOUND AT STEP      2

       OBJECTIVE FUNCTION VALUE

       1)      1618.1820
```

VARIABLE	VALUE	REDUCED COST
O11	4.000000	.000000
O21	.000000	450.000000
R11	.000000	400.000000
R21	3.636364	.000000

ROW	SLACK OR SURPLUS	DUAL PRICES
2)	.000000	-32.500000
3)	.000000	12.272730
4)	46.000000	.000000
5)	30.000000	.000000
6)	6.000000	.000000
7)	1.363636	.000000

NO. ITERATIONS= 2

RANGES IN WHICH THE BASIS IS UNCHANGED:

		OBJ COEFFICIENT RANGES	
VARIABLE	CURRENT COEF	ALLOWABLE INCREASE	ALLOWABLE DECREASE
O11	650.000000	INFINITY	400.000000
O21	720.000000	INFINITY	450.000000
R11	-250.000000	INFINITY	400.000000
R21	-270.000000	270.000000	450.000000

		RIGHTHAND SIDE RANGES	
ROW	CURRENT RHS	ALLOWABLE INCREASE	ALLOWABLE DECREASE
2	80.000000	920.000000	80.000000
3	80.000000	30.000000	80.000000
4	50.000000	INFINITY	46.000000
5	30.000000	INFINITY	30.000000
6	6.000000	INFINITY	6.000000
7	5.000000	INFINITY	1.363636

The value of the objective function is 5550+1618.182 or 7168.182.

PROBLEM 2:

Suppose AT&T wants to plan for two periods for two classes of workers. Let:

$$P_{11} = 200 \text{ days}$$
$$P_{21} = 250 \text{ days}$$
$$P_{12} = 250 \text{ days}$$
$$P_{22} = 250 \text{ days}$$
$$n_1 = 20 \text{ days}$$
$$n_2 = 22 \text{ days}$$
$$c_{11} = \$250 \text{ per day}$$
$$c_{21} = \$270 \text{ per day}$$

c_{12} = \$450 per day
c_{22} = \$500 per day
b_{11} = \$400 per worker
b_{21} = \$450 per worker
b_{12} = \$600 per worker
b_{22} = \$600 per worker
N_{11} = 6 workers
N_{21} = 15 workers
N_{12} = 10 workers
N_{22} = 10 workers
M_{11} = 50 workers
M_{21} = 30 workers
M_{12} = 20 workers
M_{22} = 20 workers
S_{11} = 6 workers
S_{21} = 5 workers
S_{12} = 10 workers
S_{22} = 10 workers

Determine the number of workers that is needed to be borrowed or released for each skill level over the two periods of time so that the worker cost function is minimized.

PROBLEM 3:

Suppose AT&T wants to plan for three periods for two classes of workers.
Let:

P_{11} = 200 days
P_{21} = 250 days
P_{31} = 250 days
P_{12} = 250 days
P_{22} = 250 days
P_{32} = 250 days
n_1 = 20 days
n_2 = 22 days
n_3 = 22 days
c_{11} = \$250 per day
c_{21} = \$270 per day
c_{31} = \$270 per day
c_{12} = \$450 per day

c_{22} = \$500 per day
c_{32} = \$500 per day

b_{11} = \$400 per worker
b_{21} = \$450 per worker
b_{31} = \$450 per worker

b_{12} = \$600 per worker
b_{22} = \$600 per worker
b_{32} = \$600 per worker

N_{11} = 6 workers
N_{21} = 15 workers
N_{31} = 12 workers

N_{12} = 10 workers
N_{22} = 10 workers
N_{32} = 10 workers

M_{11} = 50 workers
M_{21} = 30 workers
M_{31} = 10 workers

M_{12} = 20 workers
M_{22} = 20 workers
M_{32} = 5 workers

S_{11} = 6 workers
S_{21} = 5 workers
S_{31} = 5 workers

S_{12} = 10 workers
S_{22} = 10 workers
S_{32} = 1 worker

Determine the number of workers that is needed to be borrowed or released for each skill level over the three periods of time so that the worker cost function is minimized.

CHAPTER FIVE

The Simplex Method and Sensitivity Analysis

LEARNING OBJECTIVES

Upon completing Chapter 5, you should be able to:

- Understand how the simplex algorithm is used to solve linear programs.
- Set up the initial simplex tableau and use the simplex algorithm to find the optimal solution.
- Interpret slack, surplus, and artificial variables.
- Explain the meaning of the Z_j values, $C_j - Z_j$ values, and the critical ratios.
- Recognize, using the simplex tableau, when a solution is unbounded, degenerate, infeasible, or when multiple optimal solutions exist.
- Find reduced costs and dual prices from the optimal simplex tableau.
- Determine how much an objective function coefficient may change before a new basis is optimal.
- Determine the range of values for changes in the right-hand side of a constraint for which the dual price is relevant.

CHAPTER OUTLINE

5.1

INTRODUCTION

In an earlier chapter, graphical methods were used to solve linear programming problems with two decision variables. In the chapter on linear programming applications, we saw that even most small problems have more than two variables and consequently cannot be represented by a two-dimensional graph. The most commonly used technique for solving linear programming problems is the **simplex algorithm**.

Simplex algorithm
The most common technique for solving linear programming problems.

In this chapter we will present the general approach of the simplex algorithm. Examples of both a maximization problem and a minimization problem will be provided. Sensitivity analysis based on the simplex algorithm also will be presented. We will see how the upper and lower limits are calculated for objective function coefficients and right-hand side values that were observed in computer outputs in an earlier chapter.

Conceptual Description of the Simplex Algorithm

Earlier, a linear programming problem with two decision variables showed that an optimal solution will be found (if it exists) at one of the corner points and will be a basic feasible solution. With three variables, the feasible region might be viewed as a cube or other solid object with straight sides. An optimal solution would exist at one of the corner points. With four or more variables, visualizing the feasible region may be impossible, but an optimal solution still must be a basic solution.

We will study the simplex algorithm which will systematically evaluate corner points or basic solutions to find the one that is optimal. We will begin by considering the basic solution where all decision variables are set equal to zero. Computations will be performed to determine if it is possible to find another basic solution that provides a better value for the objective function. If it is possible to generate a better solution, additional calculations will be performed to find this next solution. This new solution will be evaluated to determine if yet another basic solution is better. This process will continue until it is no longer possible to get a better solution. This last point will be the optimal solution.

5.2

BEFORE BEGINNING THE SIMPLEX ALGORITHM

Slack variable
A variable added to a ≤ constraint to represent unused resources.

Surplus variable
A variable used in a ≥ constraint to represent the amount by which the right-hand side of the constraint is exceeded.

The linear programming problem must be in the standard form before we begin using the simplex algorithm. As we saw in Chapter 2, this means the right-hand side values and all variables are restricted to be nonnegative and all constraints must be expressed as equalities. To convert all constraints into equalities, a **slack variable** is added to each ≤ constraint and a **surplus variable** is subtracted from each ≥ constraint.

Artificial variables also are added to all constraints that were ≥ or = constraints. The simplex algorithm starts at the basic solution in which all decision variables are set equal to zero, and this is usually not a feasible solution if there is a ≥ or = constraint. The **artificial variables** allow us to begin at an infeasible solution and eventually move to a feasible basic solution if one exists. This will be discussed later in this chapter.

Artificial variables
Variables used with the simplex algorithm to indicate if the solution is feasible.

We will use the simplex algorithm to solve the B & B Electronics problem from Chapter 2. The steps of the simplex algorithm will be summarized after this has been presented. We then will present an example of a minimization problem.

5.3 A MAXIMIZATION EXAMPLE

Recall the B & B Electronics problem from Chapter 2. In this problem, we defined the variables as:

X_1 = number of cellular phones produced each week
X_2 = number of pagers produced each week

The linear programming model for this was:

$$\begin{aligned} &\text{Maximize profit} = 15X_1 + 20X_2 \\ &\text{Subject to: } 4X_1 + 2X_2 \le 36 \quad \text{assembly hours} \\ &\qquad X_1 + 2X_2 \le 24 \quad \text{inspection hours} \\ &\qquad X_1, X_2 \ge 0 \quad \text{nonnegativity constraints} \end{aligned}$$

All of the right-hand side values already are nonnegative, so we may now add slack variables to the problem (all of the constraints are ≤ constraints) and put the problem in the standard form. Doing this results in:

$$\begin{aligned} &\text{Maximize profit} = 15X_1 + 20X_2 \\ &\text{Subject to: } 4X_1 + 2X_2 + S_1 = 36 \quad \text{assembly hours} \\ &\qquad X_1 + 2X_2 + S_2 = 24 \quad \text{inspection hours} \\ &\qquad X_1, X_2, S_1, S_2 \ge 0 \quad \text{nonnegativity constraints} \end{aligned}$$

The slack variable S_1 represents any excess or unused assembly hours. Similarly, S_2 represents any unused inspection hours. Surplus variables are not used with the nonnegativity constraints because all variables are assumed to be nonnegative when using the simplex algorithm. The graph of this is shown in Figure 5.1. Notice there are four corner points in the feasible region. The simplex algorithm will begin by evaluating the corner point (0,0), which is identified as point A on the graph. Certain numbers found with the simplex algorithm will indicate this is not the optimal solution, and another corner point (B) then will be evaluated. Upon finding this is not the optimal corner point, another point (C) will be evaluated and it will be determined that this is the optimal solution without ever explicitly evaluating point D. Thus, the simplex algorithm will move from one corner point to an adjacent corner point, until the optimal corner point is finally found.

FIGURE 5.1

Graph of B & B Electronics Problem with No Demand Constraints

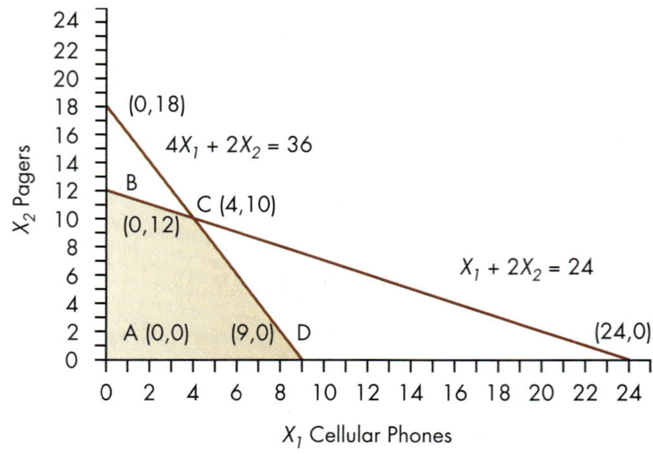

5.4

DEVELOPING THE INITIAL SIMPLEX TABLEAU

In using the simplex algorithm, we will use what is referred to as the *simplex tableau.* This simplex tableau represents the linear programming problem in a tabular format. The beginning of the initial simplex tableau for this problem is given in Figure 5.2.

Basic variables
Variables not required to have values of zero in a solution found using the simplex algorithm.

The initial simplex tableau will have one column for each of the variables plus three additional columns. One of these columns is for the right-hand side (RHS) values of the constraints. Another column is for the **basic variables**, which are variables not restricted to have values of zero, and the third column is for the objective function coefficients *(C_j)* for the basic variables.

C_j
An objective function coefficient.

The top row (referred to as the C_j row) of the simplex tableau will provide the objective function coefficients. The profit on X_1 is 15, so this is

FIGURE 5.2

Partial Initial Simplex Tableau for B & B Electronics Problem

C_j	Basic Variable	15 X_1	20 X_2	0 S_1	0 S_2	RHS Value
		4	2	1	0	36
		1	2	0	1	24
	Z_j					
	$C_j - Z_j$					

written in the X_1 column. Similarly, 20 is written above X_2 to indicate the profit for X_2. Slack variables typically represent unused resources, and these do not add anything to profit. Therefore, *the objective function coefficient for each of the slack variables (and surplus variables) is zero.*

There will be one row in the simplex tableau for each constraint. The first row represents the first constraint with the coefficients for the variables in this constraint written in the appropriate column. Similarly, the second row of the tableau gives the coefficients for the second constraint. In addition to rows for the constraints, there will be two additional rows—the Z_j row and the $C_j - Z_j$ row. These will be used later to evaluate the current solution to see if it is optimal.

Basic Variables

When using the simplex algorithm, any variable listed in the Basic Variable column is called a basic variable. The set of all basic variables is called the **basis**. Any variable not listed in the Basic Variable column is called a **nonbasic variable**. Each nonbasic variable is equal to zero. Thus, the only variables that may be greater than zero are the basic variables given in the tableau. The simplex algorithm will begin with the decision variables (X_1 and X_2) equal to zero, so they must be nonbasic variables. *In the initial simplex tableau, only slack variables and artificial variables will be basic variables.*

Basis
The set of all basic variables in a solution.

Nonbasic variable
A variable that is not in the basis and is required to equal zero. These are the variables not listed in the Basic Variables column in the simplex tableau.

Thus, looking at the first constraint we see

$$4X_1 + 2X_2 + S_1 = 36$$
$$4(0) + 2(0) + S_1 = 36$$

so

$$S_1 = 36$$

This is indicated in the initial simplex tableau with S_1 being put in the Basic Variable column in the first row. Similarly, S_2 must be equal to 24 (because $X_1 = 0$ and $X_2 = 0$), and this is placed in the Basic Variable column in the

FIGURE 5.3

Partial Initial Simplex Tableau for B & B Electronics Problem

C_j	Basic Variable	15 X_1	20 X_2	0 S_1	0 S_2	RHS Value
0	S_1	4	2	1	0	36
0	S_2	1	2	0	1	24
	Z_j					
	$C_j - Z_j$					

second row. Figure 5.3 shows the addition of these variables. Notice the coefficient for each of these variables in the objective function is written next to the basic variable in the column labeled C_j.

The values of the basic variables are given in the RHS Value column in the tableau. In this initial simplex tableau, the basic variables are S_1 and S_2, and the solution represented by this tableau is $S_1 = 36$ and $S_2 = 24$ with nonbasic variables X_1 and X_2 both equal to zero.

Basic solution

A basic solution to a set of m linear equations with n unknowns (with $m < n$) and is found by setting $n - m$ of these variables equal to zero and solving for the rest of them. This is the equivalent of a corner point solution.

The solution represented by this simplex tableau is a corner point solution (point A in Figure 5.1 above) and is referred to as a **basic solution.** In mathematical terms, a basic solution to a set of m linear equations with n unknowns (with $m < n$) is found by setting $n - m$ of these variables equal to zero and solving for the rest of them. While there may be cases with other systems of equations where such a solution does not exist, such difficulties will not arise in linear programming problems with slack, surplus, and artificial variables. In this particular problem, there are two constraints ($m = 2$) and four variables ($n = 4$) including the slack variables. There are $n - m = 4 - 2 = 2$ variables, which are set equal to zero, and these are called the nonbasic variables in the simplex algorithm. In this initial solution, we have $X_1 = 0$ and $X_2 = 0$. The two equations could be solved for the remaining two variables and we would get $S_1 = 36$ and $S_2 = 24$. While all basic solutions could be found algebraically, the simplex algorithm provides a systematic way of finding the optimal basic solution.

Substitution Rates

Substitution rates

Numbers in the simplex tableau. The substitution rate indicates how much the value of a basic variable would have to be reduced in order to bring one unit of the nonbasic variable into the solution.

The numbers in the simplex tableau below the variables are called **substitution rates.** In the initial simplex tableau, these substitution rates are simply the coefficients found in the constraints. The substitution rate indicates how much the value of a basic variable would have to be reduced in order to bring one unit of the nonbasic variable into the solution. For example, the 4 in the X_1 column in Figure 5.3 above indicates the value of S_1 (the basic variable in that row) must be reduced by 4 units if one unit of X_1 is produced. Thus, to make one cellular phone (X_1), 4 hours of assembly time will be used, which reduces the slack for assembly time (S_1) by 4 units. Similarly, the 1 in the X_1 column indicates the value of S_2 will be reduced by 1 unit if one unit of X_1 is produced. This means to produce one cellular phone, the slack for inspection hours (S_2) must be reduced by 1 hour. Because the RHS Value column gives the values for the basic variables, if one unit of X_1 is produced, the RHS value in the first row decreases by 4 units (the substitution rate) and the RHS value in the second row decreases by 1 unit (the substitution rate in that row).

Notation for Z_j and C_j

The subscript j that is used with C_j and Z_j indicates the column for this particular value. In this example, there are four columns (X_1, X_2, S_1, and S_2) in the tableau, so we will be calculating Z_1 for the first (X_1) column, Z_2 for the second (X_2) column, Z_3 for the third (S_1) column, and Z_4 for the fourth (S_2) column. Similar subscripts apply to the C_j values.

Calculating Z_j (Opportunity Cost)

Z_j
The opportunity cost of bringing in one unit of a variable into the solution.

The Z_j row in the simplex tableau indicates what must be sacrificed in the current solution to bring in one unit of the variable in that column. This might be viewed as an opportunity cost. We will use the substitution rates and the objective function coefficients (C_j values listed in the C_j column) for the basic variables to calculate this. To calculate the Z_j for a particular column, we simply multiply the substitution rate in each row by the objective coefficient in that row and add these together.

Consider the X_1 column in Figure 5.3 above. We see from the substitution rates that to produce one unit of X_1, we must reduce the amount of S_1 by 4 units and the amount of S_2 by 1 unit. Looking at the profit generated by these (in the C_j column), we see that S_1 and S_2 contribute \$0 profit per unit. We will multiply the profit (in the C_j column) for the basic variables by the number of units that must be sacrificed (substitution rate) for each basic variable and add these together. Thus to produce one unit of X_1, we must give up:

$$\begin{array}{l} (\$0 \text{ profit per unit of } S_1) \times (4 \text{ units of } S_1) \\ \underline{+(\$0 \text{ profit per unit of } S_2) \times (1 \text{ unit of } S_2)} \\ \$0 = \text{opportunity cost for } X_1 = Z_1 \end{array}$$

Thus, to make one unit of X_1 (to produce one cellular phone), we give up \$0 profit being generated with the current solution.

For the other columns, we have:

$$\begin{aligned} \text{opportunity cost for } X_2 = Z_2 &= 0(2) + 0(2) = 0 \\ \text{opportunity cost for } S_1 = Z_3 &= 0(1) + 0(0) = 0 \\ \text{opportunity cost for } S_2 = Z_4 &= 0(0) + 0(1) = 0 \\ Z_j \text{ for RHS Value column} &= 0(36) + 0(24) \quad = 0 \end{aligned}$$

The Z_j value in the RHS Value column has a different interpretation than the other Z_j values just as the other numbers in this column are not substitution rates. This Z_j in the RHS Value column gives the value of the objective function for the solution represented by this tableau.

In simplex tableaus presented later, the basic variables will change and thus the objective function coefficients (C_j) will not all be zeroes. Consequently, the Z_j values will not all be zeroes in the later tableaus.

Calculating $C_j - Z_j$ (Net Change in Objective Function Value)

$C_j - Z_j$
The net change in the objective function value that would result from bringing one unit of the corresponding variable into the solution.

The last row in the simplex tableau is the $C_j - Z_j$ row. This row represents the net change in the objective function value that would result if one unit of the variable in that column were brought into the solution. In this example, the $C_j - Z_j$ value (or $C_1 - Z_1$ because this is the first column) in the X_1 column would represent the net increase in profit that would result from making one cellular phone. The $C_j - Z_j$ value in the X_2 column (or $C_2 - Z_2$ because this is the second column) would represent the net increase in profit that would result from making one pager.

In each column, the $C_j - Z_j$ value is calculated by subtracting the Z_j value from the C_j value in the top row. Thus, in the X_1 column we have:

$$\begin{aligned} C_1 &= 15 \\ \underline{-Z_1} &= -0 \\ C_1 - Z_1 &= 15 \end{aligned}$$

Thus, if one unit of X_1 were brought into the solution (one cellular phone was produced), the objective function value (profit) would change by +$15 so it would increase by $15.

In the X_2 column we have:

$$\begin{aligned} C_2 &= 20 \\ \underline{-Z_2} &= -0 \\ C_2 - Z_2 &= 20 \end{aligned}$$

Thus, if one unit of X_2 were brought into the solution (one pager was produced), the objective function value (profit) would change by +$20 so it would increase by $20.

Continuing this with the other columns we have the values shown in Figure 5.4. This is the complete initial tableau for the B & B Electronics problem.

Evaluating the Current Solution

To determine if the solution represented by a simplex tableau is the optimal solution, we simply look at the $C_j - Z_j$ values for that tableau. *If all the $C_j - Z_j$ values for a maximization problem are negative or zero, then the current solution must be the optimal solution.* If any of these values is positive, then the objective function value (profit in this example) can still be increased so we must develop the next solution.

FIGURE 5.4

Complete Initial Simplex Tableau for B & B Electronics Problem

C_j	Basic Variable	15 X_1	20 X_2	0 S_1	0 S_2	RHS Value
0	S_1	4	2	1	0	36
0	S_2	1	2	0	1	24
	Z_j	0	0	0	0	0
	$C_j - Z_j$	15	20	0	0	

BEST PRACTICES

Optimizing Wastewater Reuse in Southern California

SOURCE: Martin, R. A., June 1993. "Thirsting for Answers: Optimization of Wastewater Reuse in Southern California Offers Possible Long-Range Hope for Drought-Plagued Area." *OR/MS Today*: 24-29.

California seems to be plagued with one natural disaster after another. In 1993, the state emerged from six consecutive years of drought, and found supplies of potable groundwater and surface waters greatly depleted. Southern California was particularly hard-hit by the drought, because most of its water supply (up to 90 percent) is imported from northern California and the Colorado River. Because the northern California reservoirs had declined to record lows, southern Californians had less water than usual. Meanwhile, the population of the area was growing by an average of 350,000 people per year; those people were getting thirsty.

Courtesy of American Water Works Company (Denver, CO)

In such times of drought, people in southern California began to explore supplemental sources of water as long-range solutions. Given legal, political, and environmental barriers to the development of new sources of water, they turned to the idea of wastewater reclamation and reuse. The basic idea behind this reclamation and reuse is to get at least a second use out of the initial drinkable water supply before the water makes it back out to sea. Secondary uses for wastewater include agricultural and landscape irrigation, ground water recharge, and industrial facilities.

The U.S. government commissioned the Southern California Comprehensive Water Reclamation and Reuse Study to analyze the political, institutional, and technical aspects of water reclamations. Other elements of the study included investigating cost-effective methods of reclaiming and transporting the water, and developing an economic distribution model to optimize the use of the reclaimed water. The manager of the study, Richard A. Martin, was at the time a Ph.D. student in operations research. He was particularly interested in the opportunity to use management science techniques for the project. He developed a model to define the optimum distribution network that will, when completed, maximize the reuse of wastewater regionwide at minimum cost. The model will be formulated as a transshipment problem, and will incorporate existing reclamation facilities and potential future projects. Policy makers will be able to use this model to evaluate future expansions based on changing technology and water supplies and demands.

5.5 DEVELOPING THE NEXT SOLUTION

If any $C_j - Z_j$ value is positive, we must continue with the simplex algorithm and find a better solution. To do this, we first determine which nonbasic variable should enter the basis. Then we decide how many units of this variable may be brought into the solution. Adjustments are made to the simplex tableau because bringing a new variable into the basis will usually impact the values for the other variables.

Selecting the Entering Variable

We are trying to maximize the value of the objective function (profit). If we select any variable with a positive $C_j - Z_j$ to enter the solution, the value of the objective function will increase. We will select the variable with the

Entering variable
The variable in the pivot column that will be in the basis of the next simplex tableau.

Pivot column
The column which contains the variable that will enter the basis. For maximization problems, this is the column with the largest positive $C_j - Z_j$ value. For minimization problems, this is the column with the most negative $C_j - Z_j$ value.

largest positive $C_j - Z_j$ value to enter the solution (become a basic variable) next. This will result in a greater increase in objective function value (profit) per unit of the variable that is brought in than any other variable. This variable will be called the **entering variable** and the column corresponding to this variable is called the **pivot column**.

In the simplex tableau given in Figure 5.4 above, we see the largest positive $C_j - Z_j$ value is for the X_2 column. The 20 in the $C_j - Z_j$ position tells us that profits will increase $20 per unit of X_2 that is brought into the solution. Thus, X_2 will be the entering variable and the X_2 column will be the pivot column.

Selecting the Leaving Variable

Critical ratio
For each row, the RHS value divided by the positive substitution rate in the pivot column for that row. The pivot row has the smallest critical ratio.

Pivot row
The row corresponding to the smallest critical ratio. The variable in this row leaves the basis.

Leaving variable
The basic variable that is in the pivot row. This will be a nonbasic variable in the next tableau.

Pivot number
The number at the intersection of the pivot row and pivot column.

Because the value of the objective function increases with each unit of the entering variable that is brought into the solution, we would like to bring in as many units of this as possible. To determine the maximum number of units this could be, we will consider the current right-hand side values and the substitution rates. Because all variables must be nonnegative, we must insure the RHS values in the simplex tableau do not become negative. We will divide the RHS values by the positive substitution rates in the pivot column (if there are negative or zero substitution rates we omit the rows from consideration). This result is called the **critical ratio**. The smallest critical ratio tells us how many units of the entering variable may be brought into the solution. The row with the smallest critical ratio is called the **pivot row**. By selecting the row with the smallest critical ratio, we guarantee that the next solution found is feasible. If any other row is selected, the next solution found would be infeasible. The basic variable in this row is called the **leaving variable** because the value of this variable will become zero and this variable will leave the basis and become a nonbasic variable. The number where the pivot row and pivot column intersect is called the **pivot number**.

In Figure 5.5 we see the critical ratios in this example are 36/2 = 18 for the first row and 24/2 = 12 for the second row. This tells us because 2 units

FIGURE 5.5

Pivot Row and Pivot Column for B & B Electronics Problem

C_j	Basic Variable	15 X_1	20 X_2	0 S_1	0 S_2	RHS Value	Critical Ratio	
0	S_1	4	**2**	1	0	36	36/2=18	
0	**S_2**	**1**	**2**	**0**	**1**	**24**	**24/2=12**	← pivot row
	Z_j	0	**0**	0	0	0		
	$C_j - Z_j$	15	**20**	0	0			
			↑ pivot column					

of S_1 must be given up to bring in one unit of X_2 and $S_1 = 36$, if we then bring 18 units of X_2 into the solution, the value for S_1 will become zero. Similarly, if we bring 12 units of X_2 into the solution, the value of S_2 will become zero. Because all variables must be nonnegative, the maximum value for X_2 will be 12 (the smallest of these ratios). The pivot row is the second row, and the leaving variable will be the basic variable in this row, which is S_2. The pivot number is 2 because this is the substitution rate where the pivot row and pivot column intersect.

The graph of this problem in Figure 5.6 gives a clear picture of why the smallest critical ratio is used. The entering variable is the X_2 variable. To increase X_2, we move up the X_2 axis, which also represents the constraint $X_1 \geq 0$, from the current solution (0,0). The corner points shown in Figure 5.6 as we move in the direction of increasing X_2 are (0,12) and (0,18). The value for X_2 is 12 at the first corner point and 18 at the second. These values are the calculated critical ratios. We must stay inside the feasible region, which means we must select the smallest of these values for X_2, which is the smallest critical ratio. If we do not select the smallest critical ratio, the next basic solution in the simplex tableau would be infeasible as the value for one of the basic variables would be negative. We see in Figure 5.6 the point (0,18) is outside the feasible region. At this point (0,18), the inspection hours constraint is violated, and there would actually be a negative slack for this constraint.

The leaving variable in this example is S_2, the basic variable in the pivot row. This variable will be replaced by the entering variable X_2. The objective function coefficient for X_2 is 20, so this number will be put in the C_j column. All other variables currently in the basis will remain in the basis. Consequently, all other basic coefficients also remain unchanged. Figure 5.7 illustrates the beginning of the next tableau.

FIGURE 5.6

Corner Points for B & B Electronics Problem

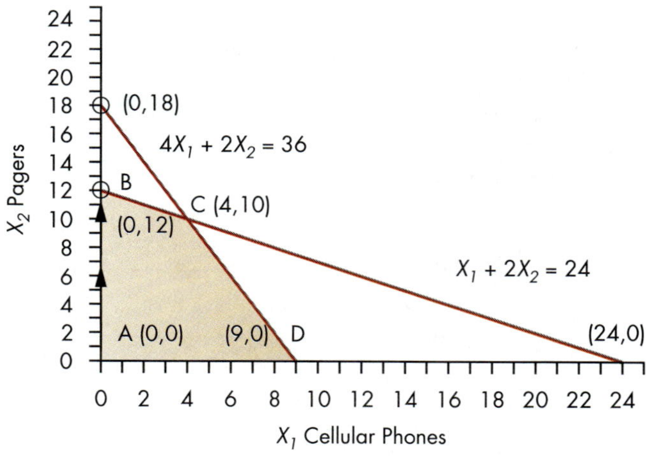

FIGURE 5.7

Basic Variable and Coefficient Replaced

C_j	Basic Variable	15 X_1	20 X_2	0 S_1	0 S_2	RHS Value
0	S_1					
20	$\mathbf{X_2}$					
	Z_j					
	$C_j - Z_j$					

Modifying the Simplex Tableau

Once the pivot column and pivot row have been determined, we must modify the rows of this tableau to reflect the new solution. To do this, we must perform particular row operations to turn the pivot number into a 1 and to make all other numbers in the pivot column equal to zero. Thus, the new X_2 column should look like the old S_2 column.

To make the pivot number a 1, we simply divide all the numbers in the pivot row by the pivot number. The pivot number in the example was 2, so we divide everything in the pivot row (row 2) by 2. Thus, we have:

old row 2:	1	2	0	1	24
new row 2:	1/2	2/2	0/2	1/2	24/2

Simplifying this we get:

new row 2:	1/2	1	0	1/2	12

Putting this in the simplex tableau results in Figure 5.8.

FIGURE 5.8

Simplex Tableau with Pivot Row Changed

C_j	Basic Variable	15 X_1	20 X_2	0 S_1	0 S_2	RHS Value
0	S_1					
20	X_2	1/2	1	0	1/2	12
	Z_j					
	$C_j - Z_j$					

Because the X_2 column was the pivot column, we must make all other numbers in the pivot column equal to zero. In this example, there is a 2 in the X_2 column in the first row. We wish to make this a zero. *To get a zero in other positions in the pivot column, we multiply the revised pivot row by whatever number is in the position we wish to be zero (2 in this example), and subtract this result from the old row.* In this example, we have:

new row 1 = (old row 1) – 2(revised pivot row)

Putting in the numbers we have

old row 1:	4	2	1	0	36
–2(revised pivot row):	–2(1/2	1	0	1/2	12)

or

old row 1:	4	2	1	0	36
–2(revised pivot row):	–1	–2	–0	–1	–24
new row 1:	3	0	1	–1	12

Putting this in the simplex tableau as the new row 1 results in Figure 5.9. Notice the substitution rate in the X_2 column is zero for the first row, and the X_2 column (X_2 is the entering variable) looks like the S_2 column (S_2 was the leaving variable) in the previous tableau.

The solution represented by this tableau must be evaluated by calculating the Z_j and $C_j - Z_j$ values as we did before. The Z_j values are found by multiplying the objective function coefficients in the C_j column by the substitution rates in each column. This gives:

$$Z_j \text{ for } X_1 \text{ column} = 0(3) + 20(1/2) = 10$$
$$Z_j \text{ for } X_2 \text{ column} = 0(0) + 20(1) = 20$$
$$Z_j \text{ for } S_1 \text{ column} = 0(1) + 20(0) = 0$$
$$Z_j \text{ for } S_2 \text{ column} = 0(-1) + 20(1/2) = 10$$
$$Z_j \text{ for RHS Value column} = 0(12) + 20(12) = 240$$

FIGURE 5.9

Second Simplex Tableau with Both Rows Changed

C_j	Basic Variable	15 X_1	20 X_2	0 S_1	0 S_2	RHS Value
0	S_1	3	0	1	–1	12
20	X_2	1/2	1	0	1/2	12
	Z_j					
	$C_j - Z_j$					

FIGURE 5.10

Second Simplex Tableau with $C_j - Z_j$ Calculated

C_j	Basic Variable	15 X_1	20 X_2	0 S_1	0 S_2	RHS Value
0	S_1	3	0	1	–1	12
20	X_2	1/2	1	0	1/2	12
	Z_j	10	20	0	10	240
	$C_j - Z_j$	5	0	0	–10	

To obtain the $C_j - Z_j$ values, subtract the Z_j from the objective function row, which results in Figure 5.10.

The solution represented by this tableau is $S_1 = 12$, $X_2 = 12$ (the basic variables are equal to the RHS values), while X_1 and S_2 are both equal to zero because they are nonbasic variables. The objective function value is 240. Notice the objective function value increased from zero in the initial tableau to 240 in this one. This change in the objective function value could have been predicted from the $C_j - Z_j$ value and the smallest critical ratio. The $C_j - Z_j$ value for X_2 was 20 indicating profits would increase $20 per unit, and the smallest critical ratio was 12 indicating 12 units of X_2 could be brought into the solution. Thus, profits should increase by $20(12) = $240.

This solution is not optimal because there is still a positive $C_j - Z_j$ value. Thus, we must continue to find another solution.

Generating the Third Simplex Tableau

Because there is a positive $C_j - Z_j$ value in Figure 5.10 above, continue and select the X_1 column as the pivot column because it has the largest positive $C_j - Z_j$ value. This means variable X_1 will enter the solution in the next tableau. The +5 in the $C_j - Z_j$ row for this means profits will increase $5 for each unit of X_1 that is brought into the solution.

To select the pivot row and find the leaving variable, we calculate critical ratios by dividing the RHS values by the substitution rates in the pivot column. We obtain the following:

$$12/3 = 4$$

and

$$12/(1/2) = 24$$

The smallest critical ratio is 4, so the first row is selected as the pivot row and the basic variable in this row, S_1, will be the leaving variable. This will be replaced by the entering variable, X_1, and the number in the C_j column is changed to 15 (the objective function coefficient for X_1). The pivot number is three because this is the substitution rate at the intersection of the pivot row and pivot column. Notice in Figure 5.6 above as we move from the corner point (0,12) in a direction of increasing X_1 (the entering variable) and along the inspection hours constraint, we would encounter the corner points (4,10) and (24,0). The values of X_1 at these points are 4 and 24 which are the values of the critical ratios. Thus, we must select the smallest of these to remain inside the feasible region.

The next step is to turn the pivot number into a 1 by dividing the pivot row by 3 (the pivot number). This gives us:

(old row 1)/3:	3/3	0/3	1/3	−1/3	12/3
= new row 1:	1	0	1/3	−1/3	4

Next we must get zeroes as the substitution rates in the pivot column for all other rows. There is only one other row (row 2), so we wish to turn the ½ in the X_1 column into a zero by multiplying the new pivot row by ½ and subtracting this from the old row 2. This gives us

new row 2 = (old row 2) – (1/2)(revised pivot row)

or

old row 2:	1/2	1	0	1/2	12
−1/2(revised pivot row):	−1/2(1	0	1/3	−1/3	4)

or

old row 2:	1/2	1	0	1/2	12
−(1/2)(new pivot row):	−1/2	−0	−1/6	+1/6	−2
= new row 2:	0	1	−1/6	2/3	10

Putting the new row 1 and the new row 2 into the simplex tableau and making the changes in the basic variable results in Figure 5.11.

FIGURE 5.11

Partial Third Simplex Tableau with New Basis

C_j	Basic Variable	15 X_1	20 X_2	0 S_1	0 S_2	RHS Value
15	X_1	1	0	1/3	−1/3	4
20	X_2	0	1	−1/6	2/3	10
	Z_j					
	$C_j - Z_j$					

We now calculate the Z_j by multiplying the basic variable coefficients by the substitution rates in each column. This yields:

$$\begin{aligned} Z_j \text{ for } X_1 \text{ column} &= 15(1) + 20(0) = 15 \\ Z_j \text{ for } X_2 \text{ column} &= 15(0) + 20(1) = 20 \\ Z_j \text{ for } S_1 \text{ column} &= 15(1/3) + 20(-1/6) = 5/3 \\ Z_j \text{ for } S_2 \text{ column} &= 15(-1/3) + 20(2/3) = 25/3 \\ Z_j \text{ for RHS Value column} &= 15(4) + 20(10) = 260 \end{aligned}$$

Putting these in the simplex tableau and subtracting them from the C_j row results in Figure 5.12. In this tableau, all of the $C_j - Z_j$ values are negative or zero, so this is the optimal solution. The values of the variables are:

$X_1 = 4$ produce 4 cellular phones
$X_2 = 10$ produce 10 pagers
$S_1 = 0$ no slack for assembly hours
$S_2 = 0$ no slack for inspection hours
profit = $260

This is precisely the solution we found using the graphical methods.

Performing Simplex Calculations with the Computer

The DSS computer software may be used to perform the simplex calculations and provide the simplex tableaus in the output. Output 5.1 illustrates this with the B & B Electronics problem. The notation used in the software is the following:

Bi: RHS value

Impr Indx: improvement index ($C_j - Z_j$)

Keycell: pivot number

Θ_i: critical ratio

You may find it helpful to check your calculations with this software.

FIGURE 5.12

Complete Third Simplex Tableau

C_j	Basic Variable	15 X_1	20 X_2	0 S_1	0 S_2	RHS Value
15	X_1	1	0	1/3	−1/3	4
20	X_2	0	1	−1/6	2/3	10
	Z_j	15	20	5/3	25/3	260
	$C_j - Z_j$	0	0	−5/3	−25/3	

OUTPUT 5.1

DSS Output with Simplex Tableaus for B & B Electronics Problem

```
Linear Programming

Z         X1        X2        Rel Op    R H S
MAX       15        20
Cons1     4         2         <=        36
Cons2     1         2         <=        24

Tableau   1
Ci        Basis       Bi          X1          X2          Slack 1    Slack 2   θi
                            Cj>>  15          20          0          0
-------------------------------------------------------------------------------
 0         Slack 1    36          4           2           1          0          18
 0         Slack 2    24          1           2           0          1          12
-------------------------------------------------------------------------------
          Zj          0           0           0           0          0
          Impr Indx               15          20          0          0
Keycell = (Slack 2 , X2        )

Tableau   2
Ci        Basis       Bi          X1          X2          Slack 1    Slack 2   θi
                            Cj>>  15          20          0          0
-------------------------------------------------------------------------------
 0         Slack 1    12          3           0           1          -1         4
 20        X2         12          .5          1           0           .5        24
-------------------------------------------------------------------------------
          Zj          240         10          20          0          10
          Impr Indx               5           0           0          -10
Keycell = (Slack 1 , X1        )

Tableau   3
Ci        Basis       Bi          X1          X2          Slack 1    Slack 2
                            Cj>>  15          20          0          0
-------------------------------------------------------------------------------
 15        X1         4           1           0           .3333333 -.3333333
 20        X2         10          0           1          -.1666667  .6666667
-------------------------------------------------------------------------------
          Zj          260         15          20          1.666667  8.333334
          Impr Indx               0           0          -1.666667 -8.333334
Keycell = None - Optimal
```

5.6

SUMMARY OF THE SIMPLEX ALGORITHM

A review and summary of the steps in this process will be presented. While only the maximization problem has been presented up to this point, the changes necessary for the minimization problem also will be presented and illustrated in the next example.

Before Beginning the Simplex Algorithm

If any of the constraints have negative right-hand side values, multiply these constraints by –1. For each ≤ constraint, add a slack variable. For each equality constraint, add an artificial variable. For each ≥ constraint, subtract a surplus variable and add an artificial variable. Objective function coefficients for slack and surplus variables will be zero. (*Note:* Objective function coefficients for artificial variables will be discussed later.) It is assumed all variables are restricted to be nonnegative.

Steps in the Simplex Algorithm

Step 1: Set up the initial simplex tableau. The basic variables in the initial solution will be slack variables and artificial variables only. For each column, calculate the Z_j value by multiplying the C_j values (in the C_j column) for the basic variables by the corresponding substitution rates in each column and adding these together. Calculate the $C_j - Z_j$ value for each column by subtracting the Z_j value from the C_j (objective function coefficient) in that same column. For a maximization problem, if all of the $C_j - Z_j$ values are less than or equal to zero, stop. Otherwise go to Step 2. (For a minimization problem, if all of the $C_j - Z_j$ values are greater than or equal to zero, stop. Otherwise go to Step 2.)

Step 2: For a maximization problem the pivot column is selected as the column with the largest positive $C_j - Z_j$ value. (For a minimization problem, the pivot column is selected as the column with the most negative $C_j - Z_j$ value. This is the value that indicates the greatest reduction in the objective function value.) The variable in this column is the entering variable.

Step 3: Calculate critical ratios by dividing the right-hand side values by the corresponding positive substitution rates in the pivot column. The pivot row is the row with the smallest critical ratio and the basic variable in this row is the leaving variable. The pivot number is the number at the intersection of the pivot row and the pivot column. If a substitution rate in the pivot column is zero or negative, this row cannot be selected as the pivot row, because dividing by zero is not defined and dividing by a negative number would make the right-hand side negative violating the nonnegativity requirement. Thus, it is not necessary to calculate the critical ratio when this occurs. Change the basic variable column by replacing the leaving variable with the entering variable. Also change the C_j column.

Step 4: To change the pivot number into a 1, divide the pivot row by the current pivot number:

revised pivot row = (old pivot row)/(pivot number)

Step 5: For each other row, change the substitution rates in the pivot column to zero by multiplying the revised pivot row by the substitution rate that is to become zero and subtracting this from the old row:

new row = (old row) – (substitution rate)(revised pivot row)

Step 6: Calculate the Z_j value for each column by multiplying each of the C_j values for the basic variables by the corresponding substitution rate in each column and adding the results.

A minimization linear program can be used by a clothing manufacturer such as Swiff Tees to determine the number of shirts to produce with special-event logos. SOURCE: Photograph courtesy of Sara Lee Corporation

Step 7: Calculate the $C_j - Z_j$ value for each column by subtracting the Z_j value from the C_j (objective function coefficient) in that same column. For a maximization problem, if all of the $C_j - Z_j$ values are less than or equal to zero, stop. Otherwise go to Step 2 to develop the next solution. (For a minimization problem, if all of the $C_j - Z_j$ values are greater than or equal to zero, stop. Otherwise go to Step 2.)

5.7 CHANGES IN THE SIMPLEX ALGORITHM FOR MINIMIZATION PROBLEMS

To solve a minimization problem, we make only two changes to the simplex algorithm used for maximization problems. Both of the changes are obvious from the interpretation of the $C_j - Z_j$ values. If we are minimizing the objective function, we stop when all of the $C_j - Z_j$ values are greater than or equal to zero. If any of the $C_j - Z_j$ values are negative we continue with Step 7, because this means the objective function value can still decrease.

The second change is in Step 2. Select as the pivot column the one that results in the greatest per unit reduction in the value of the objective function.

This means the pivot column is the one with the most negative $C_j - Z_j$ value. Thus, if the $C_j - Z_j$ values for two columns were –12 and –5, we would select the one with the –12 because this decreases the value of the objective function by $12 per unit of the variable that enters the solution while the other variable would decrease the value of the objective function by $5 per unit. All other steps in the simplex algorithm are the same for maximization and minimization problems.

An Alternative Method for Solving Minimization Problems

There is another way to solve minimization problems with the simplex algorithm. We may simply multiply the objective function for a minimization problem by –1 and solve this as a maximization problem. When doing this, the final value of the objective function must be multiplied by –1 to get the true value. To illustrate why this works, consider the following situation. Suppose a linear programming problem has three corner points, and the values of the objective function at each of these are 17, 23 and 36. If we wish to minimize this, we would simply select the smallest of these numbers, which is 17. If we were to multiply the objective function by –1, the value of the objective function for each of these would be –17, –23, and –36. Solving this as a maximization problem we select the –17, which is the largest or maximum of these numbers. The true value of the objective function is the negative of this, which is –(–17) = 17.

5.8

SURPLUS AND ARTIFICIAL VARIABLES

It is possible to have slack, surplus, and artificial variables with maximization and minimization problems. These are used with the constraints, and we may have all types of constraints for both maximization and minimization problems. The objective function coefficients for slack variables and surplus variables will be zero, because these do not affect the value of the objective function.

The artificial variables in the simplex algorithm are used to indicate the feasibility of a solution. If any artificial variable is not zero in a solution, then that solution is not feasible. Artificial variables are used to allow us to start with an infeasible initial solution. We would then like to force all artificial variables to equal zero, which would mean a feasible solution has been found. To force the simplex algorithm to do this, assign a very "bad" objective function coefficient (C_j) to each of the artificial variables so that as long as the artificial variable is not zero, the objective function value for that solution would be very poor. To do this, we may assign a coefficient of –1,000 or –10,000 to the artificial variables for maximization problems and +1,000 or +10,000 for minimization problems. The size of this coefficient should be much greater than all other objective coefficients so it dominates the objective function. Usually, the letter M is used to represent a very large number. For maximization problems a $-M$ is used and for minimization problems a $+M$ is used.

Consider the following linear programming problem:

$$\begin{aligned} &\text{Maximize profit} = 15X_1 + 25X_2 \\ &\text{Subject to: } 2X_1 + 3X_2 \geq 30 \\ &\qquad X_1 + 4X_2 \leq 36 \\ &\qquad X_1, X_2 \geq 0 \end{aligned}$$

When the slack, surplus, and artificial variables are added, we have:

$$\begin{aligned} &\text{Maximize profit} = 15X_1 + 25X_2 + 0S_1 - MA_1 + 0S_2 \\ &\text{Subject to: } 2X_1 + 3X_2 - S_1 + A_1 = 30 \\ &\qquad X_1 + 4X_2 + S_2 = 36 \\ &\qquad X_1, X_2, S_1, S_2, A_1 \geq 0 \end{aligned}$$

The $-M$ coefficient for A_1 could be viewed as –500 or –1,000. If the simplex algorithm was used to solve this, the decision variables would be equal to zero in the initial solution, so

$$\begin{aligned} X_1 &= 0 \\ X_2 &= 0 \\ S_1 &= 0 \text{ (there is no surplus in the first constraint)} \\ A_1 &= 30 \\ S_2 &= 36 \\ \text{profit} &= 15(0) + 25(0) + 0(0) - M(30) + 0(36) \\ &= -30M \end{aligned}$$

Because M is a large number, this represents a very poor profit. If we simply use a large number such as 1,000 instead of M, the profit would be –\$30,000, which obviously is not good. This initial solution would be improved considerably by forcing A_1 to equal zero because a zero profit is much better than $-30M$ (or –\$30,000). The computations involved in the simplex algorithm will automatically force this artificial variable to equal zero if any feasible solution exists.

If the objective function coefficients in this previous example had been costs instead of profits, the objective function would have been:

$$\text{Minimize cost} = 15X_1 + 25X_2 + 0S_1 + MA_1 + 0S_2$$

and the cost for the initial solution would have been $+30M$ (or \$30,000 if M were equal to 1,000). This is a very poor solution and the cost would decrease considerably if A_1 became zero. Thus, the simplex algorithm would eventually force this to a feasible solution if one exists.

5.9

A MINIMIZATION EXAMPLE

We will illustrate the use of the simplex algorithm for minimization problems with the following example.

Swiff Tees is a T-shirt manufacturing company that specializes in producing shirts for special events. Spring break for college students is approaching, and the company has decided to produce some special shirts to commemorate this year's events. Both T-shirts and tank tops will be produced, and a special logo will be attached to the shirts. The costs to manufacture these are \$4 for each T-shirt and \$5 for each tank top. It has been determined that a total of 30 shirts must be produced, and at least 10 of these must be T-shirts. A total of 100 logos have been developed, and four of these will be attached to each T-shirt and two will be attached to each tank top. The company has decided to minimize the cost of producing these.

Developing a linear programming model for this results in the following statement of the problem:

Minimize cost
Subject to:

1. The total number of shirts produced equals 30.
2. The number of T-shirts must be at least 10.
3. The number of logos used must not exceed 100.

Because decisions must be made regarding the number of T-shirts and tank tops to produce, the decision variables will be defined as:

X_1 = number of T-shirts produced

X_2 = number of tank tops produced

The mathematical formulation of the problem is:

$$\begin{aligned} &\text{Minimize cost} = 4X_1 + 5X_2 \\ &\text{Subject to: } X_1 + X_2 = 30 && \text{total production} \\ &X_1 \geq 10 && \text{T-shirt requirement} \\ &4X_1 + 2X_2 \leq 100 && \text{logo restriction} \\ &X_1, X_2 \geq 0 && \text{nonnegativity constraints} \end{aligned}$$

The graph of this is shown in Figure 5.13, where certain points are labeled for later reference. Note that point A (where $X_1 = 0$ and $X_2 = 0$, which is the initial solution using the simplex method) is not in the feasible region. Notice the feasible region consists of a line segment due to the equality constraint.

To solve this with the simplex algorithm, note that all right-hand side values are nonnegative, so it is not necessary to multiply any of the constraints by –1. Adding the slack, surplus, and artificial variables, we get:

$$\begin{aligned} &\text{Minimize cost} = 4X_1 + 5X_2 + MA_1 + MA_2 + 0S_2 + 0S_3 \\ &\text{Subject to: } X_1 + X_2 + A_1 = 30 && \text{total production} \\ &X_1 - S_2 + A_2 = 10 && \text{T-shirt requirement} \\ &4X_1 + 2X_2 + S_3 = 100 && \text{logo restriction} \end{aligned}$$

We will solve this with the simplex algorithm, which will be presented in a step-by-step fashion using the numbers presented earlier for the steps in the simplex algorithm.

FIGURE 5.13

Graph of Swiff Tees Example

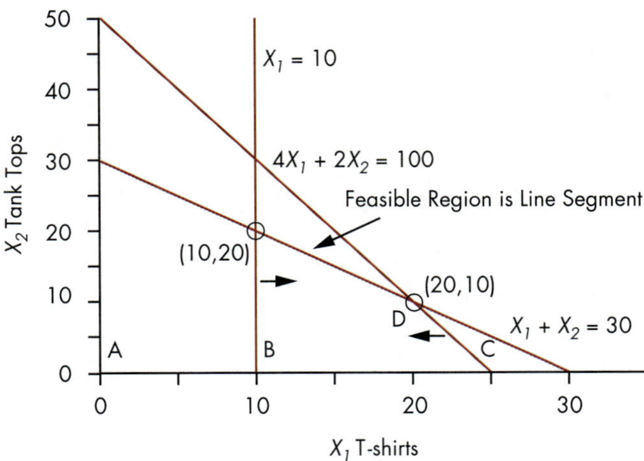

Developing the Initial Tableau

Step 1: The initial simplex tableau is shown in Figure 5.14. The initial solution (shown as corner point A in Figure 5.13 above) is:

$X_1 = 0$ (X_1 is a nonbasic variable)
$X_2 = 0$ (X_2 is a nonbasic variable)
$A_1 = 30$
$A_2 = 10$
$S_2 = 0$ (S_2 is a nonbasic variable)
$S_3 = 100$
cost = $40M$

FIGURE 5.14

Initial Simplex Tableau for Swiff Tees Example

C_j	Basic Variable	4 X_1	5 X_2	M A_1	M A_2	0 S_2	0 S_3	RHS Value
M	A_1	1	1	1	0	0	0	30
M	A_2	1	0	0	1	−1	0	10
0	S_3	4	2	0	0	0	1	100
	Z_j	2M	M	M	M	−M	0	40M
	$C_j - Z_j$	4 − 2M	5 − M	0	0	M	0	

Notice this solution is not feasible for two reasons—A_1 and A_2 are positive. In the first constraint we see $X_1 + X_2 = 0$ at this point and so this total is not equal to 30 as required by the first constraint. Thus, this constraint is not met and $A_1 = 30$. Similarly, X_1 is not at least 10 as required by the second constraint, and there is no surplus. Therefore, the variable $A_2 = 10$, which indicates this constraint is not met. For this solution, we calculate the Z_j values.

$$Z_j \text{ for } X_1 \text{ column} = M(1) + M(1) + 0(4) = 2M$$
$$Z_j \text{ for } X_2 \text{ column} = M(1) + M(0) + 0(2) = M$$
$$Z_j \text{ for } A_1 \text{ column} = M(1) + M(0) + 0(0) = M$$
$$Z_j \text{ for } A_2 \text{ column} = M(0) + M(1) + 0(0) = M$$
$$Z_j \text{ for } S_2 \text{ column} = M(0) + M(-1) + 0(0) = -M$$
$$Z_j \text{ for } S_3 \text{ column} = M(0) + M(0) + 0(1) = 0$$
$$Z_j \text{ for RHS column} = M(30) + M(10) + 0(100) = 40M$$

Thus, the objective function value (cost) for this solution is $40M$, which is a very high cost. We now calculate the $C_j - Z_j$ values.

$$C_j - Z_j \text{ for } X_1 \text{ column} = 4 - 2M$$
$$C_j - Z_j \text{ for } X_2 \text{ column} = 5 - M$$
$$C_j - Z_j \text{ for } A_1 \text{ column} = M - M$$
$$C_j - Z_j \text{ for } A_2 \text{ column} = M - M = 0$$
$$C_j - Z_j \text{ for } S_2 \text{ column} = 0 - (-M) = +M$$
$$C_j - Z_j \text{ for } S_3 \text{ column} = 0 - 0 = 0$$

Because this is a minimization problem and some of the $C_j - Z_j$ values are negative, we continue.

Developing the Second Tableau

Step 2: Select the pivot column. We select the X_1 column as the pivot column because doing so decreases the objective function value more per unit than any other column. Because M is a large number, $4 - 2M$ indicates a greater improvement than $5 - M$—if you use $M = 1000$, then $4 - 2M = -1{,}996$ and $5 - M = -995$; the $-1{,}996$ would indicate this column should be selected. The entering variable is the variable in this pivot column, which is X_1.

Step 3: Calculate the critical ratios and select the pivot row. Calculate the critical ratios by dividing the RHS values by the substitution rates, which results in:

row 1: 30/1 = 30

row 2: 10/1 = 10 ← smallest critical ratio

row 3: 100/4 = 25

The row with the smallest critical ratio is the second row, so this is the pivot row and the variable leaving the basis is A_2. We replace A_2 in the basis with the entering variable X_1 and change the basic coefficient to 4. The other variables in the basis in the first tableau stay in the basis in the second tableau. The pivot number is at the intersection of the pivot row and pivot column, and this is 1.

Step 4: The pivot number already is 1 in this solution, and dividing the numbers in this row by 1 leaves them unchanged.

Step 5: Change the substitution rates in the pivot column to zero for all of the other rows. This means both row 1 and row 3 must be changed. In doing this, we multiply the new pivot row (in this case the numbers in the new and the old pivot rows are the same) by the substitution rate in the pivot column and subtract the result from the old row.

We will first make the changes to row 1. Because there is a 1 in the pivot column of row 1, multiplying the pivot row by this number leaves it unchanged. Thus, we have:

$$\text{new row } 1 = \text{old row } 1 - 1(\text{pivot row})$$

To change row 3, we multiply the pivot row by 4 (the number in row 3 in the pivot column) and subtract this from the old row 3.

$$\text{new row } 3 = \text{old row } 3 - 4(\text{revised pivot row})$$

These calculations result in the next tableau shown in Figure 5.15. This solution (shown as point B in Figure 5.13 above) is:

$X_1 = 10$
$X_2 = 0$ (X_2 is a nonbasic variable)
$A_1 = 20$
$A_2 = 0$ (A_2 is a nonbasic variable)
$S_2 = 0$ (S_2 is a nonbasic variable)
$S_3 = 60$
cost $= 20M + 40$

Then go to Step 6 to evaluate this new solution.

FIGURE 5.15

Second Simplex Tableau for Swift Tees Example

C_j	Basic Variable	4 X_1	5 X_2	M A_1	M A_2	0 S_2	0 S_3	RHS Value
M	A_1	0	1	1	−1	1	0	20
4	X_1	1	0	0	1	−1	0	10
0	S_3	0	2	0	−4	4	1	60
	Z_j	4	M	M	−M + 4	M − 4	0	20M + 40
	$C_j - Z_j$	0	5 − M	0	2M − 4	−M + 4	0	

Step 6: The Z_j values are calculated and shown in Figure 5.15 above. Notice the cost for this solution is $20M + 40$.

Step 7: The $C_j - Z_j$ values are calculated and shown in Figure 5.15. Because not all $C_j - Z_j$ values are positive or zero, we must continue and return to Step 2.

Developing the Third Tableau

Step 2: Select the S_2 column as the pivot column. This has the most negative $C_j - Z_j$ value.

Step 3: Calculate the critical ratios. These are:

row 1: 20/1 = 20

row 2: -- the substitution rate is –1, so this row cannot be the pivot row because dividing by a negative number would result in a negative right-hand side value, which is not allowed. We do not even calculate this critical ratio.

row 3: 60/4 = 15 ← smallest critical ratio

The pivot row is row 3, and the leaving variable is S_3. The pivot number is 4. Change the basis by replacing the leaving variable (S_3) with the entering variable (S_2).

Because resources often are estimated or subject to change, the solution to a linear programming problem cannot be fully evaluated unless an analysis is performed to determine how the optimal solution would be affected by a change. SOURCE: Karla Harvill, Gold Kist, Inc., Atlanta, GA

Step 4: To get a 1 in the pivot position, divide the pivot row by 4 (the pivot number). The pivot row is row 3, so:

new row 3 = (old row 3)/4

Step 5: Change the other numbers in the pivot column to 0. In row 1, the number in the pivot column is 1. To make this zero, simply subtract the revised pivot row (row 3) from this.

new row 1 = (old row 1) – 1(revised pivot row)

In the second row, the number in the pivot column is –1. To make this zero, we multiply this by the pivot row and subtract:

new row 2 = (old row 2) – (–1)(revised pivot row)

These calculations give us the simplex tableau in Figure 5.16. The solution represented by this tableau (shown as point C in Figure 5.13 above) is:

$X_1 = 25$
$X_2 = 0$ (X_2 is a nonbasic variable)
$A_1 = 5$
$A_2 = 0$ (A_2 is a nonbasic variable)
$S_2 = 15$
$S_3 = 0$ (S_3 is a nonbasic variable)

Notice this is still not a feasible solution because the artificial variable A_1 is not equal to zero.

Step 6: The Z_j values are calculated and shown in Figure 5.16. Note that the cost of this solution is $5M + 100$.

Step 7: The $C_j - Z_j$ values are calculated and shown in Figure 5.16. Because not all $C_j - Z_j$ values are positive or zero, we continue.

FIGURE 5.16

Third Simplex Tableau for Swift Tees Example

C_j	Basic Variable	4 X_1	5 X_2	M A_1	M A_2	0 S_2	0 S_3	RHS Value
M	A_1	0	1/2	1	0	0	–1/4	5
4	X_1	1	1/2	0	0	0	1/4	25
0	S_2	0	1/2	0	–1	1	1/4	15
	Z_j	4	1/2M + 2	M	0	0	–1/4M + 1	5M + 100
	$C_j - Z_j$	0	3 – 1/2M	0	M	0	1/4M – 1	

Developing the Fourth Tableau

Step 2: Select the X_2 column as the pivot column. This has the smallest (and only) negative $C_j - Z_j$ value.

Step 3: Calculate the critical ratios. These are:

row 1: 5/(1/2) = 10 ← smallest critical ratio

row 2: 25/(1/2) = 50

row 3: 15/(1/2) = 30

Select row 1 to be the pivot row because it has the smallest critical ratio. This means the leaving variable will be A_1, which is the basic variable in this row. Thus, the next solution will be feasible because all artificial variables will be out of the basis and equal to zero. The pivot number is ½. Variable X_2 (the entering variable) will replace the leaving variable (A_1) in the basis. The C_j column also is changed.

Step 4: To get a 1 in the pivot position, divide the pivot row by the pivot number (½).

new row 1 = (old row 1)/(1/2) = 2(old row 1)

Step 5: Change the other numbers in the pivot column to 0. In the second row, the number in the pivot column is ½. To make this zero, we simply multiply the pivot row (row 1) by ½ and subtract this from the old row 2.

new row 2 = (old row 2) – (1/2)(revised pivot row)

The results are shown in Figure 5.17.

In row 3, the number in the pivot column also is 1/2, so we multiply the pivot row (row 1) by 1/2 and subtract from the old row 3.

new row 3 = (old row 3) – (1/2)(revised pivot row)

This new row is shown in Figure 5.17. The solution represented by this tableau (shown as point D in Figure 5.13 above) is:

$X_1 = 20$

$X_2 = 10$

$A_1 = 0$ (A_1 is a nonbasic variable)

$A_2 = 0$ (A_2 is a nonbasic variable)

$S_2 = 10$

$S_3 = 0$ (S_3 is a nonbasic variable)

We now go to Step 6 to evaluate this new solution.

Step 6: The Z_j values are calculated and shown in Figure 5.17. Note that the cost of this solution is $130.

Step 7: The $C_j - Z_j$ values are calculated and shown in Figure 5.17. All $C_j - Z_j$ values are positive or zero, so this is the optimal solution. It is impossible to obtain a lower cost solution than this.

Based on the solution in the optimal simplex tableau, Swiff Tees will produce 20 T-shirts ($X_1 = 20$) and 10 tank tops ($X_2 = 10$) at a

FIGURE 5.17

Fourth Simplex Tableau for Swiff Tees Example

C_j	Basic Variable	4 X_1	5 X_2	M A_1	M A_2	0 S_2	0 S_3	RHS Value
5	X_2	0	1	2	0	0	−1/2	10
4	X_1	1	0	−1	0	0	1/2	20
0	S_2	0	0	−1	−1	1	1/2	10
	Z_j	4	5	6	0	0	−1/2	130
	$C_j - Z_j$	0	0	M − 6	M	0	1/2	

total cost of $130. Thus, the first constraint is met because 20 + 10 = 30. There are 10 units of surplus in the second constraint (S_2 = 10) because the minimum number of T-shirts (10) is exceeded by 10 units. There is no slack for the last constraint (S_3 = 0), so all 100 logos are used.

Computational Note

Due to the values of the objective function coefficients for the artificial variables, once an artificial variable has left the basis it will never reenter the basis. Thus, if an artificial variable is a nonbasic variable, the column for this variable may be deleted from the simplex tableau. This may save time when doing simplex calculations by hand.

5.10 SPECIAL CONDITIONS

In using the simplex algorithm, certain unusual conditions may arise. We will look at how the simplex tableau indicates each of these.

Unbounded Solution

A linear programming problem may be unbounded, as was seen in the chapter on graphical methods for solving linear programming problems. An unbounded solution typically indicates to a manager that a constraint was omitted in the formulation of the problem. You may recognize that an unbounded solution exists if in the simplex tableau all of the substitution rates in the pivot column are negative or zero. Figure 5.18 provides an example of a maximization problem with an unbounded solution. The X_2 column would be selected as the pivot column. These substitution rates would indicate that for each unit of the variable in the pivot column brought into the solution, the RHS value in the simplex tableau actually

FIGURE 5.18

Example of Maximization Problem with Unbounded Solution

C_j	Basic Variable	5 X_1	4 X_2	0 S_1	0 S_2	0 S_3	RHS Value
5	X_1	1	–1	1	0	0	24
0	S_2	0	–2	–1	1	0	12
0	S_3	0	0	2	0	1	25
	Z_j	5	–5	5	0	0	120
	$C_j - Z_j$	0	9	–5	0	0	
			↑ pivot column				

will increase (if the substitution rate is negative) or it will stay the same (if the substitution rate is zero). Thus, there is no upper limit to the number of units of the entering variable that could be brought into the solution.

No Feasible Solution

If there is no feasible solution to a linear programming problem, an artificial variable will have a positive value in the final simplex tableau. Figure 5.19 provides an example of this situation. This is the optimal tableau for a maximization problem, but there is still an artificial variable in the basis with a positive value ($A_1 = 20$). The constraint to which this artificial variable was added would be the constraint that is violated in the last solution. The person who is using the linear program to aid in managerial decision making may wish to reevaluate the constraints, beginning with the violated constraint, to determine if they are all necessary or if some of them could be eliminated or modified.

FIGURE 5.19

Example of Problem with No Feasible Solution

C_j	Basic Variable	6 X_1	4 X_2	$-M$ A_1	0 S_1	0 S_2	RHS Value
6	X_1	1	2	0	0	1	8
$-M$	A_1	0	–4	1	–1	–2	20
	Z_j	6	$12 + 4M$	$-M$	M	$6 + 2M$	$48 - 20M$
	$C_j - Z_j$	0	$-8 - 4M$	0	$-M$	$-6 - 2M$	

Multiple Optimal Solutions

The existence of multiple optimal solutions is indicated in the simplex tableau by the $C_j - Z_j$ values in the final tableau. If the $C_j - Z_j$ value for a nonbasic variable is zero, then this column could be selected as the pivot column and another solution could be found. This $C_j - Z_j$ value of zero would indicate that the value of the objective function would not change if that column were selected as the pivot column. Thus, another basic solution also would be optimal. This would provide flexibility to the person using linear programming to help make decisions.

In Figure 5.20 we see that the tableau represents the optimal solution for a maximization problem, but the $C_j - Z_j$ value for the nonbasic variable X_1 is zero. The X_1 column could be selected as the pivot column, and another solution to the problem would be found that has exactly the same objective function value as this. Thus, there is another optimal solution.

Degenerate Solutions

Degenerate solution
A solution to a linear programming problem in which the value of one of the basic variables is zero.

The solution represented by the simplex tableau is called a **degenerate solution** if the value of one of the basic variables is zero. Thus, a right-hand side value in the simplex tableau would be zero. When two or more rows have tied for the smallest critical ratio, the solution represented by the next simplex tableau will be degenerate. This means a nonbasic variable that must have a value of zero has entered the solution as a basic variable, but it still has a value of zero. Figure 5.21 provides an illustration of this. Variable S_3 is a basic variable with a value of zero. It is possible this variable will then leave the basis, and another variable also will enter the basis of the next solution with a value of zero. Thus, the solution has not changed despite the fact that the basic variables change. If this occurs, it is theoretically possible for the simplex algorithm to continually cycle through a set of basic solutions, returning to basic solutions that previously have been evaluated. While degeneracy itself is not uncommon, cycling rarely occurs. Special rules may be included in computer codes to prevent this cycling.

FIGURE 5.20

Example of Problem with Multiple Optimal Solutions

C_j	Basic Variable	12 X_1	18 X_2	15 X_3	0 S_1	0 S_2	0 S_3	RHS Value
0	S_1	4/3	0	−7/3	1	−4/3	0	28
18	X_2	2/3	1	4/3	0	1/3	0	8
0	S_3	1/3	0	−1/3	0	−1/3	1	4
	Z_j	12	18	24	0	6	0	144
	$C_j - Z_j$	0	0	−9	0	−6	0	

FIGURE 5.21

Example of Problem with Degenerate Solution

C_j	Basic Variable	3 X_1	2 X_2	0 S_1	0 S_2	0 S_3	RHS Value
3	X_1	1	0.5	1	0	0	8
0	S_2	0	−2	−1	1	0	6
0	S_3	0	2	2	0	1	0
	Z_j	3	1.5	3	0	0	24
	$C_j - Z_j$	0	0.5	−3	0	0	

GLOBAL PERSPECTIVES

Operational Planning in Indian Railways

Indian Railways (IR) is the largest railway system under a single management in Asia, and the second largest in the world. IR's fleet includes more than 9,000 locomotives, 38,000 passenger cars, and 350,000 freight cars. These cars carry nearly 10 million passengers and one million tons of freight every day. The railway system forms the lifeline of India's economy, making operational planning of passenger trains an important issue for IR and for the country.

For operational convenience, the Indian Railway network is divided into nine zonal railways. The zonal railways are the basic operational units for planning freight and passenger services. Each zonal railway has an allotment of passenger cars and locomotives that must provide a set of services. The services must meet a given timetable and a set of maintenance and operating norms. Trains also must have a set composition between first class, sleepers, and other categories.

The Centre for Railway Information Systems commissioned the development of an optimization-based decision support system (DSS) to simplify operational planning of passenger trains. The DSS has been implemented by two of the zonal railways, which both report direct and indirect benefits. The railways have saved on passenger cars and locomotives by replacing nonoptimal routings with optimal routings, thus generating savings in production costs and operating and maintenance costs. Indirect benefits include the ability of the railways to analyze future requirements for passenger cars and locomotives easily. This ability will help IR to extend their existing services, offer new services, and meet the future needs of the people of India.

SOURCE:
Ramani K. V., and B. K. Mandal, September-October 1992. "Operational Planning of Passenger Trains in Indian Railways." *Interfaces* 22 (5): 39-51.

5.11 SENSITIVITY ANALYSIS

Once the optimal solution to a linear program has been found, we may wish to analyze the final linear programming results to determine how sensitive the optimal solution is to changes in any of the data used in formulating the problem. Because profits, costs, resources, and other factors often are estimated or subject to change, the solution to the linear programming problem cannot be fully evaluated unless an analysis is performed to determine how the optimal solution would be affected by changes in any of these. We will demonstrate how the simplex tableau can be used to determine the impact of changes in objective function coefficients and right-hand side values on the optimal solution. The simplex tableau also will be used to determine the objective coefficient ranges and the right-hand side ranges that are provided in computer solutions to a linear programming problem.

Arlington Luggage Problem

Arlington Luggage produces two models of briefcases—regular and executive. The profit and resource needs are shown in Table 5.1. Currently there are only 25 locks in inventory to be used for briefcases. Additional locks cannot be received until next week. There are 80 labor hours available this week for the production of these briefcases. Management wants to maximize profit subject to limits on labor hours and the number of locks.

To formulate this as a linear programming problem, let

X_1 = number of regular briefcases produced this week

X_2 = number of executive briefcases produced this week

The linear program is:

$$
\begin{aligned}
&\text{Maximize profit} = 30X_1 + 90X_2 \\
&\text{Subject to: } 2X_1 + 5X_2 \le 80 \quad \text{labor hours} \\
&\qquad X_1 + X_2 \le 25 \quad \text{locks} \\
&\qquad X_1, X_2 \ge 0 \quad \text{nonnegativity constraints}
\end{aligned}
$$

The optimal simplex tableau is given in Figure 5.22. The solution represented by this tableau is:

$X_1 = 0$ produce no regular briefcases

$X_2 = 16$ produce 16 executive briefcases

$S_1 = 0$ 0 slack for labor hours using all 80 hours

$S_2 = 9$ 9 locks remaining, using only 16

profit = \$1,440

TABLE 5.1

Arlington Luggage Profit and Resource Requirements

	Profit	Labor Hours	Lock Used
Regular Briefcase	\$30	2	1
Executive Briefcase	\$90	5	1

FIGURE 5.22

Optimal Simplex Tableau for Arlington Luggage Problem

C_j	Basic Variable	30 X_1	90 X_2	0 S_1	0 S_2	RHS Value
90	X_2	.4	1	.2	0	16
0	S_2	.6	0	−.2	1	9
	Z_j	36	90	18	0	1440
	$C_j - Z_j$	−6	0	−18	0	

A manager evaluating this might be concerned that no regular briefcases are being produced or that additional locks are available that are not being used. The possibility of using overtime to obtain additional hours might be considered. The manager may wish to see how the production schedule would change if the profit were modified on either type of briefcase. Sensitivity analysis will help to address each of these concerns.

5.12 CHANGES IN OBJECTIVE FUNCTION COEFFICIENTS

Range of optimality
The set of possible values for an objective function coefficient in which there is no change in the optimal basic solution (although the value of the objective function could change).

Changing an objective function coefficient has no impact on the feasible region. The objective function simply determines which basic solution (corner point) is optimal. Thus, if a coefficient is changed, either the same basic solution remains optimal or another one becomes optimal. The same basic solution remains optimal as long as the $C_j - Z_j$ values in the simplex tableau continue to indicate optimality (all $C_j - Z_j \leq 0$ for a maximization problem and all $C_j - Z_j \geq 0$ for a minimization problem). We will compute the **range of optimality**, which is the set of possible values for an objective function coefficient in which there is no change in the optimal basic solution (although the value of the objective function could change).

To find the range of optimality for an objective function coefficient for a decision variable X_k, replace the coefficient for that variable with the term C_k everywhere this appears in the final simplex tableau (in the objective function row and possibly the C_j column as well if the variable is basic). Then recompute the Z_j and $C_j - Z_j$ values, and restrict all of these $C_j - Z_j$ values to indicate optimality (≤ zero for a maximization problem). From this, determine the values of C_k for which this optimality condition exists. The result is the range of optimality.

Because the computations are trivial when evaluating changes in objective function coefficients for nonbasic variables but are not trivial when considering basic variables, we will present these two cases separately in the following examples.

Nonbasic Variables

Consider the final simplex tableau for the Arlington Luggage problem. Currently there are no regular briefcases being produced ($X_1 = 0$), and thus X_1 is a nonbasic variable. To see what the profit on regular briefcases would have to be to cause a change in the optimal solution, replace the \$30 profit for X_1 with C_1 and make the changes to the $C_1 - Z_1$ value as well. This would give the result shown in Figure 5.23. This solution will remain the optimal solution as long as all the $C_j - Z_j$ values are negative or zero. The only one of these that changed is $C_1 - Z_1$, so the current solution will be optimal as long as

$$C_1 - 36 \leq 0$$

or

$$C_1 \leq 36$$

This means there is no lower limit to the value of C_1, and the upper limit is 36. If C_1 is 36, then there would be multiple optimal solutions. If C_1 is greater than 36, then the current solution would not be optimal ($C_1 - Z_1$ would be greater than zero), and we would have to generate another basic solution. Therefore, the current profit on X_1 would have to increase by \$6 (the negative of the $C_j - Z_j$ value for X_1) before any units of this would be brought into the solution. This is the reduced cost that appears in the output of LINDO and other software packages. It indicates how much the objective function coefficient must improve before that variable would become a basic variable in the optimal solution. This reduced cost for a nonbasic variable also is seen as the allowable increase for that variable in a maximization problem.

Basic Variables

To determine the impact of a change in the profit on executive briefcases, additional computations are required because X_2 is a basic variable. Replacing the profit of \$90 with C_2 also requires a change in the C_j column

FIGURE 5.23

Evaluating Changes in Profit on X_1 for Arlington Luggage Problem

C_j	Basic Variable	C_1 X_1	90 X_2	0 S_1	0 S_2	RHS Value
90	X_2	.4	1	.2	0	16
0	S_2	.6	0	−.2	1	9
	Z_j	36	90	18	0	1440
	$C_j - Z_j$	$C_1 - 36$	0	−18	0	

as well. This is shown in Figure 5.24. The solution represented by this tableau is optimal if all the $C_j - Z_j$ values are negative or zero, so

$$30 - 0.4C_2 \leq 0$$

and

$$-0.2C_2 \leq 0$$

From the first requirement above we get

$$30 - 0.4C_2 \leq 0$$
$$-0.4C_2 \leq -30$$
$$-C_2 \leq -30/0.4$$
$$-C_2 \leq -75$$
$$C_2 \geq 75$$

and for the second requirement,

$$-0.2C_2 \leq 0$$
$$-C_2 \leq 0$$
$$C_2 \geq 0$$

Because both $C_2 \geq 75$ and $C_2 \geq 0$ must be met, we select the largest of these because if $C_2 \geq 75$ it also must be greater than the lower value (0). So the current basic solution remains optimal if the profit on executive briefcases is \$75 or more. The lower limit is \$75 and there is no upper limit because when the above restrictions on the $C_j - Z_j$ values were placed, none of these resulted in an upper limit on C_2. Because the original profit for executive briefcases is \$90, the profit on these could decrease by \$15 (\$90 – \$75) without affecting the values of the decision variables, although the amount of profit would change. Notice the profit is $16C_2$ in the simplex tableau where the calculations were performed. If the objective function coefficient for X_2 is changed by \$1, total profit will change by 16(\$1) = \$16. This occurs because 16 units of X_2 are being produced, and the \$1 change in profit applies to all of these. This total change in profit will continue to occur at the same rate as long as the change in profit on X_2 is within the allowable limits.

FIGURE 5.24

Change in Profit on X_2 for Arlington Luggage Problem

C_j	Basic Variable	30 X_1	C_2 X_2	0 S_1	0 S_2	RHS Value
C_2	X_2	.4	1	.2	0	16
0	S_2	.6	0	−.2	1	9
	Z_j	$.4C_2$	C_2	$.2C_2$	0	$16C_2$
	$C_j - Z_j$	$30 - .4C_2$	0	$-.2C_2$	0	

Interpreting the Range of Optimality

The LINDO output for this problem is shown in Output 5.2. The allowable increases and decreases in the profit for the decision variables are shown. As calculated, the profit on X_1 may decrease by any amount or increase by up to \$6 without affecting the optimal solution. Similarly, the profit on X_2 may decrease by up to \$15 or increase by any amount and the same basic solution will remain optimal while the total profit will continue to change by \$16 for each dollar change in profit on X_2.

OUTPUT 5.2

LINDO Output for Arlington Luggage Problem

```
MAX      30 X1 + 90 X2
 SUBJECT TO
        2)   2 X1 + 5 X2 <=   80
        3)   X1 + X2 <=   25
 END

LP OPTIMUM FOUND AT STEP      1

       OBJECTIVE FUNCTION VALUE

       1)      1440.0000

 VARIABLE         VALUE          REDUCED COST
       X1          .000000           6.000000
       X2        16.000000            .000000


      ROW   SLACK OR SURPLUS     DUAL PRICES
       2)          .000000         18.000000
       3)         9.000000          .000000

NO. ITERATIONS=       1

RANGES IN WHICH THE BASIS IS UNCHANGED:

                           OBJ COEFFICIENT RANGES
VARIABLE          CURRENT        ALLOWABLE        ALLOWABLE
                    COEF          INCREASE         DECREASE
      X1        30.000000         6.000000         INFINITY
      X2        90.000000         INFINITY        15.000000

                           RIGHTHAND SIDE RANGES
     ROW          CURRENT        ALLOWABLE        ALLOWABLE
                    RHS           INCREASE         DECREASE
       2        80.000000        45.000000        80.000000
       3        25.000000         INFINITY         9.000000
```

In summary, we state the following: If an objective function coefficient is within the range of optimality, there is no change in the value of any of the variables. The value of the objective function will change by the amount of change in the objective function coefficient times the value of the corresponding decision variable. Any change outside the range of optimality will cause another basic solution to be optimal.

5.13

CHANGES IN RIGHT-HAND SIDE VALUES

As was discussed in Chapter 3, changes in right-hand side values, which typically represent changes in available resources, may result in changes in the values of the decision variables at the corner points of the feasible region. As a result of this, the value of the objective function at the optimal solution may change. The dual price and shadow price for the constraint indicate the amount of change in the value of the objective as a result of a one unit change in the right-hand side of the constraint. This change will continue as long as the change in the right-hand side does not exceed certain limits. These limits are provided in the output of computer software for linear programming. We will now show how the simplex tableau may be used to find the dual prices as well as these limits.

Dual Prices and Shadow Prices

The improvement in the objective function value for a one unit change in the right-hand side of a constraint is called the dual price. As mentioned in Chapter 3, some authors and software developers call this the shadow price while others try to differentiate between these and say the shadow price is the increase (instead of improvement) in the value of the objective function per unit increase in the right-hand side. Therefore, due to a lack of consistency by authors of various software, it is best to ignore the sign of the dual price or shadow price reported in computer output and use the following rule: If the RHS of a constraint is relaxed by one unit, the objective function will improve by the absolute value of the dual price (or shadow price). If the constraint is tightened by one unit, the objective function value will worsen by the absolute value of the dual price (or shadow price).

The dual prices are found directly from the final simplex tableau. If the constraint is a $\leq$ constraint, the dual price is the Z_j for the slack variable for that constraint. If the constraint is a $\geq$ constraint, the dual price is $-Z_j$ for the surplus variable for that constraint.

To see why this information is provided by the Z_j values in the final simplex tableau, consider the Arlington Luggage problem. This problem is:

$$
\begin{aligned}
&\text{Maximize profit} = 30X_1 + 90X_2 \\
&\text{Subject to: } 2X_1 + 5X_2 \leq 80 \quad \text{labor hours} \\
&\qquad\qquad X_1 + X_2 \leq 25 \quad \text{locks} \\
&\qquad\qquad X_1, X_2 \geq 0 \quad \text{nonnegativity constraints}
\end{aligned}
$$

FIGURE 5.25

Evaluating Change in Labor-Hours Constraint

C_j	Basic Variable	30 X_1	90 X_2	**0** S_1	0 S_2	RHS Value
90	X_2	.4	1	**.2**	0	16
0	S_2	.6	0	**–.2**	1	9
	Z_j	36	90	**18**	0	1440
	$C_j - Z_j$	–6	0	**–18**	0	

First, consider the labor-hours constraint. To see the impact of obtaining additional labor hours, look at the S_1 column in the final simplex tableau, because S_1 was added to this constraint. The final simplex tableau is shown in Figure 5.25. This tableau shows the dual price for labor hours is 18 (the Z_j for the S_1 column). A reexamination of how this Z_j is calculated will help to understand this interpretation.

The substitution rates indicate how much the values of the basic variables would decrease if one unit of variable S_1 were brought into the solution. Bringing one unit of this slack into the solution is equivalent to making one less labor hour available for use in producing the briefcases (if $S_1 = 1$, then only 79 labor hours would be used). From the simplex tableau in Figure 5.25 above, the substitution rate in row 1 is 0.2. This means 0.2 units of X_2 must be given up if one unit of slack is to be made available. Because the profit on X_1 is \$90, 0.2 units generate a profit of 0.2(90) = \$18. Thus, the Z_j value for S_1 indicates how much profit would be sacrificed if one unit of S_1 were forced into the solution. This also indicates if one additional labor hour were made available (to bring the original total to 81), this additional hour could be used to increase the values of the basic variables and profit would increase. If there were 81 labor hours instead of 80, total profit would increase by \$18. If labor hours available increased from 80 to 82, total profit would increase by 2(18) = \$36. Thus, the dual price for labor hours (S_1) is 18.

To clearly see how the additional profit is generated, consider what happens if one more labor hour was made available. The 0.2 in the first row of the S_1 column indicates the number of units of the basic variable in that row (X_2) would increase by 0.2 units. Thus, to obtain the new RHS value in the final tableau given that the right-hand side of the original constraint is increased by one unit, simply add the substitution rate to the old RHS value. Thus, row 1 would have:

$$\begin{aligned}\text{new RHS value} &= (\text{old RHS value}) + (\text{substitution rate})\\ &= 16 + 0.2 = 16.2\end{aligned}$$

Because X_2 is the basic variable in row 1,

$$X_2 = 16.2$$

Similarly, the –0.2 substitution rate in row 2 (S_2 row) in this column indicates the RHS value in this final tableau would increase by –0.2, which means it would actually decrease. Thus, the new RHS value for row 2 in the final tableau would be:

$$\begin{aligned}\text{new RHS value} &= (\text{old RHS value}) + (\text{substitution rate})\\ &= 9 + (-0.2) = 8.8\end{aligned}$$

Because S_2 is the basic variable in row 2,

$$S_2 = 8.8$$

Because the objective (profit) function is

$$30X_1 + 90X_2 + 0S_1 + 0S_2$$

we would have

$$\text{profit} = 30(0) + 90(16.2) + 0(0) + 0(8.8) = 1458$$

This represents an increase of \$18 (dual price) from the current value of \$1,440. Management should consider obtaining additional labor hours if the additional cost is not more than \$18 per hour.

Consider the second constraint in this problem. In the statement of this problem, there was a limited number of locks (25) available, and more locks were not scheduled to arrive until next week. Management may consider paying an additional cost to have a next day delivery of some locks. Should this be done? To determine this, consider by how much profits would improve if one more lock was available. The dual price for locks is found in the S_2 column because S_2 was added to this constraint. The Z_j value is 0, which means the dual price is 0. Profits would not change if additional locks were available. This should be obvious to a manager because in the optimal solution, there are 9 units of slack for this constraint. This means there are 9 locks available now that are not being used. If additional locks were obtained, they would not be used and would simply increase the amount of slack for that constraint. Similarly, decreasing the number of locks available from 25 to 24 would have no impact on profit.

Right-Hand Side Ranges

The dual prices are relevant only within a certain range. Profits increase by the value of the dual price for each additional unit of the resource until some limit is reached. If too much of one particular resource becomes available, eventually there will not be enough of the other resources. At some point, profits will no longer continue to increase as additional units of the resource are obtained. Similarly, decreases in the amount of a resource will decrease the value of the objective function by the amount of the dual price until a limit is reached. We will use information in the final simplex tableau to find these limits.

Consider the Arlington Luggage problem. The dual price for labor hours is \$18. We see this additional profit is generated as the RHS values in the final tableau are changed by the values of the substitution rates in the column for the slack variable representing labor hours. Thus, we have:

$$\begin{array}{cccccc} \text{new RHS value} & = & (\text{old RHS value}) & + & (\text{substitution rate}) \\ 16.2 & = & 16 & + & 0.2 \\ 8.8 & = & 9 & + & (-0.2) \end{array}$$

If we increase the labor hours by 10 units, then

$$\begin{array}{cccccc} \text{new RHS value} & = & (\text{old RHS value}) & + & 10(\text{substitution rate}) \\ 18 & = & 16 & + & 10(0.2) \\ 7 & = & 9 & + & 10(-0.2) \end{array}$$

and profits would increase by the dual price for each of these 10 units for a total of 10($18) = $180.

This same type of change will continue as long as the RHS values are greater than or equal to zero. Because the RHS values in the final tableau represent the values for the basic variables, all of the RHS values must be nonnegative. Thus, the dual price provides useful information about changes in the original right-hand side values for the constraints as long as the change in the original right-hand side value of a constraint does not cause the RHS values to become negative in the final tableau.

To find the allowable increase and decrease for right-hand side values, we will let Δ represent the amount of change in the original right-hand side of the constraint. Then, for the final simplex tableau, we will restrict the new RHS values to be greater than or equal to zero. We use the substitution rates in the slack (or surplus) variable column and have

$$\text{new RHS value} = (\text{old RHS value}) + \Delta(\text{substitution rate}) \geq 0$$

for each of the rows. To find the limits for the labor-hours constraint, we use the S_1 column because S_1 was added to this constraint. We have:

$$\begin{array}{cccccc} \text{new RHS value} = & (\text{old RHS value}) & + & \Delta(\text{substitution rate}) & \\ \text{new RHS row 1} = & 16 & + & \Delta(0.2) & \geq 0 \\ \text{new RHS row 2} = & 9 & + & \Delta(-0.2) & \geq 0 \end{array}$$

Solving these for Δ we have

$$\begin{aligned} 16 + \Delta(0.2) &\geq 0 \\ 0.2(\Delta) &\geq -16 \\ \Delta &\geq -80 \end{aligned}$$

and

$$\begin{aligned} 9 + \Delta(-0.2) &\geq 0 \\ -0.2(\Delta) &\geq -9 \\ \Delta &\leq 45 \end{aligned}$$

Thus, the dual price is relevant as long as the change in labor hours (Δ) is not less than −80 or more than 45. Profits will increase by $18 for each additional labor hour that is added up to 45 hours. Similarly, profits will decrease by $18 per hour for each labor hour that is taken away up to an allowable decrease of 80 hours.

Performing a similar analysis on the constraint limiting the number of locks used, we have:

$$\text{new RHS value} = (\text{old RHS value}) + \Delta(\text{substitution rate})$$
$$\text{new RHS row 1} = 16 + \Delta(0) \geq 0$$
$$\text{new RHS row 2} = 9 + \Delta(1) \geq 0$$

Because Δ is multiplied by 0 in the first constraint, it doesn't affect the RHS value. Looking at the second constraint we have:

$$9 + \Delta(1) \geq 0$$
$$\Delta \geq -9$$

Thus, as long as Δ is −9 or greater, the dual price of zero is relevant. Profits will continue to change by $0 per unit change in the number of locks available as long as the number available doesn't decrease by more than nine. The allowable decrease is nine, and the allowable increase is infinity.

Because there are nine units of slack available in the final solution ($S_2 = 9$), we could simply say the shadow price is relevant as long as the right-hand side of the constraint is not reduced more than the slack that is available. This is true whenever slack is not zero for a constraint. Thus, this could have been determined without performing the calculations above.

The LINDO output for this example is shown in Output 5.2 above. Notice the reduced costs in the computer output are seen directly in the $C_j - Z_j$ values in the final simplex tableau. Similarly, the dual prices in the computer output are found in the final simplex tableau as well. The objective function coefficient ranges and the right-hand side ranges required some calculations using the information provided in the final simplex tableau.

5.14

THE DUAL PROBLEM

Primal problem
The original statement of a linear programming problem.

Dual problem
A revised form of a linear program.

The original linear programming problem is often called the **primal problem**. Related to this is another problem called the **dual problem**, and this is where the term *dual price* was developed. However, we have seen that dual prices may be found in the final simplex tableau for the primal problem. For large problems in which the primal problem has more constraints than decision variables, the dual problem will have more decision variables than constraints. This will require less space in the computer memory because slack, surplus, and artificial variables are added to constraints. Thus, for extremely large problems, there may be benefits to solving the dual problem.

Formulating the Dual Problem

If the primal problem has been formulated as a maximization problem with all ≤ constraints, the dual problem will be a minimization problem with all ≥ constraints. To formulate the dual problem, the following relationships will be used:

1. Each variable in the primal problem will be associated with a constraint in the dual. The coefficients of this variable in the

primal problem will be coefficients in the associated dual constraint. The number of constraints in the dual problem will equal the number of variables in the primal problem.

2. Each constraint in the primal problem will be associated with a variable in the dual problem. The number of variables in the dual problem will equal the number of constraints in the primal problem.
3. The right-hand side values in the primal problem will be the objective function coefficients in the dual problem.
4. The objective function coefficients in the primal problem will be the right-hand side values in the dual problem.

We will return to the Arlington Luggage problem to illustrate this. The linear programming model for this was:

$$\begin{aligned} &\text{Maximize profit} = 30X_1 + 90X_2 \\ &\text{Subject to: } 2X_1 + 5X_2 \le 80 \quad \text{labor hours} \\ &\qquad 1X_1 + 1X_2 \le 25 \quad \text{locks} \\ &\qquad X_1, X_2, \ge 0 \quad \text{nonnegativity constraints} \end{aligned}$$

We will let the dual variables be U_1, which will be associated with the labor-hours constraint, and U_2, which will be associated with the locks constraint. Writing the coefficients underneath the primal variables, it is easy to develop the dual, as shown in the following table.

X_1	X_2	RHS	
30	90		← RHS values for dual
2	5	80	U_1 ← dual variable
1	1	25	U_2 ← dual variable
		↑	

Objective function coefficients for dual

Using the primal right-hand side values, the objective function of the dual would be:

$$\text{Minimize profit} = 80U_1 + 25U_2$$

The right-hand side value for the first dual constraint is 30 and for the second dual constraint is 90. To obtain the first constraint, use the coefficients for X_1, resulting in:

$$2U_1 + 1U_2 \ge 30$$

To obtain the second dual constraint, use the coefficients for X_2 resulting in:

$$5U_1 + 1U_2 \ge 90$$

The complete dual problem is:

$$\begin{aligned} &\text{Minimize profit} = 80U_1 + 25U_2 \\ &\text{Subject to: } 2U_1 + 1U_2 \ge 30 \\ &\qquad 5U_1 + 1U_2 \ge 90 \\ &\qquad U_1, U_2 \ge 0 \end{aligned}$$

This problem now could be solved using the simplex algorithm. Certain relationships exist between the optimal solutions to the primal problem and the dual problem.

Relationships Between the Optimal Solutions to the Primal and Dual Problems

The solution to the dual problem may be found from the solution to the primal problem and the solution to the primal may be found from the dual solution. A summary of the important relationships when the primal is a maximization problem are as follows:

1. The optimal objective function value for the primal problem also is the optimal objective function value for the dual problem.
2. The absolute value of the $C_j - Z_j$ values in the primal are equal to the optimal values for the variables in the dual problem. Similarly, the absolute values of the $C_j - Z_j$ values in the dual are equal to the optimal values for the variables in the primal problem.

FIGURE 5.26

Final Simplex Tableaus for Primal and Dual Problems

Primal Problem

C_j	Basic Variable	30 X_1	90 X_2	0 S_1	0 S_2	RHS Value
90	X_2	0.4	1	0.2	0	16
0	S_2	0.6	0	−0.2	1	9
	Z_j	36	90	18	0	1440
	$C_j - Z_j$	−6	0	−18	0	
		↑ $S'_1 = 6$	↑ $S'_2 = 0$	↑ $U_1 = 18$	↑ $U_2 = 0$	

Dual Problem

C_j	Basic Variable	80 U_1	25 U_2	0 S'_1	0 S'_2	RHS Value
80	U_1	1	0.2	0	−0.2	18
0	S'_1	0	−0.6	1	−0.4	6
	Z_j	80	16	0	−16	1440
	$C_j - Z_j$	0	9	0	16	
		↑ $S_1 = 0$	↑ $S_2 = 9$	↑ $X_1 = 0$	↑ $X_2 = 16$	

Figure 5.26 provides the optimal simplex tableau for both the primal and the dual problems. We have used the notation S'_1 and S'_2 to represent the surplus variables in the dual problem so that these are not confused with S_1 and S_2 in the primal problem. Notice the values for all the variables in the primal problem may be found from the $C_j - Z_j$ values in the dual.

The primal variable X_1 is associated with the first dual constraint, and consequently it is associated with the dual surplus variable (S'_1) for the first dual constraint. Because X_1 is a nonbasic variable in the primal problem, it has a value of zero as does the $C_j - Z_j$ value for variable S'_1. Similarly, the primal variable X_2 is associated with the second dual constraint, and consequently it is associated with the dual surplus variable (S'_2) for the second dual constraint. Because $X_2 = 16$ in the primal solution, the $C_j - Z_j$ value for variable S'_2 also is 16.

The dual prices from the primal problem are simply the values for the respective dual variables. From Figure 5.26 above we see that $U_1 = 18$, so the dual price for the original labor-hours constraint is 18. Similarly, the dual price for the lock constraint is zero because $U_2 = 0$. The economic interpretation of these dual prices (or shadow prices) was provided earlier in this chapter.

The relationships between the primal and the dual problem that have been presented here are applicable whenever the primal is expressed with all ≤ constraints and all variables are restricted to be nonnegative. In situations where the primal is not expressed in this way, modifications must be made in formulating the dual problem and interpreting the results. For additional information on this, references have been provided.

5.15 ADDITIONAL TOPICS RELATED TO THE SIMPLEX ALGORITHM

What has been presented in this chapter is an introduction to the use of the simplex algorithm for solving linear programming problems. There are numerous variations of the simplex algorithm used for various computational reasons. Brief mention of these variations as well as related topics will be provided.

Revised Simplex Algorithm

The **revised simplex algorithm** helps to avoid round-off errors and reduces computer storage requirements for extremely large problems. This is found in more advanced textbooks on linear programming.

Revised simplex algorithm
A version of the simplex algorithm used both to reduce round-off errors and storage requirements in the computer.

Dual Simplex Algorithm

Sometimes the optimal solution to a linear programming problem has been obtained and additional constraints are added to the problem. The **dual**

Dual simplex algorithm A version of the simplex algorithm that begins with an existing, better than optimal infeasible solution.

simplex algorithm allows the existing solution to be the starting solution for the expanded problems even if this solution is infeasible relative to the new constraints. For large problems, this may save considerable computer time.

Unrestricted Variables

Unrestricted in sign A variable that may be positive, zero, or negative.

In all the problems worked on in this chapter, the decision variables were required to be nonnegative. If a variable is **unrestricted in sign** (i.e., it may be positive, zero, or negative), a transformation must be made before using the simplex algorithm because the simplex algorithm assumes all variables are nonnegative. For example, if X_1 is unrestricted in sign, we would let

$$X_1 = X_1' - X_1''$$

and replace X_1 by this everywhere in the linear program. If in the final solution $X_1' = 0$ and $X_1'' = 12$, this would mean

$$X_1 = 0 - 12 = -12$$

and X_1 would be negative.

5.16 SUMMARY

In this chapter we saw how to use the simplex algorithm to solve linear programming problems. This algorithm is the basis for most computer software designed for solving linear programming problems. We begin by using slack, surplus, and artificial variables in the constraints. The initial basic solution occurs where all the decision variables are set equal to zero. The simplex algorithm systematically evaluates corner points (basic solutions) until the optimal solution is reached.

Sensitivity analysis based on the simplex algorithm involves determining the impact of changing inputs in the model. Allowable increases and decreases in objective function coefficients indicate where the current basic solution remains optimal. Dual prices are found by looking at the Z_j values in the columns for the slack or surplus variables for the corresponding constraints. The allowable increases and decreases in the right-hand side values may be determined by using the substitution rates in the slack and surplus variable columns together with the RHS values.

Recognizing infeasible solutions, multiple optimal solutions, unbounded solutions, and degenerate solutions when using the simplex algorithm were discussed. More advanced topics related to linear programming were briefly mentioned, and these are more fully discussed in some of the references.

A CLOSER LOOK

Karmarkar's Algorithm

In recent years a new technique was developed to solve linear programming problems. This was developed by Narendra Karmarkar and is called **Karmarkar's Algorithm.** Instead of evaluating corner points as the simplex algorithm does, this method evaluates interior points by developing a sequence of spheres within the feasible region. The centers of these spheres represent improved solutions that are on the interior of the feasible region. This process of creating spheres continues until the center of the sphere is sufficiently close to the optimal basic solution so that it is identified as the optimal solution.

For some extremely large linear programming problems, this may be up to 50 times faster than the simplex algorithm. However, it should be noted that for problems where the number of decision variables and the number of constraints are in the hundreds or even thousands, computer software based on the simplex algorithm works efficiently and quickly. Software based on Karmarkar's Algorithm has been used by some airlines and petrochemical companies, which may have problems with tens of thousands or even hundreds of thousands of variables and constraints. Delta Air Lines with thousands of pilots and over 400 aircraft has developed linear programs to aid in setting monthly schedules for the pilots. An interior-point algorithm is used to solve these problems.

SOURCE: Hooker, J. N., 1986. "Karmarkar's Linear Programming Algorithm." *Interfaces*: 16(4): 75–90.

GLOSSARY

Karmarkar's Algorithm Another mathematical technique for solving linear programming problems.

Artificial variables Variables used with the simplex algorithm to indicate if the solution is feasible. *p. 169*

Basic solution A basic solution to a set of m linear equations with n unknowns (with $m < n$) and is found by setting $n - m$ of these variables equal to zero and solving for the rest of them. This is the equivalent of a corner point solution. *p. 172*

Basic variables Variables not required to have values of zero in a solution found using the simplex algorithm. *p. 170*

Basis The set of all basic variables in a solution. *p. 171*

C_j An objective function coefficient. *p. 170*

$C_j - Z_j$ The net change in the objective function value that would result from bringing one unit of the corresponding variable into the solution. *p. 173*

Critical ratio For each row, the RHS value divided by the positive substitution rate in the pivot column for that row. The pivot row has the smallest critical ratio. *p. 176*

Degenerate solution A solution to a linear programming problem in which the value of one of the basic variables is zero. *p. 197*

Dual problem A revised form of a linear program. *p. 208*

Dual simplex algorithm A version of the simplex algorithm that begins with an existing, better than optimal infeasible solution. *p. 212*

Entering variable The variable in the pivot column that will be in the basis of the next simplex tableau. *p. 176*

Karmarkar's Algorithm Another mathematical technique for solving linear programming problems. *p. 213*

Leaving variable The basic variable that is in the pivot row. This will be a nonbasic variable in the next tableau. *p. 176*

Nonbasic variable A variable that is not in the basis and is required to equal zero. These are the variables not listed in the Basic Variables column in the simplex tableau. *p. 171*

Pivot number The number at the intersection of

the pivot row and pivot column. *p. 176*

Pivot row The row corresponding to the smallest critical ratio. The variable in this row leaves the basis. *p. 176*

Pivot column The column which contains the variable that will enter the basis. For maximization problems, this is the column with the largest positive $C_j - Z_j$ value. For minimization problems, this is the column with the most negative $C_j - Z_j$ value. *p. 176*

Primal problem The original statement of a linear programming problem. *p. 208*

Range of optimality The set of possible values for an objective function coefficient in which there is no change in the optimal basic solution (although the value of the objective function could change). *p. 200*

Revised simplex algorithm A version of the simplex algorithm used both to reduce round-off errors and storage requirements in the computer. *p. 211*

Simplex algorithm The most common technique for solving linear programming problems. *p. 168*

Slack variable A variable added to a ≤ constraint to represent unused resources. *p. 168*

Substitution rates Numbers in the simplex tableau. The substitution rate indicates how much the value of a basic variable would have to be reduced in order to bring one unit of the nonbasic variable into the solution. *p. 172*

Surplus variable A variable used in a ≥ constraint to represent the amount by which the right-hand side of the constraint is exceeded. *p. 168*

Unrestricted in sign A variable that may be positive, zero, or negative. *p. 212*

Z_j The opportunity cost of bringing in one unit of a variable into the solution. *p. 173*

SOLVED PROBLEMS

SOLVED PROBLEM 5-1

Solve the following problem with the simplex algorithm.

$$\text{Maximize} = 18X_1 + 14X_2 + 16X_3$$

$$\text{Subject to: } 2X_1 + X_2 + 2X_3 \le 24$$

$$4X_1 + 4X_2 + 2X_3 \le 40$$

$$X_1 + X_2 + X_3 \le 14$$

$$X_1, X_2, X_3 \ge 0$$

SOLUTION

C_j		18	14	16	0	0	0	RHS	Critical
	Basic Variable	X_1	X_2	X_3	S_1	S_2	S_3	Values	Ratios
0	S_1	2	1	2	1	0	0	24	24/2 = 12
0	S_2	4	4	2	0	1	0	40	40/4 = 10 ← pivot row
0	S_3	1	1	1	0	0	1	14	14/1 = 14
	Z_j	0	0	0	0	0	0	0	
	$C_j - Z_j$	18	14	16	0	0	0		
		↑ pivot column							

C_j Basic Variable	18 X_1	14 X_2	16 X_3	0 S_1	0 S_2	0 S_3	RHS Values	Critical Ratios	
0 S_1	0	−1	1	1	−0.5	0	4	4/1 = 4	← pivot row
18 X_1	1	1	0.5	0	0.25	0	10	10/0.5 = 20	
0 S_3	0	0	0.5	0	−.25	1	4	4/0.5 = 8	
Z_j	18	18	9	0	4.5	0	180		
$C_j - Z_j$	0	−4	7	0	−4.5	0			
			↑ pivot column						

C_j Basic Variable	18 X_1	14 X_2	16 X_3	0 S_1	0 S_2	0 S_3	RHS Values	Critical Ratios	
16 X_3	0	−1	1	1	−0.5	0	4	—	
18 X_1	1	1.5	0	−0.5	0.5	0	8	8/1.5 = 12	
0 S_3	0	0.5	0	−0.5	0	1	2	2/0.5 = 4	← pivot row
Z_j	18	11	16	7	1	0	208		
$C_j - Z_j$	0	3	0	−7	−1	0			
		↑ pivot column							

C_j Basic Variable	18 X_1	14 X_2	16 X_3	0 S_1	0 S_2	0 S_3	RHS Values
16 X_3	0	0	1	0	−0.5	2	8
18 X_1	1	0	0	1	0.5	−3	2
14 X_2	0	1	0	−1	0	2	4
Z_j	18	14	16	4	1	6	220
$C_j - Z_j$	0	0	0	−4	−1	−6	

Optimal solution indicated because all $C_j - Z_j \leq 0$.

SOLVED PROBLEM 5-2

The following linear programming model represents a production problem in which three products are produced, and three resources are used to produce them. This was solved with the simplex algorithm. The final simplex tableau is provided below.

X_1 = number of units of Product #1 produced per week

X_2 = number of units of Product #2 produced per week

X_3 = number of units of Product #3 produced per week

$$\text{Maximize profit} = 82X_1 + 65X_2 + 75X_3$$

$$\begin{aligned} \text{Subject to: } 4X_1 + 4X_2 + 5X_3 &\leq 960 && \text{hours of Resource A} \\ 12X_1 + 10X_2 + 10X_3 &\leq 2100 && \text{hours of Resource B} \\ X_1 + X_2 + X_3 &\leq 250 && \text{hours of Resource C} \\ X_1, X_2, X_3 &\geq 0 \end{aligned}$$

C_j Basic Variable	82 X_1	65 X_2	75 X_3	0 S_1	0 S_2	0 S_3	RHS Values
75 X_3	0	0.4	1	0.6	−0.20	0	156
82 X_1	1	0.5	0	−0.5	0.25	0	45
0 S_3	0	0.1	0	−0.1	−0.05	1	49
Z_j	82	71	75	4	5.5	0	15,390
$C_j - Z_j$	0	−6	0	−4	−5.5	0	

Answer the following questions based on this optimal simplex tableau.

a) How much would the profit on Product #2 have to increase in order to produce any of this without sacrificing profit?

b) How much would the profit on Product #1 have to change before another basic solution would be optimal?

c) What is the dual price for each of the three resources?

d) If one additional hour of Resource B were made available, what would be the maximum possible profit?

e) If one additional hour of Resource B were made available, what would be the values for all the variables in the optimal solution?

f) Find the allowable increase and decrease for Resource B in which the dual price is relevant.

g) What is the dual price for Resource C? Find the allowable increase and decrease for Resource B in which the dual price is relevant.

SOLUTION

a) The profit on Product #2 has to increase by $6 per unit in order to produce any of this without sacrificing profit.

b) Substitute C_1 for the coefficient of X_1 in the objective function row and the C_j column. Recalculate the Z_j and $C_j - Z_j$ values and restrict all of these to be negative or zero to maintain optimality.

C_j Basic Variable	C_1 X_1	65 X_2	75 X_3	0 S_1	0 S_2	0 $S3$	RHS Values
75 X_3	0	0.4	1	0.6	−0.20	0	156
C_1 X_1	1	0.5	0	−0.5	0.25	0	45
0 S_3	0	0.1	0	−0.1	−0.05	1	49
Z_j	C_1	$30+0.5C_1$	75	$45-0.5C_1$	$-15+0.25C_1$	0	$11{,}700+45C_1$
$C_j - Z_j$	0	$35-0.5C_1$	0	$-45+0.5C_1$	$15-0.25C_1$	0	

To maintain optimality:

$$35 - 0.5C_1 \leq 0$$

$$-45 + 0.5C_1 \leq 0$$

$$15 - 0.25C_1 \leq 0$$

Solving for C_1 results in:

$$C_1 \geq 70$$

$$C_1 \leq 90$$

$$C_1 \geq 60$$

Thus:

$$70 \leq C_1 \leq 90$$

Because the original value of C_1 is 82, the allowable increase is 8 and the allowable decrease is 12.

c) The dual price for Resource A is 4, the dual price for Resource B is 5.5, and the dual price for Resource C is 0.

d) If one additional hour of Resource B were made available, the profit would increase by the dual price of 5.5, so the maximum possible profit would be \$15,395.50.
e) Adding the substitution rates from the S_2 column to the current right-hand side values results in the new values for the basic variables as shown below.

Basic Variable	RHS Value
X_3	$= 156 + 1(-0.2) = 155.8$
X_1	$= 45 + 1(0.25) = 45.25$
S_3	$= 49 + 1(-0.05) = 48.95$

All other variables would still be equal to zero.

$$\text{Profit} = 82(45.25) + 65(0) + 75(155.8) = 15{,}395.5$$

Note that the profit increased by the amount of the dual price.
f) Let Δ = allowable change for this resource. Working with the substitution rates in the S_2 column, we use the following condition which maintains feasibility:

$$\text{RHS Value} + \Delta(\text{substitution rate}) \geq 0$$

Using each of the three rows in the final simplex tableau we have:

$$156 + \Delta(-0.2) \geq 0$$

$$45 + \Delta(0.25) \geq 0$$

$$49 + \Delta(-0.05) \geq 0$$

Solving for Δ we get the following:

$$\Delta \leq 780$$

$$\Delta \geq -180$$

$$\Delta \leq 900$$

Thus, the allowable decrease is 180, and the allowable increase is 780. The dual price is relevant in this range, and the current basic variables remain in the basis for changes in this range.
g) The dual price is 0. There is no limit to the amount of increase; the slack will simply increase. The allowable decrease is 49, which is the amount of slack for this constraint.

QUESTIONS

1. Explain what the $C_j - Z_j$ values in the simplex tableau represents.
2. For a maximization problem, what would happen if the pivot row selection rule was changed to *select any column with a positive* $C_j - Z_j$ *value?*
3. What are the critical ratios used in the simplex algorithm?
4. What would happen if the row with the largest critical ratio was selected as the pivot row?
5. Without developing the next simplex tableau, how can you determine how many units of the entering variable will be brought into the solution in the next iteration?
6. In a simplex tableau for a profit maximization problem, the largest positive $C_j - Z_j$ value is four, and the smallest critical ratio is 15. How much will total profit increase in the solution represented by the next simplex tableau?
7. How does the simplex method indicate there is no feasible solution to a linear programming problem?
8. How does the simplex method indicate there is more than one solution to a linear programming problem?
9. How does the simplex method indicate a linear programming problem is unbounded?
10. Suppose the optimal solution to a linear programming problem has been found, and we are evaluating the impact of changing an objective function coefficient for a nonbasic variable. If this change is within the allowable limits, will the values of any variables change? Will the value of the objective function change?
11. Suppose the optimal solution to a linear programming problem has been found, and we are evaluating the impact of changing an objective function coefficient for a basic variable. If this change is within the allowable limits, will there be a change in the value of any variable? Will the value of the objective function change?
12. If the objective function coefficient for a basic variable is changed by an amount that does exceed the allowable limits, will there be a change in the optimal value of any variable? Will the objective function value change?
13. How can you determine the value of obtaining additional units of a particular resource from the final simplex tableau?
14. If a slack variable is basic in the optimal simplex tableau, how much may the right-hand side of the constraint corresponding to this slack variable increase without affecting the value of any of the other variables? How much may it decrease without affecting the value of any of the other variables?
15. Suppose a slack variable is nonbasic in the final solution, and a change is made in the right-hand side of the constraint associated with this slack variable. If this change is within the allowable limits, what will happen to the value of the objective function? What will happen to the values of the basic variables? What will happen to the values of the nonbasic variables?

PROBLEMS

16. The following is the initial simplex tableau for a linear program to maximize profit.

C_j Basic Variable	12 X_1	4 X_2	0 S_1	0 S_2	RHS Values
0 S_1	2	1	1	0	24
0 S_2	2	4	0	1	36
	Z_j				
$C_j - Z_j$					

a) Write the objective function and the constraints for this problem.

b) What is the solution represented by this tableau? Which variables are nonbasic variables?

c) Calculate the Z_j and the $C_j - Z_j$ values and select the pivot row.

d) Which variable will enter the basis? How much will profit increase for each unit that is brought into the solution?

e) Calculate the critical ratios and select the pivot row.

f) Which variable will leave the basis and become a nonbasic variable?

g) How many units of the entering variable will be in the next solution?

h) Using information already calculated, what will be the total profit in the next tableau?

i) Develop the next tableau. Answer the questions in parts (b) through (g) with the next tableau.

17. Consider the following linear programming problem:

$$\text{Maximize profit} = 20X_1 + 30X_2 + 15X_3$$
$$\text{Subject to: } 3X_1 + 5X_2 - 2X_3 \leq 120$$
$$2X_1 + X_2 + 2X_3 \geq 250$$
$$X_1 + X_2 + X_3 = 180$$
$$X_1, X_2, X_3 \geq 0$$

a) Add the slack, surplus, and artificial variables that would be needed if the simplex algorithm were to be used to solve this problem. Include these in the objective function with the appropriate coefficients.

b) Give the values for all the variables and the objective function for the basic solution found when all the decision variables and surplus variables are set equal to zero.

c) Set up the initial simplex tableau.

18. Solve the linear program in the previous problem using the simplex algorithm.

19. Consider the following linear programming problem:

$$\text{Minimize cost} = 5X_1 + 6X_2 + 4X_3$$
$$\text{Subject to: } 4X_1 - 5X_2 + 4X_3 \leq 230$$
$$3X_1 + 2X_2 - X_3 \geq 250$$
$$X_1 + X_2 + X_3 = 120$$
$$X_1, X_2, X_3 \geq 0$$

a) Add the necessary slack, surplus, and artificial variables to this problem. Include these in the objective function with the appropriate coefficients.

b) Give the values for all the variables and the objective function for the basic solution found when all the decision variables and surplus variables are set equal to zero.

c) Set up the initial simplex tableau.

d) If this problem were changed to a maximization problem, how would the above answers change?

20. Solve the linear program in Problem 19 using the simplex algorithm.
21. Consider the following linear programming problem:

$$\text{Maximize cost} = 12X_1 + 15X_2$$
$$\text{Subject to: } 3X_1 - 5X_2 \leq -50$$
$$2X_1 + X_2 \leq 250$$
$$X_1, X_2 \geq 0$$

a) Make any necessary changes to this problem and then add the necessary slack, surplus, and artificial variables to the problem to put it in standard form.
b) Set up the initial simplex tableau.
c) What are the values for all of the variables in this initial solution?
d) Is this initial solution feasible? Explain.

22. Consider the following linear programming problem:

$$\text{Maximize profit} = 10X_1 + 8X_2$$
$$\text{Subject to: } 4X_1 + 2X_2 \leq 80$$
$$X_1 + 2X_2 \leq 50$$
$$X_1, X_2 \geq 0$$

a) Solve this problem graphically.
b) Set up the initial simplex tableau.
c) Select the pivot row and pivot column.
d) Which variable is the entering variable? Which variable is the leaving variable?
e) Identify on the graph what the critical ratios in the initial tableau represent.
f) How many units of the entering variable will be brought into the solution in the second tableau?
g) Finish solving this problem using the simplex algorithm.
h) The solution in each simplex tableau is a corner point on the graph. Identify the corner point that is associated with each simplex tableau.

23. Formulate the dual problem for Problem 22.
24. Modify the Swiff Tees example presented in this chapter so the total production of shirts must be 40 instead of 30. The linear program is given below.

$$\text{Minimize cost} = 4X_1 + 5X_2$$
$$\text{Subject to: } X_1 + X_2 = 40 \quad \text{total production}$$
$$X_1 \geq 10 \quad \text{T-shirt requirement}$$
$$4X_1 + 2X_2 \leq 100 \quad \text{logo restriction}$$
$$X_1, X_2 \geq 0$$

This change will result in a degenerate solution at one of the basic solutions.
a) Solve this problem using the simplex algorithm.
b) Solve this problem graphically. Identify the corner points associated with the solution represented by each tableau. Identify the basic and nonbasic variables for each tableau.
c) What occurs graphically when there is a degenerate solution?

25. Three types of products (Product #1, Product #2, and Product #3) are produced using labor hours in three departments (Department A, Department B, and Department C). A linear program has been formulated to maximize the profit subject to limits on the amounts of the labor hours.

X_1 = number of units of Product #1 produced per week

X_2 = number of units of Product #2 produced per week

X_3 = number of units of Product #3 produced per week

$$\begin{aligned}
\text{Maximize profit} &= 12X_1 + 15X_2 + 14X_3 \\
\text{Subject to: } 4X_1 + 2X_2 + X_3 &\leq 60 \quad \text{hours in Department A} \\
X_1 + 2X_2 + 2X_3 &\leq 36 \quad \text{hours in Department B} \\
2X_1 + 2X_2 + 2X_3 &\leq 40 \quad \text{hours in Department C} \\
X_1, X_2, X_3 &\geq 0
\end{aligned}$$

The optimal simplex tableau for this is given below.

C_j / Basic Variable	12 X_1	15 X_2	14 X_3	0 S_1	0 S_2	0 S_3	RHS Values
0 S_1	0	0	−1	1	2	−3	12
15 X_2	0	1	1	0	1	−0.5	16
12 X_1	1	0	0	0	−1	1	4
Z_j	12	15	15	0	3	4.5	288
$C_j - Z_j$	0	0	−1	0	−3	−4.5	

a) Give the values for all of the basic and nonbasic variables for the solution represented by this tableau.
b) What are the dual prices for hours in each of the three departments?
c) How much should the company be willing to pay for additional hours in each of the three departments?
d) How much would profit on Product #3 have to increase before it could be produced without sacrificing profit?
e) What is the allowable increase and decrease for the profit on Product #1?
f) How much could labor hours be reduced without changing the profit?
g) Find the range of values for hours in Department B in which the dual price is relevant.
h) Suppose one additional hour in Department B were made available. Find the profit and the values for all of the variables for the new optimal solution.
i) Should additional hours in Department C be used if these could be obtained at a cost of $6 per hour?

26. A linear program has been formulated and solved. The final simplex tableau is provided.

$$\begin{aligned}
\text{Maximize profit} &= 80X_1 + 120X_2 + 90X_3 \\
\text{Subject to: } 12X_1 + 20X_2 + 14X_3 &\leq 800 \\
4X_1 + 2X_2 + 2X_3 &\leq 100 \\
X_1 + X_2 + X_3 &\geq 30 \\
X_1, X_2, X_3 &\geq 0
\end{aligned}$$

The optimal simplex tableau for this is given below.

C_j Basic Variable	80 X_1	120 X_2	90 X_3	0 S_1	0 S_2	0 S_3	$-M$ A_3	RHS Values
0 S_3	1	0	0	1	0.5	1	–1	20
90 X_3	4.667	0	1	–0.167	1.667	0	0	33.33
120 X_2	–2.667	1	0	0.167	–1.167	0	0	16.67
Z_j	100	120	90	5	10	0	0	5,000
$C_j - Z_j$	–20	0	0	–5	–10	0	$-M$	

a) What are the dual prices for the three constraints?

b) If the right-hand side of the first constraint were increased by 10 units, what would the new RHS values in the tableau be?

c) How much could the RHS of the third constraint increase or decrease without changing the profit?

d) If the RHS of the third constraint were increased from the current value of 30 to 45, what would be the values for all variables?

27. Formulate the dual problem for Problem 26. Using the optimal simplex tableau for the primal problem, find the values for all of the dual variables.
28. Consider the following simplex tableau for a maximization problem.

C_j Basic Variable	12 X_1	4 X_2	0 S_1	0 S_2	RHS Values
0 S_1	–2	1	1	0	24
0 S_2	–1	4	0	1	36
Z_j	0	0	0	0	0
$C_j - Z_j$	12	4	0	0	

Select the pivot column and calculate the critical ratios. What special condition exists for this problem?

29. An optimal simplex tableau for a maximization problem is given below.

C_j Basic Variable	20 X_1	30 X_2	30 X_3	0 S_1	0 S_2	0 S_3	RHS Values
0 S_1	0	0	–1	1	2	–3	26
30 X_2	0	1	1	0	1	–0.5	40
20 X_1	1	0	0	0	–1	1	50
Z_j	20	30	30	0	10	5	2,200
$C_j - Z_j$	0	0	0	0	–10	–5	

What special condition exists for this problem? Find another optimal solution to this problem.

30. The following is the simplex tableau after one iteration for a maximization problem.

C_j Basic Variable	12 X_1	8 X_2	0 S_1	0 S_2	0 S_3	RHS Values
12 X_1	1	1/2	1/4	0	0	6
0 S_2	0	1/2	–1/4	1	0	4
0 S_3	0	1/2	–3/4	0	1	0
Z_j	12	6	3	0	0	72
$C_j - Z_j$	0	2	–3	0	0	

a) What solution is represented by this tableau? Which variables are basic variables? Which variables are nonbasic variables?
b) What special condition exists for this solution?
c) Which column will be selected as the pivot column? How much will profit increase for each unit of the entering variable that is brought into the solution?
d) Develop the next tableau. How much did profit increase from the previous solution?

31. Solve the following problem using the simplex algorithm.

$$\text{Minimize cost} = 5X_1 + 2X_2$$
$$\text{Subject to: } X_1 + X_2 \geq 40$$
$$2X_1 + 4X_2 \leq 72$$
$$X_1, X_2 \geq 0$$

What special condition exists for this problem?

32. A bank has 10 million dollars that is to be used for mortgage loans, automobile loans, and government securities, although some of the money may be held as a cash reserve. The expected returns for the uses of the money are nine percent for mortgages, 12 percent for automobile loans, six percent for government securities, and zero percent for the cash reserves. While the bank would like to maximize the expected return on these dollars, there are certain restrictions related to the risk of these investments. These are:

    1. The total amount put into government securities and held as a cash reserve must be at least 50 percent of the money invested.
    2. The amount of money in automobile loans cannot exceed the amount in mortgages.
    3. At least 10 percent must be held as a cash reserve.

    Use linear programming to determine how much money to invest in each of the three areas.

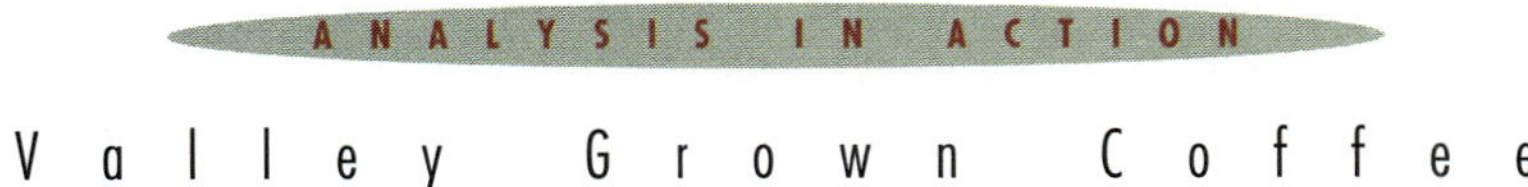

Valley Grown Coffee

Valley Grown Coffee produces two types of coffee—Regular and Gourmet. Each of these possess certain characteristics, which are important to the overall quality of the coffee. The caffeine content, acidity, and aroma are carefully monitored to guarantee the quality of the product. These characteristics are measured on a scale of 1–10 with 10 being of the highest level. The Regular coffee has been required to have a rating of no more than seven on caffeine, no more than four on acidity, but at least a seven on aroma. The Gourmet coffee has been required to have a rating of no more than six on caffeine, no more than three on acidity, but at least an eight on aroma. However, these restrictions are being investigated to determine how changes may impact the cost of production. Market research tests are being developed to determine how such changes would affect the taste of the coffees. Past studies have indicated the taste of the coffee, particularly for the Gourmet coffee, is more important to the consumer than is the price of the coffee.

These two coffees are blended from Brazilian and Colombian coffee beans. The characteristics of coffee made from each of these two types of beans are:

	Brazilian	Colombian
caffeine	7	3
acidity	4	2
aroma	5	9

The prices per pound of beans are $1.00 for Brazilian and $1.40 for Colombian. Because Valley Grown produced 80 million pounds of coffee last year, a minor change in the cost per pound of coffee may have a major impact on profits.

Use linear programming to determine how to blend the coffee beans to minimize the cost of manufacturing these two types of coffee. Prepare a managerial report indicating your recommendations. Indicate in your report how the cost would be impacted if the restrictions on caffeine, acidity, and aroma are modified.

Linear Programming Example Using Solver with Sensitivity Analysis

The linear programming problem is:

$$
\begin{aligned}
&\text{Max } z = 3x1 + 2x2 + 10x3 \\
&\text{st} \\
&\qquad 4x1 + x2 + 3x3 \le 48 \\
&\qquad 2x1 + 6x2 + 3x3 \le 60 \\
&\qquad x1 \ge 0 \\
&\qquad x2 \ge 0 \\
&\qquad x3 \ge 0
\end{aligned}
$$

To obtain sensitivity analysis, run Solver. When the solution is found, select the type of report you desire—Answer, Sensitivity, or Limits.

	A	B	C	D	E	F	G	H
1	Linear Programming Example Using Solver with Sensitivity Analysis							
2								
3								
4	Max z= 3x1 + 2x2 + 10x3							
5	st							
6	4x1+ x2 + 3x3 <= 48							
7	2x1+6x2 +3x3 <= 60							
8	x1 >= 0							
9	x2 >= 0							
10	x3 >= 0							
11								
12	objective function				constraints			
13	z	160				48	<=	48
14						48	<=	60
15	decision variables							
16	x1	1.19E-08				1.19E-08	>=	0
17	x2	0				0	>=	0
18	x3	16				16	>=	0

	A	B	C	D	E	F
1	Linear Programming					
2						
3						
4	Max z= 3x1 + 2x2 + 10					
5	st					
6	4x1+ x2 + 3x3 <=					
7	2x1+6x2 +3x3 <=					
8	x1 >= 0					
9	x2 >= 0					
10	x3 >= 0					
11						
12	objective function		constraints			
13	z	=3*B16+2*B17+10*B18		=4*B16+ B17+3*B18	<=	48
14			=2*B16+6*B17+3*B1	<=	60	
15	decision variables					
16	x1	1.18566368744862E-8		=+B16	>=	0
17	x2	0		=+B17	>=	0
18	x3	15.9999999841912		=+B18	>=	0

Microsoft Excel 4.0a Limits Report
Worksheet: LP.XLS
Report Created: 6/6/95 11:50

Cell	Target Name	Value
$BS13	z	159.9999999

Cell	Adjustable Name	Value	Lower Limit	Target Result	Upper Limit	Target Result
$BS16	x1	1.18566E-08	1.18566E-081	59.9999999	1.18566E-08	159.9999999
$BS17	x2	0	0	159.9999999	0	159.9999999
$BS18	x3	15.99999998	0	3.55699E-08	15.99999998	159.9999999

Microsoft Excel 4.0a Answer Report
Worksheet: LP.XLS
Report Created: 6/6/95 11:48

Target Cell (Max)

Cell	Name	Original Value	Final Value
$B$13	z	159.9999999	159.9999999

Adjustable Cells

Cell	Name	Original Value	Final Value
$B$16	x1	1.18566E-08	1.18566E-08
$B$17	x2	0	0
$B$18	x3	15.99999998	15.99999998

Constraints

Cell	Name	Cell Value	Formula	Status	Slack
$F$13	z	48	$F$13<=$H$13	Binding	0
$F$14		47.99999998	$F$14<=$H$14	Not Binding	12.00000002
$F$16	x1	1.18566E-08	$F$16>=$H$16	Binding	0
$F$17	x2	0	$F$17>=$H$17	Binding	0
$F$18	x3	15.99999998	$F$18>=$H$18	Not Binding	5.99999998

Microsoft Excel 4.0a Sensitivity Report
Worksheet: LP.XLS
Report Created: 6/6/95 11:50

Changing Cells

Cell	Name	Final Value	Reduced Gradient
$B$16	x1	.18566E-08	0
$B$17	x2	0	0
$B$18	x3	15.99999998	0

Constraints

Cell	Name	Final Value	Lagrange Multiplier
$F$13	z	48	3.333333333
$F$14		47.99999998	0
$F$16	x1	1.18566E-08	-10.33333826
$F$17	x2	0	-1.333338102
$F$18	x3	15.99999998	0

CHAPTER SIX

Transportation and Assignment Problems

LEARNING OBJECTIVES

Upon completing Chapter 6, you should be able to:

- Develop an initial solution to a transportation problem using the northwest corner, least cost, and Vogel's approximation methods.
- Evaluate the empty cells in a transportation problem using the steppingstone method and the modified distribution (MODI) method.
- Interpret the evaluation indices in a transportation problem.
- Recognize and deal with special cases of the transportation problem.
- Solve transportation problems using a computer.
- Use the Hungarian algorithm to solve assignment problems.
- Recognize and deal with special cases of the assignment problem.
- Solve assignment problems using a computer.

CHAPTER OUTLINE

6.1 INTRODUCTION

In an earlier chapter on linear programming applications, we saw how to formulate transportation and assignment problems as linear programming problems. These are two very specific types of linear programming problems, which because of their importance, special techniques were developed to solve them more efficiently. With the recent advances in computing power, the need for special algorithms to solve these has diminished considerably, although for very large problems the differences in computer solution times may be significant. However, even for small problems there are benefits to studying these special techniques as they provide insights into the problem.

The basic transportation problem involves trying to find the least cost way to transport items from a set of sources to a set of destinations. The sources may be factories or regional warehouses, each having a specific capacity or number of units available. The destinations may be warehouses or retail outlets, each of these would have a specific demand.

To see how important transportation costs are to a company, consider General Motors. In 1984, GM had approximately 20,000 supplier plants, 31 assembly plants, and 11,000 dealers in North America. Total transportation costs associated with both raw materials and finished products were $4.1 billion.

The basic transportation problem involves trying to find the least cost way to transport items from a set of sources to a set of destinations. SOURCE: Courtesy of GATX Corporation

In this chapter, special-purpose algorithms for both the transportation and assignment problems will be presented. A discussion of how these techniques relate to linear programming and the simplex algorithm will be presented.

6.2

AN EXAMPLE

Capitol Electric produces electric motors in each of its three factories located in Lubbock, Mobile, and Lake Charles. The Lubbock plant can produce 100 electric motors each week while the Mobile plant can produce 150 units per week and the Lake Charles plant can produce 180 per week. Each motor is shipped to one of three regional distribution centers in Miami, Dallas, and Atlanta. Based on a forecast of demand, 210 motors must be shipped to Miami, 120 motors must be shipped to Dallas, and 100 motors must be shipped to Atlanta. An analysis of the shipping cost from each source to each destination has resulted in the information in Table 6.1. While there are many ways for Capitol Electric to meet the demands at the different warehouses, management would like to minimize the shipping cost. What is the shipping schedule that will do this?

6.3

THE TRANSPORTATION ALGORITHM

While a transportation problem such as the Capitol Electric problem may be solved using normal linear programming procedures, for problems with a large number of sources and destinations it may be desirable to use a special-purpose algorithm, which is significantly faster than the simplex algorithm. As many real-world problems have been developed with thousands of variables and constraints, it is important to recognize that faster techniques are available.

Before determining a shipping schedule for Capitol Electric, we will provide an overview of the transportation algorithm that may be used with this type of problem. To begin the development of a transportation model,

TABLE 6.1

Unit Shipping Costs for Capitol Electric Problem

	To		
From	Miami	Dallas	Atlanta
Lubbock	$6	2	5
Mobile	3	8	4
Lake Charles	7	6	7

all of the information will be put into a transportation table as shown in Figure 6.1. The sources (factories) in this problem are represented by rows in this table while the destinations (warehouses) are represented by the columns in this table. The supplies and demands are seen in the margins. In the upper right-hand corner of each cell, we will put the transportation cost per unit shipped. Later the number of units shipped will be put into the middle of each cell in this table. By representing this problem in this fashion, it is easy to see all of the pertinent information, and it would be easy for a manager to quickly evaluate any solution.

In Chapter 4, we saw how to express this type of problem as a linear program. A decision variable would be defined for each cell in Figure 6.1, and a constraint would be formed for each row and column. Just as the simplex algorithm (Chapter 5) is used to find an optimal basic solution to the problem expressed as a linear program, the transportation algorithm is used to find an optimal basic solution to this problem in the format shown in Figure 6.1. Empty cells in this table will represent the nonbasic variables that must equal zero, while filled cells will represent the basic variables.

We will present a special-purpose technique for solving transportation problems using this type of format. This transportation algorithm may be used to solve any transportation problem. The steps in this algorithm are summarized in Summary Table 6.1 to provide an overview of this process.

We will use the Capitol Electric problem to illustrate this algorithm. The first step in the algorithm is to set up the transportation table as shown in Figure 6.1. Proceeding to Step 2, an initial solution must be generated. We will use the northwest corner method for this purpose.

6.4 DEVELOPING AN INITIAL SOLUTION—NORTHWEST CORNER METHOD

Northwest corner method
A method for generating an initial solution to a transportation problem.

The **northwest corner method** is a very easy technique for obtaining an initial solution to a transportation problem. This involves starting at the upper left-hand corner (the northwest corner) of the table and assigning as

FIGURE 6.1

Tabular Representation of Capitol Electric Problem

Source	Destination: Miami	Dallas	Atlanta	Supply
Lubbock	6	2	5	100
Mobile	3	8	4	150
Lake Charles	7	6	7	180
Demand	210	120	100	

SUMMARY TABLE 6.1

Summary of Transportation Algorithm

Step 1. Set up a **balanced** (total demand must equal total supply) transportation table.

Step 2. Generate an initial solution. Common techniques are the northwest corner method, the least cost method, and Vogel's approximation method (VAM).

Step 3. Calculate an evaluation index for each empty cell with either the steppingstone method or the modified distribution (MODI) method. For a minimization problem, the optimal solution occurs when all the evaluation indices are positive or zero.

Step 4. Select the empty cell that results in the greatest per unit improvement, and generate an improved solution using a steppingstone path. Return to Step 3.

Balanced

A transportation problem in which the total demand is equal to the total supply. Also, an assignment problem in which the number of rows equals the number of columns.

many units as possible to that cell. This will exhaust either the supply available in that row, the demand required in that column, or both. The next step is to move to the right if there is still some supply available in that row or down in the column if the demand has not yet been met. In this next cell, we exhaust either the row or column amount and continue. This process continues until all supplies are exhausted and all demands are met.

Figure 6.2 illustrates the northwest corner method for the Capitol Electric problem. We begin by placing as many units as possible in the northwest corner of this table. Because the supply from Lubbock is 100 and the demand at Miami is 210, the maximum number that may be assigned to this cell is 100 units, which is the entire supply from Lubbock. The next step is to move either to the right or down. Because the supply from Lubbock is exhausted, move down to the Mobile row. Miami still needs 110 units, and Mobile has 150 units available. Therefore, we will assign 110 units to this cell and exhaust the demand at Miami. The next step is to move either to the right or down, and in this case we move to the right because Mobile still has 40 units that have not been allocated. We assign 40 units to the Mobile to Dallas route and exhaust the supply from Mobile. Moving down in the Dallas column, allocate 80 units to the Lake Charles

FIGURE 6.2

Northwest Corner Method Applied to Capitol Electric Problem

Source	Destination: Miami	Dallas	Atlanta	Supply
Lubbock	100 [6]	[2]	[5]	100
Mobile	110 [3]	40 [8]	[4]	150
Lake Charles	[7]	80 [6]	100 [7]	180
Demand	210	120	100	

Dow Jones Faces a Global Transportation Problem

Dow Jones is one of the world's leading publishers of business news, information services, and community newspapers. The company's flagship publication, the *Wall Street Journal*, is published in the U.S., Europe, and Asia, with a worldwide circulation of nearly two million. Other business publications include *Barron's*, *Far Eastern Economic Review*, *National Business Employment Weekly*, *Texas Journal*, the *Asian Wall Street Journal Weekly*, the *Wall Street Journal Classroom Edition*, *SmartMoney*, and *American Demographics*. Dow Jones also has investments in newspaper and magazine publishers in North and South America, Europe, and Asia.

Publishing and distributing this broad range of publications is no simple task. Dow Jones maintains *Wall Street Journal* news bureaus in many countries. The company also publishes the *Wall Street Journal* in a variety of locations. In response to a growing demand for reporting on regional business trends and issues, Dow Jones offers weekly supplements to the *Wall Street Journal* in Texas and Asia. A quarterly magazine called the *Central European Economic Review* targets the European market. To keep readers satisfied, the company also has increased the number of areas around the world that receive early-morning home delivery (nearly one million copies of the *Journal* delivered daily).

Clearly, Dow Jones faces a global transportation problem of tremendous size. To keep operating costs low, and customers satisfied, the company must find efficient means of distributing its various publications. With numerous supply points, and more than a million demand points, the *Wall Street Journal* distribution problem alone is too large to solve optimally. However, if broken into smaller, regional subproblems, the problem could provide an exciting application of management science techniques.

SOURCE:
Dow Jones Annual Report, 1993.

---

to Dallas route and exhaust the demand at Dallas. Moving to the right, assign 100 units to the Lake Charles to Atlanta route. This exhausts both the row and the column amounts.

The derived solution in Figure 6.2 represents the initial solution to this problem using the northwest corner method. This method totally ignores the transportation costs, and consequently we would not expect this to be a very good, low-cost solution. However, it is very easy to use. The total cost for this initial solution may be found by multiplying shipping cost per unit by the number of units shipped along each route and adding the results. This is:

$$\text{total cost} = 6(100) + 3(110) + 8(40) + 6(80) + 7(100) = \$2{,}430$$

Proceeding to Step 3 of this algorithm, we must now evaluate this solution to see if it can be improved.

Steppingstone method
One way to evaluate the current solution to determine if it is optimal or if a better, lower-cost solution may be found.

Evaluation index
The net change in cost (or profit) per unit that results from using an empty cell in a transportation problem.

6.5 EVALUATING THE CURRENT SOLUTION—STEPPINGSTONE METHOD

The **steppingstone method** is one way to evaluate the current solution to determine if it is optimal or if a better, lower-cost solution may be found. We will calculate an **evaluation index** for each of the empty cells to see what would happen to the total transportation cost if one of the unused routes (empty cells) were used. The basic concept behind the steppingstone method is that if any change is made to the number of units in a cell, other changes must be made in that row and column to offset that change and ensure that supplies are not exceeded and demands are met. These other changes also will dictate that offsetting changes be made in the other rows and columns if they already have not been made.

For each empty cell we must calculate an evaluation index using a **steppingstone path**. To find the path, begin with an empty cell. Add one unit. In that same row, subtract one unit from a *filled* cell to keep the row total constant. In the column where one unit was subtracted, add one to a *filled* cell to offset that change. Continue making changes of this type alternating between row changes and column changes to *filled* cells until you are back in the column with the empty cell that is being evaluated. Thus, in every row and every column there will either be zero changes or exactly two changes. If there are two changes in a row or column, there must be one change where a unit is added and one change where a unit is subtracted. Other than the initial cell that is being evaluated, all changes must be made in cells that already are filled.

Steppingstone path

A path from an empty cell through other filled cells that is used to compute the evaluation index in a transportation problem. It also is used to determine what changes may be made in developing an improved solution.

Evaluation Indices for the Capitol Electric Problem

The initial solution found using the northwest corner method in Figure 6.2 above will be evaluated with the steppingstone method. At present, there are four empty cells representing four shipping routes that are currently not being used. These routes are Lubbock to Dallas, Lubbock to Atlanta, Mobile to Atlanta, and Lake Charles to Miami. An evaluation index must be calculated for each of the empty cells.

We will start by calculating the evaluation index for the Lubbock to Dallas route. This evaluation index will tell us what would happen to the total cost if one unit were shipped from Lubbock to Dallas. If we add one unit to this cell, it would add $2 to the total cost. However, another change must be made in the first row because Lubbock only has 100 units to ship and simply adding one to the Lubbock-Dallas cell would indicate that 101 units would be shipped from Lubbock. Therefore, we must subtract one unit from the Lubbock-Miami cell, and this will save $6 in shipping cost. This change in the Miami column now would leave only 209 units shipped to Miami if we did not make another change in the Miami column. Therefore, we must add one unit to a cell in the Miami column. Because we must add this to a cell that already is filled, we will add this to the Mobile-Miami cell that would cost an additional $3. Now we have too many units shipped from Mobile, so we must subtract one unit from the number shipped from Mobile to Dallas, and this will save $8. Notice this last change is a change in the Dallas column where the original change was made. This change in the number of units shipped to Dallas already is offset by a previous change. Thus, the number of units shipped to Dallas would remain 120 units.

The steppingstone path used to evaluate this one empty cell is shown in Figure 6.3. The evaluation index for this empty cell representing the Dallas to Lubbock route would tell us the net change in cost if one unit is

FIGURE 6.3

Steppingstone Path for Lubbock to Dallas Route

Source	Miami (Destination)	Dallas (Destination)	Atlanta (Destination)	Supply
Lubbock	− 100 [6]	+ [2]	[5]	100
Mobile	+ 110 [3]	− 40 [8]	[4]	150
Lake Charles	[7]	80 [6]	100 [7]	180
Demand	210	120	100	

added to the Lubbock to Dallas route while offsetting changes are made elsewhere. Thus, for the Lubbock-Dallas cell we have

$$\text{evaluation index} = +2 - 6 + 3 - 8 = -9$$

which means that total cost would decrease by $9 if one unit were shipped from Lubbock to Dallas. It also means that total cost decreases $9 per unit for each unit shipped on this route. Thus, the current solution represented by the table in Figure 6.3 is not the optimal solution. We also must evaluate the other empty cells to see if changes in one of these others would decrease costs even more.

All of the empty cells in the initial solution to the Capitol Electric problem will be evaluated before an improved solution is developed. These other steppingstone paths are shown in Figure 6.4. Considering the Lake Charles to Miami route, the steppingstone path shown in Figure 6.4 gives the following evaluation index:

$$\text{evaluation index} = +7 - 3 + 8 - 6 = +6$$

This means if one unit were added to this cell, total cost would increase by $6.

Using the cells in the steppingstone path for the Mobile-Atlanta cell results in:

$$\text{evaluation index} = +4 - 8 + 6 - 7 = -5$$

This means if one unit were added to this cell, total cost would decrease by $5.

The steppingstone path from Lubbock to Atlanta is more complicated than the others. If one unit is shipped from Lubbock to Atlanta, one unit must be subtracted from the Lubbock to Miami route because this is the only filled cell in this row. Then one unit is added to the Mobile to Miami route, one unit is subtracted from the Mobile to Dallas route, one unit is added to the Lake Charles to Dallas route, and one unit is subtracted from the Lake Charles to Atlanta route. This last change ends in the same

FIGURE 6.4

Steppingstone Paths in Capitol Electric Problem

Source	Miami	Dallas	Atlanta	Supply
Lubbock	100 [6]	[2]	[5]	100
Mobile	− 110 [3]	+ 40 [8]	[4]	150
Lake Charles	+ [7]	− 80 [6]	100 [7]	180
Demand	210	120	100	

Source	Miami	Dallas	Atlanta	Supply
Lubbock	100 [6]	[2]	[5]	100
Mobile	110 [3]	− 40 [8]	+ [4]	150
Lake Charles	[7]	+ 80 [6]	− 100 [7]	180
Demand	210	120	100	

Source	Miami	Dallas	Atlanta	Supply
Lubbock	− 100 [6]	[2]	+ [5]	100
Mobile	+ 110 [3]	− 40 [8]	[4]	150
Lake Charles	[7]	+ 80 [6]	− 100 [7]	180
Demand	210	120	100	

(Destination: Miami, Dallas, Atlanta)

column with the empty cell, so this finishes the steppingstone path. This gives the following result:

$$\text{evaluation index} = +5 - 6 + 3 - 8 + 6 - 7 = -7$$

This indicates that cost would decrease $7 per unit placed in this cell.

Note that for each row and each column in the tables shown in Figure 6.4 above there are exactly two changes or there are zero changes. The Lubbock to Atlanta steppingstone path is longer than the others, but the same procedure is used in developing the path.

Selecting the Empty Cell to Be Filled

Once the evaluation index for each of the empty cells has been calculated, we look to see where the greatest, if any, improvement can be made. A negative evaluation index indicates costs may be lowered by using the shipping route represented by the cell with the negative evaluation index. If there is no negative evaluation index, we would stop. However, the evaluation index for the Lubbock-Dallas cell is –9, the evaluation index for the Lubbock-Atlanta cell is –7, and the evaluation index for the Mobile-Atlanta cell is –5. Thus, if any of these empty cells were picked to fill, the total cost would decrease. We always will select the cell that has the best improvement index. Therefore, we will select the Lubbock-Dallas cell to be filled because filling this cell will result in the greatest decrease in cost per unit.

Additional Comments on the Steppingstone Path

In finding the steppingstone path for any empty cell, there are three things to remember.

1. Only filled cells may be used in the steppingstone path except for the one empty cell being evaluated.
2. After making a change in a row, the next change must occur in a column. After making a change in a column, the next change must occur in a row. You may begin with a change in either a row or a column.
3. Each row and each column in the table will have either two changes or zero changes in the steppingstone path.

There are some intuitive reasons why the steppingstone path must consist of cells already filled except for the one empty cell being evaluated. Obviously, we cannot subtract one unit from a cell that already is empty. Also, we are trying to determine the impact of using one new shipping route in conjunction with other routes that are currently being used. If more than one empty cell were included in the steppingstone path, meaning two or more empty cells were becoming filled, then the number calculated for the cell evaluation index would reflect the impact of using two or more new shipping routes instead of just one.

6.6 DEVELOPING THE NEXT SOLUTION

To develop the next solution (Step 4 of the transportation algorithm), we will make changes according to the steppingstone path that generated the evaluation index for the empty cell to be filled. The initial solution found in this problem is a basic solution, and the steppingstone method is used to develop another basic solution.

We will make changes only to the steppingstone path shown in Figure 6.3 above because these changes will result in a \$9 per unit savings. We would like to put as many units as possible in this cell while changing only the steppingstone path. Whatever is added to the Lubbock-Dallas cell will be subtracted from the Lubbock-Miami cell, added to the Mobile-Miami cell, and subtracted from the Mobile-Dallas cell. We are restricted by the cells where a subtraction is to be made. Because there are 100 units in the Lubbock-Miami cell and 40 in the Mobile-Dallas cell (the cells marked with a minus (–) sign indicating something will be subtracted), the most we can add to the Lubbock-Dallas cell is 40 units. If we try to put more than 40 units in that cell, we would have too many units sent to Dallas. We cannot change the 80 units that are currently assigned to the Lake Charles-Dallas cell because it is not in the steppingstone path. Thus, *the maximum number that may be put in the empty cell is the smallest number that is in a steppingstone path cell where a subtraction is to be made.* The changes are illustrated in Figure 6.5. The total cost for this new solution is:

$$\begin{aligned}\text{total cost} &= 6(60) + 3(150) + 2(40) + 6(80) + 7(100)\\ &= \$2{,}070\end{aligned}$$

This represents a $360 decrease ($2,430 – $2,070) in total cost from the previous solution. This could have been anticipated because the evaluation

FIGURE 6.5

Changes Made in Lubbock to Dallas Steppingstone Path

Source	Miami (Destination)	Dallas (Destination)	Atlanta (Destination)	Supply
Lubbock	– [6] 100 – 40	+ [2] 0 + 40	[5]	100
Mobile	+ [3] 110 + 40	– [8] 40 – 40	[4]	150
Lake Charles	[7]	[6] 80	[7] 100	180
Demand	210	120	100	

Source	Miami (Destination)	Dallas (Destination)	Atlanta (Destination)	Supply
Lubbock	60 [6]	40 [2]	[5]	100
Mobile	150 [3]	[8]	[4]	150
Lake Charles	[7]	80 [6]	100 [7]	180
Demand	210	120	100	

for the cell to be filled was –9, meaning that cost would decrease $9 per unit assigned to this cell. We put 40 units in this cell so the total cost should decrease by 9(40) = $360, as was calculated above.

6.7 CONTINUING TO THE OPTIMAL SOLUTION

Once a new solution is generated, it must be evaluated. This again will be done using the steppingstone path method. The evaluations for the empty cells in the new solution shown in Figure 6.5 above are:

Lubbock-Atlanta evaluation index = +5 – 2 + 6 – 7 = +2

Mobile-Dallas evaluation index = +8 – 2 + 6 – 3 = +9

Mobile-Atlanta evaluation index = +4 – 7 + 6 – 2 + 6 – 3 = +4

Lake Charles-Miami evaluation index = +7 – 6 + 2 – 6 = –3

Because there still is a negative evaluation index, we must continue.

Developing the Third Solution

Select the Lake Charles-Miami empty cell to be filled because the evaluation index of –3 indicates the greatest, and only, improvement for the empty cells. The changes to be made in the steppingstone path are indicated in Figure 6.6. We are subtracting from the Lubbock-Miami and Lake Charles-Dallas cells, which currently have 60 units and 80 units, respectively. Therefore, the most we can add to the empty cell is 60 units—the lowest of the amounts in the cells where a subtraction occurs. The new total cost should be 3(60) = $180 less than the previous total cost or $2,070 – $180 = $1,890. Calculating this by multiplying the cost per unit by the number of units yields:

$$\text{cost} = 2(100) + 3(150) + 7(60) + 6(20) + 7(100) = 1{,}890$$

which verifies that $1,890 is the new total cost.

Evaluating the Third Solution

Because this is a new solution, the evaluation index again must be calculated for each of the empty cells to see if this solution is optimal. The evaluations for the empty cells in the new solution shown in Figure 6.6 are:

Lubbock-Miami evaluation index = +6 – 2 + 6 – 7 = +3

Lubbock-Atlanta evaluation index = +5 – 2 + 6 – 7 = +2

Mobile-Dallas evaluation index = +8 – 3 + 7 – 6 = +6

Mobile-Atlanta evaluation index = +4 – 3 + 7 – 7 = +1

Because there are no negative cell evaluations, it is impossible to generate a lower-cost solution and this solution must be the optimal solution. The total cost is $1,890.

FIGURE 6.6

Changes in Solution Due to Filling the Lake Charles-Miami Cell

Source	Destination: Miami	Dallas	Atlanta	Supply
Lubbock	− [6] 60 − 60	+ [2] 40 + 60	[5]	100
Mobile	[3] 150	[8]	[4]	150
Lake Charles	+ [7] 0 + 60	− [6] 80 − 60	[7] 100	180
Demand	210	120	100	

Source	Destination: Miami	Dallas	Atlanta	Supply
Lubbock	[6]	100 [2]	[5]	100
Mobile	150 [3]	[8]	[4]	150
Lake Charles	60 [7]	20 [6]	100 [7]	180
Demand	210	120	100	

6.8 SENSITIVITY ANALYSIS

A manager who has been given the optimal solution may be interested in how the optimal solution would change if some minor changes are made in the costs in the transportation table. An analysis of the cell evaluations helps to show the impact of changes in costs. We know if we were to put one unit in one of the empty cells, the total cost would change by the amount of the cell evaluation for the cell. For example, the Lubbock to Miami route has a cell evaluation of +3. Therefore, if we were forced to use this route and made changes in the steppingstone path, the total transportation cost would be $3 per unit higher than the current cost. The goal is to minimize cost, so this route would not be used unless a way could be found to reduce its shipping costs by at least $3 per unit. If there was a reason that required us to ship some units on this route, we would know the total shipping costs would be $3 per unit more than the lowest cost solution.

If the shipping costs from a particular source to all destinations (or to a particular destination from all sources) all changed by the same amount, the cell evaluations would not change. This easily is seen because in the steppingstone path every row and column either will have zero changes or exactly two changes. If there are two changes in a row or column, in one cell we will be adding and in the other cell we will be subtracting, which results in a net change of zero in the cell evaluation. Thus, any shipping cost change in an entire row or column would have no impact on the optimal allocations, although the total cost would change.

6.9

ALTERNATIVE METHODS FOR FINDING AN INITIAL SOLUTION

While the northwest corner method is a very easy way to generate an initial solution, it totally ignores cost and usually does not provide a very low-cost solution as a starting point. With high-speed computers, it is not essential with most problems that a good starting point be found, as the optimal solution will eventually be found. For extremely large problems, however, it would be beneficial to start with a low-cost solution so that fewer iterations of the transportation algorithm would be required. There are two common methods for finding an initial solution to the transportation problem based on cost. These are the least cost method and Vogel's approximation method.

Least Cost Method

Least cost method
A method for generating an initial solution to a transportation problem.

The **least cost method** begins by simply finding the lowest-cost cell in the transportation table and putting as many units as possible in that cell. Once completed, move to the next lowest-cost cell and put as many units as possible in that cell, recognizing that some units already have been assigned. Continue doing this until all the supplies and demands are exhausted. This is illustrated in Figure 6.7 for the Capitol Electric problem. Begin by putting 100 units (at $2 per unit) in the Lubbock-Dallas cell, exhausting the supply at Lubbock and leaving 20 units of demand at Dallas. Then, move to the Mobile-Miami cell and put 150 units (at $3 per unit) in this cell. The next lowest-cost cell is Mobile-Atlanta at $4 per unit, but we already have allocated all 150 units from Mobile, so move to the next lowest-cost available cell. Because all of the units from Lubbock as well as Mobile have been allocated, we are left with units from Lake Charles. Therefore, the next lowest-cost available cell is Lake Charles-Dallas. We put 20 units there (100 of the 120 demanded are supplied by Lubbock). Then we are left with assigning 60 units from Lake Charles to Miami and 100 units from Lake Charles to Atlanta. This initial solution is shown in the last table in Figure 6.7. This procedure is summarized in Summary Table 6.2.

SUMMARY TABLE 6.2

Summary of the Least Cost Method

1. Allocate as many units as possible to the cell with the least cost, exhausting either the row or column total.
2. Go to the next lowest-cost available cell and allocate as many units as possible to this cell. Continue until all the supplies have been exhausted and all demands have been met.

FIGURE 6.7

Initial Solution Found Using Least Cost Method

Source	Miami	Dallas	Atlanta	Supply
		Destination		
Lubbock	--- [6]	100 [2]	--- [5]	~~100~~
Mobile	[3]	[8]	[4]	150
Lake Charles	[7]	[6]	[7]	180
Demand	210	120	100	

Source	Miami	Dallas	Atlanta	Supply
		Destination		
Lubbock	--- [6]	100 [2]	--- [5]	~~100~~
Mobile	150 [3]	--- [8]	--- [4]	~~150~~
Lake Charles	[7]	[6]	[7]	180
Demand	210	120	100	

Source	Miami	Dallas	Atlanta	Supply
		Destination		
Lubbock	--- [6]	100 [2]	--- [5]	~~100~~
Mobile	150 [3]	--- [8]	--- [4]	~~150~~
Lake Charles	[7]	20 [6]	[7]	180
Demand	210	~~120~~	100	

Source	Miami	Dallas	Atlanta	Supply
		Destination		
Lubbock	[6]	100 [2]	[5]	100
Mobile	150 [3]	[8]	[4]	150
Lake Charles	60 [7]	20 [6]	100 [7]	180
Demand	210	120	100	

Notice each time a cell is filled, we will eliminate a row or column from further consideration, as we will have met the demand in the column or we will have exhausted the supply from the row.

Once this initial solution using the least cost method is derived, it must be evaluated to see if a better solution can be found. In doing the evaluations we find

Lubbock-Miami evaluation index = +6 – 2 + 6 – 7 = +3

Lubbock-Atlanta evaluation index = +5 – 2 + 6 – 7 = +2

Mobile-Dallas evaluation index = +8 – 3 + 7 – 6 = +6

Mobile-Atlanta evaluation index = +4 – 3 + 7 – 7 = +1

which indicates this is the optimal solution. Thus, using the least cost method resulted in finding the best solution much more quickly than using the northwest corner method. It should be noted that the initial solution found with this method is not always the optimal solution.

Vogel's Approximation Method

Vogel's approximation method (VAM)

A method for generating an initicl solution to a transportation problem. It is based on observing the additional cost that must be paid if the lowest-cost cell from a source or to a destination is not used.

A third way to generate an initial solution to a transportation problem is with **Vogel's approximation method** (VAM). This usually provides a better, lower-cost, starting solution than either of the previous methods, although there are times when the others work better. Vogel's method is based on calculating the opportunity costs for each row or column to see what would happen if the lowest-cost cell in that row or column was not used. We calculate the opportunity cost by subtracting the lowest cost in a row or column from the next lowest cost in that same row or column.

For example, in the Lubbock row, the lowest cost is $2 which is paid if any of the electric motors are shipped to Dallas. If we don't take advantage of this low cost by shipping units from Lubbock to Dallas, the next lowest-cost shipping route is from Lubbock to Atlanta where we must pay $5 per unit. Thus, we pay 5 – 2 = $3 more for each unit shipped from Lubbock to Atlanta than we would shipped from Lubbock to Dallas, and so the opportunity cost is $3. The opportunity cost is calculated for each of the rows and columns as shown in the first table in Figure 6.8. The highest of these opportunity costs is $4, which was calculated from the second column.

To avoid having to incur this highest opportunity cost, begin by selecting the second column and assigning as many units as possible to the lowest-cost cell in this column. In this case, put 100 units in this cell as shown in the second table in Figure 6.8. Once completed, we have exhausted the total amount available from Lubbock, and may no longer consider shipping any units from Lubbock. Therefore, we must recompute the opportunity costs and continue this process. Figure 6.8 indicates the empty cells in the Lubbock row may not be considered, and the new opportunity costs are shown. The highest opportunity cost now is +4 for the Miami column. We select this column and avoid this additional cost by filling the lowest-cost available cell in that column with as many units as possible. We put 150 units here, exhausting the supply from Mobile as indicated in Figure 6.8. Now that there is only one row left with 180 units available, simply fill in the amounts needed to meet the demands in the three columns.

FIGURE 6.8

Initial Solution Using Vogel's Approximation Method

Source	Miami	Dallas	Atlanta	Supply	
	Destination				
Lubbock	6	2	5	100	5 − 2 = 3
Mobile	3	8	4	150	4 − 3 = 1
Lake Charles	7	6	7	180	7 − 6 = 1
Demand	210	120	100		
	6 − 3 = 3	6 − 2 = 4*	5 − 4 = 1		

Source	Miami	Dallas	Atlanta	Supply	
	Destination				
Lubbock	--- 6	100 2	--- 5	~~100~~	
Mobile	3	8	4	150	4 − 3 = 1
Lake Charles	7	6	7	180	7 − 6 = 1
Demand	210	120	100		
	7 − 3 = 4*	8 − 6 = 2	7 − 4 = 3		

Source	Miami	Dallas	Atlanta	Supply
	Destination			
Lubbock	--- 6	100 2	--- 5	~~100~~
Mobile	150 3	--- 8	--- 4	~~150~~
Lake Charles	60 7	20 6	100 7	180
Demand	210	120	100	

* Indicates highest opportunity cost

We need 60 units for Miami, 20 units for Dallas, and 100 units for Atlanta. This initial solution found with Vogel's approximation method is shown in the last table in Figure 6.8. After using this method to find the initial solution, we must still evaluate the empty cells just as we did with the other initial solutions. For this problem, this solution is the previously found optimal solution.

BEST PRACTICES

United Airlines Optimizes Transportation Routes

SOURCE: UAL Corporation Annual Report, 1993.

In 1993, United Airlines was facing serious competitive challenges. The U.S. recession, worldwide economic weakness, and the rapid growth of low-cost carriers in the domestic marketplace all contributed to the company's need to move to a strategy of stringent cost containment. United focused its efforts on controlling operating costs and adjusting flight schedules to eliminate unprofitable flying, while striving to maintain product quality.

United undertook several measures to control costs. Besides reducing personnel, the company cut capital expenditures for 1993-1996 in half by deferring new aircraft purchases and accelerating the retirement of older aircraft. United then was faced with the problem of developing more efficient ways to use a fleet smaller than originally forecast. Further complicating the matter, the growing competition from low-cost carriers prompted United to restructure its domestic route system.

United solved this transportation problem by focusing on its four hubs and its long-haul transcontinental flights, and eliminating less profitable routes. The company changed the focus of the Washington Dulles hub to make it function as a gateway to more profitable European and transcontinental flights. Flights to and from the Denver hub were increased, with flight times modified to serve the local market better. Meanwhile, United reduced capacity on point-to-point flights in the West Coast market in response to the saturation of low-cost carriers in the area. Similarly, flights to Orlando were reduced in response to a weakened leisure travel market. Finally, United suspended its operations in seven U.S. destinations, and added nine new, more profitable routes to its network. Overall, United reduced cost per available seat mile by three percent and increased revenue per available seat mile by three percent over the previous year by solving this transportation problem effectively.

Courtesy of United Airlines

The least cost method and Vogel's approximation method both gave the optimal solution in the initial table, although optimizing does not always occur in the initial solution. If it is not optimal, and the cell evaluations would indicate this, we must move to a better solution using the steppingstone path. Continue until the optimal solution is reached. A summary of Vogel's approximation method is given in Summary Table 6.3.

SUMMARY TABLE 6.3

Summary of Vogel's Approximation Method

Step 1. Compute opportunity loss for each row and column by subtracting lowest available cost from second lowest available cost in that row or column.

Step 2. Select the row or column with highest opportunity cost. Put as many units as possible in the lowest-cost available cell in that row or column. Go to Step 1 and recompute opportunity losses.

6.10

THE MODI METHOD FOR EVALUATING EMPTY CELLS

We used the steppingstone method to evaluate the empty cells, which is easy for small problems. For larger problems, however, finding all of the steppingstone paths may be quite tedious and time consuming. An easier way to evaluate the empty cells for large problems is the **modified distribution (MODI) method.**

Modified distribution (MODI) method

A method for evaluating empty cells in a transportation problem.

The MODI method evaluates empty cells by comparing some MODI row values and MODI column values with the shipping costs. For each row we will determine a MODI row value designated by R_i. For each column we will find a MODI column value called K_j. The shipping cost will be designated by c_{ij}. The MODI method is based on two key equations. These are

$$c_{ij} = R_i + K_j \qquad \text{for each filled cell}$$

and

$$\text{cell evaluation} = c_{ij} - R_i - K_j \text{ for each empty cell}$$

The steps of the MODI method are:

Step 1. Arbitrarily select one of the R_i or K_j values and set it equal to zero. Selecting the R_i or K_j for the row or column with the most filled cells has some benefits.

Step 2. Use the filled cells and the relationship

$$c_{ij} = R_i + K_j$$

to find the values for all of the other R_i and K_j values.

Step 3. Evaluate the empty cells using the formula:

$$\text{cell evaluation} = c_{ij} - R_i - K_j$$

If all the cell evaluations are positive or zero, stop. Otherwise, go to Step 4.

Step 4. Select the empty cell that decreases cost the most and find the steppingstone path. Using this steppingstone path, generate the next solution making changes only in the steppingstone path. Then go to Step 1. You must find all the R_i and K_j values again in Step 1 because one cell that was previously empty is now filled.

Once the evaluations are found, the next solution is generated with the same procedure used in conjunction with the steppingstone path method of evaluating the empty cells. Changes are made only in the cells in the steppingstone path. After the new solution is found, evaluate this new solution. If all the cell evaluations are positive or zero we have found the optimal solution. Otherwise, continue this process of evaluating the solution and generating a new solution until all the cell evaluations are positive or zero.

Using the Modi Method to Evaluate the Capitol Electric Problem

The MODI method will be illustrated with the initial solution to the Capitol Electric problem found using the northwest corner method. Figure 6.9 shows the northwest corner initial solution. We will arbitrarily select $K_1 = 0$. Because the cell in the first row and first column is filled, we have

$$c_{ij} = R_i + K_j$$
$$c_{11} = R_1 + K_1$$
$$6 = R_1 + 0$$

which means that $R_1 = 6$. Then, look for any other filled cells in this first column. The Mobile-Miami cell also is filled. Therefore,

$$c_{21} = R_2 + K_1$$
$$3 = R_2 + 0$$

which means $R_2 = 3$. Note that this in the second table in Figure 6.9. There are no other filled cells in the first column, so K_1 will not help us find other R_i or K_j values. However, we now know the values of R_1 and R_2, so we may use these with filled cells in these rows.

We continue using the known R_i and K_j values together with the filled cells to find the other MODI row and column values. Because $R_2 = 3$ and the cell in the second row and second column is filled, we have:

$$c_{22} = R_2 + K_2$$
$$8 = 3 + K_2$$
$$K_2 = 5$$

Using this with the filled cell in the last row we have:

$$c_{32} = R_3 + K_2$$
$$6 = R_3 + 1$$
$$R_3 = 1$$

Knowing R_3 allows us to use the filled cell in the third row and third column to find K_3. We have:

$$c_{33} = R_3 + K_3$$
$$7 = 1 + K_3$$
$$K_3 = 6$$

Figure 6.10 illustrates these last few calculations.

If we had initially selected some other MODI row or column value to equal zero to start instead of K_1, we would have found different values for these R_is and K_js. However, the cell evaluations would be exactly the same regardless of which R_i or K_j is selected to equal zero initially.

Computing the Evaluation Indices with Modi

Once all of the R_i and K_j values have been found, begin evaluating the empty cells. Use the relationship

$$\text{cell evaluation} = c_{ij} - R_i - K_j$$

FIGURE 6.9

MODI Used with Northwest Corner Solution for Capitol Electric Problem

	K_1 = 0	K_2 =	K_3 =	
		Destination		
Source	Miami	Dallas	Atlanta	Supply
R_1 = Lubbock	100 [6]	[2]	[5]	100
R_2 = Mobile	110 [3]	40 [8]	[4]	150
R_3 = Lake Charles	[7]	80 [6]	100 [7]	180
Demand	210	120	100	

	K_1 = 0	K_2 =	K_3 =	
		Destination		
Source	Miami	Dallas	Atlanta	Supply
R_1 = 6 Lubbock	100 [**6**]	[2]	[5]	100
R_2 = 3 Mobile	110 [**3**]	40 [8]	[4]	150
R_3 = Lake Charles	[7]	80 [6]	100 [7]	180
Demand	210	120	100	

	K_1 = 0	**K_2 = 5**	K_3 =	
		Destination		
Source	Miami	Dallas	Atlanta	Supply
R_1 = 6 Lubbock	100 [6]	[2]	[5]	100
R_2 = 3 Mobile	110 [3]	40 [**8**]	[4]	150
R_3 = Lake Charles	[7]	80 [6]	100 [7]	180
Demand	210	120	100	

for each of the empty cells. The empty cells and their evaluations are:

Lubbock-Dallas cell evaluation = 2 – 6 – 5 = –9

Lubbock-Atlanta cell evaluation = 5 – 6 – 6 = –7

Mobile-Atlanta cell evaluation = 4 – 3 – 6 = –5

Lake Charles-Miami cell evaluation = 7 – 1 – 0 = +6

FIGURE 6.10

MODI Method Used with Northwest Corner Solution for Capitol Electric Problem

Source	$K_1 = 0$ Miami	$K_2 = 5$ Destination Dallas	$K_3 =$ Atlanta	Supply
$R_1 = 6$ Lubbock	100 [6]	[2]	[5]	100
$R_2 = 3$ Mobile	110 [3]	40 [8]	[4]	150
$\boldsymbol{R_3 = 1}$ Lake Charles	[7]	80 **[6]**	100 [7]	180
Demand	210	120	100	

Source	$K_1 = 0$ Miami	$K_2 = 5$ Destination Dallas	$\boldsymbol{K_3 = 6}$ Atlanta	Supply
$R_1 = 6$ Lubbock	100 [6]	[2]	[5]	100
$R_2 = 3$ Mobile	110 [3]	40 [8]	[4]	150
$R_3 = 1$ Lake Charles	[7]	80 [6]	100 **[7]**	180
Demand	210	120	100	

Because there are some negative cell evaluations, this is not the optimal solution. At this point, the next solution is developed in exactly the same way as when the cells were evaluated with the steppingstone method. Select the empty cell that most improves the solution, and fill that cell making changes only to the cells in the steppingstone path associated with that empty cell. In this case, select the Lubbock-Dallas cell because costs will decrease by \$9 per unit. Find the steppingstone path that would generate the –9 evaluation and make the appropriate changes.

Once the next solution is found, evaluate the empty cells again using the MODI method and continue. Note that new R_i and K_j values must be found because these are based on the specific filled cells, and one previously empty cell is now filled and one previously filled cell is now empty. Continue evaluating and improving until finding a solution where all cell evaluations are positive or zero.

To maximize profit, General Motors transports vehicles to China via cargo ship. SOURCE: Copyright General Motors Corp., used with permission

6.11

SPECIAL CASES OF THE TRANSPORTATION PROBLEM

There are some special conditions that must be addressed with the transportation algorithm. These are unbalanced problems, degeneracy, multiple optimal solutions, and prohibited shipping routes. We also will discuss how this procedure could be easily modified to solve maximization problems instead of minimization problems. Brief examples will illustrate these.

Unbalanced Problems

A transportation problem is **unbalanced** if the total supply available is not equal to the total demand. If this situation arises we must add a "dummy row" or "dummy column" to the transportation table. This **dummy row or column** simply represents an excess supply or an unsatisfied demand. Because any units assigned to a cell in a dummy row or column will not actually be shipped anywhere, the cost for each of these cells is zero. This extra source added to the transportation problem to balance the problem is considered the **dummy source**.

To illustrate this, consider a modified version of the Capitol Electric problem. Suppose the Lubbock plant has undergone an expansion allowing 150 units to be produced at this site. Now we have a supply of 150 from Lubbock, 150 from Mobile, and 180 from Lake Charles, resulting in a total supply of 480 units. The total demand is 210 + 120 + 100 = 430 units. Because the total supply does not equal the total demand, the problem is unbalanced. To alleviate this problem, add a **dummy destination** (column)

Unbalanced transportation problem
A transportation problem in which the total demand does not equal total supply.

Dummy row or column
An extra row or column that has been added so the number of rows equals the number of columns in an assignment problem.

Dummy source
An extra source that has been added to a transportation problem to balance the problem. The cost associated with shipping from this source is zero.

Dummy destination
An extra destination added to a transportation problem to balance the problem. The cost associated with shipping to this destination is zero.

as shown in Figure 6.11. Then solve while treating the dummy column just like any other column in the transportation table. The empty cells in this column must be evaluated just like for any other column. In the final solution, we recognize anything that is put in this dummy column will simply represent an excess capacity at the factory associated with that cell (or several factories if several cells are filled in the dummy column).

Degeneracy

Degenerate
In a transportation problem this is a solution in which the number of filled cells is not equal to the number of rows plus the number of columns minus one.

In solving a transportation problem, each solution represented by a transportation table must have a specific number of filled cells or else the solution is **degenerate.** If the following condition is not true, then the solution is degenerate.

$$\text{number of filled cells} = R + C - 1$$

where

$$R = \text{number of rows}$$
$$C = \text{number of columns}$$

For example, if a transportation problem has three rows and three columns, then each solution must have five filled cells ($R + C - 1 = 3 + 3 - 1 = 5$). If a solution does not have three filled cells, it would be degenerate.

This concept of degeneracy is associated with the concept of a basic solution. In a basic solution to a linear programming problem, a specific number of variables are forced to be zero. In the transportation algorithm, a specific number of cells must be empty and the others must be filled.

If a solution is degenerate, you will be unable to evaluate all of the empty cells unless the degeneracy is removed. To remove the degeneracy, put a zero in one of the empty cells and consider this as a filled cell with zero units, as illustrated in Figure 6.12. The zero must be placed in a cell that will allow all empty cells to be evaluated. Note that in Figure 6.12 if the zero had been placed in cell #2-A, we would not be able to find a steppingstone path to evaluate cell #3-B.

FIGURE 6.11

Dummy Destination Added to Capitol Electric Problem

Source	Miami	Dallas	Atlanta	Dummy	Supply
	Destination				
Lubbock	6	2	5	0	150
Mobile	3	8	4	0	150
Lake Charles	7	6	7	0	180
Demand	210	120	100	50	

FIGURE 6.12

Example of Problem with Degenerate Solution

From	To A	To B	To C	Supply
#1	50 [7]	100 [4]	[6]	150
#2	[11]	100 [8]	[9]	100
#3	[12]	0 [6]	90 [4]	90
Demand	50	200	90	

Note: A "0" was placed in cell #3–B to remove the degeneracy.

Once the degeneracy has been removed, proceed to evaluate the empty cells as before and continue to find the optimal solution.

Multiple Optimal Solutions

It is possible that more than one optimal solution exists in a transportation problem. This would provide the manager with some flexibility as cost could be minimized in different ways. You would know that **multiple optimal solutions** exist if in the final solution using the transportation algorithm

The assignment problem involves determining the best way to assign people or machinery to jobs or tasks. SOURCE: Courtesy of Deere & Company

FIGURE 6.13

Example of Problem with Multiple Optimal Solutions

From \ To	A	B	C	Supply
X	150 [7]	100 [4]	[6]	250
Y	[11]	50 [8]	[9]	50
Z	[12]	20 [6]	90 [4]	110
Demand	150	170	90	

cell evaluation XC = +4 cell evaluation YA = 0
cell evaluation YC = +3 cell evaluation ZA = +3

total cost = 7(150) + 4(100) + 8(50) + 6(20) + 4(90) = 2,330

From \ To	A	B	C	Supply
X	100 [7]	150 [4]	[6]	250
Y	50 [11]	[8]	[9]	50
Z	[12]	20 [6]	90 [4]	110
Demand	150	170	90	

total cost = 7(100) + 4(150) + 11(50) + 6(20) + 4(90)
= 2,330

there is a cell evaluation equal to zero. This would mean a unit could be added to that empty cell and total cost would change by $0. We could select this cell to be filled, use the steppingstone path, and generate another solution. The total cost for this next solution would be the same as the total cost for the current solution. An example is provided in Figure 6.13. Notice when the first table is evaluated, an evaluation index is zero. If this cell is selected and filled using the steppingstone path method, another optimal solution is found as shown in the second table in Figure 6.13.

Maximization Problems

Many transportation-type problems exist in which we wish to maximize profit rather than minimize cost. If we have several destinations (buyers) for a product produced at several locations, the profit generated from each sale would depend not only on the selling price of the item but also on the transportation cost incurred in delivering that item to our buyers. The transportation algorithm only requires a very simple modification to maximize rather than minimize the objective function. *Stop if all the cell evaluations are negative or zero* (instead of positive or zero as in the minimization problem); and the *cell to be filled is the one with the highest evaluation index* instead of the lowest evaluation index. All other steps in the algorithm are exactly the same for maximization problems as they are for minimization problems.

Prohibited Routes

In the basic transportation problem, we assume that we may ship units of the product from any source to any destination. If there is a reason that one of the shipping routes may not be used, we refer to that particular route as a **prohibited route**. With this type of situation, the transportation algorithm may still be used. Assign a very high cost to that route if the objective is to minimize cost; a negative profit would be used for maximization problems. A very high cost relative to the other costs would result in that cell being empty in the final solution of a minimization problem.

Prohibited route

A shipping route that may not be used in a transportation problem. A shipping cost of M is assigned to this for minimization problems.

Often the letter M is used to represent a very high cost in this type of situation. This M is interpreted the same as the coefficient M assigned as the objective function coefficient for artificial variables in the simplex algorithm. If the objective is to maximize the profit, then a $-M$ would be assigned as the profit to a prohibited route.

6.12 COMPARISON OF THE SIMPLEX ALGORITHM TO THE TRANSPORTATION ALGORITHM

The transportation problem is a special type of linear programming problem. The simplex method or the special transportation algorithm could be used to solve this. Understanding the transportation algorithm may provide some insights into the simplex solution and to the transportation problem in general. Table 6.2 provides certain parts of the simplex algorithm and the corresponding parts of the transportation algorithm.

TABLE 6.2

Simplex Algorithm Counterparts in the Transportation Algorithm

Simplex Algorithm	Transportation Algorithm
Constraints	Rows and columns
Decision variables	Cells in the table
Basic variables	Filled cells
Nonbasic variables	Empty cells
$C_j - Z_j$	Evaluation index for cell
Smallest critical ratio	Smallest number of units in cells where subtraction is made
Leaving variable	Cell that becomes empty
Entering variable	Empty cell to be filled
Slack variables	Cells in dummy destination
Artificial variables	Cells in dummy source

The $C_j - Z_j$ in the simplex algorithm has exactly the same interpretation as the evaluation index in the transportation algorithm. This tells us the change in the objective function value that will occur if one unit of that variable is brought into the solution. Thus, for a minimization problem, we continue as long as there are any negative $C_j - Z_j$ values in the simplex, or any negative evaluation indices in the transportation, algorithm. The maximum number of units that may be brought into the next solution is based on maintaining a feasible solution. In the simplex algorithm, the smallest critical ratio gives this number. In the transportation algorithm, the smallest number in a cell where a subtraction is to be made determines this number.

6.13

THE ASSIGNMENT PROBLEM

The basic assignment problem involves determining the best way to assign a set of people or items, such as machinery, to a set of jobs or tasks. Generally the objective is to minimize the cost or time of completing all of the jobs. This problem may be formulated as a transportation problem with each demand and each supply equal to one. We will demonstrate this using the following example.

Erinburgh Construction Example

The Erinburgh Construction Company has three pieces of earth-moving equipment. These have been purchased over time, and each type of equipment is versatile but is best-suited for a particular type of job. Erinburgh Construction has three jobs that will be started next week. Each of these three jobs requires the use of an earth-moving machine. Nick Piccolo, the manager of Erinburgh Construction must decide which piece of equipment to assign to each of the three jobs. He has estimated the number of days required for each job using each of the three pieces of equipment, and this is given in Table 6.3. From this table we see that if Equipment A is used on Job #1, it will take 10 days to complete this job. If Equipment B is used on Job #1, it will take only 8 days to complete the job. Equipment C could be

TABLE 6.3

Days Required in Erinburgh Construction Problem

	Job		
Equipment	#1	#2	#3
A	10	14	9
B	8	16	5
C	7	14	4

used to complete Job #1 in only 7 days. The table shows that Equipment C could complete any of the three jobs in the least amount of time, but we only may assign this piece of equipment to one job.

The assignment of the machines to the jobs may be viewed as a transportation problem as shown in Figure 6.14. Notice the supplies and demands are each equal to 1. A special-purpose algorithm that takes advantage of this feature was developed to solve the assignment problem. This is a much more efficient way of solving this problem than using the transportation algorithm or the simplex algorithm.

6.14 THE HUNGARIAN ALGORITHM

The **Hungarian algorithm** (also called the assignment algorithm) is a technique that was developed to solve assignment problems. The Hungarian algorithm is based on a method normally referred to as matrix reduction. This involves determining the opportunity costs or excess costs for making less than optimal assignments and minimizing the total of these excess costs. A summary of the steps of the Hungarian algorithm is given in Summary Table 6.4.

Hungarian algorithm
A technique for solving assignment problems. Also called the assignment algorithm.

FIGURE 6.14

Assignment Problem as a Transportation Problem

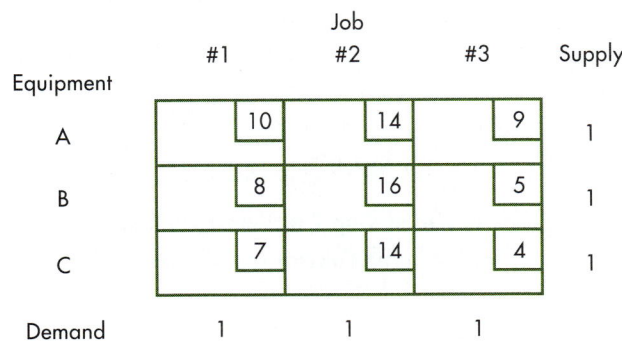

Equipment	Job #1	Job #2	Job #3	Supply
A	10	14	9	1
B	8	16	5	1
C	7	14	4	1
Demand	1	1	1	

SUMMARY TABLE 6.4

The Hungarian Algorithm

Step 1. Subtract the smallest number in each row from all numbers in that row to obtain opportunity costs. With this new matrix, subtract the smallest number in each column from all numbers in that column.

Step 2. Draw the minimum number of vertical and horizontal lines needed to cover all the zeroes in the table. If the minimum number of lines is the same as the number of rows, then an optimal assignment may be made. Make assignments on the zeroes. If the number of lines is less than the number of rows, go to Step 3.

Step 3. Subtract the smallest number not covered by one or more lines from all numbers not covered by one or more lines. Add this same number to any number covered by the intersection of two lines. Go to Step 2.

We will illustrate this using the Erinburgh Construction problem shown in Table 6.3 above. Begin by subtracting the smallest number in each row (9 in the first row, 5 in the second row, and 4 in the third row) from all the numbers in that row. This gives us the first table in Figure 6.15.

These numbers indicate what the opportunity cost or excess cost would be if the lowest-cost assignment in each row is not made.

Continuing with Step 1, subtract the smallest number in each column from all numbers in that column. This results in the second table in Figure 6.15. Notice any column that already has a zero in it will not change. These numbers represent the overall excess cost that would be incurred if the lowest-cost assignment in each row and column is not made. We wish to make assignments where there is zero excess cost.

To determine if it is possible to make assignments only where zero excess costs exist in the table, go to Step 2. Draw the minimum number of lines to cover the zeroes. To ensure that the minimum number of lines is drawn, it is helpful to look for a row or column that only has one zero. If there is a *row* that contains only one zero, draw a line through the *column* that contains that zero. By doing this, we are making an assignment in the only place in this row where there is zero excess cost. Drawing the line through the associated column indicates that this column may not be used for any other assignment. If there is a *column* that contains only one zero, draw a line through the *row* that contains that zero. Continue this process for all uncovered zeroes.

Figure 6.16 shows how to draw lines for the Erinburgh Construction problem. Because there is only one zero in column 1, draw a line through the *row* containing this zero (row 1). This indicates that Equipment A must be reserved for Job #1, and it cannot be used for any other job. Because there is only one zero in row 2, we draw a line through the column that

FIGURE 6.15

Implementation of Step 1 of Hungarian Algorithm for Erinburgh Construction Problem

	Job		
Equipment	#1	#2	#3
A	1	5	0
B	3	11	0
C	3	10	0

	Job		
Equipment	#1	#2	#3
A	0	0	0
B	2	6	0
C	2	5	0

FIGURE 6.16

Lines Drawn for Erinburgh Construction Problem

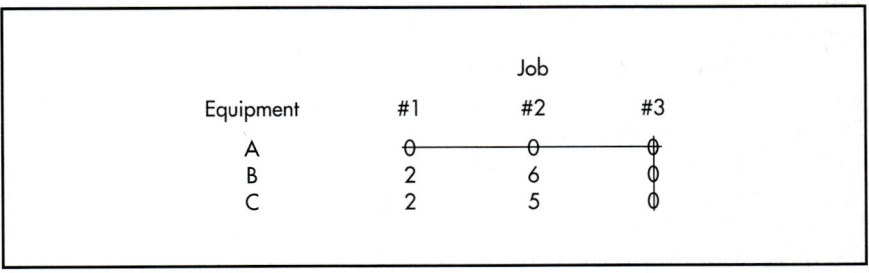

	Job		
Equipment	#1	#2	#3
A	0	0	0
B	2	6	0
C	2	5	0

contains this zero (column 3). All of the zeroes in this table are now covered as shown in Figure 6.16. Notice it only required two lines to cover all the zeros. This means if we make the assignments based on this table, only two of the assignments may be made with zero excess costs, while the other assignment will have a positive excess cost and would have to occur at a number not covered by any line.

Because there are three rows and only two lines, we must continue to the next step. In Step 3 of the Hungarian algorithm, we find the smallest number not covered by a line; in Figure 6.16, this number is 2. Subtract 2 from all numbers not covered by a line. This provides an indication of how this excess cost compares with each of the other excess costs not covered by a line. Also add this number to any excess cost number covered by two lines. Figure 6.17 shows the result.

FIGURE 6.17

Step 3 of Hungarian Algorithm for Erinburgh Construction Problem

	Job		
Equipment	#1	#2	#3
A	0	0	0+2
B	2-2	6-2	0
C	2-2	5-2	0

	Job		
Equipment	#1	#2	#3
A	0	0	2
B	0	4	0
C	0	3	0

Going to Step 2, we now draw the minimum number of lines to cover all the zeroes in this new table. Because column 2 has only one zero in it, draw a line through the row containing this zero. Then, draw lines through the other zeroes. Because there is no other row or column with a single zero, we draw the minimum number of lines to cover the remaining zeroes. There are several ways to draw these lines, but they all require a total of three lines. Because it requires three lines to cover all of the zeroes and there are three rows, an optimal assignment may be made from this table. The lines are shown in the first table in Figure 6.18.

We make assignments where zeroes are present in the final table, as this would result in zero excess cost indicating this would be the optimal solution. Look for a row or a column with a single zero and make an assignment at that position. Figure 6.18 shows we must assign Equipment A to Job #2 because this is the only zero in the Job #2 column. We then eliminate that row and column and look for another row or column with a single zero. Because there is none, we may choose to assign Equipment B to Job #1 and Equipment C to Job #3; or we could assign Equipment B to Job #3 and Equipment C to Job #1. Thus, there are two optimal solutions to this problem. To find the total cost for this solution, return to the original table and look at the costs for the assignments made. Find the following:

FIGURE 6.18

Minimum Lines Drawn and Two Optimal Assignments Made for Erinburgh Construction Problem

	Job		
Equipment	#1	#2	#3
A	0	0	2
B	0	4	0
C	0	3	0

	Job		
Equipment	#1	#2	#3
A	0	0*	2
B	0*	4	0
C	0	3	0*

	Job		
Equipment	#1	#2	#3
A	0	0*	2
B	0	4	0*
C	0*	3	0

Equipment A to Job #2	14 days
Equipment B to Job #1	8 days
Equipment C to Job #3	4 days
Total	26 days

The total number of days required to complete these jobs given these assignments is 26 days. If we make the alternate assignments we have:

Equipment A to Job #2	14 days
Equipment B to Job #3	5 days
Equipment C to Job #1	7 days
Total	26 days

Thus, there are two optimal solutions.

Were some assignments to be made other than the ones indicated here, the total cost would be higher by the amounts of the excess costs seen in the last table.

6.15 SPECIAL CASES WITH THE ASSIGNMENT PROBLEM

There are some special cases that may arise with assignment problems. These involve unbalanced problems, multiple optimal solutions, and prohibited assignments. The Hungarian algorithm also may be used to solve maximization problems with only a slight modification.

Unbalanced Problems

It often occurs that the number of machines or individuals is not the same as the number of jobs. If this occurs, then the problem is **unbalanced.** This means one or more of the machines will sit idle, or one or more of the jobs will not be completed unless additional resources are obtained. However, it would still be desirable to minimize the cost or time for completing the jobs that are performed. If a problem is unbalanced, we simply add the necessary number of rows or columns to make the problem balanced. A cost of zero is used for each of the positions in the dummy rows or columns because there is no cost associated with assignments in the dummy rows or columns. Note that it may require several rows or columns to balance a problem. Figure 6.19 demonstrates this for a situation in which there are five people to be assigned to only three jobs.

Unbalanced assignment problem

An assignment problem in which the number of rows is not the same as the number of columns.

Multiple Optimal Solutions

In minimizing costs in an assignment situation, it is possible that several sets of assignments result in exactly the same costs. This provides flexibility to the manager responsible for making the assignments. Factors other than cost may cause a manager to prefer one set of assignments over another. This was seen in the Erinburgh Construction problem.

FIGURE 6.19

Using Dummy Rows to Balance an Assignment Problem

	Person				
Job	A	B	C	D	E
#1	9	7	7	9	6
#2	5	5	4	7	7
#3	7	6	5	6	6
Dummy	0	0	0	0	0
Dummy	0	0	0	0	0

Prohibited Assignments

Prohibited assignment
An assignment that may not be made. A cost of *M* is assigned to this for minimization problems.

When machines are assigned to specific jobs, or individuals are assigned to specific tasks, we may find that one specific assignment is not possible due to the characteristics of the machine or the individual. Perhaps a person has skills necessary for most of the jobs, but lacks the necessary skills for one of them. We may consider the assignment of this individual to that job to be **prohibited.** If this occurs, we want to ensure that this assignment is not made. The assignment algorithm may be used to minimize the cost or the time by making one modification. For the prohibited assignment, an extremely high cost will be associated with that assignment. As we did with the transportation algorithm, we will use the letter M to denote this very high cost. If computer software is used, instead of using M, simply assign a value that is several times as large as the largest cost in the table and proceed in the normal manner. Figure 6.20 shows how the Erinburgh Construction problem would be modified if Equipment B could not be used on Job #3.

FIGURE 6.20

Example of Prohibited Assignment for Erinburgh Construction Problem

	Job		
Equipment	#1	#2	#3
A	10	14	9
B	8	16	M
C	7	14	4

Maximization Problems

It is very common for managers to focus on costs, and to try to minimize costs when determining assignments of machines or people to jobs. However, in some instances we may consider the profits that result from the particular assignments instead of the costs. For example, we may have five people that will be assigned as regional sales managers to five regions of the country. Based on the skills and experiences of these individuals as well as particular demographic information about each of the five regions, the projected sales would vary depending on which individual is assigned to which region.

To solve a maximization assignment problem, one modification is necessary to the Hungarian algorithm. Because maximizing profit or sales is equivalent to minimizing the opportunity cost of not making the optimal assignments, we may convert the profits or sales to opportunity costs and then minimize the result using the Hungarian algorithm. To convert the sales or profits to opportunity costs, simply subtract each number in the original table from the largest number in the table. Once this is done, proceed with the Hungarian algorithm as before. Figure 6.21 demonstrates this process. Once the table of opportunity costs has been developed, proceed with the Hungarian algorithm as a minimization problem.

FIGURE 6.21

Hungarian Algorithm for Maximization Problem

	Job			
Equipment	#1	#2	#3	Profit table (maximization)
A	21	15	19	
B	23	12	17	
C	25	14	19	

	Job			
Equipment	#1	#2	#3	
A	25 - 21	25 - 15	25 - 19	Calculating
B	25 - 23	25 - 12	25 - 17	opportunity
C	25 - 25	25 - 14	25 - 19	cost

	Job			
Equipment	#1	#2	#3	
A	4	10	6	Minimizing
B	2	13	8	opportunity cost
C	0	11	6	

6.16

COMPUTER SOLUTIONS

Output 6.1 provides the DSS output for the Capitol Electric transportation problem. The software is capable of using any of the starting solutions discussed in this chapter, and the user has the option of printing all of the transportation tables if desired.

Output 6.2 provides the DSS output for the Erinburgh Construction assignment problem. All of the tables used are printed here, although the user has the option of simply printing the final solution.

6.17

SUMMARY

In this chapter we saw how the transportation problem is a special type of linear programming problem. It may be solved either as a linear programming problem or by using a special-purpose transportation algorithm. The transportation algorithm begins by finding an initial solution using either the northwest corner method, the least cost method, or Vogel's approximation method. Once the initial solution is found it may be evaluated using

OUTPUT 6.1

DSS Output for Capitol Electric Transportation Problem

Transportation Model　　　Problem: CAPITOL.P11

Initial Problem

Min	Miami	Dallas	Atlanta	Prod Cap
Lubbock	6	2	5	100
Mobile	3	8	4	150
Lake Cha	7	6	7	180
Dest Req	210	120	100	430

Enhanced Vogel's Approximation Method

Solution: Min Z = 1890

From	To	Number	Cost	Amount
Lubbock	Dallas	100	2	200
Mobile	Miami	150	3	450
Lake Cha	Miami	60	7	420
Lake Cha	Dallas	20	6	120
Lake Cha	Atlanta	100	7	700
Total				1890

OUTPUT 6.2

DSS Output for Erinburgh Construction Assignment Problem

```
Assignment Model
Initial Problem

         MIN        #1         #2         #3
         A           10         14          9
         B           8          16          5
         C           7          14          4
Tableau  1
                                            |
         MIN        #1         #2         #3
      -> A           0  *       0          0
         B           2          6          0  *
         C           2          5          0
Tableau  2
                    |                     |
         MIN        #1         #2         #3
      -> A           0          0  *       2
         B           0  *       4          0
         C           0          3          0  *
Solution

         MIN        #1         #2         #3
         A                      14
         B           8
         C                                 4
From          To            Cost
A             #2            14
B             #1            8
C             #3            4
Total assignment:           26
** Multiple solutions exist **
```

either the steppingstone method or the MODI method. If the current solution is not optimal, a new solution is generated using a steppingstone path.

The assignment problem may be viewed as a special type of transportation problem with all demands and supplies equal to one. This may be solved as a linear programming problem, as a transportation problem, or as an assignment problem using the Hungarian algorithm.

Features of the simplex algorithm were identified and paired with the counterparts in the transportation algorithm. This should help in understanding both algorithms.

GLOSSARY

Balanced A transportation problem in which the total demand is equal to the total supply. Also, an assignment problem in which the number of rows equals the number of columns. *p. 233*

Degenerate In a transportation problem this is a solution in which the number of filled cells is not equal to the number of rows plus the number of columns minus one. *p. 252*

Dummy row or column An extra row or column

that has been added so the number of rows equals the number of columns in an assignment problem. *p. 251*

Dummy destination An extra destination added to a transportation problem to balance the problem. The cost associated with shipping to this destination is zero. *p. 251*

Dummy source An extra source that has been added to a transportation problem to balance the problem. The cost associated with shipping from this source is zero. *p. 251*

Evaluation index The net change in cost (or profit) per unit that results from using an empty cell in a transportation problem. *p. 234*

Hungarian algorithm A technique for solving assignment problems. Also called the assignment algorithm. *p. 257*

Least cost method A method for generating an initial solution to a transportation problem. *p. 242*

Modified distribution (MODI) method A method for evaluating empty cells in a transportation problem. *p. 247*

Northwest corner method A method for generating an initial solution to a transportation problem. *p. 232*

Prohibited route A shipping route that may not be used in a transportation problem. A shipping cost of *M* is assigned to this for minimization problems. *p. 255*

Prohibited assignment An assignment that may not be made. A cost of *M* is assigned to this for minimization problems. *p. 262*

Steppingstone method One way to evaluate the current solution to determine if it is optimal or if a better, lower-cost solution may be found. *p. 234*

Steppingstone path A path from an empty cell through other filled cells that is used to compute the evaluation index in a transportation problem. It also is used to determine what changes may be made in developing an improved solution. *p. 235*

Unbalanced assignment problem An assignment problem in which the number of rows is not the same as the number of columns. *p. 261*

Unbalanced transportation problem A transportation problem in which the total demand does not equal total supply. *p. 251*

Vogel's approximation method (VAM) A method for generating an initial solution to a transportation problem. It is based on observing the additional cost that must be paid if the lowest-cost cell from a source or to a destination is not used. *p. 244*

KEY EQUATIONS

(6-1) $c_{ij} = R_i + K_j$

Equation used with MODI to find R_i and K_j values. This must be true for filled cells.

(6-2) Cell evaluation index $= c_{ij} - R_i - K_j$

Equation used with MODI to find cell evaluation indices for empty cells.

SOLVED PROBLEMS

SOLVED PROBLEM 6-1

Coolbreeze, Inc. produces room air conditioners in manufacturing plants located in Houston, Texas, Phoenix, Arizona, and Memphis, Tennessee. These are sent to regional distributors in Dallas, Atlanta, and Denver. The production capacities, demands, and shipping costs are shown in the following table:

	Dallas	Atlanta	Denver	Capacity
Houston	8	12	10	850
Phoenix	10	14	9	650
Memphis	11	8	12	300
Demand	800	600	200	

Find the least expensive way to ship the required number of air conditioners. Use the northwest corner method to develop the initial solution and the steppingstone method to evaluate the empty cells.

Source	Destination: Dallas	Atlanta	Denver	Dummy	Supply
Houston	800 [8]	50 [12]	[10]	[0]	850
Phoenix	[10]	550 [14]	100 [9]	[0]	650
Memphis	[11]	[8]	100 [12]	200 [0]	300
Demand	800	600	200	200	

SOLUTION

Add a dummy destination to balance the problem.

cell evaluations =

Houston-Denver = +10 − 12 + 14 − 9 = +3

Houston-Dummy = +0 − 12 + 14 − 9 + 12 − 0 = +5

Phoenix-Dallas = +10 − 14 + 12 − 8 = 0

Phoenix-Dummy = +0 − 9 + 12 − 0 = +3

Memphis-Dallas = +11 − 8 + 12 − 14 + 9 − 12 = −2

Memphis-Atlanta = +8 − 14 + 9 − 12 = −9 * greatest improvement

The second transportation table is:

Source	Destination: Dallas	Atlanta	Denver	Dummy	Supply
Houston	800 [8]	50 [12]	[10]	[0]	850
Phoenix	[10]	450 [14]	200 [9]	[0]	650
Memphis	[11]	100 [8]	[12]	200 [0]	300
Demand	800	600	200	200	

cell evaluations =

Houston-Denver = +10 – 12 + 14 – 9 = +3

Houston-Dummy = +0 – 12 + 8 – 0 = –4

Phoenix-Dallas = +10 – 14 + 12 – 8 = 0

Phoenix-Dummy = +0 – 14 + 8 – 0 = **–6** * greatest improvement

Memphis-Dallas = +11 – 8 + 12 – 8 = +7

Memphis-Denver = +12 – 8 + 14 – 9 = +9

The third transportation table is:

Source	Destination: Dallas	Atlanta	Denver	Dummy	Supply
Houston	800 [8]	50 [12]	[10]	[0]	850
Phoenix	[10]	250 [14]	200 [9]	200 [0]	650
Memphis	[11]	300 [8]	[12]	[0]	300
Demand	800	600	200	200	

cell evaluations =

Houston-Denver = +10 – 12 + 14 – 9 = +3

Houston-Dummy = +0 – 12 + 14 – 0 = +2

Phoenix-Dallas = +10 – 14 + 12 – 8 = 0

Memphis-Dallas = +11 – 8 + 12 – 8 = +7

Memphis-Denver = +12 – 8 + 14 – 9 = +9

Memphis-Dummy = +0 – 0 + 14 – 8 = +6

total cost = 8(800) + 12(50) + 14(250) + 9(200) + 0(200) + 8(300)
= $14,700

This is an optimal solution because all improvement indices are positive or zero. There is another optimal solution because the evaluation of the cell for the Phoenix to Dallas route is 0. This alternate solution may be found by using the steppingstone path that generated this evaluation of zero, and filling this using the normal procedure. This alternate solution is:

Source	Destination: Dallas	Atlanta	Denver	Dummy	Supply
Houston	550 [8]	300 [12]	[10]	[0]	850
Phoenix	250 [10]	[14]	200 [9]	200 [0]	650
Memphis	[11]	300 [8]	[12]	[0]	300
Demand	800	600	200	200	

total cost = 8(550) + 12(300) + 10(250) + 9(200) + 0(200) + 8(300)
= $14,700

SOLVED PROBLEM 6-2

Four automobiles have entered Bubba's Repair Shop for various types of work ranging from a transmission overhaul to a brake job. Bubba must decide which mechanic to assign to each job. The experience level of the mechanics is quite varied, and Bubba would like to minimize the time required to complete all of the jobs. He has estimated the time in minutes for each mechanic to complete each job. The table below gives the estimated time (in minutes) for each mechanic on each job.

	Job #1	#2	#3	#4
Billy	400	90	60	120
Taylor	650	120	90	180
Mark	480	120	80	180
John	500	110	90	150

Use the Hungarian algorithm to determine the assignments that would minimize the total time required to complete the jobs.

SOLUTION

Beginning with the table above, subtract the smallest number in each row from all numbers in the row:

	Job #1	#2	#3	#4
Billy	340	30	0	60
Taylor	560	30	0	90
Mark	400	40	0	100
John	410	20	0	60

Subtracting the smallest number in each column results in:

	Job			
	#1	#2	#3	#4
Billy	0	10	0	0
Taylor	220	10	0	30
Mark	60	20	0	40
John	70	0	0	0

Drawing the minimum number of lines we have:

	Job			
	#1	#2	#3	#4
Billy	0	10	0	0
Taylor	220	10	0	30
Mark	60	20	0	40
John	70	0	0	0

The smallest number not covered by a line is subtracted from all uncovered numbers and added to the numbers at the intersection of two lines. This gives us:

	Job			
	#1	#2	#3	#4
Billy	0	10	10	0
Taylor	210	0	0	20
Mark	50	10	0	30
John	70	0	10	0

The minimum number of lines required to cover the zeroes is four, so optimal assignments may be made. Beginning with the only row or column with one zero, we assign Mark to Job #3. Once this row and column have been eliminated, there is only one zero left for Taylor, so Taylor is assigned to Job #2. Then John is assigned to Job #4 and Billy is assigned to Job #1. The total time required for these assignments (from the original table) is 400 + 120 + 80 + 150 = 750 minutes.

QUESTIONS

1. List three methods for generating an initial solution to a transportation problem. What are the advantages of each of these?
2. List two methods for evaluating a solution to a transportation problem.
3. Using the transportation algorithm, an empty cell is found to have a cell evaluation of +6. Explain what this means.
4. In finding the steppingstone path in a transportation problem, why must there be exactly two changes in each row or column which has changes?
5. How is the transportation algorithm modified if the objective is to maximize profit rather than minimize cost?
6. How is degeneracy in the transportation problem recognized? What problem does degeneracy create? What should be done when this is observed?
7. How do you recognize that more than one optimal solution exists in a transportation problem?
8. Would it ever be necessary to add more than one dummy row or dummy column in a transportation problem?
9. Discuss the similarities between the simplex method and the transportation algorithm.
10. Explain why a cost of *M* is assigned to a prohibited cell in a transportation problem for a minimization problem, and a –*M* is assigned to a prohibited cell if it is a maximization problem.
11. Why is a cost of zero assigned as the cost to each cell in dummy rows or columns in a transportation problem?
12. How would you modify the least cost method and Vogel's approximation method if you were using them to generate initial solutions for a maximization problem instead of a minimization problem?
13. In a transportation problem with zero costs assigned to a dummy row or column, why is it necessary to evaluate the empty cells in that row or column?
14. How is a prohibited assignment handled when using the Hungarian algorithm?
15. In the Capitol Electric problem, explain what the cell evaluation for each of the empty cells in the final solution means to management of the firm.

PROBLEMS

16. In the Capitol Electric problem presented in this chapter, suppose the supply from Lubbock is increased by 20 units. Solve using the transportation algorithm. How many units are shipped from each source to each destination? What is the total cost for this solution? If this solution is used, which source would be left with excess capacity?
17. Finnish Furniture manufactures tables in facilities located in three cities—Reno, Nevada, Denver, Colorado, and Pittsburgh, Pennsylvania. These are sent to three retail stores in Phoenix, Arizona, Cleveland, Ohio, and Chicago, Illinois. Management must determine a distribution schedule to meet the demands at the three retail stores, and the shipping cost should be kept as low as possible. The shipping cost per unit from each of the sources to each of the destinations is given in the following table.

	To		
From	Phoenix	Cleveland	Chicago
Reno	10	16	19
Denver	12	14	13
Pittsburgh	18	12	12

The available supplies are 120 from Reno, 200 from Denver, and 160 from Pittsburgh. Phoenix needs to receive 140 units, Cleveland needs 160 units, and Chicago needs 180 units.

a) Generate an initial solution to this problem using the northwest corner method. What is the cost of this initial solution?

b) Generate an initial solution to this problem using Vogel's approximation method. What is the cost of this initial solution?

c) Beginning with the northwest corner initial solution, use the transportation algorithm to determine how many units to ship from each source to each destination. What is the total cost?

18. In Problem 17, suppose the demand in Chicago has decreased and is only 150 units. What special condition would exist? What would be the minimum cost solution in this situation? Will there be any units remaining at any of the sources?
19. In Problem 17, suppose the manager of the Chicago store, which has a demand of 180 units, believes the quality of the tables produced in Denver is not as good as those in the other two facilities, and consequently she will not accept any tables from Denver. Solve this problem again with the transportation algorithm to minimize the shipping cost.
20. Consider the following transportation table for a minimization problem.

From \ To	X	Y	Z
1	1800 [6]	300 [9]	[10]
2	[11]	1100 [12]	700 [11]
3	[13]	[10]	2000 [8]

a) Verify this is the optimal solution by evaluating all of the empty cells.

b) What is the cost for this solution?

c) Currently there are no units being shipped from 3 to X. By how much would the cost of shipping from 3 to X have to decrease before this route could be used while minimizing cost?

d) Explain what the cell evaluation for cell 3–X means.

21. Refer to the transportation table in Problem 20. Suppose before this problem is solved, a truck from source 3 is loaded with 500 units and sent to destination Y. This necessitates some changes in the solution represented by the table. Make these changes and calculate the minimum total cost. Then look at the

original evaluation index for this cell and use this to determine how much the total shipping cost should increase over the cost represented by the table.

22. Cole Dare Corporation produces room air conditioners in factories located in Lubbock, Texas, Albuquerque, New Mexico, and Phoenix, Arizona. Each factory can produce 80 units per week. These are sent to regional distribution centers in San Diego, California, Houston, Texas, and Mobile, Alabama. Anticipated demand for San Diego is 100 units, for Houston is 120 units, and for Mobile is 50 units. The shipping costs are given below.

	To		
From	San Diego	Houston	Mobile
Lubbock	12	8	15
Albuquerque	10	10	16
Phoenix	8	14	17

Establish the least cost shipping schedule using the transportation algorithm. Will the demand at each location be met? Is there another solution that will give the same cost as this?

23. Refer to the Cold Dare situation in Problem 22. Suppose the cost of producing each air conditioner is $40 in Lubbock, $45 in Albuquerque, and $45 in Phoenix. The selling price is $120 in all locations. The profit generated by each air conditioner depends on the selling price, production cost, and shipping cost. Using the transportation algorithm, find the production and shipping schedule that maximizes profit.

24. David Monthly is a real estate developer who is currently building in three areas of Texas. He has hired three individuals, Simpson, Garcia, and Thomas, to manage the sales force in each location. Based on the experience of these individuals and their familiarity with the real estate markets in the different cities, Monthly has rated each individual on a scale of 1 to 10 for each location. A rating of 1 is the best rating, which means the person would sell the houses in the least possible amount of time. These ratings are in the table below.

	Simpson	Garcia	Thomas
Houston	3	5	6
Dallas	5	6	6
Austin	4	7	5

a) Use the Hungarian algorithm to make assignments that will minimize the total of the ratings. Is there another assignment that will result in the same total rating?

b) Suppose the ratings are such that a 10 is the best rating and a 1 is the worst rating. Use the Hungarian algorithm to make assignments that maximize the total rating.

25. An accounting firm has three new clients. To spread the workload around, each new client must be assigned to a different accountant. There are four accountants who are being considered for these clients. The time in days required per month by each accountant to perform the work required by each client is given in the following table.

	Accountant			
Client	Jones	Smith	Davis	Li
#1	4	5	5	3
#2	7	8	6	6
#3	10	9	10	10

a) Use the Hungarian method to make assignments that minimize the total time used for these clients. How many days in total would be allocated to these clients?
b) If the accounting firm wishes to maximize the total time charged to each client, what assignments would be made? What would the total time be?

26. Campus Construction has three pieces of heavy equipment that are used in construction. Three jobs are scheduled to start next week, each of which requires the use of one of these machines. The time (in days) required on each job by each machine is shown in the table below.

	Job		
Machine	#1	#2	#3
A	9	6	4
B	7	7	6
C	10	12	8

Which machine should be assigned to each job to minimize the total time required? Is there more than one set of assignments that will result in the same minimum time?

27. Suppose in Problem 26, a new piece of machinery has been purchased. This machine can complete Job #1 in 8 days, Job #2 in 6 days, and Job #3 in 6 days. Which machine should be assigned to each job if total time is to be minimized? Which machine will be idle?
28. Baseball umpiring crews are currently in four cities where three-game series are beginning. When these are finished the crews are needed to work games in four different cities. The distances from each of the cities where the crews are working to the cities where the new games will be starting are shown in the table below.

	To			
From	Kansas City	Chicago	Detroit	Toronto
Seattle	1800	1900	1850	2100
Arlington	500	800	950	1200
Oakland	1500	2100	2000	x
Baltimore	1300	800	600	400

The x in the Oakland to Toronto assignment means that this particular assignment may not be made.
a) Determine which crews should be sent to which cities to minimize the total distance traveled. How many miles will be traveled if these assignments are used?

b) To evaluate the potential benefit of using the optimal assignments, determine which assignments would result in the maximum possible miles being traveled.

29. Digital Industries manufactures automobile distributors for a special type of high performance automobile. The projected demand for these in the next four months is 240 for March, 400 for April, 600 for May, and 320 for June. The company may produce 300 per month using regular time, and an additional 150 per month may be produced using overtime. The cost of producing each distributor using normal procedures is $120 and this cost increases by $50 per unit if overtime is used. These distributors may be produced in advance and stored for later use, but a monthly storage cost of $20 per unit is incurred for doing this. Currently the company has 50 distributors in inventory.

    Using the techniques associated with the transportation problem, determine how many distributors to produce each month to minimize the total cost of production and storage.

30. In Problem 29, how would the production decisions change if the overtime costs were increased by $10 per unit?
31. In Problem 29, how would the production decisions change if the monthly storage cost was to increase from $20 per unit to $25 per unit?
32. In Problem 29, suppose management has decided that at least 100 units should be remaining in inventory at the end of June. How should the production schedule be modified to accommodate this at the least cost?
33. Solve Problem 20 in Chapter 4 using the Hungarian algorithm.

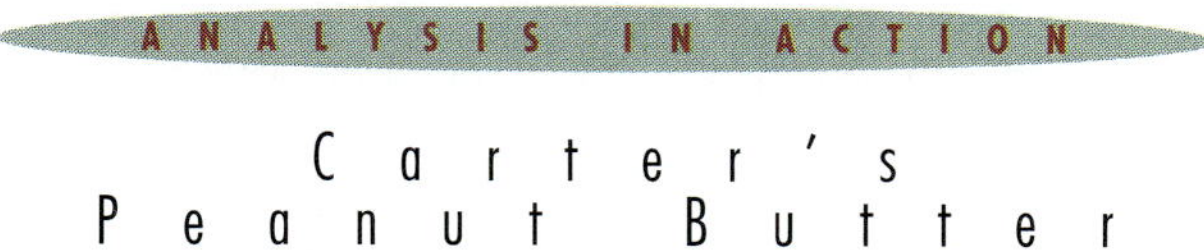

Carter's Peanut Butter

Carter's Peanut Butter is a food-processing firm, which produces peanut butter at processing plants in Columbia, South Carolina and Morgantown, Virginia. Due to increased demand, the company is considering opening a new plant. A careful evaluation of the labor supplies, taxes, and other pertinent factors has resulted in two cities being selected for consideration—Memphis, Tennessee and Atlanta, Georgia. J. R. Aimee, general manager of Carter's Peanut Butter, wishes to evaluate the overall impact each city would have on the company's costs for production and total shipping. Currently, there are two regional distribution centers where all peanut butter is sent from the processing plants. The table below provides the current weekly supplies and demands in cases as well as the shipping cost per case. The

	To		
From	Nashville	New Orleans	Supply
Columbia	$8	12	240
Morgantown	7	14	200
Demand	280	260	

production cost is $19 per case in Columbia and $22 per case in Morgantown.

The new processing plant, regardless of the location, will have a capacity of 200 cases per week. Due to labor costs in the two cities, the production cost is $21 per case in Memphis and $22 per case in Atlanta. The shipping costs are estimated in the table below.

	To	
From	**Nashville**	**New Orleans**
Memphis	6	15
Atlanta	8	13

Your job is to determine which of the two cities would result in the lowest cost for the company. (*Hint:* This is referred to as a facility location problem. Use the transportation algorithm to evaluate the addition of each one of these separately and compare the results.)

Prepare a brief managerial report indicating what you would recommend giving all pertinent information.

C H A P T E R   S E V E N

Integer Linear Programming and Goal Programming

LEARNING OBJECTIVES

Upon completing Chapter 7, you should be able to:

- Identify the three types of integer programming problems.
- Use 0-1 variables to formulate special types of integer programming problems.
- Explain how an integer programming problem differs from a linear programming problem.
- Solve integer programming problems using the Branch and Bound (B & B) Algorithm.
- Use computer software to solve integer programming problems.
- Formulate goal programming problems.
- Use weighted goals and preemptive priorities in the development of the objective function in goal programming problems.
- Solve goal programming problems using software for linear programming.

CHAPTER OUTLINE

7.1 INTRODUCTION

In previous chapters, we have seen that linear programming is a very widely used technique. However, in many situations where it appears a linear programming model might be helpful, there are conditions which prevent the use of this technique. One of the assumptions of linear programming is that the decision variables are continuous and do not have to be integer valued. If a problem satisfies the conditions for a linear programming problem except that the values for the decision variables must be integers, then we may use integer linear programming (ILP). Adding the integer requirements means new restrictions or constraints have been placed on the problem. Thus, the feasible region will be smaller and the optimal value for the integer programming problem cannot be better and is usually worse than the optimal value for the linear problem without the integer restrictions. The first part of this chapter will be devoted to integer linear programming.

The second part of this chapter will be devoted to another topic related to linear programming called goal programming. We have seen that in linear programming problems, we must have one single objective function. In many situations, management may have several objectives or goals. Perhaps the sales manager wants to maintain a large inventory of products so customer demand can be met immediately, but the production manager wants to minimize the total inventory cost of the company. Thus, there is more than one single objective, and these objectives may be conflicting. In situations such as this, goal programming may help to model the managerial problem.

In this chapter we will see how to use integer linear programming and goal programming to model many types of problems. The basic solution techniques for these types of problems will be presented, although these types of problems are normally solved with the aid of computer software.

7.2 TYPES OF ILP

There are three general types of integer linear programming problems. In all of these, a linear objective function and linear constraints are required.

Pure integer problem
An ILP problem in which all of the variables must be integer valued.

The **pure integer problem** is one in which all the variables are required to be integer valued. For example, if the decision variables in a linear programming problem were defined as the number of aircraft of different types to purchase for a fleet, all of these variables would be required to be integer valued as we cannot buy 2.75 units of any type of plane. This would be a pure integer problem.

Mixed integer linear programming problem
An ILP problem in which some but not all of the variables must be integer valued.

The **mixed integer linear programming problem** is one in which some of the variables are required to be integer valued while others are not. For example, decision variables representing the number of employees to assign to a specific job would have to be integer valued. However, in this same problem we may have other variables representing the number of hours that will be spent on the job. These variables are not required to be integers because a fraction of an hour is a possible solution. Thus, this would be a mixed integer problem.

A third class of problems that is very common is the **0–1 integer programming problem** in which the variables not only must be integer valued but they also must equal either zero or one. Variables of this type are sometimes called **binary variables** or **0-1 variables.** Variables that may have any integer values are called **general integer variables.**

The use of 0-1 variables is very important, and a large class of integer programming problems require the use of 0-1 variables, as will be seen in the following examples.

0-1 integer programming problem
A problem in which variables are required to equal either zero or one.

0-1 variables
Variables that are restricted to be either zero or one. These also are called **binary variables.**

General integer variables
Variables that are restricted to be integer valued, but are not restricted to being only zero and one.

7.3 FORMULATIONS USING 0-1 VARIABLES

In this section we will see how 0-1 variables may be used to model several diverse situations. Typically, a 0-1 variable is assigned a value of zero if a certain condition is not met and one if the condition is met. A common problem of this type, the assignment problem, involves deciding which individuals to assign to a set of jobs, as was seen in Chapter 4. In this assignment problem, a value of one indicates a person is assigned to a specific job and zero otherwise. Due to the special structure of this type of problem, it may be solved with standard linear programming software, and the values of the decision variables will be zero or one. Other types of 0-1 problems will be presented to show the wide applicability of this modeling technique.

A common capital budgeting decision may involve purchasing only one piece of equipment when budget limitations make it impossible to purchase more. SOURCE: Raceland Sugars, Inc., a subsidiary of Savannah Foods Industrial

Capital Budgeting

A common capital budgeting decision involves selecting from a set of possible projects when budget limitations make it impossible to select all of these. A separate 0-1 variable would be defined for each project. We will see this in the following example.

Quemo Chemical Company is faced with three possible investments, but capital requirements and budget limitations in the next two years prevent Quemo from investing in all of these. The net present value (the NPV is the future value of the project discounted back to the present time) of each of the investments is given in Table 7.1 together with the capital requirements and the available funds for the next two years.

To formulate this as an ILP problem, we identify the objective function and the constraints as:

Maximize net present value of investment

Subject to: Total funds used in Year 1 $\leq$ 20,000

Total funds used in Year 2 $\leq$ 16,000

We define the decision variables as:

$$X_1 = 1 \text{ if Investment 1 is made}$$
$$= 0 \text{ otherwise}$$
$$X_2 = 1 \text{ if Investment 2 is made}$$
$$= 0 \text{ otherwise}$$
$$X_3 = 1 \text{ if Investment 3 is made}$$
$$= 0 \text{ otherwise}$$

The mathematical statement of the ILP becomes:

$$\text{Maximize } 25{,}000X_1 + 18{,}000X_2 + 32{,}000X_3$$
$$\text{Subject to: } 8{,}000X_1 + 6{,}000X_2 + 12{,}000X_3 \leq 20{,}000$$
$$7{,}000X_1 + 4{,}000X_2 + 8{,}000X_3 \leq 16{,}000$$
$$X_1, X_2, X_3 = 0 \text{ or } 1$$

Computer output in Output 7.1 indicates the optimal solution to this is $X_1 = 1$, $X_2 = 0$, and $X_3 = 1$ with an objective function value of 57,000. This means that Quemo should invest in Investment 1 and Investment 3 while

TABLE 7.1

Quemo Chemical Investment Information

Investment	NPV	Year 1	Year 2
1	25,000	8,000	7,000
2	18,000	6,000	4,000
3	32,000	12,000	8,000
Available Funds		20,000	16,000

not investing in Investment 2. The net present value of these investments will be $57,000.

Limiting the Number of Alternatives Selected

Suppose in the Quemo Chemical Company example, the company is required to select no more than two of the three alternatives. This could be modeled by adding the following constraint to the problem:

$$X_1 + X_2 + X_3 \leq 2$$

If we wished to force the selection of exactly two of the three investment alternatives, the following constraint should be used:

$$X_1 + X_2 + X_3 = 2$$

This forces exactly two of the variables to have values of one while the other variable must have a value of zero.

OUTPUT 7.1

DSS Output for Quemo Chemical Capital Budgeting Example

```
Integer Programming

Node Branching Table:

       Branched
       From                                Resulting            Current Values:
Node#  Node#  Additional Constraint   'Z' Value Results  X1        X2        X3
 1      First Linear Approximation      59000     NI       1         1        .5
 2      1       X3       <=  0          43000     I        1         1         0
 3      1       X3       >=  1          57000     I <=Opt  1         0         1
BS: Bounded Suboptimum, BI: Bounded Infeasible, I: Integer, NI: Non-integer

Original Problem:

Z         X1        X2        X3
MAX       25000     18000     32000
Cons1     8000      6000      12000     <=        20000
Cons2     7000      4000      8000      <=        16000
Int Req   Z         Z         Z

Solution:
               X1        =  1
               X2        =  0
               X3        =  1

               MAX       Z         =  57000

This solution is degenerate

Slack 1        1
Slack 2        0
Additional Constraint: X3        >=  1
```

Dependent Selections

Suppose in the Quemo Chemical problem, Investment 1 could be made only if Investment 2 also was made. The following constraint would force this to occur:

$$X_1 \le X_2$$

or equivalently

$$X_1 - X_2 \le 0$$

Thus, if Investment 2 is not made, the value of X_2 is 0, and the value of X_1 also must be 0 because of this constraint. However, if Investment 2 is made (X_2 = 1), then it is possible that Investment 1 also is made, although this is not required.

If we wished for Investments 1 and 2 to either both be selected or both not be selected, we should use the following constraint

$$X_1 = X_2$$

or equivalently

$$X_1 - X_2 = 0$$

Thus, if either of these is zero, the other also must be zero. If either of these is one, the other also must be one.

Fixed Charge Problem

Often businesses are faced with decisions involving a fixed charge, which will impact the cost of future operations. Building a new factory would involve a fixed cost, which might vary depending upon the size of the factory and the location. Once a factory is built, the variable production costs will be impacted by the labor cost in the particular city where the factory is located. Consider a situation where a company is planning to build at least one new plant, and three cities are being considered. Once the plant or plants have been constructed, the company wishes to have sufficient capacity to produce at least 18,000 units each year. The costs associated with the possible locations are given in Table 7.2.

To model this as an ILP, the objective function is identified as minimize total of the fixed cost and the variable cost. The constraints are (1) total

TABLE 7.2

Costs of Building at Three Locations

Site	Fixed Cost	Variable Cost	Capacity
1	340,000	12	11,000
2	270,000	13	10,000
3	290,000	10	9,000

production capacity is at least 18,000; (2) number of units produced at Site 1 is zero if the plant is not built, and it is no more than 11,000 if the plant is built; (3) number of units produced at Site 2 is zero if the plant is not built, and it is no more than 10,000 if the plant is built; (4) number of units produced at Site 3 is zero if the plant is not built, and it is no more than 9,000 if the plant is built.

Then we define the decision variables as:

X_1 = 1 if plant is built at Site 1
= 0 otherwise
X_2 = 1 if plant is built at Site 2
= 0 otherwise
X_3 = 1 if plant is built at Site 3
= 0 otherwise
X_4 = number of units produced at plant 1
X_5 = number of units produced at plant 2
X_6 = number of units produced at plant 3

The ILP formulation becomes:

$$\text{Minimize cost} = 340{,}000X_1 + 270{,}000X_2 + 290{,}000X_3 + 12X_4 + 13X_5 + 10X_6$$

$$\text{Subject to: } X_4 + X_5 + X_6 \geq 18{,}000$$
$$X_4 \leq 11{,}000X_1$$
$$X_5 \leq 10{,}000X_2$$
$$X_6 \leq 9{,}000X_3$$
$$X_1, X_2, X_3 = 0 \text{ or } 1;\ X_4, X_5, X_6 \geq 0 \text{ and integer}$$

Notice if $X_1 = 0$ (meaning plant 1 is not built), then X_4 (number of units produced at plant 1) also must equal zero due to the second constraint. If $X_1 = 1$, then X_4 may be any integer value less than or equal to the limit of 11,000. The third and fourth constraints are similarly used to guarantee that no units are produced at plants 2 and 3 if these plants are not built.

The optimal solution found using LINDO is shown in Output 7.2. From this we see the solution is:

$X_1 = 0$ $X_2 = 1$
$X_3 = 1$ $X_4 = 0$
$X_5 = 9000$ $X_6 = 9000$
objective function value = 767,000

This means plants will be built at Sites 2 and 3. Each of these will produce 9,000 units and the total cost will be $767,000.

We have seen some examples that illustrate the use of 0-1 variables. In addition to these 0-1 integer problems, there are many other problems in which the variables must be integer valued although they do not have to be 0 or 1. We will illustrate this in the following example.

OUTPUT 7.2

LINDO Output for Fixed Charge Example

```
MIN   340000 X1 + 270000 X2 + 290000 X3 + 12 X4 + 13 X5 + 10 X6
  SUBJECT TO
         2)    X4 + X5 + X6 >=   18000
         3) - 11000 X1 + X4 <=    0
         4) - 10000 X2 + X5 <=    0
         5) - 9000 X3 + X6 <=    0
  END

        OBJECTIVE FUNCTION VALUE

        1)      767000.00

  VARIABLE        VALUE           REDUCED COST
        X1           .000000      329000.000000
        X2          1.000000      270000.000000
        X3          1.000000      263000.000000
        X4           .000000            .000000
        X5       9000.000000            .000000
        X6       9000.000000            .000000

       ROW   SLACK OR SURPLUS      DUAL PRICES
        2)           .000000       -13.000000
        3)           .000000         1.000000
        4)       1000.000000          .000000
        5)           .000000         3.000000

 NO. ITERATIONS=       11
 BRANCHES=     5 DETERM.=  1.000E    0
```

A CLOSER LOOK

Using Heuristic Techniques for Integer Programming

SOURCE: Winston, W. L., 1995. *Introduction to Mathematical Programming.* California: Duxbury Press.

For many situations that could be modeled using 0-1 integer programming, the number of variables or constraints may cause the solution time to be excessive even on the fastest computers available. For problems such as these, heuristic methods, or simply heuristics, are used.

A heuristic is a rule of thumb approach to solving problems that does not necessarily find the optimal solution, but typically finds a good solution very quickly.

The traveling salesperson problem (TSP) is often solved with heuristics. In this problem, a salesperson would leave home and travel to each of several other cities one time before returning home. The objective would be to minimize the number of miles traveled or the time spent traveling. If there were 10 cities to be visited, the number of possible ways that the visits could be scheduled is $10! = 10\ (9)\ (8) \ldots (1) = 3{,}628{,}800$. While this could be modeled as an integer program, the time required to solve such a problem using normal integer programming software would be excessive.

One heuristic for the TSP is the nearest-neighbor heuristic. We would begin by selecting a city to be visited first, and we would go from that city to the nearest city. This continues until all cities have been visited and the person returns home. Then, we would select another city as the first city and the process would be repeated. Whichever of the sequences resulted in the shortest total distance would be the solution used, although it may not be optimal.

7.4

A GENERAL INTEGER PROGRAMMING EXAMPLE

Katherine Blissit is the manager of Cypress Country, a country and western night club in Texas. Katherine has identified a specific radio station where advertising for Cypress Country will reach the target audience. With a weekly advertising budget of $1,800, Katherine wants to reach as many people as possible. The rates for ads on this particular radio station are $390 per ad during prime time and $240 per ad during other times. Each ad during prime time reaches 8,200 people, while each ad in nonprime time reaches 5,100 people. It has been determined that there should be at least two ads per week during prime time, and no more than six ads per week during the off-periods. To help determine how many of each type to use, a linear program was formulated as follows:

X_1 = number of ads per week during prime time

X_2 = number of ads per week during nonprime time

Maximize $8200X_1 + 5100X_2$

Subject to: $X_1 \geq 2$

$X_2 \leq 6$

$390X_1 + 240X_2 \leq 1800$

$X_1, X_2 \geq 0$

To maximize the number of viewers reached, an advertising manager may use general integer programming to determine how many ads to run on a particular station. SOURCE: Mike Steinberg

The solution found using computer software for linear programming, not integer programming, is shown in Output 7.3. The solution is:

$X_1 = 2$ ads during prime time
$X_2 = 4.25$ ads during other times
objective function value = 38,075 people reached

Recognizing that the number of ads must be integer valued, Katherine decides to use two ads during prime time and four ads during other times. This would reach 36,800 people per week. After considering this approach, Katherine is wondering if another solution might be better than this one. This is a situation where integer programming would be helpful. We will see graphically the difficulty with simply rounding the solution to the relaxed problem.

7.5 A GRAPHICAL SOLUTION FOR THE CYPRESS COUNTRY EXAMPLE

The graph of the feasible region (ignoring the integer restrictions) in the Cypress Country example is shown in the top graph in Figure 7.1. The optimal solution ($X_1 = 2$, $X_2 = 4.25$) and the profit line are shown on the graph. If this solution is rounded we would get $X_1 = 2$ and $X_2 = 4$. The value of the objective function would be 36,800.

In the bottom graph in Figure 7.1, the feasible region for the integer problem is shown. Notice a finite number of integer solutions exist for this

OUTPUT 7.3

LINDO Output for Cypress Country Problem Solved as Linear Rather Than as Integer Problem

```
MAX      8200 X1 + 5100 X2
 SUBJECT TO
        2)    X1 >=    2
        3)    X2 <=    6
        4)    390 X1 + 240 X2 <=    1800
 END

LP OPTIMUM FOUND AT STEP       3

       OBJECTIVE FUNCTION VALUE

       1)      38075.000

 VARIABLE          VALUE            REDUCED COST
       X1          2.000000             .000000
       X2          4.250000             .000000

      ROW    SLACK OR SURPLUS      DUAL PRICES
       2)           .000000         -87.500000
       3)          1.750000            .000000
       4)           .000000          21.250000

NO. ITERATIONS=        3
```

FIGURE 7.1

Feasible Region for LP Relaxation and ILP of Cypress Country Example

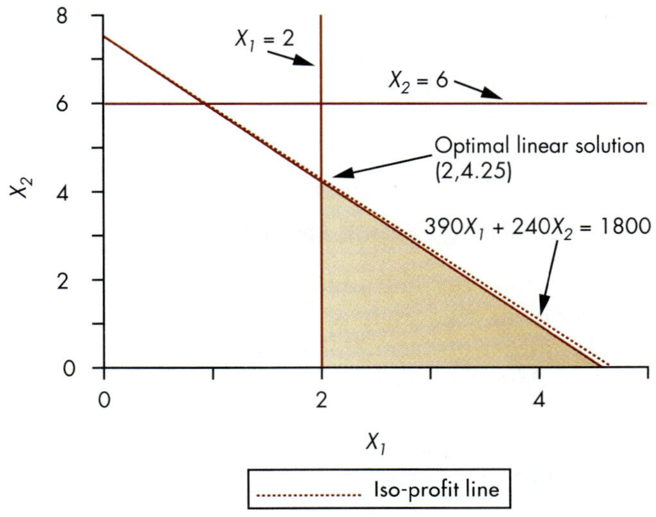

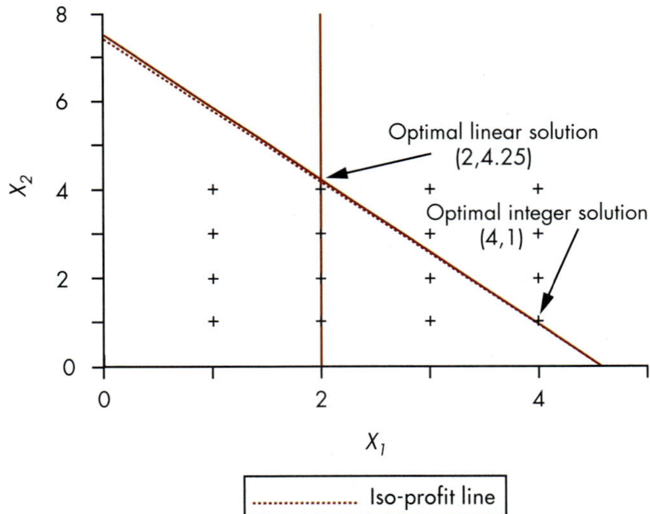

problem. Because the solution to the relaxed problem is not integer, the optimal integer solution must be found. The iso-profit method may be used for this purpose. To do this, we draw the profit line through the solution to the LP relaxation, and see that it does not touch a feasible integer point. To find a feasible integer solution, move the objective function line from the optimal point for the LP problem back towards the origin until it touches an integer point. The first one it touches is the point (4,1). Therefore, this is the optimal solution to the integer problem. The value of the objective function is 37,900. This is 1,100 higher than the value for the integer solution obtained by rounding.

While the graphical method illustrates the basic concept associated with solving ILP problems, it only may be used when there are two decision variables. For problems with more than two decision variables, other techniques must be used to find the optimal integer solution. Simply rounding off the solution to the linear problem is not sufficient.

7.6 LP RELAXATION AND ROUNDING

Linear programming (LP) relaxation
An integer linear programming problem with the integer restriction on the variables omitted.

If the integer restriction on the variables is dropped for an integer linear programming problem, the result is called the **linear programming (LP) relaxation** of the integer problem. For some problems, solving the relaxed problem and rounding the solution may provide an adequate solution to the managerial problem. However, at times this approach may provide a very poor or even an infeasible solution.

Suppose the optimal solution to a relaxed problem is $X_1 = 275.37$ and $X_2 = 454.96$. The fractional portion of these numbers is very small relative to the size of the number. These values could be rounded to 275 and 455 and a solution usable to management might be obtained. This solution might be feasible or so close to feasible that management could find a way to obtain the resources necessary to make it feasible. While it is not necessarily the optimal solution, it would likely be close to the optimal solution. However, if the solution to the relaxed problem were $X_1 = 1.45$ and $X_2 = 3.38$, rounding these numbers may have a dramatic impact on the solution. Rounding X_1 up to two instead of down to one would double the value of this decision variable. This relative difference or percentage difference between the values of one and two is considerably greater than the previous example where X_1 might be rounded to either 275 or 276. The difference between 275 and 276 is very small when expressed as a percentage of the actual value.

Thus, when the values for the decision variables are large, rounding the relaxed solution might be satisfactory from a managerial perspective, although it is not necessarily optimal. When the values of the decision variables are small, rounding the relaxed solution is not advisable. The Cypress Country example indicated how rounding the solution to the relaxed problem may lead to a less than optimal integer solution.

7.7 SOLUTION TECHNIQUES

Large linear programming problems may be solved in a very short time with the aid of a computer and the appropriate software. Solving integer linear programming problems is much more difficult and typically requires much more computer time than a comparably sized linear problem. For extremely large integer problems, the time required to reach the optimal solution may be excessive. Some software packages allow the user to specify an upper limit on the amount of computer time used on a problem. The best feasible solution that has been obtained by this time often is used even though it may not be optimal.

Two solution procedures for solving general integer linear programming problems are the cutting plane method and the Branch and Bound (B & B) Algorithm. Both of these may be used with any ILP problem.

For 0-1 problems, a complete enumeration or listing of all possible solutions may appear to be a way of finding the best solution. However, as the problem size increases, the number of possible solutions becomes extremely large. For a problem in which 10 variables must be zero or one, the number of possible solutions is $2^{10} = 1{,}024$. For a problem with n 0-1 variables, the number of possible solution is 2^n. Because there are so many possible solutions and explicit enumeration would be quite time consuming, implicit enumeration methods based on a branch and bound procedure often are used for 0-1 problems.

Cutting Plane Method

The **cutting plane method** is based on solving the linear programming relaxation of the ILP problem. If the solution to this is integer valued, then it also must be the optimal solution to the integer problem. If it is not integer valued, then a new constraint or *cut* is added to the problem that cuts off the optimal linear solution without cutting off any integer points. Because this previous optimal solution is no longer feasible, a new solution must be found. If this new solution is integer, then it must be the optimal solution. If it is not integer valued, then a new cut is generated. This process continues until an integer solution is found.

Cutting plane method
A technique for solving integer linear programming problems.

The cutting plane method is not used as widely as the branch and bound method because the number of cuts may be excessive, and thus the computer time required may be quite long. With this technique, the solutions found for the relaxed linear problems are all noninteger until the final solution is found. Because only integer solutions make sense to management, this means unless the optimal solution is found, management does not have any feasible solutions to use.

Branch and Bound Method

Most ILP software is based on the branch and bound method. The concept of branch and bound is used for many types of problems, but we will present what will be called the **Branch and Bound (B & B) Algorithm** for solving integer linear programming problems.

Branch and Bound (B & B) Algorithm
The most common technique for solving integer linear programming problems.

The Branch and Bound (B & B) Algorithm begins with the solution to the relaxation of the ILP problem. If the variables are integer valued, this also must be the solution to the ILP problem. If these variables are not integer valued, the feasible region is divided by adding constraints restricting the value of one of the variables that was not integer valued. The divided feasible region results in subproblems, which are then solved. Bounds on the value of the objective function are found and used to help determine which subproblems may be eliminated from consideration and when the optimal solution has been found. If the solution to a subproblem does not yield an optimal solution, a new subproblem is selected and branching continues.

One major advantage of this B & B procedure over the cutting plane procedure is that some very good integer solutions are usually found quickly with the B & B method. A good integer solution may provide management with something usable from a managerial perspective even if the optimal solution requires excessive time to obtain.

7.8

SOLVING THE CYPRESS COUNTRY PROBLEM WITH THE B & B ALGORITHM

Returning to the Cypress Country media selection problem that was presented earlier in this chapter, we will illustrate how the Branch and Bound Algorithm is used with a maximization problem. Expressing this problem as an integer linear programming problem we have:

X_1 = number of ads per week during prime time

X_2 = number of ads per week during nonprime time

Maximize $8200X_1 + 5100X_2$

Subject to: $X_1 \geq 2$

$X_2 \leq 6$

$390X_1 + 240X_2 \leq 1800$

$X_1, X_2 \geq 0$ and integer

Notice in the statement of the problem that the variables are specifically restricted to be integer valued. To solve this with the Branch and Bound Algorithm, first drop the integer restriction and solve the relaxation of this. We will identify this relaxation as problem *P1*. The solution to this is:

$X_1 = 2$

$X_2 = 4.25$

objective function value = 38,075

Because the value of X_2 is not integer, we must continue. We generate an upper bound and a lower bound on the value of the objective function for the ILP. Because the value of the objective function for the ILP cannot be better than the value for the LP, we may begin with an upper bound of 38,075. To generate an initial lower bound, we must find a feasible solution. In this case, if we round off the LP solution we get $X_1 = 2$ and $X_2 = 4$. Checking the constraints we see this is feasible. The objective function value at this point is:

$$8200(2) + 5100(4) = 36{,}800$$

Thus, we have a feasible, integer solution (although not necessarily the optimal solution) that may be used for comparison. This objective function value is used as the initial lower bound. If this had not been a feasible solution, another approach could be used to find a feasible integer solution to get the initial lower bound.

Returning to the LP problem *P1*, select a variable that is not integer valued and generate two constraints to divide the feasible region into two parts. Because $X_2 = 4.25$ in the LP solution, we know that in the optimal integer solution either

$$X_2 \leq 4$$

or

$$X_2 \geq 5$$

These constraints would eliminate the current noninteger value for this variable without eliminating any integer points. Add the first constraint to the original problem and create the first subproblem, which we will call *P2*.

$$\begin{aligned}
&\text{Maximize } 8200X_1 + 5100X_2 \\
&\text{Subject to: } X_1 \geq 2 \\
&X_2 \leq 6 \\
&390X_1 + 240X_2 \leq 1800 \\
&X_2 \leq 4 \\
&X_1, X_2 \geq 0
\end{aligned}$$

You may notice the constraint $X_2 \leq 4$ makes the constraint $X_2 \leq 6$ redundant, and so the problem may be simplified by dropping the constraint $X_2 \leq 6$. However, we will leave this constraint in the problem to make it easier to follow the branching process.

Solving subproblem *P2* as a linear program we get:

$$\begin{aligned}
&X_1 = 2.154 \\
&X_2 = 4 \\
&\text{objective function value} = 38061.54
\end{aligned}$$

We then add the second constraint ($X_2 \geq 5$) to the original LP and get the second subproblem, which we will call *P3*.

$$\begin{aligned}
&\text{Maximize } 8200X_1 + 5100X_2 \\
&\text{Subject to: } X_1 \geq 2 \\
&X_2 \leq 6 \\
&390X_1 + 240X_2 \leq 1800 \\
&X_2 \geq 5 \\
&X_1, X_2 \geq 0
\end{aligned}$$

Solving this we find there is no feasible solution to this problem. Figure 7.2 illustrates how to use a tree structure to keep track of the branching that is being done and presents the solutions to these problems. Notice neither of the solutions shown in Figure 7.2 is integer, so the lower bound established previously cannot be changed. However, the upper bound may be modified because the best solution for all the subproblems at the branch ends (problems *P2* and *P3*) is 38061.54, which is less than the previous upper bound. This becomes the new upper bound.

The optimal integer solution must be in the feasible region of one of the subproblems at the branch ends because when constraints are added for

FIGURE 7.2

Initial Branching for Cypress Country Example

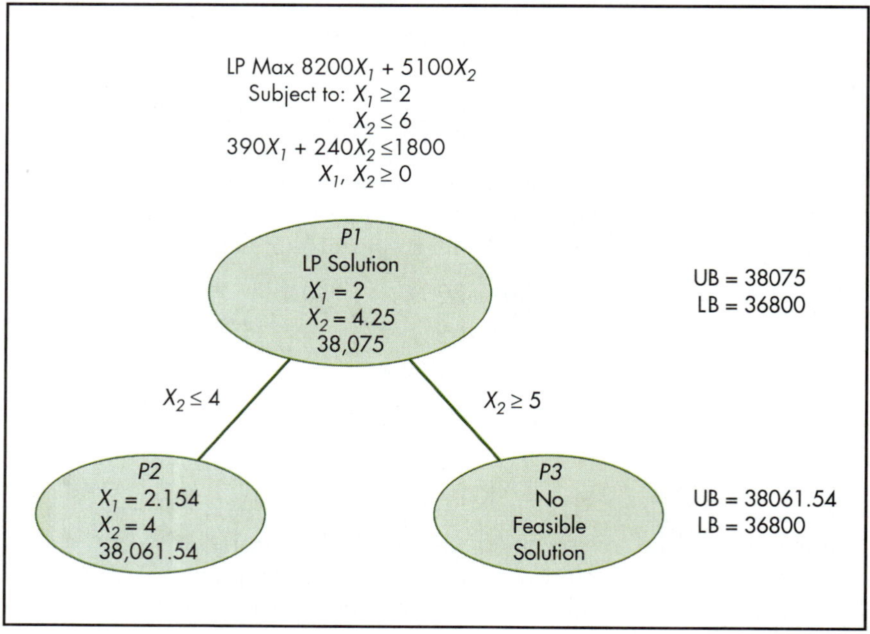

branching, the only points eliminated from the feasible region are not integers. Therefore, for maximization problems continue branching on the subproblems with feasible solutions until either:

1. an integer solution is obtained (if this is equal to the upper bound then this is the optimal solution and other branches also may be eliminated),
2. using the lower bound indicates that further branching on this particular branch is not necessary, or
3. it is determined there is no feasible solution.

In the Cypress Country example, begin with subproblem *P2* and generate constraints for variable X_2 because the value for this was not integer in the solution to *P2* ($X_2 = 2.154$). We know either $X_2 \leq 2$ or $X_2 \geq 3$. Adding these to subproblem *P2* we get two more subproblems, which will be called *P4* (with $X_1 \leq 2$) and *P5* (with $X_1 \geq 3$), as shown below.

$$
\begin{aligned}
&P4 \quad \text{Maximize } 8200X_1 + 5100X_2 \\
&\text{Subject to: } X_1 \geq 2 \\
&X_2 \leq 6 \\
&390X_1 + 240X_2 \leq 1800 \\
&X_2 \leq 4 \\
&X_1 \leq 2 \\
&X_1, X_2 \geq 0
\end{aligned}
$$

P5 Maximize $8200X_1 + 5100X_2$

Subject to: $X_1 \geq 2$

$X_2 \leq 6$

$390X_1 + 240X_2 \leq 1800$

$X_2 \leq 4$

$X_1 \geq 3$

$X_1, X_2 \geq 0$

Notice in problem *P4* the constraints $X_1 \geq 2$ and $X_1 \leq 2$ could be replaced by the single constraint $X_1 = 2$, and the constraint $X_2 \leq 6$ is redundant and could be omitted. In problem *P5*, the constraint $X_1 \geq 2$ also is redundant because of the constraint $X_1 \geq 3$.

Solving these we get the solutions shown in Figure 7.3. Notice the solution to *P4* is integer valued and is equal to the lower bound. While this is

FIGURE 7.3

Second Set of Subproblems for Cypress Country Example

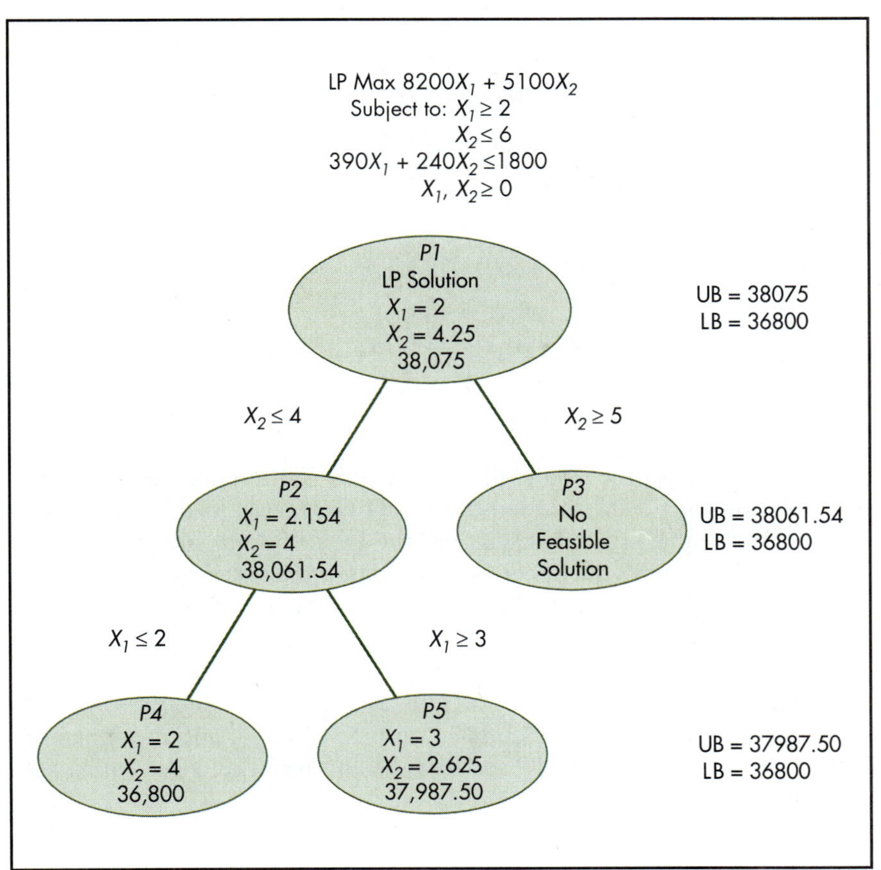

the optimal solution to the subproblem *P4*, which contains only a portion of the original feasible region, it may not be the optimal integer solution to the original ILP problem. The other branches must be considered to determine if another integer solution is better. Notice now the best objective function value for the subproblems at the bottom of all the branches (problems *P3*, *P4*, and *P5*) is 37,987.5 for subproblem *P5*. This is lower than the current upper bound, so this becomes the new upper bound.

The solution to *P5* shown in Figure 7.3 above is not integer valued, and the objective function value is higher than the lower bound of 36,800 so we must continue. If this had not been greater than the 36,800, we would not have to consider this branch any further because it would be impossible for any subproblem to be better than the current lower bound solution. We will branch on variable X_2 because it was not integer valued in *P5* ($X_2 = 2.625$). We create subproblem *P6* by adding the constraint $X_2 \leq 2$ and create *P7* by adding $X_2 \geq 3$, as shown below.

$$
\begin{aligned}
&P6 \quad \text{Maximize } 8200X_1 + 5100X_2\\
&\text{Subject to:} \quad X_1 \geq 2\\
&X_2 \leq 6\\
&390X_1 + 240X_2 \leq 1800\\
&X_2 \leq 4\\
&X_1 \geq 3\\
&X_2 \leq 2\\
&X_1, X_2 \geq 0
\end{aligned}
$$

$$
\begin{aligned}
&P7 \quad \text{Maximize } 8200X_1 + 5100X_2\\
&\text{Subject to:} \quad X_1 \geq 2\\
&X_2 \leq 6\\
&390X_1 + 240X_2 \leq 1800\\
&X_2 \leq 4\\
&X_1 \geq 3\\
&X_2 \geq 3\\
&X_1, X_2 \geq 0
\end{aligned}
$$

Solving these we get the results shown in Figure 7.4. Notice there is no feasible solution to *P7*. The solution to *P6* is not integer valued and the objective function value still is higher than the lower bound so we must continue. We also modify the upper bound because the best objective function value for the subproblems at the bottom of all the branches (problems *P3*, *P4*, *P6*, and *P7*) is 37,953.84, which is lower than the previous upper bound, so this is the new upper bound.

Select the variable that is not integer valued in the solution to *P6* and create two more subproblems. Because $X_1 = 3.385$, add the constraint $X_1 \leq 3$ creating subproblem *P8* and add the constraint $X_1 \geq 4$ creating subproblem *P9*.

FIGURE 7.4

Third Set of Subproblems for Cypress Country Example

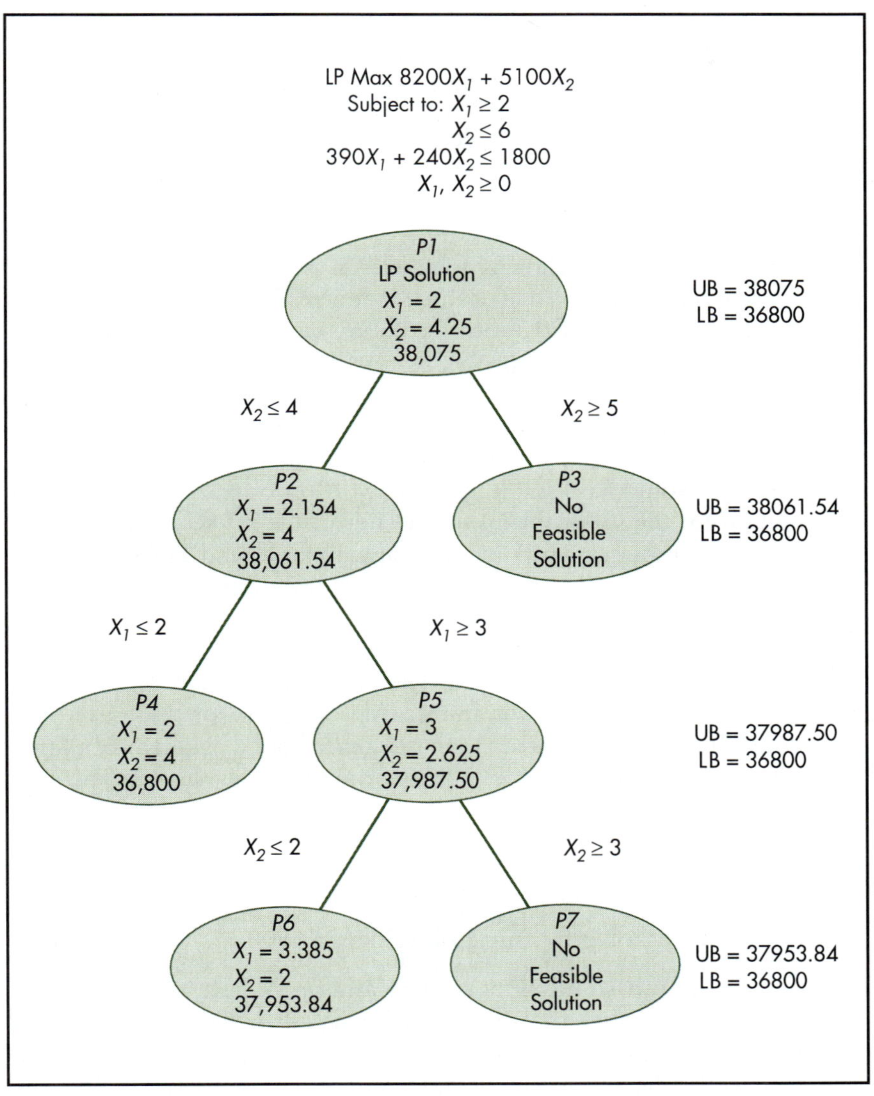

P8 Maximize $8200X_1 + 5100X_2$

Subject to:
$$X_1 \geq 2$$
$$X_2 \leq 6$$
$$390X_1 + 240X_2 \leq 1800$$
$$X_2 \leq 4$$
$$X_1 \geq 3$$
$$X_2 \leq 2$$
$$X_1 \leq 3$$
$$X_1, X_2 \geq 0$$

$$\begin{aligned} &P9 \quad \text{Maximize } 8200X_1 + 5100X_2 \\ &\text{Subject to:} \quad X_1 \geq 2 \\ &X_2 \leq 6 \\ &390X_1 + 240X_2 \leq 1800 \\ &X_2 \leq 4 \\ &X_1 \geq 3 \\ &X_2 \leq 2 \\ &X_1 \geq 4 \\ &X_1, X_2 \geq 0 \end{aligned}$$

The solutions to these are shown in Figure 7.5. In problem *P8*, the value of the objective function is 34,800, which is lower than the lower bound of 36,800. Therefore, even if the solution to *P8* were not integer valued, we would not have to create subproblems for this branch because any constraints used for branching would only reduce the value of the objective function, which already is lower than an existing integer solution. The solution to *P9* is integer valued and it is better than the previous lower bound. Therefore, we would let 37,900 be the new lower bound. This is also the best solution for the subproblems at the ends of the branches (*P3*, *P4*, *P7*, *P8*, and *P9*), and thus this becomes the new upper bound as well. Because the lower bound is equal to the upper bound, the solution that generated this lower bound must be the optimal solution.

We also could determine this solution is optimal because at this point all the branches have been evaluated. The final node on each branch either indicated an integer solution, or an infeasible solution, or a solution with an objective function value lower than the lower bound. Therefore, all possible solutions have been either explicitly or implicitly evaluated. The optimal solution is:

$$\begin{aligned} &X_1 = 4 \\ &X_2 = 1 \\ &\text{objective function value} = 37{,}900 \end{aligned}$$

Looking at what this solution means to Katherine Blissit, the manager of Cypress Country, we see that four prime time ads should be placed and only one ad at other times should be used. This results in 37,900 people being reached by the advertising. If the original solution to the LP had simply been rounded off, there would have been two prime time ads and four others. This would have reached 36,800 per week. Thus, by using integer programming to solve this problem, Katherine may reach an additional 1,100 people every week.

Output 7.4 provides the output obtained when this problem is solved using LINDO. Notice eight branches are used in solving this problem, and each branch corresponds to one of the subproblems.

The steps of the Branch and Bound Algorithm for solving integer linear programming maximization problems are provided in Summary Table 7.1. For minimization problems, only slight modifications in this algorithm are required. The terms *upper bound* and *lower bound* are simply reversed in this

FIGURE 7.5

Final Solution for Cypress Country Example

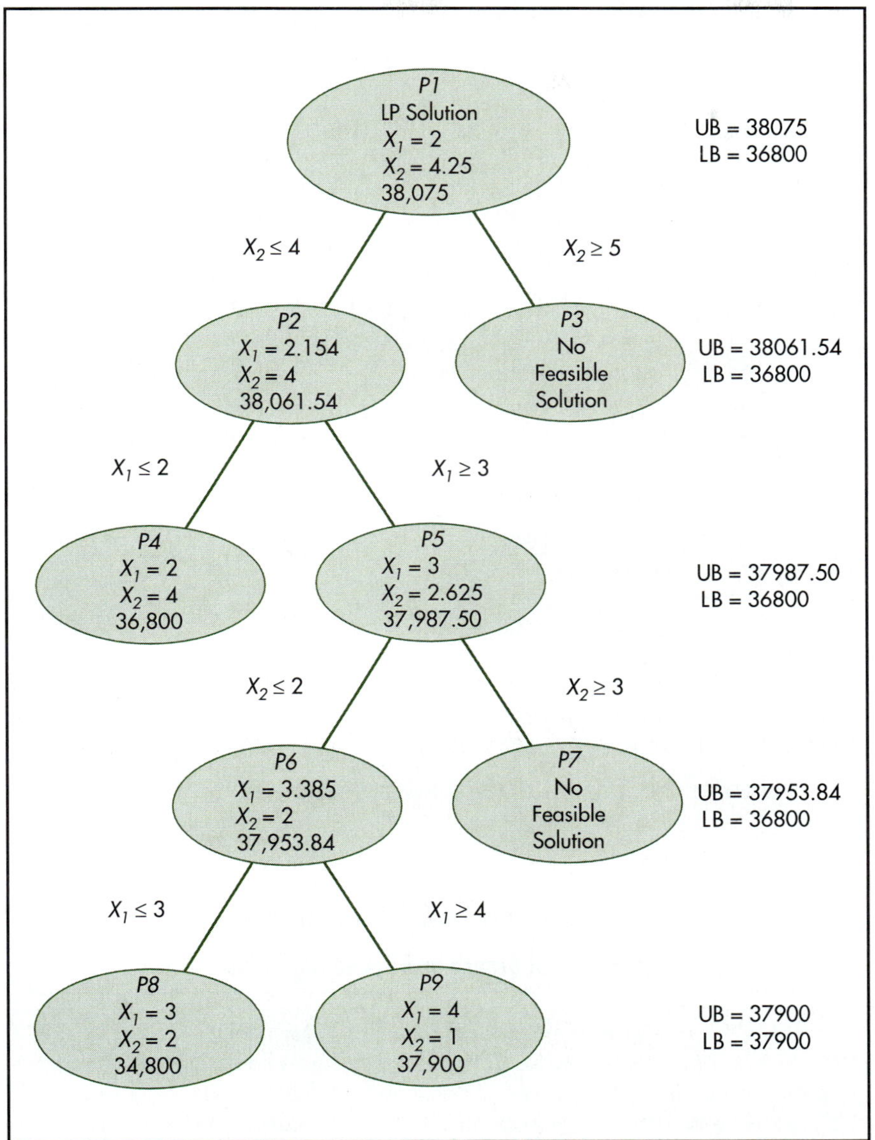

algorithm. The solution to the relaxed problem in Step 1 is used as a lower bound on the value of the objective function for the ILP problem. Also in Step 1, an upper bound instead of a lower bound is developed through inspection or other means. In Step 4, the best solution at the branch ends becomes the lower bound. In Step 5, the best integer solution to the subproblems becomes the new upper bound. The rest of the algorithm does not change.

OUTPUT 7.4

LINDO Output for the Cypress Country Example as ILP

```
MAX      8200 X1 + 5100 X2
SUBJECT TO
        2)    X1 >=   2
        3)    X2 <=   6
        4)    390 X1 + 240 X2 <=   1800
END

      OBJECTIVE FUNCTION VALUE

      1)      37900.000

VARIABLE        VALUE          REDUCED COST
      X1         4.000000         87.500000
      X2         1.000000          .000000

     ROW   SLACK OR SURPLUS     DUAL PRICES
      2)         2.000000          .000000
      3)         5.000000          .000000
      4)          .000000        21.250000

NO. ITERATIONS=       18
BRANCHES=     8 DETERM.=  1.000E    0
BOUND ON OPTIMUM:  37900.00
DELETE        X1 AT LEVEL     4
DELETE        X2 AT LEVEL     3
DELETE        X1 AT LEVEL     2
DELETE        X2 AT LEVEL     1
ENUMERATION COMPLETE. BRANCHES=     8 PIVOTS=      18

LAST INTEGER SOLUTION IS THE BEST FOUND
```

SUMMARY TABLE 7.1

Summary of Branch and Bound Algorithm

Summary of Branch and Bound (B & B) Algorithm

STEP 1. Solve the LP relaxation. Set upper bound (UB) = value of the objective function for LP relaxation. Develop a lower bound (LB) on the value of the ILP objective function by finding any feasible integer solution.

STEP 2. Select a variable that is not integer in the solution to the previous problem. Create two subproblems by restricting a variable to be less than or equal to the integer portion of its current value, and restricting it to be greater than or equal to the next higher integer. Add each of these separately to the previous problem and create two new subproblems.

STEP 3. Solve the new subproblems.

STEP 4. Set UB = the best objective function value for problems at all branch ends.

STEP 5. If the solution to a subproblem is integer valued and has an objective function value greater than the lower bound, change LB to this new value. If LB = UB, the optimal solution is the integer solution that yielded the LB. If not, continue.

STEP 6. From the subproblems with feasible, noninteger solutions, select the one with the best objective function value. Go to Step 2.

Integer Programming Helps Bellcore Optimize Research Spending

Research and development (R & D) is a key element in the race to be globally competitive. However, paying for R & D can be costly. Businesses with similar interests can sometimes overcome the high costs by joining together to establish a research company. The seven regional local telephone companies did this when they formed Bell Communications Research (Bellcore). One of Bellcore's goals is to provide the most value to its seven companies, called the Bellcore Client Companies, or BCCs.

Bellcore organizes its research into products (i.e., synchronous optical networks), each of which can contain several different projects. Although projects can contain multiple deliverables, whole projects are Bellcore's smallest unit of sale to its member companies. Some projects are funded by all seven BCCs because they are important to the overall industry infrastructure. Other projects, however, are elective. They can be funded by one to seven of the BCCs. Each BCC elects to fund projects that are most valuable to itself, and that fit within its budget. Only companies that fund a given project have access to its deliverables.

Researchers at Bellcore use nonlinear integer programming to arrange additional elective project buy-ins for each BCC. The constraints on the model require the BCCs stay within their spending targets, and that each BCC receives high-benefit projects. Using the model, Bellcore increased participation in elective projects by 30 percent, without changing the overall elective project budget. Since then, the integer programming model has become an integral part of Bellcore's budgeting process.

SOURCE:
Hoadley, B., P. Katz, and A. Sadrian, January-February 1993. "Improving the Utility of the Bellcore Consortium." *Interfaces* 23 (1): 27-43.

7.9 ADDITIONAL NOTES ON THE B & B ALGORITHM

While the Branch and Bound Algorithm is the most widely used technique for solving ILP problems and theoretically can solve any such problem, you should be aware that difficulties do exist. The example presented here was very small. For larger problems, the number of subproblems can be so large that keeping track of all of them can strain the memory limitations of computers. Because there are so many subproblems, the time required to reach the optimal solution may be excessive. Because of this, some software allows you to place limits on the total time that the problem runs or on the number of subproblems that are solved. Fortunately, good solutions usually are found rather quickly, and the manager may use the current best integer solution, the one which yields the current lower bound, even if it is not optimal. Some software packages will allow the user to specify that the problem should be terminated when the lower bound of the integer solution is within a certain percentage of the upper bound. Thus, if a solution that is within one percent or two percent of the upper bound is acceptable to the manager, this can be specified and the algorithm stops when this target is reached.

There have been many modifications of the Branch and Bound (B & B) Algorithm. Special rules have been used to determine which variable to select for branching when there are several variables that are not integer valued. Selecting the subproblem to use next for branching also has received a lot of attention, and this can have a significant impact on the time required to reach the optimal solution. (*Note:* There are references at the end of the book to indicate where additional information on these may be found.)

7.10

INTRODUCTION TO GOAL PROGRAMMING

While the LP and ILP problems examined all had a single objective, there are many times when management may have more than one objective. Perhaps management would like to maximize profit but also would like to minimize idle time in a department. We could not use linear programming and express both of these as objective functions because only one objective function is allowed. However, we could use **goal programming** to handle situations like this. Goal programming also may be helpful when we find no feasible solution to a linear programming problem.

Goal programming
A procedure based on linear programming that allows several goals to be considered instead of just one single objective.

The basic approach in goal programming is to identify specific goals to be reached. For example, a targeted profit amount may be listed as one goal while total utilization of the labor hours available may be another. The goals would be expressed as constraints in the problem, although they are flexible in that deviations from these are allowed. Variables called overachievement variables and underachievement variables allow these deviations, as will be seen in the next section. The objective function in a goal programming problem is to minimize the deviations from the goals. If the total deviation is zero, then all goals are met.

7.11

FORMULATING GOAL PROGRAMMING PROBLEMS

To illustrate how goal programming problems are formulated, consider the situation faced by management at Thompson Computers. This company produces two types of personal computers—Model BP6 and Model BP8. Table 7.3 provides information regarding the profit generated and the resource requirements for these computers. There are currently 480 hours of electronic technician time and 200 hours of assembly and packaging time available each week, although some overtime may be used if necessary. Also, management would like to minimize the amount of idle time by both the electronic technicians and the assemblers and packagers. Management has determined at least 70 computers of each type should be produced every week to meet the anticipated demand. While profit is important, management would be happy with a profit of $7,000 each week, which management has made a goal.

This may appear similar to situations where linear programming has been used. However, management does not have a single objective but rather has several goals. To formulate this as a goal programming problem,

TABLE 7.3

Profit and Resource Information for Thompson Computers

	Profit	Electronic Technician Time	Assembly & Packaging Time
Model BP6	$30	3	1
Model BP8	$70	4	2
Hours per Week		480	200

first specifically identify the goals as well as any constraints in the problem. The goals are listed below.

1. Generate a profit of at least $7,000 per week.
2. Use 480 hours of electronic technician time every week.
3. Use 200 hours of assembly and packaging time every week.
4. Produce at least 70 Model BP6 computers every week.
5. Produce at least 70 Model BP8 computers every week.

All of these have been specified as goals by management instead of rigid constraints. If there had been other strict constraints in this problem, they would be specified as constraints and the procedure for the formulation of these would have been the same procedure used in linear programming.

Developing the Constraints

Once the goals have been identified, define the decision variables and set up the problem. Each goal will be expressed as a constraint in the problem.

In this situation the decision variables will be defined as:

X_1 = number of Model BP6 computers produced each week

X_2 = number of Model BP8 computers produced each week

We will use these variables to develop mathematical expressions for each goal. Writing mathematical expressions for the five goals results in:

$30X_1 + 70X_2 \geq 7{,}000$ profit

$3X_1 + 4X_2 = 480$ electronic technician time utilization

$X_1 + 2X_2 = 200$ assembly & packaging time utilization

$X_1 \geq 70$ demand for Model BP6 computers

$X_2 \geq 70$ demand for Model BP8 computers

If these were left in the current form, they would require that the conditions be completely met. However, these are merely goals, so as to allow the possibility that this is not met. Therefore, define **deviational variables** and put these into these goal constraints. For the first goal, let:

Deviational variables
Variables used in goal programming problems to allow possible deviations from the stated goals.

d_1^+ = amount by which profit exceeds 7,000

d_1^- = amount by which profit is below 7,000

Putting these into the constraint equation results in:

$$30X_1 + 70X_2 - d_1^+ + d_1^- = 7000$$

This allows the total profit to be above or below 7,000. Deviational variables with the plus (+) sign (such as d_1^+) often are called **overachievement variables** while those with the minus (–) sign often are called **underachievement variables**. The overachievement variables are similar to surplus variables while the underachievement variables are similar to slack variables.

Overachievement variables
Deviational variables used in a goal programming problem to indicate how much a targeted amount has been exceeded.

Underachievement variables
Deviational variables used in a goal programming problem to indicate the amount by which a targeted amount is not met.

To develop the goal constraints for each of the other goals, define the following deviational variables to allow deviations from targeted goals:

d_2^+ = amount by which electronic technician time used exceeds 480 hours
d_2^- = amount by which electronic technician time used is below 480 hours
d_3^+ = amount by which assembly & packaging time used exceeds 200 hours
d_3^- = amount by which assembly & packaging time used is below 200 hours
d_4^+ = amount by which number of Model BP6 computers exceeds 70
d_4^- = amount by which number of Model BP6 computers is less than 70
d_5^+ = amount by which number of Model BP8 computers exceeds 70
d_5^- = amount by which number of Model BP8 computers is less than 70

These last four goals are then expressed as:

$3X_1 + 4X_2 - d_2^+ + d_2^- = 480$ electronic technician time
$X_1 + 2X_2 - d_3^+ + d_3^- = 200$ assembly & packaging time
$X_1 - d_4^+ + d_4^- = 70$ Model BP6 computers
$X_2 - d_5^+ + d_5^- = 70$ Model BP8 computers

Notice if all the deviational variables are equal to zero, then every goal would be met with no overachievement or underachievement. If any deviational variable is not zero, then the goal associated with that deviational variable may have some overachievement or underachievement.

Developing the Objective Function for Goal Programming Problems

Because the deviational variables must equal zero for a goal to be met, the objective function in a goal programming problem will be to minimize the total of some or all of the deviational variables.

To formulate the objective function, we must decide which deviational variables to include. The first goal is to generate at least $7,000 profit per week, but more would certainly be no problem. If the profit is more than $7,000, then d_1^+ is positive. Therefore, we would not want to minimize d_1^+, but we do want to minimize d_1^- because a positive value for this would indicate the profit is less than $7,000. For the two labor-hour goals (constraints 2 and 3), the goal is to totally utilize the hours available and to avoid overtime. Therefore, we would like the deviational variables d_2^+, d_2^-, d_3^+, and d_3^- to be minimized. For the last two constraints, management has decided there is not a problem if more than 70 computers of each type were produced, but we wish to minimize underachievement of these goals. This means that we would like d_4^- and d_5^- to equal zero if possible. Therefore, the objective function for this would be:

$$\text{Minimize } d_1^- + d_2^+ + d_2^- + d_3^+ + d_3^- + d_4^- + d_5^-$$

The complete goal programming formulation for this would be:

$$\begin{aligned}
&\text{Minimize } d_1^- + d_2^+ + d_2^- + d_3^+ + d_3^- + d_4^- + d_5^- \\
&\text{Subject to: } 30X_1 + 70X_2 - d_1^+ + d_1^- = 7000 \quad \text{profit} \\
&3X_1 + 4X_2 - d_2^+ + d_2^- = 480 \quad \text{electronic technician time} \\
&X_1 + 2X_2 - d_3^+ + d_3^- = 200 \quad \text{assembly \& packaging time} \\
&X_1 - d_4^+ + d_4^- = 70 \quad \text{Model BP6 computers} \\
&X_2 - d_5^+ + d_5^- = 70 \quad \text{Model BP8 computers} \\
&X_1, X_2, d_1^+, d_1^-, d_2^+, d_2^-, d_3^+, d_3^-, d_4^+, d_4^-, d_5^+, d_5^- \geq 0
\end{aligned}$$

Solving this using computer software for linear programming, we have the output shown in Output 7.5. Note that the deviational variables used in this computer solution are defined as O_i for overachievement of goal i and U_i as underachievement of goal i. The solution is:

$X_1 = 62.22$	Model BP6 computers
$X_2 = 73.33$	Model BP8 computers
$d_3^+ (O3) = 8.89$	overutilization of assembly & packaging time
$d_4^- (U4) = 7.78$	number of Model BP6 computers less than target of 70
$d_5^+ (O5) = 3.33$	number of Model BP8 computers more than target of 70

All other deviational variables are equal to zero.

Evaluating this solution indicates the number of computers is not integer valued, but because these represent the number produced each week, this is not a problem. The production of a computer could be started one week and finished the next, so fractional values have meaning in this problem and this does not have to be solved as an integer programming problem. There are 8.89 hours of overtime for assembly & packaging time ($d_3^+ = 8.89$), and the number of computers of each type do not exactly equal the goal of 70 ($d_4^- = 7.78$ and $d_5^+ = 3.33$). Because the other deviational variables are zero, we know the $7,000 profit generated goal is met. The electronic technician time used is equal to the 480 hours available.

This solution may cause some questions to be raised and perhaps some modifications should be made to better reflect the intentions of management. Are the goals of 70 computers each week intended to be absolute minimums that must be met if it is possible to do so? If this is the case, then the underachievement variables should be omitted from these constraints. Thus, the last two constraints could have been expressed as:

$$X_1 - d_4^+ = 70 \quad \text{Model BP6 computers}$$
$$X_2 - d_5^+ = 70 \quad \text{Model BP8 computers}$$

If the overtime for each of the departments is limited to a specific number of hours per week, we could add constraints that force this to occur. For

OUTPUT 7.5

LINDO Output for Thompson Computers Goal Programming Problem

```
MIN     U1 + O2 + U2 + O3 + U3 + U4 + U5
SUBJECT TO
       2)   U1 + 30 X1 + 70 X2 - O1 =     7000
       3) - O2 + U2 + 3 X1 + 4 X2 =    480
       4) - O3 + U3 + X1 + 2 X2 =    200
       5)   U4 + X1 - O4 =    70
       6)   U5 + X2 - O5 =    70
END

 LP OPTIMUM FOUND AT STEP      5

        OBJECTIVE FUNCTION VALUE

        1)      16.666670

 VARIABLE        VALUE          REDUCED COST
       U1         .000000           .933333
       O2         .000000           .333333
       U2         .000000          1.666667
       O3        8.888889           .000000
       U3         .000000          2.000000
       U4        7.777778           .000000
       U5         .000000          1.000000
       X1       62.222220           .000000
       X2       73.333340           .000000
       O1         .000000           .066667
       O4         .000000          1.000000
       O5        3.333333           .000000

      ROW   SLACK OR SURPLUS     DUAL PRICES
       2)         .000000         -.066667
       3)         .000000          .666667
       4)         .000000         1.000000
       5)         .000000        -1.000000
       6)         .000000          .000000

 NO. ITERATIONS=        5
```

example, if each department could only have five hours of overtime, the following two constraints would be added:

$d_2^+ \leq 5$ overtime for electronic technicians

$d_3^+ \leq 5$ overtime for assembly & packaging

If any of these had been constraints that must be met instead of goals, simply omit all deviational variables from them.

Further evaluation of this model indicates all deviational variables are equally important in the objective function despite the fact they represent different things. The variables d_1^+ and d_1^- represent dollars of profit that the solution is away from the goal, while d_4^- and d_5^- represent deviations from a goal for the number of Model BP6 and Model BP8 computers to produce. Is missing the profit goal by \$1, which is only 0.04 percent of the target profit, as important as missing the number of Model BP6 computers by one

BEST PRACTICES

Goal Programming to Plan a New CIM Facility

In 1987, the Department of Engineering Management at the University of Missouri - Rolla received 5,072 square feet of floor space to be developed into a computer integrated manufacturing (CIM) lab. The department saw the new lab as a tremendous resource that would stimulate interest in teaching and research and evolve into a center of technical excellence for industry in Missouri. The university viewed the new lab as a campus-wide resource, to be used by all engineering departments and research centers. Naturally, these conflicting viewpoints resulted in considerable debate concerning the best layout for the new facility.

The Department of Engineering Management established an in-house planning team to make recommendations to the School of Engineering. The team first used an analytic hierarchy process to rank five conflicting teaching, research, and university service goals for the CIM lab. They also identified 15 sections to be found in the CIM lab, each of which would support one or more of the goals. They then used a sequential linear goal programming (SLGP) algorithm to solve for space allocation factors for the 15 areas. To implement the algorithm, they partitioned the objective function according to priority levels based on the five goals. They solved the resulting linear programming models sequentially, and used the solution obtained at each level as a constraint on the next lower level.

The facilities-planning committee used the space allocation recommended by the SLGP model as a guide in developing the initial layout of the CIM lab. The School of Engineering accepted the department's proposals, although the current layout includes some modifications to adapt to additional equipment. Overall, the lab has fulfilled its teaching, research, and university service objectives.

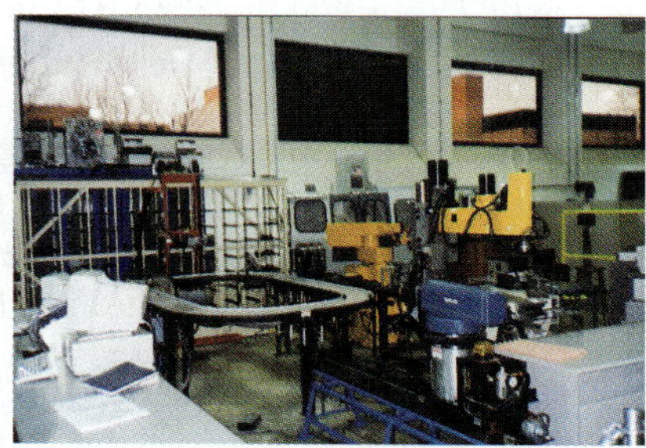

Courtesy of the Department of Engineering Management, University of Missouri - Rolla

SOURCE: Benjamin, C. O., I. C. Ehie, and Y. Omurtag, 1992. "Planning Facilities at the University of Missouri - Rolla." *Interfaces* 22 (4): 95-105.

computer, which is 4 percent of the target amount? Is missing the profit goal by $1 equivalent to utilizing one hour of overtime in the assembly & packaging process? Because the deviational variables represent different things, merely minimizing the sum of the relevant deviations may not produce what management considers satisfactory results. For this reason, we may wish to use weighted goals.

7.12 GOAL PROGRAMMING WITH WEIGHTED GOALS

If all the goals are equally important, the objective function would be to minimize the sum of the relevant deviational variables. If some goals may be expressed as being twice (or three times or another multiple) as important as another goal, then *weights* may be assigned to the relevant deviational variables. If some goals totally dominate other goals, place each goal in a priority level indicating the order of importance. A goal in the highest priority level would have to be met as closely as possible first before any other goal is even considered.

Weighted Goals

In considering the Thompson Computers problem, suppose management has decided the labor-hour goals (goals 2 and 3) are four times as important as the profit goal. Management also has decided the last two goals related to the number of computers of each type to produce are eight times as important as the profit goal. Given these relative weights for the goals, we would modify the objective function to reflect the importance of the goals by multiplying the deviational variables by these weights. The least important goal is given the weight of one, and the others are multiples of this. Thus, we would have the following goal programming problem with weighted goals:

Minimize $d_1^- + 4d_2^+ + 4d_2^- + 4d_3^+ + 4d_3^- + 8d_4^- + 8d_5^-$

Subject to:	$30X_1 + 70X_2 - d_1^- + d_1^- = 7000$	profit
	$3X_1 + 4X_2 - d_2^+ + d_2^- = 480$	electronic technician time
	$X_1 + 2X_2 - d_3^+ + d_3^- = 200$	assembly & packaging time
	$X_1 - d_4^+ + d_4^- = 70$	Model BP6 computers
	$X_2 - d_5^+ + d_5^- = 70$	Model BP8 computers

$X_1, X_2, d_1^+, d_1^-, d_2^+, d_2^-, d_3^+, d_3^-, d_4^+, d_4^-, d_5^+, d_4^- \geq 0$

Solving this with linear programming software results in the following solution:

$X_1 = 70$	Model BP6 computers
$X_2 = 70$	Model BP8 computers
$d_2^+ = 10$	overtime for electronic technicians
$d_3^+ = 10$	overtime for assemblers & packagers

All other deviational variables are equal to zero.

This solution shows 70 units of each type of computer would be produced. To do this, use 10 hours of overtime for electronic technician time and 10 hours of overtime for assembly & packaging time. The profit goal totally is met as are the goals for the number of computers of each type. This solution might be very desirable for management because only two goals are not met and the overtime hours are small relative to the total number of hours originally scheduled.

Establishing Weights to Minimize Percentage Deviations

While managers may clearly understand their goals, they may not understand how assigning weights to deviational variables may impact the final solution. In some situations a manager may say that one goal is twice as important as another goal, but due to the way the goals have been constructed, deviations from one goal may not be twice as important as deviations from another goal. Consider the profit goal in the Thompson Computers example. The original statement of this goal was:

$$30X_1 + 70X_2 - d_1^+ + d_1^- = 7000$$

A deviation of one unit ($d_1^- = 1$) means the profit goal is missed by \$1. If this profit goal had been expressed in thousands instead of in dollars, it would have been stated as:

$$0.030X_1 + 0.070X_2 - d_1^+ + d_1^- = 7$$

Now a deviation of one unit ($d_1^- = 1$) means the profit goal is missed by \$1,000. This change in scaling implicitly gives different weights to the deviations that are totally independent of the importance of the goals as stated by the manager.

To better reflect how management may view the goals and deviations from the goals, it often is appealing to minimize the total percent of deviation from the goals. One way of doing this is to assign a weight for each deviational variable equal to 1/(target amount or right-hand side value). The objective function developed in this way would actually represent proportions instead of percentages, but multiplying these weights by 100 would convert them to percentages and the optimal solution is not affected by multiplying all deviations by 100. In the Thompson Computers example, the goal programming problem would be:

$$\text{Minimize } (1/7000)d_1^- + (1/480)d_2^+ + (1/480)d_2^- + (1/200)d_3^+ + (1/200)d_3^- + (1/70)d_4^- + (1/70)d_5^-$$

Subject to:	$30X_1 + 70X_2 - d_1^+ + d_1^- = 7000$	profit
	$3X_1 + 4X_2 - d_2^+ + d_2^- = 480$	electronic technician time
	$X_1 + 2X_2 - d_3^+ + d_3^- = 200$	assembly & packaging time
	$X_1 - d_4^+ + d_4^- = 70$	Model BP6 computers
	$X_2 - d_5^+ + d_5^- = 70$	Model BP8 computers

$$X_1, X_2, d_1^+, d_1^-, d_2^+, d_2^-, d_3^+, d_3^-, d_4^+, d_4^-, d_5^+, d_5^- \geq 0$$

The LINDO output for this problem is shown in Output 7.6. The solution is:

$X_1 = 70$	Model BP6 computers
$X_2 = 70$	Model BP8 computers
d_2^+ (O2) = 10	overutilization of electronic technician time
d_3^+ (O3) = 10	overutilization of assembly & packaging time

Notice the objective function value may be found by $(1/480)d_2^+ + (1/200)d_3^+ = (1/480)10 + (1/200)10 = .0708$. Thus, this solution misses the goals by a total deviation of 7.08 percent.

There is an alternative way to do this same thing that has an advantage in the interpretation of the results. Before adding the deviational variables, divide each equation by its right-hand side value to make this right-hand side equal one. Then multiply the equation by 100 to make the right-hand side equal 100 representing 100 percent achievement of the goal. After this is done, add the deviational variables, which now will represent the percentage deviation from the goal. The value of the objective function is the

OUTPUT 7.6

LINDO Output for Thompson Computers Goal Programming Problem with Weights as Percentages of Goals

```
  MIN      0.0001428 U1 + 0.0020833 O2 + 0.0020833 U2 + 0.005 O3 + 0.005 U3   +
0.01428 U4 + 0.01428 U5
  SUBJECT TO
         2)    U1 + 30 X1 + 70 X2 - O1 =     7000
         3) - O2 + U2 + 3 X1 + 4 X2 =     480
         4) - O3 + U3 + X1 + 2 X2 =    200
         5)    U4 + X1 - O4 =    70
         6)    U5 + X2 - O5 =    70
  END

 LP OPTIMUM FOUND AT STEP       7

        OBJECTIVE FUNCTION VALUE

        1)      .70833000E-01

  VARIABLE        VALUE          REDUCED COST
        U1          .000000          .000085
        O2        10.000000          .000000
        U2          .000000          .004167
        O3        10.000000          .000000
        U3          .000000          .010000
        U4          .000000          .004767
        U5          .000000          .000000
        X1        70.000000          .000000
        X2        70.000000          .000000
        O1          .000000          .000058
        O4          .000000          .009513
        O5          .000000          .014280

       ROW   SLACK OR SURPLUS     DUAL PRICES
        2)          .000000         -.000058
        3)          .000000          .002083
        4)          .000000          .005000
        5)          .000000         -.009513
        6)          .000000         -.014280

 NO. ITERATIONS=        7
```

total of the percentage deviations from all the goals. In the Thompson Computers example, this would be:

Minimize $d_1^- + d_2^+ + d_2^- + d_3^+ + d_3^- + d_4^- + d_5^-$

Subject to: $(3000/7000)X_1 + (7000/7000)X_2 - d_1^+ + d_1^- = 100$ profit

$(300/480)X_1 + (400/480)X_2 - d_2^+ + d_2^- = 100$ electronic technician time

$$(100/200)X_1 + (200/200)X_2 - d_3^+ + d_3^- = 100 \quad \text{assembly \& packaging time}$$

$$(100/70)X_1 - d_4^+ + d_4^- = 100 \quad \text{Model BP6 computers}$$

$$(100/70)X_2 - d_5^+ + d_5^- = 100 \quad \text{Model BP8 computers}$$

$$X_1, X_2, d_1^+, d_1^-, d_2^+, d_2^-, d_3^+, d_3^-, d_4^+, d_4^-, d_5^+, d_5^- \geq 0$$

These constraints could be simplified, and the problem could be solved using available linear programming software. LINDO output for this is shown in Output 7.7. This solution is:

$X_1 = 70$	Model BP6 computers
$X_2 = 70$	Model BP8 computers
d_2^+ (O2) = 2.08	overutilization of electronic technician time
d_3^+ (O3) = 5.00	overutilization of assembly & packaging time

Notice in this solution, the deviational variables represent the percentage deviations, and the objective function value is the 7.08. Comparing this with the solution above in Output 7.6 indicates the solutions are equivalent.

There may be situations where one goal absolutely must be met if possible, and deviations from other goals only should be minimized if they do not impact deviations from the most important goal. This could be accomplished by using goal programming with preemptive priorities.

7.13 GOAL PROGRAMMING WITH PREEMPTIVE PRIORITIES

Using **preemptive priorities** in goal programming means that goals are placed in priority levels based on the importance of the goals. All goals in the most important priority level, which will be called level 1, must be met as closely as possible before other goals are considered. Once the minimum deviations from the goals in priority level 1 have been determined, then priority level 2 is considered. Deviations from the goals in level 2 are then minimized while restricting deviations from goals in level 1 to equal the minimum amount previously determined for these. Only after the first two priority levels are considered will priority level 3 be considered. This process continues until the last priority level is evaluated.

Preemptive priorities
Priorities assigned to goals that force the most important goals to be satisfied before lesser goals are considered.

The key concept with this preemptive priority approach is that once minimum deviations from goals in a particular priority level are found, additional deviations for these are not permitted as additional goals in lesser priority levels are considered.

Preemptive Priorities for Thompson Computers Example

We will illustrate the use of preemptive priorities with the Thompson Computers example previously presented. The first step is to determine what

OUTPUT 7.7

LINDO Output for Thompson Computers Goal Programming Problem with Constraints as Percentage Goals

```
 MIN     U1 + O2 + U2 + O3 + U3 + U4 + U5
 SUBJECT TO
        2)   U1 + 0.42857 X1 + X2 - O1 =    100
        3) - O2 + U2 + 0.625 X1 + 0.83333 X2 =    100
        4) - O3 + U3 + 0.5 X1 + X2 =    100
        5)   U4 + 1.42857 X1 - O4 =    100
        6)   U5 + 1.42857 X2 - O5 =    100
 END

LP OPTIMUM FOUND AT STEP      7

       OBJECTIVE FUNCTION VALUE

       1)     7.0833030

 VARIABLE        VALUE          REDUCED COST
       U1         .000002           .000000
       O2        2.083198           .000000
       U2         .000000          2.000000
       O3        5.000103           .000000
       U3         .000000          2.000000
       U4         .000000           .512498
       U5         .000000           .416668
       X1       70.000070           .000000
       X2       70.000070           .000000
       O1         .000000          1.000000
       O4         .000000           .487501
       O5         .000000           .583332

      ROW   SLACK OR SURPLUS     DUAL PRICES
       2)         .000000         -1.000000
       3)         .000000          1.000000
       4)         .000000          1.000000
       5)         .000000          -.487501
       6)         .000000          -.583332

NO. ITERATIONS=       7
```

priority will be given to each goal. Let us assume the profit goal is the most important goal and this is put in priority level 1. The labor-hour goals both will be placed in priority level 2. The goals of producing 70 Model BP6 and 70 Model BP8 computers will be placed in level 3. The statement of the problem will be:

$$\text{Minimize } P_1d_1^- + P_2d_2^+ + P_2d_2^- + P_2d_3^+ + P_2d_3^- + P_3d_4^- + P_3d_5^-$$

$$\text{Subject to: } 30X_1 + 70X_2 - d_1^+ + d_1^- = 7000 \quad \text{profit}$$

$3X_1 + 4X_2 - d_2^+ + d_2^- = 480$	electronic technician time
$X_1 + 2X_2 - d_3^+ + d_3^- = 200$	assembly & packaging time
$X_1 - d_4^+ + d_4^- = 70$	Model BP6 computers
$X_2 - d_5^+ + d_5^- = 70$	Model BP8 computers

$$X_1, X_2, d_1^+, d_1^-, d_2^+, d_2^-, d_3^+, d_3^-, d_4^+, d_4^-, d_5^+, d_5^- \geq 0$$

It is important to note that P_1, P_2, and P_3 do not represent numbers. They simply identify the priority level for each goal.

While there is software that will solve goal programming problems with preemptive priorities, we will illustrate the process using standard linear programming procedures. This process is the basis for most computer software for solving prioritized goal programming problems.

Solving Preemptive Priority Goal Programming Problems

To solve problems where preemptive priorities are used, start with the goal in priority level 1 and develop an objective function based solely on deviations from these goals. In the Thompson Computers example, only one goal is in level 1, and the wish is to minimize the underachievement of this profit goal (d_1^-). The goal programming problem for level 1 is:

Minimize d_1^-

Subject to: $30X_1 + 70X_2 - d_1^+ + d_1^- = 7000$	profit
$3X_1 + 4X_2 - d_2^+ + d_2^- = 480$	electronic technician time
$X_1 + 2X_2 - d_3^+ + d_3^- = 200$	assembly & packaging time
$X_1 - d_4^+ + d_4^- = 70$	Model BP6 computers
$X_2 - d_5^+ + d_5^- = 70$	Model BP8 computers

$$X_1, X_2, d_1^+, d_1^-, d_2^+, d_2^-, d_3^+, d_3^-, d_4^+, d_4^-, d_5^+, d_5^- \geq 0$$

Using standard linear programming software the problem is solved where the objective function value is zero. This means the profit goal is met exactly. As the deviations for the other goals are minimized, the achievement of the profit goal must be maintained. This means d_1^- must equal zero in all later problems. Therefore, we will add

$$d_1^- = 0$$

as a constraint when considering the other priority levels. The problem that will be solved for priority level 2 will have this as a constraint and the objective function will contain the deviations associated with goals in priority level 2. Because we wish to use exactly the number of hours available, we would like all the deviational variables associated with these to equal zero if possible. The objective function will be to minimize all of the deviational variables for these goals. This goal programming problem is:

Minimize	$d_2^+ + d_2^- + d_3^+ + d_3^-$	
Subject to:	$30X_1 + 70X_2 - d_1^+ + d_1^- = 7000$	profit
	$3X_1 + 4X_2 - d_2^+ + d_2^- = 480$	electronic technician time
	$X_1 + 2X_2 - d_3^+ + d_3^- = 200$	assembly & packaging time
	$X_1 - d_4^+ + d_4^- = 70$	Model BP6 computers
	$X_2 - d_5^+ + d_5^- = 70$	Model BP8 computers
	$d_1^- = 0$	priority level 1

$$X_1, X_2, d_1^+, d_1^-, d_2^+, d_2^-, d_3^+, d_3^-, d_4^+, d_4^-, d_5^+, d_5^- \geq 0$$

Solving this with the help of linear programming software and a computer results in an objective function value of 8.8889. This is the minimum possible for the sum of the deviations in this objective function.

After the solution for priority level 2 is found, add a constraint to the problem restricting the value of the objective function for priority level 2 to equal the minimum value found in this solution. This is:

$$d_2^+ + d_2^- + d_3^+ + d_3^- = 8.889$$

We develop the new objective function based on the deviations from the goals in level 3. We wish to produce at least 70 computers of each type, therefore the variables d_4^- and d_5^- should equal zero or be minimized. The variables d_4^+ and d_5^+ represent the number produced above 70, and management is not concerned if more than 70 are produced. This gives the following goal programming problem:

Minimize	$d_4^- + d_5^-$	
Subject to:	$30X_1 + 70X_2 - d_1^+ + d_1^- = 7000$	profit
	$3X_1 + 4X_2 - d_2^+ + d_2^- = 480$	electronic technician time
	$X_1 + 2X_2 - d_3^+ + d_3^- = 200$	assembly & packaging time
	$X_1 - d_4^+ + d_4^- = 70$	Model BP6 computers
	$X_2 - d_5^+ + d_5^- = 70$	Model BP8 computers
	$d_1^- = 0$	priority level 1
	$d_2^+ + d_2^- + d_3^+ + d_3^- = 8.889$	priority level 2

$$X_1, X_2, d_1^+, d_1^-, d_2^+, d_2^-, d_3^+, d_3^-, d_4^+, d_4^-, d_5^+, d_4^- \geq 0$$

Solving results in the following:

$X_1 = 62.222$	Model BP6 computers
$X_2 = 73.333$	Model BP8 computers
$d_3^+ = 8.889$	overtime for assembly & packaging

$d_4^- = 7.778$ number of Model BP6 computers less than 70

$d_5^+ = 3.333$ number of Model BP8 computers more than 70

objective function value = 7.777 deviations for level 3

all other variables = 0

Because this is the last priority level, this represents the solution to the original goal programming problem. This, and the solutions above, indicate the goal in priority level 1 is met completely (d_1^- and $d_1^+ = 0$, profit = 7,000). The goals in priority level 2 (labor utilization) have a total deviation of 8.889. The goals in priority level 3 (number of computers) have a total underachievement deviation of 7.778.

Additional Comments about Goal Programming

We have seen how to use weights and priority levels in goal programming. At times, the two techniques are combined as weights are used within priority levels. In the Thompson Computers example, if management were more concerned about using all labor hours than it was about having to use overtime, different weights would be assigned to these. Perhaps a weight of 2 would be given to the underutilization variables and the objective function for the problem involving priority level 2 would be:

$$\text{Minimize } d_2^+ + 2d_2^- + d_3^+ + 2d_3^-$$

The problem would then be solved as before.

There are difficulties in assigning weights when using weighted goal programming. A manager may know which goals are most important, but the relative importance is sometimes not so clear. Using priority levels eliminates this problem, but it essentially says that goals in level 1 are infinitely more important than goals in other levels.

In solving goal programming with priority levels using linear programming software, a person may be tempted to simply assign a very high weight to deviations from priority level 1, a smaller weight for deviations in the next priority level, and even smaller weights for deviations in the next level. This may be 1,000,000 for priority level 1, 10,000 for priority level 2, and 1,000 for priority level 3. While conceptually this may be appealing, practically it may create round-off problems in a computer and should therefore be avoided.

7.14 SUMMARY

In this chapter we saw how to formulate problems as integer linear programming problems. The use of 0-1 variables has enabled managers to develop models for many different types of situations. The Branch and Bound (B & B) Algorithm was illustrated to show how integer linear programming problems normally are solved. We noted that ILP problems are much more difficult to solve than LP problems.

Goal programming was used to model situations where multiple objectives or goals existed. In developing goal programming models, deviations from the goals are to be minimized. Assigning weights to the deviations allows management to place more importance on some goals than on others. Using preemptive priorities allows management to obtain the best possible solutions for specific goals while also giving consideration to lesser goals.

As with linear programming, it is important for a manager to carefully evaluate the final solution to see if it is appropriate for the managerial problem. While the solution found must be the best solution for the goal programming problem, the goal programming model may not accurately reflect the managerial problem. It is the responsibility of the manager to determine this.

GLOSSARY

0-1 integer programming problem A problem in which variables are required to equal either zero or one. *p. 279*

0-1 variables Variables that are restricted to be either zero or one. These also are called **binary variables.** *p. 279*

Branch and Bound (B & B) Algorithm The most common technique for solving integer linear programming problems. *p. 289*

Cutting plane method A technique for solving integer linear programming problems. *p. 289*

Deviational variables Variables used in goal programming problems to allow possible deviations from the stated goals. *p. 301*

General integer variables Variables that are restricted to be integer valued, but are not restricted to being only zero and one. *p. 279*

Goal programming A procedure based on linear programming that allows several goals to be considered instead of just one single objective. *p. 300*

Linear programming (LP) relaxation An integer linear programming problem with the integer restriction on the variables omitted. *p. 288*

Mixed integer linear programming problem An ILP problem in which some but not all of the variables must be integer valued. *p. 278*

Overachievement variables Deviational variables used in a goal programming problem to indicate how much a targeted amount has been exceeded. *p. 302*

Preemptive priorities Priorities assigned to goals that force the most important goals to be satisfied before lesser goals are considered. *p. 309*

Pure integer problem An ILP problem in which all of the variables must be integer valued. *p. 278*

Underachievement variables Deviational variables used in a goal programming problem to indicate the amount by which a targeted amount is not met. *p. 302*

QUESTIONS

1. What may happen if you attempt to obtain the solution to an integer linear programming problem by solving the LP relaxation of the problem and rounding off this answer?
2. Suppose a linear programming problem is formulated. Upon examining this, it is determined integer restrictions should be placed on all the variables. What

would happen to the feasible region of the original LP problem as a result of these integer restrictions?

3. Is it possible for the solution to an ILP problem to be better (i.e., the objective function value is better) than the solution to the LP relaxation of this problem? Explain why or why not.
4. Explain in your own words how the Branch and Bound (B & B) Algorithm solves ILP problems.
5. When the Branch and Bound Algorithm is used to solve a pure integer problem, a variable whose value is a noninteger is selected and branching on this variable results in two new linear programming subproblems. Explain why the solutions to the LP subproblems cannot have an objective function value better than the previous upper bound.
6. What does it mean if all deviational variables in a goal programming problem are equal to zero?
7. Suppose a person tries to solve a goal programming problem with preemptive priorities by assigning very high weights to the most important goals. What difficulties might this cause?
8. Explain why it is not possible for both deviational variables in one goal in a goal programming problem to be positive in the final solution (i.e., you cannot have $d_1^+ = 5$ and $d_1^- = 8$ simultaneously).
9. Suppose a preemptive priority goal programming problem is solved, and the objective function used in the priority level 1 problem was to minimize d_1^-. The objective function value for this solution is 120. Explain why it will not be possible in later stages of the problem to obtain a solution such that $d_1^- < 120$.
10. Suppose you have formulated a linear programming problem and found there is no feasible solution to this problem. How might you use goal programming to deal with this situation?

PROBLEMS

11. A real estate developer is considering three possible projects—a small apartment complex, a small shopping center, and a miniwarehouse. Each of these requires different funding over the next two years and the net present value of the investments also varies. The table below provides the required investment amounts in thousands and the net present value of each in thousands.

	NPV	Year 1	Year 2
Apartment	18	40	30
Shopping center	15	30	20
Miniwarehouse	14	20	20

The company has $80,000 to invest in Year 1 and $50,000 to invest in Year 2.

a) Develop an integer programming model to maximize the net present value in this situation.

b) Solve the problem in part (a) using available computer software. Which of the three projects would be undertaken if net present value is maximized? How much money would be used each year?

12. Refer to the real estate investment situation in Problem 11.
    a) Suppose the shopping center and the apartment would be on adjacent properties, and the shopping center only would be considered if the apartment also were built. Formulate the constraint that would stipulate this.
    b) Formulate a constraint that would force exactly two of the three projects to be undertaken.
13. Refer to the Cypress Country example in this chapter. Use the graphs in Figure 7.1. Indicate on these graphs what the feasible region is for each of the subproblems (i.e., add the constraint used to generate each subproblem) seen in Figure 7.1.
14. Consider the following integer linear programming problem.

$$\begin{aligned} &\text{Maximize } 200X_1 + 100X_2 + 100X_3 \\ &\text{Subject to: } X_1 + X_3 \geq 2 \\ &X_1 + X_2 \leq 6 \\ &91X_1 + 47X_2 + 35X_3 \leq 1200 \\ &X_1, X_2, X_3 \geq 0 \text{ and integer} \end{aligned}$$

Using linear programming software to find the solutions to the subproblems, solve this using the Branch and Bound Algorithm.

15. Consider the following integer linear programming problem.

$$\begin{aligned} &\text{Maximize } 120X_1 + 160X_2 + 170X_3 \\ &\text{Subject to: } X_1 - X_3 \geq 2 \\ &X_1 + X_2 \leq 8 \\ &8X_1 + 7X_2 + 6X_3 \leq 200 \\ &X_1, X_2, X_3 \geq 0 \text{ and integer} \end{aligned}$$

Using linear programming software to find the solutions to the subproblems, solve this using the Branch and Bound Algorithm.

16. Baseball umpiring crews are currently in four cities where three-game series are beginning. When these are finished, the crews are needed to work games in four different cities. The distances from each of the cities where the crews are working to the cities where the new games will be starting are shown in the table below.

	To			
From	**Kansas City**	**Chicago**	**Detroit**	**Toronto**
Seattle	1800	1900	1850	2100
Arlington	500	800	950	1200
Oakland	1500	2100	2000	*x*
Baltimore	1300	800	600	400

The x in the Oakland to Toronto assignment means this particular assignment may not be made. Each crew may be sent to only one city, and each city must receive exactly one crew. Use 0-1 variables to formulate this as an integer programming problem to determine which crews should be sent to which cities to minimize the total distance traveled. Using available computer software, determine which crews should go to which cities. How many miles will be traveled if the optimal assignments are made?

17. A real estate developer is currently building in three areas of a particular state. He has hired three individuals, Sam, Gerri, and Linda, to manage the sales force in each location. Based on the experience of these individuals and their familiarity with the real estate markets in the different cities, each individual is rated on a scale of 1 to 10 for each location. A rating of 1 is the best rating, which means that the person would sell the houses in the least possible amount of time. These ratings are in the table below.

Location	Sam	Gerri	Linda
#1	3	5	6
#2	5	6	6
#3	4	7	5

Use 0-1 variables to formulate this as an integer programming problem to determine which individual should be sent to each city to minimize the total of the ratings. Each city must have only one person as manager, and each person can only be sent to one city. Using available computer software, determine which assignments should be made.

18. Triangle Utilities provides electricity for three cities. The company has four electric generators, which are used to provided electricity. The main generator operates 24 hours per day, with an occasional shutdown for routine maintenance. Three other generators (#1, #2, and #3) are available to provide additional power when needed. A start-up cost is incurred each time one of these generators is started. The start-up costs are $6,000 for #1, $5,000 for #2, and $4,000 for #3. These generators are used in the following ways. A generator may be started at 6:00 A.M. and run for either eight hours or 16 hours, or it may be started at 2:00 P.M. and run for eight hours (until 10:00 P.M.). All generators except the main generator are shut down at 10:00 P.M. Forecasts indicate the need for 3,200 megawatts more than provided by the main generator before 2:00 P.M., and this need goes up to 5,700 megawatts between 2:00 P.M. and 10:00 P.M. Generator #1 may provide up to 2,400 megawatts, generator #2 may provide up to 2,100 megawatts, and generator #3 may provide up to 3,300 megawatts. The cost per megawatt used per eight hour period is $8 for #1, $9 for #2, and $7 for #3.

Formulate this problem as an integer programming problem to determine the least cost way to meet the needs of the area.

19. A Certified Financial Planner (CFP) has been asked by a client to invest $250,000. This money may be placed in stocks, bonds, or a mutual fund in real estate. The expected return on investment is 13 percent for stocks, 8 percent for bonds, and 10% for real estate. While the client would like a very high expected return, she would be satisfied with a 10 percent expected return on her money. Due to risk considerations, several goals have been established to keep the risk at an acceptable level. One goal is that at least 30 percent of the money should be put in bonds. Another goal is that the amount invested in real estate should not exceed 50 percent of the total amount invested in stocks and bonds. Under no circumstance should more than $150,000 be invested in any one of these three alternatives, and so for each investment alternative this represents a rigid constraint instead of a goal.

a) Formulate this as a goal programming problem. Assume the goals are equally important.

b) Using available software, solve this problem. How much should be invested in each of the areas? What is the expected return for this?

20. The campaign manager for a politician who is running for reelection to a political office is planning the campaign. Four ways to advertise have been selected—television ads, radio ads, billboards, and newspaper ads. The cost of these are \$900 for each TV ad, \$500 for each radio ad, \$600 for a billboard for one month, and \$180 for each newspaper ad. The audience reached by each type of advertising has been estimated to be 40,000 for each TV ad, 32,000 for each radio ad, 34,000 for each billboard, and 17,000 for each newspaper ad. The total monthly advertising budget is \$16,000. The following goals have been established:

    1. The number of people reached should be at least 1,500,000.
    2. The total monthly advertising budget should not be exceeded.
    3. Together the number of ads on either TV or radio should be at least six.
    4. No more than 10 ads of any one type of advertising should be used.

    a) Formulate this as a goal programming problem. Assume that the budget goal is twice as important as the others.

    b) Solve this with any available computer software.

    c) Which goals are completely met and which are not?

21. Refer to Problem 20. Suppose preemptive priorities are to be used with this problem. Goal 1 is the most important, while goal 2 is the next most important. Goals 3 and 4 are next and they are equally important. Formulate this as a goal programming problem and solve with available software.

22. Refer to Problem 20. Suppose the goal of having no more than 10 ads of any type is flexible, but under no circumstances can more than 12 ads of any type be used. Modify the formulation of this problem by adding the necessary constraints.

23. Consider the following goal programming problem:

$$\text{Minimize } d_1^- + d_2^- + d_2^+ + d_3^+$$
$$\text{Subject to: } 4X_1 + 3X_2 + 3X_3 + d_1^- - d_1^+ = 100$$
$$5X_1 + 8X_2 + 4X_3 + d_2^- - d_2^+ = 220$$
$$X_1 + 2X_2 + X_3 + d_3^- - d_3^+ = 90$$
$$X_1, X_2, X_3, d_1^-, d_1^+, d_2^-, d_2^+, d_3^-, d_3^+ \geq 0$$

    a) Based on the objective function, are the goals equally important?

    b) Based on the objective function, which of the goals does management wish to meet exactly (i.e., no underutilization and no overutilization)?

    c) Suppose the first goal (constraint) represents labor hours. Based on the objective function, is management trying to avoid using overtime or is management trying to avoid idle time?

24. For the goals specified in the previous problem, formulate a weighted goal programming problem in which the objective is to minimize the percentage deviations from the goals. Use the same deviational variables in the objective function that are currently in the objective function.

25. Milborne Manufacturing produces three models of electric blenders—Standard, Deluxe, and Chef's Delight. Production of the Standard model takes 1.5

hours, the Deluxe model takes 2 hours, and the Chef's Delight takes 2.5 hours. The profit generated by these are $28 for the Standard, $32 for the Deluxe, and $35 for the Chef's Delight. A total of 240 hours per week are available for production. The demand for each has been forecasted to be 60 units. Management has set the following goals (each having the same importance):

1. Utilize exactly 240 hours per week.
2. Produce at least 60 units of the Chef's Delight.
3. Produce at least 60 units of the Deluxe model.
4. Produce at least 60 units of the Standard model.
5. Generate at least $3,500 profit per week.

Formulate this as a goal programming problem. Solve with any available software.

26. Refer to Problem 25. Suppose goal 1 is twice as important as goals 2, 3, and 4, and goal 1 is three times as important as goal 5. Formulate this as a goal programming problem and solve using any available software.
27. Refer to Problem 25. Suppose the goals are equally important, but management would like to minimize the percentage deviations from the goals. Formulate this as a goal programming problem and solve using any available software.
28. A group of college students is planning a camping trip during the upcoming break. The group must hike several miles through the woods to get to the campsite, and anything that is needed on this trip must be packed in a knapsack and carried to the campsite. One particular student has identified eight items that she would like to take on the trip, but the combined weight is too great. She has decided to rate the utility of each item on a scale of 1 to 100, with 100 being the most beneficial. The item weights in pounds and their utility values are given below.

Item	1	2	3	4	5	6	7	8
Weight	8	1	7	6	3	12	5	14
Utility	80	20	50	55	50	75	30	70

Recognizing the hike to the campsite will be quite long, a limit of 35 pounds has been set as the maximum total weight of the items to be carried. Formulate this as a 0-1 programming problem to maximize the total utility of the items carried while not exceeding the weight limit. Solve this knapsack problem using any available software.

29. Refer to Carter's Peanut Butter facility location problem in the Analysis in Action section at the end of Chapter 6. Model this as a single integer programming problem that could be used to determine which plant to open and what the optimal shipping schedule would be. Solve this using any available software.

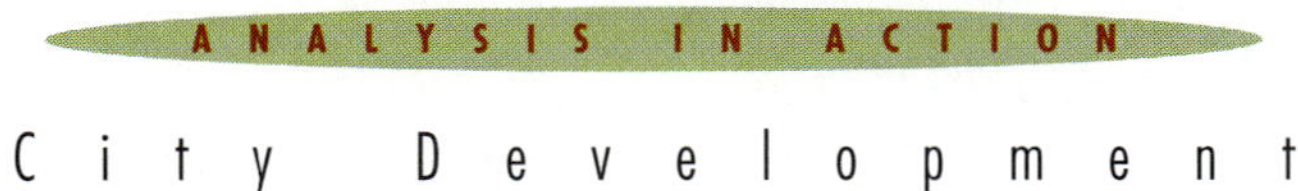

City Development

A city owns 800 acres of land that is being considered for various types of development. The city manager has been instructed to submit a plan for the best use of this land. It has been determined the best use would be defined as having the highest net present value. There are budget constraints that will restrict what can be done. Funds totalling $5,000,000 that have been received through federal grants must be spent in the first year or else future funding will be jeopardized. The city has an additional $2,000,000 that also may be spent in the first year. In the second year of the projects, at least $4,000,000 but no more than $6,000,000, may be spent.

The projects that are being considered are listed in the table below. The net present values and costs are given in thousands.

			Expenditures	
Project	Acres Needed	NPV	Year 1	Year 2
1. Park	60	–$20	$ 400	$ 300
2. Golf course	170	20	900	300
3. Low income housing	185	–30	1,300	1,700
4. Industrial park	150	65	1,400	1,200
5. Waste facility	100	90	3,900	1,000
6. Youth sports facilities	80	–10	800	200
7. Wildlife preserve	250	0	400	0

Because the election year is coming, it has been decided at least one project must be selected from Projects 1, 3, 6, and 7. If Project 5 is selected, Projects 4 or 7 also must be selected to put between Project 5 and the other projects.

Using 0-1 variables, formulate this as an integer programming problem. Solve with available software and determine which projects should be undertaken. Write a brief managerial report giving your recommendations.

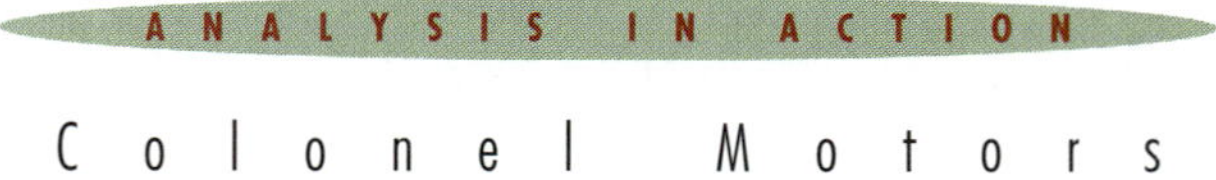

Colonel Motors

Colonel Motors, Inc. produces four types of automobiles in the United States. In the coming year, the company is planning to build exactly 300,000 automobiles. Due to federal regulations the average mileage for the automobiles produced by this company must be at least 30 miles per gallon. While the company is interested in generating as much profit as possible, it also is interested in the total sales revenue. In the next year, the company would like to generate a profit of at least $90 million and total sales of at least $800 million. The information about the four types of cars is given in the table below.

Type of Car	Profit	Price	MPG
Argon	$ 500	$ 7,500	42
Zipper	600	9,800	35
Cruiser	900	13,000	25
Luxus	1,500	20,000	18

To satisfy the anticipated demand, the company would like to produce at least 40,000 of each type of automobile, although producing less would be acceptable.

The profit goal is the most important goal. It is three times as important to achieve this as it is to achieve the total sales goal. The profit goal is five times as important as the goals related to the minimum number of automobiles. The company must meet the federal regulations for mileage, and it must produce exactly 300,000 automobiles.

Use goal programming to determine how many of each type of automobile should be produced. Prepare a brief report of your recommendations to give to management.

An Integer Programming Spreadsheet Example

Maximize $z = 2x_1 + 5x_2$

Subject to:

$x_1 + x_2 \leq 5$
$x_1 - x_2 \geq 0$
$x_1, x_2 \leq 0$ and integer

To solve an integer problem using Excel's **Solver**:

From the **Solver Parameters** screen:

Select **Add** to add a constraint for each variable that must be integer.

Specify the cell containing the value for each decision variable.

Select **Int** from the choices of <=, =, >=, and **Int**.

Select **Solve**.

	A	B	C	D	E	F
1	Integer programming example using Solver					
2						
3						
4	Max 2x1+5x2					
5	st x1+x2<=5					
6	x1-x2>=0					
7	x1>=0 and integer					
8	x2>=0 and integer					
9						
10						
11	objective function			constraints		
12	z	16		5	<=	5
13				1	>=	0
14	decision variables					
15	x1	3		3	>=	0
16	x2	2		2	>=	0

	A	B	C	D	E	F
1	Integer programming example using Solver					
2						
3						
4	Max 2x1+5x2					
5	st x1+x2<=5					
6	x1-x2>=0					
7	x1>=0 and integer					
8	x2>=0 and integer					
9						
10						
11	objective function			constraints		
12	z	=2*B15+5*B16		=+B15+B16	<=	5
13				=+B15-B16	>=	0
14	decision variables					
15	x1	3		=B15	>=	0
16	x2	2		=B16	>=	0

CHAPTER EIGHT

Project Management: PERT/CPM

LEARNING OBJECTIVES

Upon completing Chapter 8, you should be able to:

- Explain how PERT and CPM are used in project management.
- Develop a work breakdown structure for a project.
- Draw a network representation of a project.
- Find the earliest, latest, and slack times for all activities in a project and explain their meaning.
- Find the critical path in a project.
- Use three time estimates to determine the probability of completing a project by a specific time.
- Develop a budget schedule for a project.
- Determine the least cost way to crash a project.

CHAPTER OUTLINE

8.1 INTRODUCTION

Program evaluation and review technique (PERT)

A procedure that may be used to schedule activities in a project using three time estimates.

Critical path method (CPM)

A procedure for scheduling activities in a project; used when times are known with certainty.

In the late 1950s, the Polaris missile program was begun. This involved literally thousands of tasks or activities that had to be performed by a large number of contractors. In order to plan, schedule and control this massive project, **Program Evaluation and Review Technique** (PERT) was developed. About this same time, in a totally separate project, plans were being prepared for the construction and maintenance of chemical plants. J. E. Kelly of Remington Rand and M. R. Walker of Du Pont developed a technique called the **Critical Path Method (CPM)** to help the planning, scheduling, and controlling of this project. While the techniques of PERT and CPM were developed separately, the techniques and terminology have evolved over the years so that now people often refer to this basic approach as PERT/CPM. However, one distinction still is commonly made. The term CPM is used when times are known with certainty, and the term PERT is used when times are uncertain and must be estimated.

Over the years, PERT and CPM have been used to help manage such projects as launches of the space shuttle, major highway construction, software development, remodeling hospitals, and planning concert tours. In this chapter we will see that the concepts associated with PERT and CPM may be used not only to develop a schedule of when activities will begin and finish, but also to develop a budget schedule to help managers see how actual costs compare to budgeted costs at each stage of the project. We also will investigate how to evaluate the use of additional resources to finish the project in a shorter period of time.

PERT and CPM have been used to help manage projects such as the clean-up of Boston Harbor. SOURCE: Photo courtesy of Kevin Kirwin, Regina Villa Associates, Boston; courtesy of Massachusetts Water Resource Authority

8.2 GAMMA INDUSTRIES EXAMPLE

Gamma Industries is a company specializing in equipment used for a variety of medical tests. The company currently is planning the development of a new medical testing device. To stay ahead of the competition, Gamma management would like to bring this product to market as soon as possible. Based on the development of similar types of projects in the past, the company has identified what must be done to develop this product. The time required to develop and test the hardware and software is based on this past experience, and management feels confident that these times are accurate. However, because the personnel that will be involved in this project currently are finishing another project, management needs to know when each of these individuals can be scheduled to begin their work on the new project. There also is concern that part of one of these other projects is taking longer than anticipated and the people responsible for developing the documentation will not be available as early as previously anticipated. Management is trying to determine if a delay in this other project will delay the completion of the new project.

8.3 WORK BREAKDOWN STRUCTURE

In planning the Gamma Industries project, the first step is to carefully identify the activities that must be performed. In a complete **work breakdown structure** (**WBS**), all the activities are listed and broken down into subactivities, which would be on a lower level than the activities themselves. As part of this work breakdown structure, management will identify either the subcontractor or the functional group within the organization, such as systems engineering or computer programming, that will be working on this part of the project. A person responsible for this also will be designated.

Work breakdown structure (WBS)
The process of identifying the activities in a project and breaking these into finer levels of detail.

In the Gamma Industries example, assume that the activities involved in developing the new piece of equipment are those given in Figure 8.1. There are no subactivities listed in Figure 8.1 as this is a small project and there is no need for further breakdown. However, to illustrate a more complete work breakdown structure, suppose the activity of designing the system involves meeting with design engineers, surveying medical technicians for their input, and developing the design. This is shown in the diagram in Figure 8.2. Also other subactivities have been included as well to illustrate this process. Each subactivity is numbered according to which activity it belongs. If a subactivity could be subdivided further, the numbering might be 1.1.2.1 or 1.1.2.2. Thus, when the entire work breakdown structure has been developed, the numbering will clearly indicate the level of each activity.

This numbering system often is used to track costs and is thus a part of an accounting system as well. Reports may be generated for the various levels depending on what information is needed. For example, the overall project manager may only wish to have information regarding the top level of

FIGURE 8.1

Work Breakdown Structure for Highest Levels

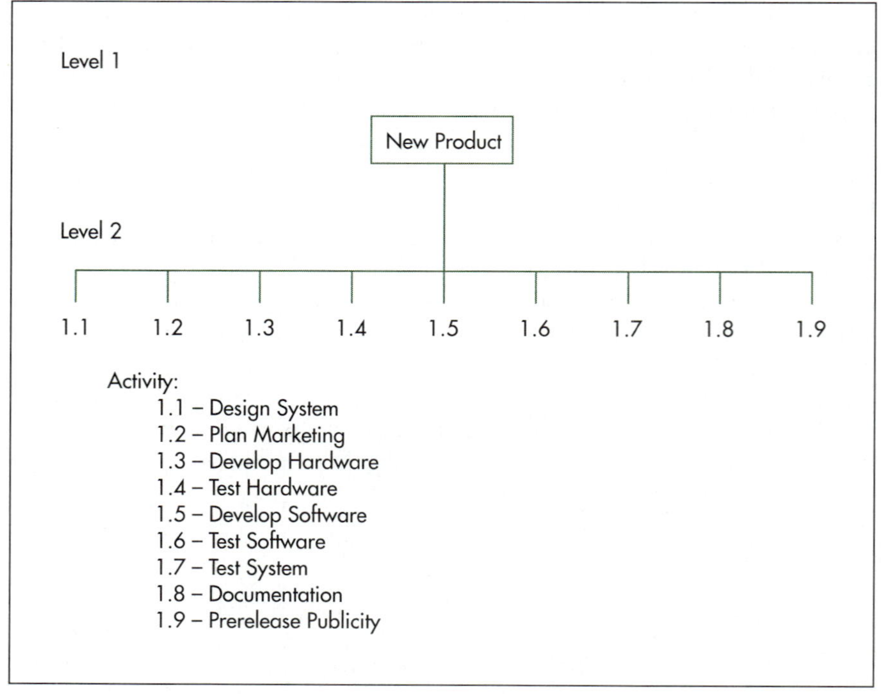

FIGURE 8.2

Work Breakdown Structure with Subactivities

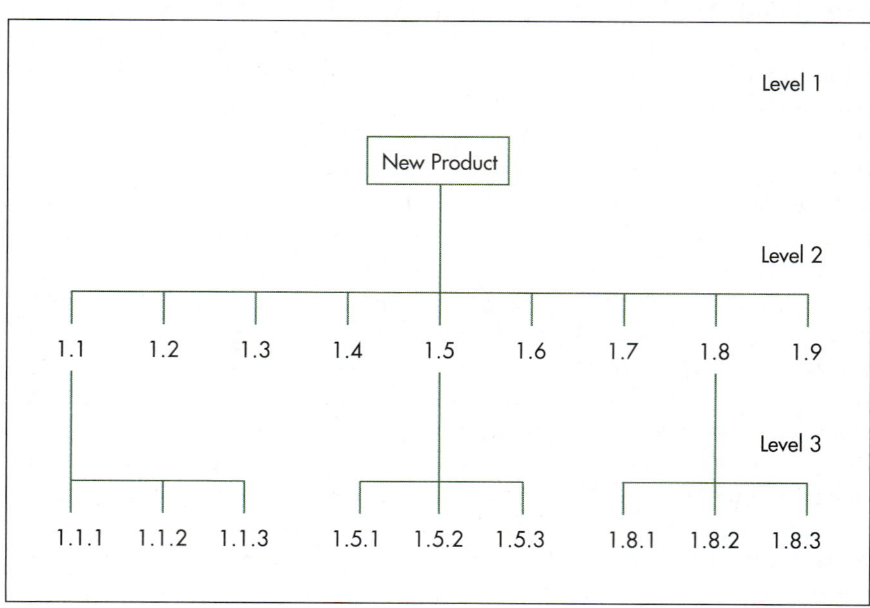

activities while supervisors for each of the activities must have detailed information on subactivities for their specific part of the project.

Determining Times and Relationships

Once the activities in a project have been identified, two things must be determined—how long each activity will take and the order in which the activities may occur. Some activities may not begin until other activities are finished.

In the Gamma Industries example, the hardware cannot be developed until the design is complete. The hardware testing may not begin until the hardware has gone through the preliminary hardware development phase. An activity that must be finished before the next activity can be started is called the **immediate predecessor**. Table 8.1 lists the activities, the immediate predecessors, and the time required for each activity in the Gamma Industries example. Assume these times are known with certainty. If they are not known with certainty, they must be estimated, and the technique used for estimating times will be given in a later section.

Immediate predecessor
An activity that must be finished before the next activity may begin.

Table 8.1 gives an idea of the overall magnitude of this particular project. To illustrate why the PERT/CPM techniques were developed, try to

Some project management activities may not begin until other activities are finished; the haulage system pictured here must be assembled prior to installation in a Virginia coal mine. SOURCE: Photo courtesy of Joy Mining Machinery

TABLE 8.1

Activities, Immediate Predecessors, and Times for Gamma Industries Example

Activity	Immediate Predecessor	Weeks
A Design System	—	20
B Plan Marketing	—	10
C Develop Hardware	A	15
D Develop Software	A	14
E Test Hardware	C	4
F Test Software	D	7
G Test System	E,F	3
H Prepare Documentation	E,F	4
I Prerelease Publicity	B,G	3

look at the table representing the Gamma Industries project and answer the following questions:

1. How long will it take to complete the entire project if all personnel are available to begin their work whenever they are needed? Note that some activities may occur simultaneously.
2. When will the people working on the documentation be needed to start their work on this project?
3. If there is a delay of two weeks in testing the hardware, will this cause a delay in the completion of the project?
4. How long may each activity be delayed without having an adverse affect on the completion time of the project?

These are just a few of the questions that a project manager might ask. While it may be possible to answer these for this small project without using PERT/CPM, for larger projects with hundreds of activities it would be virtually impossible to simply look at a presentation of the project in a form similar to Table 8.1 and answer these types of questions. However, PERT and CPM provide a systematic way of providing information about this type of project.

Activities-on-arcs
A network representation of a project in which the arcs represent the activities.

Activities-on-nodes
A network representation of a project in which the nodes represent the activities.

Activity
A specific job or task in a project.

Event
A node in a PERT/CPM network, which indicates when all the activities ending at that node will be finished.

8.4 DRAWING THE NETWORK

For PERT and CPM a network will be used to represent the project. There are two types of networks that are common—**activities-on-arcs** and **activities-on-nodes**. In this book, we will use the activities-on-arcs approach in which each **activity** in the network is represented by a directed arc or arrow. With this activities-on-arcs approach, the circles or nodes in the network represent the **events** in the project. An event represents the completion of all activities leading into a node, and it also indicates when the next activity, or activities, may begin. Each network representation of a project will have one node representing the start of the project and one node representing the completion of the entire project. Each arc is labeled to indicate which activity it represents. Each node also may be numbered as some software packages identify the activities by the beginning and ending nodes for the arc representing the activity.

Looking at the Gamma Industries example in Table 8.1, Activity A has no immediate predecessors, so this activity can begin immediately. It would be represented as:

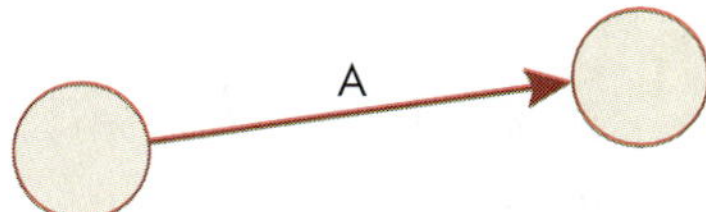

The node from which Activity A starts represents the start of the project. The node where Activity A ends represents the completion of Activity A. Because Activity B has no predecessors, it also may begin immediately. Adding this to what has been drawn for Activity A results in:

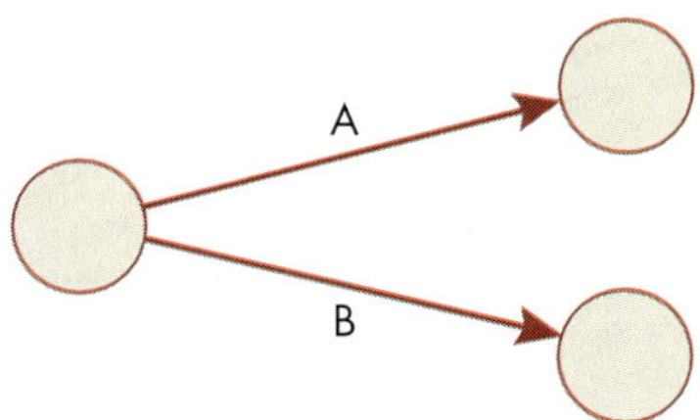

Continuing the development of this network results in the network shown in Figure 8.3. Notice Activities E and F are both predecessors for Activities H and G. This means there must be one node representing the completion of both E and F, so the arrows representing these two activities should end at the same node. In looking at Activity G, you see the importance of the direction of the arrow. If an undirected arc with no arrowhead were used for this, it would be impossible to determine if G was preceding H or I.

Also note that Activities H and I have no activities following them, and when drawing these you may be tempted to have them ending at separate nodes. However, there must be one single node that represents the completion of the project, and thus all activities with no succeeding activities must end at the same node.

Because the nodes have been numbered, Activity A might be identified as activity 1-2 (i.e., the activity starting at node 1 and ending at node 2). Similarly, Activity F could be identified as activity 4-5. This type of notation often is used with computer software specifically designed for PERT/CPM.

Dummy Activities

At times it may be necessary to use a **dummy activity** in a network. A dummy activity does not represent an actual activity but is used only to show a precedence relationship and has zero time associated with it. A

Dummy activity
An activity used in a network to show a precedence relationship. It has zero time associated with it.

FIGURE 8.3

Network Representation of Gamma Industries Example

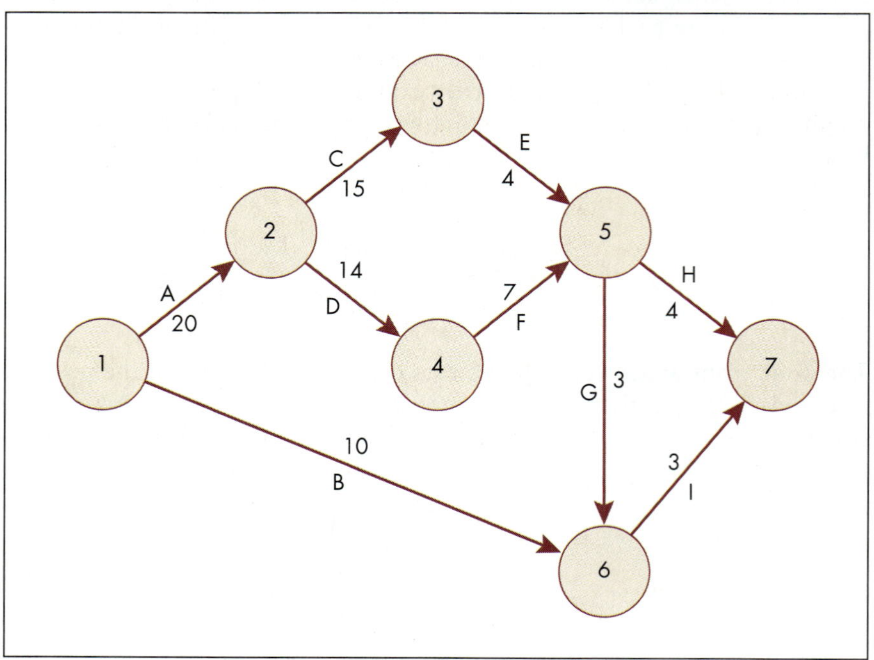

dummy activity will be necessary if two activities have exactly the same predecessors and themselves are immediate predecessors for the same activities. A dummy activity also is necessary if two activities are immediate predecessors for the same activity, and one, but not both, is a predecessor for another activity. The following examples will illustrate this.

Suppose we consider the following project:

Activity	Immediate Predecessor
A	—
B	—
C	A,B

If we try to draw the network representation of this without a dummy activity, we might have the following:

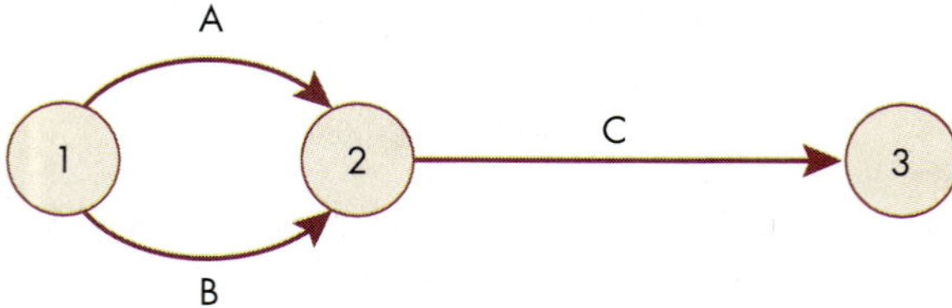

Notice Activities A and B have exactly the same immediate predecessors (none) and are both immediate predecessors for the same Activity (C). The network above shows this relationship, but the difficulty arises when we try to identify the activities by their beginning and ending nodes. Using the notation activity 1-2 is ambiguous because this could be either Activity A or Activity B as both of these activities begin at node 1 and end at node 2. Thus, to avoid this difficulty a dummy activity could be used with the following result:

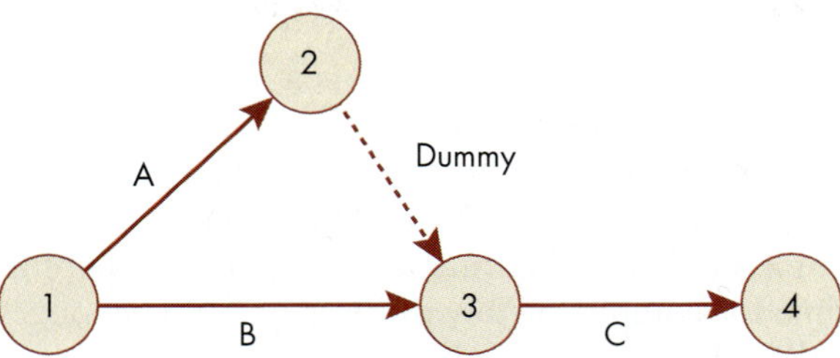

Now Activity A also is denoted by 1-2 while Activity B is denoted by 1-3. There is no ambiguity. Because the dummy activity is shown as an immediate predecessor for C, this presentation indicates Activity A also is a predecessor of C.

The other case where a dummy is necessary is shown in the following example.

Activity	Immediate Predecessor
A	—
B	—
C	A
D	B
E	B,C

Notice Activities B and C are immediate predecessors for Activity E, while B alone is an immediate predecessor for Activity D. To accurately reflect this, examine the following network:

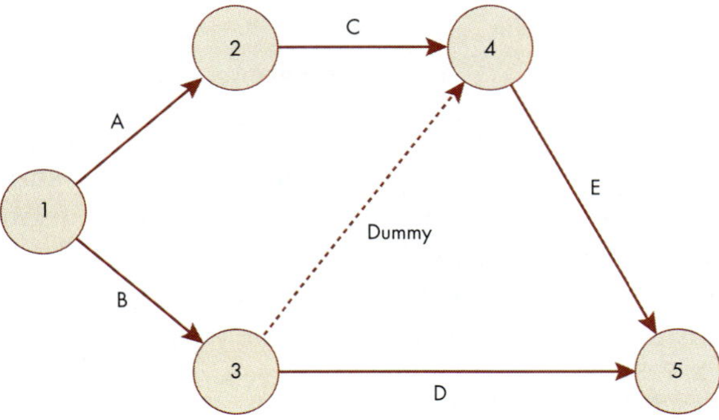

Notice if the dummy was not used, then the network would indicate that only C is a predecessor for E. If E were drawn from B we would have a similar problem. If we tried to have both B and C ending at the same node, then it would be impossible for D to be drawn with only B as the predecessor.

8.5 FINDING THE CRITICAL PATH

Critical path
The longest path from the starting node in a project to the finishing node in a project.

Once the network has been drawn, it may be used to help determine how long it will take to complete the entire project. To do this, we will find the **critical path**. A path in the network is a set of activities that connect the starting node of the project to the finishing node in the project. Adding the activity times for all the activities on the path will determine the time required for completing each path. The project is finished when all activities are completed, and the time required for completing the project is the longest time for completing any of these paths. The longest path in the network is called the critical path because completing these activities on schedule is critical to completing the project on schedule. A delay in any of these critical activities will delay the project.

For small networks you could simply list all the paths and determine the times for each one. For example, in the Gamma Industries example the paths and the time required to complete each of these would be:

ACEH	20 + 15 + 4 + 4	= 43 weeks
ADFH	20 + 14 + 7 + 4	= 45 weeks
ACEGI	20 + 15 + 4 + 3 + 3	= 45 weeks
ADFGI	20 + 14 + 7 + 3 + 3	= 47 weeks *
BI	10 + 3	= 13 weeks

This shows the critical path is ADFGI because all other paths could be finished in less time than this one. A delay in the completion of any activity in this path would cause the project to take longer than 47 weeks. The weeks required to complete each of these were found by adding the activity times for each activity in the path. However, for projects with hundreds of activities, this approach would not be feasible. Even if this was done, it still would not necessarily be possible to determine the impact of delaying activities that are not on the critical path.

Earliest Times

Earliest start time (ES)
The earliest possible time that an activity may start.

Earliest finish time (EF)
The earliest possible time that an activity may finish.

The **earliest start time** (ES) and the **earliest finish time** (EF) will be calculated for each activity. As the name implies, the earliest start time for an activity is the earliest possible time that an activity may begin. This means all immediate predecessors must have been completed. The earliest finish time is simply the earliest possible time an activity may be finished. The earliest finish is equal to the earliest start time plus the activity time. Thus,

$$t = \text{activity time}$$
$$ES = \text{largest } EF \text{ for all immediate predecessors}$$
$$EF = ES + t$$

BEST PRACTICES

Management Science and Project Management in the Persian Gulf War

The ground war in the Persian Gulf began on February 24, 1991 and lasted only 100 hours. It was, however, the culmination of a tremendous exercise in project management. The U.S. had deployed some 500,000 forces, along with another 200,000 representing allied nations. Before venturing to combat, the allied forces undertook a large logistics effort to distribute supply, repair, and medical assets in an unfriendly desert environment. Management science techniques were essential to the successful execution of the military operation.

Courtesy of General Dynamics Land Systems

Military planners responded to General Schwarzkopf's directive to keep a 60-day supply of necessary materials on-hand. They first consulted historical data and projections to obtain an initial estimate of a 26,352 short ton (STONs) supply of medical supplies. That figure was later modified based on the specifics of Operation Desert Storm. For example, the amount of saline solution required for rehydration of personnel was expected to be greater than that required in Europe. Also, insufficient refrigeration units were on-hand to store the requested 60-day supply of whole blood properly. The supply figures were adjusted accordingly. Projected requirements of diesel fuel and gasoline also were modified to suit the situation. These projections were doubled from more routine maneuvers, because the allied forces expected to be on the offensive in the Gulf.

Logistics planners played several other roles in the management of Operation Desert Storm. They were responsible for developing resupply techniques for the forward battalions, at a time when limited transportation assets and supplies were available. The planners also had to maximize the security of these assets, and minimize the time required for resupply operations. They used a technique called the Logistics Release Point (LRP) resupply technique to resupply combat brigades in record time, and contribute to the allied success in the Gulf War effort.

SOURCE: Staats, R., December 1991. "Desert Storm: A Reexamination of the Ground War in the Persian Gulf, and the Key Role Played by OR." *OR/MS Today*: 42-56.

Start the project at time 0, so for Activity A,

$$ES = 0$$
$$EF = 0 + 20 = 20$$

This will be indicated on the network by using the notation [ES,EF]. For Activity B, $ES = 0$ and $EF = 10$. Because Activity C cannot begin until Activity A is finished:

$$ES(\text{Activity C}) = EF(\text{Activity A}) = 20$$
$$EF(\text{Activity C}) = 20 + 15 = 35$$

All the earliest start and finish times are shown in Figure 8.4. Notice the earliest start time for Activity G, and also Activity H, depends on the earliest finish times for both immediate predecessors Activities E and F. Thus,

$$ES(\text{Activity G}) = \text{largest } EF \text{ for Activity E and Activity F} = 41$$

FIGURE 8.4

Earliest Times [ES,EF] for Gamma Industries Example

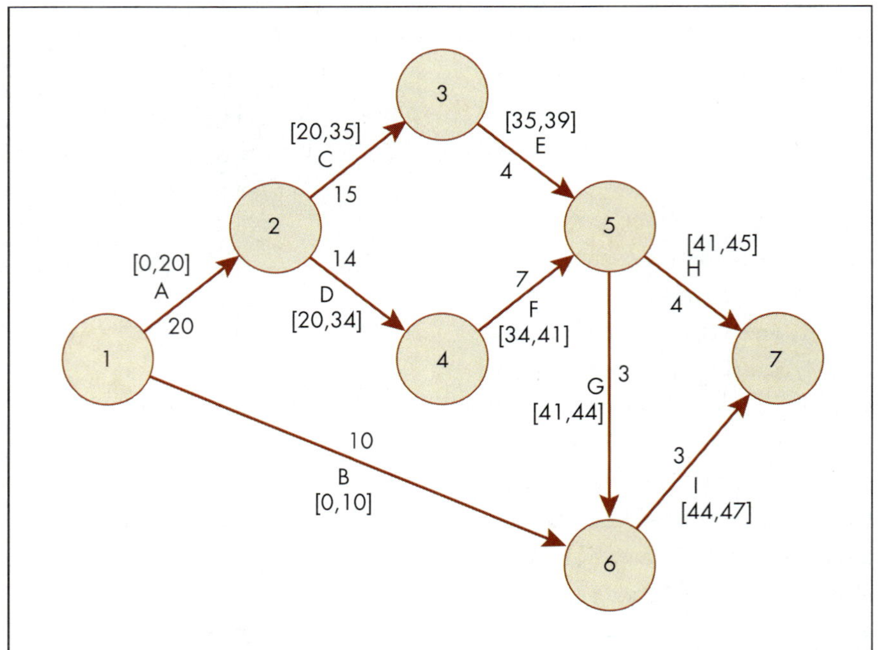

We cannot start Activity G until Week 41 and this is the earliest start time for Activity G. If we mistakenly tried to start Activity G when Activity E was finished at Week 39 (the smallest of the EF times), we would not yet be finished with Activity F and so would violate the precedence relationship.

We see from the earliest finish times that the project may be finished in 47 weeks. This is the largest of the EF times for all activities ending at the node representing the completion of the project. While Activity H may be finished at the end of 45 weeks, the project is not over until all activities are finished.

Latest Times

Latest start time (LS)
The latest time that an activity may start without delaying the completion of the project.

Latest finish time (LF)
The latest time that an activity may finish without delaying the completion of the project.

Once the earliest times are found, begin calculating the **latest start times** (LS) and the **latest finish times** (LF). The latest start time for an activity is the latest time that an activity may start without delaying the completion of the project. The latest finish time is the latest possible time that an activity may be finished without delaying the completion of the project. This means the latest finish time for an activity must be no later than the latest start time for each activity that immediately follows that activity.

In determining the ES and EF times, we started at the beginning node of the project and moved forward through the network. For the LS and LF times, begin at the ending node of the network and work backwards through the network to find all the latest times. The following relationships are used to determine these times.

$$LS = LF - t$$

$$LF = \text{smallest } LS \text{ for activities that immediately follow}$$

Assume we wish to finish the project in the minimum possible time. Looking at Figure 8.4 shows it is possible to finish the project at event node 7 in 47 weeks. Therefore, schedule the completion of the project for 47 weeks. This means both Activities H and I must be finished no later than Week 47, so the latest finish time for both of these is 47 weeks. To determine the latest start time for Activity H we have:

$$\begin{aligned} LS(\text{Activity H}) &= LF(\text{Activity H}) - t(\text{Activity H}) \\ &= 47 - 4 \\ &= 43 \end{aligned}$$

Similarly for Activity I, $LS = 47 - 3 = 44$. On the network we use the notation

$$(LS, LF)$$

to indicate the latest start and latest finish times as shown in Figure 8.5.

Figure 8.5 shows that on this network the immediate predecessors of I are B and G. Therefore, both of these must be finished no later than the latest

FIGURE 8.5

Earliest [ES,EF] and Latest [LS,LF] Times for Gamma Industries Example

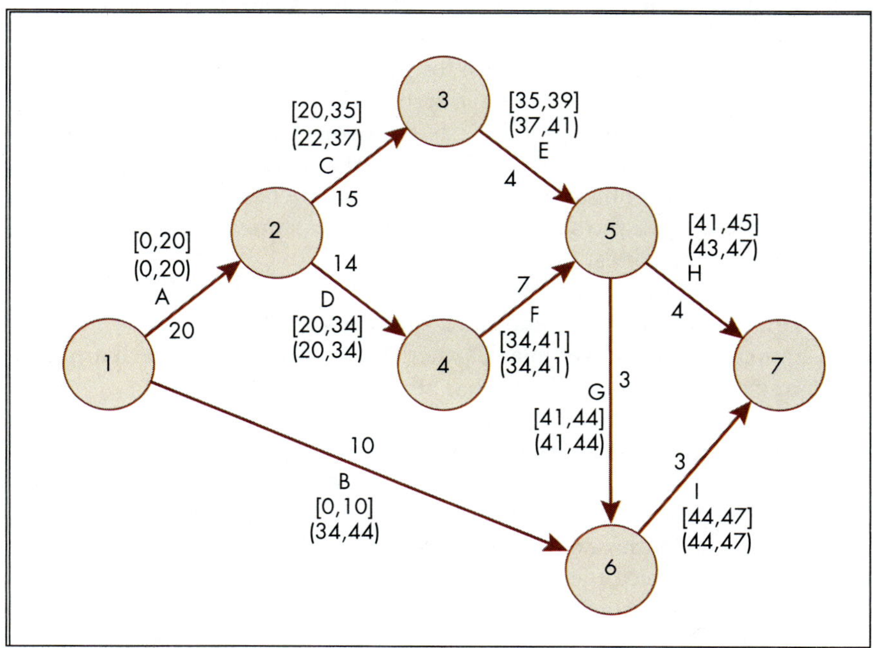

start time of I, so LF for both B and G is 44. Continuing this process results in the latest times shown in Figure 8.5. In calculating the LF for Activities E and F, note there are two activities that immediately follow these (i.e., there are two activities that start at node 5). Therefore, the LF for E and F must be the smallest of the LS times for G and H. The two LS times are 41 (for G) and 43 (for H). The LF for E and F must be 41 in order to start Activity G on time.

Slack Times

Slack (S)
The amount of time an activity may be delayed without delaying the completion of the project.

Once all the latest times are determined, determine the **slack (S)** for each activity. The slack for an activity is the time an activity may be delayed without delaying the completion of the entire project. Because the ES tells us the earliest time an activity could be started and LS tells us the latest time that activity could be started, slack is simply the difference between these two numbers. Slack also could be determined by comparing the earliest and latest finish times as well. Therefore,

$$S = LS - ES$$

or

$$S = LF - EF$$

Figure 8.5 shows that for Activity H,

$$S = LS - ES = 43 - 41 = 2$$

so there are 2 weeks of slack for Activity H. We could delay this activity 2 weeks assuming there are no delays in other activities, and the project could still be finished on schedule.

For several activities in the project, the slack is zero because the earliest and latest times are the same. If a project is scheduled to finish in the minimum possible time, the critical path for the network is the path through the network for which all activities have zero slack. A manager should pay particular attention to these activities as the project progresses because any delay in these activities will delay the project. A delay in an activity not on the critical path will not affect the completion date of the project unless the delay is greater than the slack for that activity, assuming that there are no delays in other activities.

It is sometimes convenient to use a table to keep track of the calculations for the earliest, latest, and slack times. Table 8.2 gives all of these for the Gamma Industries example. The activities on the critical path are identified, and each of these activities has zero slack.

The problems in this book assume we wish to finish the project in the minimum possible time. However, a project manager may desire to schedule the completion date of the project at a later time in order to build some slack into the project. If the project manager has the opportunity to do this, then slack for activities on the critical path would not be zero but would be the difference between the completion date set by the manager and the earliest time that the project could be finished. Therefore, the critical path would be the path consisting of the activities with the least slack.

TABLE 8.2

Earliest, Latest, and Slack Times for Gamma Industries Example

Activity	ES	EF	LS	LF	Slack	Critical Path
A	0	20	0	20	0	yes
B	0	10	34	44	34	no
C	20	35	22	37	2	no
D	20	34	20	34	0	yes
E	35	39	37	41	2	no
F	34	41	34	41	0	yes
G	41	44	41	44	0	yes
H	41	45	43	47	2	no
I	44	47	44	47	0	yes

8.6 PERT/CPM WITH UNCERTAIN TIMES

In the Gamma Industries example, it is assumed the times for each activity were known with certainty. In situations where similar projects have been done in the past and where activity times have been relatively constant, we may feel confident that the times given for the activities are accurate and are not subject to significant variability. However, for projects that involve new techniques or procedures there may be significant variability in the project completion times. For example, in the original development of the Polaris missile, there were numerous systems that did not exist and had to be developed specifically for this project. The times required to develop these systems were not known with certainty and had to be estimated.

In estimating the times for activities, it often is assumed the time required to complete an activity is a random variable that may be described by a beta distribution. Three time estimates are used to determine the time required to complete each activity. The absolute minimum possible time to complete the activity if everything goes smoothly is called the optimistic time (a) estimate. The time required under normal conditions and recognizing that things do not always proceed smoothly is called the most probable time (m) estimate. The maximum time required for completing the activity if significant problems occur would be called the pessimistic time (b) estimate. A weighted average of these three time estimates is used to find the **expected time** (t) or average time for the activity. The formula to calculate this expected time is:

Expected time (t)
The average time to complete an activity.

$$t = (a + 4m + b)/6$$

Notice the most probable time estimate is given a weight of four while the weights for the optimistic and pessimistic times are one. The denominator is six because this is the total of the weights (1+4+1).

Variance (σ^2)
A measure of the variability of the completion time of an activity.

To measure the variability of the activity completion times, a **variance** (σ^2) for each activity is estimated. This is found by using the following formula:

$$\sigma^2 = \left(\frac{b - a}{6}\right)^2$$

This is based on the fact that for any distribution of activity times or other values, a high proportion of all values are within three standard deviations of the mean. Thus, the optimistic time (a) would be used to represent the minimum possible value and would be three standard deviations below the mean. The pessimistic time (b) would represent the maximum possible value and would be three standard deviations above the mean. Thus, the total distance from the lowest number to the highest number, from a to b, would equal six standard deviations. Thus:

$$6\sigma = b - a$$

$$\sigma = (b - a)/6$$

Because the variance equals the square of the standard deviation, we have:

$$\sigma^2 = \left(\frac{b - a}{6}\right)^2$$

An Example

Returning to the Gamma Industries problem, suppose the times were not known with certainty but were estimated using the three time estimates. Table 8.3 gives the time estimates for each of the activities in the project.

The expected time and the variance for each activity will be calculated. For Activity A:

$$t_A = \frac{a + 4m + b}{6} = \frac{15 + 4(20) + 25}{6} = 20$$

TABLE 8.3

Gamma Industries Example with Three Time Estimates

Activity	*a*	*m*	*b*
A	15	20	25
B	9	10	11
C	13	14	21
D	13	14	15
E	3	4	5
F	6	7	8
G	2	3	4
H	3	4	5
I	3	3	3

$$\sigma^2 = \left(\frac{b-a}{6}\right)^2 = \left(\frac{25-15}{6}\right)^2 = 2.78$$

Doing this with each activity produces the results shown in Table 8.4.

Once the expected times are found, use them exactly the same way the times known with certainty were used before. The expected times shown in Table 8.4 are used to find the ES, EF, LS, LF, and slack times for the activities in the Gamma Industries example. The only thing that is different when times are estimated rather than known with certainty is the interpretation of what the times mean. Stated previously, the time required to complete the project was 47 weeks. If the activity times are expected times, then the 47 weeks represents the expected time or average time that it would take to finish this type of project. The actual time for this one project might be more or less than 47 weeks.

Variability in Completion Time of the Project

To determine the probability that a project will be finished in a specified amount of time, it is necessary to make certain assumptions. Assume the activity time for each activity is independent of the activity time for other activities. Also assume the project completion time is approximately normally distributed. Due to the central limit theorem in statistics, this second assumption will be met if the activity times are independent and the number of activities on each path in the project is large.

To find a probability using the normal distribution, the mean and the standard deviation of the distribution must be known. Use the following notation:

T = completion time of the project

$E(T)$ = expected time (or mean time) for the project
= total of activity times on critical path

σ_T^2 = variance of the project (critical path)
= total of variances for activities on critical path

TABLE 8.4

Expected Times and Variances for Gamma Industries Example

Activity	a	m	b	$t=(a+4m+b)/6$	$\sigma^2=((b-a)/6)^2$
A	15	20	25	20	2.78
B	9	10	11	10	0.11
C	13	14	21	15	1.78
D	13	14	15	14	0.11
E	3	4	5	4	0.11
F	6	7	8	7	0.11
G	2	3	4	3	0.11
H	3	4	5	4	0.11
I	3	3	3	3	0

Because the completion time of the project depends on the critical path, the expected time and the variance for the project are actually the expected time and variance of the critical path. The expected time for the critical path already was found to be 47 weeks. To find the variance for any path in the network, simply add the variances for all the activities on that path. To find the variance for the critical path, add the variances for the activities on the critical path.

For the Gamma Industries example, the critical path was ADFGI, which had an expected completion time of 47 weeks. Thus:

$$E(T) = t_A + t_D + t_F + t_G + t_I$$
$$E(T) = 20 + 14 + 7 + 3 + 3 = 47$$
$$\sigma_T^2 = \sigma_A^2 + \sigma_D^2 + \sigma_F^2 + \sigma_G^2 + \sigma_I^2$$
$$\sigma_T^2 = 2.78 + 0.11 + 0.11 + 0.11 + 0 = 3.11$$

A normal distribution with a mean of 47 and a variance of 3.11 will be used. The standard deviation is the square root of 3.11 so:

$$\sigma_T = 1.76$$

Software may be used to perform most of the calculations in this type of problem. Output 8.1 provides the output from the DSS software for the Gamma Industries example with the three time estimates.

With these values, the normal distribution may be used to find the probability of finishing the project by a specific time (T). Suppose we wish to determine the probability of finishing the project in 50 weeks or less. Use the Z-formula for the normal distribution, which results in the following:

$$Z = \frac{T - E(T)}{\sigma_T}$$
$$= \frac{50 - 47}{1.76} = 1.70$$

A graphical representation of this is shown in Figure 8.6. Using the probability table for the normal distribution in the appendix at the end of the book, shows that the probability associated with this Z value is 0.9554. Thus, there is approximately a 95.5% chance the project, more specifically the critical path, will be finished in 50 weeks or less.

Probability (project is finished in 50 weeks or less) =

$$P(T \leq 50) = P\left(Z \leq \frac{(50 - 47)}{1.76}\right) = P(Z \leq 1.70) = .9554$$

Caution should be taken in using this probability because it is based on several estimates and assumptions. It also may be possible that another path may have an expected completion time close to the critical path time but this other path may have a larger variability than the critical path. This path could actually have a smaller probability of being finished in this amount of time. It is possible that if one activity on this other path takes close to the pessimistic time to complete, that this other path may actually become critical. Thus, while the critical path should receive close monitoring during the project, it is not the only path that should be monitored. A good manager will not ignore the other paths and will recognize this possibility.

OUTPUT 8.1

DSS Output for Gamma Industries Example

Networks - CPM/Pert

Initial Problem

PERT	Start	End	Opt (a)	Lkly (m)	Pes (b)	Cost	Mean
A	1	2	15	20	25	0	20.00
B	1	6	9	10	11	0	10.00
C	2	3	13	14	21	0	15.00
D	2	4	13	14	15	0	14.00
E	3	5	3	4	5	0	4.00
F	4	5	6	7	8	0	7.00
G	5	6	2	3	4	0	3.00
H	5	7	3	4	5	0	4.00
I	6	7	3	3	3	0	3.00

Solution

Activity	Early Start	Early Finish	Late Start	Late Finish	Slack
*A	0.00	20.00	0.00	20.00	0.00
B	0.00	10.00	34.00	44.00	34.00
C	20.00	35.00	22.00	37.00	2.00
*D	20.00	34.00	20.00	34.00	0.00
E	35.00	39.00	37.00	41.00	2.00
*F	34.00	41.00	34.00	41.00	0.00
*G	41.00	44.00	41.00	44.00	0.00
H	41.00	45.00	43.00	47.00	2.00
*I	44.00	47.00	44.00	47.00	0.00

Expected completion: 47

Total Cost: 0

Standard deviation: 1.763834

* denotes critical path

Setting the Due Date for a Project

There are times when a person must set a due date for the completion of a project. Setting the due date to be the expected completion time of the project may seem reasonable. However, if this is done, there is only a 50 percent chance the project will actually be finished by this time if the project completion time is normally distributed. Thus, there would be 50 percent chance the project is finished late.

We may use the normal distribution to help us determine what an appropriate due date would be. Suppose in the Gamma Industries example

FIGURE 8.6

Normal Distribution Used to Find Probability of Completion by Time *T*

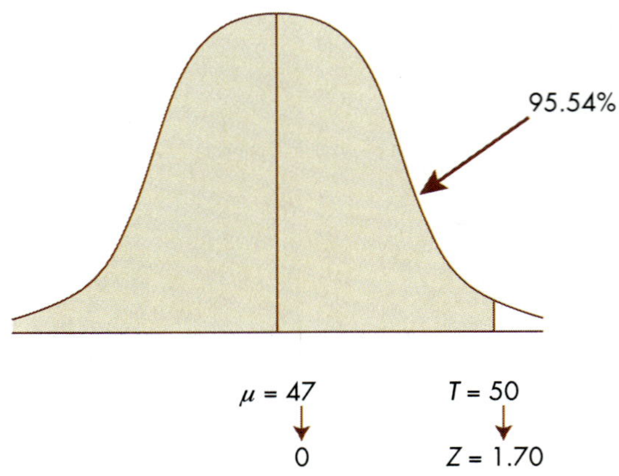

it is determined the due date should be set so there is only a 10 percent chance of being late and a 90 percent chance of finishing on schedule. Assuming the completion time is normally distributed, use the normal distribution to help find the appropriate due date. Figure 8.7 illustrates this situation. It is known the probability (area under the curve) to the left of the due date should be 90 percent. Looking up the probability 0.9000 in the normal distribution table, we find the closest probability to be 0.8997. The Z-value associated with this is 1.28. Therefore, set the due date (T) so that it has a Z-value of 1.28. Thus:

$$Z = \frac{T - E(T)}{\sigma_T}$$

$$1.28 = \frac{T - 47}{1.76}$$

or

$$T = 47 + 1.28(1.76) = 49.25$$

Given the assumptions made, there is a 90 percent chance the project will be finished in 49.25 weeks or less, so this would be the due date based on a 0.90 probability.

8.7

USING PERT/COST TO DEVELOP A BUDGET SCHEDULE

PERT/Cost
A technique used to develop a cost schedule for a project.

To this point, we have considered how to plan and schedule the activities in the project. We have only looked at the times involved in these activities. A manager also must develop a budget and schedule the cash flow so money is available when it is needed. **PERT/Cost** is very helpful in this regard. This is a technique for planning, scheduling, and monitoring costs of a project. Based on the assumption that costs for an activity are evenly

FIGURE 8.7

Determining the Due Date for a 90 Percent Probability of Completion

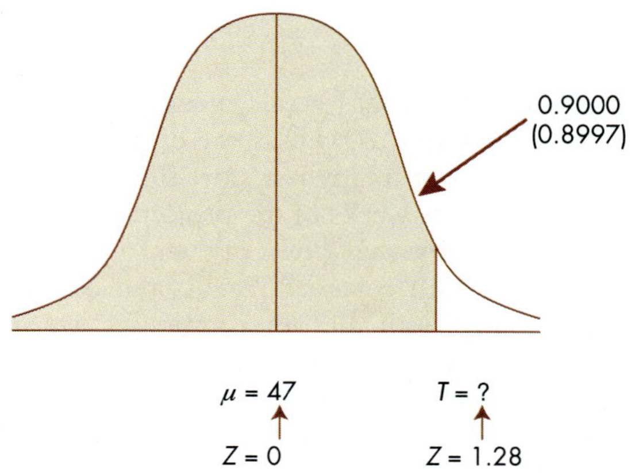

distributed over the duration of the activity, PERT/Cost allocates the costs to the specific time period when they will be incurred.

Delta Computer Consultants Example

Consider the project faced by Delta Computer Consultants. Delta is a small consulting firm that specializes in the development of customized software. The company is planning the development project shown in Figure 8.8. The

FIGURE 8.8

Network for Delta Computer Example

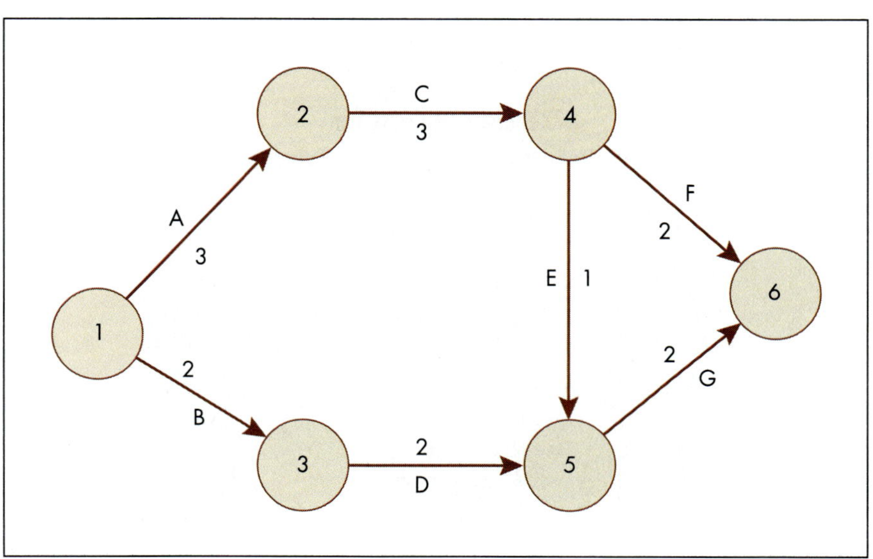

times for each activity and the costs associated with them are shown in Table 8.5. These costs are broken down on a per-week basis. For example, it is assumed the cost for Activity A is $2,500 per week for each of the three weeks required to complete this activity. If this assumption is not valid, the manager could use personal knowledge to accurately reflect the anticipated costs each week.

Output 8.2 gives the DSS output for this example. The earliest, latest, and slack times for each activity as well as the critical path are shown. Assuming each activity starts at its earliest start time, Activity A will be worked on during the first three weeks of the project. Similarly, Activity B will be worked on during the first two weeks of the project. Thus, in Weeks 1 and 2, we will be faced with costs of $2,500 and $4,000 per week, respectively. Continuing this with the other activities, we may prepare a schedule of budgeted costs based on earliest start times as shown in Table 8.6. Notice Activity D may start at the end of two weeks ($ES = 2$), so the actual work is performed beginning at the start of Week 3. The costs for D are therefore incurred in Weeks 3 and 4 if it is started at the earliest start time.

The total cost each week is shown at the bottom of the table. Also shown at the bottom is the total amount spent up to that point in time. This will enable management to compare their actual costs to the budgeted costs to determine if costs are over budget.

Because there is slack for some activities, it may be beneficial for management to delay the start of the activities until their latest start times. A cost schedule based on the latest start times is shown in Table 8.7. By delaying the start of activities until the latest start times, the company may delay the payments. This may have benefits from a cash flow perspective as well as a time value of money perspective. Comparing the total costs based on the earliest times with the total costs based on the latest times shows that at the end of the project, $41,000 will have been spent regardless of which starting times are used. However, at the end of Week 4, only $13,500 will

TABLE 8.5

Times and Costs for Delta Computer Consultants Example

Activity	t	Cost	Cost per Week
A	3	7,500	2,500
B	2	8,000	4,000
C	3	6,000	2,000
D	2	5,000	2,500
E	1	1,500	1,500
F	2	8,000	4,000
G	2	5,000	2,500
		Total 41,000	

OUTPUT 8.2

DSS Output for Delta Computer Consultants Example

Networks - CPM/Pert

Initial Problem

PERT	Start	End	Opt (a)	Lkly (m)	Pes (b)	Cost	Mean
A	1	2	15	20	25	0	20.00
B	1	6	9	10	11	0	10.00
C	2	3	13	14	21	0	15.00
D	2	4	13	14	15	0	14.00
E	3	5	3	4	5	0	4.00
F	4	5	6	7	8	0	7.00
G	5	6	2	3	4	0	3.00
H	5	7	3	4	5	0	4.00
I	6	7	3	3	3	0	3.00

Solution

Activity	Early Start	Early Finish	Late Start	Late Finish	Slack
*A	0.00	20.00	0.00	20.00	0.00
B	0.00	10.00	34.00	44.00	34.00
C	20.00	35.00	22.00	37.00	2.00
*D	20.00	34.00	20.00	34.00	0.00
E	35.00	39.00	37.00	41.00	2.00
*F	34.00	41.00	34.00	41.00	0.00
*G	41.00	44.00	41.00	44.00	0.00
H	41.00	45.00	43.00	47.00	2.00
*I	44.00	47.00	44.00	47.00	0.00

Expected completion: 47

Total Cost: 0

Standard deviation: 1.763834

* denotes critical path

have been spent if we start at the latest times, while $22,500 will have been spent if we start at the earliest start times.

While delaying starting times until the latest start time may have some benefits for the cash flow of a company, it does have the disadvantage of eliminating the slack that was present for an activity. If you start an activity at the latest time, any delay in the completion of that activity will cause it to be finished later than the latest finish time, thus delaying the completion of the entire project.

TABLE 8.6

Budgeted Costs for Delta Computer Consultants Based on Earliest Start Times (Costs are in thousands.)

	Week								
Activity	1	2	3	4	5	6	7	8	9
A	2.5	2.5	2.5						
B	4	4							
C				2	2	2			
D			2.5	2.5					
E							1.5		
F							4	4	
G								2.5	2.5
Total	6.5	6.5	5	4.5	2	2	5.5	6.5	2.5
Total to Date	6.5	13	18	22.5	24.5	26.5	32	38.5	41.0

TABLE 8.7

Budgeted Costs for Delta Computer Consultants Based on Latest Start Times (Costs are in thousands.)

	Week								
Activity	1	2	3	4	5	6	7	8	9
A	2.5	2.5	2.5						
B				4	4				
C				2	2	2			
D						2.5	2.5		
E							1.5		
F								4	4
G								2.5	2.5
Total	2.5	2.5	2.5	6	6	4.5	4	6.5	6.5
Total to Date	2.5	5	7.5	13.5	19.5	24	28	34.5	41

8.8 TIME/COST TRADE-OFFS

Crashing
The process of reducing the time required to complete an activity by using additional resources.

In planning the time required to complete a project, it often is possible to reduce the time required for the project by using additional resources of some type. This may involve the use of overtime or additional crews. Reducing the time to complete the project by using additional resources usually means the cost will increase. If it is necessary to finish a project in a time that is less than the normal completion time, the project manager must decide how to do this in the least expensive way possible. The process of reducing the time for the project is often called **crashing**, and the minimum possible time required to complete a specific activity is called the crash time for that activity. The cost of finishing an activity in the crash time is called the crash cost.

In performing this type of analysis, it is normally assumed that if an activity time can be reduced, the total time for that activity can be made to be any time between the crash time and the normal time. For example, if the crash time for Activity A is 20 weeks and the normal time is 25 weeks, this activity could be scheduled to be completed in 20 weeks, or 21 weeks, or any number up to 25 weeks. It also often is assumed the cost of crashing is linear. This means if an activity normally costs $30,000 to complete in 25 weeks but has a crash time of 20 weeks and a crash cost of $40,000, then the additional cost of $10,000 is evenly spread over the five weeks of time saved. The cost would be $2,000 per week to reduce the time. If this activity were to be completed in 24 weeks, a reduction of one week, then the additional cost would be $2,000. If these assumptions cannot be made, then some minor modifications would be required in the procedure that will now be presented.

Delta Computers Example

Suppose the project for Delta Computers can be completed in less time if additional resources are used. Table 8.8 provides all of the normal and crash times as well as the normal and crash costs for this modified situation. The cost per week for crashing also has been calculated. If this project must be completed in eight weeks instead of the originally planned nine weeks, then one of the activities must be crashed. Because the critical path is the path that requires nine weeks to complete, to reduce project completion time one of the activities on the critical path must be crashed. The critical path is ACEG. Table 8.8 indicates the time may be reduced for Activity A by one week at a cost of $2,000 per week, and the time for Activity C may be reduced by two weeks at a cost of $1,500 per week. Activities E

TABLE 8.8

Times and Costs for Delta Computer Consultants Example with Normal Times and Crash Times

	Time		Cost		Maximum Time	Cost per Week
Activity	Normal	Crash	Normal	Crash	Reduction	Reduced
*A	3	2	7,500	9,500	1	2,000
B	2	1	8,000	9,000	1	1,000
*C	3	1	6,000	9,000	2	1,500
D	2	1	5,000	6,500	1	1,500
*E	1	1	1,500	1,500	—	—
F	2	1	8,000	11,000	1	3,000
*G	2	2	5,000	5,000	—	—

* Activity on Critical Path

and G also are on the critical path but they may not be crashed. Therefore, select the activity on the critical path that has the lowest cost per week to crash. Select Activity C and crash this by one week, so the completion time is now two weeks instead of three. The cost of doing this would be an additional $1,500. Notice the cost of crashing B is only $1,000 per week, but because this is not on the critical path, crashing Activity B would not change the completion time for the project. The new times for this project are shown in Table 8.9. Notice crashing this one activity has an impact on the earliest, latest, and slack times for many of the other activities as well. If the total project time was to be reduced to seven weeks, crash C by one additional week.

When the critical path is crashed, it is possible that another path may become critical. Therefore, when crashing a project by inspection as done above, you should check the paths other than the critical path to see if the time for any of these other paths is greater than the revised time for the original critical path. For large projects, crashing by inspection is not feasible, but linear programming may be used for this purpose.

Using Linear Programming for Crashing

Linear programming may be used to determine the best way to crash a project to reduce the project completion time to any feasible desired amount. The objective is to minimize the cost of crashing, and the decision variables will represent the numbers of days to crash each activity and the time that an event will occur.

To illustrate this process, we will formulate the linear program that could be used to reduce the time for the Delta Computer example to eight weeks from the original nine weeks. Figure 8.8 above shows the relationships between the activities and the events. The statement of this problem will begin as follows:

Minimize cost of crashing
Subject to:

1. Event 1 occurs at time 0
2. Event 2 must occur after Activity A is finished

TABLE 8.9

Schedule for Delta Computer Consultants after Crashing Activity C One Week

Activity	ES	EF	LS	LF	Slack	Critical Path
A	0	3	0	3	0	yes
B	0	2	2	4	2	no
C	3	5	3	5	0	yes
D	2	4	4	6	2	no
E	5	6	5	6	0	yes
F	5	7	6	8	1	no
G	6	8	6	8	0	yes

3. Event 3 must occur after Activity B is finished
4. Event 4 must occur after Activity C is finished
5. Event 5 must occur after Activity D is finished
6. Event 5 must occur after Activity E is finished
7. Event 6 must occur after Activity F is finished
8. Event 6 must occur after Activity G is finished
9. Event 6 occurs in eight weeks

10–16. Limits on the number of days each activity is crashed

The variables will be defined as:

X_1 = time Event 1 occurs
X_2 = time Event 2 occurs
X_3 = time Event 3 occurs
X_4 = time Event 4 occurs
X_5 = time Event 5 occurs
X_6 = time Event 6 occurs
C_A = number of weeks A is crashed
C_B = number of weeks B is crashed
C_C = number of weeks C is crashed
C_D = number of weeks D is crashed
C_E = number of weeks E is crashed
C_F = number of weeks F is crashed
C_G = number of weeks G is crashed

For the sake of completeness, we include the variables for crashing Activities E and G even though these activities may not be crashed.

There is no cost for an event occurring, but there is an additional cost for crashing. Getting the cost per week crashed from Table 8.8 above, the objective function becomes:

$$\text{Minimize } 2{,}000C_A + 1{,}000C_B + 1{,}500C_C + 1{,}500C_D + 3{,}000C_F$$

The first constraint is

1. Event 1 occurs at time 0

and this is expressed as

$$X_1 = 0$$

The second through the eighth constraints are best understood by viewing the starting time of the activity as the time of the event from which the arrow in the network begins. For example, the start of Activity C is the time that Event 2 (X_2) occurs. The finish time of the activity is then the start time plus the activity time minus any crashing. For Activity C this means the finish time of C is $X_2 + 3 - C_C$. If several activities end at the same node, the event time of that node is the largest of the activity finish times, so the event time must be greater than or equal to the finishing times for all activities leading into it. This is why there are two constraints associated with Event 5.

Looking at the beginning of this network shows Activity A may begin immediately, and it ends at node (Event) 2. Thus, for Event 2:

$$\text{event time } 2 \geq \text{start time for A} + \text{activity time} - \text{crash time}$$

$$X_2 \geq X_1 + 3 - C_A$$

Rearranging these terms results in:

$$-X_1 + X_2 + C_A \geq 3$$

For the third constraint related to node (Event) 3:

$$X_3 \geq X_1 + 2 - C_B$$

Rearranging these terms results in:

$$-X_1 + X_3 + C_B \geq 2$$

The fourth through eighth constraints are constructed similarly. The ninth constraint is simply:

$$X_6 = 8$$

The last seven constraints limit the number of weeks that each activity may be crashed. For Activity A that may only be crashed one week this constraint is:

$$C_A \leq 1$$

The other constraints are similarly formulated.

The complete formulation is:

Minimize $2{,}000C_A + 1{,}000C_B + 1{,}500C_C + 1{,}500C_D + 3{,}000C_F$

Subject to:

$$\begin{aligned}
X_1 &= 0 \\
-X_1 + X_2 + C_A &\geq 3 \\
-X_1 + X_3 + C_B &\geq 2 \\
-X_2 + X_4 + C_C &\geq 3 \\
-X_3 + X_5 + C_D &\geq 2 \\
-X_4 + X_5 + C_E &\geq 1 \\
-X_4 + X_6 + C_F &\geq 2 \\
-X_5 + X_6 + C_G &\geq 2 \\
X_6 &= 8 \\
C_A &\leq 1 \\
C_B &\leq 1 \\
C_C &\leq 2 \\
C_D &\leq 1 \\
C_E &\leq 0 \\
C_F &\leq 1 \\
C_G &\leq 0 \\
\text{All variables} &\geq 0
\end{aligned}$$

This problem could be solved using any available software, which would show the activities to crash and the additional cost for crashing. You may note this problem could have been simplified by leaving out variables X_1, C_E, and C_G because each of these must be zero. They were included simply for the sake of completeness and consistency.

Once the problem has been formulated, it would be easy to evaluate the cost of crashing to seven or six or any number of weeks by simply changing the right-hand side of the ninth constraint, which specifies when to finish the project. No changes would be required in any of the other constraints.

8.9 ADDITIONAL TOPICS IN PROJECT MANAGEMENT

The tools seen in this chapter are helpful in managing a project. However, there are other very important and very helpful things for a project manager. We will briefly introduce these to you.

Gantt Charts

While network diagrams are very useful, managers often prefer to use **Gantt charts** to depict the activities of a project. A Gantt chart to represent the Delta Computer example is shown in Figure 8.9. This looks very similar to the PERT/Cost diagram in Table 8.6 above except the costs are replaced with bars to simply show when the activity is taking place.

Gantt chart
A graphical presentation of the activities in a project that clearly illustrates which activities will be occurring in each time period.

The basic Gantt chart shows clearly the activities being performed in each week of the project. Unlike PERT/CPM where the length of the arrows is not indicative of the time required for an activity, the length of a

FIGURE 8.9

Gantt Chart for Delta Computer Example

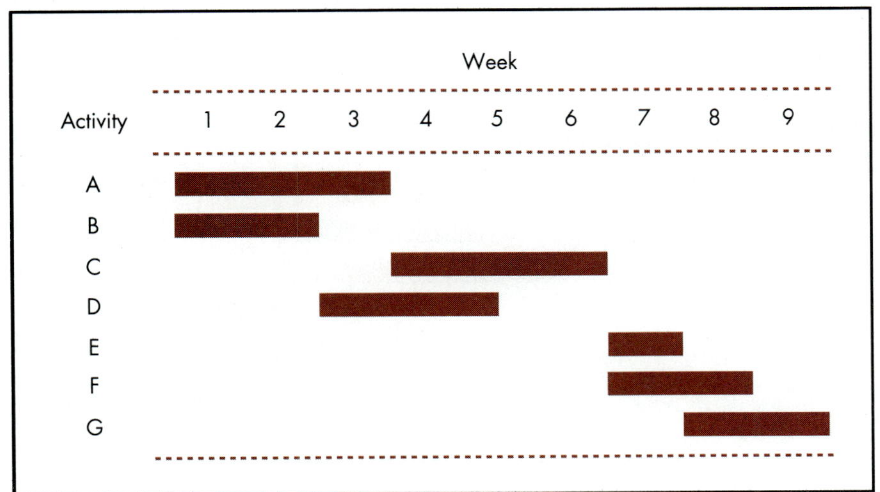

Launching the space shuttle is an extremely large project that is comprised of several smaller subactivities.
SOURCE: Courtesy NASA

FIGURE 8.10

Gantt Chart for Delta Computer Example with Slack Time Shown

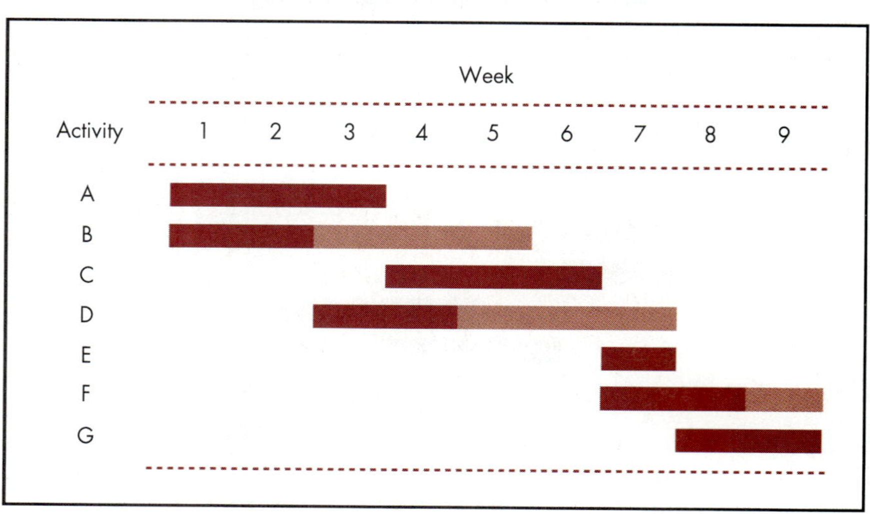

bar in a Gantt chart does indicate how long the activity will last. However, this basic Gantt chart does not show which activities must precede the others, and it does not indicate if any slack exists for the activities. Some modifications have been made with Gantt charts to indicate if slack does exist. Figure 8.10 represents this same project, but the additional lines at the ends of the bars provide an indication of the present slack.

Subprojects

For extremely large projects, an activity may be made of several smaller subactivities, and these might be viewed as a smaller project or a **subproject** of the original project. The person in charge of the activity might wish to create a PERT/CPM chart for managing this subproject.

Subproject
A set of activities that make up another activity, which is part of a larger project.

Milestones

Major events in a project are often referred to as **milestones.** These often are reflected in Gantt charts and PERT charts to highlight the importance of reaching these events.

Milestone
A major event in a project.

Resource Leveling

In addition to managing the time and costs involved in a project, a manager also must be concerned with the resources used in a project. These resources

GLOBAL PERSPECTIVES

Project Management in the United States Antarctic Program

Antarctica is the last pristine continent on Earth. The climate and location of Antarctica provide a unique opportunity for people to study the environment. Each year, approximately 2,500 Americans work in and around Antarctica as part of the United States Antarctic Program (USAP). The program draws upon the resources of various U.S. universities, federal agencies, and commercial firms. The goal of the USAP is to support research on worldwide and regional problems and to expand the fundamental knowledge of Antarctica.

In 1991, the National Science Foundation commissioned a study of the operations of McMurdo Station, America's largest Antarctic station. Logistics, planning, warehousing and staffing are critical at the station, because of its isolation from supply points. To reduce pollution by the station, the NSF wanted to identify inefficiencies and duplications in staffing. They were motivated more by environmental concerns than by cost containment, although cost issues also were considered.

The staffing analysis was conducted on three levels, each of which contained several clearly-defined steps. In the first level, each support function was evaluated individually. Responsibilities, workload, and staffing were identified for each function, and staffing and/or workload ratios were defined. Next, the support and management systems of the two major service providers for the station were examined. A proposed organization and management plan, a time-line, and a workload database were developed, along with proposed staffing levels. Finally, the impacts of various personnel reduction strategies were examined, and final recommendations were made. It is hoped this project will succeed in keeping Antarctica, the world's last frontier, in its current state for as long as possible.

SOURCE:
Hewitt, R. L., June 1992. "OR in Antarctica." *OR/MS Today*: 30-33.

might be equipment or people. In planning the project and often as part of the work breakdown structure, a manager must identify which resources are needed with each activity. For example, in a construction project there may be several activities requiring the use of heavy equipment such as a crane. If the construction company only has one such crane, then conflicts will occur if two activities requiring the use of this crane are scheduled for the same day. To alleviate problems such as this, **resource leveling** is employed. This means one or more activities is moved from its earliest start time to another time (no later than the latest start time), so the resource utilization is more even over time. If the resources are construction crews, this is very beneficial in that the crews are kept busy while overtime is minimized.

Resource leveling
The process of balancing the resource utilization over the duration of a project.

Software

There are numerous project management software packages on the market for both mainframe computers and personal computers. A few of these are listed in Summary Table 8.1. Good software is available for personal computers, and the cost ranges from a few hundred dollars to several thousand dollars. For mainframe computers, software may cost considerably more. Companies have paid several hundred thousand dollars for project management software because it helps management make better decisions and keep track of things that would otherwise be unmanageable.

In using professional software for project management, a person would input the activities, predecessors, times or three time estimates, costs, and resources for a particular project. The computer then will draw the network diagram or Gantt chart. If a resource is overutilized (i.e., scheduled at the same time for different activities), the computer will highlight this and actually level the resources for you. Most software will even check to see if this resource is being utilized on another project also at the same time. Most software will allow the user to input a calendar to indicate which days are work days and which days are not. Then, the earliest start time for an activity might not be given as *Week 8* but rather as *June 24* or whatever the actual day is. Planned start times and actual start times may be input for each activity. Thus, if the project falls behind schedule, new planned starting times for

SUMMARY TABLE 8.1

Software Tools for Project Management

1. Harvard Project Manager
2. InstaPlan
3. Mac Project II
4. Microsoft Project for Windows
5. Open Plan
6. Primavera Project Planner
7. Project Workbench
8. Quiknet Professional
9. Super Project Expert
10. Time Line
11. ViewPoint

A CLOSER LOOK

Graphical Evaluation and Review Technique (GERT)

In addition to PERT and CPM, other techniques are available to help manage projects. One technique that is closely related to these is the graphical evaluation and review technique (GERT). With this, it is possible that certain activities may not occur and each activity is given a probability of occurring. If a previous activity has not been successfully completed, the activities that follow may change. It also is possible in GERT for some activities to be repeated, whereas in PERT, each activity must occur exactly one time. Thus, GERT may prove to be the appropriate method for modeling when certain conditions required for PERT are not met.

While GERT is not new, it was developed later than PERT and CPM. With the constant advances in both computer graphics and computer software, GERT one day may be as widely utilized as these other project management tools.

SOURCE: Meredith, J. R. and S. J. Mantel, Jr., 1989. *Project Management: A Managerial Approach*. 2nd ed. NY: John Wiley & Sons, Inc.

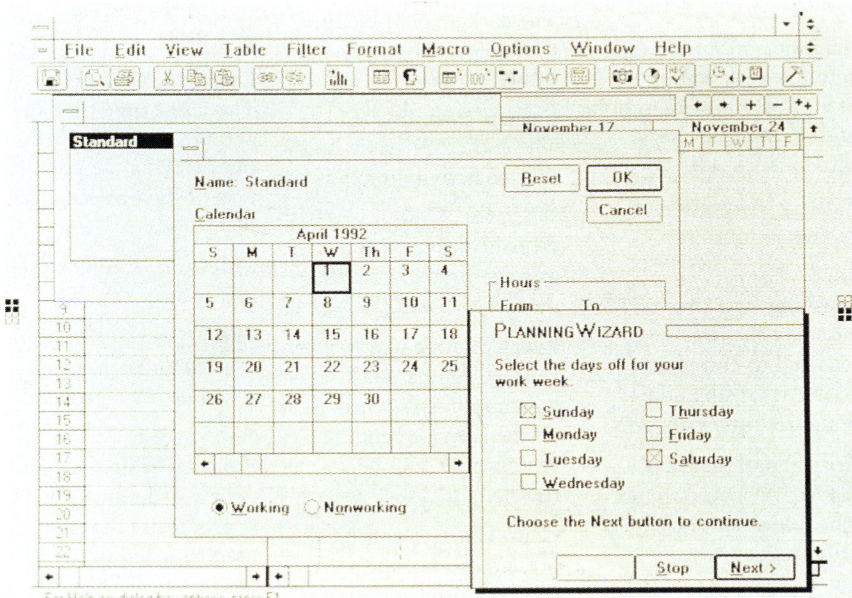

Microsoft Project 4.0 is one of the many project management software packages available. SOURCE: Reprinted with permission from Microsoft Corporation

later activities immediately may be determined by the computer. Many software packages will allow the user to specify up to four or more levels of subprojects. The level of detail on reports provided by the software may be at whatever level would be appropriate for that level of management.

8.10 SUMMARY

We have seen how a project manager may use PERT and CPM to plan, schedule, and control a project. With the aid of a network representation it was shown how to determine the earliest, latest and slack times for each activity in a project. Using PERT/Cost showed how to develop a budget schedule for a manager to use in tracking costs for a project. The use of additional resources may be considered to crash a project and finish it in an earlier time than normal.

Modern computer software takes the drudgery out of the work involved with techniques used for project management. The knowledge of project management techniques together with available software allows a project manager to use his or her time more efficiently and more productively.

GLOSSARY

Activities-on-arcs A network representation of a project in which the arcs represent the activities. *p. 330*

Activities-on-nodes A network representation of a project in which the nodes represent the activities. *p. 330*

Activity A specific job or task in a project. *p. 330*

Crashing The process of reducing the time required to complete an activity by using additional resources. *p. 348*

Critical path method (CPM) A procedure for scheduling activities in a project; used when times are known with certainty. *p. 326*

Critical path The longest path from the starting node in a project to the finishing node in a project. *p. 334*

Dummy activity An activity used in a network to show a precedence relationship. It has zero time associated with it. *p. 331*

Earliest finish time (EF) The earliest possible time that an activity may finish. *p. 334*

Earliest start time (ES) The earliest possible time that an activity may start. *p. 334*

Expected time (*t*) The average time to complete an activity. *p. 339*

Event A node in a PERT/CPM network, which indicates when all the activities ending at that node will be finished. *p. 330*

Gantt chart A graphical presentation of the activities in a project that clearly illustrates which activities will be occurring in each time period. *p. 353*

Immediate predecessor An activity that must be finished before the next activity may begin. *p. 329*

Latest finish time (LF) The latest time that an activity may finish without delaying the completion of the project. *p. 336*

Latest start time (LS) The latest time that an activity may start without delaying the completion of the project. *p. 336*

Milestone A major event in a project. *p. 355*

PERT/Cost A technique used to develop a cost schedule for a project. *p. 344*

Program evaluation and review technique (PERT) A procedure that may be used to schedule activities in a project using three time estimates. *p. 326*

Resource leveling The process of balancing the resource utilization over the duration of a project. *p. 356*

Slack (S) The amount of time an activity may be

delayed without delaying the completion of the project. *p. 338*

Subproject A set of activities that make up another activity, which is part of a larger project. *p. 355*

Variance (σ^2) A measure of the variability of the completion time of an activity. *p. 340*

Work breakdown structure (WBS) The process of identifying the activities in a project and breaking these into finer levels of detail. *p. 327*

KEY EQUATIONS

(8-1) t = activity time

(8-2) ES = largest EF for all immediate predecessors
earliest start time for activity

(8-3) $EF = ES + t$
earliest finish time for activity

(8-4) $LS = LF - t$
latest start time for activity

(8-5) LF = smallest LS for activities that immediately follow
latest finish time for activity

(8-6) $t = (a + 4m + b)/6$
expected completion time for activity with three time estimates

(8-7) slack $= LF - EF = LS - ES$

(8-8) variance for activity $\sigma^2 = ((b - a)/6)^2$

(8-9) σ_T^2 = sum of variances on critical path
variance of the project (critical path)

(8-10) σ_T = square root of variance of critical path
standard deviation for critical path

(8-11) $Z = [T - E(T)]/\sigma_T$
Z-value for use with normal distribution. T = project completion time.
$E(T)$ = expected (mean) completion time for project.

SOLVED PROBLEMS

SOLVED PROBLEM 8-1

A project is being planned and the following activities, relationships, and times have been identified:

Activity	Immediate Predecessor	Weeks
A	—	4
B	—	3
C	A	8
D	A	2
E	B,D	3
F	B,D	2
G	E	1
H	C,G	4
I	F	2

a) Draw the CPM network to represent this project.
b) Calculate all the earliest, latest, and slack times.
c) Identify the critical path. What is the minimum possible time required for completing this project?
d) What would happen if Activity B actually took seven weeks to complete instead of three weeks as planned?

SOLUTION

a)

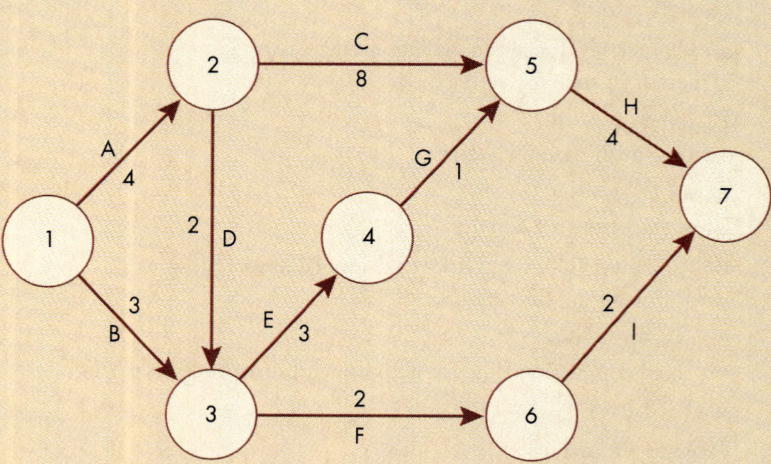

b)

Activity	ES	EF	LS	LF	Slack	Critical Path
A	0	4	0	4	0	yes
B	0	3	5	8	5	no
C	4	12	4	12	0	yes
D	4	6	6	8	2	no
E	6	9	8	11	2	no
F	6	8	12	14	6	no
G	9	10	11	12	2	no
H	12	16	12	16	0	yes
I	8	10	14	16	6	no

c) The critical path is ACH. The minimum possible time for completing the project is 16 weeks (the time required to complete the critical path).
d) Because B has five weeks of slack, the project would not be delayed and could still be finished in 16 weeks even if Activity B was delayed by four weeks.

SOLVED PROBLEM 8-2

The following times, in weeks, have been estimated for a project.

Activity	Immediate Predecessor	*a*	*m*	*b*
A	—	2	3	4
B	—	2	3	4
C	A	2	3	10
D	A	6	7	8
E	B,C	9	10	11
F	A	5	7	9
G	E,F	3	4	5
H	E,F	7	8	9
I	D,G	1	2	3

a) Draw the network to represent this project.
b) What is the expected completion time of the project?
c) What is the probability the project will be finished in 27 weeks or less?

SOLUTION

a)

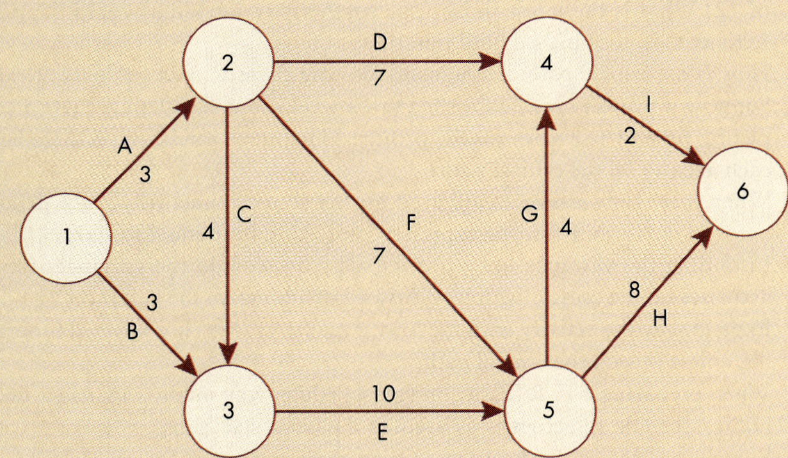

b)

Activity	*a*	*b*	*c*	$t = (a+4m+b)/6$	$\sigma^2 = ((b-a)/6)^2$
*A	2	3	4	3	0.111
B	2	3	4	3	0.111
*C	2	3	10	4	1.778
D	6	7	8	7	0.111
*E	9	10	11	10	0.111
F	5	7	9	7	0.444
G	3	4	5	4	0.111
*H	7	8	9	8	0.111
I	1	2	3	2	0.111

*Critical path is ACEH. Expected completion time is 25 weeks.

c) The project (critical path) variance is found by adding the variances on the critical path. This is:

$$0.111 + 1.778 + 0.111 + 0.111 = 2.111$$

The standard deviation is 1.45.

$$Z = \frac{T - E(T)}{\sigma_T} = \frac{27-25}{1.45} = 1.38$$

$$P(T \le 27) = P(Z \le 1.38) = 0.9162$$

Thus, there is about a 92 percent probability the project will be finished in 27 weeks or less.

QUESTIONS

1. What is an immediate predecessor? Why is it not necessary to list all predecessor activities in a project?
2. In a PERT network, how is the latest finish time for an activity determined?
3. Suppose Activity C is the only immediate predecessor for Activities E and F. Activity E has a latest start time of eight and Activity F has a latest start time of 12. What is the latest finish time for Activity C? What would happen if Activity C is not finished until time 12?
4. How is the critical path determined? Why are these activities called critical?
5. Suppose a project may be finished in 14 weeks, but the manager sets a completion time of 16 weeks for the project. How much slack would there be for each activity on the critical path?
6. When three time estimates are used for the activity time, why is the denominator in the formula for the expected completion time equal to six?
7. In finding the variance for a project, why do we add the variances for the activities on the critical path used instead of adding all the variances?
8. Explain why the activity with the lowest cost to crash is not selected for crashing unless it is on the critical path.
9. When preparing a PERT/Cost budget schedule, why might a manager decide not to schedule all activities to begin at the latest start time?
10. Explain the differences between a Gantt chart and a PERT chart.

PROBLEMS

11. Using the Gamma Industries example in this chapter, answer the following questions:
    a) When should you schedule the workers to begin the work of preparing the documentation?
    b) What would happen if these workers were not available until Week 42?
    c) Would the project be delayed if testing the hardware was delayed two weeks and developing the documentation also was delayed two weeks?
    d) Would the project be delayed if developing the hardware was delayed two weeks and testing the hardware also was delayed two weeks?
12. Calculate the earliest, latest, and slack times for the project represented by the following network. Which activities are on the critical path? What are the immediate predecessors for Activity H? What are the immediate predecessors for Activity G?

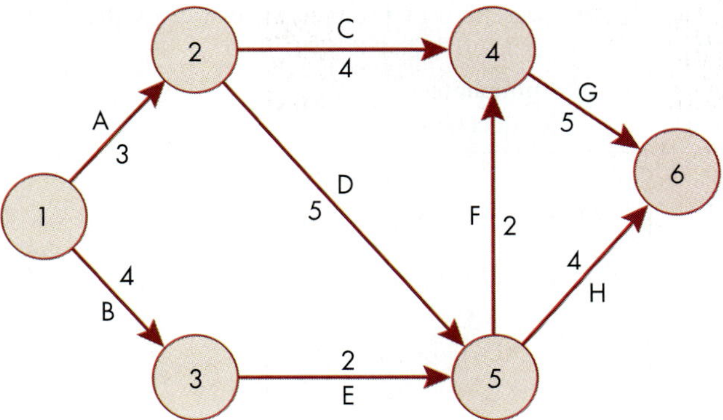

13. Calculate the earliest, latest, and slack times for the project represented by the following network. Which activities are on the critical path? What is the dummy activity in this network indicating?

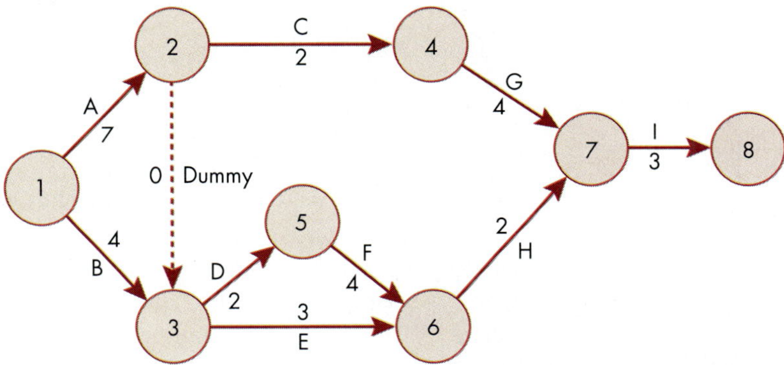

14. For the project represented by the table below, draw the network.

Activity	Immediate Predecessor
A	—
B	—
C	A
D	B
E	C,D
F	A
G	E,F

15. The following are the activity times for the project in Problem 14 above. Find the slack time for each activity and find the critical path.

Activity	Time in Weeks
A	3
B	7
C	4
D	2
E	5
F	6
G	3

16. For the project represented by the table below, draw the network.

Activity	Immediate Predecessor
A	—
B	—
C	—
D	B
E	A,C
F	D
G	E

17. The following are the activity times for the project in Problem 16 above. Find the slack time for each activity and find the critical path.

Activity	Time in Days
A	5
B	2
C	7
D	6
E	5
F	4
G	2

18. For the project represented by the table below, draw the network.

Activity	Immediate Predecessor
A	—
B	—
C	A
D	B,C
E	C

19. For the project represented by the table below, draw the network.

Activity	Immediate Predecessor
A	—
B	—
C	A,B
D	C
E	A

20. The expected completion time of a project is 80 weeks with a standard deviation of five weeks. Find the probability that the project is finished in:
a) 90 weeks or less
b) 88 weeks or less
c) 78 weeks or less

21. The expected completion time of a project is 80 weeks with a standard deviation of five weeks. Management has decided to set the due date so there is only a 15 percent chance the project will be finished later than the due date. What due date should be set?
22. A project was planned using PERT with three time estimates. The expected completion time of the project was determined to be 40 weeks. The variance of the critical path is four.
    a) What is the probability the critical path will be finished in 40 weeks or less?
    b) What is the probability the critical path takes longer than 40 weeks?
    c) What is the probability the critical path will be finished in 44 weeks or less?
    d) What is the probability the critical path takes longer than 44 weeks?
    e) There is only a _____ percent chance the critical path will take longer than 44 weeks.
    f) There is only a 10 percent chance the critical path will take longer than _____ weeks.
    g) If the project manager wishes to set the due date for the completion of the project so there is a 90 percent chance of finishing on schedule, what due date should be set?
23. The estimated times and immediate predecessors for the activities in a project are given in the table below.

Activity	Immediate Predecessor	*a*	*m*	*b*
A	—	9	10	11
B	—	4	10	16
C	A	9	10	11
D	B	5	8	11

    a) Calculate the expected time and variance for each activity.
    b) What is the expected completion time of the critical path? What is the expected completion time of the other path in the network?
    c) What is the variance of the critical path? What is the variance of the other path in the network?
    d) If the time to complete path AC is normally distributed, what is the probability this path will be finished in 22 weeks or less?
    e) If the time to complete path BD is normally distributed, what is the probability this path will be finished in 22 weeks or less?
    f) Explain why the probability the critical path will be finished in 22 weeks or less is not necessarily the probability the project will be finished in 22 weeks or less.

24. The estimated times and immediate predecessors for the activities in a project are given in the table below.

Activity	Immediate Predecessor	*a*	*m*	*b*
A	—	9	10	11
B	—	8	10	12
C	A	7	8	9
D	A	3	5	13
E	B,C	8	9	10
F	D	3	9	15
G	D	4	5	14
H	E,F	5	8	11

a) Calculate the expected completion time and variance for each activity.
b) Find all the ES, EF, LS, LF, and slack times.
c) Which activities are on the critical path?
d) What is the expected completion time and variance of the critical path?
e) What is the probability the critical path is finished in 37 weeks or less?
f) What is the probability the project is not finished in 37 weeks or less?
g) If the project manager wishes to set the due date of the project so there is only a five percent chance of not finishing by this time, what due date should be set?

25. The following costs have been estimated for the activities in a project.

Activity	Immediate Predecessors	Time	Cost
A	—	8	8,000
B	—	4	12,000
C	A	3	6,000
D	B	5	15,000
E	C,D	6	9,000
F	C,D	5	10,000
G	F	3	6,000

a) Develop a cost schedule based on earliest start times.
b) Develop a cost schedule based on latest start times.
c) Suppose it has been determined the $6,000 for Activity G is not evenly spread over the three weeks. Instead, the cost for the first week is $4,000 while the cost is $1,000 per week for each of the last two weeks. Modify the cost schedule based on earliest start times to reflect this situation.

26. The following table provides information about the development of a computerized accounting system. The company is concerned about having this system in place before the busy tax season begins. The times in the table are in weeks.

Activity	Immediate Predecessor	Time		Cost	
		Normal	Crash	Normal	Crash
A	—	3	2	8,000	9,800
B	—	4	3	9,000	10,000
C	A	6	4	12,000	15,000
D	B	2	1	5,000	5,500
E	A	5	3	7,500	8,700
F	C	2	1	8,000	9,000
G	D,E	4	2	6,000	7,400
H	F,G	5	3	5,000	6,600

a) Using normal times, what is the minimum time required for completing the project? What is the total cost of the project using normal times?
b) Suppose the project must be finished in 16 weeks. Determine by inspection which activity or activities should be crashed to do this at the minimum additional cost. How much does this increase the cost of the project?
c) List all the paths in the network. After the crashing in part (b) has been done, what is the time required to complete each path? If the project completion time must be reduced another week so the total time is 15 weeks, which activity or activities should be crashed? Solve this by inspection. Note that it is sometimes better to crash an activity that is not the least cost for crashing if it is on several paths rather than crashing several activities on separate paths when there is more than one critical path.

27. Refer to the situation in Problem 26. Formulate the linear programming problem that would be used to crash this project so it is finished in 16 weeks? What change would have to be made if we wished to finish the project in 14 weeks?

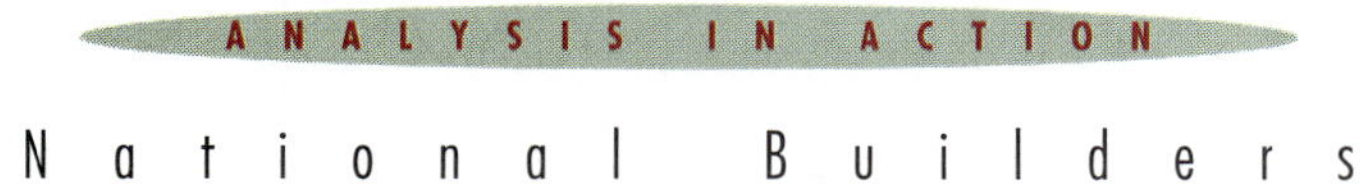

National Builders

National Builders specializes in the construction of single family houses. Recent plans to move into the Phoenix area have strained the resources of the company and new personnel have been hired to help in this new venture. Before beginning a new housing development, management has decided to prepare a typical PERT chart to help the new project managers gain familiarity with the construction practices in this new area. As many houses will be under construction simultaneously and a limited number of subcontractors are available, careful planning is essential.

A recent college graduate, Bill Door, has been assigned the task of developing a basic plan for the construction schedule. Drawing upon his knowledge about project scheduling, he has decided to use the critical path method in this task. He has developed the following table based on previous experience and other information about the availability of materials.

Activity	Immediate Predecessor	Time
Prepare Land	—	2
Forms & Plumbing	Prepare Land	3
Pour Foundation	Forms & Plumbing	1
Frame & Roof	Pour Foundation	7
Wiring in Walls	Frame	3
Rough Plumbing	Frame	4
Dry-in	Frame	3
Heating/AC Ducts	Dry-in	5
Sheetrock/Plaster	Heating/AC Ducts	8
Kitchen Fixtures	Sheetrock/Plaster	3
Finish Plumbing	Sheetrock/Plaster	2
Finish Interior Walls	Sheetrock/Plaster	6
Finish Roof	Frame & Roof	2
Bricks	Frame & Roof	6
Gutters	Finish Roof, Bricks	1
Floors	Finish Interior Walls	5
Finish Electrical	Finish Interior Walls	3
Driveway	Bricks	3
Landscape & Clean-up	Driveway	4
Inspection	Landscape & Clean-up	1

Upon seeing this information, the vice president for construction has questioned Bill about several things that seem to be missing. Bill has explained these are included in the activities listed in the table, although several subcontractors may be involved in a single activity. Bill agrees some of these activities could be broken into subactivities if further detail is needed.

Assuming the information in this table is accurate, prepare a managerial report indicating when these activities could take place. Include information about the slack time available. Also include any suggestions for improving this table.

CASE TWO

Network Programming at AT&T

As described in the previous case study on Linear Programming, AT&T's Production Planning and Control (PP & C) Group uses linear programming to help make annual staffing decisions based on demand forecasts and pending projects. Meanwhile, workloads at regional offices are updated every day given the latest information from the planning, project management, and marketing organizations within AT&T's Network Services Division (NSD). John Zuk, the manager of the PP & C group, and his team help decide which offices should do what work when, to minimize overall cost.

This daily office scheduling problem is not simple. Hundreds of offices and thousands of workers are involved. Meanwhile, the environment is constantly changing in both inputs and resources. Marketing plans change. The deployment of internal experts changes. People go on vacation. Blizzards or floods cripple the system. Solving this problem by hand is hard to imagine. Even finding a feasible solution on a given day would be difficult, let alone finding any kind of optimal solution. Even if it were possible, circumstances would change from one day to the next, and the problem would have to be resolved. John Zuk and his team tackle this office assignment problem with the help of network programming.

Each individual problem is driven by the tasks that must be done. These tasks include maintenance of equipment, addition of equipment for capacity reasons (so that more calls can be processed), addition of equipment for capability reasons (so that new services can be offered), and change of equipment (so that new technologies can be used). Ultimately, AT&T needs to know where each task will be performed, and what extra staff members will be assigned to each location for what period. The constraints for the problem are related mainly to the workforce. There are daily fluctuations due to illness and vacations. There also are skill set restrictions (i.e., who can do which tasks). Finally, there are geographic

With the help of Network Programming, AT&T tackles an immense daily office scheduling and assignment problem.
CREDIT: AT&T Network Operations Center

constraints. The PP & C team tries not to move people too far from their homes, which also helps minimize transportation costs.

A simplified version of the types of network problems solved by AT&T at this level is next described. In the example, demands for service are divided between four regions, East, Southeast, Midwest, and West. Each region needs a certain number of hours of support for each of three different types of work. Table 1 shows the support demands for the different regions in hours.

TABLE 1

Demands

	East	Southeast	Midwest	West
Capacity Support	100	200	75	100
Maintenance Support	150	300	200	100
Planning Support	75	200	100	300

There are six regional offices. Each office has an available capacity for each type of support, as shown in Table 2.

TABLE 2

Supply

	Boston	Atlanta	Austin	Phoenix	Chicago	Seattle
Capacity	50	100	50	200	50	50
Maintenance Support	250	150	100	100	75	75
Planning Support	100	175	50	150	100	100

This problem can be formulated as a series of three separate transportation networks, one corresponding to each type of work. The network for capacity support is shown below. The costs associated with each office satisfying the demands for each region are shown in Table 3. In general, the costs become larger for performing tasks further away from the source of the demand.

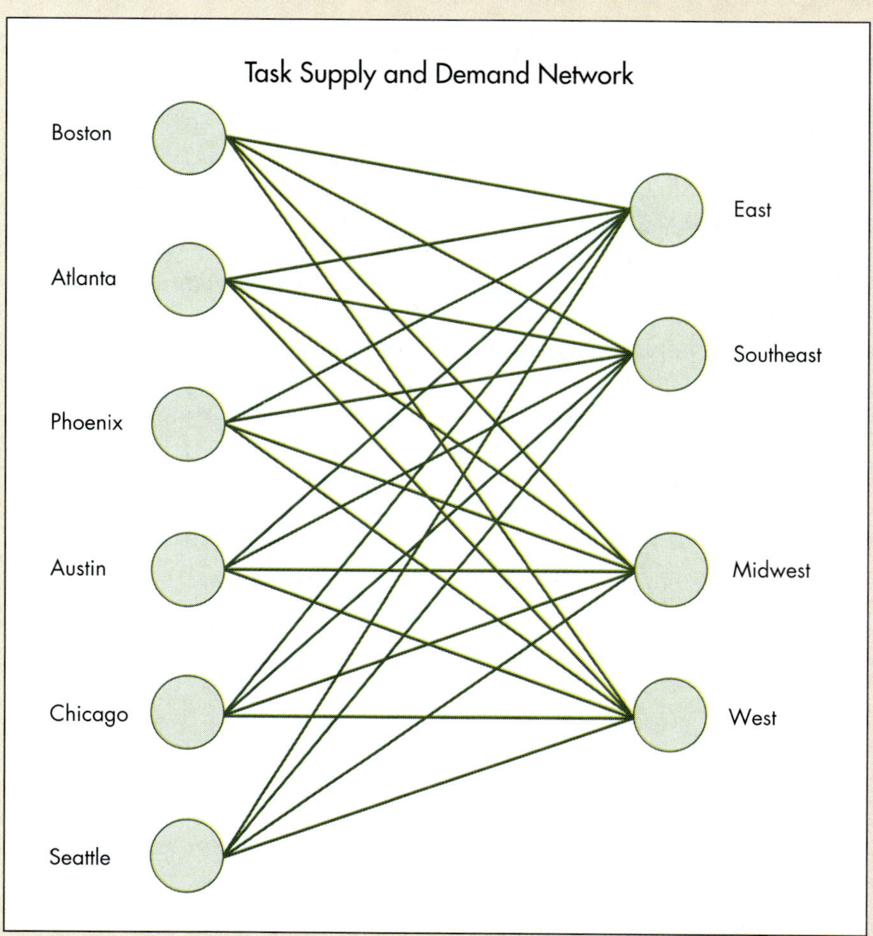

TABLE 3

Costs

	East	Southeast	Midwest	West
Boston	5	7	10	20
Atlanta	6	4	8	18
Austin	10	7	7	10
Phoenix	12	10	6	4
Chicago	7	10	5	9
Seattle	20	20	7	7

The above can be readily solved as a minimum cost network flow problem using the computer software provided with this book. The variables will be worker hours provided by each office to support each region's demands. Various extensions could be added to this example, while still allowing it to be solved as a network problem.

For example, arcs could be added between the local offices showing the assignment of workers to other locations. Sending a worker from Boston to Atlanta for the duration of a project might be less expensive than bringing the work up to Boston. Geographic restrictions on how far a worker could be asked to travel easily could be modeled by not including arcs for unacceptable assignments.

Another extension that would bring the model closer to the reality of planning for AT&T would be to model technicians who can perform multiple types of tasks (i.e., doing planning work or maintenance work). This extension would mean that the problem could no longer be broken into three unrelated networks. Weights would have to be added to each type of job, to show which jobs should be assigned workers first. At AT&T, capacity installation holds the highest priority, followed by maintenance of existing equipment, and then planning tasks.

The problem can be written as three separate transportation problems. A solution will be obtained for capacity support. This may be modeled as a linear program and solved with LINDO, Excel, or DSS. It also may be solved as a transportation problem as follows:

```
Using DSS, select Transportation Method, the formulation and the
solution are:
Transportation Model        06-13-1995 at 13:12:38     Problem:
case2.P11

Initial Problem

          Min       Dest1     Dest2     Dest3     Dest4     Prod Cap
          Srce1      5         7         10        20        50
          Srce2      6         4         8         18        100
          Srce3      10        7         7         10        50
          Srce4      12        10        6         4         200
          Srce5      7         10        5         9         50
          Srce6      20        20        7         7         50
          Dest Req   100       200       75        100       500

Enhanced Vogel's Approximation Method

Initial solution degenerate -  1  zero cell(s) entered initial
solution

Solution: Min Z =  2725

From          To             Number         Cost          Amount

Srce1         Dest1           50             5             250
Srce1         Dest2           0              7             0
Srce2         Dest2           100            4             400
Srce3         Dest2           50             7             350
Srce4         Dest2           50             10            500
Srce4         Dest3           50             6             300
Srce4         Dest4           100            4             400
Srce5         Dest1           50             7             350
Srce6         Dest3           25             7             175
Srce6         Dummy           25             0             0

Total                                                      2725

** Multiple solutions exist
```

PROBLEM 2

Solve the other two transportation network problems for the case. That is, assign the maintenance and planning support staff to the different geographic regions.

PROBLEM 3

Due to a contractual agreement the Seattle office cannot assign workers to the Midwest. How should the assignments of the three classifications of workers be made? What is the impact on the total assignment cost?

CHAPTER NINE

Network Models

LEARNING OBJECTIVES

Upon completing Chapter 9, you should be able to:

- Identify the different types of networks commonly used to aid in decision making.
- Find the minimal spanning tree that connects all the nodes in a network.
- Determine the maximal flow capacity from the source node to the sink node in a network.
- Find the shortest route from the origin node to each of the nodes in a network.
- Use computer software to perform the calculations in the three network models.

CHAPTER OUTLINE

9.1

INTRODUCTION

Businesses often are faced with problems that may be modeled using networks. Chapter 8 illustrated the use of a network as an important part of PERT and CPM. This chapter will show how using a minimal spanning tree may help to determine the best way to connect computers in a local area network. We will see how the maximal flow technique may help in designing a freeway system to maximize the number of cars that can use it or in designing a pipeline system to maximize the amount of oil that could flow through it. Also, the shortest route technique, which could be used to determine the least cost or least distance way to get from one location to another, will be explored.

9.2

MINIMAL SPANNING TREE

J. T. Thompson is the computer services manager at Connexus University. Thanks to a donation from a wealthy alumnus, a major expansion of the computing capabilities of the university is being planned. As a part of this

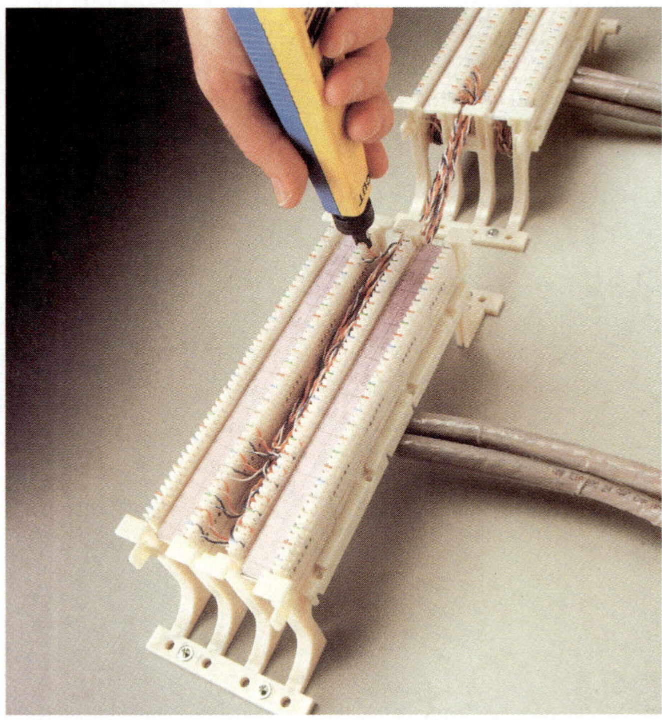

To determine the minimum total length of cable required to connect nodes on a computer network the minimal spanning tree technique may be used. SOURCE: Courtesy of AMP Incorporated

expansion, several buildings on campus will be connected into a computer network. The cables that must be run are expensive, and Thompson would like to minimize the total length of the cables used. There are eight buildings that must be connected, and Figure 9.1 shows the distances, in hundreds of feet, between the buildings where it is feasible to run cables. Notice there is no arc connecting certain nodes, such as nodes 2 and 3, because it has been determined physical restrictions prevent these connections. Given this situation, Thompson would like to determine the minimum total length of cabling required to connect these buildings.

The **minimal spanning tree technique** is a method that may be used to determine the minimum distance required to connect a set of nodes. The method is summarized below:

Minimal spanning tree technique
A method that may be used to determine the minimum distance required to connect a set of nodes (points).

STEP 1. Select any node in the network. Connect this node to the closest unconnected node.

STEP 2. Find the unconnected node that is nearest to a connected node, and connect these two nodes. If there is a tie, arbitrarily select one of them to be connected.

STEP 3. If all nodes are connected, stop. Otherwise, repeat STEP 2 until each node is connected to another node.

Applying this technique to the Connexus University problem illustrated in Figure 9.1, in STEP 1 arbitrarily select node 1. The shortest distance to any other node is one, which would connect node 1 with node 2. This is shown as the first network in Figure 9.2.

In STEP 2, look at the unconnected nodes to see which is closest to one of the connected nodes, currently nodes 1 and 2. Node 4 has a distance of two to node 1, and this is lower than the other choices. Therefore, node 4 is connected to node 1 as seen in the second network in Figure 9.2.

FIGURE 9.1

Connexus University Spanning Tree Problem

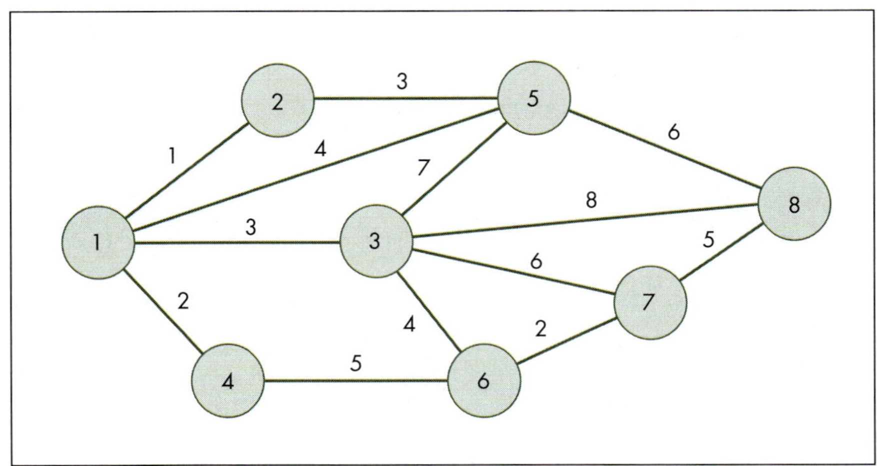

FIGURE 9.2

Connexus University Spanning Tree Problem with First Three Connections

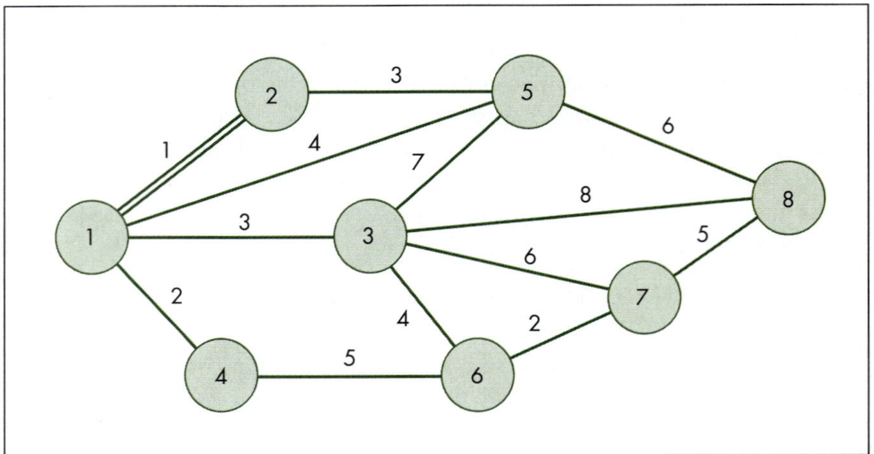

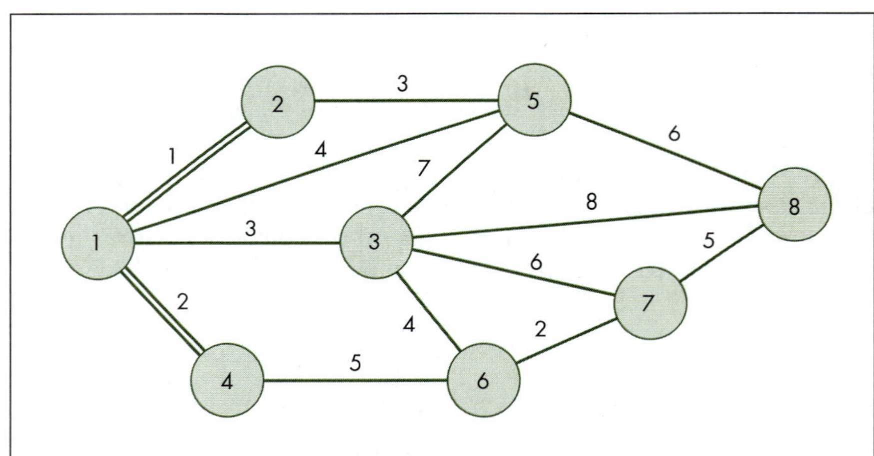

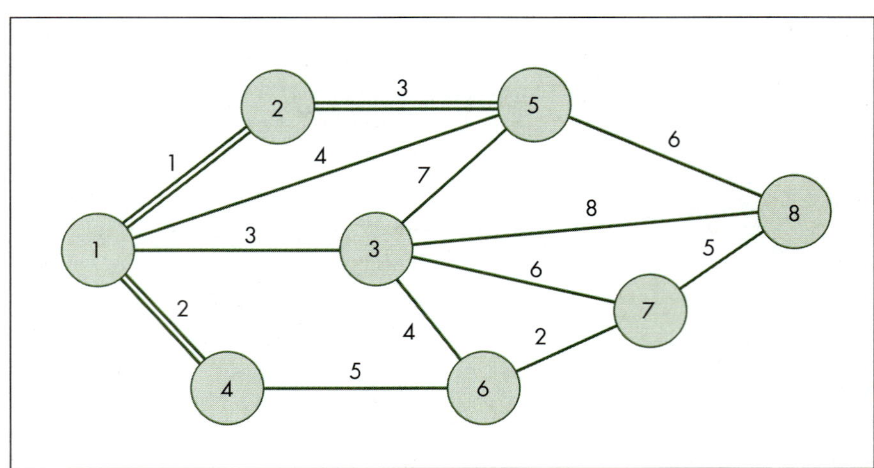

Returning to STEP 2, look at all the unconnected nodes to find the one closest to a connected node. There is a tie because the distance from node 1 to node 3 and the distance from node 2 to node 5 is the same. Arbitrarily select node 5 to be connected to node 2, as shown in the last network in Figure 9.2.

Selecting the next unconnected node closest to a connected node shows node 3 is connected to node 1 because the distance is 3. After this, the shortest distance from an unconnected node to a connected node is four units, which is the distance from node 3 to node 6. Selecting the next unconnected node that is closest to a connected node, choose node 7 to connect to node 6. These connections are seen in Figure 9.3.

Once these connections have been made, the only unconnected node is node 8, and we connect it to node 7, which is the closest one as shown in the first network in Figure 9.4. The second network in Figure 9.4 clearly shows the minimal spanning tree that connects all of the buildings (nodes) in the Connexus University example. From this the following nodes would be connected:

nodes 1-2

nodes 1-3

nodes 1-4

nodes 2-5

nodes 3-6

nodes 6-7

nodes 7-8

The total distance for doing this would be:

$$1 + 3 + 2 + 3 + 4 + 2 + 5 = 20$$

There is no way to connect these nodes that would result in a lower total distance.

This problem may be solved using computer software. Using DSS, the output shown in Output 9.1 would be obtained.

Additional Notes on Minimal Spanning Tree

The choice of which node to use initially is totally arbitrary. Regardless of which node is connected first, the optimal distance always will be found using this technique.

If multiple optimal solutions exist, then the selection of the arcs for connection when a tie occurs may determine which optimal solution is found.

This problem may be formulated as a 0-1 integer linear programming problem. However, it is not recommended for large problems as the number of variables and constraints can be quite large, and the minimal spanning tree method is very efficient. Software readily is available for solving this type of problem.

FIGURE 9.3

Connexus University Spanning Tree Problem with Fourth, Fifth, and Sixth Connections

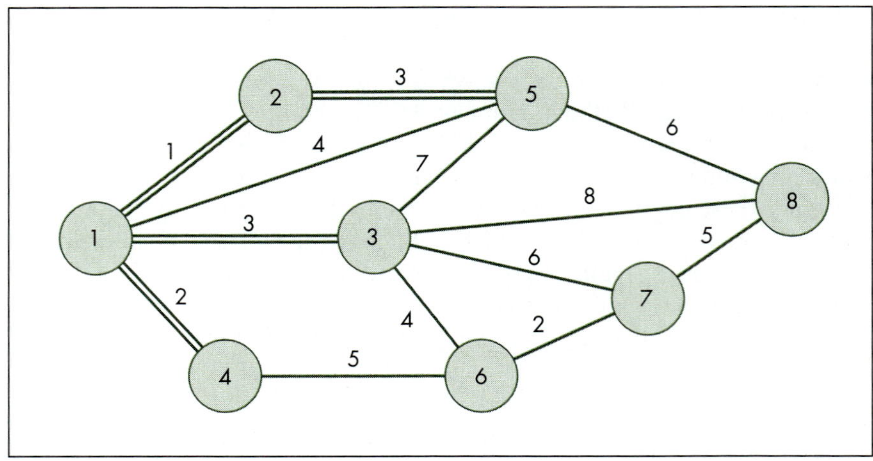

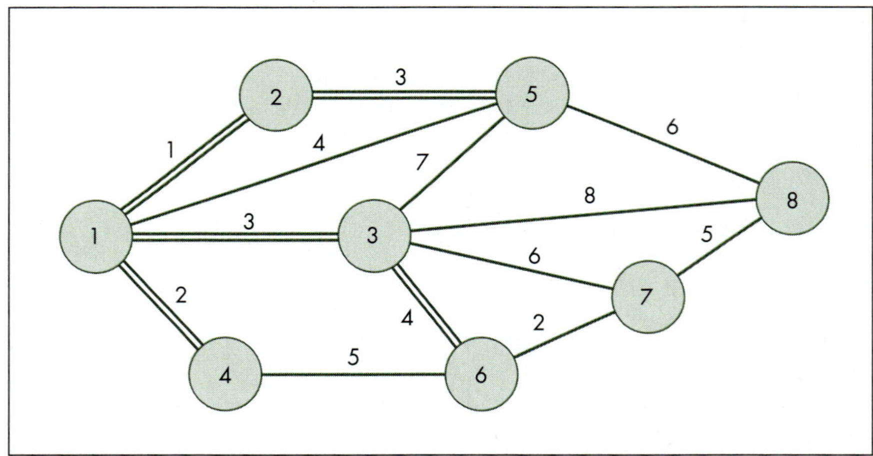

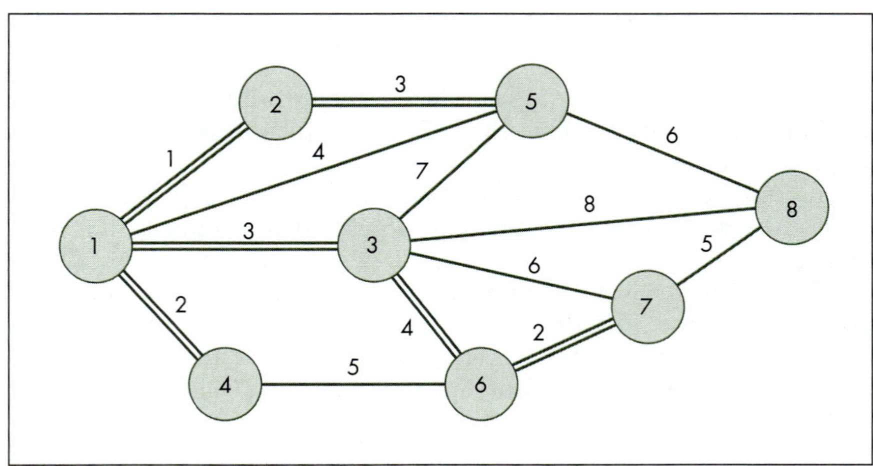

FIGURE 9.4

Final Solution to Connexus University Spanning Tree Problem

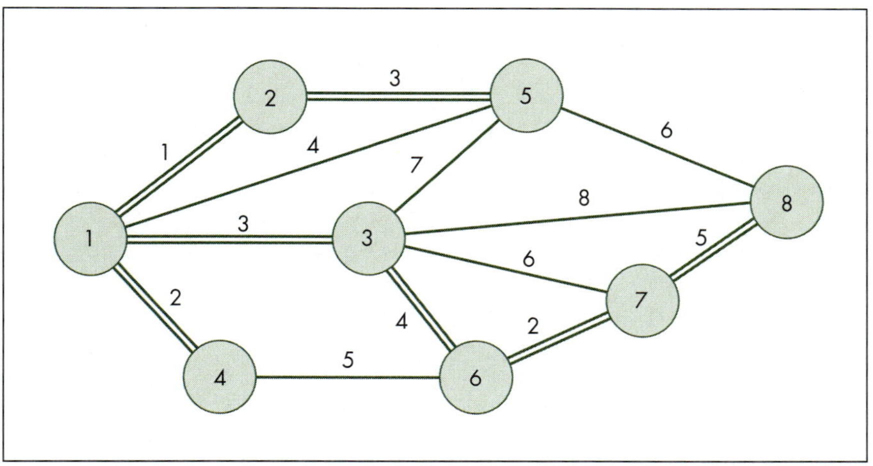

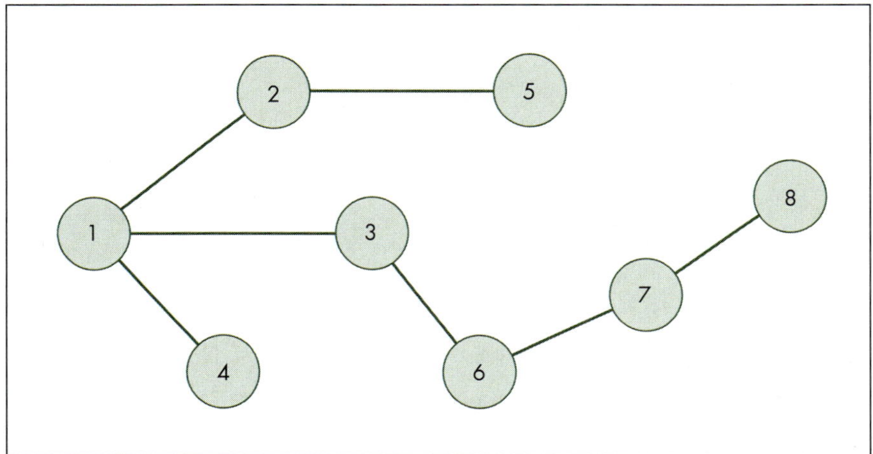

9.3 MAXIMAL FLOW TECHNIQUE

The **maximal flow technique** is concerned with allocating flows in a network in order to provide the maximum possible flow from a single input or **source node** to one single output or **sink node.** Such a procedure may be used with an oil pipeline to determine how much oil could flow from the source to the sink. It may be used to determine how many automobiles could travel over a set of roads. This technique also has been used to determine the capacity of a telephone or computer communication network.

For each arc in the network, the flow capacity in a particular direction will be indicated on the arc next to the node from which it is flowing. Unlike an arc, a node has no specific capacity. However, we will assume **conservation of flow,** which means that the flow into a particular node

Maximal flow technique
A method of finding the maximum amount of flow possible from a source node to a sink node.

Source node
The input node or origin in a maximal flow network.

Sink node
The output node or final node in a maximal flow network.

Conservation of flow
An assumption in the maximal flow technique that the flow out of a node must equal the flow into that node.

OUTPUT 9.1

DSS Output for Connexus Example

Networks - Minimum Spanning Tree

Initial Problem

From\To	Node1	Node2	Node3	Node4	Node5	Node6	Node7	Node8
Node1	x	1*	3*	2*	4	x	x	x
Node2	1*	x	x	x	3*	x	x	x
Node3	3*	x	x	x	7	4*	6	8
Node4	2*	x	x	x	x	5	x	x
Node5	4	3*	7	x	x	x	x	6
Node6	x	x	4*	5	x	x	2*	x
Node7	x	x	6	x	x	2*	x	5*
Node8	x	x	8	x	6	x	5*	x

Solution

From	To	Cost
Node1	Node2	1
Node1	Node4	2
Node1	Node3	3
Node2	Node5	3
Node3	Node6	4
Node6	Node7	2
Node7	Node8	5
	Total Cost:	20

*** Multiple optimal solutions exist ***

must equal the flow out of that same node. The flow into the source node and the flow out of the sink node will be the same and will indicate the maximum flow through the network.

Consider the Westex Pipeline Company that has a pipeline linking a major oil field to a refinery where the oil is sent to be processed. Figure 9.5 provides a network representation of this situation. The number of barrels per minute that may flow from one node to the next is given in the network. As seen in Figure 9.5, the flow from the source node (number 1) to node 2 is eight. The zero at the end of this arc indicates there is zero flow from node 2 to node 1. If there had been a positive number for flow in the reverse direction, it would be possible to have flow in the reverse direction as well as the original direction. This would mean that oil could flow in either direction depending on which is needed. To determine the maximum amount of oil that may flow through this pipeline from the source to the sink, use the maximal flow algorithm presented below.

BEST PRACTICES

A Network Model Helps Yellow Freight Control their Transportation System

Yellow Freight Systems is a national motor carrier with approximately 500 terminals handling 15 million shipments annually. The company's mission is to provide solutions to the ever-changing needs of current and future customers. To do this requires managing tens of thousands of shipments daily, across a huge and varying network. To accomplish their mission, YFS uses an operational planning tool called SYSNET.

SYSNET is a large-scale interactive optimization system for shipment routing and terminal network design. YFS uses SYSNET to anticipate system-wide needs for drivers, tractors, trailers, and facility capacity by graphically displaying the information down to individual terminals. System conditions are updated hourly so dispatchers can respond promptly to changes. With the program, YFS can adjust the network system to meet the specific needs of customers quickly. Such responsiveness allows the company to remain competitive in the transportation industry.

With SYSNET, YFS has made substantial cost savings from operations improvements. SYSNET also has improved the company's planning responsiveness to a rapidly changing business environment. By using the model, YFS can evaluate the impact of new ideas on the system as a whole. This lets managers make decisions more quickly, and allows analysts the freedom to try more new ideas. Overall, SYSNET has yielded significant improvements in transit times and service reliability for YFS's customers.

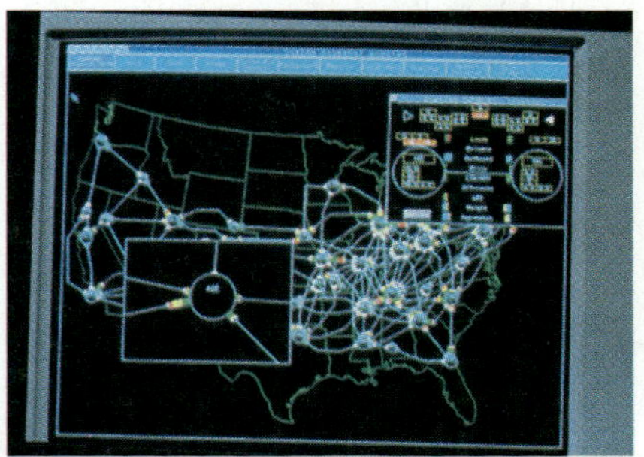

Photo courtesy of Yellow Freight Systems

SOURCE: Braklow, J. W., June 1993. "Keep on Truckin': Yellow Freight's SYSNET Planning System Provides Control of Transportation Network." *OR/MS Today*: 30-32.

FIGURE 9.5

Westex Pipeline Maximal Flow Network

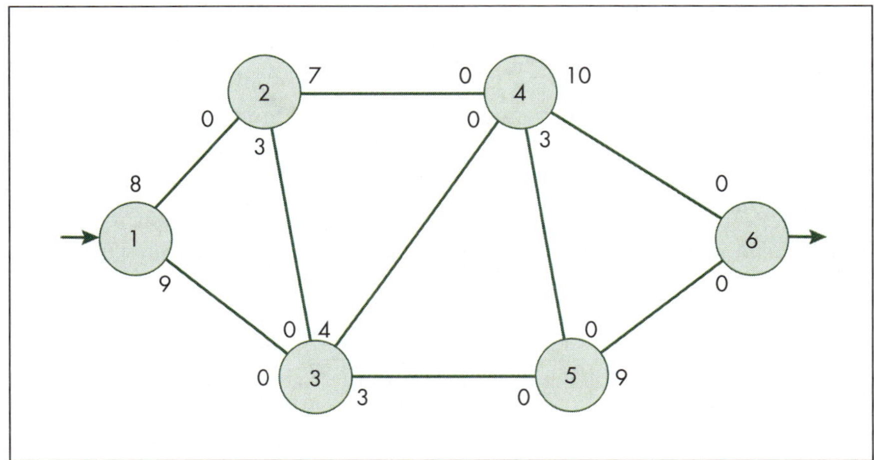

The maximal flow technique may be used with an oil pipeline to determine how much oil could flow from the oil field to the refinery. SOURCE: © 1991 Texaco Inc.; reprinted with permission from Texaco Inc.

MAXIMAL FLOW ALGORITHM

STEP 1. Find any path from the source node to the sink node with a nonzero flow capacity at each arc on the path. If no path exists with nonzero flow capacity for each arc, then the optimal solution has been reached.

STEP 2. Once the path has been selected, find the arc with the smallest flow capacity available. Call this capacity C. This capacity represents the maximum additional amount that can now be allocated to flow along this path.

STEP 3. Decrease the current flow capacity on each arc in the path by the amount C. This will cause one of these arcs now to have an available flow capacity of zero.

STEP 4. Increase the flow capacity in the reverse direction by the amount C for each arc in the path. This is to allow for later adjustments that might result in greater overall flow. Return to STEP 1.

To illustrate this process, consider the network in Figure 9.5. Beginning with STEP 1, arbitrarily select the path 1-3-4-5-6, although any path with a positive flow for each arc could be selected.

STEP 2 indicates the smallest flow capacity in this path is for arc 4-5, which has a capacity of three. Therefore, the maximum amount that may flow along this path is three, and let $C = 3$.

In STEP 3, subtract three from the flow capacity of each arc in this path. In STEP 4, add three to the flow capacity in the reverse direction for each arc in this path. The result is shown as the first network in Figure 9.6. Notice the amount of the flow into the network at the source and out of the network at the sink is shown to be three units. This amount will be modified each time a new path is found and capacities are revised.

FIGURE 9.6

Paths 1-3-4-5-6, 1-2-3-5-6, and 1-3-4-6 Adjusted for Westex Example

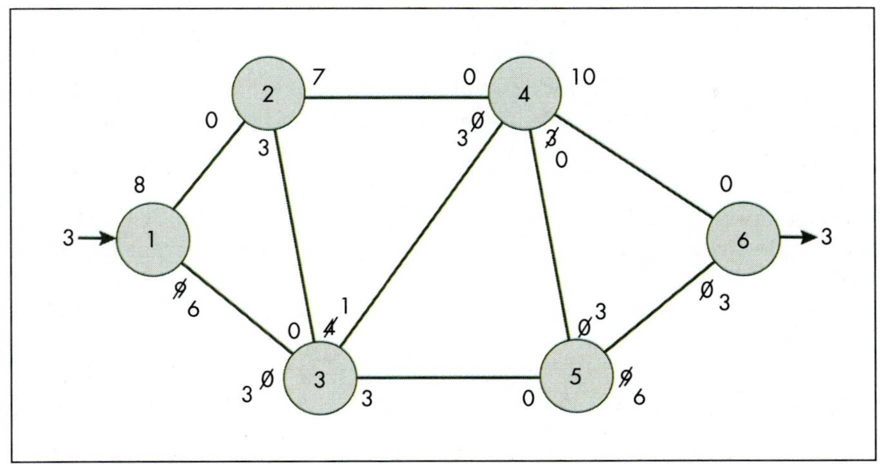

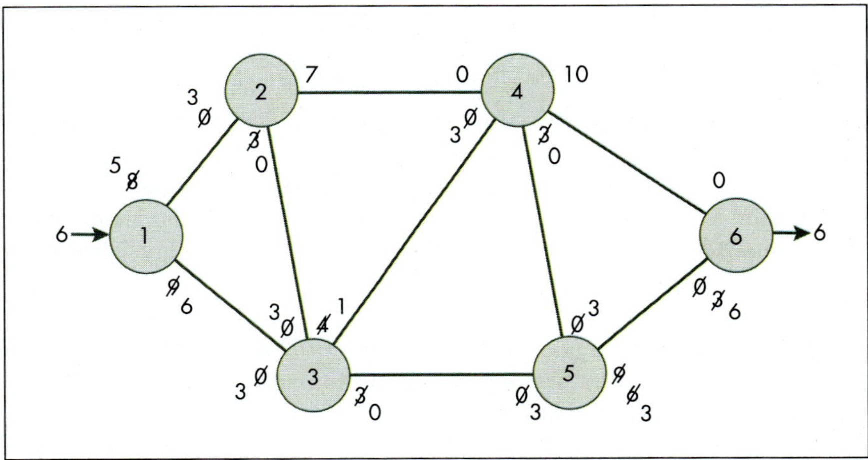

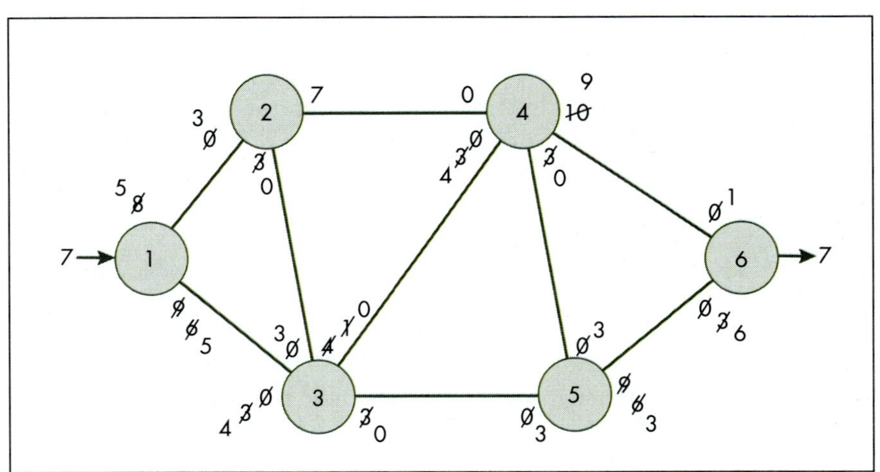

Returning to STEP 1, arbitrarily select another path, 1-2-3-5-6. In STEP 2, we find the smallest flow is three for arcs 2-3 and 3-5. Thus, $C = 3$.

In STEP 3, subtract three from the flow capacity of each arc in this path. In STEP 4, add three to the flow capacity in the reverse direction for each arc in the path. The result is shown as the second network in Figure 9.6.

Returning to STEP 1, arbitrarily select path 1-3-4-6. In STEP 2, the smallest flow capacity is one for arc 3-4, so $C = 1$. In STEP 3, subtract one from each flow capacity in the path, and in STEP 4, add one to the flow capacity in the reverse direction. This results in the third network in Figure 9.6.

Again, return to STEP 1 and arbitrarily select path 1-2-4-6. In STEP 2, the smallest flow capacity is five, so $C = 5$. In STEP 3, subtract five from the flow capacity for each arc in the path. In STEP 4, add five to the flow capacity in the reverse direction. The result is given as the first network in Figure 9.7.

Going to STEP 1, the only path with a positive flow is the path 1-3-2-4-6. While the flow from arc 2-3 is zero, the reverse flow (from node 3 to node 2) is positive. Without allowing for this reverse flow, we mistakenly would have assumed this current solution was the optimal solution. However, the use of the reverse flow indication allows some of the flow from arc 2-3 that was allocated previously to be redirected to allow for a greater overall flow. Going to STEP 2, the smallest flow is two from node 2 to node 4. With $C = 2$, go to STEP 3 and subtract two from the flow for each of these arcs in the path. In STEP 4, add two to the reverse flow for each of these. The result is shown in the second network in Figure 9.7.

Notice in the second network in Figure 9.7 there is no path from the source node to the sink node, which has a positive flow. At least one of the arcs in any path that is selected will have a zero flow capacity. Therefore, the maximum possible flow has been found.

Looking at the last network in Figure 9.7, we can see how the flow occurs. Because there was zero reverse flow in the initial statement of the problem, look at the numbers indicating the amount of the reverse flow to determine how much flow is allocated to each arc. We see that eight units are flowing from node 1 to node 2. The reverse flow from node 2 to node 4 is seven, so seven units flow from node 2 to node 4. Similarly, the reverse flow from node 2 to node 3 is one, so one unit is flowing from node 2 to node 3. Notice the flow into node 2 from node 1 is eight, and the total flow out of this node also is eight (7+1). The other reverse flow amounts may be inspected to see the other flow amounts through the nodes as well. The total flow into node 1 is 14, and the total flow out of node 6 is 14. Therefore, the maximum possible flow from the source to the sink is 14 barrels per minute. If the company needs more flow than this, additional pipes would be needed.

Output 9.2 provides the DSS output for this problem. Notice the flow is 14 but it is obtained by sending seven barrels from node 1 to node 2 and seven barrels from node 1 to node 3. One barrel is sent from node 2 to node 3 so seven barrels will flow from node 3. This is different than the solution obtained manually, and it indicates there is more than one way to obtain a flow of 14 barrels.

FIGURE 9.7

Paths 1-2-4-6 and 1-3-2-4-6 Adjusted for Westex Example

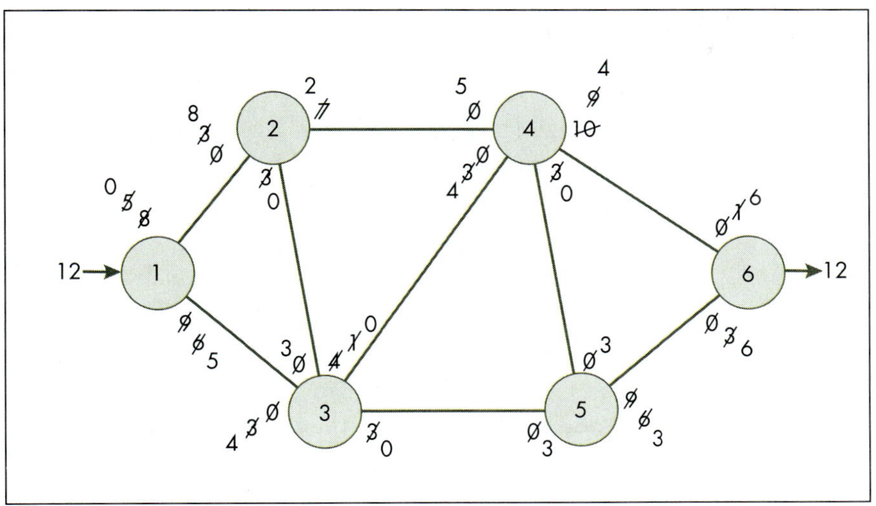

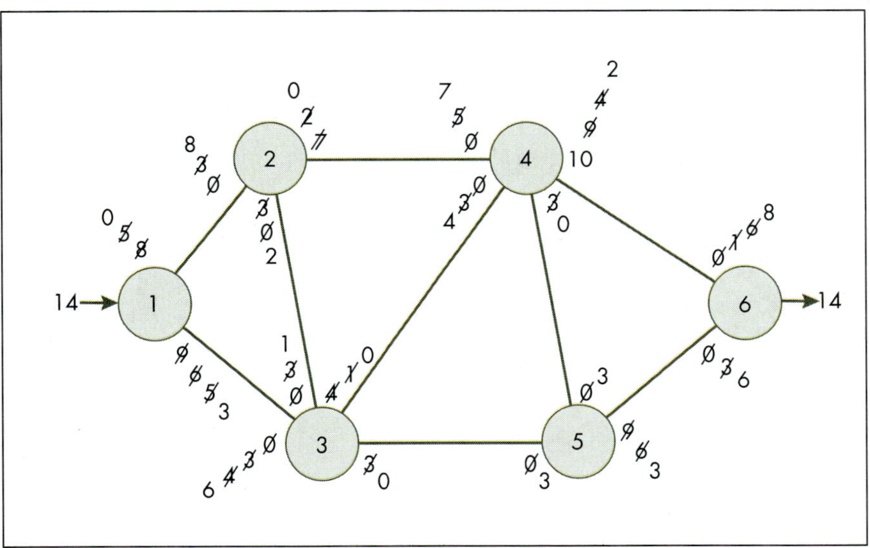

Additional Notes on the Maximal Flow Technique

Computer software is available to solve this type of problem, so performing the calculations manually is not usually necessary. However, it is important you understand the terminology that is used so you may understand what information is necessary to input this into the computer. It also is important to understand the types of applications where this is helpful.

This technique is very useful in planning highway maintenance. If a portion of a highway is to be closed for repairs, automobiles are normally

OUTPUT 9.2

DSS Output for Westex Maximal Flow Example

Networks - Maximum Flow/Min Cut

Initial Problem

From\To	Node1	Node2	Node3	Node4	Node5	Node6
Node1	x	8	9	x	x	x
Node2	0	x	3	7	x	x
Node3	0	0	x	4	3	x
Node4	x	0	0	x	3	10
Node5	0	0	0	0	x	9
Node6	0	0	0	0	0	x

Solution

From\To	Node1	Node2	Node3	Node4	Node5	Node6
Node1		7	7			
Node2			0	7		
Node3				4	3	
Node4					3	8
Node5						6
Node6						

Solution:	From	To	Amount	Capacity	Unused
	Node1	Node2	7	8	1
	Node1	Node3	7	9	2
	Node2	Node3	0	3	3
	Node2	Node4	7	7	0
	Node3	Node4	4	4	0
	Node3	Node5	3	3	0
	Node4	Node5	3	3	0
	Node4	Node6	8	10	2
	Node5	Node6	6	9	3

Maximum Flow = 14

diverted to alternate routes. An evaluation using the maximal flow technique will indicate the maximum number of automobiles that may be handled by these alternate routes.

Directed arc
An arc in a flow network in which flow is possible in only one direction.

Undirected arc
An arc in a flow network in which flow is possible in both directions.

The example considered in this chapter had a possible flow in only one direction. An arc with this characteristic is sometimes called a **directed arc.** If flow is possible in either direction, such as on a two-way street, the arc would be called an **undirected arc.** The simplest way to handle situations with undirected arcs is to create two separate arcs—one with flow in one direction and the other with flow in the reverse direction.

A Network Optimization Model for Freight Transportation

Even while opening new market opportunities, the North American Free Trade Agreement (NAFTA) has placed tremendous pressure on intercity freight motor carriers. They need to be able to adjust prices and services rapidly to compete in this less tightly regulated environment. They need to generate efficient operations schedules that meet both cost minimization and service criteria.

Two researchers from the University of Montreal, Quebec, Canada, developed a network optimization model to help motor carriers make routing decisions within this expanded North American transportation network. They have focused their initial efforts on less-than-truckload (LTL) carriers, who haul shipments weighing from 100 to 10,000 pounds, combining shipments to make up the 30,000 to 50,000 pounds that can fit in a typical trailer. Demands for shipments are rarely known in advance, and vary daily and seasonally. Often dispatching a trailer to a city to make a single delivery is not economical. Instead, freight is consolidated into trailers going to intermediate terminals, and then loaded with other materials going to the final destination. Overall, the process is highly labor intensive, and the decisions concerning the routing of freight through the network are critical.

The researchers have used the network optimization model to evaluate transportation networks for two Canadian LTL trucking companies, CN Express and Transport Brazeau Inc. They have examined variations in global demand, and in specific market demand, in terms of their impact on freight transportation and handling costs. With NAFTA, these and other trucking companies expect more changes in demands. The model network model will help in responding efficiently to these changes, and allowing companies to take advantage of new marketing opportunities.

SOURCE:
Roy, J. and T. G. Crainic, May-June 1992. "Improving Intercity Freight Routing with a Tactical Planning Model." *Interfaces* 22 (3): 31-44.

9.4 SHORTEST ROUTE TECHNIQUE

The **shortest route technique** is designed to find the shortest route from an origin to each of several points. In a network, we are trying to determine how far each node is from the initial node. Each node will be assigned a **label** to indicate how far it is from the starting node and which node is the preceding node in the route used to get to this point. For example, a label for node 6 might be (12,4), which would indicate this node is 12 miles (or whatever the units may be) from the origin and node 4 was the last node along this route before reaching node 6.

Shortest route technique
A technique for determining the route representing the minimum distance from the origin node to other nodes in a network.

To keep track of the calculations in the shortest route technique, two types of labels will be used—a **temporary label** and a **permanent label.** Temporary labels are given to nodes to indicate the distance from the origin to that node, although this distance indicated by the temporary label is not necessarily the closest possible distance. Temporary labels will become permanent labels when it is established that the distance indicated by the temporary label is the minimum possible distance from the origin to this node. Permanent labels are found by selecting from a particular set of temporary labels as will be seen in the examples that follow. For the sake of clarity of notation, use ( ) to indicate a label is temporary and use [ ] to indicate the label is permanent. The shortest route algorithm is summarized here:

Label
An indication of the distance from the origin and the preceding node in the route used to obtain this distance in a shortest route network.

Temporary label
A label which may or may not represent the shortest distance to the origin.

Permanent label
A label used when the shortest route to the node has been determined.

The shortest route algorithm can be used to find the shortest route from an origin to each of several points. SOURCE: Mark IV Industries, Inc.

SHORTEST ROUTE ALGORITHM

STEP 1. Assign the permanent label [0,S] to the starting node.
STEP 2. Assign temporary labels to all nodes that are adjacent or directly connected by a single arc to nodes with permanent labels.
STEP 3. Find the temporary label that has the smallest distance to the origin. Make this label a permanent label. If all labels are permanent, stop. Otherwise, go to STEP 2.

Because the labels indicate the originating node and the distance, the shortest route is found by looking at the permanent label for the final destination and tracing the route backwards until the origin is reached.

An Example of the Shortest Route Algorithm

Consider the Rhodes Concrete Company that delivers truckloads of concrete to various construction projects in a particular city. Figure 9.8 shows the distance in miles from the Rhodes office to each of the sites. Node 1 represents the office, which will be the origin in this problem.

A CLOSER LOOK

Dynamic Programming

Many of the techniques used to solve network problems may be viewed as dynamic programming approaches to problem solving. Richard Bellman developed dynamic programming in the 1950s while investigating sequential decision making in inventory control problems. This technique has been used with production scheduling, capital budgeting, and the allocation of funds for research and development.

While there is no specific form for a dynamic programming problem, there are certain characteristics that generally exist. A dynamic programming problem can be broken down into smaller problems or stages. Each stage usually has several states associated with it, and a decision is made at each stage about which state to enter at the next stage. In viewing the shortest route algorithm as a dynamic programming approach, the determination of a permanent label would represent a stage. The states would be the nodes that could be assigned temporary labels at each stage.

The dynamic programming approach is based on the principle of optimality which says that the optimal decisions for the remaining stages in a problem do not depend on any of the previous decisions. In the shortest route algorithm this would mean that at any node with a permanent label, the decisions to find the shortest route from that point to the final destination do not depend on how that node was reached.

SOURCE:
Bellman, Richard E., 1957. *Dynamic Programming*. Princeton: Princeton University Press.

In STEP 1, assign the permanent label [0,S] to node 1. This is shown as the first network in Figure 9.9. In STEP 2, assign a temporary label to each node that is adjacent to a permanently labeled node. Because nodes 2, 3, and 4 are connected directly with a single arc to node 1, assign temporary labels to these. Node 2 is four miles from node 1, so it is given the temporary label

FIGURE 9.8

Network Representation of Rhodes Concrete Company Example

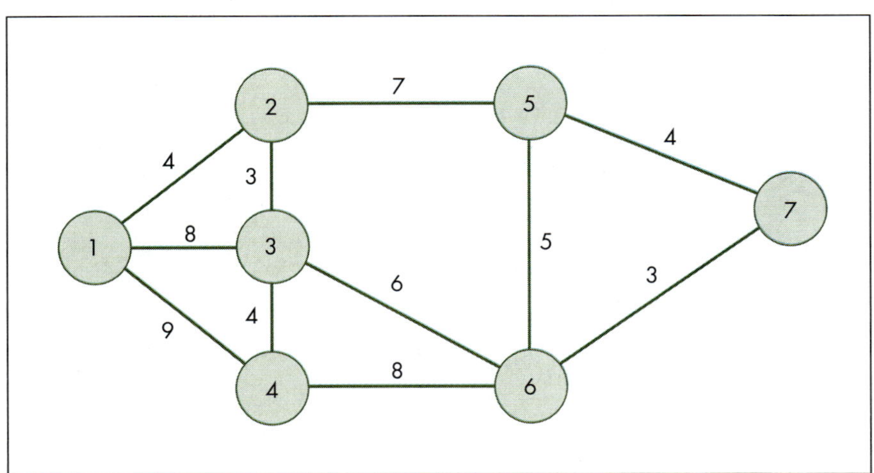

FIGURE 9.9

Node 1 Permanently Labeled; Temporary Labels for Nodes 2, 3, and 4; and Permanent Label for Node 2

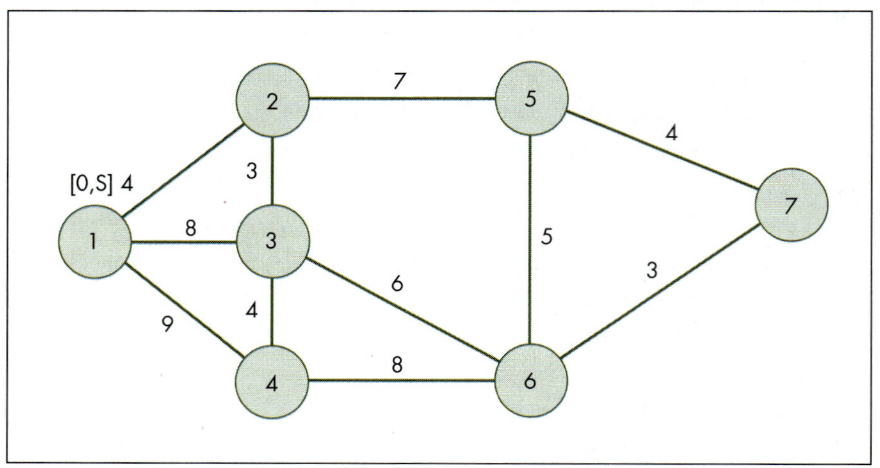

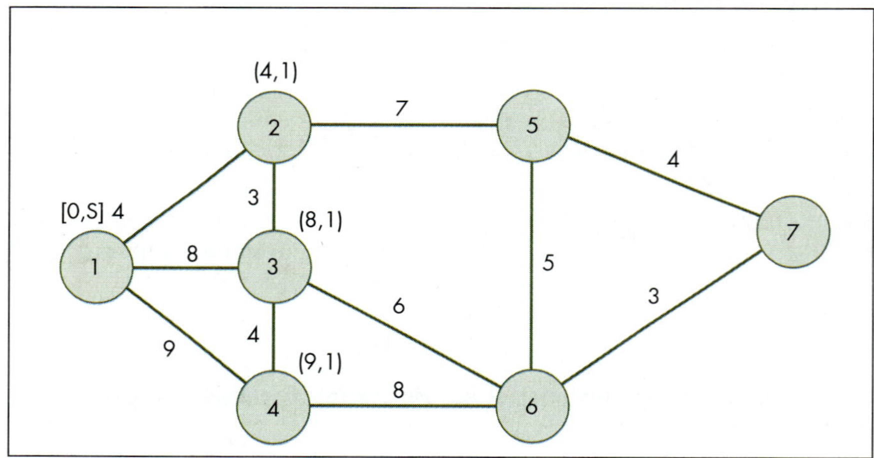

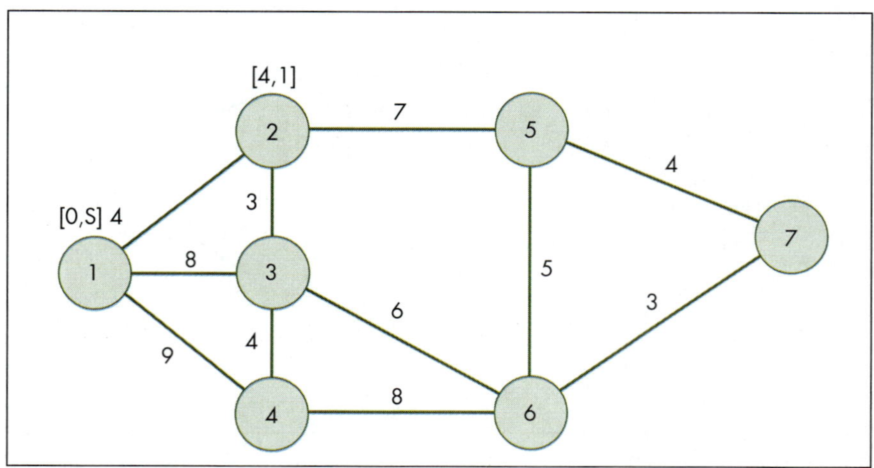

(4,1). Node 3 is eight miles from node 1, so it receives the label (8,1). Similarly, node 4 receives the label (9,1) because it is nine miles from node 1. This is shown as the second network in Figure 9.9.

In STEP 3, select the temporary label that has the smallest distance from node 1, and make this a permanent label. Thus, select (4,1) and indicate this is now a permanent label so it becomes [4,1]. This is shown as the third network in Figure 9.9.

Returning to STEP 2, now assign temporary labels to all nodes that are adjacent to any permanently labeled node (nodes 1 and 2). Because node 3 is adjacent to both nodes 1 and 2, label this using the temporary label (7,2) because this route is closer to the origin than the route indicated by (8,1). By going from node 1 to node 2 and then to node 3, the total distance is seven miles, as indicated by the temporary label. There is no way to get to node 3 by going fewer than seven miles. Notice this temporary label for node 3 is better than the temporary label (8,1) that was assigned to this node when only node 1 had a permanent label.

Continuing with this stage of the example, the temporary label (9,1) is assigned to node 4 because it is nine miles from node 1 to node 4. Node 5 is given the temporary label (11,2), which means that the distance from the origin to node 5 is 11 miles, and the last node that is passed through before reaching node 5 is node 2. These are shown in the first network in Figure 9.10. In STEP 3, select from the temporary labels (7,2), (9,1), and (11,2), and choose the one with the smallest distance to node 1. Thus, select the label (7,2) and make this label permanent for node 3.

Returning to STEP 2, assign temporary labels to all nodes adjacent to a permanently labeled node (nodes 1, 2, and 3). These are shown in the second network in Figure 9.10. Notice the temporary label for node 4 is (9,1) rather than (11,3) because this results in a shorter route from the origin. In STEP 3, select the temporary label with the smallest distance from the origin, choose the label (9,1) for node 4 and make this label permanent.

Returning to STEP 2, create temporary labels for all nodes connected to permanently labeled nodes, as seen in the last network in Figure 9.10. In STEP 3, make the label for node 5 permanent because it has the smallest distance from the origin.

Returning to STEP 2, create temporary labels for the nodes connected to permanently labeled nodes, as shown in the first network in Figure 9.11. In STEP 3, make the label (13,3) for node 6 permanent.

In STEP 2, then create the temporary label (15,5) for node 7. Because this is the last node, this temporary label becomes permanent as shown in the second network in Figure 9.11. This represents the final solution to the Rhodes Concrete Company example.

You may find it helpful to keep track of the labels with the use of a table. Table 9.1 illustrates how this might be done with the Rhodes Concrete Company example.

Interpreting the Final Result

The final solution in Figure 9.11 shows the shortest route from node 1 to node 7 is 15 miles. To find what this route is, backtrack through the network. Because the label is [15,5], go back to node 5. At node 5 the label is

FIGURE 9.10

Node 2 Permanently Labeled and Temporary Labels for Nodes 3, 4, and 5; Node 3 Permanently Labeled and Temporary Labels for 4, 5, and 6; and Permanent Label for Node 4 and Temporary Labels for Nodes 5 and 6

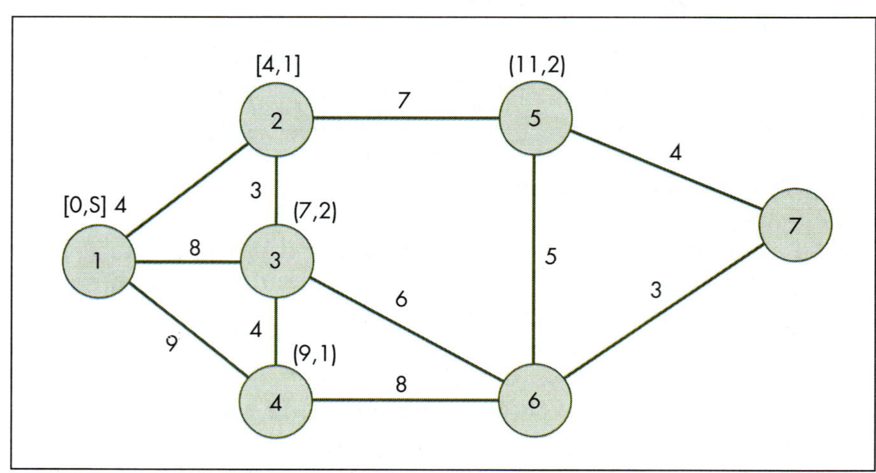

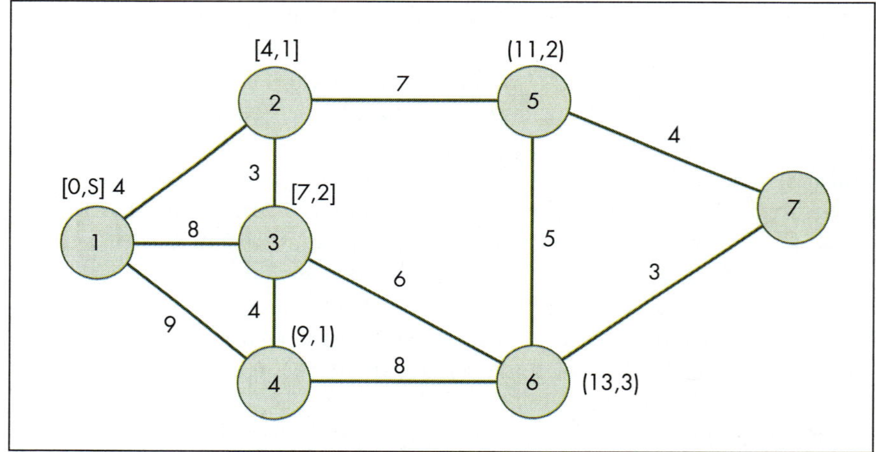

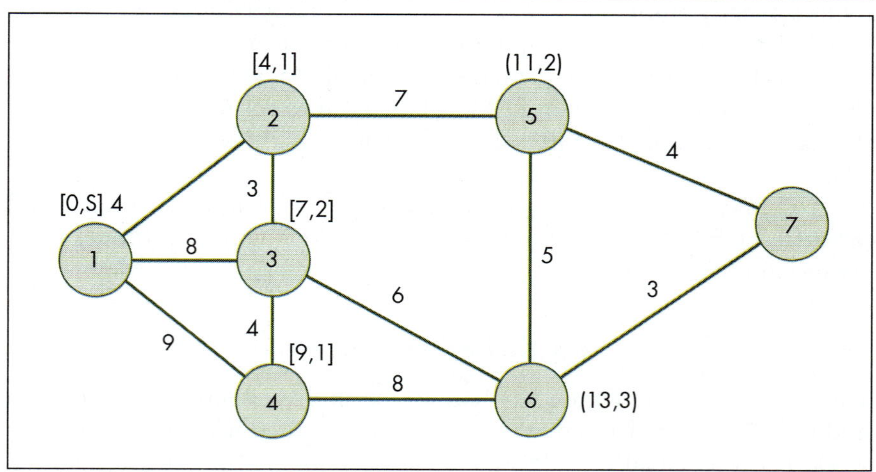

FIGURE 9.11

Node 5 Made Permanent; Temporary Labels for Nodes 6 and 7; and Nodes 6 and 7 Made Permanent Giving Final Solution

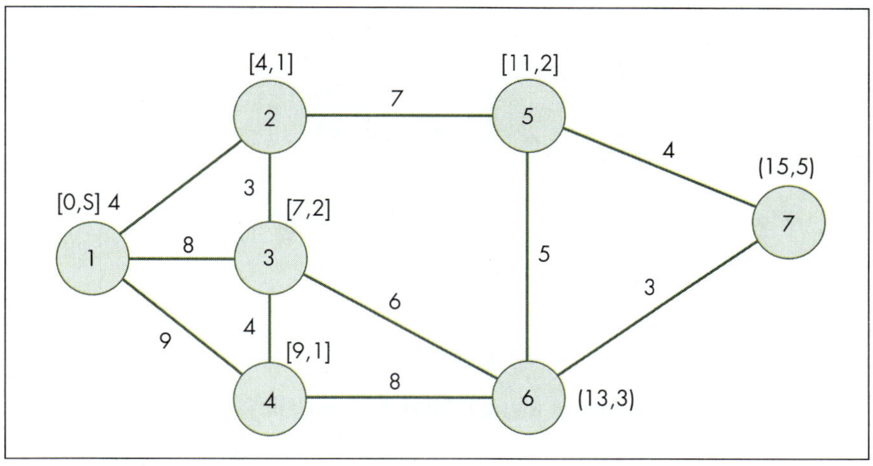

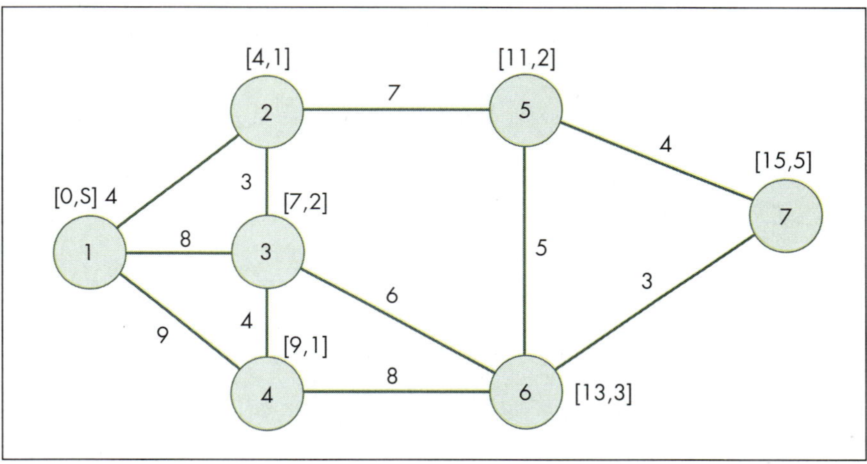

TABLE 9.1

Temporary and Permanent Labels for Nodes at Each Iteration of the Rhodes Concrete Company Example

Iteration		1	2	3	4	5	6
Node	1	[0,S]					
	2	[4,1]					
	3	(8,1)	[7,2]				
	4	(9,1)	(9,1)	[9,1]			
	5		(11,2)	(11,2)	[11,2]		
	6			(13,3)	(13,3)	[13,3]	
	7					(15,5)	[15,5]

TABLE 9.2

Shortest Routes to Each Node

Node	Distance	Route
1	0	Starting Node
2	4	1-2
3	7	1-2-3
4	9	1-4
5	11	1-2-5
6	13	1-2-3-6
7	15	1-2-5-7

OUTPUT 9.3

DSS Output for the Rhodes Concrete Company Example

```
Networks - Shortest Route

Initial Problem with solution indicated

Segment    Start     End       Measure    Best Cumulative Measure

*Seg1      1         2         4           4
 Seg2      1         3         8           8
 Seg3      1         4         9           9
 Seg4      2         3         3           7
 Seg5      3         4         4           11
*Seg6      2         5         7           11
 Seg7      3         6         6           13
 Seg8      4         6         8           17
 Seg9      5         6         5           16
*Seg10     5         7         4           15
 Seg11     6         7         3           16

          Total Objective Measure: 15

* denotes shortest path
```

[11,2], so we go back to node 2. The label at node 2 is [4,1], so go from here back to node 1. Thus, the shortest route from node 1 to node 7 goes from node 1 to node 2 to node 5 to node 7. A similar backtracking procedure will find the shortest routes from all of the nodes. These are summarized in Table 9.2.

This problem could have been solved using the Decision Support Software. Output 9.3 provides the DSS output for this problem.

9.5 SUMMARY

In this chapter we saw three common network models—the minimal spanning tree, the maximal flow technique, and the shortest route technique. All of these have numerous applications in business today. The techniques presented in this chapter are very efficient methods, and the calculations involved are quite simple. For large problems, you should consider using available software to eliminate the tedious calculations.

GLOSSARY

Conservation of flow An assumption in the maximal flow technique that the flow out of a node must equal the flow into that node. *p. 381*

Directed arc An arc in a flow network in which flow is possible in only one direction. *p. 388*

Label An indication of the distance from the origin and the preceding node in the route used to obtain this distance in a shortest route network. *p. 389*

Maximal flow technique A method of finding the maximum amount of flow possible from a source node to a sink node. *p. 381*

Minimal spanning tree technique A method that may be used to determine the minimum distance required to connect a set of nodes (points). *p. 377*

Permanent label A label used when the shortest route to the node has been determined. *p. 389*

Shortest route technique A technique for determining the route representing the minimum distance from the origin node to other nodes in a network. *p. 389*

Sink node The output node or final node in a maximal flow network. *p. 381*

Source node The input node or origin in a maximal flow network. *p. 381*

Temporary label A label which may or may not represent the shortest distance to the origin. *p. 389*

Undirected arc An arc in a flow network in which flow is possible in both directions. *p. 388*

SOLVED PROBLEMS

SOLVED PROBLEM 9-1

For the network given below, use the minimal spanning tree technique to determine which nodes to connect to minimize the total distance.

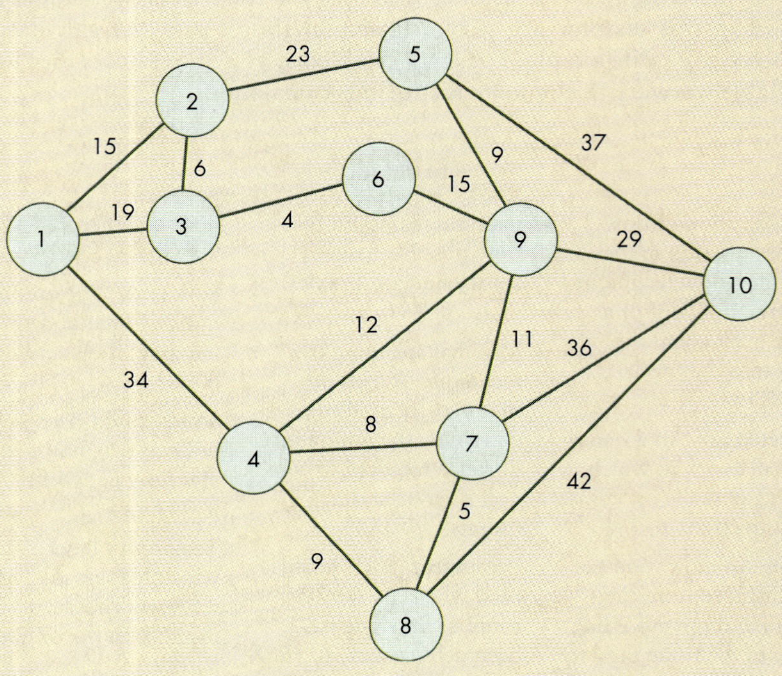

SOLUTION

Connect Arcs 1-2, 2-3, 3-6, 6-9, 9-5, 9-7, 7-8, 7-4, 9-10.
Total distance = 15 + 6 + 4 + 15 + 9 + 11 + 5 + 8 + 29 = 93

SOLVED PROBLEM 9-2

In the network given below, the distances between cities is given in miles. Determine the shortest route from city 1 to city 12.

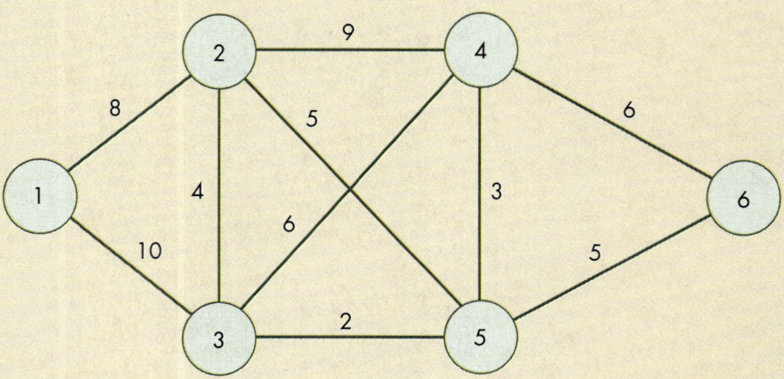

SOLUTION

The temporary and permanent labels for nodes at each iteration of this method are shown below. The starting node is labeled [0,S] in STEP 1 of the first iteration. In each column, the node labeled with [ ] is the one that originally has a temporary label in STEP 2 but which is made permanent in STEP 3.

Iteration	1	2	3	4	5
Node 1	[0,S]				
2	[8,1]				
3	(10,1)	[10,1]			
4		(17,2)	(16,3)	[15,5]	
5		(13,2)	[12,3]		
6				(17,5)	[17,5]

QUESTIONS

1. Explain the objectives of the minimal spanning tree, shortest route, and maximal flow techniques.
2. In the maximal flow technique, if the reverse flow is initially zero for all arcs, what does the reverse flow in the final solution indicate?
3. The conservation of flow assumption is normally associated with the nodes in the maximal flow network. Is there also conservation of flow for the entire network (i.e., is the total flow into the network equal to the total flow out of the network)?
4. If there is an undirected arc in a maximal flow network, what changes would be necessary if the maximal flow algorithm were to be used to solve this?
5. In the shortest route algorithm, what do the numbers in the label represent?
6. In using the shortest route algorithm, which nodes are assigned temporary labels?
7. How are permanent labels in a shortest route network determined?
8. If one node in a shortest route network is connected to several nodes with permanent labels, how is the temporary label determined for this node?
9. A student is planning a trip by automobile to Ft. Lauderdale for spring break. Which of the techniques presented in this chapter would be most helpful to this student in planning the trip?
10. Repairs on the major interstate highway passing through a small city north of Ft. Lauderdale currently is creating traffic problems within the city. The city manager is concerned about the number of cars passing through his city during the upcoming spring break, and wishes to plan alternate routes if possible. If the city manager wishes to determine how many cars per hour could pass through the city given the current detours through the city streets, which of the techniques in this chapter would be most helpful?

PROBLEMS

11. Use the minimal spanning tree technique to find how to connect the following sites in a communication network if the total distance is to be minimized.

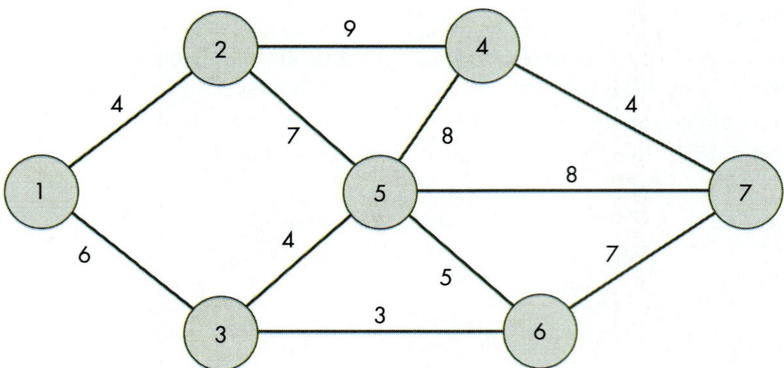

12. Use the minimal spanning tree technique to determine the minimum distance required to connect the locations in this network. Which nodes would be connected in the optimal solution?

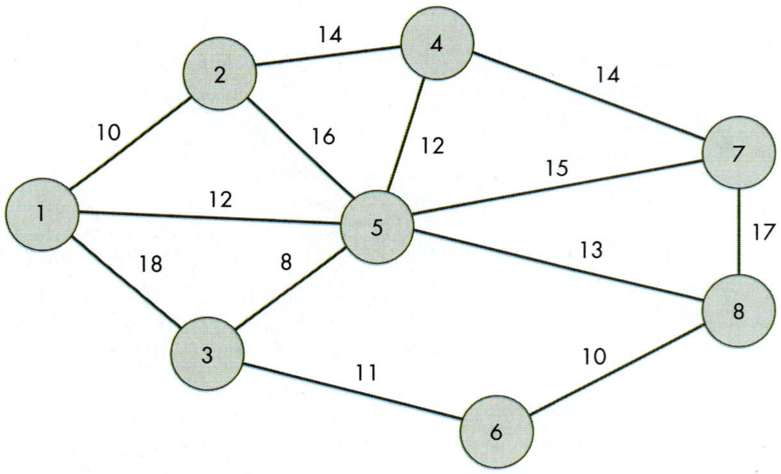

13. The following represents a network with the arcs identified by their starting and ending nodes. Draw the network and use the minimal spanning tree technique to find the minimum distance required to connect these nodes.

Arc	Distance
1-2	12
1-3	8
2-3	7
2-4	10
3-4	9
3-5	8
4-5	8
4-6	11
5-6	9

14. Use the maximal flow algorithm to determine the capacity of this network. How much flow would be provided by each arc in the optimal solution?

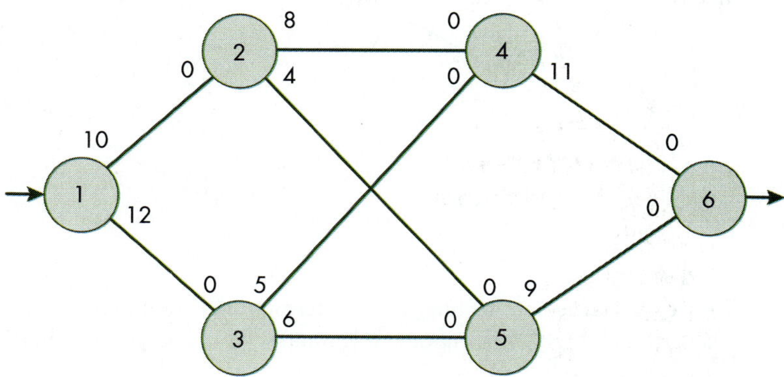

15. The following network represents streets of a city with the indicated number of cars per hour that can travel these streets. Find the maximum number of cars that could travel per hour through this system. How many cars would travel on each street (arc) to allow this maximum flow? How would the maximum number of cars be affected if the street from node 3 to node 6 were temporarily closed?

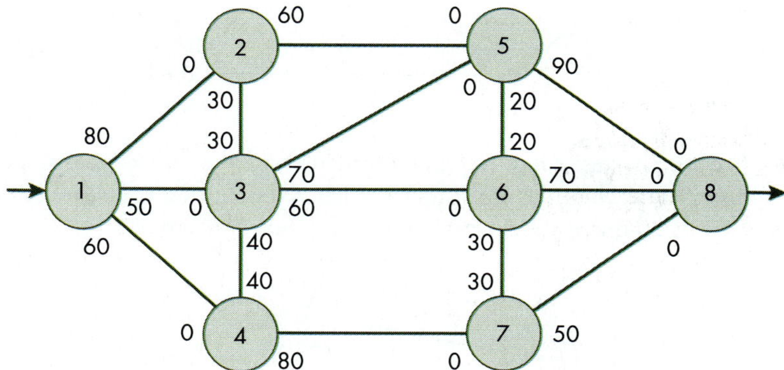

16. The following network gives the maximum flow in barrels per minute of a pipeline. Determine the maximum possible flow per minute through this network. How many barrels of oil would flow through each arc per minute?

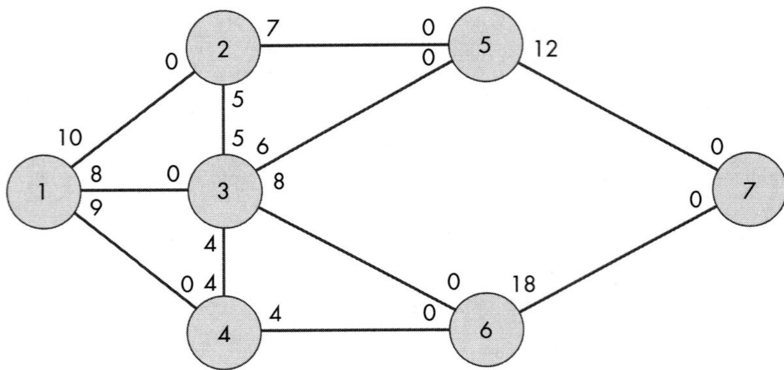

17. Use the shortest route technique to determine the minimum distance from node 1 to each of the other nodes. What nodes would be included in the shortest route from node 1 to node 7?

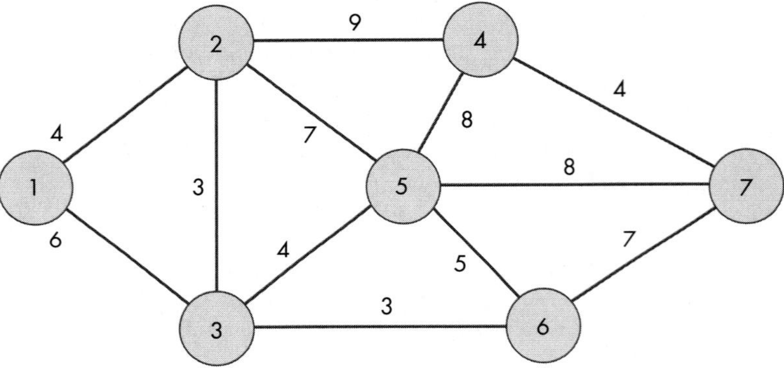

18. Use the shortest route technique to determine the minimum distance from node 1 to each of the other nodes. What is the shortest route from node 1 to node 12? What is the shortest route from node 1 to node 8?

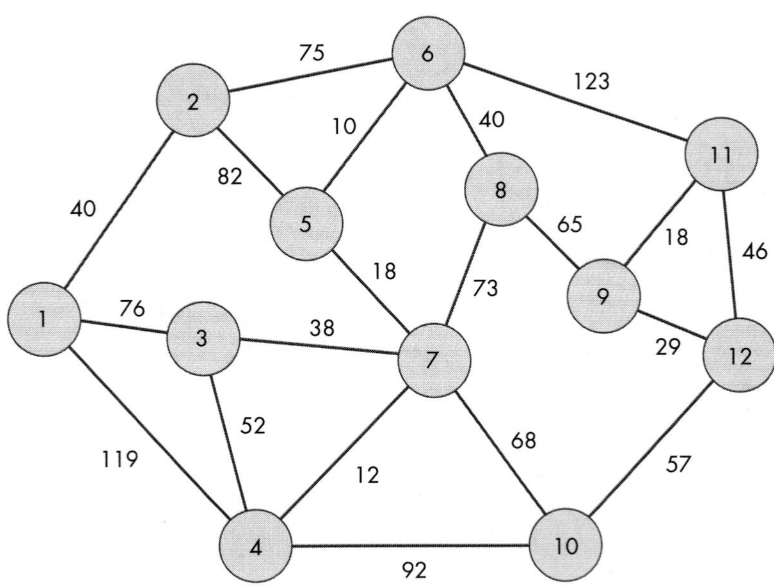

19. Safe Waste is a company specializing in the handling and disposal of hazardous waste. When contracted to pick up and dispose of dangerous materials, Safe Waste always evaluates the alternate routes to the disposal site. While Safe Waste has never had an accident, the company policy is to select the least populated route to minimize potential liabilities.

    A recent contract has been obtained which calls for weekly pick-ups (node 1) of an extremely hazardous material. This is to be taken to a disposal site (node 10) on the other side of the state. The network below indicates the possible routes and the population (in thousands) along each of these routes. Find the route which would minimize the number of people along the route.

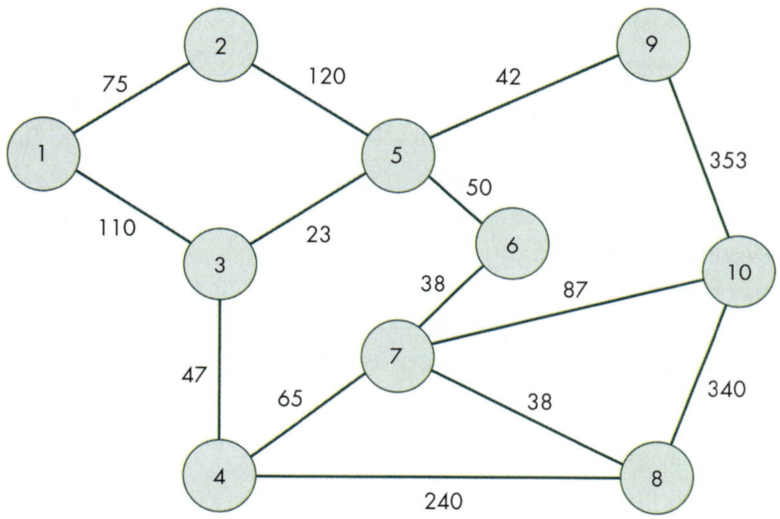

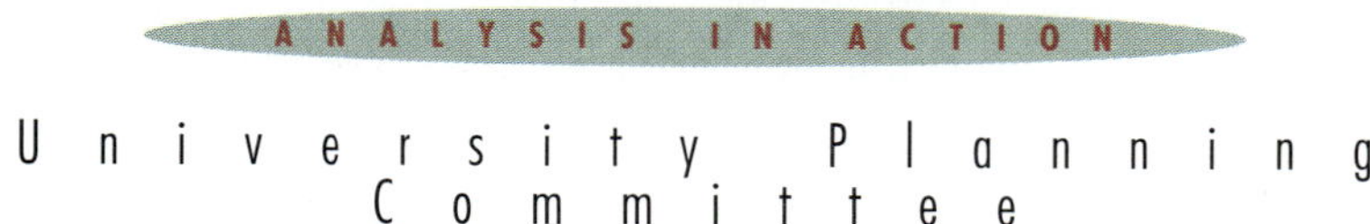

University Planning Committee

A new football stadium is being planned for a university located in a small town. The stadium is to be built on land north of the campus. Due to the influx of alumni on football weekends, major traffic problems are expected. Based on traffic projections, the university would like to have sufficient capacity so 35,000 cars per hour could travel from the stadium to the interstate highway.

To alleviate the anticipated traffic problems, some of the current streets leading from the university to the interstate highway are being considered for widening to increase the capacity. The current street configuration with the number of cars (in thousands) per hour are shown below. Because the major problem will be after the game, only the flows away from the stadium are indicated. These flows include some streets closest to the stadium being transformed into one-way streets for a short period after each game with police officers directing traffic.

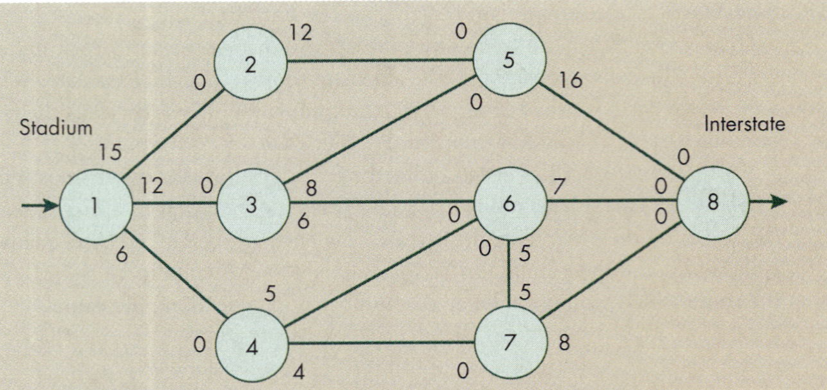

A member of the university planning committee has said that a quick check of the road capacities in the diagram below indicates that the total number of cars per hour that may leave the stadium (node 1) is 33,000. The number of cars that may go from nodes 2, 3, and 4 is 35,000 per hour, and the number of cars that may go from nodes 5, 6, and 7 to the interstate (node 8) per hour is 33,000. Therefore, she has suggested it appears that the current capacity is 33,000 cars per hour. She also has suggested a recommendation be made to the city manager that whichever route from the stadium to the highway is cheapest to expand should be expanded to permit an additional 2,000 cars per hour. If the expansion is not made, it is felt the traffic problem would be a manageable nuisance.

Based on past experience, it is believed that as long as the street capacity is within 2,500 cars per hour of the number that leave the stadium, the problem is not too severe. However, the severity of the problem grows dramatically for each additional 1,000 cars that are added to the streets.

Using techniques learned in this chapter, determine the maximum number of cars that may actually travel from the stadium to the interstate per hour. Why is this number not equal to 33,000 as the planning committee member suggested? Which street(s) would you recommend expanding to increase the capacity to 33,000? If the cost for expanding a street is the same for each street (arc), which streets would you recommend expanding to get the total capacity of the system to 35,000 per hour? Prepare a brief report that may be presented to the university planning committee.

CHAPTER TEN

Inventory Models

LEARNING OBJECTIVES

Upon completing Chapter 10, you should be able to:

- Explain the purposes for carrying inventory.
- Identify the costs associated with inventory.
- Calculate inventory costs when certain conditions exist.
- Determine the economic order quantity.
- Calculate the minimum cost order quantity when quantity discounts exist.
- Calculate the minimum cost production quantity.
- Explain the use of safety stock and how this affects the reorder point.
- Use marginal analysis to determine the best order quantity.
- Use ABC analysis to identify important inventory items.
- Use MRP to plan inventory orders when several inventory items are used in the production of a single product.
- Explain the benefits and limitations of a just-in-time system.

CHAPTER OUTLINE

10.1 INTRODUCTION

The term inventory refers to idle resources, materials, and products that a company maintains for use in the future. This may include raw materials, work in process, finished products, or even people (labor hours). While basic inventory principles apply to all of these types of inventory, discussions in this chapter will focus on goods that a company purchases from a supplier or produces itself to be sold to the public.

There are costs associated with inventory that may have a dramatic impact on the profitability of a firm. The money invested in inventories each year in the United States totals about 20 to 25 percent of the gross domestic product (GDP). Managing inventory wisely and making good decisions regarding how much to order and when to order may be the difference between the success and failure of a firm.

In this chapter we will identify the reasons a company maintains inventory. We will explore the costs normally associated with inventory and see how these may be calculated. Conditions will be described in which one of the most common inventory models, the economic order quantity, may be used to minimize inventory costs for a company. As this model is only appropriate if certain assumptions are met, we will determine what modifications should be made to the inventory policy when the assumptions are not met.

There are other important topics related to inventory management that also will be presented in this chapter. These topics should help a manager understand the best way to use inventory to meet the needs of the organization.

10.2 PURPOSES FOR HOLDING INVENTORY

There are several reasons why a company may wish to carry inventory of a product. Among the major reasons for carrying inventory are:

1. to serve as a buffer between supply and demand
2. to obtain efficiencies of scale
3. to store resources
4. to act as a hedge against inflation or unexpected outages

Buffer between Supply and Demand

Inventory may serve as a buffer between supply and demand, both of which may be variable. For example, most agricultural products have a limited harvest season, but the demand for these products is not seasonal. Thus, when the crop is harvested, it must be stored for use later.

Even if the supply of a product is constant, a company may not be able to predict the demand for that product. In order to make this product available when the customer wants it, an inventory of this product is held.

In order to make a product available when customers want it, an inventory of the product is held. SOURCE: Photo courtesy of Detroit Diesel Corporation

Buffers also may be needed at the workstations on an assembly line. The first station cannot begin unless the materials needed already are present. A company will normally have this on-hand to allow production to begin. If the company schedules the material to arrive exactly when the line is to start production, the company faces a serious problem if the delivery is late. At later stages on the assembly line, a delay at a previous station will not cause a later station to be idle if an inventory of work in process has been established.

Efficiencies of Scale

Discounts often are available if large quantities of a product are ordered. To take advantage of these discounts, a company may order a large quantity of the product and put the extra amount in inventory to be used later.

If a company is producing an item, a production line must be set up for this item each time it is produced. The equipment may need special cleaning when the production is finished. Therefore, it often is better to continue production of this product until a large number have been produced rather than to produce a few units each day and have to spend time preparing the equipment.

At times a delivery charge may be imposed regardless of the size of the order. Thus, it may be beneficial to order and store several items rather than pay the delivery charge each time another item is needed.

Storing Resources

For a company that is producing a product to be sold to the public or to wholesalers, the company may be faced with a demand known to be very high at certain times of the year and very low at other times. If the company wishes to maintain little or no inventory, it would have to expand production greatly at certain times of the year, and restrict production considerably at other times. The cost of hiring and training workers who will only be used for a short period of time could be prohibitive. Therefore, a prudent manager would try to smooth out the production rate so the labor hours utilized would be relatively constant over time. This would mean at times there would be a build up of inventory to be used later.

Hedge against Inflation or Unexpected Outages

If the price of a product is anticipated to increase in the near future, a company may wish to order additional units of this product before the price rises. This would mean the inventory level rises, but this savings in purchase cost could make this desirable.

At times a company may wish to keep a large inventory of the item to prevent problems if a shortage of the product were to occur. A strike at the manufacturing plant or at the trucking firm might prevent additional units from being received for a long period of time. Unexpected weather conditions might cause an agricultural product to be in short supply. Any of these would cause a manager to be thankful that an inventory of the product was available.

10.3 COSTS ASSOCIATED WITH INVENTORY

Inventory decisions for a company typically involve how many units to order and when to order. A company may want to do this in a way that minimizes total costs associated with inventory. Even if the company does not minimize costs, it is important for a manager to know what these costs are. There are typically four costs associated with inventory. These costs are:

1. purchase
2. holding or carrying
3. ordering
4. stockout

Purchase cost
The cost of obtaining or purchasing a good.

The **purchase cost** is simply what must be paid to obtain the product. Unless there is a quantity discount available, this often is relatively constant

A manager may carry additional units of windshield wipers and antifreeze in anticipation of poor weather conditions.
SOURCE: Courtesy of Masco Corporation

and may not impact a company's inventory policy. If a price increase is anticipated, a company may wish to order extra units now to avoid paying more later.

Holding (or carrying) cost
The cost associated with holding inventory, such as the cost of capital, insurance, taxes, and storage costs.

The **holding cost** or **carrying cost** is a cost a company incurs whenever it has inventory. As the amount of inventory increases, the total holding cost would increase. A company that carries a large inventory also will have a lot of money invested in this inventory. This money could be used elsewhere to earn interest or to generate other revenues. Thus, there is a cost of having this money in inventory that increases with the amount of inventory. Also, if the inventory level is high, the insurance required also would be high. For large inventories, other costs, such as taxes, warehouse personnel costs, and possible spoilage, also could be very high. Therefore, holding costs would include such things as the cost of capital, insurance, warehouse or storage costs, taxes, spoilage, theft, and obsolescence.

Ordering cost
The cost associated with placing an order. This cost is incurred regardless of the size of the order.

The **ordering cost** is a cost incurred each time an order is placed. This generally involves personnel time used to place the order, receive the order, enter the order into the bookkeeping system, pay the bill, and other tasks associated with purchasing. These costs do not vary as the size of the order changes. For example, whether 10 units of a product or 1,000 units of that product are ordered, the time involved in processing the paperwork is the same. One purchase order is used, one entry is made in the bookkeeping system, and one bill is paid. The time and cost involved in doing this does not depend on the size of the order.

Stockout cost
The cost to a company of not having an item when it is needed.

A **stockout cost** is the cost that occurs when an inventory item is out of stock. This cost may be difficult to determine. If a customer comes to buy an item that currently is not in inventory, that customer may go to a competitor and buy the item there. This represents a lost sale. If this happens too often, this customer may go to the competition first in the future, and thus future sales also would be lost. This cost of lost future sales is difficult to estimate. There are times when a stockout means a sale is not lost, but an additional cost must be paid to expedite the delivery of the item (using an overnight delivery service) so customer goodwill is not lost. This extra cost may be viewed as a stockout cost. For a firm that produces a product on an assembly line, a stockout of a part necessary for production may halt the entire assembly line until that part is obtained. The wages involved in this assembly line would represent an extremely high stockout cost.

Given these four inventory costs, quantitative techniques may be used to determine the optimal or minimum cost policy when certain conditions are met. To determine how this is done, we will begin by making some rather restrictive assumptions. These assumptions will then be relaxed to consider how a manager may modify his or her actions if the assumptions are not met. This will be illustrated with the following example.

10.4 MILLER GRAPHICS EXAMPLE

Miller Graphics produces a variety of products in a production facility in northern Colorado. One particular chemical, LX95, is used extensively and is supplied by a small firm in Arizona. Whenever the inventory of this product is low, an order is placed and the shipment is received in four days. A review of the records from the last two years indicates the usage of this product is relatively constant throughout the year, and Miller Graphics uses 2,000 cases per year. An evaluation of the overall inventory policies of the company is being performed, and costs associated with inventory have been determined. Every time an order is placed, the time spent placing the order, checking the order when it arrives, placing the cases in the storage room and paying the bills costs the company $20 of personnel time. The company also has found the cost of capital for the company as well as insurance, spoilage, and other factors costs the company 10 percent of the value or cost of the inventory. Each case of LX95 costs $80, and there are no discounts available for ordering large quantities.

In the past, Miller has placed orders for 40 cases every week; the company is open five days per week and 50 weeks per year. Now it is considering reducing the number of orders per year by ordering more cases each time an order is placed. Under consideration is the policy of placing 25 orders per year, although management is open to other suggestions.

Inventory Modeling at Bausch & Lomb

Bausch & Lomb's corporate focus is on the global healthcare and optics markets. The company relies on advanced technology, low production costs, and established brand names to remain competitive in these markets. Bausch & Lomb offers a variety of over-the-counter products, including oral care products, eye care products, and nonprescription medicines. The company's medical sector makes contact lenses, periodontal equipment, hearing aids, and other prescription products. The biomedical sector supplies products and services to customers involved in pharmaceutical research and genetic engineering. Finally, Bausch & Lomb's optics segment sells vision enhancement products such as sunglasses, binoculars, and telescopes.

Regions outside the U.S. represent 48 percent of Bausch & Lomb's corporate revenues. The company has manufacturing or marketing organizations in 33 countries. Overall, Bausch & Lomb's products are distributed in more than 100 nations. Managing such a widespread system requires constant innovation. Bausch & Lomb uses employee-directed problem solving teams to improve the way products are made. The teams focus on issues including finance, distribution, production control, and inventory management.

For example, Kmart in 1992 challenged Bausch & Lomb to provide better service and contribute to higher profit margins. A cross-functional team was formed to address this challenge. The most significant contribution of the team was starting Kmart's Partners in Merchandise Flow Program. With this program, Kmart gives Bausch & Lomb all the information necessary to manage inventory levels at Kmart's distribution centers. Bausch & Lomb can then replenish inventory in a timely manner.

Other teams also have helped Bausch & Lomb's strategic focus. One team developed a Total Quality Management program to improve customer service in Tokyo. Another developed inventory management systems that help eye care specialists run their practices more effectively. Overall, by focusing on inventory management, Bausch & Lomb has kept customer satisfaction levels high, and remained in the forefront of the worldwide optics industry.

SOURCE:
Bausch & Lomb, Healthcare and Optics Worldwide, 1992 Annual Report.

10.5 CALCULATING INVENTORY COSTS

To help Miller Graphics with this inventory problem, first determine which of the inventory costs are relevant and which will impact the decisions made regarding the inventory policy. The four inventory costs were identified as the purchase cost, holding cost, ordering cost, and stockout cost. To simplify the presentation of this material, we will define the following variables:

D = annual demand
Q = order quantity
C = purchase cost per unit
C_o = cost of placing an order
C_h = cost of holding one unit in inventory for one year
TPC = total annual purchase cost
THC = total annual holding cost
TOC = total annual ordering cost

The order quantity is the number of units ordered each time an order is placed. Assume every order is for this same amount.

Total Purchase Cost

The total annual purchase cost will be what is paid for the number of units purchased during the entire year (i.e., annual demand). Thus:

$$\text{total purchase cost} = (\text{annual demand})(\text{purchase cost per unit})$$
$$TPC = DC$$

Notice this cost does not depend on the number of units that are ordered each time an order is placed. If a total of D units are needed during the year, eventually a total of DC will have been paid for these units.

Total Ordering Cost

The total annual ordering cost is the number of orders per year times the cost of placing an order. Because the annual demand is D and the order quantity is Q, we have:

$$\text{number of orders per year} = D/Q$$

Thus, the total annual ordering cost (TOC) is calculated as:

$$TOC = (\text{orders per year})(\text{cost of placing an order})$$
$$TOC = (D/Q)C_o$$

Total Holding Cost

To determine the total annual holding cost, something must be known about the inventory levels for the company. The holding cost per unit (C_h) indicates what the cost would be if one unit were held in inventory for one entire year. However, usually one unit is not left in the inventory for the entire year. Rather, units are placed in inventory until they are needed, and then they are sold or used. When the inventory levels fall to a certain amount, the inventory is replenished. Because the inventory level fluctuates throughout the year, the average inventory level will be used to calculate the annual holding cost. Thus, we have:

$$\text{total annual holding cost} = THC$$
$$THC = (\text{average inventory})(\text{cost of holding one unit})$$
$$THC = (\text{average inventory})C_h$$

The average inventory depends on how many units are ordered each time an order is placed, when the order is received, and the demand pattern of the product. Certain assumptions will be made to allow this average inventory to be found.

10.6

THE ECONOMIC ORDER QUANTITY

In addition to assumptions necessary to find the average inventory, there are other assumptions that implicitly have been made. When these assumptions are met, the economic order quantity (EOQ) formula may be used to find the order quantity that will minimize the total annual inventory costs. The assumptions necessary for using the EOQ model are:

1. Purchase cost is known and constant.
2. Holding and ordering costs are known and constant.
3. Demand is known and constant.
4. Lead time is known and constant.
5. Entire order arrives at one time.
6. Orders will be placed to avoid stockouts.

If these assumptions are met, the average inventory and the total inventory costs may be calculated. Before presenting the EOQ formula, look at the assumptions and determine why they are necessary.

The first assumption of a constant purchase cost means what is paid for the product does not vary throughout the year, and does not depend on the size of the order. This means there are no quantity discounts available. The purchase cost must be known in order to calculate the total purchase cost for the year. We will later relax this assumption and consider how to evaluate the option of quantity discounts.

The second assumption that holding and ordering costs are known and constant is necessary to calculate the total annual holding cost and the total annual ordering cost. In most instances, these costs would not be expected to change very much during a year. If minor changes did occur, it would not have a major impact on the inventory policy.

The third assumption of a known and constant demand is necessary to determine the total annual holding costs. These costs are based on the average inventory, and cannot be found unless the demand pattern is known. While this assumption usually is not met exactly, in many instances demand may be relatively constant with minor variations from week to week. We will look at how to deal with nonconstant demand later in this chapter.

The next two assumptions relate to how the order is delivered and the timing of the order. The **lead time** is simply the time that elapses between the placement of the order and the receipt of the order. If this is known and constant, the order may be scheduled to arrive when the inventory level falls to zero. The assumption that the entire order arrives at one time is necessary to determine the average inventory. There may be situations where the entire order is not delivered together but in batches. For example, if 1,000 units were ordered and the supplier did not have this many, these may be shipped as they are produced. Thus, 200 units per day for five days may be received. This would have an impact on the average inventory level and will be discussed later.

Lead time
The time that elapses from ordering a product to the receipt of that product.

The last assumption simply indicates how management plans to operate. With the other assumptions, this may be ensured by ordering at the proper time.

Determining the Average Inventory

Consider Figure 10.1 that presents a graph of the inventory pattern for Miller Graphics' current policy when these assumptions are met. Miller is ordering 40 cases whenever an order is placed, so:

$$Q = 40$$

FIGURE 10.1

Inventory Pattern for Miller Graphics

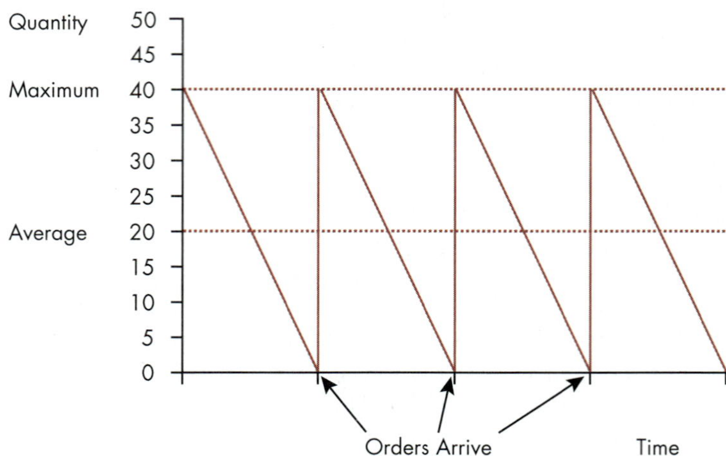

The order is placed so it arrives when the inventory level falls to zero. Because of the constant demand assumption, we know when the inventory level will be at zero, and because of the constant lead time assumption we know the order will arrive at this time. When the order does arrive, all 40 units arrive at the same time so the inventory level immediately rises from zero to 40 units. Thus, the maximum inventory level is 40. Thus, we know:

$$\text{maximum inventory level} = Q = 40$$

Also because of these assumptions, we know the average inventory will be exactly one half of the maximum inventory level. Thus:

$$\text{average inventory} = (\text{maximum inventory})/2 = Q/2$$

This gives us the following formula for the total annual holding cost:

$$\text{total annual holding cost} = THC = (Q/2)C_h$$

Relevant Inventory Costs for EOQ Situation

The total relevant inventory costs, if purchase costs are constant and if stockouts are avoided, would be the total of the holding costs and the ordering costs. This would be:

$$\text{total relevant cost} = THC + TOC$$
$$= (Q/2)C_h + (D/Q)C_o$$

Figure 10.2 illustrates how these costs vary as the order quantity changes. Notice the graph of the total holding cost is a straight line that increases as Q increases. The graph of the total ordering cost decreases as Q increases. Because we would like to minimize the total of these two costs, they are added together to get the third cost curve in this graph. Notice the lowest point on this total cost curve coincides with the point where $TOC = THC$.

FIGURE 10.2

Inventory Costs as a Function of the Order Quantity

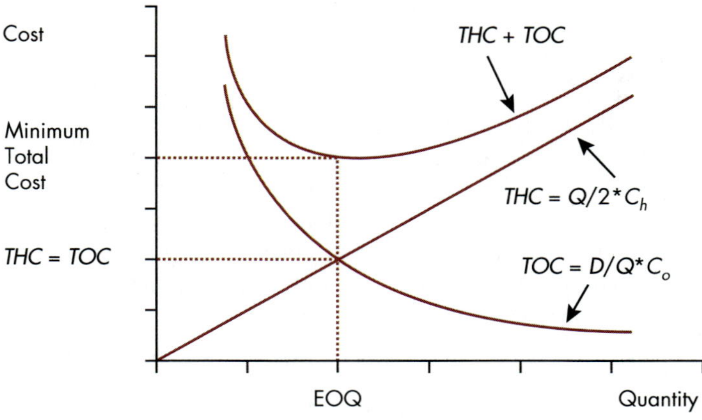

Miller Graphics Example

Let's return to the Miller Graphics example. Recall the company had a policy of ordering 40 units each time an order was placed ($Q = 40$) and this policy was not based on minimizing cost. Thus, the following information and costs are indicated:

$$
\begin{aligned}
D &= 2000 \text{ units} \\
Q &= 40 \text{ units} \\
C &= \$80 \text{ per case} \\
C_o &= \$20 \text{ per order} \\
C_h &= 10\%(\$80) = \$8 \text{ per unit per year} \\
TPC = DC &= 2000(80) = 160{,}000 \\
THC = (Q/2)C_h &= (40/2)8 = \$160 \text{ per year} \\
TOC = (D/Q)C_o &= (2000/40)20 = \$1{,}000 \text{ per year}
\end{aligned}
$$

The average inventory is $Q/2 = 40/2 = 20$ units. The number of orders per year is $D/Q = 2000/40 = 50$. Because the purchase cost is constant, the total relevant cost is:

$$
\begin{aligned}
\text{total cost} &= THC + TOC \\
&= (Q/2)C_h + (D/Q)C_o \\
&= 160 + 1000 = \$1{,}160
\end{aligned}
$$

If management decides to change to the number of orders per year from 50 to 25, then 80 units would be ordered each time an order is placed. This would result in the following costs:

$$
\begin{aligned}
TPC = DC &= 2000(80) = 160{,}000 \\
THC = (Q/2)C_h &= (80/2)8 = \$320 \text{ per year} \\
TOC = (D/Q)C_o &= (2000/80)20 = \$500 \text{ per year} \\
\text{total cost} = THC + TOC &= 320 + 500 = 820
\end{aligned}
$$

This clearly shows that total costs would decrease if fewer orders were placed.

The EOQ Formula

While a trial and error process might be used to determine if costs could be lowered by ordering some other quantity, it is not necessary to use this method. A mathematical formula can be used to find the quantity that will give the minimum possible total cost. To obtain this formula, notice in Figure 10.2 above that the total cost curve is lowest when $THC = TOC$. If these two quantities are set equal and we solve for Q, this results in the order quantity that minimizes inventory costs. This quantity that minimizes the total inventory costs when the assumptions are met is called the **economic order quantity** (EOQ).

Economic order quantity (EOQ)
The quantity that will minimize total inventory cost when certain conditions are met.

$$THC = TOC$$

$$\frac{Q}{2}C_h = \frac{D}{Q}C_o$$

$$Q^2 = \frac{2DC_o}{C_h}$$

$$Q = \sqrt{\frac{2DC_o}{C_h}}$$

Thus:

$$\text{economic order quantity} = EOQ = Q = \sqrt{\frac{2DC_o}{C_h}}$$

In the Miller Graphics example this becomes:

$$Q = \sqrt{\frac{2DC_o}{C_h}} = \sqrt{\frac{2(2000)20}{8}} = 100 \text{ units}$$

If Q = EOQ = 100 units, then:

$$THC = (Q/2)C_h = (100/2)8 = \$400 \text{ per year}$$

$$TOC = (D/Q)C_o = (2000/100)20 = \$400 \text{ per year}$$

$$\text{total relevant cost} = THC + TOC = 400 + 400 = 800$$

Figure 10.3 presents the cost curve to illustrate the Miller Graphics example. Notice the EOQ is indicated in this graph as the point where the THC line and the TOC cost curve intersect. From this we can see what happens to total cost if the EOQ is not used.

10.7 SENSITIVITY ANALYSIS

If the quantity used in the Miller Graphics example is 80 units per order instead of 100 units as specified by the EOQ model, the total inventory cost

FIGURE 10.3

Inventory Costs for Miller Graphics as a Function of Order Quantity

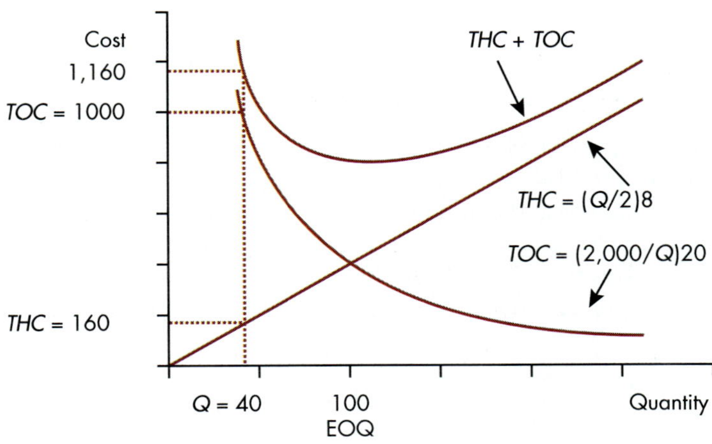

would increase. However, the increase only would be $20 per year. The graph in Figure 10.3 shows the cost curve is relatively flat around the minimum point. This means order quantities reasonably close to the EOQ will have costs very close to the minimum possible cost. Thus, a manager who wishes to use factors other than cost in determining the order quantity may do so without sacrificing much in terms of costs as long as it is not drastically different from the EOQ. For example, in a particular situation the EOQ might indicate that 11 orders per year should be placed, but a manager may wish to order once a month (12 times per year) because this may fit the work routine better.

Another important feature to note about the economic order quantity is that small changes in the numbers used in the EOQ formula (D, C_o, C_h) will have a very minor impact on the quantity calculated. This means while the demand and costs are often estimated and may not be completely accurate, using the EOQ formula with these estimates still will result in a quantity very close to the true EOQ. Thus, a manager should have confidence in using this if the assumptions are close to being met.

10.8

DETERMINING WHEN TO ORDER

The importance of determining how much to order using the EOQ model has been shown. As a part of this model, the receipt of the order is scheduled to occur exactly when the inventory level falls to zero. This will happen only if the constant demand and constant lead time assumptions are met and only if the order is placed at the right time. The **reorder point** is used to determine when to place an order. This is based on the inventory position of a firm, the lead time, and the demand rate. The **inventory position** is defined as the amount of inventory on-hand plus any inventory that

Reorder point
The amount of inventory on-hand or on-order that indicates that a new order should be placed.

Inventory position
The amount of inventory on-hand plus the amount of inventory that is on-order.

may be on-order. An order should be placed whenever the inventory position is equal to the inventory that would be used during the lead time. Thus:

$$\text{reorder point} = (\text{daily demand})(\text{lead time})$$
$$= d \times L$$
$$\text{where } d = \text{daily demand}$$
$$L = \text{lead time in days}$$

When the inventory position reaches the reorder point, an order is placed.

Consider the Miller Graphics example in which the lead time was given as four days. Because the annual demand is 2,000 cases and there are 250 working days per year, the daily demand is eight cases per day. Thus, during the four days that elapse from the time the order is placed until the time the order is received, a total of 32 cases will be used. Therefore:

$$d = 8$$
$$L = 4$$
$$\text{reorder point } (ROP) = dL = (8)(4) = 32$$

If an order is placed when the inventory position is at 32, the order will arrive when the inventory drops to zero.

BEST PRACTICES

Inventory Management in the Mail-Order Camera Business

SOURCE: LaPlante, A., August 2, 1993. "Camera Business Eyes Inventory Management; Integrated Inventory/Financial Application Gives Start-Up an Edge Over its Competitors." *Infoworld* 15 (31): 66.

Mail-order businesses typically operate on very low margins. To remain profitable, mail-order companies must be highly efficient. One way to do this is to use information technology to maintain close control over inventory levels, to keep them as low as possible.

Atlanta-based Wolf Camera, Inc. started a mail-order photographic equipment subsidiary called Peach State Photo in the early 1990s. Although new ventures in the photo industry typically take a year or two to generate profit, Peach State had a healthy income statement within a few months. The company was able to do this by keeping overhead as low as possible. The key to maintaining this low overhead lies in the use of a sophisticated inventory model.

The model Peach State uses maintains inventory data for 180 Wolf Camera locations around the United States. At the end of each business day, each store uploads a file of detailed inventory information to a computer network. This information is then downloaded into the inventory database. Whenever a Peach State customer places an order that is not in stock at the Atlanta warehouse, the customer service representative can do a search to find the nearest supply of the item. Peach State also can use the data in the model to set future inventory levels for the Atlanta warehouse, and determine when to place an order for additional stock.

Courtesy of Peach State Photo, Atlanta, GA

10.9

QUANTITY DISCOUNTS

One assumption of the EOQ models was that the purchase cost was constant throughout the year regardless of the number of units ordered. What if this assumption is not met? There are two ways this assumption could be violated. If the purchase cost varies during the year, the assumption would not be valid. However, as long as the price fluctuations are minor, using the EOQ formula still would yield very good results.

The second way that the constant purchase cost assumption may be violated is by the presence of quantity discounts. Often suppliers will sell a product at a lower price if it is ordered in large quantities. The savings in production and delivery costs are passed along to the buyer.

To determine how many units to order when a quantity discount is available, the total purchase becomes a relevant inventory cost because this changes as the order quantity changes. It also should be recognized that changing the purchase price changes the holding costs per unit (C_h) because this is based on the value of the inventory.

If all the other assumptions of the EOQ are met, the EOQ formula may be used with the different C_h values to determine the minimum cost order quantity for each price category. Within each price category there will be one quantity that should be considered. If the EOQ for a category qualifies for the discount, it should be used. If the EOQ does not qualify for the discount, then the quantity that does qualify for the discount should be considered and that is closest to the EOQ amount. This would be the minimum quantity necessary for the discount. The total relevant cost should be calculated for these quantities, and the best solution is selected.

The total relevant costs are the total holding cost, the total ordering cost, and the total purchase cost. Thus, we have:

$$\begin{aligned}\text{total relevant cost} &= THC + TOC + TPC \\ &= (Q/2)C_h + (D/Q)C_o + DC\end{aligned}$$

This will be illustrated in the following example.

An Example

The supplier for Miller Graphics has just announced that a discount is available for orders of 200 cases or more. If one to 199 cases are ordered, the price is still $80 per case. However, if 200 or more cases are ordered, the cost drops to $75 per case; and if 500 or more cases are ordered, the price drops to $72 per case. Management is considering ordering more cases to save money on the purchase cost. However, in doing so, the total holding cost will increase because more cases must be stored for a longer period of time. What should be done?

Table 10.1 gives the quantities, purchase costs, and holding costs for this situation. Using the different C_h values to calculate the EOQ values results in:

TABLE 10.1

Purchase Costs and C_h for Miller Graphics with Discounts

Category	Quantity	Cost	C_h = 10%C
1	1–199	$80	.10(80)=8
2	200–499	$75	.10(75)=7.5
3	500 or more	$72	.10(72)=7.2

$$EOQ_1 = Q = \sqrt{\frac{2DC_o}{C_h}} = \sqrt{\frac{2(2000)20}{8}} = 100 \text{ units}$$

$$EOQ_2 = Q = \sqrt{\frac{2DC_o}{C_h}} = \sqrt{\frac{2(2000)20}{7.5}} = 103.2 \text{ units}$$

$$EOQ_3 = Q = \sqrt{\frac{2DC_o}{C_h}} = \sqrt{\frac{2(2000)20}{7.2}} = 105.4 \text{ units}$$

Notice in the second category, the EOQ was 103.2. This means if the holding cost is $7.5 and the purchase cost is $75, cost would be minimized by ordering 103.2 units. However, if less than 200 units are ordered, the discount is not received. Therefore, do not consider this EOQ (103.2) but rather consider the minimum quantity (Q = 200) to get the discount.

Similarly, in the third category the EOQ was 105.4, but this quantity must be at least 500 to qualify for the discount. Therefore, 105.4 cannot be ordered at $72, so consider the quantity 500 instead.

Figure 10.4 illustrates how the costs are changing as the purchase cost changes. The dotted lines indicate what the entire cost curve would look

FIGURE 10.4

Total Cost Curves for Different Purchase Costs

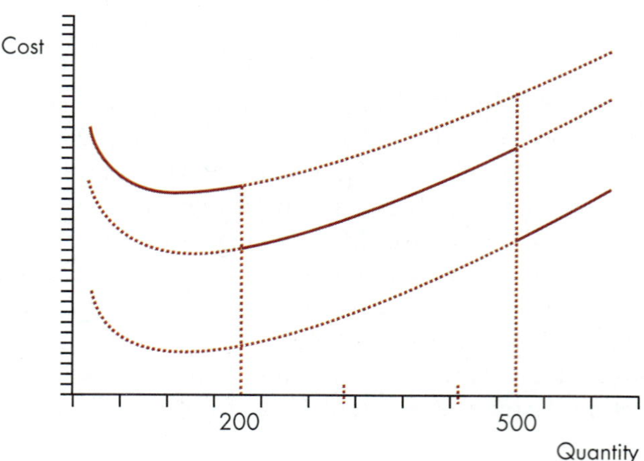

like if the purchase costs were relevant over all quantities. You see the lowest point (EOQ) on each of the last two curves is not enough to qualify for the discount. To obtain the discounts, more than the EOQ amounts must be ordered.

Once it is decided which quantity to consider in each category (either the EOQ for that category or the minimum quantity in that category), simply calculate the total relevant costs and select the quantity with the lowest cost. The quantities to consider are 100, 200, and 500 units. The cost calculations are shown below. Notice both C and C_h vary for each of the three quantities. The total relevant cost is:

$$TC = (Q/2)C_h + (D/Q)C_o + DC$$

For $Q = 100$

$$TC = (100/2)8 + (2000/100)20 + 2000(80) = 160{,}800$$

For $Q = 200$

$$TC = (200/2)7.5 + (2000/200)20 + 2000(75) = 150{,}950$$

For $Q = 500$

$$TC = (500/2)7.2 + (2000/500)20 + 2000(72) = 145{,}880$$

The lowest of these is $145,880 so 500 units at $72 per unit would be ordered each time an order is placed. A summary of these costs is shown in Table 10.2.

10.10 PRODUCTION RUN MODEL

One of the assumptions of the EOQ model was that the entire order arrived at one time. There are many situations in which this assumption is not met. A company may be producing a product for its own use, and there may be a limited daily production rate. When the production of this item begins, the production continues until the order quantity, or production quantity Q, is produced. While this violates one of the assumptions of the EOQ model, if the other EOQ assumptions are met, it is possible to determine the inventory costs and the production quantity that will minimize these costs. This type of situation often is called the **production run model** or the **continuous rate EOQ model.**

Production run model or continuous rate EOQ model

An inventory model that may be used to determine the production quantity that will minimize inventory costs when demand is constant and other assumptions are met.

TABLE 10.2

Evaluating Discounts for Miller Graphics

Quantity	Cost	C_h	EOQ or Minimum for Discount	Total Cost
1–199	$80	8	100	160,800
200–499	$75	7.5	~~103.2~~ 200	150,950
500 or more	$72	7.2	~~105.4~~ 500	145,880 ← minimum cost

The concept of a holding cost is the same whether the inventory is bought from a supplier or produced by the firm itself. However, the average inventory level must be calculated differently because the entire order is not received at one time but rather it is received over several days.

In a production situation, the specific costs defined for an ordering cost may not be relevant. There may not be a purchase order or bills to pay, but there is an equivalent type of cost—the **set-up cost**. Each time a production line is used, it must be set up to produce a specific item. When the production of this item is complete, there may be a cost to clean the machinery. These costs are incurred if one item is produced or if 1,000 items are produced. Therefore, these set-up costs are equivalent to ordering costs in that they do not depend on the size of the order or production run. Therefore, the term ordering cost or set-up cost may be used to refer to this cost.

Set-up cost
The cost associated with preparing the production of a product.

For ease of presentation, the following variables are defined:

$$p = \text{daily production rate}$$
$$d = \text{daily demand rate}$$
$$C_s = \text{cost to set up for production}$$
$$TSC = \text{total annual set-up cost}$$
$$\text{total holding cost} = (\text{average inventory})C_h$$
$$\text{total set-up cost} = (\text{number of set ups per year})(\text{cost to set up})$$
$$TSC = (D/Q)C_s$$

To determine the average inventory, remember some of the items being produced are used on the day they are produced. Figure 10.5 illustrates how the inventory builds up over time. Notice the production continues until production is complete, and then the inventory level falls as before. The

FIGURE 10.5

Inventory Level Over Time for Production Model

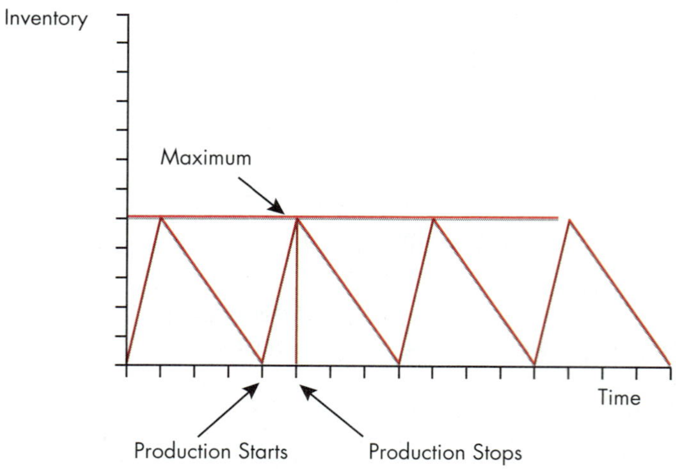

number of new units in inventory at the end of a day of production is the number produced minus the number used (daily demand) or:

$$\text{number of units added to inventory each day} = p - d$$

Dividing this quantity by p results in the proportion of items produced that are added to the inventory. Therefore, for the production model, the inventory will be at its maximum when production stops and this quantity will be:

$$\text{maximum inventory} = Q\frac{p-d}{p} = Q\left(1 - \frac{d}{p}\right)$$

The average inventory will be:

$$\text{average inventory} = \frac{Q}{2}\left(1 - \frac{d}{p}\right)$$

The total holding cost will be:

$$THC = \frac{Q}{2}\left(1 - \frac{d}{p}\right)C_h$$

As the relevant costs are *THC* and *TSC*, the total is minimized when these two costs are equal. Setting these equal and solving for Q, determines the optimum production quantity, which will be indicated by Q^* to be:

$$Q^* = \sqrt{\frac{2DC_s}{C_h\left(1 - \frac{d}{p}\right)}}$$

The following example illustrates the use of this production run model.

Production Run Model Example

R. C. Mills is a chiropractor who, in addition to his chiropractic business, produces cold packs used in chiropractic treatment. Orders arrive daily, and the production department ships these out as soon as orders arrive. The annual demand for this product is 3,000 cases, and demand seems to be constant throughout the year. An analysis of this holding cost indicates there is a cost of $2 per case per year to keep these in inventory. The cost of preparing for production has been found to be $40. In the past, one production run per month has been used, and 250 cases per month are made. Given the size of the operation, only 25 cases per day can be made, and Mills only works 250 days per year. What is the total annual inventory cost for this current policy? How does this compare to the minimum cost policy?

This situation indicates the following:

D = 3,000 units

C_s = \$40 per set up

C_h = \$2 per unit per year

Q = 250 units in production run

p = 25 units per day

d = 3000/250 = 12 units per day

Because the current policy is to produce 250 units ($Q = 250$) in each production run, the following results:

$$\text{maximum inventory} = Q\left(1 - \frac{d}{p}\right) = 250\left(1 - \frac{12}{25}\right) = 130$$

$$\text{average inventory} = \frac{Q}{2}\left(1 - \frac{d}{p}\right) = \frac{250}{2}\left(1 - \frac{12}{25}\right) = 65$$

$$\begin{aligned} THC &= (\text{average inventory})C_h \\ &= (65)2 \quad = 130 \\ TSC &= (D/Q)C_o = (3000/250)40 \\ &= (12)40 \quad = 480 \end{aligned}$$

Thus, the total cost for the current policy is:

$$130 + 480 = 610$$

To minimize total cost, use the formula given above, which results in:

$$Q^* = \sqrt{\frac{2DC_s}{C_h\left(1 - \frac{d}{p}\right)}} = \sqrt{\frac{2(3000)40}{2\left(1 - \frac{12}{25}\right)}} = 480.4$$

Thus, to minimize the total cost, the production run quantity should be 480.4 or rounded off to 480. If this was done, the costs would be:

$$\begin{aligned} \text{average inventory} &= (480/2)(1\text{–}12/25) = 214.8 \\ THC &= (\text{average inventory})C_h \\ &= (124.8)2 = 249.6 \\ TSC &= (D/Q)C_o = (3000/480.4)40 \\ &= (6.25)40 = 250 \end{aligned}$$

The slight difference between these two values is due to round-off error. The total cost using the optimal production quantity is therefore approximately \$500. Thus, if 480 units are produced in each production run, the total inventory cost will decrease from \$610 for the current policy ($Q = 250$) to \$500 with the minimum cost policy ($Q = 480$) for a savings of \$110 per year.

Additional Comments

If the daily production rate (p) is much greater than the daily demand rate (d), then the production run model almost is the same as the EOQ. Intuitively this makes sense because the number produced each day would be very large, so the daily demand would be almost insignificant when compared to the amount produced. Mathematically this is shown by the fact that the production run model is the same as the EOQ model except the denominator of the EOQ model is multiplied by the factor $1 - d/p$. If p is large relative to d, the d/p almost is zero, so $1 - d/p$ is almost one. Therefore, when the denominator of the EOQ model is multiplied by a number that is almost one, there is virtually no change at all.

10.11

STOCKOUTS, SERVICE LEVELS, AND SAFETY STOCK

If inventory is totally depleted and additional units do not arrive immediately, there will be a stockout, and a stockout cost is incurred. With the EOQ assumptions, this would never happen. However, if the EOQ assumption of a known and constant demand is not met or if the assumption of a known and constant lead time is not met, then stockouts may occur. A company may wish to carry extra inventory so if the demand during the lead time is higher than normal, or if the lead time itself is longer than normal, the company will have the inventory available to meet this demand and avoid a stockout. This extra inventory is called **safety stock.**

Safety stock
Extra inventory used to prevent a stockout.

At times, the cost of an item, and consequently the holding cost of that item, may be so high the company is willing to accept the possibility of an occasional stockout. Perhaps the company is willing to be out of stock 10 percent of the time so that 90 percent of the time the company will not be out of stock. The probability the company is not out of stock is called the **service level** of the company. Thus:

Service level
The percentage of time a company is not out of stock when an item is wanted by a customer.

$$\text{service level} = 1 - \text{probability of a stockout}$$

The desired service level is determined by management based on holding costs, stockout costs, and perhaps other factors. If the stockout cost is high and holding cost is low, it may be desirable to maintain a high service level. If the stockout cost is low and holding cost is high, then a lower service level may be appropriate. However, at times a company may base its marketing on the fact it always has what the customer wants when the customer wants it. Thus, in this case the service level is not based strictly on costs but also is influenced by other factors important to the company.

If the assumption of a constant demand or the assumption of a constant lead time is not met, safety stock is used to maintain the service level that management has set for the company. To determine how much safety stock to carry in order to yield a specific service level, management must have information about the variability in demand or the variability in lead time. Based on the probability distributions for these, it is then possible to determine how much safety stock is necessary to maintain a particular service level.

Once the service level has been established and the safety stock has been determined, the reorder point is found by adding the safety stock (SS) to the expected demand during the lead time. Thus:

$$\text{reorder point} = \text{expected lead time demand} + \text{safety stock}$$
$$ROP = dL + SS$$

In figuring the cost of carrying the safety stock, it is important to remember safety stock represents extra inventory not normally depleted. Therefore, if a company has decided to carry 100 units of safety stock, the average amount of safety stock is 100 units. In considering the cost of maintaining this level of safety stock, a commonly used calculation for determining the cost of holding this safety stock is:

$$\text{cost of holding safety stock} = (SS)C_h$$

Note how this differs from the EOQ situation for normal inventory where the average inventory is one half of the order quantity. While this formula is based on several implicit assumptions and always may not be correct, it normally provides a close approximation to the true holding cost for safety stock.

An Example when Demand Is Normally Distributed

The following inventory information has been collected from historical records:

$$D = 4{,}000$$
$$C_h = 9$$
$$C_o = 45$$
$$d = 16$$

An EOQ of 200 units has been calculated. While most of the EOQ assumptions are met, the demand is not constant. However, based on past sales data, it is found that sales during the lead time are normally distributed and the average demand during the five day lead time period is 80 units with a standard deviation of 12 units. After considering the stockout costs and the holding costs, management has decided to maintain a 90 percent service level. What reorder point would provide this?

Because the assumption is that the demand during the lead time is normally distributed, use the following notation:

μ = mean demand during lead time
σ = standard deviation of demand during lead time
X = reorder point

This leads to the situation shown in Figure 10.6. It is known the probability or area under the curve to the left of the reorder point should be 90 percent. Looking up the probability 0.9000 in the normal distribution table in the appendix at the end of the book, the closest probability is found to be 0.8997 for a Z-value of 1.28. Thus, set the reorder point so it has a Z-value of 1.28. Using the Z-formula for the normal distribution, results in

$$Z = (X - \mu)/\sigma$$
$$Z = (ROP - \text{expected demand})/(\text{standard deviation of demand})$$
$$1.28 = (ROP - 80)/12$$

or

$$ROP = 80 + 1.28(12) = 80 + 15.36 = 95.36$$

The average demand during lead time is 80 and the safety stock would be 15.36. Thus, given the assumptions made, if a reorder point of 95.36 is used there is a 90 percent chance that demand can be met during this lead time. The cost of carrying this safety stock is:

$$\text{cost} = (SS)C_h = 15.36(9) = \$138.24$$

In general, when it is appropriate to use the normal distribution to determine the amount of safety stock, use the following formula:

FIGURE 10.6

Determining the Reorder Point for a 90 Percent Service Level

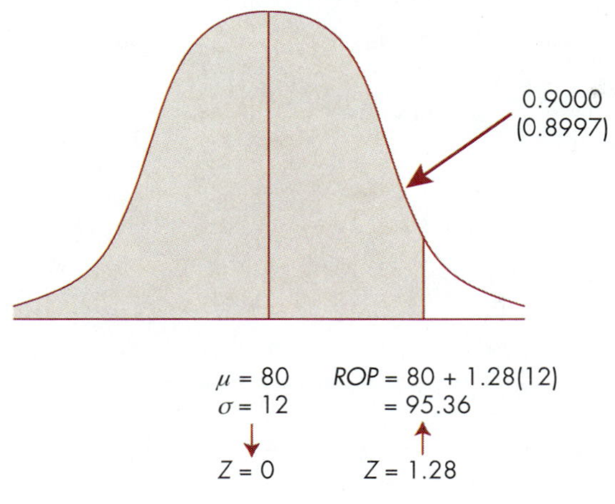

$$SS = Z\sigma$$

where the Z-value is found from the normal distribution tables based on the desired service level.

10.12 SINGLE PERIOD INVENTORY—THE NEWSBOY PROBLEM

A common type of inventory problem involves determining how many units to order or produce to meet the demand in one particular time period. For example, a newspaper must decide how many newspapers to produce each day. Any papers not sold that day have very little value, and they may not be held in inventory to be used later. Also, once the production run for papers has stopped, it is impossible to produce additional papers if the demand is higher than expected.

The type of problem described above often is referred to as the *newsboy problem.* Similar situations are faced by magazine publishers who are unsure how many copies will sell. Buyers for clothing stores must order seasonal clothes for delivery many months in advance, and it usually is not possible to obtain additional units if demand is high. Toys sold during the holiday season of November and December are ordered many months in advance, and stores often sell out a toy that becomes unexpectedly popular, such as dolls or other toys associated with television programs.

For inventory problems of this type, an approach based on marginal analysis often is used. This type of approach is related to other decision making concepts that will be seen in Chapter 12. However, because it so often is used in inventory situations, we will present a brief description here.

The marginal profit is the additional profit to be obtained if one additional unit is stocked and sold. The marginal loss is the loss that occurs if

A single period inventory problem is constantly faced by supermarket managers who must decide how much fresh produce to order. SOURCE: Courtesy of The Lubrizol Corporation

one additional unit is stocked but not sold. An additional unit should be stocked if the expected marginal profit of stocking that unit is greater than the expected marginal loss. Let:

MP = marginal profit of adding one more unit

ML = marginal loss if additional unit is not sold

p = probability of selling additional unit

$1 - p$ = probability of not selling additional unit

Therefore, with this:

$$\text{expected marginal profit} = p(MP)$$

$$\text{expected marginal loss} = (1 - p)(ML)$$

Add the additional unit if:

$$\text{expected marginal profit} \geq \text{expected marginal loss}$$

$$pMP \geq (1 - p)ML$$

Solving this for p yields:

$$p \geq ML/(ML + MP)$$

Thus, add an additional unit as long as the probability of selling that additional unit is at least *ML/(ML + MP)*.

A Newsboy Example with a Discrete Distribution

The *Daily News* stocks vending machines around the city with the daily paper. The cost of each paper is $0.10 and each paper sells for $0.40. Any paper not sold by the end of the day is sold to a recycling plant for $0.02. The daily demand at one particular vending machine location varies according to the probability distribution below:

Demand	24	25	26	27
Probability	0.23	0.30	0.32	0.15

How many papers should be stocked each day? For this situation:

$$MP = 0.40 - 0.10 = 0.30$$
$$ML = 0.10 - 0.02 = 0.08$$
$$p \geq ML/(ML + MP) = 0.08/(0.08 + 0.30) = 0.21$$

Thus, the goal is to have at least a 21 percent chance of selling the last paper stocked. It is known that:

$$P(\text{demand} \geq 24) = 0.23 + 0.30 + 0.32 + 0.15 = 1.00$$
$$P(\text{demand} \geq 25) = 0.30 + 0.32 + 0.15 = 0.77$$
$$P(\text{demand} \geq 26) = 0.32 + 0.15 = 0.47$$
$$P(\text{demand} \geq 27) = 0.15$$

Thus, 26 papers should be stocked. If the 27th paper is stocked, the probability of selling it is only 0.15, which is less than 0.21.

A Newsboy Example with the Normal Distribution

A national sports magazine is planning a special issue that features the Superbowl champions. Past history indicates that the sales of this type of issue follow a normal distribution with a mean of 80,000 and a standard deviation of 10,000. The marginal cost of producing the magazine is $1.00, and the profit is $4.00.

To determine how many copies to produce, calculate:

$$p \geq ML/(ML + MP) = 1/(1 + 4) = 0.20$$

Therefore, enough copies should be produced so there is at least a 20 percent chance of selling the last copy.

Because the assumption is that the demand is normally distributed, let:

$$\mu = \text{mean demand}$$
$$\sigma = \text{standard deviation of demand}$$
$$X = \text{number of units to produce}$$
$$Z = (X - \mu)/\sigma$$

This situation is illustrated in Figure 10.7. Looking up the Z-value for 0.8000 (the closest probability is 0.7995) in the normal tables, gives $Z = 0.84$. Thus:

$$Z = (X - \mu)/\sigma$$
$$0.84 = (X - 80{,}000)/10{,}000$$

or

$$X = 80{,}000 + 0.84(10{,}000) = 88{,}400$$

Therefore, 88,400 copies of this issue should be produced.

10.13 ABC ANALYSIS

Using the EOQ formula and the other inventory management techniques mentioned in this chapter may be beneficial to management. However, for a company which has numerous products, it is not feasible to spend a lot of time forecasting demand, determining the demand distribution, determining the pattern of lead time, and calculating the ordering cost and holding cost for hundreds or thousands of products. However, for certain high cost items, which carry with them a high holding cost, inventory costs may be reduced greatly by careful management of these items. It is important to determine which inventory items have the greatest impact on the inventory cost. Spend more time developing good inventory policies for the items which represent the greatest cost.

FIGURE 10.7

Determining the Production Quantity for a 20 Percent Probability of Selling the Last Unit

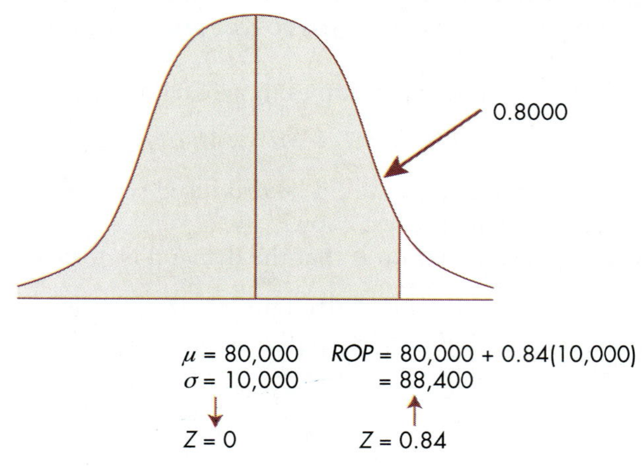

ABC analysis A method of classifying inventory items based on their dollar value.

ABC analysis is a method of categorizing inventory items based on their value. Inventory items are classified in three categories—A, B, and C. Category A items are the very expensive inventory items. Because of the value of these items, their holding cost is high, and consequently, careful management of these is warranted. Often, only 10 percent of all inventory items would be in this category, but the value of these may be 70 percent of the total dollar investment in inventory.

Category B items are less expensive than Category A items, but these are moderately expensive. Less time should be spent managing these because there is less potential for savings. These items may account for 20 percent of all inventory items, and the value of these may be 20 percent of the total value of inventory.

Category C items are the low cost inventory items. While 70 percent of all items in inventory would be in this category, the total value of these may be only 10 percent of the value of inventory. Thus, the company would not have much money invested in these, and there are so many that if a manager spent much time on each one there would be no time to do anything else.

Table 10.3 illustrates these categories for ABC analysis. The percentages should not be considered as absolute numbers, but rather they should give you a general idea of the magnitude of these numbers. The number of items in Category A might be 5 percent or 15 percent, and the value of these items might be more or less than 70 percent. The important thing is the concept that relatively few items account for a very large portion of the investment in inventory.

A prudent manager will spend most of his or her time with the Category A items. Careful management of these may produce significant savings in the holding cost. Because there are so few of these items, there is time to carefully forecast demand and determine a good policy. Some time should be spent on the Category B items, but not as much time as on the Category A items. There are more of these and yet they represent less value than the Category A items. Carrying additional safety stock on these is not nearly as expensive as it is for carrying additional safety stock for the Category A items. The Category C items are so numerous and inexpensive that a manager might develop a simple policy to ensure that stockouts do not occur. Because the value of these is so low, the holding cost also is very low. Thus, carrying safety stock does not cost much. While these items are

TABLE 10.3

Categories for ABC Analysis

Inventory Category	Dollar Value (%)	Number of Items (%)
A	70	10
B	20	20
C	10	70

A CLOSER LOOK

Closed-Loop MRP, MRP II, and DRP

SOURCE: Schonberger, R. J. and E. M. Knod, Jr., 1994. *Operations Management: Continuous Improvement*. 5th ed. Boston: Richard D. Irwin, Inc.

Using materials requirements planning (MRP) to develop a schedule does not guarantee the schedule can be followed. Problems may be experienced when several products utilize the same resources. Adjustments in the master schedule sometimes are necessary after a plan has been developed with an MRP system. When an automatic feedback mechanism is implemented within an MRP system, it is referred to as a *closed-loop MRP*. This closed-loop system may include the production planning, master production scheduling, capacity requirements planning, and the distribution system as well.

The inclusion of other functional areas, such as marketing and finance, into an integrated information system related to materials planning has been called *manufacturing resources planning* or *MRP II*. This inventory management system may include information not only about the quantities of a product but also about the materials costs, labor hours, or any other type of resource.

A *distribution resource planning (DRP)* system is a logical extension of the MRP concept. With DRP, an overall forecast of the demand of a product is developed. This forecast rather than the receipt of an order is used as a basis of the gross requirement of an item in an MRP system. This forecast would include parts that may be needed for repairs as well as those parts that are actually used in production.

inexpensive, they are still important to customers and thus they are important to the company.

The Two-Bin System

Two-bin system
An inventory control system in which an item is removed from one bin until it is empty, at which time an order is placed and the second bin is used.

The **two-bin system** may be a good way to manage the Category C items. In this system, two bins or containers are filled with the item. One container is used until it is empty. At this time an order is placed for a predetermined amount, and the second container is used until the order arrives. When the order arrives, the empty container is filled and any remaining items are put in the container that currently is being utilized. The reorder point in this situation is the point at which one bin is empty and the other is starting to be used. A modification of this is to use two different sized bins. A large bin is used until it is emptied at which time an order is placed and the small bin is used. When the order arrives, the small bin is filled and set aside, and the larger bin is used until it is empty. Thus, the small bin would represent the amount of inventory normally needed during the lead time plus any safety stock that is desired.

10.14 MATERIALS REQUIREMENTS PLANNING

In discussing inventory up to this point, inventory items that were independent from one another were discussed. When the demand for each item is independent of the demand for other items, each item is managed independently. In production situations, there is a dependent demand situation in which the demand for one item depends on the demand for another item.

For example, an automobile manufacturer knows that the demand for steering wheels this week depends on the number of automobiles to be produced this week. In forecasting the demand for all of the different parts that go into the production of an automobile, a determination may be made from the number of automobiles scheduled for production. **Materials requirements planning** (MRP) is an inventory system that ties all of these together. A **bill of materials** normally presents the information concerning the number of components needed for a product and how these items are related.

Materials requirements planning (MRP)
An inventory management technique that is very beneficial when there is a dependent demand situation, as in a manufacturing situation.

Bill of materials
A listing of the components of a product.

In a production environment, the master production schedule for the final product together with the bill of materials can be used to develop demand schedules for all of the component parts. As the demand (production schedule) for the product is not constant, the reorder point for the component parts should be based on when they are needed for production. By doing this, the inventory for each of these is minimal until it is needed.

An MRP system is typically a computerized system in which the demand for each component is tied to the demand for the final product, the inventory position for each component is entered into the system, and information about the lead time for each component also is entered. Thus, when a production schedule is set by management, this is entered into the computer and purchase orders are generated by the computer for the necessary number of parts. These purchase orders will indicate not only when the materials are needed but also when they should be placed based on the lead time.

An Example

Outdoor Products produces several types of barbecue grills. In planning for the production of one particular product, which we will simply call Item A, a bill of materials was developed as shown in Figure 10.8. The numbers in

FIGURE 10.8

Bill of Materials for Outdoor Products Example

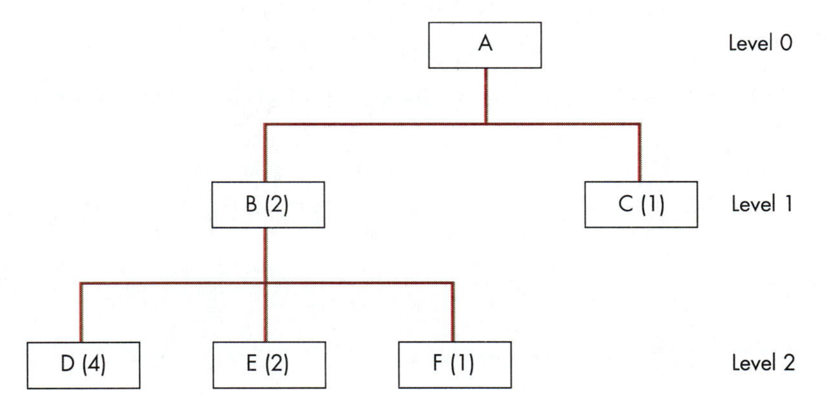

parentheses indicate how many of each part is used in production. Two units of Part B and one unit of Part C are used in making Item A. Four units of Part D, two units of Part E, and one unit of Part F go into the production of one unit of Part B.

An order for 250 units of Item A has been received for delivery in five weeks. Management is planning the production of this product, and the materials requirements are being determined. An inspection of existing inventory as well as scheduled receipts for parts that already have been ordered result in the information in Table 10.4. Also included in this table is the lead time or assembly time for each product. This shows production should start on Item A one week before it is due. An order for Part E should be placed two weeks prior to the time work on Part B starts.

A materials requirements plan, such as the one shown in Figure 10.9, is used in scheduling the orders. In creating this, begin with the schedule of production for the top level product, and use it to determine the needs for the parts. Looking at the top chart in Figure 10.9 shows that 250 units of Part A are needed in Week 5. This is called the gross requirement for the item. The net requirements are the gross requirements less any on-hand inventory and any scheduled receipts. Because there are 50 units on-hand and none scheduled to be received, the net requirement for Part A is 200 units. The lead time of one week means an order release is planned for Week 4 so 200 more units of Part A will be available in Week 5.

From the planned order release for 200 units of Part A and the bill of materials, the need for 400 units of Part B in Week 4 and 200 units of Part C in Week 3 is determined. Put this as the gross requirements in the appropriate spot on the schedules. Then determine the net requirements for these parts as shown in Figure 10.9. Using the lead times, plan the order releases for these products. Then use the planned order release for Part B to determine the gross requirements for Parts D (4 x 340), E (2 x 340), and F (1 x 340). Continuing this process results in the requirement plans for Parts D, E, and F.

This process becomes more complicated when several products use the same type of part, but the basic concept still applies. Computer software is used for this process, and with the recent advances in computer hardware, MRP is becoming increasingly prevalent.

TABLE 10.4

On-Hand Inventory and Scheduled Receipts for Outdoor Products Example

	Item					
	A	B	C	D	E	F
On-Hand	50	20	0	100	0	0
Scheduled Receipts	0	40	20	200	90	40
Lead/Assembly Time (Weeks)	1	1	2	1	2	1

FIGURE 10.9

Requirements Planning Chart for Outdoor Products Example

Part A Week	1	2	3	4	5
Gross Requirements					250
On-Hand 50					50
Scheduled Receipts 0					
Net Requirements					200
Planned Order Receipt					200
Planned Order Release				200	

Part B Week	1	2	3	4	5	
Gross Requirements				400		←2 × 200 From A
On-Hand 20				20		
Scheduled Receipts 40				40		
Net Requirements				340		
Planned Order Receipt				340		
Planned Order Release			340			

Part C Week	1	2	3	4	5	
Gross Requirements				200		←1 × 200 From A
On-Hand 0				0		
Scheduled Receipts 20				20		
Net Requirements				180		
Planned Order Receipt				180		
Planned Order Release		180				

Part D Week	1	2	3	4	5	
Gross Requirements			1,360			←4 × 340 From B
On-Hand 100			100			
Scheduled Receipt 200			200			
Net Requirements			1,060			
Planned Order Receipt			1,060			
Planned Order Release		1,060				

(continued)

FIGURE 10.9

(continued)

Part E Week	1	2	3	4	5
Gross Requirements			680		
On-Hand 0			0		
Scheduled Receipts 90			90		
Net Requirements			590		
Planned Order Receipt			590		
Planned Order Release	590				

←2 × 340 From B

Part F Week	1	2	3	4	5
Gross Requirements			340		
On-Hand 0			0		
Scheduled Receipts 40			40		
Net Requirements			300		
Planned Order Receipt			300		
Planned Order Release		300			

←1 × 340 From B

10.15 JUST-IN-TIME

Just-in-time system
A Japanese system of inventory control based on minimizing the amount of inventory.

Push system
A production system in which work in process is produced and pushed along to the next workstation even if it is not needed.

Pull system
A production system in which items are not produced and sent unless the next station needs these items.

The Japanese have taken some of the concepts from MRP, basic inventory theory, and concern for quality and effectively implemented an approach to inventory management called the **just-in-time system**. A basic premise of this type of system is that inventories should be kept low. The product should be produced at the time it is needed and it should be of good quality.

In discussing the just-in-time system, it helps to understand the difference between a push system and a pull system. A **push system** is one in which the demand for the final product is forecasted, and then production begins. The raw materials enter the system and proceed to the first station in a manufacturing process. Here work is performed and the item or batch of items is then pushed to the next station and a new batch begins. This process continues whether or not stations down the line are ready for additional units of the work in process. This work in process may build up at a station or be put into inventory for use at a later time. A **pull system** is one in which the last station sends a request (i.e., it orders a specific quantity)

TRINOVA Corporation has implemented a just-in-time inventory system; parts are made to order and shipped immediately.
SOURCE: Photo provided courtesy of TRINOVA Corporation

to the previous station for a specific number of units. If necessary, this request is sent back through each station in the system to the very beginning so the production process may begin. With this system, items are not sent along the assembly line until they are needed and requested. Thus, they are pulled through the system when they are needed. As a result of this, there is no unplanned build up of inventory.

An additional advantage of the pull system is that very small quantities are sent from one station to the next, and it is easier to find problems with quality before a large inventory of poor quality items builds up. Because there is no build up of inventory, there is no safety stock, which means it is imperative the quality of each item is good. It becomes the responsibility of each worker to maintain quality.

Kanban
A Japanese system of using cards to control the flow of inventory through a production system.

The Japanese use **kanbans** or cards attached to containers of parts to implement the just-in-time system. This may be viewed as a logical extension of the two-bin system in a production process. There may be two containers (bins) at a particular workstation, which we will call station number 5. When one container is empty, it is sent along with the kanban attached to it back to the previous station (station number 4) to be replenished. Station number 4 sends forward to station number 5 a full container with the kanban attached. At this time, station 4 also must send an empty container with a kanban back to station number 3 to be replenished with the work in process that is used at station number 4. This procedure continues throughout the entire assembly process. While this illustration uses two containers, the inventory manager may control this process as needed by providing additional kanbans at certain stations on the line or removing a kanban at other points on the line to keep the production line moving smoothly.

When the kanban system is working properly, there is a continual flow through the production line, and the final product is sent to its final destination with minimal inventory build up. This continuous, smooth flow along the production line may be achieved by properly designing and balancing a pull system, but it also could be achieved by properly designing a push system. However, with the pull system there typically is more control of the system and problems often are more easily avoided.

In putting the just-in-time system in perspective with what was presented earlier in this chapter, let's consider the first purpose that was listed for holding inventory—to serve as a buffer between supply and demand. The just-in-time philosophy negates the need for this buffer in production situations. If production can rely on the items to be delivered when they are needed and to be of good quality, then this buffer is not needed.

Also, delivering small quantities is the key to maintaining low inventories in the just-in-time system. This means the ordering cost or set-up cost must be kept low. By reducing the set-up time, the set-up cost is lowered, and smaller lot sizes become more economical.

While these discussions of the just-in-time system have focused on the production line within a manufacturing company, it also applies to the receipt of materials from vendors who are supplying parts to the manufacturing firm. There is almost a continuous flow from the suppliers to the user just as there is a continuous flow along the assembly line. For example, a Toyota manufacturing plant receives automobile parts to be assembled at the plant. The vendors are expected to deliver these just-in-time to start production, and they are expected to be of good quality. Long-term relationships between the auto manufacturer and the parts manufacturers allow this system to be effectively utilized.

10.16

USING SOFTWARE WITH INVENTORY PROBLEMS

The DSS software can be used with several of the inventory models presented in this chapter. The DSS output for the Miller Graphics example of an EOQ situation is provided in Output 10.1. This software allows the holding cost to be expressed as the percentage of the purchase cost or as the holding cost per unit per year. It also calculates the daily demand if the user specifies the number of working days per year. This same module can be used with a discount problem by specifying the last two input items (discount price and minimum quantity for discount) shown in the figure. The DSS output for the Mills example of the production lot size problem is seen in Output 10.2.

OUTPUT 10.1

DSS Output for Miller Graphics Example

```
Production & Inventory - EOQ w/ Discounts

Inputs:

     Average Annual Holding Cost per Unit (Ch) *OR*        $ 8
  Average Annual Holding Cost as a % of Unit Cost (Cp)     %
 Please enter    ┌    Annual Demand in Units per Year (A) ┐ 2000
 any two of      │    Number of Working Days per Year (D) │ 250
 inputs (A D d)  └  Daily Sales Rate in Units per Day (d) ┘
               Ordering Cost Per Order (Co)                $ 20
             Lead Time on Orders in Days (TL)
               Purchase Price per Unit (Cp)                $
          Quantity Discount Price per Unit (Cp')           $
      Minimum Quantity to qualify for discount (Q')

Outputs:

Q* =  100 units/order
N* =  20 orders/year
T* =  12.5 days/cycle
QR =  0 units
Annual Holding Cost (AHC) = $       400.00/year
Annual Ordering Cost (AOC) = $       400.00/year
Annual Purchasing Cost (APC) = $         0.00/year
Total Annual Cost = $        800.00/year
```

10.17 SUMMARY

In this chapter we have looked at the basic purposes of carrying inventory and the costs associated with this. As inventory represents a major cost to a firm, it is important to try to minimize these costs. The economic order quantity was presented as a means of minimizing costs when certain assumptions are met. We saw how inventory management may change if these assumptions are not met. If quantity discounts are available and the other EOQ assumptions are met, the total costs for certain quantities may be calculated to find the best order quantity. If items are added to inventory over time as in a production situation while the other EOQ assumptions are met, then an optimal production quantity may be found. Safety stock is used when demand or lead time is variable, and stockout costs are weighed against holding costs to help determine the service level and to determine how much safety stock to carry. ABC analysis was seen as a way of determining how much attention and time should be given to managing different items in inventory. Materials requirements planning (MRP) was seen as an effective tool when dealing with dependent demand situations as in many production situations. The use of the just-in-time system has proven to be an effective tool for the Japanese in reducing inventories and maintaining quality in manufacturing operations.

OUTPUT 10.2

DSS Output for Mills Production Lot Size Example

```
Production & Inventory - Production Lot Size

Inputs:

    Average Annual Holding Cost per Unit (Ch) *OR*          $ 2
  Average Annual Holding Cost as a % of Unit Cost (Cp)      %
 Please enter   ┌  Annual Demand in Units per Year (A)    ┐ 3000
 any two of     │  Number of Working Days per Year (D)    │ 250
 inputs (A D d) └ Daily Sales Rate in Units per Day (d)   ┘
          Setup Cost per Production Run (Cs)                $ 40
          Lead Time for setup in Days (TL)
          Manufacturing cost per Unit (Cp)                  $
     Daily Production Rate in Units per Day (p)               25

Outputs:

Q* =  480.3845 units/lot
QMax =  249.7999 units
N* =  6.244998 orders/year
T* =  40.03204 days/cycle
QR =  0 units
Production Time =  19.21538 days
Annual Holding Cost (AHC) = $       249.80/year
Annual Setup Cost (ASC) = $       249.80/year
Annual Purchasing Cost (APC) = $          0.00/year
Total Annual Cost = $       499.60/year
```

GLOSSARY

ABC analysis A method of classifying inventory items based on their dollar value. *p. 431*

Bill of materials A listing of the components of a product. *p. 433*

Economic order quantity (EOQ) The quantity that will minimize total inventory cost when certain conditions are met. *p. 416*

Holding (or carrying) cost The cost associated with holding inventory, such as the cost of capital, insurance, taxes, and storage costs. *p. 409*

Inventory position The amount of inventory on-hand plus the amount of inventory that is on-order. *p. 417*

Just-in-time system A Japanese system of inventory control based on minimizing the amount of inventory. *p. 436*

Kanban A Japanese system of using cards to control the flow of inventory through a production system. *p. 437*

Lead time The time that elapses from ordering a product to the receipt of that product. *p. 413*

Materials requirements planning (MRP) An inventory management technique that is very beneficial when there is a dependent demand situation, as in a manufacturing situation. *p. 433*

Ordering cost The cost associated with placing an order. This cost is incurred regardless of the size of the order. *p. 409*

Production run model or continuous rate EOQ model An inventory model that may be used to determine the production quantity that will minimize inventory costs when demand is constant and other assumptions are met. *p. 421*

Pull system A production system in which items are not produced and sent unless the next station needs these items. *p. 436*

Purchase cost The cost of obtaining or purchasing a good. *p. 408*

Push system A production system in which work in process is produced and pushed along to the next workstation even if it is not needed. *p. 436*

Reorder point The amount of inventory on-hand or on-order that indicates that a new order should be placed. *p. 417*

Safety stock Extra inventory used to prevent a stockout. *p. 425*

Service level The percentage of time a company is not out of stock when an item is wanted by a customer. *p. 425*

Set-up cost The cost associated with preparing the production of a product. *p. 422*

Stockout cost The cost to a company of not having an item when it is needed. *p. 410*

Two-bin system An inventory control system in which an item is removed from one bin until it is empty, at which time an order is placed and the second bin is used. *p. 432*

KEY EQUATIONS

(10-1) D = annual demand
Q = order quantity
C = purchase cost per unit
C_o = cost of placing an order
C_h = cost of holding one unit in inventory for one year
p = daily production rate
d = daily demand rate
C_s = cost to set up for production
TPC = total annual purchase cost
THC = total annual holding cost
TOC = total annual ordering cost
TSC = total annual set-up cost

(10-2) Economic order quantity (EOQ)

$$EOQ = \sqrt{\frac{2DC_o}{C_h}}$$

Average inventory = $Q/2$

(10-3) Cost formulas when EOQ assumptions are met

$$TPC = DC$$
$$THC = (Q/2)C_h$$
$$TOC = (D/Q)C_o$$

(10-4) Reorder point with no safety stock

$$ROP = dL$$

(10-5) Reorder point with safety stock

$$ROP = dL + SS$$

(10-6) Production run model

$TPC = DC$

$TSC = (D/Q)C_s$

(10-7) $\text{maximum inventory} = Q\frac{p-d}{p} = Q\left(1 - \frac{d}{p}\right)$

(10-8) $\text{average inventory} = \frac{Q}{2}\left(1 - \frac{d}{p}\right)$

(10-9) $THC = \frac{Q}{2}\left(1 - \frac{d}{p}\right)C_h$

(10-10) Optimal production quantity Q^*

$$Q^* = \sqrt{\frac{2DC_s}{C_h\left(1 - \frac{d}{p}\right)}}$$

(10-11) Safety stock assuming demand is normally distributed

$SS = Z(\text{standard deviation of demand during lead time}) = Z\sigma$

(10-12) Marginal analysis for newsboy problem

MP = marginal profit of adding one more unit

ML = marginal loss if additional unit is not sold

p = probability of selling additional unit

$1 - p$ = probability of not selling additional unit

Stock additional unit if $p \geq ML/(ML + MP)$

SOLVED PROBLEMS

SOLVED PROBLEM 10-1

The annual demand for a product is 5,000 units per year, and this is assumed to be constant throughout the year. The holding cost is $9 per unit per year, and the ordering cost is $36 per order. The lead time is three days, and there are 250 working days per year. The company wishes to minimize annual inventory costs.

a) How many units should be ordered each time an order is placed?
b) How many orders per year would be placed?
c) What is the reorder point?
d) Calculate the total holding cost and the total ordering cost.

SOLUTION

We know:

$$D = 5{,}000$$
$$C_o = \$36$$
$$C_h = \$9$$

a) If the assumptions of the EOQ are met, we minimize costs by ordering the economic order quantity:

$$EOQ = Q = \sqrt{\frac{2DC_o}{C_h}} = \sqrt{\frac{2(5000)36}{9}} = 200 \text{ units}$$

b) With $Q = 200$, the number of orders per year will be:

$$D/Q = 5000/200 = 25 \text{ orders per year}$$

c) To calculate the reorder point, we find the daily demand:

$$d = 5{,}000/250 = 20$$

Then,

$$ROP = dL = (20)3 = 60 \text{ units}$$

d) If

$$Q = 200 \text{ units}$$

then

$$THC = (Q/2)C_h = (200/2)9 = \$900 \text{ per year}$$

$$TOC = (D/Q)C_o = (5000/200)36 = \$900 \text{ per year}$$

SOLVED PROBLEM 10-2

The demand for a product is normally distributed, but all the other assumptions of the EOQ model are met. It has been determined the annual demand is 10,000, and there are 250 working days per year. The ordering cost is \$32 per order, and the holding cost is \$4 per unit per year. During the five-day lead time, sales are normally distributed with a mean of 200 units and a standard deviation of 40 units. A service level of 95 percent has been established based on holding costs and stockout costs.

a) How many units should be ordered to minimize cost?
b) How much safety stock should be carried?
c) What is the reorder point?
d) What is the average annual cost for holding the safety stock?

SOLUTION

a) We minimize cost by using the EOQ formula under these conditions.

$$EOQ = Q = \sqrt{\frac{2DC_o}{C_h}} = \sqrt{\frac{2(10{,}000)32}{4}} = 400 \text{ units}$$

b) For a 95 percent service level, the Z-value is approximately 1.64. Thus, the amount of safety stock should be:

$$SS = Z\sigma = 1.64(40) = 65.6$$

Rounding this, we would use a safety stock of 66 units.

c) The reorder point is:

$$ROP = \text{expected demand during lead time} + \text{safety stock}$$
$$= 200 + 65.6 = 265.6 \text{ or approximately 266 units}$$

d) The average cost of holding 66 units of safety stock is:

$$C_hSS = \$4(66) = \$264$$

QUESTIONS

1. Why does a company carry inventory?
2. What are the costs associated with inventory? Discuss how changing the order quantity affects each of these.
3. If the assumptions for the economic order quantity model are met and a person orders more than the EOQ amount, how will the total annual ordering cost compare with the total annual holding cost?
4. In the quantity discount model with one discount available, a person has suggested the order quantity that minimizes costs always will be the minimum quantity to obtain the discount and can never be more than this amount. Explain why this person is wrong.
5. If the daily production rate is very high relative to the daily demand, how does the production run model compare to the economic order quantity model?
6. When a just-in-time system is used in a manufacturing situation, inventory is not held to serve as a buffer between supply and demand although this is a common reason for holding inventory. Discuss the conditions that would have to exist to negate the need for this buffer.
7. It has been said ABC analysis is more of a time management tool than an inventory model. Explain this.
8. A company has found that due to a change in competition, the stockout cost for a product has suddenly increased dramatically. How should the company react to this?
9. In an EOQ situation, the average inventory level is one half of the maximum inventory level. However, if safety stock is carried, the average amount of the safety stock is equal to the maximum amount of safety stock. Explain why this is true.
10. What factors should influence a company's decision to carry safety stock?
11. Suppose the EOQ assumptions are met and a company has decided to order 400 units each time an order is placed. The annual demand is 1,000 units, so the company needs to place 2.5 orders per year. How is this fractional part of an order achieved? Is the total annual ordering cost formula presented in the chapter relevant in this situation?

PROBLEMS

12. The annual demand for a product is 5,000 units, and the demand is constant throughout the year. This item costs $80 and the holding cost per unit per year is 20 percent of the cost of the item. The ordering cost is $25 per order. There are 250 working days per year. Currently the company has an order quantity of 500 units each time an order is placed. Lead time is five days.
    a) Under the current policy, what is the maximum inventory level? What is the average inventory level? How many orders per year are placed?
    b) Under the current policy, calculate the total annual holding cost, total annual ordering cost, total annual purchase cost.
13. In the previous problem, suppose the company wishes to minimize the total annual inventory cost.
    a) How many units should be ordered each time an order is placed? How many orders per year would be used?

b) If the economic order quantity is used instead of the current policy, how much would the total annual inventory cost decrease?
c) What is the reorder point if the current policy is used? What is the reorder point if the EOQ is used?

14. Hays Hardware sells 9,000 gallons of a popular brand of wall paint each year. Demand has been relatively constant for this product that costs $15 per gallon. The cost of placing each order has been determined to be $30 per order, and the cost of holding this is 10 percent of the value of the paint. Once an order is placed, it takes the distributor five days to deliver this to Hays Hardware. There are 300 working days per year.

    Hays Hardware has a computerized system in which items are scanned for their stock number and price as they are sold. Thus, there is a continual count of remaining gallons of paint in inventory.
    a) If Hays Hardware is to minimize total annual inventory cost, how many gallons should be ordered each time an order is placed? How many orders per year would be required if this policy is used?
    b) Calculate the total holding cost, total ordering cost, and total purchase cost for the inventory policy that minimizes cost.
    c) What is the daily demand for this paint?
    d) How many gallons of paint will be sold during the lead time?
    e) What is the reorder point in this situation?

15. The supplier of paint in Problem 14 has offered a discount of 5 percent of the purchase price for orders of 1,000 gallons or more. Hays Hardware does have room to store up to 1,500 gallons of paint, so the possibility of ordering 1,000 gallons or more is being considered.
    a) If Hays Hardware were to order 1,000 gallons of paint, what would be the holding cost per unit?
    b) If Hays Hardware were to order 1,000 gallons of paint, what would be the purchase cost per unit?
    c) To minimize the total annual inventory cost, how many gallons of paint should Hays Hardware order each time an order is placed?

16. Evermore Appliances produces all types of major appliances that are sold nationwide. One particular product is a refrigerator that has an annual demand of 8,000 units. These are produced in a plant that has a capacity of 200 units per day. Each time that production of these begins, it costs the company $120 to move materials into place, reset the assembly line, and clean the equipment. The holding cost of a refrigerator has been determined to be $50 per year. The company operates 250 days per year, and demand is constant throughout the year.

    The current production plan calls for 400 refrigerators to be produced in each production run.
    a) What is the daily demand for this product?
    b) If the company were to produce 400 refrigerators each time production started, how many days would production continue?
    c) Under the current policy, how many production runs per year would be required? What would be the total annual set-up cost?
    d) If the current policy continues, how many refrigerators would be in inventory when production stopped? What would be the maximum inventory level? What would be the average inventory level?

17. Consider the Evermore Appliances situation in Problem 16. Suppose the company wishes to minimize the total annual inventory cost.
a) How many refrigerators should be produced each time production starts?
b) If the optimal production quantity is used instead of the quantity used in the current policy, how much would the company save in inventory costs each year?
c) Suppose it takes two days to prepare to start production, and the company plans to start production when the inventory level is at zero. How many refrigerators would remain in inventory when the company begins to set up for production?
18. The annual demand for a product is 1,200 units and is constant throughout the year. The holding cost has been determined to be 18 percent of the cost of the item, and each unit costs \$80. The ordering cost is \$40 per order.
a) Calculate the economic order quantity.
b) Suppose changing economic conditions indicate the holding cost is 20 percent rather than 18 percent. Calculate the new EOQ.
c) Suppose changing economic conditions indicate the holding cost is 22 percent rather than 18 percent. Calculate the new EOQ.
19. An auto parts store annually sells 600 alternators of a particular type, and demand has been relatively constant for this product. This alternator is supplied by a wholesaler who will provide a discount for large orders as shown in the table below:

Order Quantity	Cost per Unit
1–199	\$50
200–399	48
400 or more	47

The holding cost is 20 percent of the unit cost, and the ordering cost is \$30 per order. If the company wishes to minimize total annual inventory cost, how many alternators should be ordered each time an order is placed?
20. An office supply company has a chain of stores in a major metropolitan area. Every year the company sells 2,000 boxes of toner cartridges for laser printers, and the demand for these is constant throughout the year. These are purchased from a distributor who has set the price at \$80 per box. However, if 400 boxes or more are ordered, a \$2 discount is provided. The company has determined the holding cost is 15 percent of the purchase cost, and the ordering cost is \$30 per order.
a) How many boxes should be ordered to minimize total annual inventory cost? What is the total cost of doing this?
b) If the company orders 400 boxes each time an order is placed, what would the total annual inventory cost be?
21. Suppose the annual demand for a product is 5,000 and the ordering cost is \$40 per order. Calculate the economic order quantity for each of the following situations:
a) holding cost is \$10 per unit per year
b) holding cost is \$20 per unit per year
c) holding cost is \$40 per unit per year
22. The demand for a product is normally distributed, but all the other assumptions of the EOQ model are met. It has been determined the annual demand is

10,000, and there are 250 working days per year. The ordering cost is $48 per order, and the holding cost is $6 per unit per year. The lead time is usually six days, and during this time sales are normally distributed with a mean of 240 units and a standard deviation of 80 units. A service level of 90 percent has been established based on holding costs and stockout costs.

a) How many units should be ordered to minimize cost?

b) How much safety stock should be carried?

c) What is the reorder point?

23. A company has established the following inventory policy: whenever the inventory level falls to 90 units, an order for 360 units is placed. There appears to be no particular seasonal pattern to the sales, but sales do fluctuate daily. The sales pattern does seem to approximate a normal distribution. Historically, the lead time has been four days, and the average sales during a four-day period is 72 units with a standard deviation of 10 units. There are 250 working days per year. How much safety stock is the company carrying? What service level is implied by this policy?

24. After the National Basketball Association (NBA) championship series every year, a T-shirt company produces a special T-shirt with the winning team's logo and the words *World Champions* on it. The company has a contract for the use of the printing machines used on these shirts for three days, and then the printing machines are used for other projects. These T-shirts are sold at special outlets beginning the day after the last game and continue for four weeks. The cost of the T-shirt and the printing is $6, and the shirt sells for $12. Any shirts that are not sold during this four-week period are sold to a discount warehouse store for $4 each. History provides the following sales information about this T-shirt:

Sales (in Thousands)	Probability
10	0.05
11	0.08
12	0.13
13	0.14
14	0.19
15	0.17
16	0.14
17	0.10

How many T-shirts should the company produce?

25. The Webster Manufacturing Company produces a type of serving cart that is very popular. This product, the SL27 is made from the following parts: one unit of Part A, one unit of Part B, and one unit of Part C. Each unit of Part C is made up of two units of Part D, four units of Part E, and four units of Part F. The lead time for each of these is one week except for Part B which has a lead time of two weeks. Develop a bill of materials tree diagram for this situation.

26. Refer to the Webster Manufacturing Company situation in Problem 25. An order has been received for delivery of 800 units of the SL27 in five weeks. Develop an MRP net requirements chart showing when the orders for each part should be placed. Assume that currently there are no units of any parts in inventory and none are scheduled to arrive.

27. For the Webster Manufacturing Company situation in Problem 26, assume there are currently 80 units of the SL27, 50 units of Part C, and 250 units of Part F in inventory. In addition, an order has been placed for 200 units of Part C and this will be received at the beginning of next week. Modify the net requirements chart to reflect this new information.
28. The annual swimsuit edition of a popular sports magazine is being planned. This typically results in very high sales at newsstands. Past sales records for this issue shows the sales are normally distributed with a mean of 250,000 copies and a standard deviation of 50,000 copies. The cost of printing the magazine is \$1.20 and any magazines not sold have negligible value. The magazine sells on newsstands for \$3.50. How many magazines should be printed?
29. December Trees sells Christmas trees and operates several Christmas tree lots in the state of Texas between Thanksgiving and December 25. Orders are placed months in advance, and it is rare that additional trees can be ordered later if demand is higher than anticipated. Each tree costs \$8 and is sold for \$25. If past sales figures indicate sales are normally distributed with a mean of 60,000 and a standard deviation of 12,000, how many trees should be stocked?
30. One source of revenue for a professional football team is the sale of souvenir programs, which give the date, current rosters, and other information about the teams playing that game. Each program has a printing cost of \$1.25 and sells for \$4.00. Any program not sold is donated to a charity, which sells the programs to a recycling center. Past sales of this program for games involving the current visiting team have been approximately normally distributed with a mean of 15,000 and a standard deviation of 5,000. How many programs should be printed for the game? If 25,000 programs were printed, what is the chance that they will all be sold? What service level would be implied by printing 25,000 programs?
31. The Danville Works produces two types of computer desks. Each of these is produced in a production facility using the same production line, and some materials are the same for both products. Desk A is made up of one unit of Part C, two units of Part D, and four units of Part E. Desk B is made up of one unit of Part D, two units of Part E and four units of Part F. Part F is made up of two units of Part G. The company would like to implement an MRP system that will indicate when the parts should be ordered. The fact that Parts D and E are used in both means the gross requirements for these items will be determined by the production schedule for both products.

    The lead time for all items is one week. Currently there are 200 units of Part E and 100 units of Part F in inventory. Scheduled for receipt next week are 300 units of Part D. The master production schedule indicates 800 units of Desk A must be delivered in Week 5, and 500 units of Desk B must be delivered in Week 6. Develop a net materials requirements plan that may be used to determine when to place orders for the parts.
32. Prove that if the EOQ conditions are met and a company chooses to let the order quantity Q equal the EOQ, then the total of the holding cost and the ordering cost is given by the following:

$$TOC + THC = \sqrt{2DC_oC_h}$$

    (*Hint*: Because $TOC = THC$ under these conditions, the total of these two costs is $2TOC$. Substitute the EOQ formula for Q, and simplify.)

ANALYSIS IN ACTION

Ellsworth Products

Ellsworth Products produces a steel casing used in factories from Mexico to Canada. This along with two other products is produced in a facility in the southern part of New Mexico. Steve Ellsworth, the founder and chief operating officer of the company, is very pleased that sales have been steady, and for the foreseeable future should continue to be so. However, increasing supply and labor costs seem to be cutting into the firm's profit margin. While Ellsworth Products have a reputation for quality, Steve is concerned that passing the cost increases along to the customers may cause some of them to turn to a competitor.

While looking at the decreasing profit margin, Steve has decided to evaluate his current inventory policy on the steel casings. A quick check of the monthly sales records over the past year reveals the following:

Month	Sales (Units)
January	480
February	520
March	540
April	470
May	510
June	490
July	530
August	500
September	470
October	510
November	480
December	500

These sales represent the actual demand for this product as there always are extra units in inventory if a customer needs some. Years ago it was decided that once a month the production line would be used to produce this product. The number of units produced each month would be simply 550 minus the number of units remaining in inventory when production begins. Thus, even though the average monthly sales are only 500 units, Ellsworth has been prepared for sales of 550 if necessary.

In preparing for production, three workers spend eight hours each to get the equipment ready. The average labor cost per worker including salary and benefits is $30 per hour. Given the cost of capital, insurance, and other factors, the holding cost is set at 15 percent of the value of the inventory. With the materials that are used and the labor that goes into each casing, the cost of each casing is placed at $80.

Because the production line is shared with two other products, it is not always possible to start production of the casings when desired. In fact, due to the variability in the demand for the other two products, if the inventory of casings indicates that production should begin on this item, it may be a week before production can actually start. Weekly demand averages 125 units per week with a standard deviation of 10 units.

Prepare a brief managerial report indicating your recommendations for managing this production operation. Include all pertinent information that would be of interest.

EOQ Spreadsheet Example

The demand for a product is 10,000 units per year. The cost of a unit is $5, the ordering cost is $144 per order, and the holding cost is $18 per unit. Find the order quantity, the total ordering cost, the total carrying cost, and the total cost.

Demand	10000 units	
C	$5/case	TPC = 50000
C_o	$144/order	THC = 3600 per year
C_h	$18/unit/year	TOC = 3600

Formulas:

$$Q = (2DC_o/C_h)^{1/2}$$
$$TC = DC + C_o(D/Q) + C_h(Q/2)$$

	A	B	C	D	E	F	G
1	Economic Order Quantity Example						
2							
3							
4	Demand	10000	units	Q=	400	units per order	
5	C	5	per case	TPC=	50000		
6	Co	144	per order	THC=	3600	per year	
7	Ch	18	per unit per year	TOC=	3600		
8				Total cost	57200	per year	

	A	B	C	D	E	F
1	Economic Order Quantity Example					
2						
3						
4	Demand	10000	units	Q=	=+(2*B4*B6/B7)^0.5	units per order
5	C	5	per case	TPC=	=+B5*B4	
6	Co	144	per order	THC=	=+B7*E4/2	per year
7	Ch	18	per unit per year	TOC=	=+B6*B4/E4	
8				Total cost	=+E5+E6+E7	per year

ELS Spreadsheet Example

The demand for a product is 10,000 units per year. One hundred units can be produced per day. The cost of a unit is $10, the ordering cost is $250 per order, and the holding cost is $25 per unit. Find the lot size, the maximum inventory, and the total annual inventory cost. Assume 250 days per year.

$D = 10{,}000$ units/year
$d = 40$ units/day
$p = 100$ units/day
$C_o = 250$/order
$C_h = \$25$/unit/year
$C = \$10$/unit

Formulas:

$$Q = [(2DC_o/(C_h(1 - d/p))]^{1/2}$$
$$TC = C_o(D/Q) + C_h(Q/2)(p - d)/p + DC$$

Maximum Inventory = $Q(p - d)/p$

	A	B	C	D	E	F	G
1	Economic Lot Size Example						
2							
3							
4	Demand	10000	units per year	Q=	577.35	units per order	
5	Production	100	units per day	TPC=	100000		
6	C	10	per unit	THC=	4330	per year	
7	Co	250	per order	TOC=	4330	per year	
8	Ch	25	per unit per year	TC=	108660	per year	
9				Max Inv	346.4102		
10	Demand	40	units per day				

	A	B	C	D	E	F
1	Economic Lot Size Example					
2						
3						
4	Demand	10000	units per year	Q=	=(2*B4*B7/(B8*(1-B10/B5)))^0.5	units per order
5	Production	100	units per day	TPC=	=B4*B6	per year
6	C	10	per unit	THC=	=B8*E4/2*(B5-B10)/B5	per year
7	Co	250	per order	TOC=	=B7*B4/E4	per year
8	Ch	25	per unit per year	TC=	=E5+E6+E7	
9				Max Inv	=E4*(B5-B10)/B5	
10	Demand	=+B4/250	units per day			

CHAPTER ELEVEN

Queuing Models

LEARNING OBJECTIVES

Upon completing Chapter 11, you should be able to:

- Identify the elements of a queuing system.
- Describe the important characteristics of queuing systems related to the arrivals, the queue, and the service facility.
- Use Kendall notation to describe specific types of queuing systems.
- Explain why the Poisson distribution and exponential distribution are important in analyzing queuing problems.
- Explain the operating characteristics usually associated with queuing models.
- Calculate the operating characteristics for some basic queuing models.
- Perform an economic analysis of a queuing solution to compare the waiting costs with the service costs.
- Use computer software to find the operating characteristics for queuing systems.

CHAPTER OUTLINE

11.1 INTRODUCTION

Queue
A waiting line.

In everyday life, we constantly are faced with standing in a waiting line or **queue**. At a grocery store we must wait in a line to pay for the groceries. At a fast food restaurant we must stand in line to place an order, pay for the food, and receive our order. We place phone calls for hotel and airline reservations, and often are placed on hold until a person is free to handle the call. Airplanes arriving at a busy airport must wait in a holding pattern while other planes land. Automobiles must wait until a traffic light turns green before proceeding through an intersection. Jobs submitted to be processed on a computer may have to wait until other jobs have been completed. These are just a few of the many types of queuing situations that we may face every day. Understanding the basic concepts associated with queues may help a manager to plan a system or modify a system to result in a more profitable situation with increased customer satisfaction.

In this chapter we will study the basic characteristics of a queuing model. For certain situations we will see how to calculate measures of performance of the system, such as average waiting time and average length of the line. We will look at the costs associated with queuing systems to determine the best way to design queuing systems to meet the needs of the company.

11.2 COLONIAL CRAFTS EXAMPLE

Susan Lewis operates Colonial Crafts, which is a small mail-order company that sells a variety of handmade items. While small, Colonial Crafts has experienced a continual growth for the last two years, Susan has decided it is time to expand further. She has established a toll free phone line to allow customers to place orders by phone instead of by mail. One employee has been given the task of answering this phone and taking orders. This phone line is available eight hours per day. Calls have been arriving at the rate of 10 per hour. If the employee is busy with another order, the caller hears a recorded message and is placed on hold. On the average, it takes four minutes to handle a call.

It has been noted recently that some customers who have been placed on hold are becoming upset with the wait and hanging up before they place an order, and it is not known if they call back later. Susan is considering using an improved computerized system to reduce the average time for each call, but this would require additional training and a salary increase for this employee. Another option being considered is adding a second employee to assist in this operation. What should be done?

Before analyzing this situation, we will introduce the major concepts in queuing theory. Then we will return to this situation to see how these concepts can help Susan Lewis with this question.

11.3

BASIC ELEMENTS OF QUEUING MODELS

There are three important parts to any queuing situation—the arrivals, the queue, and the server or service facility. Each of these has several features that are important to the analysis of the queuing problem.

Arrival Characteristics

Arrivals into the system come from the **calling population.** (*Note*: early work in queuing theory was done by A. K. Erlang, a Danish telephone engineer. Thus, some queuing terminology relates to telephone calls.) This calling population may either be finite or infinite. For many situations, the calling population is so large the assumption of an infinite calling population is reasonable. However, in other situations this certainly is not valid. Consider the case of machines belonging to a particular firm breaking down and being repaired by a single repairperson employed by the company. The arrivals into the repair system are the machines breaking down and waiting to be repaired in the service facility. The number of machines in the company is fixed, so the calling population is finite. This means the number of machines waiting to be repaired can be no larger than the size of the calling population.

Calling population
The population from which arrivals are generated.

The behavior of the arrivals is very important to management. Arrivals are classified as **patient** if they enter the queue regardless of the length and if they stay in the system until service is received. Arrivals are said to **balk** if they do not enter the line when it is too long. Arrivals are said to **renege** if they enter the line but leave before service is received. Customers in a fast food restaurant may renege if the wait takes too long.

Patient arrival
An arrival that will enter the system regardless of the queue length and will remain in the system until service is complete.

Balk
A situation in which an arrival refuses to enter the queue.

Renege
A situation in which an arrival that has entered the queue leaves the queue and the system before receiving service.

Another important factor associated with the arrivals into a queuing system is the pattern of these arrivals. The arrival rate may be constant or random. Items moving on an automated assembly line would be arriving at the next station at a constant rate. Customers arriving at a restaurant would arrive in a random pattern. For random arrivals, various probability distributions may describe the particular pattern of arrivals. The Poisson distribution has been found to accurately describe the arrival pattern in many queuing situations. However, at times the number of arrivals per time period may best be described with a uniform or other distribution. Statistical tests for goodness-of-fit may be used to verify that the selected probability distribution is appropriate for a given situation.

Queue Characteristics

Once an arrival has been generated that arrival typically must enter a queue. The maximum possible queue length may be infinite or it may be finite. Most queuing situations are such that it is assumed the queue length may be infinite, although some queues are restricted in length. A telephone system that places callers on hold may limit the number placed on hold and if this number is met, then additional calls receive a busy signal and do not enter the system at this time.

Queue discipline
The method used to determine the order in which customers in the queue receive service.

First-in, first-out (FIFO)
A queue discipline in which an arrival does not receive service until all earlier arrivals have been serviced.

The **queue discipline** refers to the method used for determining the order of service for the members of the queue. A common one is the **first-in, first-out** or **FIFO** queue discipline. This also is called the first-come, first-served system. With this method, new arrivals go to the back of the line and do not begin receiving service until after all earlier arrivals have been handled. An example of this would be a grocery store with a single checkout line. However, an emergency room at a hospital may use a preemptive priority system whereby a new arrival may go to the front of the line and may even cause service to earlier arrivals to be interrupted if the seriousness of the new arrival's medical problem warrants it. Jobs submitted to be run on a computer may be assigned priorities based upon the importance or characteristics of the particular job. A last-in, first-out or LIFO system is common on airplanes, which are typically loaded by allowing passengers with seats in the rear of the plane to enter first, and which are unloaded by allowing the people at the front of the plane to leave first.

Channel
A service facility.

Single channel (single server) system
A queuing system where only one arrival can receive service at a time.

Multichannel (multiserver) system
A queuing system in which there are multiple service facilities.

Service System Characteristics

The reason arrivals enter a queuing system is to receive some type of service. The service facility or **channel** is where this happens. The queuing system is referred to as a **single channel** or **single server** model if only one arrival can be receiving service at a time. A **multiserver** or **multichannel** system is one in which several arrivals may receive service simultaneously. An example of this would be a post office where there are several postal clerks stationed at separate positions helping the customers.

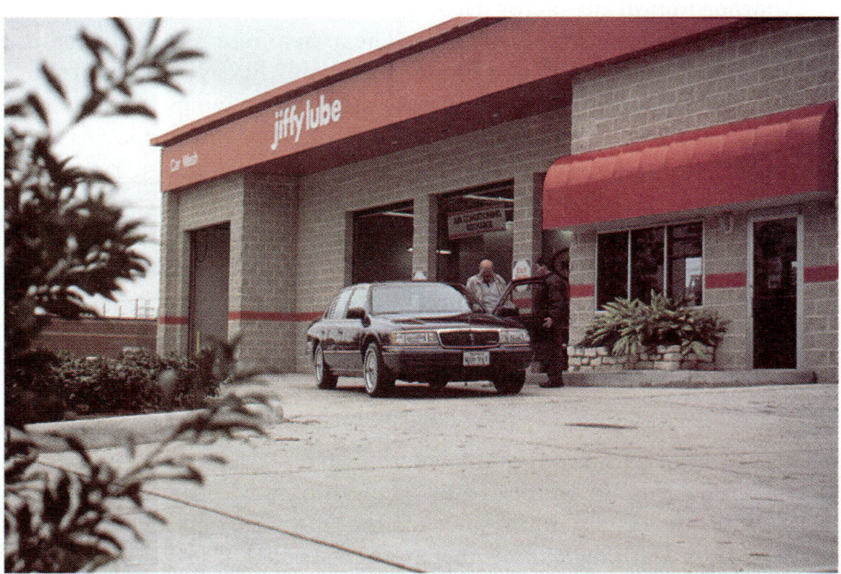

A first-in, first-out or first-come, first-served system is a method used at many services. SOURCE: Courtesy of Jiffy Lube International, Inc.

A **single-phase** or **single-stage** system is one in which the customers leave the system once they are finished at the service facility. A **multiphase** or **multistage** system is one in which the customers, upon leaving the service facility, enter another queue to receive service at another type of service facility. The drive-through at a fast food restaurant would exemplify this. A customer enters a line and places an order at the first service facility. Once the order is taken, the customer drives forward to another service facility to pay for and receive the food. Only then does this customer leave the system.

Single-phase (single-stage) system

A queuing system in which the customers leave once they are finished at the service facility.

Multiphase (multi-stage) system

A queuing system in which the arrivals must go through several service facilities in sequence.

Figure 11.1 illustrates some basic queuing configurations, although there are other possible configurations as well.

Another important characteristic of a queuing system is the pattern of service times. As with the pattern of arrivals, these may be constant or

FIGURE 11.1

Typical Queuing Configurations

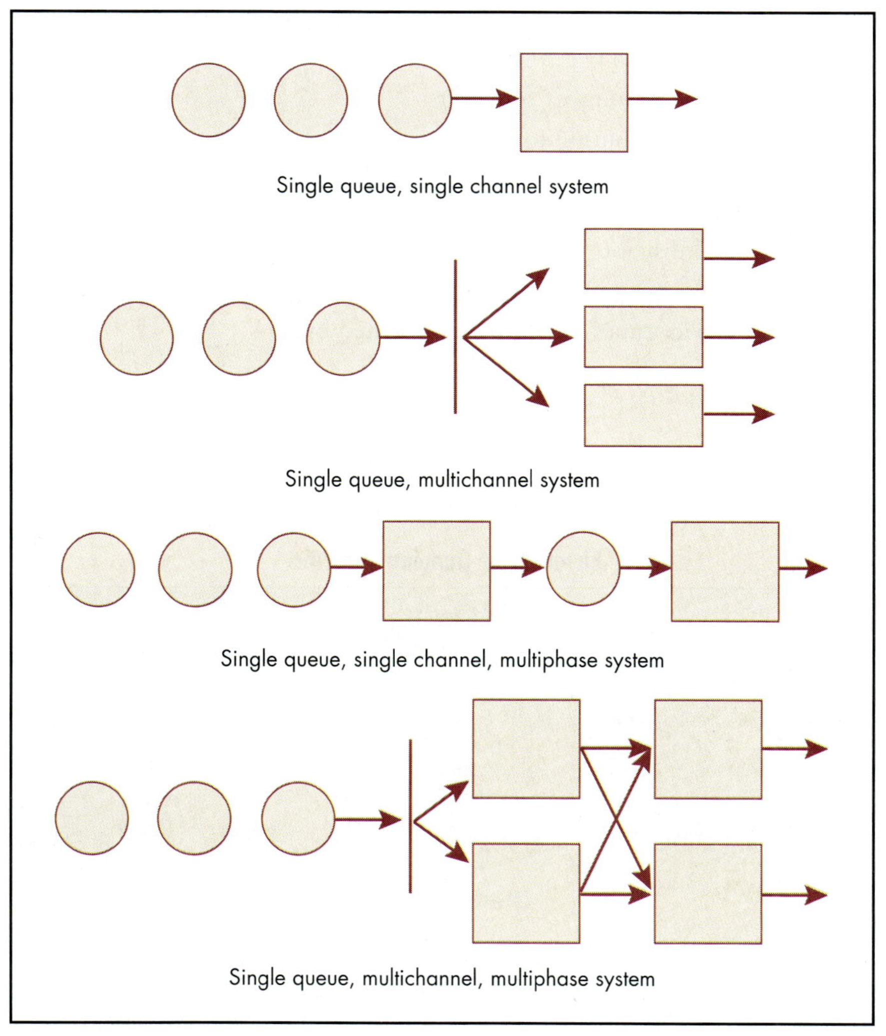

random. An automated assembly process may have a constant service rate, while the time to transact business at a bank or grocery store would be random. For random service times, several probability distributions may be appropriate. Statistical goodness-of-fit tests may be used to determine if a particular distribution is appropriate for a specific situation. While at times the uniform and normal distributions may be appropriate, the exponential distribution has been shown to be applicable in many queuing situations.

Summary Table 11.1 provides a summary review of the important features of these queuing systems.

Identifying Models Using Kendall Notation

Kendall notation
A system of identifying the arrival pattern, service pattern, and number of channels in a queuing system.

D. G. Kendall developed a notation that has been widely accepted for specifying the pattern of arrivals, the service time distribution, and the number of channels in a queuing model. This notation often is seen in software for queuing models. The basic three-symbol **Kendall notation** is in the form

arrival pattern/service pattern/number of servers

where specific letters are used to represent specific distribution. The following are commonly used in Kendall notation:

- k indicates the number of servers
- M Poisson distribution for number of occurrences, or exponential times
- D Constant rate
- G General distribution with mean and variance known

Thus, the single queue, single channel model with Poisson arrivals and exponential service times would be represented by:

$$M/M/1$$

SUMMARY TABLE 11.1

Elements of Queuing Systems

ARRIVALS
Calling population — finite or infinite Pattern — constant or random Behavior — patient or balking and reneging
QUEUE
Maximum length — finite or infinite Discipline — FIFO, LIFO, priority
SERVICE FACILITY
Number of channels Number of phases Times — constant or random

When a second channel is added, the representation would be:

$$M/M/2$$

If k channels are used, the Kendall notation would be $M/M/k$. More detailed Kendall notation would include three additional terms. The fourth term would indicate the queue discipline, the fifth term would give the maximum number in the system for a finite queue situation. The sixth term would represent the population size. When these are omitted, it is generally assumed the queue discipline is FIFO and there is no limit to the queue length or the population size.

11.4

THE POISSON AND EXPONENTIAL DISTRIBUTIONS

Most of the queuing models discussed in this chapter assume the arrivals are random and may be described by a Poisson distribution. Most of these models also assume the service times may be described by the exponential distribution. We will briefly present these distributions.

The Poisson Distribution

Assume the number of arrivals (X) per time period may be described by a **Poisson distribution.** The probability that the number of arrivals in any time period is equal to a value of x is given by the following formula:

Poisson distribution
A probability distribution that is commonly used in queuing systems to describe the number of arrivals per time period.

$$P(x) = \frac{e^{-\lambda}\lambda^x}{x!} \text{ for } x = 0, 1, 2, \ldots$$

where x = number of arrivals

λ = average number of arrivals per time period

e = 2.7183

$x! = x(x - 1)(x - 2) \ldots (2)(1)$

and $0! = 1$ by definition.

This formula may now be used to determine the probability that any number of arrivals occur during a particular time period. For example, if the average number of arrivals per hour is two ($\lambda = 2$), the probability of zero, one, or two arrivals in the next hour could be determined by the following:

$$P(0) = \frac{e^{-2}2^0}{0!} = 0.135$$

$$P(1) = \frac{e^{-2}2^1}{1!} = 0.271$$

$$P(2) = \frac{e^{-2}2^2}{2!} = 0.271$$

Thus, the probability that no arrivals occur in the next hour is 0.135 while the probability that one arrival occurs is 0.271 and the probability that two arrivals occur also is 0.271. Many of the models in this chapter are based on this distribution. Table 11.1 provides the values for $e^{-\lambda}$ for selected values of λ for use with this distribution and the exponential distribution.

A graph of the Poisson probability distribution for $\lambda = 2$ is shown in Figure 11.2. The highest probabilities are associated with values of x close to λ, and smaller probabilities are associated with values of x further from λ.

TABLE 11.1

Values of $e^{-\lambda}$ for Selected Values of λ

λ	$e^{-\lambda}$	λ	$e^{-\lambda}$
0.10	0.9048	4.00	0.0183
0.20	0.8187	4.10	0.0166
0.30	0.7408	4.20	0.0150
0.40	0.6703	4.30	0.0136
0.50	0.6065	4.40	0.0123
0.60	0.5488	4.50	0.0111
0.70	0.4966	4.60	0.0101
0.80	0.4493	4.70	0.0091
0.90	0.4066	4.80	0.0082
1.00	0.3679	4.90	0.0074
1.10	0.3329	5.00	0.0067
1.20	0.3012	5.10	0.0061
1.30	0.2725	5.20	0.0055
1.40	0.2466	5.30	0.0050
1.50	0.2231	5.40	0.0045
1.60	0.2019	5.50	0.0041
1.70	0.1827	5.60	0.0037
1.80	0.1653	5.70	0.0033
1.90	0.1496	5.80	0.0030
2.00	0.1353	5.90	0.0027
2.10	0.1225	6.00	0.0025
2.20	0.1108	7.00	0.0009
2.30	0.1003	8.00	0.0003
2.40	0.0907	9.00	0.0001
2.50	0.0821	10.00	0.0000
2.60	0.0743		
2.70	0.0672		
2.80	0.0608		
2.90	0.0550		
3.00	0.0498		
3.10	0.0450		
3.20	0.0408		
3.30	0.0369		
3.40	0.0334		
3.50	0.0302		
3.60	0.0273		
3.70	0.0247		
3.80	0.0224		
3.90	0.0202		

FIGURE 11.2

Poisson Probability Distribution

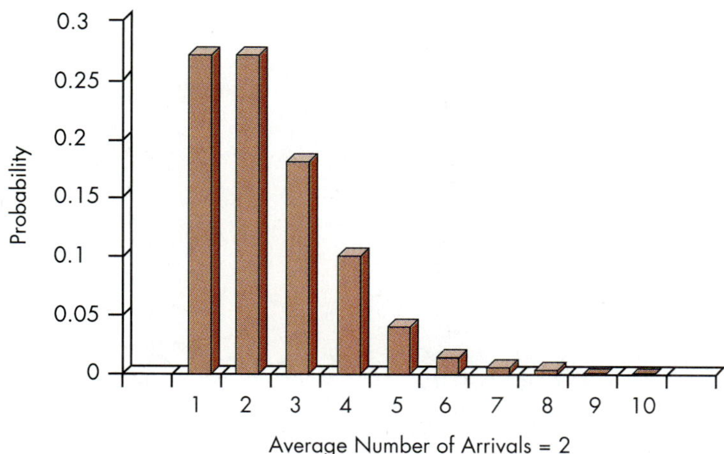

The Exponential Distribution

Exponential distribution
A probability distribution that commonly is used in queuing systems to describe the service times.

The **exponential distribution** very often is used in queuing situations to represent the service time distribution. The exponential distribution, which is a continuous distribution, and the Poisson distribution, which is a discrete distribution, are related. If the number of arrivals per time period is described by a Poisson distribution, then the time between arrivals may be described by an exponential distribution. For example, if the number of arrivals per hour follows a Poisson distribution with an average of 10 per hour, then the time between these arrivals would follow an exponential distribution with an average of 1/10 of an hour.

If the exponential distribution is appropriate for use in representing the service times, the probability the service time does not exceed a time t may be found by using:

$$P(\text{time} \leq t) = 1 - e^{-\mu t}$$

where

$$\mu = \text{the average number served per time period}$$

and, thus

$$1/\mu = \text{the average service time}$$

The probability the service time exceeds a time t is given by:

$$P(\text{time} > t) = e^{-\mu t}$$

If the average number of customers served per hour is 12, then the probability the service time is less than 10 minutes or 10/60 = 1/6 of an hour would be:

$$P(\text{time} \leq 1/6) = 1 - e^{-12(1/6)} = 1 - e^{-2} = 0.865$$

FIGURE 11.3

P (time > t) for Exponential Probability Distribution

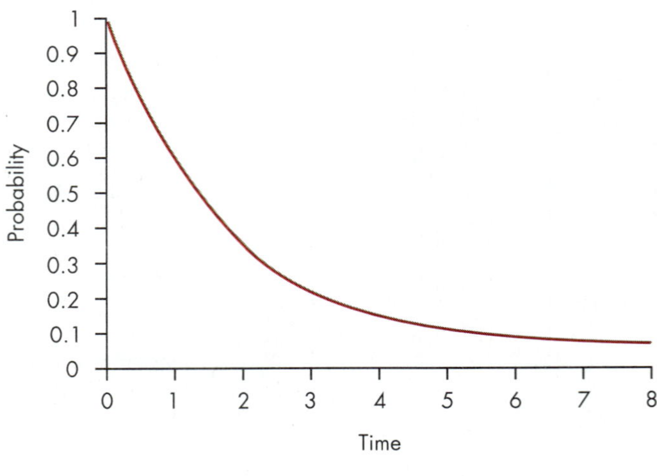

Note that if μ is expressed in hours, the time units for which the probability is to be found also must be in hours.

A graph of the exponential distribution showing the probability the time (t) exceeds an amount is shown in Figure 11.3. Notice the probability gets very small as the time increases.

11.5 MEASURES OF SYSTEM PERFORMANCE

A manager who has represented a particular situation using a queuing model normally would be concerned with how the customers (arrivals) view the operation, because customer satisfaction often depends on how the system is operating. Such things as the average time spent waiting in the queue, the average time spent in the entire system, the average length of the queue, the average number in the system, and the percentage of time that the line gets too long are important in this regard. These measures of performance often are called **operating characteristics.**

Operating characteristics
Measures of the performance of a queuing system, such as average length of the line, average number in the system, average time in line, and average time in the system.

This manager also should be concerned with the servers or service facility as it may be very expensive to have many servers sitting idle. The percentage of the time the system is totally empty and the percentage of time the server(s) is being utilized are important from this perspective.

Steady state, or stationary, condition
A condition of a queuing system in which the entire system has stabilized.

Transient condition
A changing condition in a queuing situation.

For certain types of queuing systems, formulas have been derived to provide information about these measures of system performance. These formulas are applicable once a queuing system has reached a **steady state** or **stationary condition.** This usually occurs in most systems after an initial **transient condition** where things are not yet operating in the normal

BEST PRACTICES

Queuing Models Improve Fire Department Productivity

SOURCE:
Swersey, A. J., L. Goldring, and E. D. Geyer, January-February 1993. "Improving Fire Department Productivity: Merging Fire and Emergency Medical Units in New Haven." *Interfaces* 23 (1): 109-129.

In times of shrinking municipal budgets and increasing demands on city services, administrators often must make painful decisions. Some of the most difficult involve public safety. Firehouses and ambulance services are expensive to maintain. However, attempts to reduce services generate fierce opposition from fire unions, local residents, and political leaders. New Haven, Connecticut's city administrators faced this situation in 1990. The recession had contributed to a decline in the region's manufacturing sector and therefore in tax revenues, even as crime and drug-related activities were climbing. Meanwhile, political power in the city was highly decentralized.

The city's chief administrator turned to management science techniques to help make objective decisions. He asked two consultants to study the current distribution of fire units to see if any unit could be eliminated with an acceptably small risk to the public. New Haven had 15 fire fighting units, located in 10 stations throughout the city. Each unit (known as a company) consisted of four fire fighters and a fire truck. There also was a tactical unit responsible primarily for auto wrecks, and four emergency medical units.

The consultants first used a deterministic computer model (developed for previous, similar applications) with historical demand data. They found only one of the companies could be eliminated with small risk to the public. However, follow-on analysis showed having separate emergency medical units was not justified from either a cost or an effectiveness standpoint. They learned that existing fire fighting personnel (most already were correctly trained) also could

Photo: Michael Vanacore, New Haven Fire Department

provide emergency medical services with no increase in personnel costs. They called this the fire/medic plan. The idea is analogous to pooling servers in a queuing system.

The consultants developed a spatial queuing model to estimate the improvements in emergency medical travel time under the fire/medic plan. The use of a queuing model was particularly appropriate because its speed allowed for timely analysis under the pressures of the city budgeting cycle. With the model, the consultants computed the average travel time, in minutes, to each part of the city under several possible configurations of the new system. They gave this information to city officials, who used it to help select the final plan. The final plan improved productivity by both reducing cost and improving public safety. Although there was a small loss of fire protection, it was considered offset by large decreases in emergency medical response time. The yearly savings attributed to the plan are $1.4 million.

routine. For example, a retail store may have a number of customers waiting when the door opens, so the number of arrivals during the first minutes will be much greater than arrivals during a similar time period later in the day. Once these initial arrivals are serviced, the system would usually settle down to a normal routine and a steady state would be achieved.

For a steady state condition, certain operating characteristics may be calculated for many types of situations. Some of these characteristics will relate just to the queue, while others relate to the entire system (the queue plus the service facility).

This traffic engineer is using an advanced transportation management system that can change an individual signal or coordinate several signals to improve the flow of traffic. SOURCE: Courtesy of Mark IV Industries, Inc. and its subsidiary, Automatic Signal/Eagle Signal Corp.

Operating Characteristic Relationships

Certain relationships exist among specific operating characteristics for any queuing system that is in a steady state. To introduce these, we will define the following variables:

λ = average number of arrivals into the system per time period
μ = average number served per time period
L_q = average number in the queue (or average length of the queue)
L = average number in the system
W_q = average time spent in the queue (average waiting time in line)
W = average time spent in the system

Little's formula
The equation $L = \lambda W$ that is true for queuing systems in which a steady state is reached.

Using these definitions, the relationships shown in Table 11.2 always will hold. The first of these is sometimes referred to as **Little's formula** because John D. C. Little developed the proof of this. A similar proof resulted in the second equation. The third equation simply says the average time spent in the system must equal the average time in the queue plus the average service time ($1/\mu$). The advantage of these formulas is that once one of these four characteristics is known, the other characteristics easily may be found. This is important because for certain queuing models, one of these may be much easier to determine than the others. We will be using these when appropriate with the presentation of several different queuing models.

TABLE 11.2

Relationships for all Queuing Models when Steady State Has Been Reached

(1)	$L = \lambda W$	(or $W = L/\lambda$)
(2)	$L_q = \lambda W_q$	(or $W_q = L_q/\lambda$)
(3)	$W = W_q + 1/\mu$	(or $W_q = W - 1/\mu$)

11.6 SINGLE QUEUE, SINGLE CHANNEL MODEL (*M/M/*1)

One of the most common queuing models is the single queue, single channel model. For this model, assume:

1. The calling population is infinite.
2. Arrivals are patient.
3. Arrivals are random and described by a Poisson distribution.
4. There is no limit to the queue length.
5. A FIFO queue discipline is used.
6. Service times are random and follow an exponential distribution.
7. The average number served per time period is greater than the average number of arrivals per time period.

For this situation, the following set of equations provides measures of system performance. To use these, find the average number (λ) of arrivals into the system per time period, and the average number (μ) that may be served during this same time period. The formulas are presented in the order that results in the easiest computations.

λ = average number of arrivals into the system per time period

μ= average number served per time period

where

$\mu > \lambda$

1. The average time spent in the system is:

$$W = \frac{1}{(\mu - \lambda)}$$

2. The average number in the system is:

$$L = \lambda W = \lambda \frac{1}{\mu - \lambda} = \frac{\lambda}{\mu - \lambda}$$

3. The average time spent in the queue (average waiting time in line) is:

$$W_q = W - \frac{1}{\mu} = \frac{\lambda}{\mu(\mu - \lambda)}$$

4. The average number in the queue (or average length of the queue) is:

$$L_q = \lambda W_q = \frac{\lambda^2}{\mu(\mu - \lambda)}$$

5. The probability the system is empty (or the percent idle time for the server) is:

$$P_0 = 1 - \frac{\lambda}{\mu}$$

6. The utilization rate of the service facility (or the probability the server is busy) is:

$$\rho = \frac{\lambda}{\mu}$$

7. The probability the number in the system is n is:

$$P_n = \left(\frac{\lambda}{\mu}\right)^n P_0$$

In looking at these formulas, consider how the system would be operating if the average arrival rate were equal to or greater than the average service rate. The average time in the line and in the system would approach infinity. Certainly this would be an undesirable situation to have.

Colonial Crafts Example

To illustrate the use of these formulas, consider the problem faced by Susan Lewis with Colonial Crafts described earlier in this chapter. The calls were arriving at a rate of 10 per hour, so $\lambda = 10$, and assume the number of arrivals per hour is described by the Poisson distribution. The average time required to handle a call was four minutes, and assume this service time may be described by the exponential distribution. Because λ is expressed as the number per hour, μ must be expressed as the average number served per hour. Because the calls average four minutes each, on the average 15 calls per hour could be handled by the employee. Therefore, this is an *M/M/*1 system, and the formulas just presented may be used to measure the performance of this system. Thus:

$$\lambda = 10 \text{ calls per hour}$$
$$\mu = 15 \text{ calls per hour}$$

1. The average time spent in the system is:

$$W = \frac{1}{(\mu - \lambda)} = \frac{1}{15 - 10} = 0.2 \text{ hours (12 minutes)}$$

Note that W (and W_q) are times, and the units for these are the same time units used in describing λ and μ. In this example, these are hours.

2. The average number in the system is:

$$L = \lambda W = 10(0.2) = 2$$

3. The average time spent in the queue (average waiting time in line) is:

$$W_q = W - \frac{1}{\mu} = 0.2 - \frac{1}{15}$$
$$= 0.1333 \text{ hours (8 minutes)}$$

4. The average number in the queue (or average length of the queue) is:

$$L_q = \lambda W_q = 10(0.1333) = 1.333$$

5. The probability the system is empty (or the percent idle time for the server) is:

$$P_0 = 1 - \frac{\lambda}{\mu} = 1 - \frac{10}{15} = 0.333$$

6. The utilization rate of the service facility (or the probability the server is busy) is:

$$\rho = \frac{\lambda}{\mu} = \frac{10}{15} = 0.667$$

7. The probability the number in the system is *n* for some selected values of *n* is:

$$P_n = \left(\frac{\lambda}{\mu}\right)^n P_0 = \left(\frac{10}{15}\right)^n \frac{1}{3}$$

$$P_1 = \left(\frac{10}{15}\right)^1 \frac{1}{3} = 0.222$$

$$P_2 = \left(\frac{10}{15}\right)^2 \frac{1}{3} = 0.148$$

$$P_3 = \left(\frac{10}{15}\right)^3 \frac{1}{3} = 0.099$$

$$P_4 = \left(\frac{10}{15}\right)^4 \frac{1}{3} = 0.066$$

These provide a good indication of how this system should be operating.

11.7

SINGLE QUEUE, MULTICHANNEL MODEL (*M/M/k*)

While there are many situations similar to the example just presented, there also are many situations similar to this but with more than one server or channel. A set of formulas exist for describing the operating characteristics of this type of system if the following set of assumptions are met:

1. The calling population is infinite.
2. Arrivals are patient.
3. Arrivals are described by a Poisson distribution.
4. There is no limit to the queue length.
5. A FIFO queue discipline is used.

6. Service times follow an exponential distribution, and the average service time for each server is the same.
7. The combined average number served per time period for all servers is greater than the average number of arrivals per time period.

The formulas for this situation are:

$$k = \text{number of servers}$$
$$\lambda = \text{average number of arrivals per time period}$$
$$\mu = \text{average number served per time period}$$

where

$$k\mu > \lambda$$

1. The probability the system is empty is:

$$P_0 = \frac{1}{\sum_{n=0}^{k-1} \frac{(\lambda/\mu)^n}{n!} + \frac{(\lambda/\mu)^k}{k!}\left(\frac{k\mu}{k\mu - \lambda}\right)}$$

2. The average number in the queue (or average length of the queue) is:

$$L_q = \frac{(\lambda/\mu)^k \lambda\mu}{(k-1)!\ (k\mu - \lambda)^2} P_0$$

3. The average time spent in the queue (average waiting time in line) is:

$$W_q = \frac{L_q}{\lambda}$$

4. The average time spent in the system is:

$$W = W_q + \frac{1}{\mu}$$

5. The average number in the system is:

$$L = \lambda W$$

6. The utilization rate of the service facility is:

$$\rho = \frac{\lambda}{k\mu}$$

7. The probability the number in the system is n is:

$$P_n = \frac{(\lambda/\mu)^n}{n!} P_0 \text{ for } n \leq k$$

$$P_n = \frac{(\lambda/\mu)^n}{k!k^{(n-k)}} P_0 \text{ for } n > k$$

The use of software for queuing analysis or the development of spreadsheet formulas is recommended to ease the computational task. In working problems without the aid of a computer, the value of P_0 for selected values λ/μ is given in Table 11.3. You may calculate λ/μ and find P_0 from this table.

TABLE 11.3

Values of P_0 for Selected Values of λ/μ

	Number of Servers k				
λ/μ	1	2	3	4	5
0.10	0.9000	0.9048	0.9048	0.9048	0.9048
0.15	0.8500	0.8605	0.8607	0.8607	0.8607
0.20	0.8000	0.8182	0.8187	0.8187	0.8187
0.25	0.7500	0.7778	0.7788	0.7788	0.7788
0.30	0.7000	0.7391	0.7407	0.7408	0.7408
0.33	0.6667	0.7143	0.7164	0.7165	0.7165
0.35	0.6500	0.7021	0.7046	0.7047	0.7047
0.40	0.6000	0.6667	0.6701	0.6703	0.6703
0.45	0.5500	0.6327	0.6373	0.6376	0.6376
0.50	0.5000	0.6000	0.6061	0.6065	0.6065
0.55	0.4500	0.5686	0.5763	0.5769	0.5769
0.60	0.4000	0.5385	0.5479	0.5487	0.5488
0.65	0.3500	0.5094	0.5209	0.5219	0.5220
0.67	0.3333	0.5000	0.5122	0.5133	0.5134
0.70	0.3000	0.4815	0.4952	0.4965	0.4966
0.75	0.2500	0.4545	0.4706	0.4722	0.4724
0.80	0.2000	0.4286	0.4472	0.4491	0.4493
0.85	0.1500	0.4035	0.4248	0.4271	0.4274
0.90	0.1000	0.3793	0.4035	0.4062	0.4065
0.95	0.0500	0.3559	0.3831	0.3863	0.3867
1.00		0.3333	0.3636	0.3673	0.3678
1.10		0.2903	0.3273	0.3321	0.3328
1.20		0.2500	0.2941	0.3002	0.3011
1.30		0.2121	0.2638	0.2712	0.2723
1.40		0.1765	0.2360	0.2449	0.2463
1.50		0.1429	0.2105	0.2210	0.2228
1.60		0.1111	0.1872	0.1993	0.2014
1.70		0.0811	0.1657	0.1796	0.1821
1.80		0.0526	0.1460	0.1616	0.1646
1.90		0.0256	0.1278	0.1453	0.1487
2.00			0.1111	0.1304	0.1343
2.20			0.0815	0.1046	0.1094
2.40			0.0562	0.0831	0.0889
2.60			0.0345	0.0651	0.0721
2.80			0.0160	0.0502	0.0581
3.00				0.0377	0.0466
3.20				0.0273	0.0372
3.40				0.0186	0.0293
3.60				0.0113	0.0228
3.80				0.0051	0.0174
4.00					0.0130
4.20					0.0093
4.40					0.0063
4.60					0.0038
4.80					0.0017

An Example

Returning to the situation faced by Susan Lewis in the Colonial Crafts example, evaluate the impact of adding a second worker to answer the telephones and process orders. Assume both workers work at the same rate. Based on the earlier discussion, this may be represented as an *M/M/2* model and the formulas just given are appropriate for this situation. Thus:

k = 2 servers

λ = 10 arrivals per hour

μ = 15 served per hour for each server

where

$$k\mu > \lambda \text{ gives } 2(15) > 10$$

1. The probability the system is empty is:

$$P_0 = \frac{1}{\sum_{n=0}^{2-1} \frac{(10/15)^n}{n!} + \frac{(10/15)^2}{2!}\left(\frac{2(15)}{2(15) - 10}\right)} = 0.50$$

   Notice $\lambda/\mu = 10/15 = 0.67$ and we may obtain $P_0 = 0.50$ from Table 11.2 above.

2. The average number in the queue is:

$$L_q = \frac{(10/15)^2 10(15)}{(2-1)!\,(2(15)-10)^2}(0.50) = 0.0833$$

3. The average time spent in the queue is:

$$W_q = \frac{L_q}{\lambda} = \frac{0.0833}{10} = 0.00833 \text{ hours (0.5 minutes)}$$

4. The average time spent in the system is:

$$W = W_q + \frac{1}{\mu} = 0.00833 + \frac{1}{15} = 0.075 \text{ hours (4.5 minutes)}$$

5. The average number in the system is:

$$L = \lambda W = 10(0.075) = 0.75 \text{ units}$$

6. The utilization rate of the service facility is:

$$\rho = \frac{\lambda}{k\mu} = \frac{10}{2(15)} = \frac{1}{3} = 0.333$$

7. The probability the number in the system is n = 1, 2, and 3: for n = 1 and 2, $n \leq k$ which is 2:

$$P_n = \frac{(\lambda/\mu)^n}{n!}P_0 = \frac{(10/15)^n}{n!}(0.50) \text{ for } n \leq 2$$

$$P_1 = \frac{(10/15)^1}{1!}(0.50) = 0.333$$

$$P_2 = \frac{(10/15)^2}{2!}(0.50) = 0.111$$

Queuing Theory Helps to Implement Time-Based Competitive Studies

Helkama Bica Oy is a Finnish manufacturer of communication cables and bicycles. Traditionally, the company has competed by offering short delivery times and high quality. In 1990, however, the fortunes of Helkama struggled along with the fortunes of the Finnish economy. Finland suffered from a rapid increase in competition due to the European integration, and the loss of the Soviet Union as a customer. The resulting economic downturn put pressure on Finnish companies like Helkama.

Helkama's response to increased competitive pressures has been to increase its emphasis on short delivery times, while keeping spending as low as possible. Previously, Helkama had used static models to estimate capacity in the traditional sense of maximum equipment utilizations. However, company managers were not able to explore the impact of high utilizations on customer waiting times with these traditional models. Helkama now uses queuing theory to identify the highest leverage activities, calculate expected manufacturing lead times, and aid in capacity planning. Queuing theory was particularly attractive to the company because of its short execution times.

The queuing model allowed Helkama to test out a variety of changes before making them in the factory. For example, the model was used to investigate the impacts of running smaller lot sizes, reducing set-up times, and changing operation shifts for machines. Besides showing whether the changes would be beneficial, the model also helped gain the *buy in* of manufacturing personnel. By quantifying the potential gain from a small reduction in set-up times, for example, the model inspired plant personnel to be more receptive to making set-up changes.

Finally, Helkama used the queuing model to evaluate what manufacturing changes would allow them to enter new international markets. The marketing manager identified a product that showed a high profit potential for international distribution, if the product could be manufactured with a shorter lead time. Analysts then used the model to identify a capital expenditure that would make the lead time reduction feasible. Because upper-level management had faith in the model, the expenditure was approved, and Helkama extended its marketing reach outside Finland.

SOURCE:
De Treville, S., October 1992. "Time is Money." *OR/MS Today:* 30-34.

For $n = 3$, $n > k$ so:

$$P_n = \frac{(\lambda/\mu)^n}{k!k^{(n-k)}}P_0 = \frac{(10/15)^n}{2!2^{(n-2)}}(0.50)$$

$$P_3 = \frac{(10/15)^3}{2!2^{(3-2)}}(0.50) = 0.037$$

Our focus up to this point has been on determining the operating characteristics of a queuing system. However, a manager may use this information as well as information about the costs to determine the best way to meet the needs of the organization.

11.8 MANAGERIAL OBJECTIVES IN QUEUING SYSTEM DESIGN

In using queuing models, a manager usually has one of two objectives. The first of these is to achieve some specified level of performance as measured by the operating characteristics of the system. For example, a manager may

A bank manager may wish to design a system so that the average time in line for a customer is no more than 5 minutes.
SOURCE: Photo courtesy of Bank of America NT&SA

wish to design a system so the average time in line for a customer at a bank is no more than five minutes. The average time in line could be computed for systems with one, two, three, or more servers until one is found that achieves this goal. Looking at this particular characteristic as well as others, such as the average length of the line, may allow a manager to determine how many servers to use to obtain the best overall performance.

The second objective often associated with queuing models is to minimize the overall cost of the system. When costs are available and one operating characteristic is identified as the relevant measure of performance, we may wish to use an economic analysis of the system to determine the best design.

Economic Analysis of Queuing Situations

The costs associated with queuing models are typically of two types—waiting time cost and service cost. Customers who have to wait too long may become disgruntled and leave before making a purchase, or if the line appears to be too long, they may balk at entering the system. One way to prevent this is to have several servers working to reduce the waiting time, but the salary and benefits for the workers may make this too expensive. A prudent manager will consider both types of costs.

Depending upon the particular situation, the waiting time cost could be based on the time spent waiting in line or the entire time spent in the system. In some circumstances, a customer only is concerned about time spent in line before reaching the server, but once the server begins taking care of the business for that customer, the customer may not mind that time is elapsing because the customer is receiving the undivided attention of the server. For a customer at a bank who has several transactions to be handled at one time, the customer may even expect this time to be longer than average. At other times, a customer may have certain expectations about the service time and become irritated if this is too long, such as at a fast food restaurant. The manager must understand the system that is being modeled so the appropriate waiting time information can be determined.

A typical pattern of the costs associated with a queuing system is shown in Figure 11.4. Notice the service cost is increasing at a constant rate while the waiting time cost decreases in a nonlinear fashion. A manager may wish to minimize the total of the two costs, although at times a manager may simply wish to know what these costs are while making a decision based on other factors. It should be noted the point where total costs are minimized may or may not be where the waiting time cost is equal to the service cost.

To find these costs, let:

$$C_s = \text{service cost (labor cost) per hour}$$
$$C_w = \text{waiting time cost per hour}$$
$$k = \text{number of servers}$$

With this, the total service time cost per time period is:

$$\begin{aligned}\text{total service cost} &= (\text{number of servers})(\text{cost per server})\\ &= kC_s\end{aligned}$$

The total waiting time cost is found by determining how much time is spent waiting and multiplying this by the waiting time cost per time period. If the relevant waiting time is the time in the queue, then:

$$\begin{aligned}\text{total time} &= (\text{number of customers})(\text{average wait per customer})\\ &= \lambda W_q\end{aligned}$$

FIGURE 11.4

Typical Cost Curves for Queuing Systems

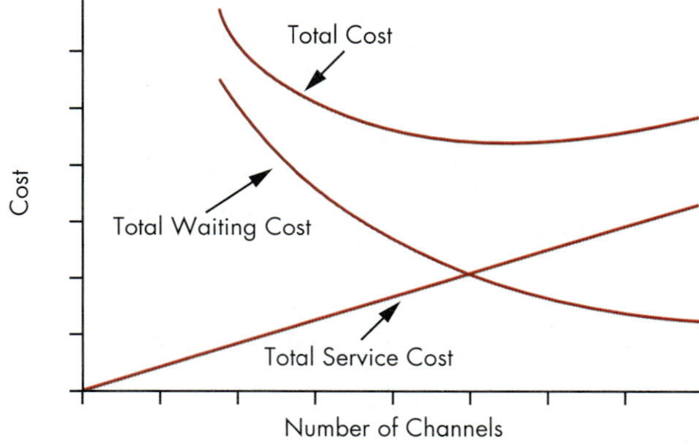

If the relevant time is the time in the system, replace W_q with W. If the time in the queue is the relevant operating characteristic, the waiting time cost is given by:

$$\text{total waiting time cost} = C_w(\text{total waiting time}) = C_w(\lambda W_q)$$

If the time in the system is the relevant operating characteristic, the waiting time cost is given by:

$$\text{total waiting time cost} = C_w(\lambda W)$$

Thus, the total cost (TC) is given by:

$$TC = \text{service cost} + \text{waiting time cost}$$

$$TC = kC_s + C_w(\lambda W_q) \text{ (cost based on time in queue)}$$

or

$$TC = kC_s + C_w(\lambda W) \text{ (cost based on time in system)}$$

Due to Little's formula, we may substitute L_q for λW_q and L for λW_q making the computations simpler. We will illustrate the formulas for the *M/M/k* model with the following example.

Colonial Crafts Example

Susan Lewis is considering the possibility of adding one or two more employees to answer the telephones for the toll free service being offered at Colonial Crafts. She has estimated the cost to the company is \$25 in lost sales and lost goodwill for each hour of time customers are placed on hold. The labor cost is \$8 per hour for each employee. Susan would like to minimize the total cost to the company.

In this problem:

C_s = \$8 per hour service cost (labor cost)

C_w = \$25 per hour cost for waiting in the queue

k = number of servers

Because the time in the queue is the relevant measure of waiting time, the total cost is:

$$TC = \text{total service cost} + \text{total waiting time cost}$$

$$TC = kC_s + C_w(\lambda W_q)$$

We must find W_q for the model with one, two, and three servers. From the formulas previously given, W_q has been calculated for $k = 1$ and 2. Perform the same computation for $k = 3$ or use computer software to obtain W_q. Doing this would yield the following:

for $k = 1$: $W_q = 0.1333$ hours

for $k = 2$: $W_q = 0.0083$ hours

for $k = 3$: $W_q = 0.0009$ hours

Using these in the total cost formula yields:

$$TC = kC_s + C_w(\lambda W_q)$$

$$\text{for } k = 1\text{: } TC = 1(8) + 25(10(0.1333))$$
$$= 8 + 33.33 = \$41.33$$
$$\text{for } k = 2\text{: } TC = 2(8) + 25(10(0.0083)) = \$2.08$$
$$= 16 + 2.08 = 18.08$$
$$\text{for } k = 3\text{: } TC = 3(8) + 25(10(0.0009))$$
$$= 24 + 0.23 = 24.23$$

Therefore, to minimize the total cost, there should be two employees staffing the telephones. This information is summarized in Table 11.4.

Using the Computer for the Colonial Crafts Problem

The computer could help with some of these calculations. A sample of the computer output obtained using DSS is shown in Output 11.1. This shows the results obtained for the Colonial Crafts example with $k = 2$. Both W and W_q are expressed in minutes. To determine the probability the queue length is any value, specify the conditions in the inputs to this problem. In this example, we used lengths from zero to four to illustrate this.

Enhancing the Queuing Environment

When a problem exists in a queuing situation, a manager should try to modify the system to allow the system to work as efficiently as possible. However, even when a system is working efficiently, it is possible customers may become upset due to the long waits. One way to try to reduce the total cost of waiting is to somehow make waiting, or the **queuing environment**, less unpleasant to the customers. There are magazines in the waiting room of doctors' offices for patients to read while waiting. There are magazines and tabloids on display by the checkout lines in grocery stores, and customers read the headlines to pass time while waiting. Music often is played while telephone callers are placed on hold. At major amusement parks there are video screens and television in some of the queue lines to make the

Queuing environment
The physical conditions surrounding a queue that affect the perception of the wait.

TABLE 11.4

Cost Analysis for Colonial Crafts with One, Two, and Three Employees

Number of Servers (k)	1	2	3
Cost per Hour per Server (C_s)	\$8	8	8
Total Hourly Service Cost (kC_s)	8	16	24
Average Waiting Time/Arrival (W_q)	0.1333	0.0083	0.0009
Number of Arrivals per Hour (λ)	10	10	10
Total Waiting Time ($W_q\lambda$)	1.333	0.083	0.009
Waiting Time Cost per Hour (C_w)	\$25	25	25
Total Waiting Time Cost ($W_q\lambda C_w$)	33.33	2.08	0.23
Total Cost ($kC_s + W_q\lambda$)	41.33	18.08	24.23

wait more interesting. For some of these, the waiting line is so entertaining it is almost an attraction itself.

All of these things are designed to keep the customer busy so it appears time is passing more quickly than it actually is. Consequently, the cost of waiting (C_w) becomes lower and the total cost of the queuing system is reduced. Sometimes reducing the total cost in this way is easier than reducing the total cost by lowering W or W_q.

11.9 OTHER QUEUING MODELS

We will present two additional queuing models that also are quite common. While both of these have arrival rates described by the Poisson distribution, the service times are not exponentially distributed. Some more advanced books on queuing listed in the references will provide additional models for the interested reader.

OUTPUT 11.1

DSS Output for Colonial Crafts Example with Two Servers

```
Queues

Inputs:

Number of Servers                                              2
Mean Time Between Arrivals (MTBA) - in minutes                 6
*OR* Arrival Rate (A) - in units/hour                          10
Mean Service Time (MST) - in minutes per server                4
*OR* Service Rate (S) - in units/hour per server               15
# in system for Probability Analysis - from                    0
                                     - to                      4

Outputs:

'Traffic Density' (A/NS) =  33.33334 %
Average Time in System (ATS) =  4.5 minutes
Average Time in the Queue (ATQ) =  .5 minutes
Average Number in the System (ANS) =  .75 units
Average Number in the Queue (ANQ) =  8.333334E-02 units
Probability of a wait with  2 servers =  .1666667


Probable Status of Queue and System at any Time

# in System   # in Queue    Probability   Cum. Probability
 0             0                 0.500              0.500
 1             0                 0.333              0.833
 2             0                 0.111              0.944
 3             1                 0.037              0.981
 4             1                 0.012              0.994
```

M/G/1 Model

For a queuing situation with a Poisson arrival rate and the service rate being described by an arbitrary distribution with a known mean and standard deviation:

λ = average number of arrivals per time period
μ = average number served per time period
$1/\mu$ = average service time
σ = standard deviation of service time

1. The probability the system is empty is:

$$P_0 = 1 - \frac{\lambda}{\mu}$$

2. The average number in the queue is:

$$L_q = \frac{\lambda^2\sigma^2 + (\lambda/\mu)^2}{2(1 - \lambda/\mu)}$$

3. The average time in the queue is:

$$W_q = \frac{L_q}{\lambda}$$

4. The average time in the system is:

$$W = W_q + \frac{1}{\mu}$$

5. The average number in the system is:

$$L = \lambda W$$

If the service times are random, the operating characteristics easily may be found if the mean and the standard deviation of the service times are known. These easily could be found or estimated by simply collecting data on service times as the system is operating.

An Example of the *M/G/1* Model

Cars arrive at the drive-through of a fast food restaurant at the rate of 60 per hour following a Poisson distribution. The average time to serve a customer is 45 seconds or 0.75 minutes. The standard deviation of the service time is 15 seconds or 0.25 minutes. If we wish to find the operating characteristics of this *M/G/1* system, express the arrival rate and service rate in common units. These will be expressed as:

λ = 1 per minute
$1/\mu$ = 0.75 minutes
μ = 1/0.75 = 1.333 per minute
σ = 0.25 minutes

1. The probability the system is empty is:

$$P_0 = 1 - \frac{\lambda}{\mu} = 1 - \frac{1}{1.333} = 0.25$$

2. The average number in the queue is:

$$L_q = \frac{\lambda^2\sigma^2 + (\lambda/\mu)^2}{2(1 - \lambda/\mu)} = \frac{1^2(0.25)^2 + (1/1.333)^2}{2(1 - 1/1.333)} = 1.25$$

3. The average time in the queue is:

$$W_q = \frac{L_q}{\lambda} = \frac{1.25}{1} = 1.25 \text{ minutes}$$

4. The average time in the system is:

$$W = W_q + \frac{1}{\mu} = 1.25 + \frac{1}{1.333} = 2 \text{ minutes}$$

5. The average number in the system is:

$$L = \lambda W = 1(2) = 2$$

M/D/1 Model

If the arrival rate is described by the Poisson distribution and the service rate is constant, the following formulas may be used:

1. The average time in the queue is:

$$W_q = \frac{\lambda}{2\mu(\mu - \lambda)}$$

2. The average number in the queue is:

$$L_q = \lambda W_q$$

3. The average time in the system is:

$$W = W_q + \frac{1}{\mu}$$

4. The average number in the system is:

$$L = \lambda W$$

You may notice this is a special case of the *M/G/*1 model in which the standard deviation of service times is zero. It is possible to show that by using a standard deviation of zero in the *M/G/*1 formulas, we can get the formulas for the *M/D/*1 model.

An Example of the *M/D/1* Model

An automatic car wash takes exactly one minute to wash each car. On a particular day, cars arrive at the rate of 40 per hour. To determine the operating characteristics of this system, use the *M/D/*1 model with:

$$\lambda = 40 \text{ per hour}$$

$$\mu = 60 \text{ per hour}$$

This gives the following results:

1. The average time in the queue is:

$$W_q = \frac{\lambda}{2\mu(\mu - \lambda)} = \frac{40}{2(60)(60 - 40)} = \frac{1}{60} \text{ hour}$$

2. The average number in the queue is:

$$L_q = \lambda W_q = 40\left(\frac{1}{60}\right) = \frac{2}{3}$$

3. The average time in the system is:

$$W = W_q + \frac{1}{\mu} = \frac{1}{60} + \frac{1}{60} = \frac{1}{30} \text{ hour}$$

4. The average number in the system is:

$$L = \lambda W = 40\left(\frac{1}{30}\right) = 1.333$$

11.10 SUMMARY

In this chapter we have considered the basic concepts associated with queuing models. Such characteristics as the size of the calling population, the arrival pattern, the queue discipline, the service rate, the number of channels, and the number of phases determine how a particular system operates. When a steady state has been reached, certain formulas may be used with some queuing models to provide the operating characteristics of the system. Kendall notation was used to identify certain types of queuing models. Examples were presented for the *M/M/*1, *M/M/k*, *M/G/*1, and *M/D/*1 models. An economic analysis illustrated the costs associated with queuing systems. Enhancing the queuing environment is one way to improve the customers' perception of the wait, and this may reduce waiting time cost.

For queuing systems that are more complex or do not meet the assumptions of the models presented in this chapter, computer simulation models often are used. These will be presented in a later chapter.

GLOSSARY

Balk A situation in which an arrival refuses to enter the queue. *p. 457*

Calling population The population from which arrivals are generated. *p. 457*

Channel A service facility. *p. 458*

Exponential distribution A probability distribution that commonly is used in queuing systems to describe the service times. *p. 463*

First-in, first-out (FIFO) A queue discipline in which an arrival does not receive service until all earlier arrivals have been serviced. *p. 458*

Kendall notation A system of identifying the arrival pattern, service pattern, and number of channels in a queuing system. *p. 460*

Little's formula The equation $L = \lambda W$ that is

true for queuing systems in which a steady state is reached. *p. 466*

Multichannel (multi-server) system A queuing system in which there are multiple service facilities. *p. 458*

Multiphase (multistage) system A queuing system in which the arrivals must go through several service facilities in sequence. *p. 459*

Operating characteristics Measures of the performance of a queuing system, such as average length of the line, average number in the system, average time in line, and average time in the system. *p. 464*

Patient arrival An arrival that will enter the system regardless of the queue length and will remain in the system until service is complete. *p. 457*

Poisson distribution A probability distribution that is commonly used in queuing systems to describe the number of arrivals per time period. *p. 461*

Queue discipline The method used to determine the order in which customers in the queue receive service. *p. 458*

Queue A waiting line. *p. 456*

Queuing environment The physical conditions surrounding a queue that affect the perception of the wait. *p. 477*

Renege A situation in which an arrival that has entered the queue leaves the queue and the system before receiving service. *p. 457*

Single channel (single server) system A queuing system where only one arrival can receive service at a time. *p. 458*

Single-phase (single-stage) system A queuing system in which the customers leave once they are finished at the service facility. *p. 459*

Steady state, or stationary, condition A condition of a queuing system in which the entire system has stabilized. *p. 464*

Transient condition A changing condition in a queuing situation. *p. 464*

KEY EQUATIONS

(11-1) Kendall notation

arrival pattern/service pattern/number of servers

M Poisson distribution for number of occurrences or exponential times

D Constant rate

G General distribution with mean and variance known

(11-2) Poisson distribution

$$P(x) = \frac{e^{-\lambda}\lambda^x}{x!} \text{ for } x = 0, 1, 2, \ldots$$

x = number of arrivals

λ = average number of arrivals per time period

e = 2.7183

$x! = x(x-1)(x-2)\ldots(2)(1)$

and $0! = 1$ by definition.

(11-3) Exponential distribution

$P(\text{time} \le t) = 1 - e^{-\mu t}$

$P(\text{time} > t) = e^{-\mu t}$

μ = the average number served per time period

$1/\mu$ = the average service time

(11-4) Operating characteristics of queuing system

λ = average number of arrivals into the system per time period

μ = average number served per time period

L_q = average number in the queue (or average length of the queue)

L = average number in the system

W_q = average time spent in the queue (average waiting time in line)

W = average time spent in the system

(11-5) Little's formula and other relationships that are true for all queuing systems where values exist

$L = \lambda W$ (or $W = L/\lambda$)

$L_q = \lambda W_q$ (or $W_q = L_q/\lambda$)

$W = W_q + 1/\mu$ (or $W_q = W - 1/\mu$)

(11-6) Operating characteristics for $M/M/1$ system

λ = average number of arrivals into the system per time period

μ = average number served per time period

where $\mu > \lambda$

$$W = \frac{1}{(\mu - \lambda)}$$ average time spent in the system

$$L = \lambda W = \lambda \frac{1}{\mu - \lambda} = \frac{\lambda}{\mu - \lambda}$$ average number in the system

$$W_q = W - \frac{1}{\mu} = \frac{\lambda}{\mu(\mu - \lambda)}$$ average time spent in the queue

$$L_q = \lambda W_q = \frac{\lambda^2}{\mu(\mu - \lambda)}$$ average number in the queue

$$P_0 = 1 - \frac{\lambda}{\mu}$$ probability the system is empty

$$\rho = \frac{\lambda}{\mu}$$ utilization rate

$$P_n = \left(\frac{\lambda}{\mu}\right)^n P_0$$ probability the number in the system is n

(11-7) Operating characteristics for $M/M/k$ system

k = number of servers

λ = average number of arrivals per time period

μ = average number served per time period

where $k\mu > \lambda$

$$P_0 = \frac{1}{\sum_{n=0}^{k-1} \frac{(\lambda/\mu)^n}{n!} + \frac{(\lambda/\mu)^k}{k!}\left(\frac{k\mu}{k\mu - \lambda}\right)}$$ probability the system is empty

$$L_q = \frac{(\lambda/\mu)^k \lambda\mu}{(k-1)!\,(k\mu - \lambda)^2} P_0$$ average number in the queue

$$W_q = \frac{L_q}{\lambda}$$ average time spent in the queue

$$W = W_q + \frac{1}{\mu}$$ average time spent in the system

$L = \lambda W$ average number in the system

$\rho = \dfrac{\lambda}{k\mu}$ utilization rate of the service facility

probability the number in the system is n

$$P_n = \frac{(\lambda/\mu)^n}{n!}P_0 \text{ for } n \le k$$

$$P_n = \frac{(\lambda/\mu)^n}{k!k^{(n-k)}}P_0 \text{ for } n > k$$

(11-8) Operating characteristics for $M/G/1$ system

λ = average number of arrivals per time period

μ = average number served per time period

$1/\mu$ = average service time

σ = standard deviation of service time

$$P_0 = 1 - \frac{\lambda}{\mu}$$

$$L_q = \frac{\lambda^2\sigma^2 + (\lambda/\mu)^2}{2(1 - \lambda/\mu)}$$

$$W_q = \frac{L_q}{\lambda}$$

$$W = W_q + \frac{1}{\mu}$$

$$L = \lambda W$$

(11-9) Operating characteristics for $M/D/1$ system

$W_q = \dfrac{\lambda}{2\mu(\mu - \lambda)}$ average time in the queue

$L_q = \lambda W_q$ average number in the queue

$W = W_q + \dfrac{1}{\mu}$ average time in the system

$L = \lambda W$ average number in the system

(11-10) Total cost (TC) formulas

C_s = service cost (labor cost) per hour

C_w = waiting time cost per hour

k = number of servers

TC = service cost + waiting cost

$TC = kC_s + C_w(\lambda W_q)$ waiting cost based on time in queue

or

$TC = kC_s + C_w(\lambda W)$ waiting cost based on time in system

SOLVED PROBLEMS

SOLVED PROBLEM 11-1

Automobiles arrive at the bank drive-through window at the rate of four every ten minutes. The average service time is two minutes. The Poisson distribution is appropriate for the arrival rate and service times are exponentially distributed.

a) What is the average time a car is in the system?
b) What is the average number of cars in the system?
c) What is the average number of cars waiting to receive service?
d) What is the average number of cars in line behind the customer receiving service?
e) What is the probability there are no cars at the window?
f) What percentage of the time is the teller busy?
g) What is the probability there are exactly two cars in the system?

SOLUTION

This problem may be modeled as an *M/M/*1 queuing system.

$$\lambda = 4 \text{ per ten-minute time period}$$
$$\mu = 5 \text{ per ten-minute time period}$$

a) $W = \dfrac{1}{(\mu - \lambda)} = \dfrac{1}{5-4} = 1$ ten-minute period

b) $L = \lambda W = 4(1) = 4$

c) $W_q = \dfrac{\lambda}{\mu(\mu - \lambda)} = \dfrac{4}{5(5-4)} = 0.8$ ten-minute periods

d) $L_q = \lambda W_q = 4(0.8) = 3.2$

e) $P_0 = 1 - \dfrac{\lambda}{\mu} = 1 - \dfrac{4}{5} = 0.2$

f) $\rho = \dfrac{\lambda}{\mu} = \dfrac{4}{5} = 0.8$

g) $P_2 = \left(\dfrac{\lambda}{\mu}\right)^2 P_0 = \left(\dfrac{4}{5}\right)^2 0.2 = 0.128$

SOLVED PROBLEM 11-2

A department store has estimated that every hour of customer time spent waiting in line for the sales clerk to become available costs the store $100 in lost sales and goodwill. Customers arrive at the checkout counter at the rate of 30 per hour, and the average service time is three minutes. The arrivals are described by the Poisson distribution and the service times are exponentially distributed. The number of sales clerks can be either two, three, or four, with each one working at the same rate. The salary and benefits for each clerk is $10 per hour. The store is open 10 hours per day.

a) Find the average time in the line if two, three, and four clerks are used?
b) What is the total time spent waiting in line each day if two, three, and four clerks are used?
c) Calculate the total of the daily waiting cost and the service cost each day if two, three, and four clerks are used. What is the minimum total daily cost?

SOLUTION

These may be modeled as *M/M/2*, *M/M/3*, and *M/M/4* systems. The average number served for each sales clerk is 20 per hour. Thus:

$$\lambda = 30 \text{ per hour}$$
$$\mu = 20 \text{ per hour}$$
$$k = 2, 3, \text{ and } 4$$

a) To find W_q in the *M/M/k* model, the formula is:

$$W_q = \frac{L_q}{\lambda}$$

We must find L_q, which is given by:

$$L_q = \frac{(\lambda/\mu)^k \lambda\mu}{(k-1)!\,(k\mu-\lambda)^2} P_0$$

and we may find P_0 by using the formula, a computer, or Table 11.3 above. If we use the table, we know:

$$\lambda/\mu = 30/20 = 1.5$$

for $k = 2$, $P_0 = 0.1429$

$$L_q = \frac{(30/20)^2(30)(20)}{(2-1)!\,(2(20)-30)^2} 0.1429 = 1.9292$$

for $k = 3$, $P_0 = 0.2105$

$$L_q = \frac{(30/20)^3(30)(20)}{(3-1)!\,(3(20)-30)^2} 0.2105 = 0.2368$$

for $k = 4$, $P_0 = 0.2210$

$$L_q = \frac{(30/20)^4(30)(20)}{(4-1)!\,(4(20)-30)^2} 0.2210 = 0.0448$$

Using the formula $W_q = L_q/\lambda$ results in:

for $k = 2$, $W_q = 1.9292/30 = 0.0643$ hours
for $k = 3$, $W_q = 0.2368/30 = 0.0079$ hours
for $k = 4$, $W_q = 0.0448/30 = 0.0015$ hours

b) Because W_q represents the average time in line per customer, the total time for the 10-hour day is $\lambda W_q 10 = \lambda(L_q/\lambda)10 = 10L_q$

for $k = 2$, total time is 10(1.9292) = 19.292 hours
for $k = 3$, total time is 10(0.2368) = 2.368 hours
for $k = 4$, total time is 10(0.0448) = 0.448 hours

c) To get the total cost for a 10-hour day:

$$TC = \text{service cost} + \text{waiting cost}$$
$$= 10(k)C_s + C_w(\text{total waiting time})$$

for $k = 2$: $TC = 10(2)(\$10) + \$100(19.292) = \$2,129.2$

for $k = 3$: $TC = 10(3)(\$10) + \$100(2.368) = \$536.8$

for $k = 4$: $TC = 10(4)(\$10) + \$100(0.448) = \$444.8$

Thus, there should be four sales clerks working to minimize cost. Notice the waiting time cost with four servers is only $44.80. The cost of one additional clerk for the day is $100, which is more than the waiting time cost. Therefore, even if we could have five clerks, the cost of adding the fifth clerk would be more than the possible savings in waiting time cost.

QUESTIONS

1. Describe the basic components of a queuing system.
2. Give an example where the FIFO queue discipline may not be appropriate.
3. In a single channel queuing model, the utilization rate plus the probability the system is empty must add to one. Explain why this is not true for a multichannel model.
4. Give an example of a situation where the calling population is finite.
5. Describe the relationship between the Poisson distribution and the exponential distribution.
6. Give an example of a situation where the service times may be constant.
7. Explain why at times W is used in performing an economic analysis of a queuing system instead of W_q.
8. Describe what the $M/M/3$ queuing system is.
9. Explain what a steady state is.
10. Why is it always assumed the total service rate (μ or $k\mu$) is greater than the arrival rate (λ)?

PROBLEMS

11. The arrivals into a queuing system are random and may be described by a Poisson distribution. The average number of arrivals per minute is two. Find the probability the number of arrivals in the next minute would be:
    a) 0
    b) 1
    c) 2
    d) 3
    e) 3 or less
12. The arrivals into a queuing system average 0.5 per minute, and are defined by a Poisson distribution.
    a) What is the average number of arrivals per hour?
    b) What is the average number of arrivals in a 10-minute time interval?
    c) What is the probability there will be exactly six arrivals in the next 10 minutes?

13. The average time to serve a customer is three minutes, and service times are exponentially distributed.
    a) What is the average number of customers served per minute?
    b) What is the probability a customer would be served in three minutes or less?
    c) What is the probability a customer would be served in five minutes or less?
14. The average time between arrivals in a store is five minutes, and it is appropriate to use the exponential distribution to describe the time between arrivals.
    a) On the average, how many customers arrive per minute?
    b) What is the probability the next arrival will be in five minutes or less?
    c) What is the probability there will be no arrivals in the next five minutes (i.e., the time until the next arrival is greater than five minutes)?
    d) On the average, how many customers arrive in a five-minute time interval?
    e) Using the Poisson distribution and $\lambda = 1$ per five-minute interval, find the probability of zero arrivals in a five-minute time period.
    f) Compare the answers for parts (c) and (e) above.
15. Buster's Burger is a hamburger restaurant where customers form a single line for the one cashier. The average number of arrivals is one per minute and the Poisson distribution accurately defines this rate. The average time to serve a customer is 30 seconds and the exponential distribution may be used to describe the distribution of service times.
    a) What are λ and μ in this situation?
    b) Using Kendall notation, what type of queuing system is this?
    c) What percentage of time is the cashier busy?
    d) What percentage of time is the cashier idle?
    e) What is the average length of the line?
    f) How many minutes does the average customer spend waiting in line?
    g) How many minutes typically elapse from the time the person enters the line until the person gets the food and leaves the system?
16. Customers arrive at a corner grocery store at a rate of three per minute and the Poisson distribution accurately defines this rate. A single cashier works at the store, the average time to serve a customer is 15 seconds, and the exponential distribution may be used to describe the distribution of service times.
    a) What are λ and μ in this situation?
    b) Using Kendall notation, what type of queuing system is this?
    c) What percentage of time is the cashier busy?
    d) What percentage of time is the cashier idle?
    e) What is the average length of the line?
    f) How many minutes does the average customer spend waiting in line?
    g) How many minutes typically elapse from the time the person enters the line until the person pays the cashier and leaves the system?
    h) Find the probability the number in the system is one, two, and three.
17. Consider a single queue, single server queuing system with Poisson arrivals and exponential service times. The average number of arrivals per hour is four, and the average service time is 12 seconds. Assume this system is open eight hours each day.
    a) On the average, how many customers arrive per hour?
    b) On the average, how many customers arrive each day?
    c) What is the average time spent in the system by a single customer?

d) What is the total time spent in the system by all the customers in a typical day?

e) If the waiting time cost is $20 per hour in the system, what would the total waiting time cost per day be for this system?

18. Suppose the waiting time cost in Problem 17 is determined to be $20 per hour in the queue instead of in the system. What would be the total waiting time cost per day for this system?

19. Arnold's Bank is the only bank in a small town in Arkansas. On a typical Friday, an average of 10 customers per hour arrive at the bank to transact business. There is one single cashier at the bank, and the average time required to transact business is four minutes. It is assumed service times may be described by the exponential distribution. While this is the only bank in town, some people in the town have begun using the bank in a neighboring town about 20 miles away. Arnold's is considering adding a second cashier who would work at the same rate as the first to reduce the waiting time for customers. The bank assumes this will cut the waiting time in half. A single line would be used, and the customer at the front of the line would go to the first available bank teller. If a single cashier is used, find:
(1) the average time in the line
(2) the average number in the line
(3) the average time in the system
(4) the average number in the system
(5) the probability the bank is empty

20. Refer to the Arnold's Bank situation in Problem 19. If a second cashier is added, find:
(1) the average time in the line
(2) the average number in the line
(3) the average time in the system
(4) the average number in the system
(5) the probability the bank is empty

21. For the Arnold's Bank situation in Problems 19 and 20, the salary and benefits for a teller would be $12 per hour. The bank is open 8 hours each day. It has been estimated the waiting time cost per hour is $25 per hour in the line.
a) How many customers would enter the bank on a typical day?
b) How much total time would the customers spend waiting in line during the entire day if one cashier is used?
c) What is the total daily waiting time cost for the bank if one teller is used?
d) How much total time would the customers spend waiting in line during the entire day if two tellers are used? What is the total waiting time cost?
e) If Arnold's wishes to minimize the total waiting time and personnel cost, how many tellers should be used?

22. The Corner Quick Stop is a small convenience store owned and operated by William Anderson and his sons. Mr. Anderson is planning to add a gasoline pump to his operation. He has estimated the number of cars arriving at the pump would be 20 per hour. Two types of gasoline pumps are being considered. The regular pump dispenses gasoline at a slower rate than the deluxe pump. The average time to pump gasoline with the regular pump is two minutes, while the average time to pump gasoline with the deluxe pump is one minute. Mr. Anderson is considering purchasing either one regular pump, two regular pumps, or one deluxe pump.

a) Determine the average time each customer would have to wait in line before getting to the pump for each of the three possible systems.
b) Based on the average time in the line, which system would be best?
c) Determine the average time each customer would be in the line or at the pump for each of the three possible systems.
d) Based on the average time in the system, which would be best?
e) Explain how it is possible a two-channel system with half the service rate of a fast one-channel system can be considered better based on one measure of performance, while the one-channel system can be considered better based on another measure. (*Hint*: Think about $W = W_q + 1/\mu$.)

23. An automatic car wash can wash a car in exactly 90 seconds. If cars arrive at the wash at the average rate of one every two minutes following an exponential distribution, find:
    (1) the average time each car is waiting in the line
    (2) the average number of cars in the line
    (3) the average time a car spends in the system
    (4) the average number in the system
24. A high school band is having a car wash as a fund raiser. The average time to wash a car is four minutes, and the standard deviation is one minute. Cars arrive at the wash at the average rate of one every five minutes. Find:
    (1) the average time each car is waiting in the line
    (2) the average number of cars in the line
    (3) the average time a car spends in the system
    (4) the average number in the system
25. Show that the formula for W_q in the *M/D/*1 model is the same as the formula for W_q in the *M/G/*1 model with $\sigma = 0$.
26. Table 11.3 above gave the values of P_0 in the *M/M/k* model for selected values of λ/μ. Show that the formula for P_0 in this model may be written as:

$$P_0 = \frac{1}{\sum_{n=0}^{k-1} \frac{(\lambda/\mu)^n}{n!} + \frac{(\lambda/\mu)^k}{(k-1)!\,(k-\lambda/\mu)}}$$

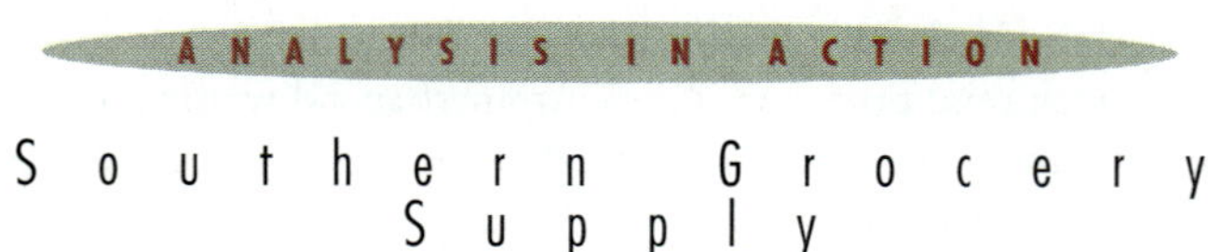

ANALYSIS IN ACTION

Southern Grocery Supply

Southern Grocery Supply provides a variety of products to grocery stores throughout the Southwest (U.S.). The company operates its own warehouses and trucking system. Recent changes in the economy have made generating a profit even more difficult in this very competitive industry. Southern Grocery is looking at possible ways to improve efficiency and reduce costs of its operations.

One particular area being studied by management is the operation of the loading docks at the warehouses. When a truck arrives at a loading dock, the truck is unloaded by a single worker. While the truck is being unloaded, the truck driver sits idle, although he or she is still drawing a salary of $15 per hour. Loading dock workers are paid $9 per hour and sit idle when there are no trucks at the dock. Management is considering the possibility of adding a second or even a third worker at each loading dock to reduce the waiting time that has been observed. Another option being investigated at certain warehouses is the possibility of adding additional loading docks. While this is impossible at some of the warehouses, it is possible to add one additional dock to some of the other warehouses. Management would like to determine the impact of adding additional workers or additional docks before actually making these decisions.

An analysis of the loading dock operation at one warehouse indicates trucks arrive at a loading dock at the rate of three per hour. With the current operation, each truck is unloaded by a single worker. The average time required to load or unload a truck is 15 minutes with a single worker. An experiment was performed and it was found the time required to unload a truck with two workers working on the same dock was eight minutes. If three workers were used at the same dock, it was estimated the average time to unload the truck was six minutes. If a second dock is added, it is anticipated the loading and unloading time would be the same at both docks. Trucks would form a single line and go to the next available dock.

Prepare a brief report to management indicating your recommendations. Include all pertinent cost information.

Spreadsheet Queuing Example M/M/1

Suppose that customers arrive at a service window at the average rate of 10 per hour. Average service takes 4 minutes; an average of 15 customers are served per hour. Determine the performance of the system.

average arrival rate 10 per hour
average service rate 15 per hour

	A	B	C	D	E	F	G	H
1								
2	Queuing Example M/M/1							
3								
4								
5	average arrival rate	10	per hour					
6	average service rate	15	per hour					
7								
8	average time in system		W		0.2	hours	12	minutes
9	average number in system		L		2			
10	average time spent in queue		Wq		0.133333333	hours	8	minutes
11	average number in queue		Lq		1.333333333			
12								
13	probability the system is empty		Po		0.333333333			
14	the utilization rate		rho		0.666666667			
15								
16	probability number in the system is			1	0.222222222			
17	probability number in the system is			2	0.148148148			
18	probability number in the system is			3	0.098765432			
19	probability number in the system is			4	0.065843621			
20	probability number in the system is			5	0.043895748			
21	probability number in the system is			6	0.029263832			
22	probability number in the system is			7	0.019509221			
23	probability number in the system is			8	0.013006147			

	A	B	C	D	E	F	G	H
1								
2	Queuing Example M/M/1							
3								
4								
5	average arrival rate	10	per hr					
6	average service rate	15	per hr					
7								
8	average time in system		W		=1/(B6-B5)	hrs	=+E8*60	minutes
9	average number in system		L		=+B5*E8			
10	average time spent in queue		Wq		=+E8-1/B6	hrs	=+E10*60	minutes
11	average number in queue		Lq		=+B5*E10			
12								
13	probability the system is empty		Po		=1-B5/B6			
14	the utilization rate		rho		=+B5/B6			
15								
16	probability number in the system is			1	=+($B$5/$B$6)^D16*$E$13			
17	probability number in the system is			=+D16+1	=+($B$5/$B$6)^D17*$E$13			
18	probability number in the system is			=+D17+1	=+($B$5/$B$6)^D18*$E$13			
19	probability number in the system is			=+D18+1	=+($B$5/$B$6)^D19*$E$13			
20	probability number in the system is			=+D19+1	=+($B$5/$B$6)^D20*$E$13			
21	probability number in the system is			=+D20+1	=+($B$5/$B$6)^D21*$E$13			
22	probability number in the system is			=+D21+1	=+($B$5/$B$6)^D22*$E$13			
23	probability number in the system is			=+D22+1	=+($B$5/$B$6)^D23*$E$13			

Spreadsheet Queuing Example M/G/1

Suppose that customers arrive at a service window at an average rate of 10 per hour. Average service takes 4 minutes; an average of 15 customers are served per hour. The standard deviation of the service time is .1 hours. Find the operating characteristics of the M/G/1 queuing system.

	A	B	C	D	E	F	G
1	Queuing Example M/G/1						
2							
3							
4	average arrival rate	10	per hour				
5	average service rate	15	per hour				
6	standard deviation	0.1	hours				
7							
8	probability the system is empty		Po	0.333333			
9	average number in queue		Lq	2.166667			
10	average time spent in the queue		Wq	0.216667	hours or	13	minutes
11	average time spent in the system		W	0.283333	hours or	17	minutes
12	average number in the system		L	2.833333			

	A	B	C	D	E	F	G
1	Queuing Example M/G/1						
2							
3							
4	average arrival rate	10	per hour				
5	average service rate	15	per hour				
6	standard deviation	0.1	hours				
7							
8	probability system is empty		Po	=1-B4/B5			
9	average number in queue		Lq	=+((B4*B6)^2+(B4/B5)^2)/(2*(1-B4/B5))			
10	average time in the queue		Wq	=+D9/B4	hours or	=+D10*60	minutes
11	average time in the system		W	=+D10+1/B5	hours or	=+D11*60	minutes
12	average number in system		L	=+B4*D11			

CASE THREE

Queuing Theory at AT&T's Wafer Fabrication Facility

Wafer fabrication is the first step in the manufacture of integrated circuits, which are the heart of the multibillion dollar electronics industry. A semiconductor wafer fabrication facility (fab) is a complex environment, in which each product may require 300-400 processing steps, and where many different end products often are produced in the same facility. A wafer fab often has between 150 and 200 different pieces of processing equipment. Processing at this equipment may be by single wafer, by single lot (groups of 24 to 48 wafers), or by batches (groups) of lots, depending on the type of operation being performed. Further complicating matters is the phenomenon of reentrant flow in wafer fabs. Each wafer starts as a blank piece of silicon, onto which up to 20 layers are built to make an integrated circuit. Each layer is produced through a particular series of operations. For each new layer, a wafer revisits the same sequence of machines, thus reentering the same machine many times in the process.

AT&T's Orlando wafer fab makes several products for AT&T's internal and external customers. These include custom chip sets and memory devices. Many managerial decisions must be made concerning the operation of the facility. High-level, strategic decisions direct what products the Orlando fab will produce. More tactical decisions also are made by the management of the Orlando fab. These decisions might involve what machines to buy, and how many wafers to produce. Finally, operational decisions are made within the fab every day. These include such questions as what lots to complete on a given day.

To make the above decisions, AT&T needs to evaluate the performance of the fab. They need to know how many lots are produced of each type of product in a given period, called product throughput. They also need data concerning the average cycle times (total time to produce a lot) of the different products, and the average inventory levels within the fab. Information about how highly utilized the different tools are also is helpful. The factory computer integrated manufacturing (CIM) system reports this type of information for actual production. However, many questions faced by management involve "what-if" analysis. There are questions like "What

AT&T uses queuing models to estimate work-in-process (WIP), cycle times, equipment utilization, and factory throughput in their semiconductor wafer fabrication facilities. CREDIT: AT&T Allentown IC Group

will happen to the cycle times if we buy this new machine?" Or, "What will happen to the throughput of the other products if we add this new product?" Historical data is not available to address these questions.

Experimenting on the actual fab would be tremendously costly, if it were feasible at all. Instead, AT&T uses management science tools to model factory performance and to assess the impact of changes within the fab. Much of this analysis work is done initially using spreadsheet-based capacity planning models. These models contain information about the number of pieces of each type of equipment, the demand placed on each type of equipment by each product, and the volume and mix of product required. The models also include data on how much time each type of equipment is unavailable, either from a failure or due to preventive maintenance or set ups. The models then make a static computation to determine whether enough pieces of equipment are available to satisfy the demand. "What-if" analyses are fairly easy to conduct with spreadsheet models and can be done quickly.

The problem with spreadsheet models, however, is that they cannot be used to estimate cycle times, or average work-in-process (WIP). This is because they are first of all static and cannot model time-dependent system behavior, such as two lots competing for the same machine. Also, spreadsheet models are deterministic and do not model random elements such as variable failures. Because these dynamic and stochastic effects have a significant impact on factory performance, AT&T uses queuing network models to capture them.

AT&T's factory-level queuing model requires inputs similar to those of their spreadsheet models. Additional assumptions also are needed about the distribution of time between failures, time between lot releases into the factory, and processing times. Unlike spreadsheet models, queuing models can yield significantly different results depending on assumptions about variability. For example, a queuing model that assumes a highly variable failure distribution (i.e., exponential distribution) will yield higher cycle time estimates than a model that assumes a lower variability distribution.

From the product mix and processing specifications for each product, the queuing model estimates an overall arrival rate and service rate for each equipment group. The service rate then is modified to reflect time that the machine is unavailable for processing (due to failures and to set ups for different products). From the arrival and service characteristics of each equipment group, and the number of servers in each group, the model then estimates the long-term behavior of the equipment group. This long-term behavior includes average queue lengths and queue times at the workstation. From this workstation-level behavior, and the number of visits to each workstation by each product, the model then estimates the overall factory WIP and cycle time by product.

Output from the queuing model includes estimates of overall equipment utilizations including downtime and set ups, queue times and queue lengths at the different equipment groups, and overall factory cycle times and WIP. These values are obtained by solving a set of equations for the queuing network and predict the long-term behavior of the system. Queuing models can be used easily for doing "what-if" analyses, because the time required to solve the queuing equations is typically not long.

At AT&T, the speed of queuing models is particularly helpful for the sales force. Sales people can run models to estimate the impact of a customer's order on the existing system. Depending on how much capacity is available, they can accept or defer the order. Sometimes, they may lower the price of the requested item if extra capacity is available. They also can sometimes give the customer an estimate of what the cycle time might be to complete that type of order.

In some cases, AT&T also might use queuing models to evaluate the performance of a single tool group. For example, the equipment engineers might be considering a change to the preventive maintenance schedule of the bottleneck machine in the fab. Their intuition might say that instead of taking the machine down for two hours every 10 hours, taking the machine down for six hours every 30 hours would be better. From a static standpoint, this schedule change would not affect the capacity of the factory. However, they could use a queuing model to investigate the impact of this change on the average cycle time of lots passing through the machine.

The system could be treated as an *M*/*D*/1 queuing system with deterministic failures. This is a reasonable approximation to use for a semiconductor workstation application. The times between arrivals to a workstation tend to be highly variable, but processing times and preventive maintenance schedules are nearly constant. For this system, the deterministic service time is one hour per lot and the exponentially distributed arrival rate is varied between 0.4 and 0.72 lots per hour. The maximum arrival rate for the system is 0.8 lots per hour because the system is down 20% of the time (either two out of every 10 hours, or six out of every 30). Table 1 shows the estimated cycle time results for the series of queuing approximations. Figure 1 shows a graph of the cycle time versus start rate for the two systems. At every arrival rate, the average cycle time is greater for the system with six hour repair times than for the system with two hour repair times. The increase in cycle time shows that the longer maintenance events are more disruptive to the system than shorter, more frequent maintenance events. These results might very well convince the engineer not to select the six hour maintenance schedule.

TABLE 1

Average Cycle Time Results from Queuing Approximations

Observed Start Rate	2 Hour Repair Time	6 Hour Repair Time
0.40	1.93	2.73
0.44	1.99	2.79
0.48	2.06	2.86
0.52	2.14	2.94
0.56	2.24	3.04
0.60	2.35	3.30
0.64	2.71	6.74
0.68	3.45	10.25
0.72	4.24	13.85

FIGURE 1

Cycle Time versus Start Rate from Queuing Approximations

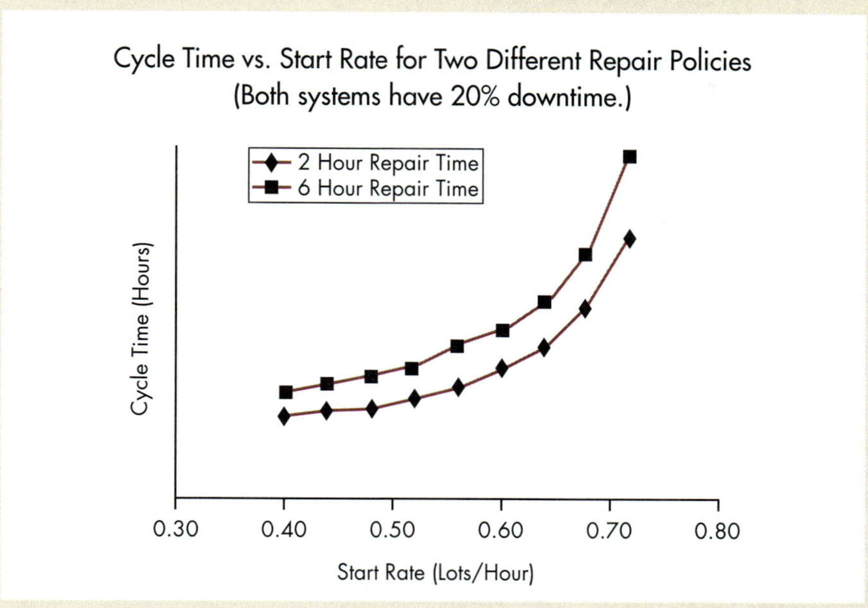

PROBLEM 1

Given an arrival rate that can vary from .4 lots per hour to .72 lots per hour, a deterministic service time of one hour, and the need for periodic maintenance, management needs to know how to schedule the repair time. Management has two options: close down the production line for two hours every 10 hours or close the line for six hours every 30 hours. In order to determine the appropriate repair policy, the average time that a lot is in the system must be found.

To find the average time in the system or cycle time:

1. Find W, the average time in the system.
2. Find L, the average number in the system.
3. Find the average number of lots that will arrive prior to the periodic maintenance. For Policy I, that is arrivals in the first seven hours. For Policy II, it is arrivals in the first 23 hours.
4. Find the expected number of hours the arrivals found in Step 3 are expected to spend in the system.
5. For the arrivals found in Step 3, find the time in the system over eight or 24 hours.
6. Find the expected number of lots in the system that will arrive before the 8th (24th) hour but will remain in the system for over 8 (24) hours. Divide the result of Step 5 by the expected time in the system for an arrival (Step 1).
7. Find the expected time of delay for the lots found in Step 6. This is calculated by taking the result of Step 5 and multiplying by the result of Step 6.

8. Find the expected number of arrivals that must wait for service. For Policy I, it is three times the arrival rate. For Policy II, it is seven times the arrival rate.
9. Find the expected time in the system for the arrivals found in Step 8.
10. Find the total number of lots that arrive in 10 or 30 hours.
11. Find the total time spent in the system for all arrivals. This number is the sum of the results of Steps 4, 7, and 9.
12. Find the average time in the system. Divide the total time in the system by the total number in the system. This is the cycle time.

Policy I: Repair Two Hours Out of Every 10 Hours

mu = 1 lambda	*W*	*L*	Arrivals in 7 Hrs.	Time in System	Time Over 8 Hrs.	# Over 8 Hrs.	Expected Delay Due to Repair
0.40	1.33	0.53	2.80	3.73			
0.44	1.39	0.61	3.08	4.29			
0.48	1.46	0.70	3.36	4.91			
0.52	1.54	0.80	3.64	5.61			
0.56	1.64	0.92	3.92	6.41			
0.60	1.75	1.05	4.20	7.35			
0.64	1.89	1.21	4.48	8.46	0.46	0.24	0.49
0.68	2.06	1.40	4.76	9.82	1.82	0.88	1.76
0.72	2.29	1.65	5.04	11.52	3.52	1.54	3.08

lambda	Arrivals in 3 Hrs.	Time in System	Total # in System	Total Time in System	Mean Time in System
0.40	1.20	4.00	4.00	7.73	1.93
0.44	1.32	4.48	4.40	8.77	1.99
0.48	1.44	4.98	4.80	9.90	2.06
0.52	1.56	5.53	5.20	11.14	2.14
0.56	1.68	6.11	5.60	12.52	2.24
0.60	1.80	6.75	6.00	14.10	2.35
0.64	1.92	8.41	6.40	17.36	2.71
0.68	2.04	11.88	6.80	23.46	3.45
0.72	2.16	15.91	7.20	30.51	4.24

Policy II: Repair Six Hours Out of Every 30 Hours

mu = 1 lambda	*W*	*L*	Arrivals in 24 Hrs.	Time in System	Time Over 24 Hrs.	# Over 24 Hrs.	Expected Delay Due to Repair
0.40	1.33	0.53	9.20	12.27			
0.44	1.39	0.61	10.12	14.10			
0.48	1.46	0.70	11.04	16.14			
0.52	1.54	0.80	11.96	18.44			
0.56	1.64	0.92	12.88	21.08			
0.60	1.75	1.05	13.80	24.15	0.15	0.09	0.51
0.64	1.89	1.21	14.72	27.80	3.80	2.01	12.08
0.68	2.06	1.40	15.64	32.26	8.26	4.00	24.02
0.72	2.29	1.65	16.56	37.85	13.85	6.06	36.36

lambda	Arrivals in 7 Hrs.	Time in System	Total # in System	Total Time in System	Mean Time in System
0.40	2.80	20.53	12.00	32.80	2.73
0.44	3.08	22.77	13.20	36.87	2.79
0.48	3.36	25.07	14.40	41.21	2.86
0.52	3.64	27.45	15.60	45.89	2.94
0.56	3.92	29.93	16.80	51.01	3.04
0.60	4.20	34.71	18.00	59.37	3.30
0.64	4.48	89.48	19.20	129.37	6.74
0.68	4.76	152.72	20.40	209.00	10.25
0.72	5.04	225.01	21.60	299.23	13.85

PROBLEM 2

Suppose the arrival rates and service rate remain the same. Determine the cycle times if management takes the machine down one hour every five hours. Determine the cycle time for this policy.

PROBLEM 3

Suppose the service rate (deterministic) increases to two hours. Determine the cycle time for Policies I and II, two hour repair every ten hours and six hours every 30 hours.

	A	B	C	D	E	F	G	H	I	J	K	L	M
1													
2													
3	2 HOUR REPAIR EVERY 10 HOURS							Expected Delay					
4	MU=1			Arrivals	Time in	Time	# Over	Due to	Arrivals	Time in	Total # in	Total Time	Mean Time
5	LAMBDA	W	L	in 7 Hrs.	System	Over 8 Hrs.	8 Hrs.	Repair	in 3 Hrs.	System	System	in System	in System
6	0.40	1.33	0.53	2.80	3.73	0.00	0.00	0.00	1.20	4.00	4.00	7.73	1.93
7	0.44	1.39	0.61	3.08	4.29	0.00	0.00	0.00	1.32	4.48	4.40	8.77	1.99
8	0.48	1.46	0.70	3.36	4.91	0.00	0.00	0.00	1.44	4.98	4.80	9.90	2.06
9	0.52	1.54	0.80	3.64	5.61	0.00	0.00	0.00	1.56	5.53	5.20	11.14	2.14
10	0.56	1.64	0.92	3.92	6.41	0.00	0.00	0.00	1.68	6.11	5.60	12.52	2.24
11	0.60	1.75	1.05	4.20	7.35	0.00	0.00	0.00	1.80	6.75	6.00	14.10	2.35
12	0.64	1.89	1.21	4.48	8.46	0.46	0.24	0.49	1.92	8.41	6.40	17.36	2.71
13	0.68	2.06	1.40	4.76	9.82	1.82	0.88	1.76	2.04	11.88	6.80	23.46	3.45
14	0.72	2.29	1.65	5.04	11.52	3.52	1.54	3.08	2.16	15.91	7.20	30.51	4.24
15													
16	6 HOUR REPAIR EVERY 30 HOURS							Expected Delay					
17	MU=1			Arrivals	Time in	Time	# Over	Due to	Arrivals	Time in	Total # in	Total Time	Mean Time
18	LAMBDA	W	L	in 24 Hrs.	System	Over 24 Hrs.	24 Hrs.	Repair	in 7 Hrs.	System	System	in System	in System
19	0.40	1.33	0.53	9.20	12.27	0.00	0.00	0.00	2.80	20.53	12.00	32.80	2.73
20	0.44	1.39	0.61	10.12	14.10	0.00	0.00	0.00	3.08	22.77	13.20	36.87	2.79
21	0.48	1.46	0.70	11.04	16.14	0.00	0.00	0.00	3.36	25.07	14.40	41.21	2.86
22	0.52	1.54	0.80	11.96	18.44	0.00	0.00	0.00	3.64	27.45	15.60	45.89	2.94
23	0.56	1.64	0.92	12.88	21.08	0.00	0.00	0.00	3.92	29.93	16.80	51.01	3.04
24	0.60	1.75	1.05	13.80	24.15	0.15	0.09	0.51	4.20	34.71	18.00	59.37	3.30
25	0.64	1.89	1.21	14.72	27.80	3.80	2.01	12.08	4.48	89.48	19.20	129.37	6.74
26	0.68	2.06	1.40	15.64	32.26	8.26	4.00	24.02	4.76	152.72	20.40	209.00	10.25
27	0.72	2.29	1.65	16.56	37.85	13.85	6.06	36.36	5.04	225.01	21.60	299.23	13.85
28													
29													
30													
31													
32													
33	Observed Start Rate				2 Hour Repair Time		6 Hour Repair Time						
34	0.40				1.93			2.73					
35	0.44				1.99			2.79					
36	0.48				2.06			2.86					
37	0.52				2.14			2.94					
38	0.56				2.24			3.04					
39	0.60				2.35			3.30					
40	0.64				2.71			6.74					
41	0.68				3.45			10.25					
42	0.72				4.24			13.85					
43													
44	Table 1.		Average Cycle Time Results from Queuing										
45			Approximations										

	A	B	C	D	E
1					
2					
3	2 HOUR REPAIR EVERY 10 HOURS				
4	MU=1			Arrivals	Time in
5	LAMBDA	W	L	in 7 Hrs.	System
6	0.4	=+(2*$B$4-A6)/(2*$B$4*($B$4-A6))	=+A6*B6	=7*A6	=B6*D6
7	=+A6+0.04	=+(2*$B$4-A7)/(2*$B$4*($B$4-A7))	=+A7*B7	=7*A7	=B7*D7
8	=+A7+0.04	=+(2*$B$4-A8)/(2*$B$4*($B$4-A8))	=+A8*B8	=7*A8	=B8*D8
9	=+A8+0.04	=+(2*$B$4-A9)/(2*$B$4*($B$4-A9))	=+A9*B9	=7*A9	=B9*D9
10	=+A9+0.04	=+(2*$B$4-A10)/(2*$B$4*($B$4-A10))	=+A10*B10	=7*A10	=B10*D10
11	=+A10+0.04	=+(2*$B$4-A11)/(2*$B$4*($B$4-A11))	=+A11*B11	=7*A11	=B11*D11
12	=+A11+0.04	=+(2*$B$4-A12)/(2*$B$4*($B$4-A12))	=+A12*B12	=7*A12	=B12*D12
13	=+A12+0.04	=+(2*$B$4-A13)/(2*$B$4*($B$4-A13))	=+A13*B13	=7*A13	=B13*D13
14	=+A13+0.04	=+(2*$B$4-A14)/(2*$B$4*($B$4-A14))	=+A14*B14	=7*A14	=B14*D14
15					
16	6 HOUR REPAIR EVERY 30 HOURS				
17	MU=1			Arrivals	Time in
18	LAMBDA	W	L	in 24 Hrs.	System
19	0.4	=+(2*$B$4-A19)/(2*$B$4*($B$4-A19))	=+A19*B19	=23*A19	=+B19*D19
20	=+A19+0.04	=+(2*$B$4-A20)/(2*$B$4*($B$4-A20))	=+A20*B20	=23*A20	=+B20*D20
21	=+A20+0.04	=+(2*$B$4-A21)/(2*$B$4*($B$4-A21))	=+A21*B21	=23*A21	=+B21*D21
22	=+A21+0.04	=+(2*$B$4-A22)/(2*$B$4*($B$4-A22))	=+A22*B22	=23*A22	=+B22*D22
23	=+A22+0.04	=+(2*$B$4-A23)/(2*$B$4*($B$4-A23))	=+A23*B23	=23*A23	=+B23*D23
24	=+A23+0.04	=+(2*$B$4-A24)/(2*$B$4*($B$4-A24))	=+A24*B24	=23*A24	=+B24*D24
25	=+A24+0.04	=+(2*$B$4-A25)/(2*$B$4*($B$4-A25))	=+A25*B25	=23*A25	=+B25*D25
26	=+A25+0.04	=+(2*$B$4-A26)/(2*$B$4*($B$4-A26))	=+A26*B26	=23*A26	=+B26*D26
27	=+A26+0.04	=+(2*$B$4-A27)/(2*$B$4*($B$4-A27))	=+A27*B27	=23*A27	=+B27*D27
28					
29					
30					
31					
32					
33	Observed Start Rate				2 Hour Repai
34	0.4				=+M6
35	=A34+0.04				=+M7
36	=A35+0.04				=+M8
37	=A36+0.04				=+M9
38	=A37+0.04				=+M10
39	=A38+0.04				=+M11
40	=A39+0.04				=+M12
41	=A40+0.04				=+M13
42	=A41+0.04				=+M14
43					
44	Table 1.		Average Cycle Time Results from Queuing		
45			Approximations		

	F	G	H	I	J	K	L	M
1								
2								
3			Expected Delay					
4	Time	# Over	Due to	Arrivals	Time in	Total # in	Total Time	Mean Time
5	Over 8 Hrs.	8 Hrs.	Repair	in 3 Hrs.	System	System	in System	in System
6	=+(2*$B$4-E6)/(2*$B$4*($B$4-E6))	=F6/B6	=2*G6	=A6*3	=(B6+2+H6)*I6	=I6+D6	=E6+J6+H6	=L6/K6
7	=+(2*$B$4-E7)/(2*$B$4*($B$4-E7))	=F7/B7	=2*G7	=A7*3	=(B7+2+H7)*I7	=I7+D7	=E7+J7+H7	=L7/K7
8	=+(2*$B$4-E8)/(2*$B$4*($B$4-E8))	=F8/B8	=2*G8	=A8*3	=(B8+2+H8)*I8	=I8+D8	=E8+J8+H8	=L8/K8
9	=+(2*$B$4-E9)/(2*$B$4*($B$4-E9))	=F9/B9	=2*G9	=A9*3	=(B9+2+H9)*I9	=I9+D9	=E9+J9+H9	=L9/K9
10	=+(2*$B$4-E10)/(2*$B$4*($B$4-E10))	=F10/B10	=2*G10	=A10*3	=(B10+2+H10)*I10	=I10+D10	=E10+J10+H10	=L10/K10
11	=+(2*$B$4-E11)/(2*$B$4*($B$4-E11))	=F11/B11	=2*G11	=A11*3	=(B11+2+H11)*I11	=I11+D11	=E11+J11+H11	=L11/K11
12	=+(2*$B$4-E12)/(2*$B$4*($B$4-E12))	=F12/B12	=2*G12	=A12*3	=(B12+2+H12)*I12	=I12+D12	=E12+J12+H12	=L12/K12
13	=+(2*$B$4-E13)/(2*$B$4*($B$4-E13))	=F13/B13	=2*G13	=A13*3	=(B13+2+H13)*I13	=I13+D13	=E13+J13+H13	=L13/K13
14	=+(2*$B$4-E14)/(2*$B$4*($B$4-E14))	=F14/B14	=2*G14	=A14*3	=(B14+2+H14)*I14	=I14+D14	=E14+J14+H14	=L14/K14
15								
16			Expected Delay					
17	Time	# Over	Due to	Arrivals	Time in	Total # in	Total Time	Mean Time
18	Over 24 Hrs.	24 Hrs.	Repair	in 7 Hrs.	System	System	in System	in System
19	=+(2*$B$4-E19)/(2*$B$4*($B$4-E19))	=F19/B19	=6*G19	=A19*7	=(B19+6+H19)*I19	=I19+D19	=E19+J19+H19	=L19/K19
20	=+(2*$B$4-E20)/(2*$B$4*($B$4-E20))	=F20/B20	=6*G20	=A20*7	=(B20+6+H20)*I20	=I20+D20	=E20+J20+H20	=L20/K20
21	=+(2*$B$4-E21)/(2*$B$4*($B$4-E21))	=F21/B21	=6*G21	=A21*7	=(B21+6+H21)*I21	=I21+D21	=E21+J21+H21	=L21/K21
22	=+(2*$B$4-E22)/(2*$B$4*($B$4-E22))	=F22/B22	=6*G22	=A22*7	=(B22+6+H22)*I22	=I22+D22	=E22+J22+H22	=L22/K22
23	=+(2*$B$4-E23)/(2*$B$4*($B$4-E23))	=F23/B23	=6*G23	=A23*7	=(B23+6+H23)*I23	=I23+D23	=E23+J23+H23	=L23/K23
24	=+(2*$B$4-E24)/(2*$B$4*($B$4-E24))	=F24/B24	=6*G24	=A24*7	=(B24+6+H24)*I24	=I24+D24	=E24+J24+H24	=L24/K24
25	=+(2*$B$4-E25)/(2*$B$4*($B$4-E25))	=F25/B25	=6*G25	=A25*7	=(B25+6+H25)*I25	=I25+D25	=E25+J25+H25	=L25/K25
26	=+(2*$B$4-E26)/(2*$B$4*($B$4-E26))	=F26/B26	=6*G26	=A26*7	=(B26+6+H26)*I26	=I26+D26	=E26+J26+H26	=L26/K26
27	=+(2*$B$4-E27)/(2*$B$4*($B$4-E27))	=F27/B27	=6*G27	=A27*7	=(B27+6+H27)*I27	=I27+D27	=E27+J27+H27	=L27/K27
28								
29								
30								
31								
32								
33		6 Hour Re						
34			=M19					
35			=M20					
36			=M21					
37			=M22					
38			=M23					
39			=M24					
40			=M25					
41			=M26					
42			=M27					
43								
44								
45								

CHAPTER TWELVE

Decision Models I

LEARNING OBJECTIVES

Upon completing Chapter 12, you should be able to:

- Recognize the three decision making environments.
- Identify states of nature and alternatives, and use them in constructing payoff tables.
- Apply the optimistic, pessimistic, Hurwicz, and equally likely criteria when making decisions under uncertainty.
- Apply the expected value criterion when making decisions under risk.
- Construct an opportunity loss table and apply the minimax regret and expected opportunity loss criteria.
- Compute and explain the importance of the expected value of perfect information.
- Use a marginal analysis approach to making decisions about certain types of inventory problems.

CHAPTER OUTLINE

12.1

INTRODUCTION

Being a manager means making decisions. Should a company expand its existing facility or build an entirely new facility to better serve customers in the future? Which of several investment alternatives would be best to select? How many employees should be hired to service new clients? Should a new product be marketed nationally or should it be tested in a smaller area first? These illustrate a few of the many decisions faced by managers. In addition to managerial decision making, individuals may make decisions about purchasing insurance, investing for retirement or college funds, and even buying lottery tickets. Concepts to be discussed in this chapter will be applicable to all of these types of decisions.

12.2

EXAMPLE

Fotochem, Inc. is a chemical manufacturing firm that specializes in photography chemicals. Some of these chemicals have a very short shelf life and are no good six days after production. Thus, it is impossible to carry a large inventory of this product. A new product, KD85, has been developed for use in developing very high-speed film. It has been projected that demand for this item will be either six, seven, or eight cases per week. The company must decide on Monday morning how many cases to produce for the week. Due to economies of scale, the cost per case is $30 for each case produced during the normal production run. However, if demand exceeds the number produced on Monday, an additional production run is needed and the cost rises to $60 per case for additional cases produced later in the week. A case of KD85 sells for $50, and the company has a policy of always meeting the demand, even if it means selling a case for $50 when it cost $60. On the other hand, if seven or eight cases are produced and demand is for less than this, the excess cases must be thrown away. At the present time, management is unable to determine exactly what the demand will be. How many cases should be produced on Monday? We will return to this situation later in this chapter.

Payoff table
A table that lists the alternatives, states of nature, and payoffs for a decision making situation.

Alternative
A possible choice that the decision maker may select.

State of nature
An event or occurrence over which the decision maker has no control.

Payoff
The actual measure of performance that is achieved when a particular alternative is selected and a specific state of nature occurs.

12.3

PAYOFF TABLES

A convenient way to structure a decision making situation is to use a **payoff table**. A payoff table lists the possible **alternatives** or choices that are being considered. It also lists the possible **states of nature** or future events that may occur and impact the payoff for each decision. A payoff table also gives the appropriate **payoff**, such as profit or total sales, that is associated with the outcome or result of each possible situation.

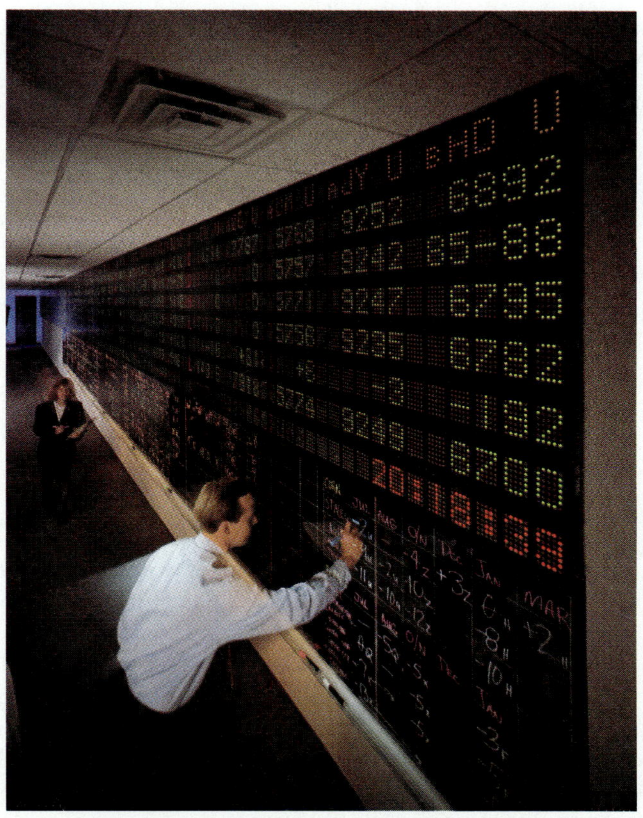

Grain merchandisers use the information provided by this electronic quote board to aid in marketing and investment decisions.
SOURCE: Archer Daniels Midland, Co.

Typical alternatives may be to invest in stocks, bonds, or government securities when facing investment decisions. The states of nature for this would be the economic conditions in the future that would impact the return on the investment. The payoff would typically be the profit or return on investment.

Perhaps a company is trying to determine the best use for a particular piece of real estate. The alternatives may be to construct an office building or to construct an apartment complex. The states of nature would be the future economic conditions that could impact the demand for office or apartment space. The payoffs would be the profits generated by each decision in each state of nature.

The payoffs in other situations may be profits, total sales, market share, cost, or any measure that management is using to measure performance. In using a payoff table, a single type of payoff measure is the basis for making a decision. If there are several payoff measures with which management is concerned, the use of a single payoff table with a single measure for the payoff may not be appropriate. However, one payoff table could be created for each type of payoff. While these may lead to different decisions, doing this forces the manager to carefully identify the alternatives that are being considered. It also forces the manager to think about the possible states of nature that may occur to influence the payoffs. Then, a manager may use multicriteria techniques discussed in the next chapter to help evaluate the information that is available and make a decision.

A manager's responsibility is to make decisions. The decision models we will see in this chapter and other chapters are only used to help in this process.

Table 12.1 provides an example of a typical payoff table. The following notation is used in this table:

$$a_i = \text{alternative } i$$
$$s_j = \text{state of nature } j$$
$$V_{ij} = \text{value of payoff for alternative } i \text{ in state of nature } j$$

Fotochem, Inc. Example

We will now return to the Fotochem, Inc. example and develop the payoff table for that situation. The company must determine how many cases of KD85 to produce each Monday. It has been projected that the demand will be either six, seven, or eight cases, and these represent the possible states of nature. If the demand is either six, seven, or eight cases, it makes sense to produce either six, seven, or eight cases each Monday. These will be the alternatives for the payoff table shown in Table 12.2. Once the alternatives and states of nature have been determined, we must determine what the payoffs would be in each situation.

The payoff that is of concern to management in this situation is assumed to be total profit. Therefore, the profit for each alternative with each state of nature must be found. Profit is simply the total revenue minus the total cost.

Beginning with the alternative of producing six cases, if demand is for six cases, then:

$$\begin{aligned} \text{profit} &= \text{total revenue} - \text{total cost} \\ &= 6(50) - 6(30) = 300 - 180 = 120 \end{aligned}$$

TABLE 12.1

Example of Payoff Table

	States of Nature		
Alternatives	s_1	s_2	s_3
a_1	V_{11}	V_{12}	V_{13}
a_2	V_{21}	V_{22}	V_{23}
a_3	V_{31}	V_{32}	V_{33}

TABLE 12.2

Fotochem, Inc. Payoff Table Listing States of Nature and Alternatives

	States of Nature		
Alternatives	**(s_1) Demand is 6 cases**	**(s_2) Demand is 7 cases**	**(s_3) Demand is 8 cases**
Produce 6 cases (a_1)			
Produce 7 cases (a_2)			
Produce 8 cases (a_3)			

If six cases are produced but demand is for seven cases, the cost for the first six cases is \$30 while the cost for the last case is \$60 giving a profit of:

$$\begin{aligned} \text{profit} &= \text{total revenue} - [\text{total cost}] \\ &= 7(50) - [6(30) + 1(60)] = 350 - [180 + 60] \\ &= 350 - 240 = 110 \end{aligned}$$

Similarly, if six cases are produced on Monday and demand is for eight, the following results:

$$\begin{aligned} \text{profit} &= \text{total revenue} - [\text{total cost}] \\ &= 8(50) - [6(30) + 2(60)] = 400 - [180 + 120] = 100 \end{aligned}$$

If the alternative of producing seven on Monday were selected, then the following profits are derived for each demand level:

$$\begin{aligned} &\text{demand of 6: profit} = 6(50) - 7(30) &&= 90 \\ &\text{demand of 7: profit} = 7(50) - 7(30) &&= 140 \\ &\text{demand of 8: profit} = 8(50) - [7(30)+1(60)] &&= 130 \end{aligned}$$

If the alternative of producing eight on Monday were selected, then the following profits are derived for each demand level:

$$\begin{aligned} &\text{demand of 6: profit} = 6(50) - 8(30) = 60 \\ &\text{demand of 7: profit} = 7(50) - 8(30) = 110 \\ &\text{demand of 8: profit} = 8(50) - 8(30) = 160 \end{aligned}$$

These payoffs are entered into the payoff table shown in Table 12.3. This provides a convenient way to quickly see what would happen with each decision in each state of nature. This payoff table will be used with most of the decision making criteria discussed in this chapter. Before actually determining which decision should be chosen, we will look at some of the conditions under which decisions must be made.

TABLE 12.3

Fotochem, Inc. Payoff Table with Payoffs Entered

	States of Nature		
Alternatives	**Demand is 6 cases**	**Demand is 7 cases**	**Demand is 8 cases**
Produce 6 cases	$120	110	100
Produce 7 cases	90	140	130
Produce 8 cases	60	110	160

12.4

DECISION MAKING ENVIRONMENTS

Decision making environment
The conditions surrounding a decision making situation that determine how much information the decision maker has about the state of nature that will occur. Three environments are certainty, uncertainty, and risk.

Decision making under certainty
A decision making environment in which the decision maker knows the state of nature that will occur and the outcome of each decision with total certainty.

Decision making under uncertainty
A decision making environment in which the decision maker does not know and cannot assign probabilities to the various states of nature.

Decision making under risk
A decision making environment in which the decision maker can assign probabilities to the various states of nature.

The **decision making environment** refers to the knowledge that a person has regarding the results of each decision alternative. **Decision making under certainty** refers to a situation where the state of nature that will occur is known before the decision is made. **Decision making under uncertainty** refers to a situation where a person does not know which of several states of nature will occur, and that person has no way of estimating the probabilities for the various states of nature. **Decision making under risk** refers to the situation where a decision maker does not know which of several states of nature will occur, but the probabilities of each state of nature are known or may be accurately estimated.

A number of different criteria have been developed for the three decision making environments. We will look at some of these criteria to try to understand how and why certain alternatives are selected.

12.5

DECISION MAKING UNDER CERTAINTY

If certainty exists regarding the state of nature that will occur, then a person would simply select the alternative that results in the best payoff. For example, a person who has decided to put money in a six-month certificate of deposit (CD) knows with certainty what the profit will be. If three different banks offered insured six-month CDs with rates of 7 percent, 7.25 percent, and 7.4 percent, a person would simply select the one with the highest rate.

In the Fotochem, Inc. example, if the decision maker knew the demand this week would be seven cases, then the alternative of producing seven cases would be selected because this would yield the highest profit. If demand is known to be eight cases, then eight cases would be produced.

However, in most situations, it is not known with certainty what state of nature will occur.

12.6 DECISION MAKING UNDER UNCERTAINTY

Many decisions must be made where uncertainty exists about the future events that may impact the payoff for a decision. Decision making under uncertainty refers to a situation where nothing is known about the probabilities of the different states of nature. Several decision making criteria have been suggested for this type of situation. We will consider these and discuss the rationale and limitations of each.

Optimistic (Maximax) Criterion

The **optimistic (maximax) criterion** considers only the best possible payoff for each decision. A decision maker using this approach would determine the best payoff for each decision and select the alternative that represented the best of these. If the payoff is to be maximized, this means selecting the alternative that has the *maxi*mum of these *max*imum payoffs. Thus, it is sometimes called the *maximax* criterion.

Optimistic (maximax) criterion
A decision making criterion in which only the best (maximum) payoff for each decision is considered, and the alternative with the best (maximum) of these best payoffs is selected.

Consider the Fotochem, Inc. example shown in Table 12.4. The maximum (best) payoff for each decision is shown in the margin of this table. The maximum of these maximums is $160, and so the decision maker using the optimistic criterion would produce eight cases. By doing this, it is possible this highest payoff may be achieved, although it also is possible that when eight cases are produced, profits will be $60 (if demand is for six cases) or $110 (if demand is for seven cases).

In using the optimistic criterion, the best payoff for each decision is used, and all other payoffs are ignored. Many entrepreneurs are optimistic. However, in some situations, the alternative with the highest possible payoff also may have some very bad payoffs for the other states of nature.

TABLE 12.4

Optimistic Criterion for Fotochem, Inc. Example

	States of Nature			
Alternatives	Demand is 6 cases	Demand is 7 cases	Demand is 8 cases	Maximum
Produce 6 cases	$120	110	100	120
Produce 7 cases	90	140	130	140
Produce 8 cases	60	110	160	160*

Pessimistic (Maximin) Criterion

Pessimistic (maximin) criterion
A decision making criterion in which only the worst (minimum) payoff for each decision is considered, and the alternative with the best (maximum) of these worst payoffs is selected.

Another criterion that may be used for making decisions under uncertainty is called the **pessimistic (maximin) criterion.** A decision maker using this approach would determine the worst payoff for each decision and select the alternative that had the best of these. If the payoff is something to maximize, such as profit, then the worst payoff would be the minimum payoff. The alternative corresponding to the *maxi*mum of the *min*imum payoffs would be selected. Thus, this criterion is sometimes called the *maximin* criterion.

Table 12.5 illustrates the pessimistic criterion for the Fotochem, Inc. example. The worst or minimum payoff for each decision is presented in the margin. A manager looking only at these payoffs would see that the maximum of these is 100, so the alternative of producing six cases would be selected. By doing this, the decision maker is guaranteed that the payoff will be at least $100. It may be higher than $100 if the demand is for six or seven cases. If any other alternative were selected, it would be possible that a payoff lower than $100 might be realized.

Using the pessimistic criterion means that only the worst possible payoff is considered for each alternative. As with the optimistic criterion, much of the available information is ignored.

Hurwicz Criterion

Hurwicz criterion
A decision making criterion in which a weighted average of the best and the worst possible payoffs for each decision is used.

Coefficient of optimism (α)
Used with the Hurwicz criterion, this is a measure of the degree of optimism that the decision maker possesses.

A criterion that considers both the best and the worst payoffs for each decision is the **Hurwicz criterion**, which uses a weighted average of the best and the worst payoffs. The alternative with the highest weighted average is selected. A value called the **coefficient of optimism** (α) is used as the weight for the best payoff while $(1 - \alpha)$ is used as the weight for the worst payoff. This coefficient of optimism is between zero and one, and a value of one would indicate that the person is totally optimistic. A value of zero for the

TABLE 12.5

Pessimistic Criterion for Fotochem, Inc. Example

	States of Nature			
Alternatives	Demand is 6 cases	Demand is 7 cases	Demand is 8 cases	Minimum
Produce 6 cases	$120	110	100	100*
Produce 7 cases	90	140	130	90
Produce 8 cases	60	110	160	60

coefficient of optimism would indicate the person is totally pessimistic and this becomes the pessimistic criterion.

If the Hurwicz criterion is applied to the Fotochem, Inc. example, first select α. If we are somewhat optimistic, we may select α to be 0.7. Then $(1 - \alpha) = (1 - 0.7) = 0.3$. Then calculate the following weighted values for each alternative:

Alternative	Weighted Value α(best payoff) + $(1 - \alpha)$(worst payoff)
Produce 6 cases	0.7(120) + 0.3(100) = 114
Produce 7 cases	0.7(140) + 0.3(90) = 125
Produce 8 cases	0.7(160) + 0.3(60) = 130

This is shown in Table 12.6. The highest value is 130, so select the alternative of producing eight cases. A different value for α may result in a different decision.

Because selecting $\alpha = 1$ is equivalent to the optimistic criterion and selecting $\alpha = 0$ is equivalent to the pessimistic criterion, this criterion uses not only the information used in each one of these individually, it includes more information. However, this method, as well as the other two methods, ignores some information that is available. The next criterion to be presented will use all the information that is available.

Equally Likely Criterion

Equally likely (LaPlace) criterion
A decision making criterion in which each state of nature is assumed to have the same likelihood of occurring. The alternative with the highest average payoff is selected.

Another criterion for making decisions under uncertainty is the **equally likely** or **LaPlace criterion**. With this method, all states of nature are assumed to have the same likelihood or probability of occurring. An average payoff is calculated for each alternative based on this assumption by multiplying each payoff by the assumed probability and adding these together. The alternative with the highest average is selected.

In the Fotochem, Inc. example there are three possible states of nature. Therefore, using the equally likely criterion, each of these is given a one-third

TABLE 12.6

Hurwicz Criterion for Fotochem, Inc. Example

	States of Nature			
Alternatives	**Demand is 6 cases**	**Demand is 7 cases**	**Demand is 8 cases**	**Hurwicz 0.7(best) + 0.3(worst)**
Produce 6 cases	$120	110	100	114
Produce 7 cases	90	140	130	125
Produce 8 cases	60	110	160	130*

chance of occurring. With this assumption an average payoff for each alternative is found as follows:

Alternative	Average Payoff
Produce 6 cases	1/3(120) + 1/3(110) + 1/3(100) = 110
Produce 7 cases	1/3(90) + 1/3(140) + 1/3(130) = 120
Produce 8 cases	1/3(60) + 1/3(110) + 1/3(160) = 110

Based on these averages, choose to produce seven cases because this results in the highest average payoff as shown in Table 12.7.

While this procedure does include all the available information (unlike the optimistic, pessimistic, and Hurwicz methods), it is not always realistic to assume each state of nature is equally likely to occur. However, in making decisions under uncertainty, the probabilities of the different states of nature are not known.

Which Criterion Is Best

Now that several different criteria have been suggested for decision making under uncertainty, which of these should be used? There is no simple answer. An individual's attitude towards risk has a major impact on which alternative a person would select, and consequently, this attitude towards risk may impact which criterion a person feels comfortable in using.

At times a person may create a decision making process that uses features from all of these. For example, a person may eliminate some possible alternatives because the worst payoff is too bad. However, once these have been eliminated so the individual could tolerate the worst payoff for any of the remaining alternatives, the person may like to take chances and use an optimistic approach for the remaining choices. The concept of utility (discussed in the next chapter) helps to illustrate how this type of approach is a logical extension of the criteria just presented.

All of these techniques may be used with decision making under uncertainty where probabilities for the states of nature are not known. If we do

TABLE 12.7

Equally Likely Criterion for Fotochem, Inc. Example

	States of Nature			
Alternatives	**Demand is 6 cases**	**Demand is 7 cases**	**Demand is 8 cases**	**Equally Likely (Average) Value**
Produce 6 cases	$120	110	100	110
Produce 7 cases	90	140	130	120*
Produce 8 cases	60	110	160	110

GLOBAL PERSPECTIVES

E-Systems Turns Data into Information for Decision Making

E-Systems is one of the largest designers, developers and producers of advanced electronic software in the world. The company supplies intelligence, reconnaissance, and communications systems to government and private sector clients in the U.S. and in foreign countries. A major goal of these systems is to give decision makers the information they need to cope with ever changing environments.

For example, E-Systems has developed a Picture Archiving and Communications System (PACS) that gives healthcare facilities the capability for image digitization, storage, distribution, and display at workstations. Hospitals can use the PACS to review images, such as X-rays and ultrasound results, thus increasing their efficiency in making diagnoses. Another system developed by the company is the Flight Service Automation System (FSAS). This system gives general aviation pilots all available flight information, including weather briefings, navigational aids, and Notices to Airmen.

The Gulf War highlighted the continuing need for fast, reliable information in decision making. E-Systems has developed precision electronic warfare systems, ultra-sophisticated military communication systems, and early warning security systems. The company also has experience with "tamper-proof" communication systems incorporating data encryption. Although the Cold War is over, the United States continues to face complex global security concerns. The need for decision making aids is unlikely to diminish.

Overall, more and more data is available around the world today. The health, airline, and defense industries are just a few of the industries confronted by this data. E-Systems' job is to help convert data into information, so it can be used to make the right decisions.

SOURCE:
E-Systems Annual Report, 1993.

know or have some way of estimating the probabilities, then the decision making environment would be risk rather than uncertainty.

12.7 DECISION MAKING UNDER RISK

If probabilities may be assigned to the states of nature and we are making decisions under risk, then more information is available to the decision maker. The probabilities may come from historical data, from knowledge about a particular process, from some subjective assessment of the situation by an expert, or from some other forecasting method.

For example, past sales records may give an indication of the probability that sales next month will be low, medium, or high. Probabilities a machine will break down in the next year and need to be replaced may be based on knowledge about the breakdown rate for machines subjected to the type of load anticipated for the equipment. The probability a firm receives a government contract may be based on a subjective assessment of the relative merits of various proposals.

When probabilities are available, a rational decision maker should use this information. One criterion that makes use of all this information is the expected value criterion.

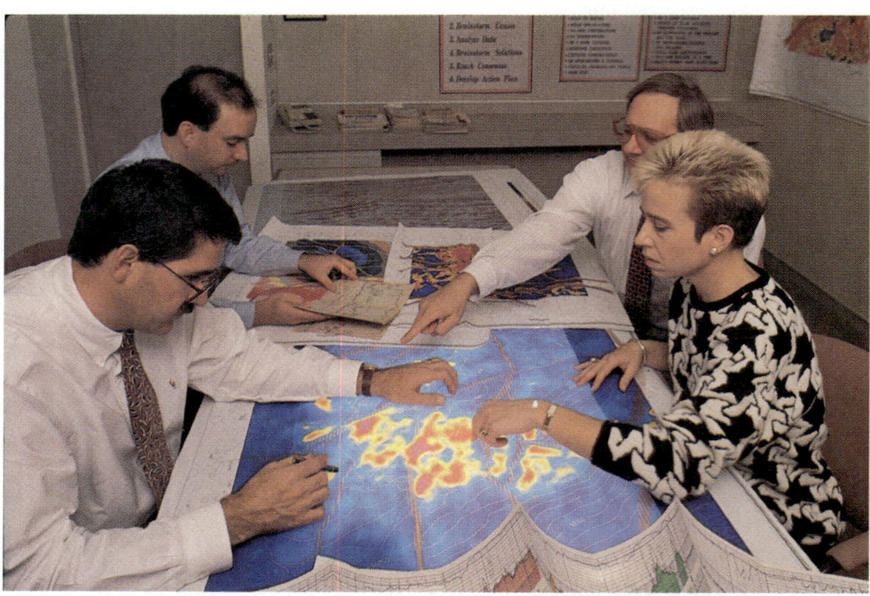

Computer-generated 3-dimensional seismic images of underground formations are used by experts to identify drilling prospects for oil. SOURCE: ©1992 Texaco Inc.; reprinted with permission from Texaco Inc.

Expected Value (EV) Criterion

Expected value (EV) The long run average value that would occur if a decision were repeated a large number of times.

The **expected value** (EV) of a decision is the long run average payoff for that particular decision. The term *expected* is used here in a statistical sense. If the decision were repeated numerous times, the average payoff for these decisions would approach the expected value. Other terms commonly used for the expected value of a decision include expected payoff, expected profit (if the payoffs are profits), and expected monetary value.

The expected value of a decision is computed by multiplying the payoff for each state of nature times the probability of that state of nature occurring and adding these together. This is essentially a weighted average approach where the weights are the probabilities. The computations are similar to the computations in the equally likely criterion. A mathematical statement of this using the notation previously presented is the following:

$$a_i = \text{alternative } i$$
$$s_j = \text{state of nature } j$$
$$V_{ij} = \text{value of payoff for alternative } i \text{ in state of nature } j$$
$$EV(\text{alternative } i) = \Sigma\text{Payoff(probability)}$$
$$EV(a_i) = \Sigma V_{ij}\, P(s_j)$$

In the Fotochem, Inc. example, let's assume the probabilities have been determined to be 0.6 for demand of six cases, 0.3 for the demand of seven cases, and 0.1 for the demand of eight cases. With these probabilities calculate the following expected values:

$$EV(\text{Produce } 6) = 0.6(120) + 0.3(110) + 0.1(100) = 115$$
$$EV(\text{Produce } 7) = 0.6(90) + 0.3(140) + 0.1(130) = 109$$
$$EV(\text{Produce } 8) = 0.6(60) + 0.3(110) + 0.1(160) = 85$$

Based on these expected values, a decision is made to produce six cases each week as this gives the highest expected value.

Table 12.8 gives the expected value for each of these decisions as well as the individual payoffs. The expected value for each decision is the long run average payoffs that would be achieved if this decision were repeated many times. If the decision to produce six cases were repeated each week, about 60 percent of the time profits would be $120, about 30 percent of the time profits would be $110, and about 10 percent of the time profits would be $100. These would average out to be the expected value of $115 per week. Note that if six cases are produced, the actual profits in any particular week will not equal the expected value of $115; they must either be $120, $110, or $100 in that one particular week.

When to Use the Expected Value Criterion

The expected value criterion is appropriate to use when a decision is repeated many times or when many similar types of decisions are being made. For a one time decision where the magnitude of the possible payoffs is extremely large relative to the payoffs for other types of decisions, the long run average value may not be appropriate. While a manager may wish to calculate this to aid in the decision making process, it would probably not be appropriate to base the decision on this criterion alone.

For many decisions, such as building a new factory or spending money to develop a new product, there are usually several factors that impact the decision. The expected value (profit or cost) is just one of the factors that a manager would consider in making a decision.

TABLE 12.8

Expected Value Criterion for Fotochem, Inc. Example

	States of Nature			
Alternatives	**Demand is 6 cases (0.6)**	**Demand is 7 cases (0.3)**	**Demand is 8 cases (0.1)**	**Expected Value**
Produce 6 cases	$120	110	100	115*
Produce 7 cases	90	140	130	109
Produce 8 cases	60	110	160	85

Expected Value of Perfect Information (EVPI)

At times it is possible to use market research of some type to obtain additional information about which state of nature will occur. The result of the market research is typically a forecast of the future conditions. With this additional information, a manager would have more information with which to make a decision and should be able to increase the expected payoff.

Expected value with perfect information
The long run average payoff that would be achieved if perfect information about the future were available.

Expected value of perfect information (EVPI)
The increase in expected value that would result from having perfect information. This is the difference between the expected value with perfect information and the best expected value without perfect information.

Information that would predict with 100 percent accuracy which state of nature will occur is called perfect information. The long run average profits that would be realized if perfect information is available is called the **expected value with perfect information.** Comparing this value to the best expected value without additional information allows us to determine the increase in the expected payoff. This increase in expected payoff is called the **expected value of perfect information** (**EVPI**) and should help determine the maximum amount a manager would pay for a perfect forecast of the future.

Consider the Fotochem, Inc. example and assume market research provides perfect information about the future state of nature that will occur. If this market research was used and it was known in advance that demand would be for six cases, the highest possible profit in this situation would be \$120 and six cases would be produced. If the information said the state of nature would be a demand of seven cases, then the highest profit would be \$140 and seven cases would be produced. Similarly, if the perfect information said the state of nature would be a demand of eight cases, the highest possible profit would be \$160 and eight cases would be produced. These are shown in Table 12.9. Thus, if perfect information could be obtained about the state of nature, the profits would be either \$120, \$140, or \$160.

When it is decided to pay for the market research (perfect information) it is not known which state of nature will be forecast. However, it is known there is a 60 percent chance that demand would be for six cases, and so

TABLE 12.9

Expected Value with Perfect Information for Fotochem, Inc. Example

	States of Nature			
Alternatives	**Demand is 6 cases (0.6)**	**Demand is 7 cases (0.3)**	**Demand is 8 cases (0.1)**	**Expected Value**
Produce 6 cases	\$120	110	100	115
Produce 7 cases	90	140	130	109
Produce 8 cases	60	110	160	85
With Perfect Information	120	140	160	130

there is a 60 percent chance the forecast will be for six cases. Therefore, there is a 60 percent chance profits will be \$120. Similarly, there is a 30 percent chance that demand and the forecast will be for seven cases resulting in a profit of \$140. There is a 10 percent chance that demand and the forecast will be for eight cases resulting in a profit of \$160. Computing the expected value with perfect information results in:

$$\text{EV with PI} = 0.6(120) + 0.3(140) + 0.1(160) = 130$$

This means if perfect information is used in making the decision each week, the long run average profits would be \$130. Without this perfect information the highest expected profit was \$115. Therefore, the expected value of perfect information (EVPI) or the increase in expected value is:

$$\text{EVPI} = (\text{EV with PI}) - (\text{best EV without PI})$$
$$\text{EVPI} = 130 - 115 = 15$$

If perfect information were available at a cost of less than \$15, it should be used as there would be a net increase in the expected value. If the information costs exactly \$15, the net expected value would be the same with the perfect information or without the perfect information.

Why should we calculate the expected value of perfect information if such information is rarely, if ever, available? One reason is this value provides an upper limit on the amount we should be willing to pay for any information—perfect or imperfect. In the next chapter we will see how to determine the value of imperfect or sample information.

12.8 OPPORTUNITY LOSS (REGRET)

At times a manager may look back on a decision once a particular state of nature has occurred and wish that another alternative had been selected because a better payoff could have been achieved for that state of nature. The difference between the best possible payoff for a particular state of nature and the actual payoff achieved with the selected alternative is called the **opportunity loss** or **regret**. For maximization problems, this may be expressed as

$$O_{ij} = V^*(s_j) - V_{ij}$$

where

O_{ij} = opportunity loss for alternative i in state s_j

$V^*(s_j)$ = best payoff for state of nature s_j

V_{ij} = payoff for alternative i in state of nature j

It is possible to make decisions based on the opportunity losses instead of the payoffs. The **minimax regret criterion** may be used when making decisions under uncertainty and the minimum **expected opportunity loss** (*EOL*) criterion may be used when making decisions under risk. An opportunity loss table is helpful when considering these.

Opportunity loss
The difference between the best possible payoff for a particular state of nature and the payoff that actually would be achieved for the decision being considered.

Regret
An opportunity loss.

Minimax regret criterion
A decision making criterion in which the maximum regret for each alternative is considered, and the alternative with the minimum of these maximums is selected.

Expected opportunity loss (*EOL*)
The long run average opportunity loss that would be achieved if a decision were repeated a large number of times.

TABLE 12.10

Best Payoffs for each State of Nature in Fotochem, Inc. Example

	States of Nature		
Alternatives	**Demand is 6 cases**	**Demand is 7 cases**	**Demand is 8 cases**
Produce 6 cases	**$120**	110	100
Produce 7 cases	90	**140**	130
Produce 8 cases	60	110	**160**

Opportunity Loss Example

We will construct an opportunity loss table to reflect the decision making situation in the Fotochem, Inc. example. The opportunity loss table has the same alternatives and states of nature that were seen in the payoff table. Compute the opportunity loss for each alternative with each state of nature. Beginning with the first state of nature of a demand for six cases, look to see what the best possible payoff would be. Table 12.10 highlights the highest payoffs for each state of nature. If demand is six cases, the highest possible payoff would be $120. If the decision had been to produce six cases, then the profit would have been $120 and there would be a zero opportunity loss. If the decision had been made to produce seven cases but demand was only six, then the payoff would have been $90 but it could have been $120 with a different decision. Therefore, if demand is for six cases:

$$\text{opportunity loss (produce 7 cases)} = 120 - 90 = \$30$$

This means had a different selection been made, the profits could have been $30 higher than they would be if seven cases were produced. If demand is for six cases and eight cases are produced, then:

$$\text{opportunity loss (produce 8 cases)} = 120 - 60 = \$60$$

If the state of nature is a demand of seven cases, then the highest possible payoff is $140, and all payoffs are compared to this. If demand is eight cases, the highest possible payoff is $160, and all payoffs are compared to this. The calculations and resulting opportunity loss table is shown in Table 12.11.

When making decisions based on opportunity losses, two criteria are common. The minimax regret criterion is used when making decisions under uncertainty, and the expected opportunity loss criterion is used when making decisions under risk.

TABLE 12.11

Opportunity Loss Table for Nature in Fotochem Inc. Example

Alternatives	States of Nature: Demand is 6 cases	Demand is 7 cases	Demand is 8 cases
Produce 6 cases	120 – 120 = **0**	140 – 110 = **30**	160 – 100 = **60**
Produce 7 cases	120 – 90 = **30**	140 – 140 = **0**	160 – 130 = **30**
Produce 8 cases	120 – 60 = **60**	140 – 110 = **30**	160 –160 = **0**

Minimax Regret Criterion

Because a zero opportunity loss for a decision indicates the highest possible payoff was achieved for the particular state of nature that occurred, we would like the opportunity loss to be as low as possible. The minimax regret criterion is a somewhat pessimistic approach in that the consideration is for the maximum possible regret that may occur for each decision, and the selection is for the alternative with the lowest of these maximums. The term minimax regret indicates the selected alternative corresponds to the *mini*mum of the *max*imum regrets.

Table 12.12 shows the minimax regret criterion applied to the Fotochem, Inc. example. The maximum regrets are 60 for producing six cases, 30 for producing seven cases, and 60 for producing eight cases. The minimum of these maximums is 30, so choose to produce seven cases based

TABLE 12.12

Minimax Regret Criterion for Fotochem Inc. Example

Alternatives	States of Nature: Demand is 6 cases	Demand is 7 cases	Demand is 8 cases	Maximum
Produce 6 cases	0	30	60	60
Produce 7 cases	30	0	30	30*
Produce 8 cases	60	30	0	60

on the minimax regret criterion. This would mean that regardless of which state of nature occurs, the regret would be no more than 30, and it could be less.

It is interesting to note that while the maximin criterion used with payoff tables and the minimax regret criterion used with regret tables both take a pessimistic view, they lead to different decisions. Recall that when the pessimistic criterion was used, the decision was to produce six cases. This guaranteed the payoff achieved would be at least 100 regardless of the state of nature that occurs, although this decision could lead to a regret of 60 if demand is for eight cases. With the minimax regret criterion, the choice was to produce seven cases. This guarantees that regardless of the state of nature that occurs, the payoff will be within 30 of the best possible payoff, although this decision could lead to a payoff of only 90 if demand is for six cases. We see that the maximin criterion is pessimistic with regards to the actual payoff, while the minimax regret criterion is pessimistic with respect to the regret that might occur.

Expected Opportunity Loss (*EOL*)

A decision making criterion based on opportunity loss that may be used when probabilities are known is the minimum expected opportunity loss (*EOL*) criterion. As with expected values, the expected opportunity loss would represent the long run average opportunity loss that would be realized if a decision were repeated many times. In computing the *EOL* for each decision alternative, the opportunity losses are multiplied by the probabilities and added together. This is expressed as:

$$EOL(\text{alternative } i) = \Sigma(\text{opportunity loss})(\text{probability})$$
$$EOL(a_i) = \Sigma O_{ij}\, P(s_j)$$

where

$$O_{ij} = \text{regret for alternative } i \text{ in state of nature } j$$
$$P(s_j) = \text{probability of state of nature } j \text{ occurring}$$

Returning to the Fotochem, Inc. example, calculate the expected opportunity loss for each decision.

$$EOL(a_i) = \Sigma O_{ij}\, P(s_j) = O_{i1}\, P(s_1) + O_{i2}\, P(s_2) + O_{i3}\, P(s_3)$$
$$= O_{i1}\, 0.6 + O_{i2}\, 0.3 + O_{i3}\, 0.1$$

$$EOL(\text{produce 6 cases}) = 0(0.6) + 30(0.3) + 60(0.1) = 15$$
$$EOL(\text{produce 7 cases}) = 30(0.6) + 0(0.3) + 30(0.1) = 21$$
$$EOL(\text{produce 8 cases}) = 60(0.6) + 30(0.3) + 0(0.1) = 45$$

These are shown in Table 12.13. The minimum of these is 15, and thus the selection would be to produce six cases based on minimizing the expected opportunity loss. This 15 means the opportunity loss would average $15 in the long run if this decision is repeated numerous times.

TABLE 12.13

Expected Opportunity Loss Criterion for Fotochem, Inc. Example

	States of Nature			
Alternatives	**Demand is 6 cases (0.6)**	**Demand is 7 cases (0.3)**	**Demand is 8 cases (0.1)**	***EOL***
Produce 6 cases	0	30	60	15*
Produce 7 cases	30	0	30	21
Produce 8 cases	60	30	0	45

BEST PRACTICES

Decision Support for Library Budget Allocations

Every year, public libraries in the United States spend more than $850 million on the acquisition of new materials. Each library system must allocate a set budget across various categories. Traditionally, this has been a tedious process. Many calculations must be made, using data on circulation, acquisitions, stocks, turnover rates, and discards for the different categories of library materials. Two researchers from Indiana University developed a decision support system (DSS) that organizes this data, and uses it to produce materials acquisitions budgets.

The DSS allocates a library's budget across categories, with the objective of maximizing the expected use of the materials. It has four modules. The first is a database that compiles data and produces various statistics, such as mean per item cost and turnover rate (circulation/stock). The second module is a forecasting module that uses time series techniques to make cost and circulation forecasts. Next is a budget-allocation module that calculates trial budgets based on a linear programming algorithm. The LP model can be solved iteratively. It has provisions for setting bounds on deviations from the allocations of previous years and from "fair" allocations (proportional to the category's share of expected circulation). Finally, a scenario-testing module calculates future stock by budget category.

Boston Public Library/Courtesy of Shepley Bulfinch Richardson and Abbott

The staffs of two Indiana public library systems helped to develop the DSS. Librarians have used the system to allocate budgets for the Monroe County Public Library ($437, 854 in 1993). They found a process that traditionally took several days could be completed in about four hours with the new system. They also judged the results to be better than traditional budgets. Particularly pleasing was a projected 7.5 percent increase in expected use over what would have resulted from a traditional, incremental budget. Both the librarians and university professors expressed optimism about using and extending the model as more refined data becomes available.

SOURCE:

Gleeson M. E., and J. R. Ottensmann, 1994. "A Decision Support System for Acquisitions Budgeting in Public Libraries." *Interfaces* 24 (5): 107-117.

OUTPUT 12.1

DSS Output for Fotochem, Inc. Example

```
Decision Analysis

MAX            Demand 6       Demand 7       Demand 8
Prod. 6        120            110            100
Prod. 7        90             140            130
Prod. 8        60             110            160
Prob's         .6             .3             .1

Decisions under Uncertainty:

  * Criterion of Optimism (MaxiMax or MiniMin)
              Prod. 6          120
              Prod. 7          140
              Prod. 8          160          <<<Optimum

  * Criterion of Pessimism (MaxiMin or MiniMax)
              Prod. 6          100          <<<Optimum
              Prod. 7          90
              Prod. 8          60

  * Hurwicz Criterion (Alpha =  .7 )
              Prod. 6          114
              Prod. 7          125
              Prod. 8          130          <<<Optimum

  * Savage Criterion (MiniMax Regret)

  - Regret Matrix values
                             Demand 6       Demand 7       Demand 8
              Prod. 6         0              30             60
              Prod. 7         30             0              30
              Prod. 8         60             30             0
```

EVPI and Opportunity Loss

The minimum expected opportunity loss always will equal the EVPI. When the EVPI was calculated previously by calculating the expected value with perfect information and subtracting the best expected value without the information, a value of $15 also was obtained. Using the minimum *EOL* criterion always will result in the same decision as using the expected value criterion.

Computer Solutions

The DSS software may be used to perform the calculations for each of these decision making criteria. Output 12.1 provides an illustration of the output for the Fotochem, Inc. example. The EVPI may be obtained in this output from the minimum expected value of regret (minimum *EOL*).

OUTPUT 12.1

```
               Prod. 6        60
               Prod. 7        30            <<<Optimum
               Prod. 8        60

Decisions under Risk:

  * Laplace Criterion (all outcomes equally likely)

    Optimize Expected Value of Payoff
               Prod. 6        110
               Prod. 7        120           <<<Optimum
               Prod. 8        110

    Minimize Expected Value of Regret
               Prod. 6        30
               Prod. 7        20            <<<Optimum
               Prod. 8        30

  * Expected Value Criterion (probabilities given in input)

    Optimize Expected Value of Payoff
               Prod. 6        115           <<<Optimum
               Prod. 7        109
               Prod. 8        85

    Minimize Expected Value of Regret
               Prod. 6        15            <<<Optimum
               Prod. 7        21
               Prod. 8        45
```

12.9 MARGINAL ANALYSIS

For inventory problems similar to the Fotochem, Inc. example, we often have many possible alternatives. In that example, we assumed demand would be six, seven, or eight cases. In some situations demand might be any value from zero to 20 or more. With a large number of alternatives it often is helpful to use **marginal analysis** to determine the best alternative. In using marginal analysis, we are facing a situation in which we must decide how many units to produce or stock, and once this decision is made, additional units may not be obtained. If only six units are produced but demand is for eight units, the number that will be sold is only six.

With marginal analysis, assume units that are not sold result in a **marginal loss.** Units that are produced and sold result in a **marginal profit.**

The basic reasoning in marginal analysis is that additional units should be produced as long as the expected value of adding one more unit is positive. If the expected value of adding an additional unit is negative, then

Marginal analysis
A method for determining which alternative will yield the maximum expected payoff by comparing the marginal profit of selling an additional unit with the marginal loss that is incurred if a unit is stocked but not sold.

Marginal loss
The loss incurred when one additional unit is produced but not sold.

Marginal profit
The additional profit generated by selling one additional unit.

producing the extra unit reduces the expected profit, so it cannot be the best alternative. Begin by defining the following:

$$MP = \text{marginal profit of selling one more unit}$$
$$ML = \text{marginal loss if additional unit is not sold}$$
$$p = \text{probability of selling additional unit}$$
$$1 - p = \text{probability of not selling additional unit}$$

Using this notation, create the payoff table shown in Table 12.14 to determine whether or not to stock one additional unit. Notice the marginal loss is indicated as negative profit by using $-ML$ in the payoff table. The decision rule is to stock an additional unit if:

$$\text{EV(stock unit)} \geq \text{EV(do not stock)}$$
$$pMP + (1 - p)(-ML) \geq 0$$

Solving this for p results in:

$$p \geq ML/(ML + MP)$$

We will keep adding an additional unit as long as the probability of selling that additional unit is at least $ML/(ML + MP)$.

Sunrise Donuts Example

Sunrise Donuts makes donuts at a bakery each morning, and some of these are taken on a truck to be sold at numerous construction sites in the city. Because these sites are not close to the shop, it is not possible to return to

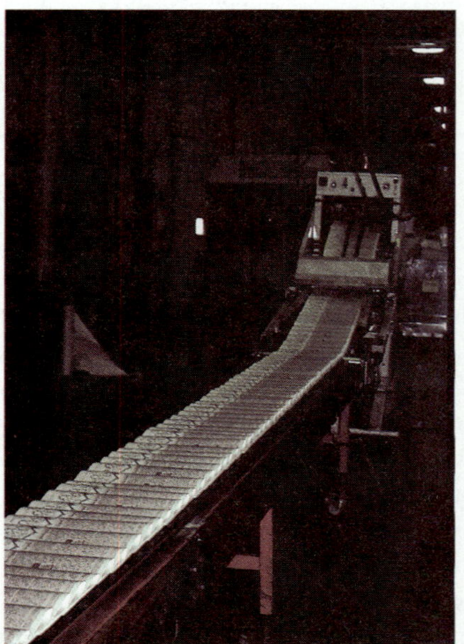

Marginal analysis can be used to help determine the number of newspapers to print each day. Papers not sold result in a marginal loss because they have little value the next day. SOURCE: Abigail Reip

TABLE 12.14

Payoff Table Illustrating Marginal Analysis

	States of nature		
Alternatives	**Sell unit** p	**Do not sell unit** $1 - p$	***EV***
Stock additional unit	*MP*	*−ML*	$p(MP) + (1 - p)(-ML)$
Do not stock unit	0	0	0

the shop for additional donuts if the demand exceeds the number available on the truck. Due to a reputation for freshness, Sunrise Donuts will not sell any donuts left on the truck after deliveries are made. The manager must decide how many donuts to put on the truck each morning.

Past records indicate demand will be at least 20 dozen but no more than 30 dozen. The demand pattern is shown in Table 12.15. The cost to manufacture one dozen donuts is \$2.00 and the selling price is \$5.00 per dozen. Therefore \$2 for each box of donuts that doesn't sell is lost, and a profit of \$3 is made for each one that does sell. Thus:

$$\text{marginal loss} = ML = 2$$
$$\text{marginal profit} = MP = 3$$

TABLE 12.15

Demand for Donuts in Sunrise Donuts Example

Demand (Dozens)	Probability
20	0.05
21	0.08
22	0.10
23	0.12
24	0.16
25	0.18
26	0.11
27	0.08
28	0.06
29	0.04
30	0.02

The decision rule is to continue putting donuts on the truck as long as:

$$p \geq ML/(ML + MP)$$

or

$$p \geq 2/(2 + 3) = 2/5 = 0.40$$

An additional dozen donuts will be put on the truck as long as the demand for an additional dozen is more than 0.40. Table 12.16 shows the probability that demand would be sufficient to sell the various quantities. For example, if 28 dozen are stocked, these will all sell if demand is for 28, 29, or 30. The probability that demand is 28 or more is:

$$\begin{aligned} P(\text{demand} \geq 28) &= P(\text{demand} = 28) + P(\text{demand} = 29) + P(\text{demand} = 30) \\ &= 0.06 + 0.04 + 0.02 = 0.12 \end{aligned}$$

Because we wish the probability to be at least 0.40, producing 28 dozen would be too many. Looking at the other probabilities, we would stock 25 dozen for which the probability is 0.49 that demand will be at least this high. If we stock 26 dozen, there is only a 0.31 probability that the last box would sell, so this is too many and we should only stock 25.

While this discussion of marginal analysis has focused on a discrete distribution of demand, the same concept applies to demand patterns described by continuous distributions as well.

Marginal Analysis and the Normal Distribution

Often the demand for a product is approximately normally distributed. If past sales data indicates this is true, the mean and the standard deviation are used to find the demand that yields a probability that is at least *ML/(ML + MP)*. Consider the following example.

TABLE 12.16

Probabilities for Sales in Sunrise Donuts Example

Demand (Dozens)	Probability	Probability that Demand is at Least this Level
20	0.05	1.00
21	0.08	0.95
22	0.10	0.87
23	0.12	0.77
24	0.16	0.65
25	0.18	0.49
		← 0.40
26	0.11	0.31
27	0.08	0.20
28	0.06	0.12
29	0.04	0.06
30	0.02	0.02

The *City Daily News* is trying to determine how many newspapers to produce for sale in vending machines and at newsstands. Past records of sales indicate the demand pattern has been normally distributed with a mean of 20,000 and a standard deviation of 3,000. The cost of producing a paper is eight cents and each paper sells for 25 cents. How many papers should *City Daily News* produce each day for the nonsubscription sales?

Using a marginal analysis approach results in:

$$ML = 8$$
$$MP = 25 - 8 = 17$$

Papers should be produced as long as:

$$p \geq ML/(ML + MP)$$

or

$$p \geq 8/(8 + 17) = 8/25 = 0.32$$

Demand is normally distributed with:

$$\mu = 20{,}000$$
$$\sigma = 3{,}000$$

Figure 12.1 shows the normal distribution for this situation. If there is to be a 32 percent chance demand will exceed the number produced, there will be a 68 percent chance demand will be less than this amount. Find a Z-value for this using the table at the end of the book and look for a probability of 0.68. This Z-value is:

$$Z = 0.47$$

Thus:

$$\text{number of papers} = \mu + Z\sigma = 20{,}000 + 0.47(3{,}000) = 21{,}410$$

FIGURE 12.1

Normal Distribution for *City Daily News* Example

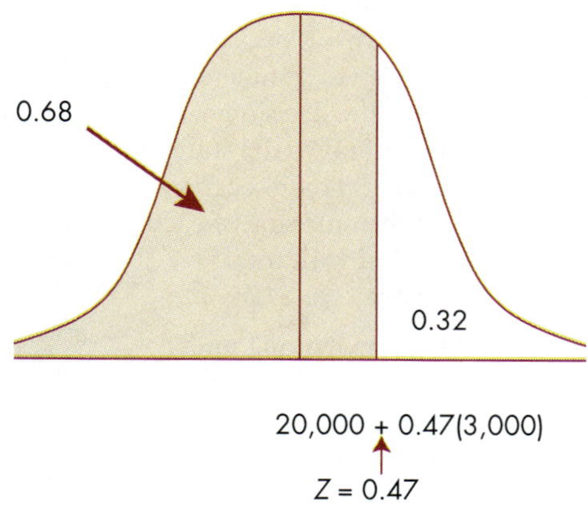

Therefore, *City Daily News* should produce 21,410 papers each day to maximize the long run average profits. However, management may wish to consider other important factors, such as advertising revenues and the impact of stockouts on future demand, when making the final decision.

12.10 SUMMARY

In this chapter we considered decision making under three environments—certainty, uncertainty, and risk. Several criteria were discussed for making decisions using a payoff table and an opportunity loss table.

For making decisions under uncertainty where the payoff is to be maximized, the following criteria may be used when making decisions under uncertainty: optimistic (maximax), pessimistic (maximin), Hurwicz, and equally likely (LaPlace). When probabilities are known, the decision making environment is risk, and the expected value criterion was used to maximize the long run average payoffs.

In comparing the possible payoffs to the best payoff for each state of nature, an opportunity loss table was created. With this, the minimax regret criterion was used when making decisions under uncertainty, and the expected opportunity loss criterion was used when making decisions under risk.

When using the expected value criteria, the expected value of perfect information was examined as a measure of the worth of a perfect forecast of the future. This may be found from the payoff table or the opportunity loss table.

Marginal analysis was seen as being helpful when making a decision regarding the number of units to produce if there is a large number of possible demand values.

GLOSSARY

Alternative A possible choice that the decision maker may select. *p. 508*

Coefficient of optimism (α) Used with the Hurwicz criterion, this is a measure of the degree of optimism that the decision maker possesses. *p. 514*

Decision making under uncertainty A decision making environment in which the decision maker does not know and cannot assign probabilities to the various states of nature. *p. 512*

Decision making under certainty A decision making environment in which the decision maker knows the state of nature that will occur and the outcome of each decision with total certainty. *p. 512*

Decision making under risk A decision making environment in which the decision maker can assign probabilities to the various states of nature. *p. 512*

Decision making environment The conditions surrounding a decision making situation that determine how much information the decision maker has about the state of nature that will occur. Three environments are certainty, uncertainty, and risk. *p. 512*

Equally likely (LaPlace) criterion A decision

making criterion in which each state of nature is assumed to have the same likelihood of occurring. The alternative with the highest average payoff is selected. *p. 515*

Expected value (EV) The long run average value that would occur if a decision were repeated a large number of times. *p. 518*

Expected value with perfect information The long run average payoff that would be achieved if perfect information about the future were available. *p. 520*

Expected opportunity loss (*EOL*) The long run average opportunity loss that would be achieved if a decision were repeated a large number of times. *p. 521*

Expected value of perfect information (EVPI) The increase in expected value that would result from having perfect information. This is the difference between the expected value with perfect information and the best expected value without perfect information. *p. 520*

Hurwicz criterion A decision making criterion in which a weighted average of the best and the worst possible payoffs for each decision is used. *p. 514*

Marginal analysis A method for determining which alternative will yield the maximum expected payoff by comparing the marginal profit of selling an additional unit with the marginal loss that is incurred if a unit is stocked but not sold. *p. 527*

Marginal loss The loss incurred when one additional unit is produced but not sold. *p. 527*

Marginal profit The additional profit generated by selling one additional unit. *p. 527*

Minimax regret criterion A decision making criterion in which the maximum regret for each alternative is considered, and the alternative with the minimum of these maximums is selected. *p. 521*

Opportunity loss The difference between the best possible payoff for a particular state of nature and the payoff that actually would be achieved for the decision being considered. *p. 521*

Optimistic (maximax) criterion A decision making criterion in which only the best (maximum) payoff for each decision is considered, and the alternative with the best (maximum) of these best payoffs is selected. *p. 513*

Payoff The actual measure of performance that is achieved when a particular alternative is selected and a specific state of nature occurs. *p. 508*

Payoff table A table that lists the alternatives, states of nature, and payoffs for a decision making situation. *p. 508*

Pessimistic (maximin) criterion A decision making criterion in which only the worst (minimum) payoff for each decision is considered, and the alternative with the best (maximum) of these worst payoffs is selected. *p. 514*

Regret An opportunity loss. *p. 521*

State of nature An event or occurrence over which the decision maker has no control. *p. 508*

KEY EQUATIONS

(12-1) Expected value criterion for decision making under risk

a_i = alternative i

s_j = state of nature j

V_{ij} = value of payoff for alternative i in state of nature j

$EV(\text{alternative } i) = \sum \text{Payoff}(\text{probability})$

$$EV(a_i) = \sum V_{ij}\, P(s_j)$$

(12-2) Expected Value with Perfect Information

EV with PI = Σ(best payoff for state of nature)(probability)

Expected Value of Perfect Information (EVPI)

EVPI = EV with PI – best EV without PI

(12-3) Expected opportunity loss (EOL)

EOL(alternative i) = Σ(opportunity loss)(probability)

$EOL(a_i) = \Sigma O_{ij} P(s_j)$

O_{ij} = regret for alternative i in state of nature j

$P(s_j)$ = probability of state of nature j occurring

EVPI = Minimum EOL

(12-4) Marginal analysis

MP = marginal profit of adding one more unit

ML = marginal loss if additional unit is not sold

p = probability of selling additional unit

$1 - p$ = probability of not selling additional unit

$p \geq ML/(ML + MP)$

SOLVED PROBLEMS

SOLVED PROBLEM 12-1

An investor is considering four possible investment options. The state of the economy next year will have an impact on the return on some of these investments. The anticipated payoffs for each of these are given in the table below.

	States of Economy			
Alternatives	Poor	Fair	Good	Very Good
#1	–200	100	200	300
#2	20	20	20	20
#3	200	30	–100	–200
#4	–40	80	150	200

a) What decision would result from the use of each of the following criteria: optimistic, pessimistic, Hurwicz (with $\alpha = 0.6$), and equally likely?

b) If the probabilities for the possible states of the economy are 0.2 for poor, 0.4 for fair, 0.3 for good, and 0.1 for very good, what decision would be made to maximize the expected profits?

c) Using the probabilities in part (b) above, what is the expected value of perfect information?

SOLUTION

a) Optimistic criterion

	States of Economy				
Alternatives	Poor	Fair	Good	Very Good	Maximum
#1	–200	100	200	300	300
#2	20	20	20	20	20
#3	200	30	–100	–200	200
#4	–40	80	150	200	200

Choose #1

Pessimistic criterion

	States of Economy				
Alternatives	Poor	Fair	Good	Very Good	Minimum
#1	–200	100	200	300	–200
#2	20	20	20	20	20
#3	200	30	–100	–200	–200
#4	–40	80	150	200	–40

Choose #2

Hurwicz $\alpha = 0.6$

	States of Economy				
Alternatives	Poor	Fair	Good	Very Good	α(best) + (1 – α)(worst)
#1	–200	100	200	300	0.6(300) + 0.4(–200) = 100
#2	20	20	20	20	0.6(20) + 0.4(20) = 20
#3	200	30	–100	–200	0.6(200) + 0.4(–200) = 40
#4	–40	80	150	200	0.6(200) + 0.4(–40) = 104

Choose #4

Equally likely

	States of Economy				
Alternatives	Poor	Fair	Good	Very Good	Average Payoff
#1	–200	100	200	300	(–200 + 100 + 200 + 300)/4 = 100
#2	20	20	20	20	(20 + 20 + 20 + 20)/4 = 20
#3	200	30	–100	–200	(200 + 30 – 100 – 200)/4 = –17.5
#4	–40	80	150	200	(–40 + 80 + 150 + 200)/4 = 97.5

Choose #1

b) Expected value

	States of Economy			
Alternatives	Poor 0.2	Fair 0.4	Good 0.3	Very Good 0.1
#1	–200	100	200	300
#2	20	20	20	20
#3	200	30	–100	–200
#4	–40	80	150	200

EV(#1) = 0.2(–200) + 0.4(100) + 0.3(200) + 0.1(300) = 90
EV(#2) = 0.2(20) + 0.4(20) + 0.3(20) + 0.1(20) = 20
EV(#3) = 0.2(200) + 0.4(30) + 0.3(–100) + 0.1(–200) = 2
EV(#4) = 0.2(–40) + 0.4(80) + 0.3(150) + 0.1(200) = 89

Choose #1

c) Expected value of perfect information

	States of Economy			
Alternatives	Poor 0.2	Fair 0.4	Good 0.3	Very Good 0.1
#1	–200	100	200	300
#2	20	20	20	20
#3	200	30	–100	–200
#4	–40	80	150	200
with PI	200	100	200	300

EV(with PI) = 0.2(200) + 0.4(100) + 0.3(200) + 0.1(300) = 170

EVPI = EV(with PI) – best EV = 170 – 90 = 80

SOLVED PROBLEM 12-2

Use the payoff table from Solved Problem 12-1 and answer the following questions:
a) Construct an opportunity loss table for the payoff table given above.
b) What decision would be made if the minimax regret criterion were used?
c) What decision would be made if the minimum expected opportunity loss criterion were used?

SOLUTION

a) Opportunity loss table

	States of Economy			
Alternatives	Poor	Fair	Good	Very Good
#1	400	0	0	0
#2	180	80	180	280
#3	0	70	300	500
#4	240	20	50	100

b) Minimax regret criterion

Alternatives	States of Economy				
	Poor	Fair	Good	Very Good	Maximum
#1	400	0	0	0	400
#2	180	80	180	280	280
#3	0	70	300	500	500
#4	240	20	50	100	240

Choose #4

c) Minimum *EOL* criterion

	States of Economy				
Alternatives	Poor 0.2	Fair 0.4	Good 0.3	Very Good 0.1	*EOL*
#1	400	0	0	0	80
#2	180	80	180	280	150
#3	0	70	300	500	168
#4	240	20	50	100	81

$EOL(\#1) = 0.2(400) + 0.4(0) + 0.3(0) + 0.1(0) = 80$
$EOL(\#2) = 0.2(180) + 0.4(80) + 0.3(180) + 0.1(280) = 150$
$EOL(\#3) = 0.2(0) + 0.4(70) + 0.3(300) + 0.1(500) = 168$
$EOL(\#4) = 0.2(240) + 0.4(20) + 0.3(50) + 0.1(100) = 81$

Choose #1

QUESTIONS

1. Describe how a payoff table is constructed.
2. How does decision making under uncertainty differ from decision making under risk?
3. An optimistic manager has selected a particular alternative because the maximum profit for that decision was \$15,000. Does this mean the profit for this one decision will be \$15,000? Explain.
4. The worst payoff for a particular decision is \$500. This decision was made based on the maximin criterion. Explain what this \$500 means.
5. Explain what using the word *expected* with expected value or expected payoff or expected profit actually means.
6. What is the expected value of perfect information and how is it calculated from a payoff table?
7. What is opportunity loss and how is it calculated?
8. How may an opportunity loss table be used to determine the expected value of perfect information?
9. Give an example in which the equally likely criterion would not be appropriate.
10. An alternative was selected based on the minimax criterion. The maximum regret for that decision alternative was \$100. Explain what this means.

PROBLEMS

11. Consider the following payoff table where the payoffs represent profits:

	States of Nature		
Decision Alternatives	A	B	C
#1	40	50	20
#2	30	30	30
#3	–10	60	80

a) What decision would be made based on the optimistic criterion?
b) What decision would be made based on the pessimistic criterion?
c) What decision would be made based on the equally likely criterion?
d) What decision would be made based on the Hurwicz criterion with a coefficient of optimism of 0.3?

12. Using the payoff table in Problem 11, suppose the probabilities of the three states of nature are:

$$P(A) = 0.2$$
$$P(B) = 0.3$$
$$P(C) = 0.5$$

a) What decision would be made based on the expected value criterion? What are the expected profits for this decision?
b) If a perfect forecast of the future were available and were used, what would the expected profits be?
c) Calculate the expected value of perfect information.

13. Use the payoff table in Problem 11 to answer the following:
a) What would the opportunity loss be if a person selected alternative #2 and state of nature B occurred?
b) Construct the opportunity loss table.
c) What decision would be made using the minimax regret criterion?
d) If the probabilities of states of nature A, B, and C are 0.2, 0.3, and 0.5 respectively, as in Problem 12, what decision would be made using the expected opportunity loss criterion?
e) What is the expected value of perfect information?

14. Consider the following payoff table where the payoffs represent profits:

	States of Nature		
Decision Alternatives	s_1	s_2	s_3
#1	120	60	–20
#2	90	80	100
#3	81	81	81
#4	–50	90	110

The probabilities for the states of nature are:

$$P(s_1) = 0.8$$
$$P(s_2) = 0.1$$
$$P(s_3) = 0.1$$

a) Without using any specific criterion other than your own intuition, does alternative #2 appear to be a good choice? Why or why not?
b) What decision would be made based on the optimistic criterion?
c) What decision would be made based on the pessimistic criterion?
d) What decision would be made based on the expected value criterion?
e) Develop the opportunity loss table and use the minimax regret criterion to find the best decision. Compare this to your answer in part (a) of this problem.

15. Consider the following payoff table:

Decision Alternatives	States of Nature s_1	s_2
#1	100	–20
#2	60	40
Probability	0.5	0.5

a) Calculate the expected value for each alternative.
b) Suppose the profit for alternative #1 in state of nature s_1 is not \$100. What is the smallest this profit could be that would cause a person to select alternative #1 based on the expected value criterion?

16. The following payoff table gives the profits that would be realized for three investment alternatives:

Decision Alternatives	States of Nature Good Economy	Poor Economy
Stock Market	80,000	–20,000
Bonds	30,000	20,000
CDs	23,000	23,000
Probability	0.5	0.5

a) What decision would maximize expected profits?
b) What is the maximum amount that should be paid for a perfect forecast of the economy?
c) Suppose the probabilities given above are not considered accurate. If the expected value criterion is used, what probability of a good economy would cause a person to be indifferent between the first two alternatives (i.e., the expected value for stock would equal the expected value for bonds)?

17. Consider the following payoff table where the payoffs represent profits:

Decision Alternatives	States of Nature A	States of Nature B
#1	100	20
#2	90	30

a) What decision would be made based on the optimistic criterion?
b) Suppose the payoff for alternative #1 with state of nature B was changed from 20 to –1,000. What decision would be made based on the optimistic criterion?
c) Using the original payoffs for alternative #1, suppose the payoff for alternative #2 in state of nature B was 90. What decision would be made based on the optimistic criterion?
d) Looking at the answers to parts (a), (b), and (c), what is a major weakness of the optimistic criterion?

18. Consider the following payoff table where the payoffs represent profits:

Decision Alternatives	States of Nature A	States of Nature B
#1	100	20
#2	90	30

a) What decision would be made based on the Hurwicz criterion with $\alpha = 0.6$?
b) Suppose the payoff for alternative #1 with state of nature B were changed from 20 to –1,000. What decision would be made based on the Hurwicz criterion with $\alpha = 0.6$?
c) Using the original payoffs for alternative #1, suppose the payoff for alternative #2 in state of nature B was 90. What decision would be made based on the Hurwicz criterion with $\alpha = 0.6$?

19. Consider the following payoff table where the payoffs represent profits:

Decision Alternatives	States of Nature A	States of Nature B
#1	100	20
#2	90	25

a) What decision would be made based on the pessimistic criterion?
b) Suppose the payoff for alternative #1 with state of nature A was changed from 100 to 10,000. What decision would be made based on the pessimistic criterion?
c) Using the original payoffs for alternative #1, suppose the payoff for alternative #2 in state of nature A was 25. What decision would be made based on the pessimistic criterion?

d) Looking at the answers to parts (a), (b), and (c), what is a major weakness of the pessimistic criterion?

20. Consider the following payoff table where the payoffs represent profits:

Decision Alternatives	States of Nature A	States of Nature B
#1	100	20
#2	90	25

a) What decision would be made based on the Hurwicz criterion with $\alpha = 0.4$?
b) Suppose the payoff for alternative #1 with state of nature A was changed from 100 to 10,000. What decision would be made based on the Hurwicz criterion with $\alpha = 0.4$?
c) Using the original payoffs for alternative #1, suppose the payoff for alternative #2 in state of nature A was 25. What decision would be made based on the Hurwicz criterion with $\alpha = 0.4$?

21. In the Sunrise Donuts example in this chapter, it was determined that 25 dozen donuts should be stocked. There is a 0.49 probability all 25 dozen will be sold and a marginal profit of $3 will be achieved on the last dozen. This means there is a 0.51 probability a marginal loss of $2 will be incurred on this last dozen.
a) Calculate the expected marginal profit and the expected marginal loss for the 25th dozen produced.
b) Is the expected marginal profit for the 25th dozen higher than the expected marginal loss for that last dozen?
c) Suppose 26 dozen donuts were stocked. What would be the probability of selling the 26th case?
d) Calculate the expected marginal profit and the expected marginal loss for the 26th dozen produced. Which of these is higher? What does this mean to management?

22. Each morning, daily newspapers are placed in an automatic vending machine. The newspaper costs 10 cents to manufacture and sells for 25 cents each. Any newspapers not sold by the end of the day are of little value and are sent for recycling. If the newspapers are all sold, the machine is not replenished until the next day. In the past, on 40 percent of the days demand has been for 15 newspapers, on 40 percent of the days demand has been for 16 newspapers, and on 20 percent of the days demand has been for 17 newspapers.
a) Develop a payoff table for this situation.
b) What decision making criterion should be used with this situation? Why?
c) Which alternative should be selected based on the expected value criterion?

23. Returning to the newspaper situation in the previous problem, suppose the demand in the past has been as low as 10 and as high as 19. Management is currently in the process of collecting information about the probabilities for the different demand levels. Using marginal analysis, develop a decision rule that management may use to determine how many newspapers to put in the machine once the probabilities are known.

24. Sal's Pizza specializes in a thick crust pizza that requires special procedures. The dough used for the crust must be prepared and allowed to sit for at least 12 hours before it is cooked. Therefore, at the end of each day, dough is prepared for use the next day. Anything not used must be discarded at the end of the day.

In the past the demand for this type of pizza has been from 10 to 20 pizzas. The cost of preparing the dough is $1, while the profit generated by each of these pizzas is $4. Based on history, the following probabilities have been developed:

Demand	Probability
10	0.03
11	0.05
12	0.11
13	0.12
14	0.17
15	0.17
16	0.14
17	0.10
18	0.07
19	0.03
20	0.01

a) Using marginal analysis, develop a decision rule that will tell Sal how to plan for the next day.
b) Based on the decision rule in part (a), how much dough should Sal prepare each day?
c) Using marginal analysis guarantees the long run average (expected) profits will be maximized assuming the probabilities are correct. Why might a manager want to prepare more dough than the amount based on the marginal analysis? (*Hint:* Think about the impact of stockouts on these probabilities in the future.)

25. Marcus Incerto inherited some land recently and is trying to determine what to do with it. Due to personal financial conditions, Marcus knows he will be unable to hold onto this property for an extended period of time. He has been offered $200,000 for the land and may accept this offer. Another option he is considering is the development of a small apartment complex. Marcus intends to sell the complex once it is complete. If demand for apartments is high and the complex is fully occupied when he sells it, he would make a profit of $400,000. However, if demand for apartments in the future is low, he will be forced to sell at a loss of $50,000. He believes there is a 60 percent chance that demand for apartments will be high and he will make $400,000, and he believes there is only a 40 percent chance demand will be low and he will lose $50,000.
a) What should Marcus do if he wishes to maximize his expected profits?
b) Do you believe the expected value criterion is the appropriate criterion for Marcus to use? Explain.
c) If it were possible to use market research to obtain a perfect forecast of future market conditions, how much should Marcus be willing to pay?

d) Suppose the estimated profit of $400,000 is not correct. What is the smallest this value could be that would cause Marcus to build the complex based on the expected value criterion?

26. Forever Life Insurance Company sells a term life insurance policy. If the policy holder dies during the year of the policy, the company pays $100,000. If the person does not die, the company pays out nothing and there is no further value to the policy. The company uses actuarial tables to determine the probability a person with certain characteristics will die during the coming year. For a particular type of individual, it is determined there is a 0.001 chance the person will die and the company will pay out $100,000. There is a 0.999 chance that the person will live and the company will pay out nothing.

    a) What is the expected payout for the insurance company for this type of policy?

    b) Suppose Forever Life Insurance has determined that the overhead costs and profit for each policy should be $75. How much should the company charge as the premium for this policy?

ANALYSIS IN ACTION

Study Time

Raquel Covington is a graduate student majoring in environmental management. In one particular class, Raquel has maintained a low A average throughout the semester, and she needs an A or a high B on the final exam to receive an A as the final grade in the course. In this course, three cases were added to the reading assignment in the last week of class, and the instructor has said there will be a 25 point question on the final exam related to one of these cases. The instructor has given no indication about which case is most likely to be included on the exam. Unexpected travel for a job interview has limited Raquel's study time in preparing for final exams, and she has not had time to read these cases. She feels prepared for the other material to be covered on this exam, and based on her experience on the other tests, she believes she will miss at most 10 points on questions related to this other material.

There are three hours remaining before the final exam in this course begins. Raquel is considering three study strategies related to the cases she has not read. The first strategy is to spend one hour on each case. She believes this will enable her to get 10 out of the possible 25 points regardless of which case is included on the exam. Another strategy is to select two of the three cases and spend one hour and thirty minutes on each. She believes this will enable her to get 15 out of a possible 25 points if either of these two cases is on the exam. If the third case is on the exam, she will get zero points. A third strategy is to spend all three hours studying one case. If she does this and the case she studies is on the exam, she believes she will get all 25 points. If it is not selected, she will get zero points.

Analyze this situation using techniques discussed in this chapter. Prepare a brief report indicating what you believe Raquel Covington should do in preparing for this exam. Include an indication of any assumptions upon which your recommendation is based.

Expected Value Criterion Spreadsheet Example

An investor has the opportunity to invest in one of three mutual funds. The stock market will either rise, go down, or stay the same. Determine which investment should be selected using the expected value criterion. Find the expected value of sample information and the expected opportunity loss for each decision.

The payoff table giving the return on investment for each fund is given below:

	State of nature Market movement		
Decision	**up**	**stay same**	**down**
Fund 1	32	15	5
Fund 2	24	18	6
Fund 3	18	16	8

	A	B	C	D	E
1					
2	Expected Value Criterion Example				
3					
4		Return on investment			
5		States of nature: market movement			
6					
7	decision	up	stay same	down	EV
8	fund 1	32	15	5	13.4
9	fund 2	24	18	6	13.2
10	fund 3	18	16	8	12.4
11					
12	probability	0.2	0.3	0.5	
13	with perfect information	32	18	8	15.8
14					
15	Expected value of perfect information =				2.4
16					
17		Opportunity loss table			
18	decision	up	stay same	down	EOL
19	fund 1	0	3	3	2.4
20	fund 2	8	0	2	2.6
21	fund 3	14	2	0	3.4

	A	B	C	D	E
1					
2	Expected Value				
3	Criterion Example				
4		Return on investment			
5		States of nature: market movement			
6					
7	decision	up	stay same	down	EV
8	fund 1	32	15	5	=$B$12*B8+$C$12*C8+$D$12*D8
9	fund 2	24	18	6	=$B$12*B9+$C$12*C9+$D$12*D9
10	fund 3	18	16	8	=$B$12*B10+$C$12*C10+$D$12*D10
11					
12	probability	0.2	0.3	0.5	
13	with perfect information	=MAX(B8:B10)	=MAX(C8:C10)	=MAX(D8:D10)	=$B$12*B13+$C$12*C13+$D$12*D13
14					
15	EV of perfect information =				=+E13-MAX(E8:E10)
16					
17		Opportunity loss table			
18	decision	up	stay same	down	EOL
19	fund 1	=+$B$13-B8	=+$C$13-C8	=+$D$13-D8	=$B$12*B19+$C$12*C19+$D$12*D19
20	fund 2	=+$B$13-B9	=+$C$13-C9	=+$D$13-D9	=$B$12*B20+$C$12*C20+$D$12*D20
21	fund 3	=+$B$13-B10	=+$C$13-C10	=+$D$13-D10	=$B$12*B21+$C$12*C21+$D$12*D21

CHAPTER THIRTEEN

Decision Models II

LEARNING OBJECTIVES

Upon completing Chapter 13, you should be able to:

- Construct a decision tree and use this tree to analyze problems.
- Understand prior and posterior probabilities.
- Use the Bayes Theorem to revise probabilities.
- Understand the concept of utility.
- Know how to assign utilities to payoffs.
- Understand how expected utilities are used to aid in decision making.
- Develop pairwise comparison matrices to be used with the analytic hierarchy process (AHP).
- Understand the process of normalizing a comparison matrix in AHP.
- Use AHP to aid in decision making.

CHAPTER OUTLINE

13.1 INTRODUCTION

In the previous chapter we investigated some basic decision models and used payoff tables and opportunity loss tables to help in making decisions. In this chapter, we will see that decision trees may be used instead of payoff tables. These trees are particularly helpful when a sequence of decisions is to be made.

In the previous chapter we calculated the expected value of perfect information. In this chapter, we will consider how sample or imperfect information may be incorporated into the decision making process, and we will calculate the expected value of this sample information.

There are occasions when people make decisions that at first appear to be irrational based on expected value or expected profits. We will see how utility theory helps to explain why these decisions are made and why they are not irrational or inconsistent.

With the decision making criteria that have been considered previously, a single payoff or factor was considered. However, there are many situations in which several payoffs or factors are important in the decision making process. We will briefly look at how we might incorporate several of these into the decision making process.

13.2 EXAMPLE

Primetime Properties is a real estate development firm in the Southwest (U.S.). In the last 10 years, Primetime has been a major part of over 300 real estate projects with investments ranging from \$200,000 to over \$3,000,000. Currently management of Primetime is considering building an apartment complex on a particular parcel of land. If Primetime builds a large apartment complex, the profit is projected to be \$200,000 if the market is good when the project is finished. If economic conditions cause the market to be poor, Primetime will lose \$100,000. A smaller apartment complex also is being considered. This smaller complex will yield a profit of \$80,000 in a good market and a profit of \$50,000 in a poor market.

Additional market research is being considered by the firm, but the cost of this would be \$10,000. Data from past projects indicates the market research is quite accurate, although there have been times when it proved to be less than perfect. There have been times when the market research indicated or predicted a good market when the market actually turned out poor. On a few occasions, the market research predicted a poor market, and the market turned out to be good. Without this additional information, the probability of a good market is estimated to be 0.50 while the probability of a poor market is estimated to be 0.50. Management at Primetime Properties must decide whether or not to perform the market research and what to do with this property.

13.3 DECISION TREES

A **decision tree** may be used in place of a payoff table to help in the decision making process. All the information contained in a payoff table is included on a decision tree. In constructing a decision tree, a square or box is used to represent a decision point where a decision is made. Lines or branches on the tree starting at these decision points represent the alternatives from which the decision maker must choose. A circle is used to represent an event where one of several states of nature must occur. Lines or branches on the tree starting at these event nodes represent the states of nature that may occur. The decision points and the event points are often referred to as **nodes** on the tree. Figure 13.1 illustrates the basic structure of a decision tree.

Decision tree
A graphical representation of a decision making situation. This is particularly helpful when a sequence of decisions is to be made.

Nodes
Points on decision trees representing decision points or events.

Primetime Properties Decision Tree

Returning to the Primetime Properties example, let's first analyze the situation without the possibility of obtaining additional information using market research. The techniques in the previous chapter could be used to develop a payoff table for this as shown in Table 13.1. Building the large complex will be designated as Alternative a_1 and building the small complex as Alternative a_2. A good market will be designated as State of Nature s_1 while a poor market will be designated as State of Nature s_2. This also may be represented by a decision tree as will be illustrated.

FIGURE 13.1

Basic Structure of Decision Tree

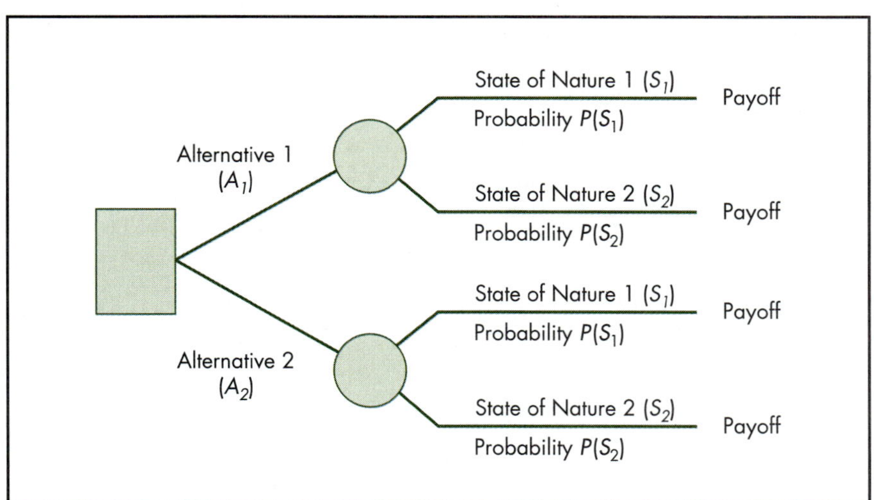

TABLE 13.1

Payoff Table for Primetime Properties

Alternatives	States of Nature Good Market (s_1)	Poor Market (s_2)	Expected Value
Build Large Complex (a_1)	200,000	−100,000	50,000 = EV(a_1)
Build Small Complex (a_2)	80,000	50,000	65,000 = EV(a_2)
Probability	$P(s_1) = 0.5$	$P(s_2) = 0.5$	

In drawing this tree, put the first decision point at the left of the page and, moving to the right, draw branches representing the possible alternatives. At the end of each branch have either an event point, another decision point, or a payoff. In our example, one branch represents the alternative of building a large apartment complex and one branch represents building a small apartment complex. At the end of these branches an event node is used because after building the complex, we would wait to see what state of nature would occur. Two branches representing the states of nature are drawn from this event node, and the probabilities are included for these states of nature. The payoffs are then put at the ends of the branches and the decision tree is complete as shown in Figure 13.2. We are ready to use this to perform our analysis.

FIGURE 13.2

Decision Tree for Primetime Properties

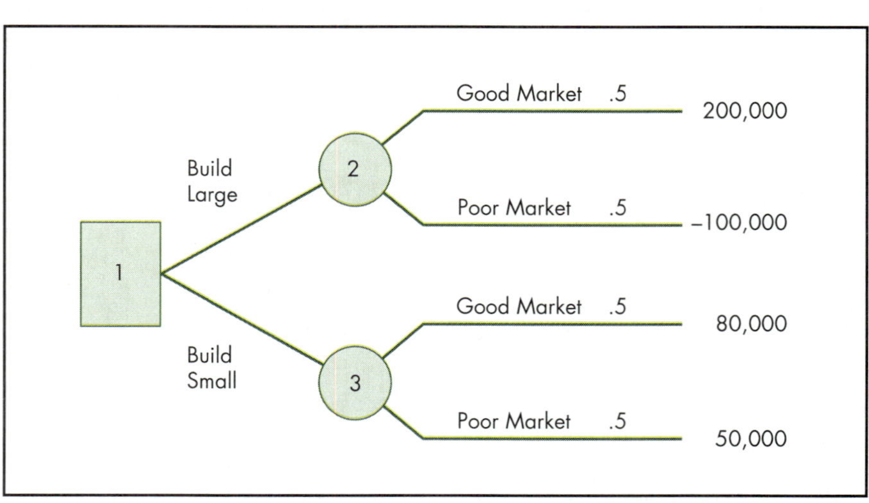

Notice there is one box in this tree, and it represents one payoff table. In general, a box on a decision tree indicates that a payoff table could be set up at that point. The number of branches emanating from that box is simply the number of alternatives available. The number of branches emanating from each circle in a tree indicate the number of states of nature possible at that point. All nodes, boxes and circles, have been numbered for the sake of reference. With some computer software, the nodes must be numbered in order to identify the inputs that are used with the software.

Analysis with a Decision Tree

Once a tree has been drawn, begin the analysis. While we proceeded from the left and moved to the right when the tree was drawn, in performing the calculations we will begin at the right and move to the left. While a decision tree may be helpful regardless of the decision making criterion being used, assume throughout our discussion of decision trees that we wish to maximize the expected value. *Therefore, at each circle an expected value will be calculated and at each box, the best alternative will be selected based on the expected value.*

Returning to the Primetime Properties example in Figure 13.2 above, at event node 2 there is a 50 percent chance the payoff is \$200,000 and a 50% chance the payoff is –\$100,000. In calculating the expected value:

$$\text{EV(Large)} = 0.5(200{,}000) + 0.5(-100{,}000) = 50{,}000$$

Put this value on the tree near event node 2. Performing a similar calculation at event node 3, the expected value is:

$$\text{EV(Small)} = 0.5(80{,}000) + 0.5(50{,}000) = 65{,}000$$

FIGURE 13.3

Primetime Properties Decision Tree with Expected Values

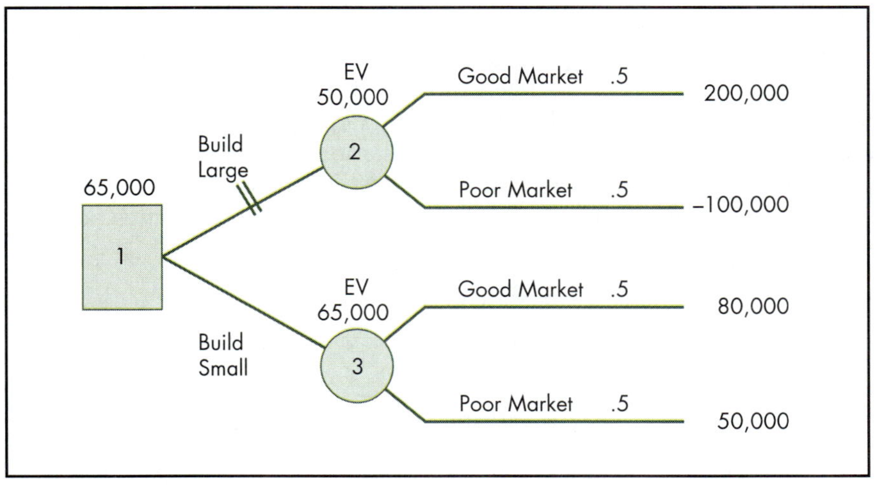

Continuing to move backwards (to the left) in the tree, the next node to be considered in the tree is decision point 1. Here simply choose the best decision based on the expected value for each alternative. Because $65,000 is greater than $50,000, we will choose to build a small complex, and will bring this value back to decision point 1 as shown in Figure 13.3 above. Notice all the information that was provided in the payoff table in Table 13.1 above also is provided on this decision tree. Notice in this figure that lines have been drawn (\\\) through the branch representing the alternative of building a large complex. These lines *cut off* that particular branch to indicate this branch will not be selected.

13.4

USING ADDITIONAL INFORMATION

The decision tree that has been drawn for the Primetime Properties example does not include the possibility of using market research to obtain additional information. Often the use of some type of market research may provide valuable information to a decision maker. Typically, this research will affect two things in a payoff table or decision tree. The research will cost money so this must be taken into consideration when calculating the payoffs, and the results of the research will cause a change in the probabilities of the states of nature.

Prior probabilities
Probabilities assigned to states of nature before any additional information is obtained.

Posterior probabilities
Conditional probabilities for states of nature that are found based on sample information.

The probabilities that are used if additional information is not obtained are called **prior probabilities**. The new probabilities used after the market research information is available are called **posterior probabilities**. Bayes Theorem is used to obtain these posterior probabilities.

Revising Probabilities Using Bayes Theorem

Bayes Theorem
A mathematical formula that may be used to revise prior probabilities based on sample information. The results are called the posterior probabilities.

The posterior probabilities used in the decision tree are based on two things—the prior probabilities and the historical accuracy of the type of sample information being used. The additional information obtained through market research or other means causes us to revise the prior probabilities upwards or downwards. If the particular type of information is extremely accurate based on past experience, a significant modification of the prior probabilities would be expected. If the additional information is only moderately accurate, then the revision in probabilities would not be as great. **Bayes Theorem** is used to obtain posterior probabilities based on both the prior probabilities and the accuracy of the information source.

To aid in the presentation of Bayes Theorem, the following variables are defined as:

$$s_1 = \text{state of nature 1}$$
$$s_2 = \text{state of nature 2}$$
$$I_1 = \text{information outcome 1}$$
$$I_2 = \text{information outcome 2}$$
$$P(s_1) = \text{prior probability of } s_1$$
$$P(s_2) = \text{prior probability of } s_2$$

If there are two states of nature and two possible outcomes from the sample information, then Bayes Theorem may be stated as:

$$P(s_j|I_k) = P(s_j \text{ and } I_k)/P(I_k)$$
$$= P(I_k|s_j)P(s_j)/[P(I_k|s_1)P(s_1)+P(I_k|s_2)P(s_2)]$$

Returning to the Primetime Properties example, the variables are defined as:

s_1 = state of nature 1 (good market)
s_2 = state of nature 2 (poor market)
I_1 = information outcome 1 (favorable research results)
I_2 = information outcome 2 (unfavorable research results)
$P(s_1)$ = prior probability of s_1 (good market)
$P(s_2)$ = prior probability of s_2 (poor market)

In order to use Bayes Theorem, these prior probabilities and the following conditional probabilities must be known:

$P(I_1|s_1) = P$(favorable research results given good market)
$P(I_2|s_1) = P$(unfavorable research results given good market)
$P(I_1|s_2) = P$(favorable research results given poor market)
$P(I_2|s_2) = P$(unfavorable research results given poor market)

These probabilities provide an indication of the accuracy of the information source in the past. The values for these probabilities usually may be obtained from previous research performed in similar situations. If this research is to be performed by a market research firm, that firm should have information about their past success.

Let's assume the following probabilities have been obtained from past data:

$P(s_1) = 0.5$ $\quad$ $P(s_2) = 0.5$
$P(I_1|s_1) = 0.9$ $\quad$ $P(I_1|s_2) = 0.3$
$P(I_2|s_1) = 0.1$ $\quad$ $P(I_2|s_2) = 0.7$

Using these probabilities, find the following posterior probabilities to put in the decision tree:

$P(s_1|I_1) = P$(good market given favorable research results)
$P(s_2|I_1) = P$(poor market given favorable research results)
$P(s_1|I_2) = P$(good market given unfavorable research results)
$P(s_2|I_2) = P$(poor market given unfavorable research results)

Using Bayes Theorem, the posterior probabilities may be obtained. For example:

$$P(s_1|I_1) = P(s_1 \text{ and } I_1)/P(I_1)$$
$$= P(I_1|s_1)P(s_1)/[P(I_1|s_1)P(s_1) + P(I_1|s_2)P(s_2)]$$
$$= 0.9(0.5)/[0.9(0.5) + 0.3(0.5)]$$
$$= 0.45/0.60$$
$$= 0.75$$

From the calculations for $P(s_1|I_1)$, it is now known $P(I_1) = 0.60$. To find $P(s_2|I_1)$, use this in the following formula:

$$\begin{aligned} P(s_2|I_1) &= P(s_2 \text{ and } I_1)/P(I_1) \\ &= P(I_1|s_2)P(s_2)/P(I_1) \\ &= 0.3(0.5)/0.60 = 0.15/0.60 = 0.25 \end{aligned}$$

This probability must be 0.25 because given that information I_1 (favorable results) occurred, either s_1 or s_2 must occur, so:

$$P(s_1|I_1) + P(s_2|I_1) = 1$$

and

$$P(s_2|I_1) = 1 - P(s_1|I_1) = 1 - 0.75 = 0.25$$

Calculating Posterior Probabilities in a Tabular Format

You may find it helpful to create a table similar to Table 13.2 to help in the computations for the posterior probabilities. This illustrates how the probabilities associated with state of nature I_1 would be obtained. In this table, the first two columns of probabilities are known. The third column is obtained by multiplying the probabilities in the previous two columns. Adding the values in this third column results in the probability of I_1 occurring. The prior probabilities are divided by this value to obtain the posterior probabilities shown in the last column.

TABLE 13.2

Table Used for Calculations Associated with Bayes Theorem for I_1 (Favorable Research Results)

Table for Information Outcome I_1 (Favorable Research Results)				
s_j	$P(s_j)$	$P(I_1\|s_j)$	$P(I_k \text{ and } s_j) = P(s_j)P(I_1\|s_j)$	$P(s_j\|I_k) = P(s_j)/P(I_1)$
s_1	$P(s_1)$	$P(I_1\|s_1)$	$P(s_1 \text{ and } I_1) = P(s_1)P(I_1\|s_1)$	$P(s_1)/P(I_1) = P(s_1\|I_1)$
s_2	$P(s_2)$	$P(I_1\|s_2)$	$P(s_2 \text{ and } I_1) = P(s_2)P(I_1\|s_2)$	$P(s_2)/P(I_1) = P(s_2\|I_1)$
			$P(I_1) = P(s_1 \text{ and } I_1) + P(s_2 \text{ and } I_1)$	

Table for Information Outcome I_1 (Favorable Research Results)				
s_j	$P(s_j)$	$P(I_1\|s_j)$	$P(I_k \text{ and } s_j) = P(s_j)P(I_1\|s_j)$	$P(s_j\|I_k) = P(s_j)/P(I_1)$
s_1	0.5	0.9	0.5(0.9) = 0.45	0.45/0.60 = 0.750
s_2	0.5	0.3	0.5(0.3) = 0.15	0.15/0.60 = 0.250
			$P(I_1) = 0.45 + 0.15 = 0.60$	

In using these tables, one table is made for each possible information outcome because we wish to obtain posterior probabilities for each of these possible information outcomes. In this situation there are two possible outcomes for the sample information—favorable research (I_1) and unfavorable research (I_2). This requires two tables, and the table for I_2 is shown in Table 13.3. If there had been three possible information outcome results, three tables would have been needed to obtain the posterior probabilities.

Now the posterior probabilities are:

$P(s_1|I_1) = P(\text{good market}|\text{favorable research results}) = 0.750$

$P(s_2|I_1) = P(\text{poor market}|\text{favorable research results}) = 0.250$

$P(s_1|I_2) = P(\text{good market}|\text{unfavorable research results}) = 0.125$

$P(s_2|I_2) = P(\text{poor market}|\text{unfavorable research results}) = 0.875$

Put these in a decision tree to determine what decisions should be made.

Expanded Decision Tree for Primetime Properties Example

The decision tree that would be drawn for the Primetime Properties example with the possibility of using market research is shown in Figure 13.4. Notice the first decision to be made is whether or not to use the market research. If the research is used, the research results must be available before we decide which size complex to build. Given the results are favorable (I_1), the posterior probabilities of 0.75 and 0.25 are placed on the appropriate branches

TABLE 13.3

Table Used for Calculations Associated with Bayes Theorem for I_2 (Unfavorable Research Results)

Table for Information Outcome I_2 (Unfavorable Research Results)

s_j	$P(s_j)$	$P(I_2|s_j)$	$P(I_k \text{ and } s_j) = P(s_j)P(I_2|s_j)$	$P(s_j|I_k) = P(s_j)/P(I_2)$
s_1	$P(s_1)$	$P(I_2|s_1)$	$P(s_1 \text{ and } I_2) = P(s_1)P(I_2|s_1)$	$P(s_1)/P(I_2) = P(s_1|I_2)$
s_2	$P(s_2)$	$P(I_2|s_2)$	$P(s_2 \text{ and } I_2) = P(s_2)P(I_2|s_2)$	$P(s_2)/P(I_2) = P(s_2|I_2)$
			$P(I_2) = P(s_1 \text{ and } I_2) + P(s_2 \text{ and } I_2)$	

Table for Information Outcome I_2 (Unfavorable Research Results)

s_j	$P(s_j)$	$P(I_2|s_j)$	$P(I_2 \text{ and } s_j) = P(s_j)P(I_2|s_j)$	$P(s_j|I_2) = P(s_j)/P(I_2)$
s_1	0.5	0.1	0.5(0.1) = 0.05	0.05/0.40 = 0.125
s_2	0.5	0.7	0.5(0.7) = 0.35	0.35/0.40 = 0.875
			$P(I_2) = 0.05 + 0.35 = 0.40$	

Decision Tree for Primetime Properties with Additional Information Available

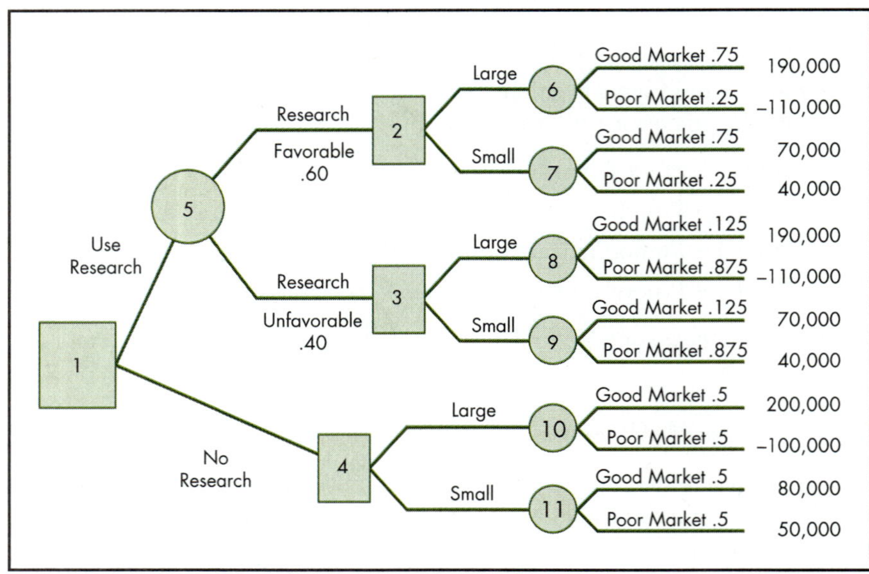

after the branch for favorable research. Similarly, given the research is unfavorable (I_2), the posterior probabilities of 0.125 and 0.875 are placed on the appropriate branches following the unfavorable research branch. Notice the payoffs for the branches after the research is used are all \$10,000 (the cost of the research) less than the payoffs without using the research. Notice if the research is not used the decision making situation is the same as that depicted in Figure 13.3 above in which no research was considered. Thus, nodes 4, 10, and 11 are exactly the same as nodes 1, 2, and 3 in Figure 13.3.

Once the decision tree is drawn, begin the analysis. Beginning at the ends of the branches with the payoffs and working backwards (to the left), first compute the expected values at the event nodes nearest to these payoffs. Then move backwards to the decision points and select the best alternative, bringing the expected payoff for this alternative back to the decision point. This is shown in Figure 13.5. At event node 5, there is a 60 percent chance the expected payoff will be \$115,000, and there is a 40 percent chance the expected payoff is \$43,750. The expected value is \$86,500, and this is written at event node 5. Continuing moving backwards we arrive at node 1 where we select to use the market research study because the expected value for this (\$86,500) is higher than the expected value with no research (\$65,000).

Figure 13.5 shows at a glance what the decisions will be in the different situations. We would choose to use the market research, and then wait for the results of the research. If the results are favorable, build a large complex, and if they are unfavorable, build a small complex.

If the market research had been capable of providing perfect information instead of imperfect information, the same approach could be used.

FIGURE 13.5

Primetime Properties Decision Tree with Expected Values

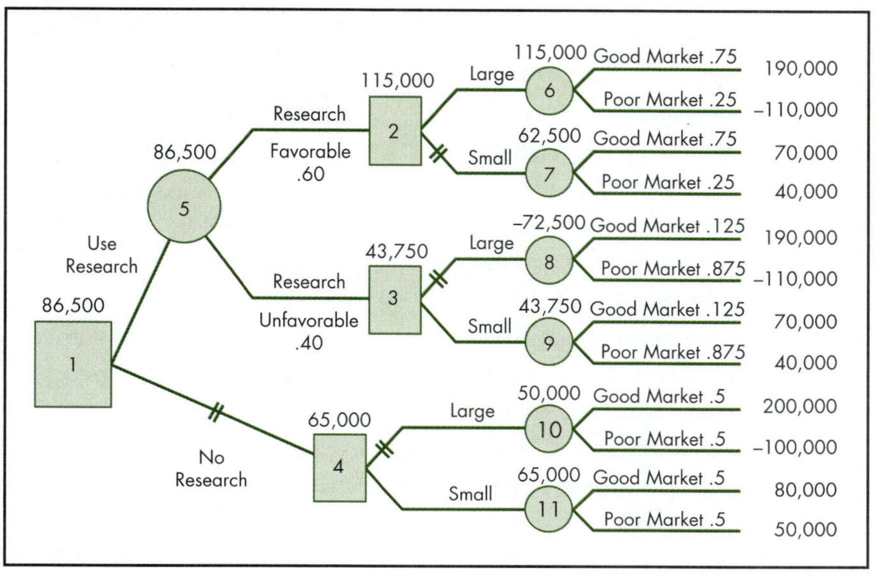

The only difference would be the posterior probabilities. If the research results provided perfect information, then if the research results are favorable the market must be good and the probability of a good market given a favorable research result would be 1.0. The probability of a poor market given this favorable research result would be 0.0. If the research results were unfavorable with perfect information, the posterior probability of a good market given the unfavorable research would be 0.0 while the probability of a poor market would be 1.0.

Expected Value of Sample Information

The increase in expected value that results from using sample information indicates how much we should be willing to pay for the sample information. This amount is called the **expected value of sample information (EVSI)**. Because the cost of the information was subtracted before computing the expected value with sample information, this amount must be considered in the calculations.

Expected value of sample information (EVSI)
The increase in expected value that results from using sample information assuming there is no cost for the sample information.

In the Primetime Properties example, if sample information was used, at a cost of $10,000, the expected value was $86,500. The best expected value without the sample information was $65,000. Thus, the expected value increased by $21,500 as a result of sample information costing $10,000. Therefore, we should be willing to pay up to $21,500 more, or a total of $31,500, for this sample information. Thus, the EVSI is $31,500.

The expected value of sample information is computed as follows:

$$\text{EVSI} = (\text{EV with SI}) + (\text{information cost}) - (\text{EV without SI})$$

BEST PRACTICES

Decision Making at Pfizer

SOURCE: Pfizer Annual Report, 1993.

Pfizer, Inc. is a research-based global health care company. The company's four business segments span a wide range of marketing areas. The healthcare unit develops prescription pharmaceuticals and hospital products. Nonprescription healthcare products, such as Visine eye drops and Plax dental rinse, are offered by the consumer healthcare segment. An up-and-coming area, the food science segment, produces specialty ingredients for foods and beverages (i.e., fat substitutes). Finally, the animal health unit provides proprietary medicines for animals.

To remain competitive in today's challenging business environment, Pfizer must constantly develop innovative products. At the same time, healthcare systems are undergoing significant changes. The trend is toward lower-cost, managed care organizations. Pfizer has responded to the growing emphasis on cost containment by undertaking more than 80 outcomes research studies. These studies show both the economic and therapeutic benefits of new products.

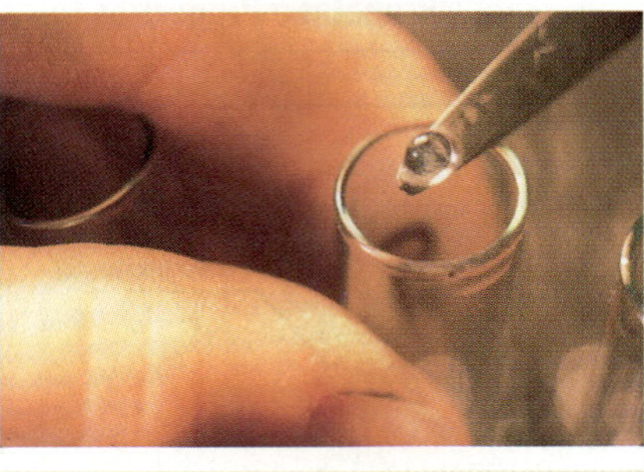

Courtesy of Pfizer, Inc.

Pfizer uses outcomes research to explore the ability of new medical devices to meet medical needs and improve the quality of patients' lives. Other areas studied include minimally invasive surgery, angioplasty, and certain types of orthopedic implants. Outcomes research helps, for example, in identifying which emerging procedures will be less risky and traumatic for the patient. This in turn results in speedier recovery times and lower overall costs.

In the Primetime Properties example:

$$\text{EVSI} = 86{,}500 + 10{,}000 - 65{,}000 = 31{,}500$$

Our expected value with the research will be higher than it will be without the research if the cost of the research is less than this EVSI.

13.5 UTILITY THEORY

There are many occasions in which people make decisions that would appear to be inconsistent with the expected value criterion. When people buy insurance, the amount of the premium is greater than the expected payout to them from the insurance company because the expected payout, overhead costs, and profit are all used in determining the premium. A person managing a business may select an alternative that does not provide the highest expected value if this decision allows the possibility, even with an extremely low probability, of a negative payoff that would bankrupt the company. When a lottery ticket is purchased, the expected return to the purchaser is negative. Casino games of all types have a negative expected return to the player. Why do people make decisions that seemingly are irrational based on the expected value criterion? The reason is the worth of the decision includes something other than the monetary value of the payoffs.

This total worth of a particular payoff or outcome often is called **utility**. An insurance policy provides peace of mind to the purchaser of the policy. The possibility of going bankrupt is such a terrible consequence that this overrides all other considerations. The anticipation of possibly winning an extremely high payoff from a lottery is part of the utility a person gains from buying a lottery ticket. Playing a casino game may have an entertainment value to the person choosing to play the game.

Utility
The total worth of a particular payoff or outcome.

Thus, when a rational person chooses to select an alternative that does not maximize the expected value of the decision, that person may be acting perfectly rationally by maximizing the expected utility. Assigning a utility value to each outcome in a decision making situation would allow expected utilities to be calculated for each decision, and would show that people maximize the expected utility of their decisions. However, assigning accurate utilities is not an easy task and depends on the subjective assessment of the payoffs by the decision maker. Another decision maker may assign different utility values. Fortunately, when monetary payoffs are the primary concern in a decision making situation, unless one payoff is extremely high or extremely low relative to all other payoffs, the monetary values often are very good approximations for utilities of each outcome.

While the utility of a monetary payoff varies among individuals, the utility of a particular amount of money also may vary within one individual. For example, the utility of an additional $10 may be very high when considering a decision in which the maximum possible payoff is currently $15, whereas the utility of an additional $10 would be much lower if the maximum possible payoff for a decision is $1,000. Thus, the utility of a

The anticipation of possibly winning an extremely high payoff from a lottery is part of the utility that a person gains from buying a lottery ticket. SOURCE: Courtesy New York State Lottery

specific monetary value may depend on the specific set of possible payoffs as well as the individual decision maker.

Assigning Utilities to Payoffs

When utility values are assigned to monetary payoffs in a particular decision making situation, the highest and lowest possible payoffs are given a maximum and minimum utility. Usually the maximum is one and the minimum is zero. However, utilities values do not have to be on a scale of zero to one. Other scales, such as zero to 10 or zero to 100, also may be used.

Certainty equivalent (CE)
A guaranteed payoff of the amount under consideration.

To assign utilities to a particular payoff, the decision maker is presented with two alternatives. The first alternative is a guaranteed payoff of the amount under consideration. The value is normally called the **certainty equivalent** (CE). The second alternative will result in a payoff of either the maximum or minimum possible payoff. The decision maker is then asked to decide what probability of receiving the maximum payoff would cause him or her to select the second alternative instead of the certainty equivalent. This probability value of p is assigned as the probability of receiving the maximum possible payoff and a probability of $1 - p$ is assigned to the probability of receiving the minimum possible payoff as shown in Table 13.4.

An Example of Utility Assignments

To illustrate the assignment and use of utilities, consider the following example. Suppose you are faced with the two possible investment alternatives shown in Table 13.5. The probabilities are shown and the expected values have been calculated. Based on the expected values, the decision would be to select Alternative #1. However, you may feel uncomfortable with this as you may lose $1,000 with this decision, while the other decision always results in a positive profit. In fact, you may feel that Investment #2 is the best choice. To see that this is a perfectly rational choice, consider the utilities of the possible payoffs and see that this choice may maximize the expected utility.

Assign utility to each of these payoffs. The best possible payoff in this problem is $3,000 and will have a utility of one, and the worst possible

TABLE 13.4

Payoff Table Used to Establish Utility Value for Amount of Certainty Equivalent (CE)

	States of Nature		
Alternatives	**#1**	**#2**	**Expected Value**
#1	CE	CE	CE
#2	maximum	minimum	p(maximum) + $(1 - p)$(minimum)
Probability	p	$1 - p$	
CE = certainty equivalent			

TABLE 13.5

Payoff Table for Utility Example

	Poor Economy	Fair Economy	Good Economy	Expected Value
Investment #1	–1,000	0	3,000	600
Investment #2	200	400	600	400
Probability	0.3	0.4	0.3	

payoff is –\$1,000 and will have a utility of zero. Letting U(payoff) represent the utility of a payoff, this means:

$$\text{Utility}(3{,}000) = U(3{,}000) = 1$$
$$\text{Utility}(-1{,}000) = U(-1{,}000) = 0$$

The other payoffs in this problem are \$0, \$200, \$400, and \$600, and utilities will be assigned for each of these payoffs.

In finding the utility of \$600, develop the payoff table shown below to compare a certain payoff of \$600 with the possibility of achieving the best and the worst payoff. This is shown in Table 13.6. You, as the decision maker, are asked to specify a value of p that would cause the two alternatives to be equally desirable. Suppose you feel this probability should be 0.7. This means if $p = 0.7$ the two alternatives would have the same expected utility, although not necessarily the same expected profit. Create a table indicating the utilities as shown below:

	States of Nature		
	#1	#2	Expected Utility
Alternative #1	$U(600)$	$U(600)$	$U(600)$
Alternative #2	$U(3{,}000)$	$U(-1{,}000)$	$pU(3{,}000) + (1 - p)U(-1{,}000)$
Probability	p	$1 - p$	

In Alternative #2, the utility of the best payoff will be one, and the utility of the worst payoff is zero. In the example, for a payoff of \$600, $p = 0.7$

TABLE 13.6

Payoff Table to Establish the Utility for \$600

	States of Nature		
	#1	#2	Expected Payoff
Alternative #1	600	600	600
Alternative #2	3,000	–1,000	$p(3{,}000) + (1 - p)(-1{,}000)$
Probability	p	$1 - p$	

when the two expected utilities are the same. This results in the following table:

	States of Nature		
	#1	#2	Expected Utility
Alternative #1	$U(600)$	$U(600)$	$U(600)$
Alternative #2	1	0	0.7
Probability	0.7	0.3	

If the two alternatives are equally desirable, set the two expected utilities equal and have:

$$\text{expected utility (CE)} = \text{expected utility (Alternative \#2)}$$
$$U(600) = 0.7$$

By choosing to use values of zero to one for the utility values, the utility for each payoff would be equal to the probability selected that would make the two alternatives equally desirable. Thus, in finding the other utilities, simply find this probability.

Suppose you are asked what probability would make the certainty equivalent and the possibility of the maximum or the minimum payoff equally desirable in each of these other instances, and you respond as follows:

Payoff	Probability
0	0.4
200	0.5
400	0.6

Repeating the process demonstrated for a payoff of $600 would result in:

$$U(0) = 0.4$$
$$U(200) = 0.5$$
$$U(400) = 0.6$$

To maximize the expected utility in this situation, create a payoff table for these utilities as shown in Table 13.7. Calculating the expected utilities shows the decision with the highest expected utility would be Investment

TABLE 13.7

Payoff Table with Utilities as Payoffs

	Poor Economy	Fair Economy	Good Economy	Expected Utility
Investment #1	0	0.4	1	0.46
Investment #2	0.5	0.6	0.7	0.60
Probability	0.3	0.4	0.3	

#2. Thus, while this decision does not have the highest expected profit, it does have the highest expected utility.

Utility Curves

A graph of utility values and their associated payoffs provides an indication of the decision maker's attitude towards risk. Such a graph is called a **utility curve.** In this example, graphing these utilities against the payoffs results in the utility curve in Figure 13.6. A graph of the utilities provides a clear picture of the decision maker's attitude towards risk.

Utility curve
A graph of utility values and their associated payoffs.

The shape of a utility curve gives an indication of the decision maker's attitude towards risk. Figure 13.7 shows the general shape for utility curves

FIGURE 13.6

Utility Curve for Utility Values and Associated Payoffs

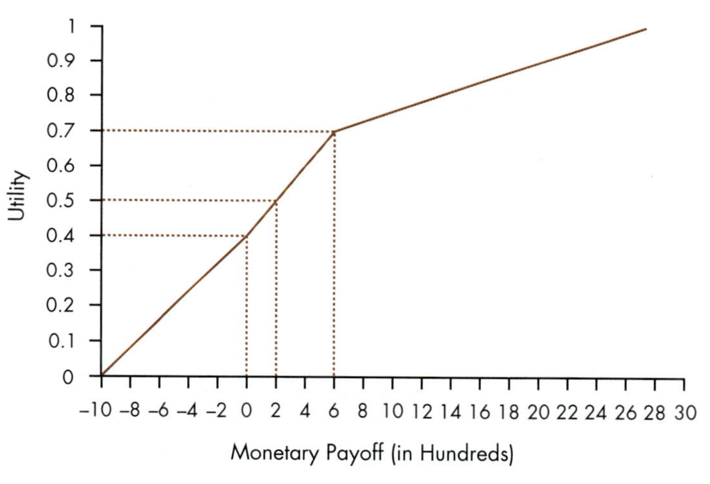

FIGURE 13.7

Utility Curves for Different Attitudes Toward Risk

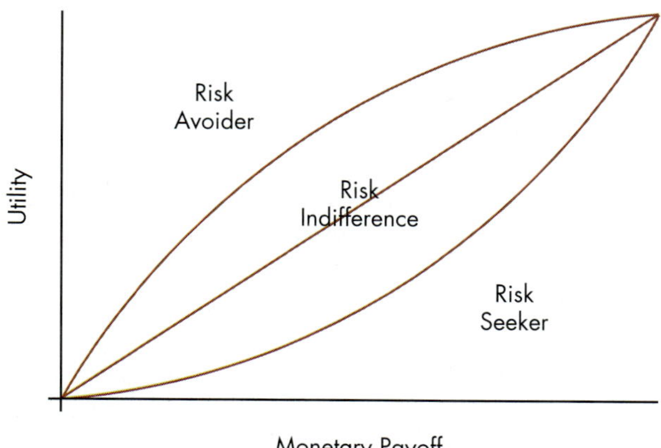

Decision Analysis for Environmental Policy Decisions in Finland

Politicians often are called upon to make important decisions about complex issues. Sometimes, the issues are far beyond the decision makers' technical experience. Most politicians are accustomed to making value trade-offs in the face of incomplete information. To ease this problem, public policy makers in Finland have incorporated decision-analytical approaches into some of their political processes.

Members of the parliament of Finland, for example, used decision analysis to assist in making policy decisions regarding nuclear energy. Their aim was to help the political debate by providing decision structuring and explicit preference comparisons. The National Energy Committee also used decision analysis to help create a comprehensive framework for comparing future energy options for Finland.

Finland's National Board of Waters and the Environment develops policy proposals for a variety of controversial issues. The board considers such matters as setting standards for water level changes in lakes due to energy production and developing measures to mitigate acid rain. Staff members of the board have actively sought ways to use decision analysis to put problems into clear frameworks for politicians.

The prime minister of Finland was impressed by the role of decision analysis in clarifying environmental policy issues. In fact, he supported using a similar analysis to analyze Finland's decision regarding joining the European Common Market. Although that analysis never was done, due to political pressures to decide very quickly, the example points to the potential of decision analysis as a public policy-making tool of the future.

SOURCE:
Hamalainen, R. P., June 1992. "Politics & Policy, Decision Analysis Makes its Way into Environmental Policy in Finland." *OR/MS Today*: 40-43.

in which the decision maker is risk averse, risk neutral, or a risk taker. At times an individual may be a risk taker when the dollar values are small, but that person may be risk averse when the dollar values are large. For example, a person may be willing to pay $1 to buy a chance at winning $1,000. However, that same person may be reluctant to spend $1,000 on a chance to win $1,000,000 even if the odds are the same as with the smaller amounts.

13.6 DECISION MAKING WITH MULTIPLE FACTORS

All of the decision models discussed to this point have involved decision making based on a single factor or criterion. However, many decisions involve several factors. When a person decides what kind of automobile to purchase, factors such as price, miles per gallon, performance, safety features, style, and other items are considered. In making a decision about where to open a new factory, the cost of land, the cost of labor, access to transportation routes, availability of resources, and even quality of life in the community may be important.

Several techniques have been used for making decisions when multiple factors must be considered. An earlier chapter discussed how goal

In making a decision about what type of automobile to buy, factors such as safety features, price, and fuel economy may be considered. SOURCE: Courtesy of American Honda Motor Co./Fleishman Hillard Inc.

programming could be used for certain types of multicriteria problems. Two other multicriteria techniques are the weighted average of the utilities technique and the analytic hierarchy process. We will illustrate these with the following example.

Example

Clunie Industries is planning to build a new production facility to meet the growing demand for its products. Upon careful evaluation of tax considerations, availability and cost of transportation, and availability of raw materials, three cities have been deemed to be acceptable and are relatively equal on these considerations. Management has decided one of these three cities will be selected.

In making the final decision, management now will rate the cities on three important factors. One factor that management has decided to consider is the quality of life in each area because existing managerial personnel will be moving to this new city. Another factor is the initial cost of the new facility's construction. The third factor is the labor supply in each location. In evaluating the three cities, it is found none of the three is considered the best for all three factors. What should be done?

13.7

WEIGHTED AVERAGE OF THE UTILITIES

One approach that may be used for including multiple factors is to assign ratings or utilities as payoffs on each factor for each alternative. These utilities will be subjectively assigned based on the judgment of management. Weights are assigned to each factor, which measure the importance of each. A weighted average of the ratings or utilities then is used.

In the Clunie Industries example, let's suppose management has decided to rate each city on a scale of one to 100 on each of the factors. Management rates the first city as 85 on the quality of life, while the other two cities are rated 60 and 80 on quality of life. Management would then rate the three cities on the other two factors as well. The results are shown in Table 13.8. The subjective assessment of the relative importance of each factor results in weights assigned by management of 0.3, 0.2, and 0.5. A weighted average would be computed for these as shown in Table 13.8. Based on these results, select City 3.

In selecting a city based on the weighted average of the utilities, it is important to recognize that these ratings and probabilities have been subjectively assigned. Minor deviations may cause a different alternative to be selected. Table 13.8 shows that while City 3 has the highest weighted average of the utilities, City 1 has an average that is very close to this.

13.8

ANALYTIC HIERARCHY PROCESS (AHP)

Analytic hierarchy process (AHP)
A procedure that may be used to make decisions when multiple factors are being considered. Pairwise comparisons are an integral part of this process.

Another approach that has been suggested for using multiple criteria in decision making is the **analytic hierarchy process (AHP)**. Like the weighted average of the utilities method, AHP also uses a weighted average approach. However, AHP uses a method for assigning ratings and weights

TABLE 13.8

Ratings for Factors in Clunie Industries Example

	Factor			
	Quality of Life	Initial Cost	Labor Supply	Weighted Average
City 1	85	70	75	77
City 2	60	80	70	69
City 3	80	75	80	79
Weights	0.3	0.2	0.5	

that is generally more reliable and consistent than the weighted average of the utilities technique.

The analytic hierarchy process is based on pairwise comparisons of the alternatives for each of the factors to obtain the ratings. Similar pairwise comparisons are used to determine the relative importance of the different factors and this yields the weights.

In using AHP, a manager must determine the overall goal, identify the factors or criteria used in the evaluation, and identify the alternatives to be considered. At times some subcriteria also are considered. In the Clunie Industries example, the goal would be to select the best city to locate the facility. The criteria would be the quality of life, initial cost of construction, and the labor supply. Subcriteria for the labor supply might be the cost of labor, availability of labor, and skill level of the local labor force. The alternatives would be the three cities that still are being considered. Once these alternatives have been identified, begin making comparisons. A summary of the AHP method is given in Summary Table 13.1. We will illustrate this with the Clunie Industries example.

Pairwise Comparisons

For the AHP process, pairwise comparisons are made based on the descriptions shown in Table 13.9. The manager of Clunie Industries would be asked to compare Cities 1 and 2, 1 and 3, and 2 and 3 on each of the three factors. Suppose on the quality of life factor, the manager says that City 1 is extremely strongly preferred to City 2. A numerical value of 9 would be assigned to this as shown in Table 13.10. Reading across in the row, the number shows how preferred the city in the row is to the city in the column. Thus, the rating for the City 2 row and the City 1 column is 1/9 because City 2 is not preferred over City 1. Note that the numerical values of 1 are assigned along the diagonal of this table because each city is being

SUMMARY TABLE 13.1

Summary of Steps in Analytic Hierarchy Process

1. Develop ratings for each alternative on each factor.
   A. Develop a pairwise comparison matrix for each factor.
   B. Normalize the matrix.
   C. Average the values in each row to obtain ratings.
   D. Calculate consistency ratio. Modify if necessary.
2. Develop weights for the factors.
   A. Develop a pairwise comparison matrix to compare factors.
   B. Normalize the matrix.
   C. Average the values in each row to obtain weights.
   D. Calculate consistency ratio. Modify if necessary.
3. Calculate a weighted average of the ratings. Select alternative with highest average value.

TABLE 13.9

AHP Pairwise Comparison Scale

Numerical Rating	Verbal Description of Judgment
1	Equally preferred
2	Equally to moderately preferred
3	Moderately preferred
4	Moderately to strongly preferred
5	Strongly preferred
6	Strongly to very strongly preferred
7	Very strongly preferred
8	Very strongly to extremely strongly preferred
9	Extremely strongly preferred

TABLE 13.10

AHP Pairwise Comparison Table with City 1 Compared to City 2 on Quality of Life

	City 1	City 2	City 3
City 1	1	9	
City 2	1/9	1	
City 3			1

compared to itself in this position. If City 1 is then compared to City 3 on this same factor, and City 3 is moderately preferred to City 1, put a 3 in the row for City 3 and column for City 1. Also put a 1/3 in the row for City 1 and the column for City 3. With the final comparison for the quality factor, suppose City 3 is strongly preferred to City 2. Put a 5 and 1/5 in the appropriate positions as shown in Table 13.11.

Synthesis
The process in AHP of obtaining the overall priority or rating for each alternative.

Once the pairwise comparisons have been made, computations are performed to determine the ratings for, and the weights to be used with, each alternative. This process is called the **synthesis** of the AHP model. The calculations involved in this synthesis use mathematics beyond the scope of this text. However, approximations are commonly used in practice, and usually are quite good. The computations that follow are approximations of the true AHP values.

Normalized matrix
A pairwise comparison matrix in the AHP method in which the columns of the matrix have been transformed so that the numbers in each column add to 1.

Normalize the Matrix

Once pairwise comparisons have been made, the matrix is normalized by totaling the numbers in each column. Each number in the column is then divided by this total. The result is called the **normalized matrix**.

TABLE 13.11

AHP Pairwise Comparisons for Quality of Life in Clunie Industries Example

	City 1	City 2	City 3
City 1	1	9	1/3
City 2	1/9	1	1/5
City 3	3	5	1

For column 1:

$$\text{total} = 1 + 1/9 + 3 = 4.111$$

To normalize the first column:

$$1/4.111 = 0.243$$
$$(1/9)/4.111 = 0.027$$
$$3/4.111 = 0.730$$

The totals for each column are shown in Table 13.12. Just as all values in the City 1 column are divided by the column total of 4.111, all values

TABLE 13.12

Normalization of Quality of Life Matrix

Pairwise Comparison Matrix			
	Quality of life		
	City 1	City 2	City 3
City 1	1	9	1/3
City 2	1/9	1	1/5
City 3	3	5	1
Total	4.111	15	1.533

Normalized Matrix				
	Quality of Life			
	City 1	City 2	City 3	Row Average (Rating)
City 1	0.243	0.600	0.217	0.354
City 2	0.027	0.067	0.130	0.075
City 3	0.730	0.333	0.652	0.572

in the City 2 column are divided by 15, and all values in the City 3 column are divided by 1.533. This results in the normalized matrix shown in Table 13.12 above.

Obtaining the AHP Ratings

Once the matrix has been normalized, average the values in each row to obtain the **rating** or **priority** for each alternative on the factor being considered. For the quality of life factor, this is shown in Table 13.12. For City 1 (row 1):

$$(0.243 + 0.600 + 0.217)/3 = 0.354$$

Thus, City 1 would have a rating of 0.354 on quality of life. Similar calculations are performed for the other cities. On this factor, City 2 would have a rating of 0.075 and City 3 would have a rating of 0.572.

At this point, calculate the consistency ratio to determine if the pairwise comparisons are consistent. In looking at these normalized matrices, if a set of ratings is consistent, all normalized values in a row would be approximately the same. The consistency ratio will tell us if any differences are large enough to be significant. However, the computations for the consistency ratios are tedious, so we will demonstrate the consistency calculations after all the other normalized matrices have been developed.

Developing Other Comparison Matrices and Selecting Best Alternative

The decision maker now would be asked to make pairwise comparisons on the other two factors—cost of construction and labor supply. This would result in the pairwise comparison tables shown in Table 13.13. The columns would be totaled and normalized. The rows would be averaged to yield the ratings also shown in Table 13.13. Now ratings have been generated for all cities on all factors. The weights to be used must be found.

Management now would compare the three factors to determine their relative importance. Table 13.14 illustrates these comparisons. These are normalized and the row averages provide the relative weights for the three factors.

Once all the ratings and weights have been found, compute a weighted average for each alternative. For City 1 this is:

$$0.360(0.354) + 0.128(0.075) + 0.512(0.572) = 0.4295$$

Similar calculations for the other cities yield the results shown in Table 13.15. Based on the pairwise comparisons that were made and the calculations that followed, management would choose to locate the facility in City 3. It should be noted that City 1 has a weighted average almost as high as that of City 3.

To insure the comparisons were consistent, calculate consistency ratios for each of the normalized matrices that were developed.

TABLE 13.13

AHP Comparison Tables for Relative Importance of the Cost and Labor Supply

Pairwise Comparison Matrix Cost			
	City 1	City 2	City 3
City 1	1	1/5	1/2
City 2	5	1	4
City 3	2	1/4	1
Total	8	1.45	5.5

Normalized Matrix Cost				
	City 1	City 2	City 3	Row Average (Rating)
City 1	0.125	0.138	0.091	0.118
City 2	0.625	0.690	0.727	0.681
City 3	0.250	0.172	0.182	0.201

Pairwise Comparison Matrix Labor Supply			
	City 1	City 2	City 3
City 1	1	2	1/4
City 2	1/2	1	1/7
City 3	4	7	1
Total	5.5	10	1.393

Normalized Matrix Labor Supply				
	City 1	City 2	City 3	Row Average (Rating)
City 1	0.182	0.200	0.179	0.187
City 2	0.091	0.100	0.103	0.098
City 3	0.727	0.700	0.718	0.715

TABLE 13.14

AHP Comparison Tables for Relative Importance of the Three Factors

Pairwise Comparison Matrix for Comparing Factors to Obtain Weights			
	Life	Cost	Labor
Life	1	4	1/2
Cost	1/4	1	1/3
Labor	2	3	1
Total	3.25	8	1.833

Normalized Matrix for Comparing Factors to Obtain Weights				
	Life	Cost	Labor	Row Average (Weights)
Life	0.308	0.500	0.273	0.360
Cost	0.077	0.125	0.182	0.128
Labor	0.615	0.375	0.545	0.512

TABLE 13.15

Weighted Average of AHP Ratings Found Using AHP Weights

	Life	Cost	Labor	Weighted Average
City 1	0.354	0.075	0.572	0.4295
City 2	0.118	0.681	0.201	0.2326
City 3	0.187	0.098	0.715	0.4459
Weights	0.360	0.128	0.512	

Calculating Consistency Ratios

There are four pairwise comparison matrices and a consistency ratio must be calculated for each of these. This will be demonstrated with the quality of life matrix. This original matrix and the average normalized ratings were given as:

	Quality of Life			
	City 1	City 2	City 3	Average (Rating)
City 1	1	9	1/3	0.354
City 2	1/9	1	1/5	0.075
City 3	3	5	1	0.572

We will illustrate the steps in computing the consistency index using this information.

Step 1. Create a weighted sum for each row. The weights for the values in each column are the average ratings obtained for the corresponding row. Thus, column 1 was City 1, so the weight for this column is the average rating for the City 1 row. This yields:

$$0.354(1) + 0.075(9) + 0.527(1/3) = 1.2165$$
$$0.354(1/9) + 0.075(1) + 0.527(1/5) = 0.2283$$
$$0.354(3) + 0.075(5) + 0.527(1) = 2.0059$$

Step 2. Divide each weighted sum by the average rating for that row.

$$1.2165/0.354 = 3.4408$$
$$0.2283/0.075 = 3.0563$$
$$2.0059/0.572 = 3.5084$$

Step 3. Compute the average of the values in Step 2. This will be denoted by λ.

$$\lambda = (3.4408 + 3.0563 + 3.5084)/3 = 3.3352$$

Step 4. Compute the **consistency index** (*CI*):

$$CI = (\lambda - n)/(n - 1)$$

where n is the number of items being compared (i.e., the number of rows in the matrix).

$$CI = (3.3352 - 3)/(3 - 1) = 0.1676$$

Step 5. Compute the **consistency ratio** (*CR*):

$$CR = CI/RI$$

where *RI* is the **random index** based on n and found in the table below.

n:	2	3	4	5	6	7	8	9	10
RI:	0.0	0.58	0.90	1.12	1.24	1.32	1.41	1.45	1.51

Thus:

$$CR = 0.1676/0.58 = 0.2889$$

If the *CR* is larger than 0.10, then there are inconsistencies in the ratings and you should go back and make modifications to the original comparison matrix. The easiest way to find these inconsistencies is to look at the normalized matrix. The normalized values in each row all should be the same or close to the same value. The consistency ratio indicates when the differences are large enough to create a problem. In this case, looking at the normalized matrix in Table 13.12 above shows that for both the City 1 row and the City 3 row, the middle value is quite different from the others. The

Consistency index
A value computed in the AHP method and used in finding the consistency ratio.

Consistency ratio
A measure of the consistency of AHP comparisons. If this is less than 0.10, the comparisons are considered consistent.

Random index
A value associated with AHP that is used to compute the consistency ratio.

person making the comparisons should be asked to review the original comparison and make a modification.

Software for AHP

While these calculations are tedious, this does illustrate how the analytic hierarchy process works. It should be noted these calculations provide an approximation of the values used with AHP. However, these approximations may be sufficient in many situations. A spreadsheet could be developed to perform these calculations for you.

There also is user friendly software available such as Expert Choice that will perform these calculations associated with AHP. Inputs are similar to the pairwise comparisons just made.

Comparison of the Weighted Utility Approach and AHP

While both the weighted utility approach and the AHP approach may be used with multiple factors, each has an advantage. The weighted utility approach is much simpler to use and understand by management. The AHP approach may be more consistent and has a consistency measure to indicate if the numerical preference ratings should be reexamined, but the computations are quite difficult. For both of these techniques, a manager should realize that subjective assessments have been made on the desirability of the different results. Thus, while a single number or rating is calculated to determine which alternative is best, any alternative with a rating close to the optimal also would be a good choice.

13.9 SUMMARY

We have seen that using decision trees instead of payoff tables may be very helpful when a sequence of decisions is to be made. The criterion for making decisions in the decision tree is typically the expected value.

In using additional information, we revised the prior probabilities using Bayes Theorem to obtain posterior probabilities that are conditioned upon the sample results. These posterior probabilities then may be used in decision tree analysis.

At times, payoffs in dollars may not accurately reflect the desirability of outcomes. An extremely bad outcome may be so terrible that it outweighs all other considerations. Assigning utility values may help in the decision making process. An alternative that has the highest expected utility may not be the alternative that has the highest expected monetary value.

When multiple factors are being considered, the weighted average utility or weighted average rating method may be used to determine the best outcome. The analytic hierarchy process is another method for making decisions based on multiple factors. This is based on pairwise comparisons and includes the calculation of a consistency ratio that may highlight a problem with a preference pattern assigned by the decision maker.

GLOSSARY

Analytic hierarchy process (AHP) A procedure that may be used to make decisions when multiple factors are being considered. Pairwise comparisons are an integral part of this process. *p. 566*

Bayes Theorem A mathematical formula that may be used to revise prior probabilities based on sample information. The results are called the posterior probabilities. *p. 552*

Certainty equivalent (CE) A guaranteed payoff of the amount under consideration. *p. 560*

Consistency ratio A measure of the consistency of AHP comparisons. If this is less than 0.10, the comparisons are considered consistent. *p. 573*

Consistency index A value computed in the AHP method and used in finding the consistency ratio. *p. 573*

Decision tree A graphical representation of a decision making situation. This is particularly helpful when a sequence of decisions is to be made. *p. 549*

Expected value of sample information (EVSI) The increase in expected value that results from using sample information assuming there is no cost for the sample information. *p. 557*

Nodes Points on decision trees representing decision points or events. *p. 549*

Normalized matrix A pairwise comparison matrix in the AHP method in which the columns of the matrix have been transformed so that the numbers in each column add to 1. *p. 568*

Posterior probabilities Conditional probabilities for states of nature that are found based on sample information. *p. 552*

Prior probabilities Probabilities assigned to states of nature before any additional information is obtained. *p. 552*

Random index A value associated with AHP that is used to compute the consistency ratio. *p. 573*

Synthesis The process in AHP of obtaining the overall priority or rating for each alternative. *p. 568*

Utility The total worth of a particular payoff or outcome. *p. 559*

Utility curve A graph of utility values and their associated payoffs. *p. 563*

KEY EQUATIONS

(13-1) Decision tree computations

1. At event node, compute expected value (EV)

   $EV = \Sigma(\text{Payoff})\text{Probability}$

2. At decision node, select alternative with best EV

(13-2) Bayes Theorem for two states of nature and two information results:

s_1 = state of nature 1

s_2 = state of nature 2

I_1 = information outcome 1

I_2 = information outcome 2

$P(s_1)$ = prior probability of s_1

$P(s_2)$ = prior probability of s_2

$$P(s_j|I_k) = P(I_k|s_j)P(s_j)/[P(I_k|s_1)P(s_1)+P(I_k|s_2)P(s_2)]$$

(13-3) Computing consistency ratio (CR) for AHP

Step 1. Create a weighted sum for each row of the pairwise comparison matrix. The weights for the values in each column are the average ratings obtained for the corresponding row.

Step 2. Divide each weighted sum by the average rating for that row.

Step 3. Compute the average of the values in Step 2. This will be denoted by λ.

Step 4. Compute the consistency index (CI):

$$CI = (\lambda - n)/(n - 1)$$

where n is the number of items being compared (i.e., the number of rows in the matrix).

Step 5. Compute the consistency ratio (CR):

$$CR = CI/RI$$

where RI is the random index based on n and found in the table below.

n:	2	3	4	5	6	7	8	9	10
RI:	0.0	0.58	0.90	1.12	1.24	1.32	1.41	1.45	1.51

If $CR > 0.10$, look for inconsistencies.

SOLVED PROBLEMS

SOLVED PROBLEM 13-1

David Dyess has just developed a new software product and is ready to bring this product to market. Based on an analysis of the current market conditions, David believes there is a 20 percent chance the product will be a major success and he will make $150,000. There is a 70 percent chance the product will be a moderate success and he will earn $40,000. There is a 10 percent chance the product will be a failure and David will lose $50,000. Before David can begin marketing the product, a major software developer has offered to buy the rights to this product for $45,000.

Develop a decision tree that could be used to help David make his decision. Perform the necessary calculations and make your recommendation.

SOLUTION

The tree is shown below. The expected value of not selling is:

$$0.2(150{,}000) + 0.7(40{,}000) + 0.1(-50{,}000) = 53{,}000$$

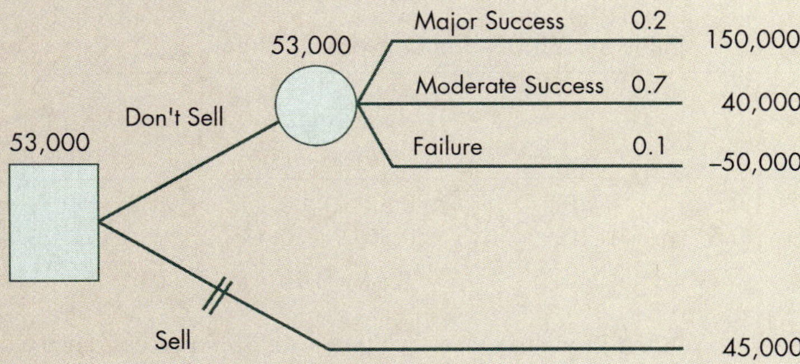

Because this is more than $45,000, David should not sell.

SOLVED PROBLEM 13-2

Policy Pollsters is a market research firm specializing in political polls. Records indicate in past elections, when a candidate was elected, Policy Pollsters had accurately predicted this 80 percent of the time and were wrong 20 percent of the time. Records also show for losing candidates, Policy Pollsters accurately predicted they would lose 90 percent of the time and were only wrong 10 percent of the time.

In the upcoming election, a particular candidate is believed to have a 50 percent chance of winning the election and a 50 percent chance of losing the election. The candidate is considering hiring Policy Pollsters to project a winner.

Use Bayes Theorem to find the probabilities of winning and losing if Policy Pollsters predicts a victory and if they predict a loss.

SOLUTION

Let

s_1 = victory s_2 = loss

I_1 = predict victory I_2 = predict loss

$P(s_1) = 0.5$ $P(s_2) = 0.5$

$P(I_1|s_1) = P$(predict victory given victory) = 0.80

$P(I_2|s_1) = P$(predict loss given victory) = 0.20

$P(I_1|s_2) = P$(predict victory given loss) = 0.10

$P(I_2|s_2) = P$(predict loss given loss) = 0.90

Table for Information Outcome I_1 (Predict victory)

s_j	$P(s_j)$	$P(I_1\|s_j)$	$P(I_k \text{ and } s_j) = P(s_j)P(I_1\|s_j)$	$P(s_j\|I_k) = P(s_j)/P(I_1)$
s_1	0.5	0.8	0.5(0.8) = 0.40	0.40/0.45 = 0.889
s_2	0.5	0.1	0.5(0.1) = 0.05	0.05/0.45 = 0.111
			$P(I_1) = 0.40 + 0.05 = 0.45$	

Table for Information Outcome I_2 (Predict loss)

s_j	$P(s_j)$	$P(I_2\|s_j)$	$P(I_2 \text{ and } s_j) = P(s_j)P(I_2\|s_j)$	$P(s_j\|I_2) = P(s_j)/P(I_2)$
s_1	0.5	0.2	0.5(0.2) = 0.10	0.10/0.55 = 0.182
s_2	0.5	0.9	0.5(0.9) = 0.45	0.45/0.55 = 0.818
			$P(I_2) = 0.10 + 0.45 = 0.55$	

Thus, if Policy Pollsters predicts a victory, there is an 88.9 percent chance of winning and an 11.1 percent chance of losing. If a loss is predicted, there is an 18.2 percent chance of winning and an 81.8 percent chance of losing.

QUESTIONS

1. When are decision trees preferable to payoff tables?
2. What are prior and posterior probabilities?
3. In a decision tree, what do boxes (squares) represent? What do circles represent?
4. What information is needed to use Bayes Theorem?
5. Describe the procedure used in performing an analysis with a decision tree.
6. Explain why a manager may select an alternative that doesn't maximize the expected monetary value.
7. Explain in your own words how utilities may be assigned to monetary payoffs.
8. Describe the shape of a utility curve associated with a risk taker? Describe the shape of a utility curve associated with a risk avoider?
9. Briefly describe the analytic hierarchy process.
10. Suppose the analytic hierarchy process is used in making decisions, and the consistency ratio for one particular factor is greater than 0.10. How is the normalized matrix used to locate the cause of the inconsistency?

PROBLEMS

11. A financial advisor has recommended two possible investment alternatives (a_1 and a_2). The return that will be achieved by each of these depends on whether the economy is good (s_1) or poor (s_2) in the next year. A payoff table has been constructed to illustrate this situation.

	States of Nature	
Decision Alternatives	s_1	s_2
a_1	2,000	–800
a_2	900	400
Probability	0.5	0.5

    a) Draw a decision tree to represent this situation.
    b) Perform the necessary calculations to determine which alternative would yield the highest expected return.
12. Refer to the situation in Problem 11. Suppose a question has arisen about the probability of a good market occurring. What probability of a good market would cause a person to be indifferent between the two alternatives based on the expected value criterion (i.e., the expected values for the two alternatives are the same)?
13. Refer to the situation in Problem 11. Using the original probabilities, suppose there is a question about the payoff for Alternative a_1 in State of Nature s_2. It may not be –800 as originally thought. What payoff would cause a person to be indifferent between the two alternatives based on the expected value criterion?
14. Suppose a financial newsletter will provide additional information about the state of the economy in Problem 11. This newsletter costs $200. If the newsletter predicts a good economy, there is a 70 percent chance it will be good. If the newsletter predicts a poor economy, there is an 90 percent chance it will be

poor. It is believed there is a 40 percent chance the newsletter will predict a good economy and a 60 percent chance it will predict a poor economy.

a) Draw a decision tree to represent this situation.

b) If the newsletter is purchased and it predicts a good market, what would the expected profits be?

c) If the newsletter is purchased and it predicts a poor market, what would the expected profits be?

d) Should the newsletter be purchased? Why or why not?

e) What is the expected value of sample information in this problem?

f) For a newsletter that provides this type of information with this accuracy, what is the maximum amount that should be paid? Why?

15. A financial advisor has recommended two possible investment alternatives (a_1 and a_2). The return that will be achieved by each of these depends on whether the economy is good (s_1), fair (s_2), or poor (s_3) in the next year. A payoff table has been constructed to illustrate this situation.

Decision Alternatives	States of Nature s_1	s_2	s_3
a_1	1,000	200	–500
a_2	600	400	0
Probability	0.2	0.3	0.5

a) Draw a decision tree to represent this situation.

b) Perform the necessary calculations to determine which alternative would yield the highest expected return.

c) Suppose there is a question about the payoff for Alternative a_1 in State of Nature s_3. What payoff would cause a person to be indifferent between the two alternatives based on the expected value criterion?

16. Cecil Development Company is planning to build a shopping center on a particular piece of land. This shopping center can be small, medium, or large. The anticipated profit for each depends on the local economy in the next few years. A payoff table has been developed giving the profits in thousands for this situation.

	States of Economy Poor	Fair	Good
Small	–20	40	60
Medium	–40	80	120
Large	–120	100	300
Probability	0.3	0.5	0.2

Draw a decision tree and use this to determine which type of shopping center to build.

17. Two states of nature exist for a particular situation. The first of these is a good market (s_1) for a product and the second one is a poor market (s_2) for that product. Market research may be performed to obtain more information about what market conditions actually will occur. The market research results

may be positive (I_1) or negative (I_2). The following probabilities are known in this situation:

$P(s_1) = 0.5$ $\quad P(s_2) = 0.5$

$P(I_1|s_1) = 0.7$ $\quad P(I_2|s_1) = 0.3$

$P(I_1|s_2) = 0.1$ $\quad P(I_2|s_2) = 0.9$

a) What are the prior probabilities in this problem?
b) What is the probability the market research results are positive (i.e., find $P(I_1)$)?
c) What is the probability that the market research results are negative (i.e., find $P(I_2)$)?
d) Use Bayes Theorem to find the following posterior probabilities:

$$P(s_1|I_1),\ P(s_2|I_1),\ P(s_1|I_2),\ P(s_2|I_2)$$

e) If the market research results are positive, what is the probability of a good market for the product?
f) If the market research results are negative, what is the probability of a good market for the product?
g) If *perfect information* were available, and this information indicated the market would be good, what is the probability the market actually will be good?

18. Two states of nature exist for a particular situation. The first of these is a good economy (s_1) and the second one is a poor economy (s_2). An economic analysis may be performed to obtain more information about what economic conditions actually will occur. The economic analysis results may forecast a good economy (I_1) or they may forecast a poor economy (I_2). Currently it is believed there is a 60 percent chance the economy will be good and a 40 percent chance it will be poor. In the past, whenever the economy actually was good, the forecast was for a good economy 80 percent of the time. Whenever the economy was poor, the forecast was for a poor economy 90 percent of the time.

    If I_1 represents a forecast of a good economy and I_2 represents a forecast of a poor economy, answer the following questions.
    a) What are the following probabilities?
    $P(s_1)$, $P(s_2)$, $P(I_1|s_1)$, $P(I_2|s_1)$, $P(I_1|s_2)$, $P(I_2|s_2)$
    b) What are the prior probabilities in this problem?
    c) Find the following probabilities:
    $P(s_1|I_1)$, $P(s_2|I_1)$, $P(s_1|I_2)$, $P(s_2|I_2)$, $P(I_1)$, $P(I_2)$
    d) If the economic analysis gives a forecast of a good economy, what is the probability of a good economy?
    e) If the economic analysis gives a forecast of a poor economy, what is the probability of a good economy?
    f) What is the probability the economic analysis gives a forecast for a good economy?
    g) What is the probability the economic analysis gives a forecast for a poor economy?

19. For the situation described in Problem 18, suppose the alternatives and the payoffs are given in the following table:

Decision Alternatives	States of Nature s_1	s_2
a_1	10,000	2,000
a_2	5,000	4,000

a) If the cost of the economic forecast is $2,000, draw a decision tree for this problem.
b) If the economic analysis were used and the results were negative, what would the expected profits be?
c) What is the expected value of sample information?

20. The following payoff table gives the profits that would be achieved by two alternatives.

Decision Alternatives	States of Nature s_1	s_2
#1	10,000	0
#2	6,000	3,000
Probability	0.7	0.3

a) What are the expected profits for the two alternatives? Which decision would be made if we wished to maximize the expected profits?
b) If utilities are to be assigned to these, which payoff would be assigned a utility of one? Which payoff would be assigned a utility of zero?
c) Set up the payoff table that would be used to find the utility of $6,000. What is the certainty equivalent in this problem? Use your own judgment and attitude toward risk to find the utility you would place on $6,000.
d) Suppose you wish to find the utility of $3,000. What is the certainty equivalent in this problem? Use your own judgment and attitude toward risk to find the utility you would place on $3,000.
e) Suppose a utility of 0.5 was found for $6,000 and a utility of 0.2 was found for $3,000. Do these utilities reflect the attitude of a person who is a risk taker or one who is risk averse?
f) Use the utilities of 0.5 for $6,000 and 0.2 for $3,000 to find the expected utility of Alternative #1 and the expected utility of Alternative #2? What decision would be made based on the expected utility?

21. Linda Price is a student who will be graduating soon and is planning to go to graduate school to work for an MBA. Linda has been accepted at three universities and must decide which one to attend. She has rated each university on cost, program reputation, and quality of life. These ratings are summarized below (one is a poor rating and 10 is perfect):

	University A	B	C
Cost	4	8	7
Reputation	9	5	6
Quality of Life	7	7	3

Linda has decided cost is the overriding factor. She has given cost a weight of 0.6, program reputation a weight of 0.2, and quality of life a weight of 0.2. Which university should Linda select?

22. Refer to the situation faced by Linda Price in Problem 21. Upon reevaluating the situation, Linda is not comfortable with her ratings. Therefore, she has decided to compare the universities two at a time. On cost, B is strongly preferred to A, B is moderately preferred to C, and C is moderately preferred to A. On program reputation, A is very strongly preferred to B, C is moderately preferred to B, and A is strongly preferred to C. On quality of life, A and B are equally preferred. A is strongly preferred to C, and B is very strongly preferred to C. On the three factors, cost is very strongly preferred to quality of life, cost is moderately preferred to program reputation, and program reputation is equally to moderately preferred to quality of life.

    Develop the pairwise comparison matrices that would be used with the analytic hierarchy process.
23. Normalize the matrices in Problem 22. What university should Linda select?
24. In searching for a new car, Gina Fox, a college student, has found three types of automobiles that are affordable and provide a basic mode of transportation. In evaluating these three cars, the student believes there is a difference in the cost, appearance, and quality of each car. A rating of 100 is the best possible rating. The three cars are rated by the student on each of these factors as shown in the table below:

	Cost	Appearance	Quality
Car A	65	90	80
Car B	80	50	65
Car C	70	80	70

    Cost is the most important factor, and the student gives this a weight of 0.5. Appearance is next most important and it is given a weight of 0.3. Quality is given a weight of 0.2. Calculate the overall weighted rating for each car and determine which one should be selected.
25. Suppose the analytic hierarchy process was to be used with Problem 24. Gina has compared the cars on the three factors and has made the following observations: On cost:

    Car B is strongly preferred to Car A.

    Car B is moderately preferred to Car C.

    Car C is moderately preferred to Car A.

    On appearance:

    Car A is moderately preferred to Car C.

    Car A is extremely strongly preferred to Car B.

    Car B is moderately to strongly preferred to Car C.

    On quality:

    Car A is moderately to strongly preferred to Car C.

    Car C is moderately preferred to Car B.

    Car A is strongly preferred to Car B.

a) Use the AHP pairwise comparison scale presented in this chapter to develop pairwise comparison tables for the factors of cost, appearance, and quality.
b) Looking at these preferences, does there appear to be any inconsistency? If so, what change(s) would you recommend?

26. For the AHP situation in Problem 25, Gina has performed comparisons of cost, appearance, and quality. The following table was developed using the AHP pairwise comparison scale:

	Cost	Appearance	Quality
Cost	1	4	6
Appearance	1/4	1	1/2
Quality	1/6	2	1

Describe in your own words how this student views the relative importance of each of the three factors.

27. Normalize the pairwise comparison matrices that were developed in Problems 25 and 26. What are the relative ratings that would be assigned to each of the three cars? What are the weights that should be used for each of the factors? What car should Gina select?

28. Calculate the consistency ratios for Problem 27. Are any inconsistencies present? Identify them if there are any.

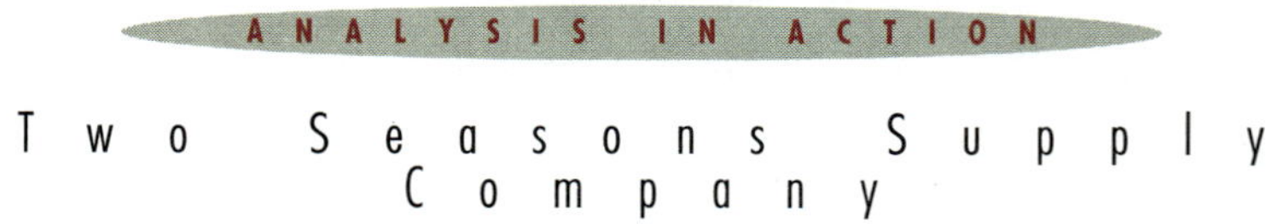

Two Seasons Supply Company

Two Seasons Supply Company is an air conditioning and heating supply company based in southern New Mexico. The company has been moderately successful, although new competition has entered the market and the management of Two Seasons has decided to start an aggressive marketing campaign.

A major source of revenue for Two Seasons is the sale of a four-ton air conditioning compressor. This compressor is sold individually or as part of a completely new air conditioning system. The manufacturer of the compressor provides a one year warranty on parts and labor. Because Two Seasons is an authorized service facility for this product, if a problem occurs during the first year, a service technician from Two Seasons will repair the unit and the compressor manufacturer then will pay Two Seasons for the cost of labor and materials.

Two Seasons is considering providing a three-year warranty on parts and labor for this product either at no cost to the buyer or at a very low rate. This is intended as an incentive to boost sales, although a high cost for this will not help sales. With this warranty, if the unit fails during the first year, the manufacturer pays for the repairs, and if it fails in years two or three, Two Seasons will pick up the cost. The management of Two Seasons would like to determine how much this will cost the company in the future if the warranty is provided.

The cost to Two Seasons for the air compressor is $300 and it is sold to independent service contractors for $400. It is also sold to the public for $750, but this includes the installation cost of $190. When the unit breaks, the average labor cost for repairing the unit is $80 for minor repairs and $120 for major repairs. The materials cost for the repairs is usually either about $50 if a minor repair is needed or about $300 for a major repair as the entire unit is replaced. Past records indicate that about 10 percent of all these units fail during the first year. Once one of the units has been repaired during the first year, it is extremely rare it would fail again in less than four more years. If a unit doesn't have a breakdown in the first year, there is a five percent chance it will break down in year two. If it doesn't have a breakdown in the first two years, there is an eight percent chance it will break down in year three. About 80 percent of all breakdowns involve minor repairs, and 20 percent involve major repairs.

Prepare a brief managerial report indicating what your recommendation would be. Include what this will cost Two Seasons if the warranty is provided at no charge, and how much Two Seasons should charge if management wishes to breakeven. Discuss other considerations management should assess in making this decision.

Weighted Average of the Utilities Spreadsheet Example

Jack is going out to a restaurant for supper. He has three restaurants to choose from. In evaluating the restaurants he is interested in the cost, quality and atmosphere. Jack's ratings on each of the three factors are given in the table below. The ratings are from 1 to 100, with 100 being the highest rating.

Restaurant	Cost	Quality	Atmosphere
A	80	70	60
B	75	85	55
C	60	90	80

	Cost	Quality	Atmosphere
Weight factor	0.4	0.35	0.25

	A	B	C	D	E	F
1	Weighted Average of					
2	Utilities Example					
3						
4	Restaurant	Cost	Quality	Atmosphere		Weighted Average
5	A	80	70	60		71.5
6	B	75	85	55		73.5
7	C	60	90	80		75.5
8						
9	Weights	0.4	0.35	0.25		

	A	B	C	D	E	F
1	Weighted Average of					
2	Utilities Example					
3						
4	Restaurant	Cost	Quality	Atmosphere		Weighted Average
5	A	80	70	60		=+$B$9*B5+$C$9*C5+$D$9*D5
6	B	75	85	55		=+$B$9*B6+$C$9*C6+$D$9*D6
7	C	60	90	80		=+$B$9*B7+$C$9*C7+$D$9*D7
8						
9	Weights	0.4	0.35	0.25		

CHAPTER FOURTEEN

Forecasting

LEARNING OBJECTIVES

Upon completing Chapter 14, you should be able to:

- Identify the different types of forecasting models.
- Explain the components of a time series.
- Develop forecasts using several time series models.
- Calculate three measures of forecast accuracy and explain how these are used in determining the best technique.
- Use regression analysis to develop a forecasting model.
- Interpret the coefficient of correlation and coefficient of determination.
- Compute seasonal indices and use them in adjusting forecasts.
- Develop a forecast for a time series that has a trend component.

CHAPTER OUTLINE

14.1

INTRODUCTION

Managers are faced with uncertainty on a daily basis. In order to plan for the future, forecasts are made to help reduce the uncertainty. A company must forecast demand for a product in order to plan production. Total revenue in the next year is forecast by corporations so budgets may be prepared. Local and state governments must forecast tax revenues for the coming year so the budget may be balanced. Changes in technology may impact the entire market for a product, and forecasts are needed so a company may react accordingly.

A good manager with experience may be able to simply use intuition or judgment to forecast certain things, particularly where the required level of accuracy is not high. However, even the most experienced manager may find the level of accuracy of the forecasts improved by using formal forecasting techniques. A manager may be optimistic about future sales for the company and may tend to overestimate what the sales will be. Other managers may tend to be pessimistic and approach the future in a more conservative manner causing the company to not adequately plan for a growth in demand. Even if the manager has good intuition, using a formal technique may highlight some possible trends that otherwise may be overlooked.

14.2

TYPES OF FORECASTING MODELS

Forecasting models typically are classified as either quantitative or qualitative models. If a forecast is made based on past quantitative or numerical data, the technique is referred to as a **quantitative model**. If the forecast is made based on judgment or other factors that are not quantitative in nature, the model is referred to as a **qualitative model**. Table 14.1 provides a typical classification scheme for some common forecasting models.

Quantitative model
A forecasting model in which numerical data is used.

Qualitative model
A forecasting model based on judgment and nonnumerical information.

Quantitative techniques are further classified as either time series models or causal models. A **time series** is a set of values that are observed at specific intervals of time. Some examples are daily stock prices, monthly sales figures, quarterly profits, and annual housing starts. All of these are recorded at specific time intervals. A time series forecasting model is one in which the only information used in forecasting future values is the past values for the variable to be forecast. Quantitative forecasting techniques that use things other than prior observations of the variable to be forecast are called **causal models**. For example, in forecasting monthly sales for a product, it is reasonable to expect that sales will be influenced by factors such as advertising expenditures and selling price. If the advertising budget for next month is relatively high, sales would be expected to be higher than average. If a major price reduction is being planned for next month, expect a greater demand for the product. A causal model would try to incorporate factors such as these into the forecast for the next month's sales.

Time series
A set of values that are observed at specific intervals of time.

Causal model
A forecasting model in which the forecast for one variable is based on the value of one or more other variables.

Reynolds Metals Company must forecast demand for beverage cans. To meet demand, they opened a new recycling facility that tripled their capacity to process used cans. SOURCE: Photo courtesy Reynolds Metals Company

TABLE 14.1

Classification of Forecasting Models

Quantitative Models
Time Series
1. Naive
2. Moving average
3. Weighted moving average
4. Exponential smoothing
Causal
1. Regression models
2. Econometric models
Qualitative Models
1. Expert Panel
2. Delphi Method

14.3 QUALITATIVE MODELS

Forecasting models that do not use mathematical models but rather use expert judgment or opinion are called qualitative models or judgmental models. These often are used when little or no historical data is available.

They also are commonly used when forecasting far into the future where advances in technology may cause significant changes in the pattern of data. For example, the inventions of the automobile and the telephone had significant impacts on lifestyles that could not have been predicted using historical data.

One common qualitative approach is to hold a meeting with experts or managers knowledgeable in a particular area. Through discussions of this group, a forecast is developed. However, due to the group dynamics and individual personalities, one person may tend to overly influence the results, thereby negating the benefits of using several experts. To eliminate this difficulty, the Delphi Method often is used.

Delphi Method
A qualitative forecasting method aimed at reaching a group consensus among a group of experts through written responses instead of through a group meeting.

The **Delphi Method** of forecasting relies on the judgment of a panel of experts, but the individuals never meet as a group. A questionnaire is developed and sent to each of the experts selected. The experts are asked not only to provide forecasts but also to identify reasons for their forecasts. The responses to the questionnaires are summarized and if a consensus is not reached, the results along with the reasoning are mailed to the same group of experts. Given the new information about answers from other experts, the individuals are asked if they wish to revise their original forecasts due to the new information. This continues until a consensus is reached.

Advances in computer hardware and software have allowed the use of group decision support systems to implement a Delphi-like approach. With these systems, the group of experts may meet together in a room with personal computers that form a network, or they may log on to a network from remote locations. Each expert types responses and explanations to questions that appear on the screen. The tabulated results and reasoning then are displayed on the computer screen in front of each expert. Additional comments then are typed, and this continues until the group leader feels sufficient time has elapsed to allow feedback and responses. As with the Delphi Method, this prevents dominant personalities from influencing the group. However, this is much faster than using the Delphi Method.

There are numerous other types of qualitative methods of forecasting, and these often are used in marketing research. Consumer preferences are very important in determining the future sales and success for a particular product. Thus, consumer surveys, focus groups, and other methods of this type are used to provide forecasts related to the success of a product.

14.4 TIME SERIES

A time series often is broken down into four components. These are a trend, a seasonal pattern, a cyclical pattern, and random or irregular variation. A particular time series may possess some or all of these components. A **scatter diagram** is a graph of the values of the time series over time, and may be very helpful in illustrating the pattern of the data.

Scatter diagram
A graph of the values of the time series over time. May be helpful in illustrating the pattern of data.

A **trend** is an overall increase or decrease in the data over time. An upward trend would mean that over a period of time, the values generally are increasing. Even if there is an upward trend in the data it is possible for values to decrease from one period to the next due to random or seasonal

Trend
An overall increase or decrease in values over time.

variations. Figure 14.1 provides two scatter diagrams to illustrate upward and downward trends.

Seasonal pattern
Variations in data that occur repetitively at particular points in a time series.

A **seasonal pattern** is a variation in the data at certain times of the year (or other time intervals) that may be expected to be repeated regularly. For example, sales of fertilizer, garden hoses, and lawn equipment normally are higher during the spring and summer months. Sales of coats, gloves, and other winter goods are expected to be higher during the fall and winter months. Some companies traditionally have higher revenues during particular quarters of the year. Many retail stores have very high sales on Saturdays while sales on other days of the week are lower. Restaurants have more customers during particular hours of the day, and the typically higher or lower number of customers at different hours of the day represents seasonal variations. Thus, the term *season* does not necessarily refer to seasons of the year. A season may be a specific hour of the day when analyzing hourly data; it may be a specific day of the week when analyzing daily data; it may be a specific quarter of the year when analyzing quarterly data; and it may

FIGURE 14.1

Examples of Time Series with Positive Trend and Negative Trend

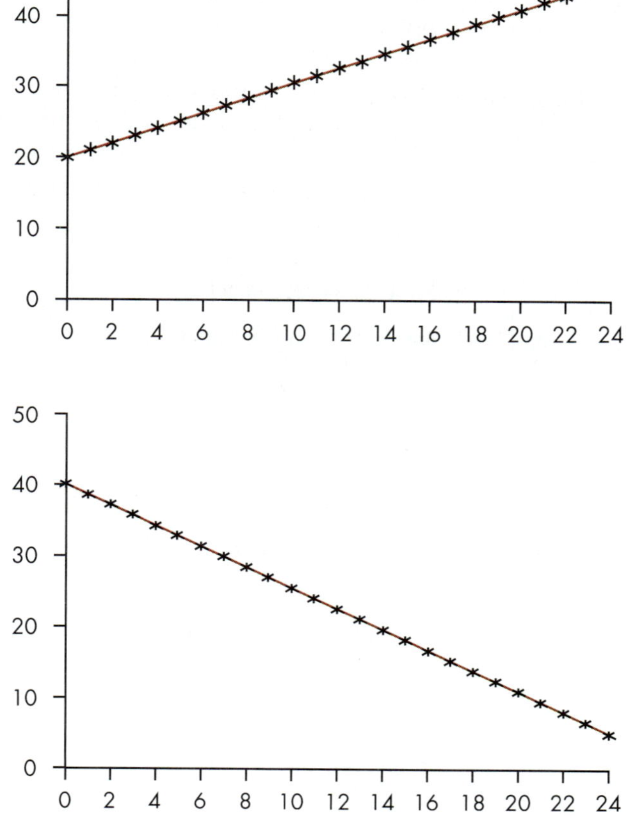

be a specific week of the month when referring to weekly data. Figure 14.2 provides a scatter diagram of time series that have seasonal variations.

Cyclical patterns
Variations in data over long periods of time that are associated with business cycles.

Random or irregular variations
Variations in the data that exist after taking into consideration any cyclical, trend, and seasonal variations.

Cyclical patterns are the variations in the data from year to year that are attributed to the general condition of the economy. Economists often speak of a business cycle when the general economy has some upswings and downswings over periods of years. You may view a cyclical variation as similar to a seasonal variation over a much longer period of time.

Random or **irregular variations** are the irregular or random variations in the data that cannot be predicted. When the trend, seasonal, and cyclical variations have been taken into consideration in making a forecast for a time series, the difference between the forecast and the actual value of the time series is attributed to the random variation. Figure 14.3 shows some scatter diagrams illustrating random fluctuations with certain combinations of a trend and seasonal patterns. We will illustrate some common time series models with the following example.

An Example

Field Fresh Foods is a distributor of numerous types of canned vegetables and other food products. A study is being performed of the company's inventory policies to see if costs of inventory may be lowered by more careful planning. Coffee is of particular concern to the company due to the recent increase in the price. While demand for coffee has been relatively stable over time, there are fluctuations from month to month. Table 14.2 provides the monthly demand for coffee in thousands of pounds for the last six months. Management would like to use this data to help forecast the demand for coffee next month.

A scatter diagram is shown in Figure 14.4. From this little data, it is difficult to determine if there is a trend, and it is impossible to determine if there is any seasonal pattern because there is not even one year of data. Coffee sales will be forecast in the next month using several different methods.

FIGURE 14.2

Example of Time Series with Seasonal Variation

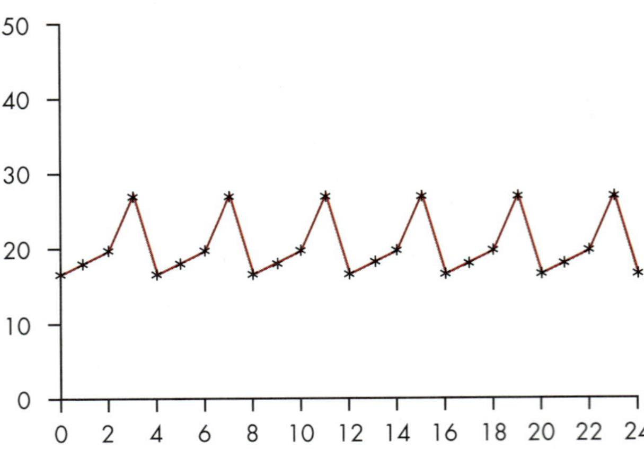

FIGURE 14.3

Random Fluctuations with and without Trend and Seasonal Components

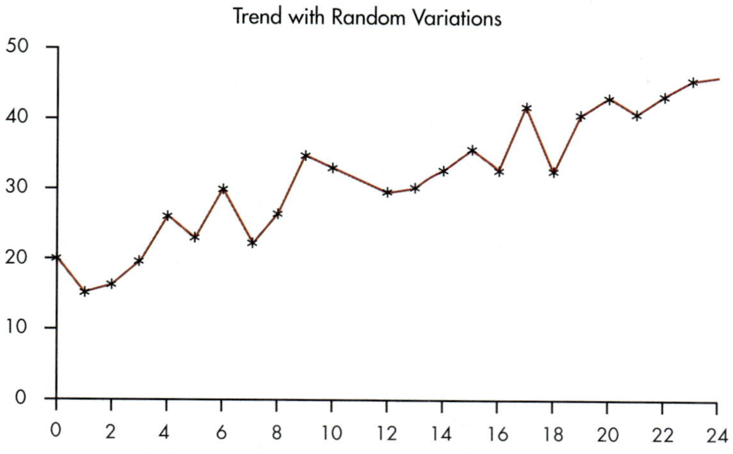

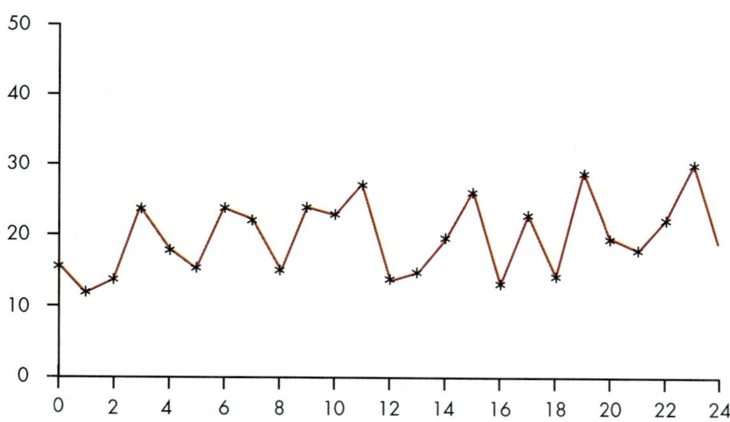

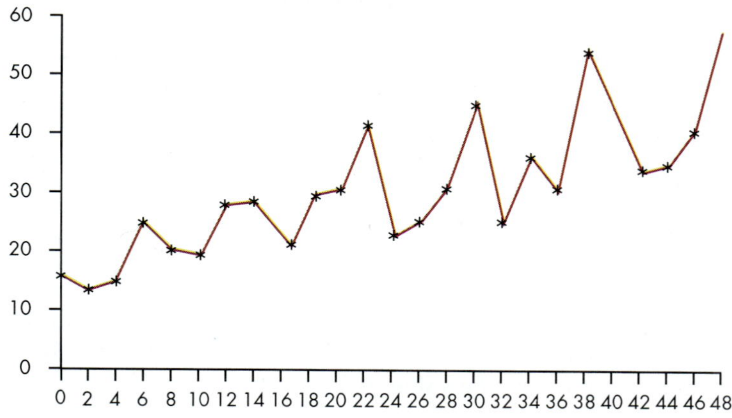

TABLE 14.2

Monthly Demand for Coffee in Field Fresh Foods Example

Month	Demand (in Thousands of Pounds)
1	28
2	18
3	22
4	30
5	23
6	28

FIGURE 14.4

Scatter Diagram of Field Fresh Foods Data

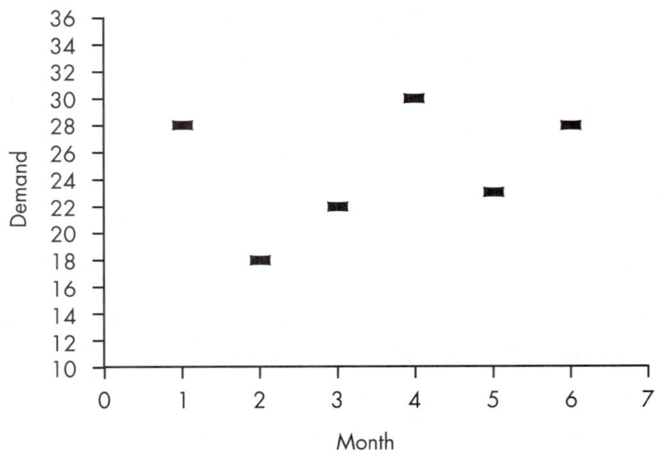

Time Series Models

There are four time series models that we will consider in this chapter. These are the naive model, moving averages, weighted moving averages, and exponential smoothing. All of these will be illustrated with the Field Fresh Foods data given in Table 14.2 above. To help in the presentation of these models, the following variables are defined:

F_t = forecast for time period t

Y_t = actual value of item being forecast in time period t

Table 14.3 shows how the variables for the actual values would be defined in the Field Fresh Foods example. The next time period for which sales are not known is Month 7, so the value of Y_7 will be forecast.

A CLOSER LOOK

Further Developments in Exponential Smoothing

In using exponential smoothing, a tracking signal often is used to monitor the forecast errors over time to determine if an adjustment in the value of the smoothing constant is necessary. The most common tracking signal is the cumulative sum of the errors divided by the mean absolute deviation of the errors. If this is close to zero, the positive errors are being canceled out by the negative errors. If the errors are consistently positive or consistently negative over time, the tracking signal will not be close to zero and may be outside some control limits. This would indicate that some adjustment should be made and the person responsible for making the forecast should check the model.

A step beyond the use of tracking signals is the use of adaptive-control methods. These are methods that automatically adjust or adapt the value of the smoothing constant based on the value of the tracking signal, thereby eliminating the need for human intervention in the forecasting system. Such adaptive methods have been very popular with practitioners. However, studies comparing adaptive-control methods to constant parameter methods have been unable to conclusively prove that adaptive methods are better.

A much more complex method of forecasting time series is the Box-Jenkins method. While this requires at least 50 periods of past data and is more difficult than exponential smoothing, in several studies exponential smoothing has been shown to be at least as accurate as Box-Jenkins.

SOURCE: Gardner, E. S., Jr., 1985. "Exponential Smoothing: The State of the Art." *Journal of Forecasting* 4: 1-28.

TABLE 14.3

Monthly Sales (in Thousands of Pounds) for Field Fresh Foods Example

Month Time = t	Demand (Y_t)
$t = 1$	$Y_1 = 28$
$t = 2$	$Y_2 = 18$
$t = 3$	$Y_3 = 22$
$t = 4$	$Y_4 = 30$
$t = 5$	$Y_5 = 23$
$t = 6$	$Y_6 = 28$
$t = 7$	$Y_7 = ?$

Naive Model

The **naive model** is perhaps the simplest forecasting model. The forecast for the next time period is simply the actual value for the current time period. This is expressed as:

Naive model
A time series forecasting model where the forecast for the next period is the actual value for the current period.

$$\text{forecast for time period } t = \text{actual value for period } t - 1$$

$$F_t = Y_{t-1}$$

To forecast for Month 7 (i.e., $t = 7$) in the Field Fresh Foods example:

$$F_7 = Y_{7-1} = Y_6 = 28$$

Thus, the forecast would be that demand in Month 7 would be 28 thousand pounds.

The naive model often is used because it is easy and may provide forecasts that are sufficiently accurate for many purposes. However, this technique ignores all prior data except data for the period immediately prior to the one being forecast. If that time period had an extremely high or low value relative to all other periods (i.e., the random variation was very high), this might not provide the best forecast. We may wish to incorporate the demand in other prior months into our forecast as well. This would smooth out the forecast and large random fluctuations in the data would not cause drastic changes in the forecast from one month to the next.

Moving Averages

One way to smooth out the forecast and use more past data is to take a simple average of all prior observations. However, if the number of prior periods is extremely large, this may involve averaging twenty years of monthly data. The data that is several years old may not be very relevant to what is happening in the current year due to changes in the conditions surrounding the demand. Managerial judgment is necessary to determine the relevancy of this past data. Also, if there are too many numbers in the average, the forecast would respond very slowly to any changes in the pattern of the data that may be occurring. A technique that averages a specific number (n) of the most recent periods is called a **moving average** technique. The model for an n-period moving average is:

Moving average model

A time series forecasting model that averages a specific number of the most recent observations.

forecast for time period t = average of previous n actual values

$$F_t = (Y_{t-1} + Y_{t-2} + \ldots + Y_{t-n})/n$$

where

n = number of periods to be averaged

In the Field Fresh Foods example, a forecast for Month 7 using a two-month moving average would be:

$$F_7 = (Y_{7-1} + Y_{7-2})/2 = (Y_6 + Y_5)/2 = (28 + 23)/2 = 25.5$$

A forecast based on a three-month moving average would be:

$$F_7 = (Y_6 + Y_5 + Y_4)/3 = (28 + 23 + 30)/3 = 27$$

Thus, if we are forecasting demand for Month 7, forecast 25.5 thousand pounds if the two-month moving average was used and 27 thousand pounds if the three-month moving average was used.

With the moving average approach, each of the last n periods is given equal weight ($1/n$). There may be occasions when it is believed the most recent observations are most relevant and should be given greater weight while still giving some consideration to earlier observations.

Weighted Moving Average

A **weighted moving average** model is a moving average model that assigns weights to the values being averaged. Typically, the most recent values are given a greater weight than earlier values. The weighted moving average forecasting model is:

Weighted moving average model
A moving average model in which weights are assigned to each of the observations that are averaged.

$$F_t = w_{t-1}Y_{t-1} + w_{t-2}Y_{t-2} + \ldots + w_{t-n}Y_{t-n}$$

where

$$n = \text{number of periods to be averaged}$$
$$w_{t-i} = \text{weight assigned to the observation}$$

and

$$\text{sum of weights} = 1$$

A three-month weighted moving average with weights of 0.5 for the most recent value, 0.3 for the next most recent and 0.2 for the next most recent value in the Field Fresh Foods example would be:

$$F_7 = 0.5Y_6 + 0.3Y_5 + 0.2Y_4$$
$$= 0.5(28) + 0.3(23) + 0.2(30) = 26.9$$

In assigning weights, if the weights are not initially expressed so the sum is one, modify them so the sum is one. Divide each number indicating a weight by the total of the numbers and use the result as the modified weight. For example, if a person wished to give the most recent observation a weight of three, the next most recent a weight of two, and the third most recent a weight of one, total these numbers:

$$\text{sum of numbers} = 3 + 2 + 1 = 6$$

Then, divide each number by this result to obtain the weights that would be used. This yields:

$$w_1 = 3/6 = 0.5$$
$$w_2 = 2/6 = 0.333$$
$$w_3 = 1/6 = 0.167$$

Notice the sum of the weights is one.

Both the moving average and the weighted moving average models require the last n values be known in order to forecast for the next period. If n is large and there are numerous different variables (i.e., demand for several different products) to be forecast, the amount of data that must be known may be quite significant.

Exponential Smoothing

Exponential smoothing
A time series forecasting technique that develops a new forecast by using the previous forecast with an adjustment for the error observed.

Forecast error
The difference between the actual value and the forecasted value.

One simple yet often very effective time series forecasting technique that requires very little data is **exponential smoothing**. An exponential smoothing forecast for a particular time period is the previous forecast with an adjustment made to the new forecast based on the accuracy of the previous forecast. **Forecast error** is the difference between the actual value and the forecasted value. If the previous forecast is too low, the next forecast automatically will be made higher. If the previous forecast is too high, the next forecast automatically will be made lower. The exponential smoothing model is:

$$\text{forecast for time period } t = (\text{forecast for previous period}) + (\text{adjustment for error in previous period})$$

$$F_t = F_{t-1} + \alpha(\text{forecast error in period } t-1)$$

$$F_t = F_{t-1} + \alpha(\text{actual} - \text{forecast in period } t-1)$$

$$F_t = F_{t-1} + \alpha(Y_{t-1} - F_{t-1})$$

where

$$Y_{t-1} = \text{actual value in period } t-1$$

$$\alpha = \text{smoothing constant } (0 \le \alpha \le 1)$$

In using this model, the forecaster selects a value of the smoothing constant (α) between zero and one. In the Field Fresh Foods example, a forecast of demand is needed for Month 7. If α is selected to be 0.4 and the forecast for the previous month was 24.8, the model would be:

$$F_7 = F_{7-1} + \alpha(Y_{7-1} - F_{7-1})$$

$$F_7 = F_6 + 0.4(Y_6 - F_6)$$

$$F_7 = 24.8 + 0.4(28 - 24.8)$$

$$= 24.8 + 0.4(3.2)$$

$$= 24.8 + 1.28$$

$$= 26.08$$

Notice in period 6, the actual value observed was 28 while the forecast was 24.8. Thus, the forecast was 3.2 units too low meaning the error was positive 3.2. When this is multiplied by α and added to the previous forecast, the new forecast is higher than the previous forecast. If the error had been negative, the new forecast would be lower than the previous forecast.

The choice of the smoothing constant may have a dramatic impact on the effectiveness of the model. If alpha is close to one, more weight is given to the previous actual value, and less weight is given to earlier values. To more clearly see this, consider the following rearrangement of the model:

$$F_t = F_{t-1} + \alpha(Y_{t-1} - F_{t-1})$$

$$F_t = F_{t-1} + \alpha Y_{t-1} - \alpha F_{t-1}$$

$$F_t = (1 - \alpha)F_{t-1} + \alpha Y_{t-1}$$

If α is close to one, relatively more weight is given to the previous actual value than to the previous forecast. If alpha is close to zero, then less weight is given to the previous actual value and more weight is given to the previous forecast. If the data is assumed to be relatively stable with random fluctuations from one period to the next, it is better to choose a low value for alpha to provide a smoother forecast—one that doesn't react strongly to random changes from one period to the next. However, if you select a value of alpha that is too low, the model will be slow to respond to any change that might occur in the pattern of the data. In the next section we will see how measures of forecast accuracy will help to determine which value of alpha should be used in specific instances.

BEST PRACTICES

Forecasting U.S. Physician Workforce Requirements

Proposals for health care reform in the United States have provoked considerable discussion. While nothing is settled, it is expected that in the future more people will receive care from integrated managed care networks. This will cause a significant change in the requirements on the U.S. physician workforce.

The Council on Graduate Medical Education (COGME) commissioned a study to assess how staffing patterns of health maintenance organizations (HMOs) will affect future U.S. physician workforce requirements. The study was conducted by extrapolating current patterns of staffing within managed care plans to the anticipated system and population of the year 2000.

Forecasting models were used in two phases of the analysis. First, the models were used to predict physician staffing levels for different types of expected health care providers, including HMOs and other types of plans. Estimates were then made of the proportion of Americans likely to be cared for by each type of provider. This resulted in a forecast of the overall U.S. physician requirements in the year 2000, broken down by type of physician.

The demand forecast was compared with the federal government's forecast of physician supply under three different sets of training assumptions. In all three cases, the overall supply of physicians was projected to be higher than the demand forecast by the study. While the primary care physician supply balanced well with the demand, the study predicted a significant surplus of specialists. This has been cited as evidence that primary care providers will be in high demand compared with specialists.

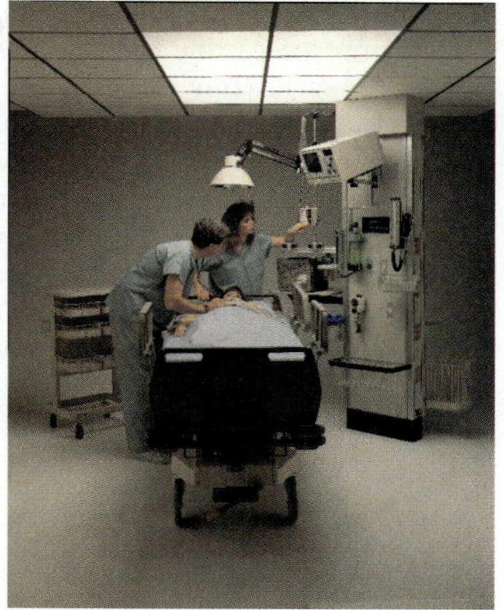

Photo courtesy of Hill-Rom, Batesville, IN.

Health care reform is likely to have a significant effect on the U.S. workforce. The results of this forecasting model may help the government to make informed policy decisions regarding health care. They also may help today's medical students in deciding whether or not to specialize.

SOURCE: Welner, J. P., 1994. "Forecasting the Effects of Health Reform on U.S. Physician Workforce Requirement: Evidence from HMO Staffing Patterns." *Journal of the American Medical Association*, 272 (3): 222-230.

14.5 MEASURES OF FORECAST ACCURACY

To determine how well a particular forecasting technique works for a particular set of data, or to determine which of several forecasting models is best to use with this set of data, it is helpful to have a measure of the accuracy of the model. Three common measures of forecast accuracy are mean absolute deviation (MAD), mean squared error (MSE), and mean absolute percent error (MAPE). All of these provide a measure of the error involved in the forecast. The term *deviation* refers to the deviation of the forecast from the actual value. Thus, the term deviation means the same as error in this context.

Each of the measures of accuracy provides an indication of how well a particular forecasting would have worked on a set of data if it had been used in the past. To calculate any of these measures of accuracy, begin by applying the forecasting technique to all of the past data to provide a forecast for the earlier time periods. The error is calculated by comparing each of these forecasted values to the actual values that occurred.

Suppose the intent is to see how well the naive model works on the Field Fresh Foods data. Table 14.4 provides the naive forecasts for this data. Notice in Month 1, there is no forecast because this was the first value. Begin the forecast in Month 2. For each month with a forecast and an actual value, the calculated error is shown in the table. Notice for Month 7, there is no error because the actual value of the demand for that month is not known.

Mean forecast error
The average of the forecast errors.

The total of the errors is zero because the negative errors are canceling out the positive errors. The **mean forecast error** is the average of the errors, and is given by:

$$\text{mean forecast error} = \Sigma(\text{errors})/n = \Sigma(Y_t - F_t)/n$$

where

$$n = \text{number of errors calculated}$$

In this particular example, the mean forecast error is zero. This is not a good measure of accuracy because large negative errors cancel large positive errors making it impossible to determine how close the forecasts were to the actual value.

Mean absolute deviation (MAD)
A measure of forecast accuracy. The average of the absolute value of the errors.

One way to eliminate the difficulty of negative errors canceling positive errors is to average the absolute value of the errors. This result is called the **mean absolute deviation** (**MAD**) and is given by:

$$\text{mean absolute deviation} = \text{MAD} = \Sigma|\text{errors}|/n = \Sigma|Y_t - F_t|/n$$

This is illustrated with the naive model in Table 14.5. This does provide an effective measure of the accuracy of the forecasting technique.

TABLE 14.4

Mean Forecast Errors for Naive Model

Month Time = t	Demand (Y_t)	Naive Forecast F_t	Error (Deviation) $Y_t - F_t$
1	28	—	—
2	18	28	18 – 28 = –10
3	22	18	22 – 18 = 4
4	30	22	30 – 22 = 8
5	23	30	23 – 30 = –7
6	28	23	28 – 23 = 5
7	—	28	—
			Sum of errors = 0
			Mean forecast error = 0

Another way to prevent negative errors from canceling out positive errors is to square the errors and average the results. This is called the **mean squared error** (**MSE**) and is given by the formula:

Mean squared error (MSE)

A measure of forecast accuracy. The average of squared forecast error.

$$\text{mean squared error} = \text{MSE} = \Sigma(\text{errors})^2/n = \Sigma(Y_t - F_t)^2/n$$

This also is illustrated for the naive model in Table 14.5.

Simply knowing the magnitude of the MAD or the MSE for a particular forecasting technique applied to a specific set of data may not give you enough information to judge the effectiveness of the technique. If the MAD in a particular situation is calculated to be 1,000, would this be considered a high value or a low value? The answer depends on the magnitude of the numbers being forecast. If the attempt is to forecast monthly revenues that range from 100,000 to 300,000, a MAD of 1,000 would be excellent. However, if the attempt is to forecast the number of orders received each month and the number varies from 500 to 3,000, then a MAD of 1,000 would not be very good. To provide more meaning to the measure of accuracy, the **mean absolute percent error** (**MAPE**) is used. The MAPE is the average of the absolute values of the errors expressed as a percentage of the actual value. The formula for this is:

Mean absolute percent error (MAPE)

A measure of forecast accuracy. The average of the absolute value of the errors expressed as a percentage of the actual value.

$$\text{MAPE} = \Sigma|\text{error/actual}|/n = \Sigma|(Y_t - F_t)/Y_t|/n$$

Table 14.6 provides this with the naive model for Field Fresh Foods. This shows that, on the average, the naive model missed the actual value by 29.7 percent of the actual value.

Selecting the Most Accurate Model

If a forecasting technique worked perfectly, all forecasts would equal the actual values. This would result in MAD = 0, MSE = 0, and MAPE = 0. If several different forecasting techniques were being evaluated to determine which one would have worked best with the data set, either the MAD, the

TABLE 14.5

Mean Absolute Deviation (MAD) and Mean Squared Error (MSE) for Naive Model

Month Time = t	Demand (Y_t)	Naive Forecast F_t	Absolute Error (Deviation) $\lvert F_t - Y_t\rvert$	Squared Error $(F_t - Y_t)^2$
1	28	—	—	—
2	18	28	$\lvert 18 - 28\rvert = 10$	$(-10)^2 = 100$
3	22	18	$\lvert 22 - 18\rvert = 4$	$(4)^2 = 16$
4	30	22	$\lvert 30 - 22\rvert = 8$	$(8)^2 = 64$
5	23	30	$\lvert 23 - 30\rvert = 7$	$(-7)^2 = 49$
6	28	23	$\lvert 28 - 23\rvert = 5$	$(5)^2 = 25$
7	—	28	—	
			$\Sigma\lvert\text{errors}\rvert = 34$	$\Sigma(\text{errors})^2 = 254$
			MAD = 34/5 = 6.8	MSE = 254/5 = 50.8

TABLE 14.6

Mean Absolute Percent Error (MAPE) for Naive Model

Month Time (t)	Demand (Y_t)	Naive Forecast F_t	Absolute % Error $(\lvert(F_t - Y_t)/Y_t\rvert)100\%$
1	28	—	—
2	18	28	$\lvert(18 - 28)/18\rvert 100\% = 55.5\%$
3	22	18	$\lvert(22 - 18)/22\rvert 100\% = 18.2\%$
4	30	22	$\lvert(30 - 22)/30\rvert 100\% = 26.7\%$
5	23	30	$\lvert(23 - 30)/23\rvert 100\% = 30.4\%$
6	28	23	$\lvert(28 - 23)/28\rvert 100\% = 17.8\%$
7	—	28	—
			$\sum\lvert \%\text{ errors}\rvert = 148.6\%$
			MAPE = 148.6/5 = 29.7%

MSE, or the MAPE could be calculated for each of the techniques. The technique with the lowest value for the measure of accuracy that is used would be selected. For example, if we are using exponential smoothing and wish to base the choice of the model on the MAD, try several different smoothing constants and select the one that resulted in the lowest MAD.

Which of the three measures of accuracy (MAD, MSE, MAPE) should be used? In many cases it doesn't matter as all three often will result in the same conclusion about which technique is best. The MAD does give a clear indication of how far the forecast missed the actual value on the average. However, the MSE is sometimes preferred because the act of squaring the numbers inherently gives a greater weight to large errors. A manager often is faced with situations in which small errors are no problem but one large error may have severe consequences, as in planning inventory decisions. When this occurs, the MSE is the preferred measure of accuracy.

14.6 CAUSAL MODELS AND REGRESSION ANALYSIS

A second category of quantitative forecasting models is the causal model. Models in this category include regression models, econometric models, and a few others. All of these attempt to forecast the value of one variable based on values for one or more other variables. We will illustrate the use of regression analysis, and provide references at the end of the book for the other topics.

Simple Linear Regression

The basic regression model often is called a simple linear regression model. The model itself is the equation of a straight line hence the term *linear*. This will be represented as:

$$\hat{Y} = a + bX$$

where

$\hat{Y}$ = predicted value of the dependent or response variable (pronounced Y-hat)

X = independent variable

a = intercept

b = slope of the regression line

The **dependent variable** (Y) or **response variable** is the variable to be predicted. A hat (ˆ) is written over the Y to indicate it is a predicted value. The variable used to help predict Y is called the **independent variable** (X). For example, if the belief is that sales of a product are affected by advertising expenditures, then develop a model to predict sales based on advertising expenditures. The dependent variable (Y) would be sales because the belief is that this *depends* on the amount of the advertising expenditures (X).

Dependent (response) variable

A variable in a regression model that is predicted based on the value of another variable. It usually is denoted by Y.

Independent variable

A variable in a regression model that is used to help predict the value of another variable. It usually is denoted by X.

If the belief is that a linear relationship exists, then the line that best fits a particular set of values should be found. While there may be many lines (values of the intercept and slope) that could be found to represent the relationship between X and Y, the line found using regression analysis is the line that results in the lowest mean squared error (MSE). Thus, this regression line often is called the *least-squares line*.

Two measures are associated with each regression model—the **coefficient of determination** (**r^2**) and the **coefficient of correlation** (**r**), which is the square root of the coefficient of determination. Both provide an indication of the strength of the relationship between the variables. The coefficient of determination may be interpreted as the proportion of variability in the dependent variable (Y) that may be explained by the changes in the independent variable (X). The range of values for these are:

Coefficient of determination (r^2)

The proportion of variability in the dependent variable in a regression model that is explained by the model.

Coefficient of correlation (r)

A measure of the relationship between two variables.

$$0 \le r^2 < 1$$

$$-1 \le r \le 1$$

A perfect relationship (MSE = 0) would exist between X and Y if $r^2 = 1$ and if $r = -1$ or $+1$. A good regression model would have a high r^2 value.

Example

City Manufacturing produces water heaters at a manufacturing facility in eastern Michigan. Management of City Manufacturing is developing a budget for the coming year, and a question has been raised about the estimates used for the cost of plant utilities. In an attempt to get a better forecast of costs for the coming year, management has begun evaluating the costs of electricity in the past five months. It is clear the monthly electric bill is higher whenever more units are produced because electricity is used in the manufacture of the product. Table 14.7 provides the monthly costs (in hundreds of dollars) for electricity and the number of units (in thousands) produced in each of these months.

A regression model may be developed to predict the monthly electric costs based on the number of units produced. The dependent variable is the cost of electricity, and the independent variable is the number of units

TABLE 14.7

Data for City Manufacturing Example

Month	Electricity Cost (in Hundreds of Dollars)	Units Produced (in Thousands)
1	12	5
2	16	7
3	9	4
4	18	8
5	17	9

produced. The model is:

$$Y = \text{monthly electricity cost (in hundreds of dollars)}$$
$$X = \text{units produced (in thousands)}$$
$$\text{predicted cost} = \text{intercept} + \text{slope(units)}$$
$$\hat{Y} = a + bX$$

To find the slope (b) and the intercept (a), use either computer software or the formulas provided in the next section. Output 14.1 provides the DSS output for this example. This yields:

$$\text{intercept} = a = 2.96$$
$$\text{slope} = b = 1.73$$

The model becomes:

$$\hat{Y} = 2.96 + 1.73X$$

To predict the electricity cost in a month when 6,000 units ($X = 6$) are produced, we would have:

$$\hat{Y} = 2.96 + 1.73(6) = 13.34 \text{ (in hundreds of dollars)}$$

Thus, the electricity cost in this month would be predicted at $1,334.

The computer output could provide the value of the coefficient of determination (r^2), which is 0.90. This indicates that 90 percent of the variability in monthly electric costs can be attributed to changes in the monthly production quantity.

While this regression model may be used to predict electricity cost for the company, further examination provides additional information to management. Electricity costs for a manufacturing company may be classified as a semi-variable cost because there is a fixed, and a variable, portion to this cost. In this model, the intercept is 2.96. This means if no units are produced ($X = 0$), the monthly electric cost is estimated to be $296. This is the fixed cost portion of the electric bill. The slope is 1.73 which indicates for each one unit increase in X, or 1,000 units produced, the electricity cost increases by 1.73 or $173. This may be viewed as the variable cost portion of the electric bill.

OUTPUT 14.1

DSS Output for City Manufacturing Example

Forecasting - Simple Linear Regression

Obs	Ind (X)	Dep (Y)	X*Y	X**2	Y**2	Y^	Y - Y^	(Y-Y^)**2
1	5.00	12.00	60.00	25.00	144.00	11.6279	0.3721	0.1385
2	7.00	16.00	112.00	49.00	256.00	15.0930	0.9070	0.8226
3	4.00	9.00	36.00	16.00	81.00	9.8953	-0.8953	0.8016
4	8.00	18.00	144.00	64.00	324.00	16.8256	1.1744	1.3793
5	9.00	17.00	153.00	81.00	289.00	18.5581	-1.5581	2.4278
Sum	33.00	72.00	505.00	235.00	1094.00	72.0000	0.0000	5.5698
Avg	6.60	14.40	101.00	47.00	218.80	14.4000	0.0000	0.5570

```
a =             2.9651
b =             1.7326              Regression Equation:
R**2 =          0.9026               Y^ =  2.965113  +  1.732559 X
R =             0.9501
Std Error =     1.3626
```

Special statistical and management science software packages have sophisticated regression capabilities. Most popular spreadsheet software programs also have this as a package feature. We will usually rely on a computer to perform the calculations required in regression. However, we will provide the formulas in a later section for the interested reader.

Multiple Regression

If it is believed that more than one independent variable helps to explain the variability in the dependent variable, additional variables may be included in a **multiple regression model**. A multiple regression model is a regression model with more than one independent variable. A model with two independent variables could be written as:

Multiple regression model

A regression model in which there are several independent variables.

$$\hat{Y} = a + b_1X_1 + b_2X_2$$

In the City Manufacturing example, it is reasonable to expect that a large portion of the electric cost could be explained by the use of air conditioning equipment. The average daily temperature of the month may be used as a variable to incorporate this into the forecast as well. Once the average daily temperature in the sample months is found, input this information together with the previous information about costs and units produced. The computer would then provide values for a, b_1, and b_2, which would be put into the model.

Mathematical Computations for Regression

We will present the formulas for calculating the intercept and the slope for a simple linear regression model. The computations for multiple regression almost always are performed on a computer and consequently will not be presented here.

To perform the calculations in a simple linear regression model, it is helpful to prepare a table similar to Table 14.8, which may be used to calculate the following:

ΣX

ΣY

ΣX^2

ΣXY

With these totals, the following may be computed:

$$b = \frac{\Sigma XY - \frac{1}{n}\Sigma X \Sigma Y}{\Sigma X^2 - \frac{1}{n}(\Sigma X)^2}$$

$$a = \frac{1}{n}\Sigma Y - b\frac{1}{n}\Sigma X$$

Table 14.8 provides the following information for the City Manufacturing example:

$$\Sigma X = 33$$
$$\Sigma Y = 72$$
$$\Sigma X^2 = 235$$
$$\Sigma XY = 505$$

Therefore:

$$b = \frac{505 - \frac{1}{5}(33)(72)}{235 - \frac{1}{5}(33)^2} = 1.733$$

$$a = \frac{1}{5}(72) - (1.733)\frac{1}{5}(33) = 2.962$$

These are the same values generated by the computer and used previously with this example.

TABLE 14.8

Calculations for City Manufacturing Example

Month	Y Cost (in Hundreds of Dollars)	X Units (in Thousands)	X^2	XY
1	12	5	25	60
2	16	7	49	112
3	9	4	16	36
4	18	8	64	144
5	17	9	81	153
	$\Sigma Y = 72$	$\Sigma X = 33$	$\Sigma X^2 = 235$	$\Sigma XY = 505$

Forecasting Trends in the Greeting Card Industry

American Greetings is the world's largest publicly owned distributor of greeting cards and related products. The company has international subsidiaries in Canada, the United Kingdom, France, and Mexico. With the help of these subsidiaries, American Greetings distributes products across a global network of 97,000 retail outlets in more than 50 countries.

Managers at American Greetings pride themselves on meeting the diverse needs of their customers. They target specific age groups in specific countries, and offer cards in 16 different languages. They tailor their products to match emerging trends and societal changes to meet various market niches. For example, they have individual lines of cards targeted to busy parents, African-Americans, college students, people with sight impairment, and pet lovers. To take this micromarketing one step further, they offer Create-A-Card booths, which allow individuals to design their own cards.

Remaining competitive in the greeting card industry today requires constant innovation and attention to the whims of the market. American Greetings develops forecasts based on demographics, trends, fashions, and past sales. The company used these forecasts to inspire new design concepts for cards, and to estimate the need for different types of inventory. For example, American Greetings monitors trends in sales by capturing sales data directly from retailers' cash registers. This allows them to react swiftly to update marketing schemes and restock individual stores. In turn, rapid response times allow the company to maintain low inventory levels and increase productivity, thus maintaining a leadership position in the greeting card industry.

SOURCE:
American Greetings Annual Report, 1993.

14.7 TREND AND SEASONAL TIME SERIES MODELS

While seasonal patterns and trends were mentioned in an earlier section, we have not incorporated these into any of our time series forecasts. However, these may be included in any of the time series techniques previously mentioned. The most common type of model for incorporating trend and seasonal patterns into a forecast is the multiplicative model, although there is an additive model as well. The **multiplicative time series model** is based on the assumption that the data inherently has the following structure:

Multiplicative time series model
A forecasting model that incorporates seasonal and cyclical variations into the forecast by multiplying the forecast by seasonal and cyclical indices.

$$Y_t = T_t \times S_t \times I_t$$

where

Y_t = actual value in time t

T_t = trend component for time period t

S_t = seasonal component for time period t

I_t = irregular (random) component for time period t

The **additive time series model** is based on the assumption that the data inherently has the following structure:

Additive time series model
A forecasting model that incorporates seasonal and cyclical variations into the forecast by adding the forecast's seasonal and cyclical components.

$$Y_t = T_t + S_t + I_t$$

In developing a forecasting model to predict Y_t, recognize that the irregular or random component cannot be forecast. The trend component (T_t) is the

Service establishments in Saratoga, N.Y. experience heightened demand every August during the "racing season" and can use data from previous seasons to forecast demand. SOURCE: Photo courtesy of New York Racing Association

forecast of the value where an adjustment has been made for trend. If there is no trend, this simply would be the forecast of the value before adjusting for a seasonal component. For the multiplicative model, the seasonal component (S_t) is actually an index expressing the size of the particular time period being considered relative to the average size for all time periods.

Computing the Seasonal Index

To calculate a seasonal index, it is best to have data on several repetitions of each time period so random fluctuations are not interpreted as seasonal variations. For example, if we have monthly data or quarterly data, we would like to have several years worth of data. If we have daily data and believe values on certain days of the week tend to have higher or lower values than normal, we would like to have several weeks of data.

Let's suppose we have monthly data for sales with no trend and we wish to find the seasonal index for January. Find the average sales for all months and find the average sales for all the January's in the sample. Then:

S_{Jan} = seasonal index for January

S_{Jan} = (average January sales)/(average monthly sales)

This computational process would be repeated for all months to obtain a seasonal index for all 12 months. If a trend is present, then the average monthly sales in the denominator of the formula should include monthly sales for the year centered around the month being analyzed. That is, an equal number of periods before January should be used with an equal number of periods after January. By doing this, any trend effect is eliminated when the monthly average is calculated. This will be illustrated in the following example.

Turner Industries Example

Table 14.9 provides quarterly sales data in $100,000 for Turner Industries for each of five years. Figure 14.5 provides the scatter diagram for this. Notice some quarters typically have high sales while others typically have low sales. The overall average monthly sales are 128.3. If no trend were present, the seasonal index for the first quarter would be:

$$S_1 = \text{(average Quarter 1 sales)/(average quarterly sales)}$$

Compute:

$$\text{average Quarter 1 sales} = (108.4 + 110.5 + 93.0 + 119.0 + 102.0)/5 = 106.58$$

$$S_1 = 106.58/128.3 = 0.83$$

Similar computations would result in the following:

$$S_2 = 0.99$$
$$S_3 = 1.08$$
$$S_4 = 1.09$$

These indices show that typically sales in the first quarter of the year are lower than average, in the second quarter are close to average, and in the last two quarters are higher than average sales.

If a trend is known to exist or if a trend is suspected, the above method may not be accurate as some variations due to the trend would be attributed to seasonal patterns. A change in sales from one quarter to the next would have a seasonal component combined with a trend component. Eliminate the trend effect by comparing the actual sales in each quarter to a moving average of quarterly sales centered about that particular quarter.

Table 14.10 illustrates how this is done. There must be an equal number of periods before and after each quarter with which to work so any trend is averaged out of the data. In this example, for Quarter 3 in Year 1, a moving average is calculated to be 132.0 by averaging the four quarters of Year 1. This average is not centered around Quarter 3 but is between Quarter 2 and Quarter 3. Another moving average is calculated to be 132.5 by averaging the last three quarters of Year 1 and the first quarter of Year 2. This is centered after Quarter 3. Averaging these two numbers results in a moving average that is centered about Quarter 3. Then compute a seasonal ratio that is the Quarter 3 sales divided by the centered moving average, which yields the following:

$$\text{seasonal ratio} = 152.9/132.2 = 1.156$$

Repeating this process with the other quarters gives the seasonal ratios shown in the last column in Table 14.10.

To minimize the impact of random variations, compute the seasonal index for each of the four quarters by averaging each of the seasonal ratios.

TABLE 14.9

Quarterly Sales Data for Turner Industries

Year	Quarter	Sales (in Hundred Thousands of Dollars)
1	1	108.4
	2	125.8
	3	152.9
	4	140.7
2	1	110.5
	2	131.1
	3	128.7
	4	139.4
3	1	93.0
	2	129.1
	3	137.9
	4	149.3
4	1	119.0
	2	128.7
	3	129.4
	4	128.8
5	1	102.0
	2	123.3
	3	143.3
	4	145.3
		Average = 128.3

FIGURE 14.5

Scatter Diagram for Turner Industries Example

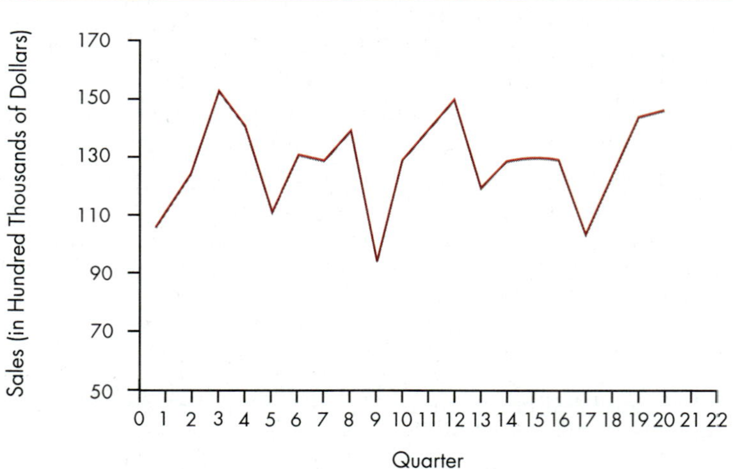

TABLE 14.10

Quarterly Sales Data for Turner Industries with Centered Moving Averages and Seasonal Ratios

Year	Quarter	Sales	MA	CMA	Seasonal Ratio (Sales/CMA)
1					
	1	108.4			
	2	125.8			
			132.0		
	3	152.9		132.2	1.156
			132.5		
	4	140.7		133.1	1.057
			133.8		
2	1	110.5		130.8	0.845
			127.8		
	2	131.1		127.6	1.028
			127.4		
	3	128.7		125.2	1.028
			123.1		
	4	139.4		122.8	1.135
			122.6		
3	1	93.0		123.7	0.752
			124.9		
	2	129.1		126.1	1.024
			127.3		
	3	137.9		130.6	1.056
			133.8		
	4	149.3		133.8	1.116
			133.7		
4	1	119.0		132.7	0.897
			131.6		
	2	128.7		129.0	0.997
			126.5		
	3	129.4		124.4	1.041
			122.2		
	4	128.8		121.6	1.060
			120.9		
5	1	102.0		122.6	0.832
			124.4		
	2	123.3		126.4	0.975
			128.5		
	3	143.3			
	4	145.3			

MA = moving average
CMA = centered moving average

This is shown in Table 14.11. The seasonal indices should add up to the number of periods to force an average period to have a seasonal index of one. Because there are four quarters, the seasonal indices should add up to four. If they do not, divide each seasonal index by the total and divide by four to force this to occur. In this example, this is not necessary.

Deseasonalizing the Data

Once the seasonal indices are found, they are used to deseasonalize the data. This is done by dividing each number by the seasonal index, as shown in Table 14.12. A graph of the original data and the deseasonalized data are shown in Figure 14.6. Looking at the first quarter of Year 5 shows that while sales in this quarter were lower than sales in the quarters immediately before and after it, the sales were quite high for a first quarter.

Adjusting the Forecast Using the Seasonal Index

The seasonal index is used to adjust the forecasts. In adjusting for a seasonal component, develop the forecast for a time series using the deseasonalized data. Use one of the techniques discussed previously and multiply this result by the appropriate seasonal index. To forecast quarterly sales for the first quarter of Year 6 in the Turner Industries example with a four-quarter moving average, average the deseasonalized data for the previous four quarters:

$$\text{4-quarter moving average} = (133.3 + 133.9 + 122.1 + 122.7)/4$$
$$= 128$$

Multiply this by the seasonal index for Quarter 1, which results in:

$$\text{forecast} = (\text{4-quarter moving average})S_1$$
$$= (128)0.83 = 106.24$$

Winter's Model
An exponential smoothing model that includes an adjustment for trend and seasonal components.

Forecasts using methods other than the moving average would incorporate the seasonal index in a similar fashion.

An exponential smoothing model that incorporates a trend and a seasonal pattern in this way is called **Winter's Model**. The interested reader is

TABLE 14.11

Seasonal Indices for Turner Industries Example

	Quarterly Ratios				Quarterly Index (Average of Ratios)
Quarter 1	0.845	0.752	0.897	0.832	0.83
Quarter 2	1.028	1.024	0.997	0.975	1.01
Quarter 3	1.156	1.028	1.056	1.041	1.07
Quarter 4	1.057	1.135	1.116	1.060	1.09
				Total	4.00

TABLE 14.12

Deseasonalized Values for Turner Industries Quarterly Sales Data

Quarter	Sales ÷ Index = Deseasonalized Value
1	108.4 ÷ 0.83 = 130.6
2	125.8 ÷ 1.01 = 124.6
3	152.9 ÷ 1.07 = 142.9
4	140.7 ÷ 1.09 = 129.1
1	110.5 ÷ 0.83 = 133.1
2	131.1 ÷ 1.01 = 129.8
3	128.7 ÷ 1.07 = 120.3
4	139.4 ÷ 1.09 = 127.9
1	93.0 ÷ 0.83 = 112.0
2	129.1 ÷ 1.01 = 128.8
3	137.9 ÷ 1.07 = 128.9
4	149.3 ÷ 1.09 = 137.0
1	119.0 ÷ 0.83 = 143.4
2	128.7 ÷ 1.01 = 127.4
3	129.4 ÷ 1.07 = 120.9
4	128.8 ÷ 1.09 = 118.2
1	102.0 ÷ 0.83 = 122.7
2	123.3 ÷ 1.01 = 122.1
3	143.3 ÷ 1.07 = 133.9
4	145.3 ÷ 1.09 = 133.3

FIGURE 14.6

Graph of Original Data and Deseasonalized Data for Turner Industries Example

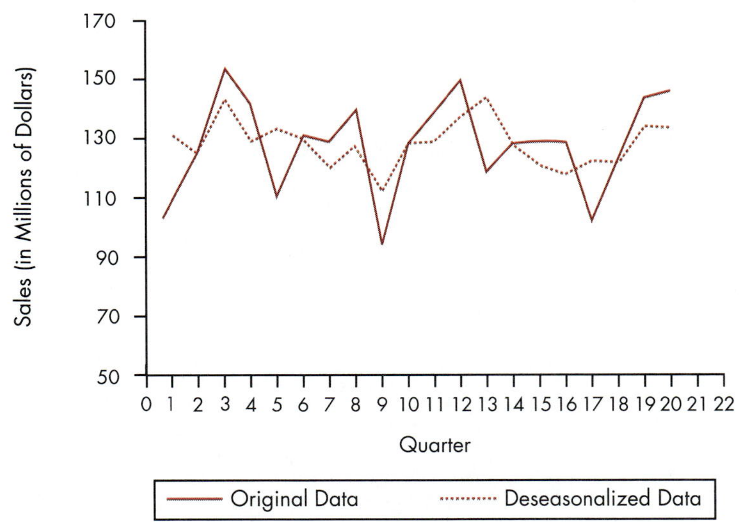

referred to the references at the end of the book. This approach is available in many software packages.

Adjusting for Trend

Holt's Model
An exponential smoothing model that includes an adjustment for trend.

There are two common approaches to forecasting time series where trend is present. If exponential smoothing is used, there is a special exponential smoothing model called Holt's Linear Exponential Smoothing Model or simply **Holt's Model**. This is an additive type of model in which the trend is estimated and this value simply is added to the normal forecast. For example, if it is found that the average increase from one time period to the next is 12 units, and the original forecast without trend for time period 7 was 680 units, then the adjusted forecast for time period 7 would be 680 + 12 = 692. The details of this approach are available in references provided at the end of the book. This method is available in numerous exponential smoothing software packages.

Another approach to incorporating trend into a forecast is to use regression analysis where the independent variable is time. This also is an additive model. The basic regression model is:

$$\hat{Y} = a + bX$$

If X = time, then this model is automatically making an adjustment for time.

For example, suppose the monthly sales (in Thousands of Dollars) for a company for the last six months are the values given in Table 14.13. A graph of this is shown in Figure 14.7. From the graph, it appears there is a trend in the data. Use either the formulas given for regression analysis earlier in the chapter or use the computer. Figure 14.9 provides the output from DSS. It shows:

$$a = 234.60$$
$$b = 8.26$$

Therefore the regression model is:

$$\hat{Y} = 234.60 + 8.26X$$

TABLE 14.13

Monthly Sales for Trend Example Using Regression

Month (X)	Sales (in Thousands of Dollars) (Y)
1	240
2	256
3	254
4	269
5	284
6	278

FIGURE 14.7

Graph of Sales Data for Regression Trend Example

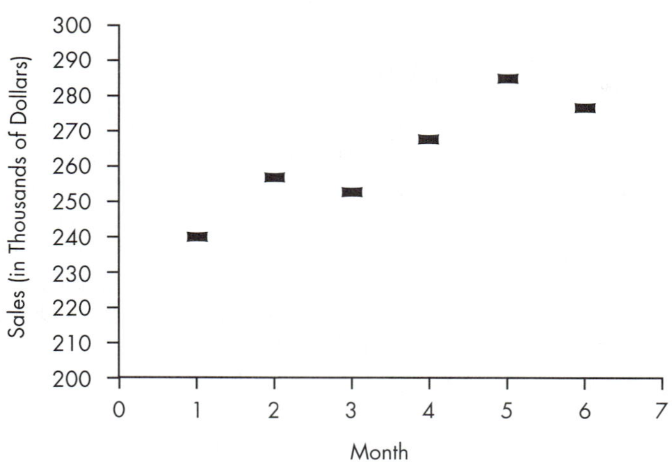

OUTPUT 14.2

DSS Output for Regression Trend Example

```
Forecasting - Simple Linear Regression

Obs  Ind (X)  Dep (Y)     X*Y    X**2     Y**2        Y^       Y - Y^  (Y-Y^)**2
 1    1.00    240.00   240.00    1.00  57600.00  242.8571  -2.8571     8.1633
 2    2.00    256.00   512.00    4.00  65536.00  251.1143   4.8857    23.8702
 3    3.00    254.00   762.00    9.00  64516.00  259.3714  -5.3714    28.8523
 4    4.00    269.00  1076.00   16.00  72361.00  267.6286   1.3714     1.8808
 5    5.00    284.00  1420.00   25.00  80656.00  275.8857   8.1143    65.8417
 6    6.00    278.00  1668.00   36.00  77284.00  284.1429  -6.1429    37.7346

Sum  21.00   1581.00  5678.00   91.00 417953.00 1581.0000   0.0000   166.3429
Avg   3.50    263.50   946.33   15.17  69658.84  263.5000   0.0000    16.6343

a =           234.6000
b =             8.2571                   Regression Equation:
R**2 =          0.8776                    Y^ =  234.6  +  8.257143 X
R =             0.9368
Std Error =     6.4487
```

To forecast the sales for Month 7 ($X = 7$):

$$\hat{Y} = 234.6 + 8.26(7) = 292.42$$

To forecast the sales for Month 10 ($X = 10$), we would have

$$\hat{Y} = 234.6 + 8.26(10) = 317.20$$

Caution should be used with this trend method when trying to forecast too far into the future. The trend may not continue indefinitely and managerial judgment is needed to determine whether this should be used for more than a few time periods into the future.

14.8

SELECTING THE APPROPRIATE TECHNIQUE

Many things may impact the type of forecasting model that is appropriate for a particular situation. In this chapter we looked at some of the common forecasting techniques that are available and saw how to measure the accuracy of the forecasting model. However, to measure the accuracy of the methods, it is necessary to actually develop the model. With a large number of items to forecast and with large sets of data, it is helpful to identify the models that might best fit a particular situation before spending the time and money to develop the models.

The items listed in Summary Table 14.1 have been identified as being very helpful in matching the forecasting method to the situation. A brief description of these will be provided, although further details are available in the references at the end of the book.

Some forecasts are used to plan for the future while others are used for control purposes to determine if a process is out of control. When a forecast is used for control, it is important the technique quickly identify changes in the pattern of the data.

The level of detail necessary may vary significantly depending on who is using the results. The policy makers in a corporation may be interested in a forecast of the aggregate performance of all products and division within the company, while the production manager must have forecasts for demand for each individual product.

While an accurate forecast is certainly wanted by management, a very rough forecast may suffice. In planning the food purchases for a restaurant, a forecast for the number of customers is needed, but it does not have to be extremely accurate as some of the food can be used on a later day. However, if a banquet is being planned by that same restaurant, a very accurate forecast is needed so the correct number of place settings and meals can be planned in advance.

The time horizon is important because some techniques are better suited for forecasting short-term (a few months), while others are better for medium-term (a few months to one or two years), and still others are better for long-term (more than one or two years). The time series methods of this chapter typically are used for short-term forecasting. Regression models often are used for short- and medium-range forecasts. Qualitative models often are used for long-term forecasts.

The type of data refers to the underlying pattern of the data. If trend and seasonal patterns are present, an appropriate model should be selected.

If the data is not available when it is needed, a forecasting model may be useless. This should be considered in selecting the model.

The cost of a forecast involves the cost of developing the model, collecting the data, and running the model. If new software must be developed or bought, the cost of this may cause one to use a different model for which software is already available.

SUMMARY TABLE 14.1

Things to Consider when Selecting a Forecasting Technique

Purpose of the forecast
Level of detail required
Accuracy required
Time horizon
Type of data
Availability of data
Cost of forecasting method

A combination of time series, causal, and judgmental models are used to forecast weather. SOURCE: Photo courtesy of National Oceanic and Atmospheric Administration

14.9 SUMMARY

In this chapter we explored several quantitative forecasting techniques that were classified as time series methods and causal methods. The time series models discussed included the naive model, moving averages, weighted moving averages, and exponential smoothing. Regression analysis was discussed as a common causal forecasting model. Both seasonal and trend patterns may be incorporated into all of these models if necessary.

Measures of accuracy are used to determine how well a technique might be expected to work with a particular set of data as they measure past performance on the data set. The mean absolute deviation, mean squared error, and mean absolute percent error are some common measures of accuracy.

The qualitative models for forecasting rely on expert judgment. The Delphi Method is helpful in reducing the impact of individual personalities in preparing forecasts. Other qualitative models very often are used in marketing research.

While there are many different forecasting techniques that are available, a manager should consider several things when trying to determine which one is best to use in a specific situation. These include the purpose of the forecast, the level of detail required, the time horizon for the forecast, the type and availability of the data, and the cost of preparing the forecast.

GLOSSARY

Additive time series model A forecasting model that incorporates seasonal and cyclical variations into the forecast by adding the forecast's seasonal and cyclical components. *p. 609*

Causal model A forecasting model in which the forecast for one variable is based on the value of one or more other variables. *p. 590*

Coefficient of correlation (*r*) A measure of the relationship between two variables. *p. 605*

Coefficient of determination (r^2) The proportion of variability in the dependent variable in a regression model that is explained by the model. *p. 605*

Cyclical patterns Variations in data over long periods of time that are associated with business cycles. *p. 594*

Delphi Method A qualitative forecasting method aimed at reaching a group consensus among a group of experts through written responses instead of through a group meeting. *p. 592*

Dependent (response) variable A variable in a regression model that is predicted based on the value of another variable. It usually is denoted by *Y*. *p. 605*

Exponential smoothing A time series forecasting technique that develops a new forecast by using the previous forecast with an adjustment for the error observed. *p. 599*

Forecast error The difference between the actual value and the forecasted value. *p. 599*

Holt's Model An exponential smoothing model that includes an adjustment for trend. *p. 616*

Independent variable A variable in a regression model that is used to help predict the value of another variable. It usually is denoted by *X*. *p. 605*

Mean forecast error The average of the forecast errors. *p. 602*

Mean absolute deviation (MAD) A measure of forecast accuracy. The average of the absolute value of the errors. *p. 602*

Mean squared error (MSE) A measure of forecast accuracy. The average of squared forecast error. *p. 603*

Mean absolute percent error (MAPE) A measure of forecast accuracy. The average of the absolute value of the errors expressed as a percentage of the actual value. *p. 603*

Moving average model A time series forecasting model that averages a specific number of the most recent observations. *p. 598*

Multiple regression model A regression model in which there are several independent variables. *p. 607*

Multiplicative time series model A forecasting model that incorporates seasonal and cyclical variations into the forecast by multiplying the forecast by seasonal and cyclical indices. *p. 609*

Naive model A time series forecasting model where the forecast for the next period is the actual value for the current period. *p. 597*

Qualitative model A forecasting model based on judgment and nonnumerical information. *p. 590*

Quantitative model A forecasting model in which numerical data is used. *p. 590*

Random or irregular variations Variations in the data that exist after taking into consideration any cyclical, trend, and seasonal variations. *p. 594*

Scatter diagram A graph of the values of the time series over time. May be helpful in illustrating the pattern of data. *p. 592*

Seasonal pattern Variations in data that occur repetitively at particular points in a time series. *p. 593*

Time series A set of values that are observed at specific intervals of time. *p. 590*

Trend An overall increase or decrease in values over time. *p. 592*

Weighted moving average model A moving average model in which weights are assigned to each of the observations that are averaged. *p. 599*

Winter's Model An exponential smoothing model that includes an adjustment for trend and seasonal components. *p. 614*

KEY EQUATIONS

(14-1) F_t = forecast for time period t
Y_t = actual value of item being forecast in time period t

(14-2) Naive forecast
forecast for time period t = actual value for period $t - 1$
$F_t = Y_{t-1}$

(14-3) Moving average forecast
forecast for time period t = average of previous n actual values
$F_t = (Y_{t-1} + Y_{t-2} + \ldots + Y_{t-n})/n$
where
n = number of periods to be averaged

(14-4) Weighted moving average forecast
$F_t = w_{t-1}Y_{t-1} + w_{t-2}Y_{t-2} + \ldots + w_{t-n}Y_{t-n}$
where
n = number of periods to be averaged
w_{t-i} = weight assigned to the observation
and
sum of weights = 1

Exponential smoothing forecast
$F_t = F_{t-1} + \alpha(Y_{t-1} - F_{t-1})$
α = smoothing constant
$0 \leq \alpha \leq 1$

(14-5) Measures of forecast accuracy

1. Mean forecast error = $\Sigma(\text{errors})/n = \Sigma(Y_t - F_t)/n$

   where

   n = number of errors calculated

2. Mean absolute deviation = MAD = $\Sigma|\text{errors}|/n = \Sigma|Y_t - F_t|/n$
3. Mean squared error = MSE = $\Sigma(\text{errors})^2/n = \Sigma(Y_t - F_t)^2/n$
4. Mean absolute percent error

   MAPE = $\Sigma|\text{error/actual}|/n = \Sigma|(Y_t - F_t)/Y_t)|/n$

(14-6) Regression models

$$\hat{Y} = a + bX$$

$$b = \frac{\Sigma XY - \frac{1}{n}\Sigma X \Sigma Y}{\Sigma X^2 - \frac{1}{n}(\Sigma X)^2} \qquad \textit{(slope)}$$

$$a = \frac{1}{n}\Sigma Y - b\frac{1}{n}\Sigma X \qquad \textit{(intercept)}$$

SOLVED PROBLEM

Weekly sales (in ten thousands of dollars) for a popular magazine over the past five weeks are given below:

Week:	1	2	3	4	5
Sales:	12	15	13	17	18

Use exponential smoothing with $\alpha = 0.3$ to forecast sales for Week 6. Calculate the mean absolute deviation to determine how accurate this was in the past. Assume the forecast for Week 1 was 12.

SOLUTION

Week	Sales (in Ten Thousands of Dollars) Y_t	Forecast $F_t = F_{t-1} + 0.3(Y_{t-1} - F_{t-1})$
1	12	$F_1 = 12$
2	15	$F_2 = 12 + 0.3(12 - 12) = 12$
3	13	$F_3 = 12 + 0.3(15 - 12) = 12.9$
4	17	$F_4 = 12.9 + 0.3(13 - 12.9) = 12.93$
5	18	$F_5 = 12.93 + 0.3(17 - 12.93) = 14.15$
6	–	$F_6 = 14.15 + 0.3(18 - 14.15) = 15.305$

The forecast for Week 6 is 15.305.

To calculate the mean absolute deviation:

Week	Sales (in Ten Thousands of Dollars)	Forecast	|Deviation|
1	12	12	$|12 - 12| = 0$
2	15	12	$|15 - 12| = 3$
3	13	12.9	$|13 - 12.9| = 0.1$
4	17	12.93	$|17 - 12.93| = 3.07$
5	18	14.15	$|18 - 14.15| = 3.85$
			MAD = 10.02/5 = 2.004

QUESTIONS

1. What is a time series? Which techniques are used to forecast time series?
2. What are some measures of forecast accuracy? What values of these would indicate perfect forecasts?
3. In a regression model, what would it mean if $r^2 = 1$? What would the MSE be if this occurred?
4. What does r^2 represent?
5. Describe the steps of the Delphi Method.
6. The selection of alpha in an exponential smoothing model influences the weight placed on recent values relative to earlier values. How should alpha be selected if you wish to smooth the forecast more and give relatively less weight to the most recent observation?
7. Describe the three measures of forecast accuracy.
8. Why is the mean forecast error not a good measure of accuracy?
9. Use the formulas provided in this chapter to compare each of the following to the naive forecasting model:
   (a) a one-month moving average forecast
   (b) a three-month weighted moving average forecast with weights of one (most recent), zero, and zero
   (c) an exponential smoothing model with alpha = 1
10. Explain what it means if the seasonal index for a period is equal to one; greater than one; less than one.

PROBLEMS

11. Weekly sales (in hundreds of dollars) for a grocery product are given in the table below.

Week:	1	2	3	4	5	6
Sales:	12	14	10	13	15	17

   Forecast sales for Week 7 using:
   a) a naive forecast
   b) a two-week moving average
   c) a two-week weighted moving average with weights of two (most recent) and one
   d) exponential smoothing with a smoothing constant of 0.4 (i.e., assume the forecast for Week 1 is 12).
12. Determine which of the four techniques in Problem 11 would have worked best on the data by calculating the mean absolute deviation for each of these. Which technique was most accurate?
13. Use the mean squared error to compare the four models used in Problem 11. Which technique was most accurate based on this measure of accuracy?
14. Quarterly sales revenues (in millions of dollars) for Bigtown Industries for the last eight quarters are given in the table below.

Year:	1994				1995			
Quarter:	1	2	3	4	1	2	3	4
Sales:	23	24	21	24	25	27	23	25

a) Forecast sales for the first quarter of 1996 using exponential smoothing with a smoothing constant of 0.2. Assume the forecast for the first quarter of 1994 was 23.

b) Create a scatter diagram of this data. Does there appear to be any trend or seasonal patterns?

15. Using the data in Problem 14, calculate:

a) the average quarterly sales

b) the average quarterly sales for each quarter

c) a seasonal index for each of the four quarters using your answers to parts (a) and (b) of this problem

d) a seasonal index for each of the four quarters based on a centered moving average

16. The time series data in the table below represent the daily sales of automobiles at a new car dealership.

Day:	1	2	3	4	5
Sales:	10	12	9	11	13

Forecast sales for Day 6 using:

a) a naive model

b) a one-month moving average

c) exponential smoothing with a smoothing constant of one

17. A real estate appraiser has developed a regression model to help appraise residential housing in Lake Charles, Louisiana. This model was developed using recent sales in a particular neighborhood. It bases the price of the house (Y) on the total square footage (X) of the house. The model is:

$$\hat{Y} = 13{,}473 + 37.65X$$

The coefficient of correlation for this model was 0.63.

a) Use the model to predict the selling price of a house that has 1,860 square feet.

b) An 1,860 square-foot house in this neighborhood just sold for $95,000. Explain why this value is not what was predicted using the model.

c) If a multiple regression model were to be used for appraisal, what other quantitative variables might be included in the model to better predict the selling price?

d) What is the coefficient of determination for this problem?

18. The data in the table below provide information regarding total monthly sales of a product and total monthly advertising expenditures for that product in each of the five randomly selected months.

Month	Sales (in Thousands of Dollars)	Advertising (in Hundreds of Dollars)
1	4	2
2	6	3
3	5	3
4	7	5
5	4	3

a) Develop the regression model that could be used to predict sales based on advertising expenditures.

b) Use the model developed in part (a) to predict sales in a month when $400 is spent on advertising.

19. Consider the time series data in the table below.

Month:	1	2	3	4	5
Sales:	35	42	39	45	47

a) Does there appear to be a trend in the data?

b) Develop a regression model with time as the independent variable to serve as a trend equation.

c) Using the regression trend equation in part (b), forecast sales for Month 6.

d) Using the regression trend equation in part (b), forecast sales for Month 7.

20. The U.S. Bureau of Labor Statistics creates a consumer price index (CPI) for various types of products and services. One particular CPI is used to measure the cost of medical services. In the table below are CPIs for medical services for five years.

Year	CPI
1	93
2	101
3	107
4	113
5	122

a) Forecast the CPI for Year 6 using exponential smoothing with $\alpha = 0.3$. Assume the forecast for Year 1 was 93.

b) Forecast the CPI for Year 6 using exponential smoothing with $\alpha = 0.8$. Assume the forecast for Year 1 was 93.

c) Compute the MAD for the forecasts in parts (a) and (b) of this problem. Which of the two appears to be the better model?

d) This data has an obvious trend. Which of the two models adjusted more quickly? What implications are there related to the selection of α when a trend is present?

21. Using the CPI data in Problem 20, develop a regression model to forecast the CPI with time as the independent variable. Use this model to predict the CPI for Years 6 and 7.

22. Students in a management science class have just received their grades on the first test of the semester. The instructor has provided information about grades on the first test from a class the previous semester as well as the final averages in the course for that same class. The information is provided in the table below.

First Test Grade	Final Average
98	93
77	78
88	84
80	73
96	84
61	64
66	64
95	95
69	76

a) Develop a regression model that could be used to predict the final average in the course based on the grade from the first test.

b) Predict the final average for a student who made 83 on the first test.

23. The New York Stock Exchange industrial stock price index for Years 1985 to 1994 is provided in the table below.

Year	NYSE Industrial Price Index
1985	124
1986	156
1987	195
1988	181
1989	216
1990	226
1991	258
1992	285
1993	300
1994	315

Develop a trend model to forecast the value of this index for the Years 1995, 1996, and 2000.

24. If the model for forecasting the NYSE industrial price index in Problem 23 had been applied to each of the numbers in the 10-year sample, what would the MAD be?
25. Use the naive model to forecast the NYSE industrial price index in Problem 23. Calculate the MAD and compare this solution with the MAD in Problem 24.
26. Annual unemployment rates in the United States during the Years 1985 – 1994 are given in the table below.

Year	Unemployment Rate
1985	7.2
1986	7.0
1987	6.2
1988	5.5
1989	5.3
1990	5.5
1991	6.7
1992	7.4
1993	6.8
1994	6.1

Use a naive model to forecast unemployment in 1995. Calculate the mean absolute deviation for this.

27. Develop an exponential smoothing model to forecast unemployment using the data in Problem 26. Use $\alpha = 0.4$ and assume the forecast for 1985 was 7.2. Calculate the MAD and compare this with the MAD using the naive model.

ANALYSIS IN ACTION

Sales Tax in Texas

A major source of revenue in Texas is a state sales tax on certain types of products and services. Texas has compiled information on sales in a variety of industries by quarter. These figures are categorized according to gross sales and amount of sales subject to taxes. The state comptroller uses this data to project future revenues that are used in the development of the state budget. This data also is broken down by zip code and is available to local governments who use this for local planning purposes.

One particular category of goods is classified as Retail Trade. In many areas, items in this category are subject to a local sales tax as well as state sales tax. Data for one particular location in southeast Texas is shown in the table below.

Year	Quarter	Taxable Sales of Retail Trade (in Millions of Dollars)
1990	1	218
	2	247
	3	243
	4	292
1991	1	225
	2	254
	3	255
	4	299
1992	1	234
	2	265
	3	264
	4	327
1993	1	250
	2	283
	3	289
	4	356

Using this data, develop forecasts for taxable sales in each of the four quarters of 1994. Prepare a report indicating your forecasts and provide an indication of the accuracy of these forecasts. Include any other relevant comments that may be of interest to the local budget director.

Simple Regression Spreadsheet Example

Given the prime rate and unemployment rates, develop a linear regression model to estimate unemployment rates for a given prime rate.

Prime Rate	Unemployment Rate
0.03	0.3
0.05	0.35
0.07	0.7
0.06	0.71
0.075	0.9
0.08	0.1
0.0675	0.65

To run a regression program in Excel:

1. Enter range of X values (A4 to A10) and Y values (B4 to B10).
2. Select **Tools**. From this menu, select **Data Analysis.** (If this does not appear on the **Tools** menu, select **Add-ins** and add this to the tool menu.)
3. Select **Regression.**
4. Input the **X Range** (A4 to A10); input the **Y Range** (B4 to B10); input the cell where the **Output Range** begins (A12). When this is finished, select **OK**. The column widths may be adjusted to get appropriate display of the numbers.

The model obtained from this spreadsheet is:

$$Y = 0.2402 + 4.6904X$$

	A	B	C	D	E	F	G
1	Simple Regression Example						
2							
3	x	y					
4	0.03	0.3					
5	0.05	0.35					
6	0.07	0.7					
7	0.06	0.71					
8	0.075	0.9					
9	0.08	0.1					
10	0.0675	0.65					
11							
12	SUMMARY OUTPUT						
13							
14	*Regression Statistics*						
15	Multiple R	0.2831041					
16	R Square	0.080148					
17	Adjusted R Sq	-0.103822					
18	Standard Error	0.2980284					
19	Observations	7					
20							
21	ANOVA						
22		*df*	*SS*	*MS*	*F*	*Significance F*	
23	Regression	1	0.0387	0.0387	0.4357	0.5384	
24	Residual	5	0.4441	0.0888			
25	Total	6	0.4828				
26							
27		*Coefficients*	*Standard Error*	*t Stat*	*P-value*	*Lower 95%*	*Upper 95%*
28	Intercept	0.2402	0.4533	0.5299	0.6188	-0.9250	1.4054
29	X Variable 1	4.6904	7.1061	0.6600	0.5384	-13.5765	22.9572

Multilinear Regression Spreadsheet Example

Suppose y is a function of two variables x_1 and x_2. Develop a multilinear regression model.

x_1	x_2	y
0.03	3.00	0.30
0.05	4.50	0.35
0.07	6.00	0.70
0.06	7.00	0.71
0.075	7.10	0.90
0.08	10.10	0.10
0.0675	7.20	0.65

To run a multiple regression program in Excel:

1. Enter range of X values (A4 to B10) and Y values (C4 to C10).
2. Select **Tools.** From this menu, select **Data Analysis.** (If this does not appear on the **Tools** menu, select **Add-ins** and add this to the tool menu.)
3. Select **Regression.**
4. Input the **X Range** (A4 to B10); input the **Y Range** (C4 to C10); input the cell where the **Output Range** begins (A12). When this is finished, select **OK.**

The model obtained from this spreadsheet is:

$$Y = 0.0909 + 24.9642X_1 - 0.1720X_2$$

	A	B	C	D	E	F	G
1	Multiple Regression Example						
2							
3	x1	x2	y				
4	0.03	3	0.30				
5	0.05	4.50	0.35				
6	0.07	6.00	0.70				
7	0.06	7.00	0.71				
8	0.075	7.10	0.90				
9	0.08	10.10	0.10				
10	0.0675	7.20	0.65				
11							
12	SUMMARY OUTPUT						
13							
14	*Regression Statistics*						
15	Multiple R	0.6725					
16	R Square	0.4522					
17	Adjusted R Square	0.1784					
18	Standard Error	0.2571					
19	Observations	7					
20							
21	ANOVA						
22		*df*	*SS*	*MS*	*F*	*Significance F*	
23	Regression	2	0.2183	0.1092	1.6512	0.3000	
24	Residual	4	0.2645	0.0661			
25	Total	6	0.4828				
26							
27		*Coefficients*	*Standard Error*	*t Stat*	*P-value*	*Lower 95%*	*Upper 95%*
28	Intercept	0.0909	0.4014	0.2263	0.8320	-1.0237	1.2054
29	X Variable 1	24.9642	13.7427	1.8165	0.1435	-13.1917	63.1201
30	X Variable 2	-0.1720	0.1043	-1.6484	0.1746	-0.4617	0.1177

CHAPTER FIFTEEN

Computer Simulation

LEARNING OBJECTIVES

Upon completing Chapter 15, you should be able to:

- Explain the steps involved in performing a computer simulation.
- Determine when it is appropriate to use a fixed time increment simulation model and when it is appropriate to use a variable time increment simulation model.
- Develop a cumulative probability distribution and use random numbers to perform a Monte Carlo simulation.
- Perform a manual simulation of a queuing problem.
- Perform a manual simulation of an inventory problem.
- Explain the advantages and disadvantages of using simulation models.

CHAPTER OUTLINE

15.1 INTRODUCTION

Simulation
The process of developing a representation of a real-world situation and using this to experiment with various decisions.

Many of the chapters in this book have dealt with determining the optimum solution to a problem using mathematical models. In this chapter, computer **simulation** will be seen as a means of representing a real-world situation and evaluating different solutions, but it does not find an optimum solution to a problem. It merely aids in the evaluation of possible decisions or choices specified by the user of the model.

Complex computer simulation models have been developed to represent such diverse things as the operation of the space shuttle, the United States economy, a trucking system, and a 10 kilometer race. Traditional business applications include capital budgeting, corporate planning, environmental impacts, cost analysis, and foreign exchange modeling. Working with the simulation model allows managers to see how decisions would affect the overall system without having to actually make the decisions and possibly suffer the consequence of poor decisions.

In this chapter we will look at the steps involved in preparing a simulation model and running this model. Part of this process uses the Monte Carlo method of simulation, which will be illustrated through some examples. We will see that there are advantages and disadvantages of using simulation. Two examples will be presented to illustrate how a basic simulation is performed. Special-purpose software has been developed for certain types of systems, and some of the most widely used software will be identified.

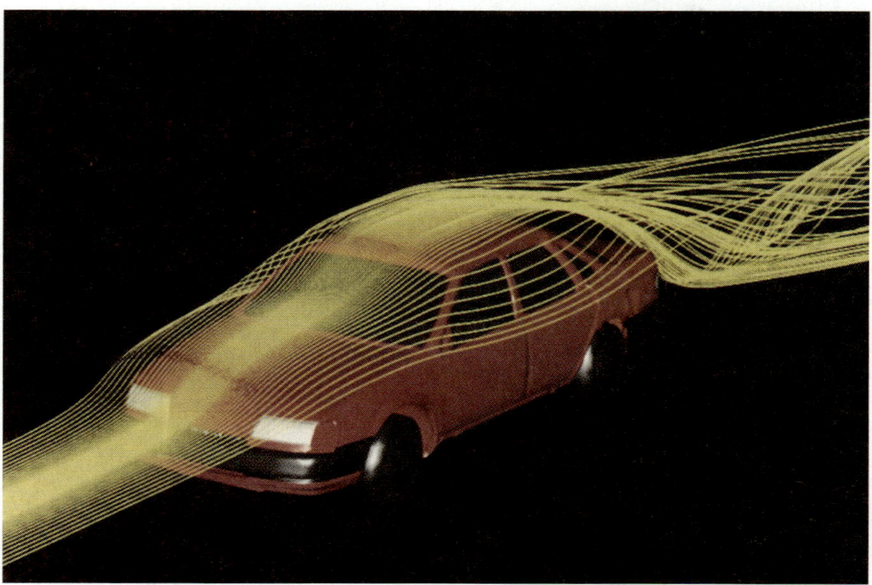

Automobile designers can use simulation to determine how various shapes will affect aerodynamic flow.
SOURCE: Photo courtesy of Ford Motor Company

15.2

EXAMPLE

The Buy Low Auto Parts Superstore is an automobile parts retail store that provides a full range of parts to both the public and to automobile repair shops. An effort is currently being made to reduce inventory costs. While several possible changes in ordering policies are being considered, management would like to have more information about the possible impact of these changes before actually implementing them.

A careful study of one particular product, a distributor used on many common vehicles, has begun. Records over the past year indicate the daily demand for this product varies from zero to four units. Whenever inventory gets too low, an order is placed. It takes from one to three days for delivery of the order. The probability distributions for the demand and for the lead time are shown in Table 15.1.

Using the available information on demand and lead time, management would like to determine the impact of using different reorder points on the costs of stockouts and holding safety stock. As the product is very expensive, a large safety stock may not be good for the company. However, stockouts result in lost sales as well as lost goodwill. Based on information about the actual cost of a stockout and the cost of holding inventory, it is estimated the holding cost per unit per day is $0.05 while the cost of a stockout is $25. The cost of placing an order is found to be $15. To find the actual costs, management would like to find the average daily inventory and the number of stockouts that would occur with different reorder point decisions.

15.3

USING COMPUTER SIMULATION FOR MANAGERIAL DECISION MAKING

Before helping Buy Low with their problem, we will provide an overview of simulation, and will then use the Buy Low Example to illustrate this procedure. Summary Table 15.1 provides a summary of the steps involved

TABLE 15.1

Probability Distributions for Demand and Lead Time in Buy Low Auto Parts Example

Daily Demand	Probability	Lead Time	Probability
0	0.30	1	0.35
1	0.35	2	0.45
2	0.20	3	0.20
3	0.10		
4	0.05		

BEST PRACTICES

The United States Postal Service Uses Simulation for Equipment and Facility Planning

SOURCE:

Cebry, M. E., A. H. DeSilva, and F. J. DiLisio, January-February 1992. "Management Science in Automated Postal Operations: Facility and Equipment Planning in the United States Postal Service." *Interfaces* 22 (1): 110-130.

By the year 2000, the U.S. Postal Service will deliver over 261 billion pieces of mail per year, with a workforce of one million employees. Currently, the U.S. Postal Service handles one fourth of the world's volume, at the lowest per unit cost in the world. However, the postal service faces increasing competition from alternate delivery companies, other advertising media, and the information superhighway. Postal service leaders identified automation technology as the only way to remain price competitive, while handling the expected volume, and maintaining service goals.

They required sophisticated modeling tools to study the complex environment of the USPS. Automated equipment influences other types of equipment, as well as facility layout, the workforce, and the costs of operation. The USPS and a consultant, Kenan Systems Corporation, developed a national simulation model called model for evaluating technology alternatives (META) in 1985. META quantifies the impacts of changes in mail processing and delivery options. It models how the entire nationwide mail-processing system would function given a certain set of inputs. The model gives results on capacity utilization, total pieces of mail handled, and work hours and costs required. The USPS has used it to analyze various strategies, including rate discounts, technology advances, and changes to processing operations. Ultimately, they used META to formulate a corporate automation plan (CAP) for use from 1988 through 1995.

The postal service has adapted and expanded META to help local sites find their specific needs for equipment, workforce, and facility space to carry out the CAP. When the CAP is fully implemented, the postal service expects to save over $4 billion per year. The value of management science tools has been recognized by staff at the highest levels of the USPS. They plan to continue to use the models developed as part of their planning and budgeting process, so they can implement future technologies more easily.

Courtesy of United States Postal Service

in using simulation. Each of these are crucial in the simulation process. We will provide a brief description of each of these steps, but a more detailed explanation of developing the simulation model (Step 2) will be presented in a later section.

Defining the Real-World Problem

A manager must clearly understand the problem and the interactions of the system surrounding this problem. The inputs over which management has control as well as the measures of performance of concern to management

SUMMARY TABLE 15.1

Steps in Performing a Computer Simulation

1. Define the real-world problem.
2. Develop the simulation model.
3. Test and validate the simulation model.
4. Design the experiments to be run on the model.
5. Run the simulation.
6. Evaluate the results.
7. Implement the results.

are identified. Data is collected and the scope and limitations of the simulation are defined.

In the Buy Low example, management is concerned with inventory costs related to safety stock. These costs include both stockout costs and holding costs. Thus, information about the number of stockouts and the average inventory level should be collected in the model. The measures of performance could be the number of stockouts and the average inventory (from which management could calculate costs), or they could be the actual costs of these.

Develop the Simulation Model

This step will be explained and illustrated in detail in the next section. Briefly, this step may involve selecting the simulation language, developing the overall structure of the model perhaps with the aid of a flowchart, generating random numbers for use in Monte Carlo simulation, and actually writing the program to be used.

As a part of this step, the developer of the model must decide which type of timekeeping mechanism to use in the model. A **fixed time increment** model is used to update the record of occurrences at fixed time intervals. For example, in simulating an inventory problem, we simply need to know if a lost sale occurred during the day due to a stockout; we do not need to know when during the day this occurred for each lost sale. The other type of timekeeping mechanism is the **variable time increment model** (also called a **next event model**) in which we keep records on each event as it occurs. This would be necessary in simulating a queuing problem where the need is to know how long each arrival waits in line, how much time the server is idle, and so forth. While it is possible to use very small fixed time increments to obtain information similar to what is found with variable time increment models, to do so is needlessly tedious and cumbersome. In determining which of the two methods to use, you should ask yourself what information is needed to compute the performance measures. Is the measure based on the number of occurrences per time period, such as stockouts *per day*, or is it based on a measurement of each event, such as the average

Fixed time increment model
A simulation model in which the record of occurrences are made at fixed time intervals.

Variable time increment model
A simulation model in which the record of each event is made as it occurs. Also called a next event model.

Next event model
A simulation model in which the record of each event is made as it occurs. Also called a variable time increment model.

time in line *per unit*? Examples of the two types of models are provided in later sections.

Test and Validate the Simulation Model

The simulation model is checked to see if it is valid. The validity of a simulation model may be checked in various ways. The model should appear to make sense to the user. It should have a logical structure that imitates the real-world operations. When the model is run numerous times with past data, it should provide results that are not too different from what actually occurred. The random number generator used in the model also should be verified as some random number generators tend to start repeating values after a relatively short period of time. For a complete discussion of this, see one of the references on simulation at the end of the book.

Design the Experiments to Be Run on the Model

In designing the experiments to be run, stipulate the values of input variables to be used. For example, decide which values of the reorder point in the Buy Low example to use in the simulation. Then set the initial conditions in a simulation so the simulation results reflect the normal operations of the system. In the Buy Low example, do not start collecting simulation results with no units currently in the store, which means a stockout would exist for every day until the first order is placed and received. This would not be representative of the typical situation. Either run the simulation for a number of days and throw these results out before recording the results or set the initial inventory at an average level. After several days of simulated results, the system approaches equilibrium or a steady state condition representing normal operations of the system. Before this condition is reached, the system is said to be in a transient or changing condition. Unless the purpose of the simulation is to study the system during the transient state, this normally is not included in the statistics computed for the simulation.

In designing the experiments, also determine the number of time periods to be simulated (the sample size) based on both the anticipated statistical analysis to be used on the final results and the cost of running the simulation. References at the end of the book provide a detailed discussion of this.

Run the Simulation

When we have developed the model, validated the model, and designed the experiments to be run, we are ready to actually run the simulation. The results are recorded for the evaluation that follows.

Evaluate the Results

The results are examined to see how well each of the managerial decisions would have performed. However, the results obtained from a simulation of 1,000 days for one single managerial decision are not necessarily the same as the results for another 1,000 days of simulation for that same decision. Statistical tests are used to see if the differences in the results of various decisions are statistically significant or if they occur merely due to random fluctuations in the simulation. From the evaluation of the results, management may decide to modify the model or try different values for the input variables under managerial control.

Implement the Results

Once the results are evaluated, the manager makes decisions based on the results. These are then implemented by management in the same way that decisions based on analytical techniques are implemented.

15.4 DEVELOPING A MONTE CARLO SIMULATION MODEL

While all parts of this simulation process are very important, the major focus of this chapter is on the second step of this process—the development of the simulation model. In the development of the model, the Monte Carlo process is a key part of the process. A **Monte Carlo simulation model** is one in which random numbers are generated and used to represent the occurrence of real-world events, such as the demand that occurs during a particular day. While random numbers could be assigned to particular values of a variable based on the probability distribution instead of the cumulative probability distribution for that variable, the procedure for performing a Monte Carlo simulation described in Summary Table 15.2 is recommended.

Monte Carlo simulation
A simulation in which random numbers are generated and used to represent the occurrence of events.

This Monte Carlo process often is used for many different variables in one simulation. For example, in the Buy Low example use Monte Carlo to generate random daily demands and also use it to generate random lead times for the deliveries. We will illustrate this now with the demand variable in the Buy Low example. In this example, use a fixed time increment model as the need is to record the number of units demanded each day and not when each unit is sold during the day.

SUMMARY TABLE 15.2

Steps in a Monte Carlo Simulation

1. Construct a cumulative probability distribution for the variable of interest.
2. Using cumulative probability distribution, assign an interval of random numbers to each value of the variable.
3. Generate the random number.
4. Determine the value of the variable based on the value of the random number.

Cumulative Probability Distribution

Cumulative probability distribution
A probability distribution that gives the probability a variable is less than or equal to a particular value.

A **cumulative probability distribution** gives the probability that a variable is less than or equal to a particular value. Table 15.2 shows the probability distribution for demand in the Buy Low example as well as the cumulative probabilities.

Assigning Random Numbers

Because all the probabilities in this example are expressed in two decimal places, use two-digit random numbers. If only one decimal place were used, use a one-digit random number. If three decimal places were used, use a three-digit random number.

Any random numbers could be used as long as the percentage of numbers assigned to the value of the demand corresponds to the probability of that demand. For example, 30 percent of the two-digit numbers must be assigned to demand = 0, 35 percent of the two-digit numbers must be assigned to demand = 1, and so forth. It is easiest to use consecutive

TABLE 15.2

Cumulative Probability Distribution for Demand in Buy Low Auto Parts Example

Daily Demand	Probability *P*(demand = __)	Cumulative Probability *P*(demand ≤ __)
0	0.30	0.30
1	0.35	0.65 = 0.30 + 0.35
2	0.20	0.85 = 0.30 + 0.35 + 0.20
3	0.10	0.95 = 0.30 + 0.35 + 0.20 + 0.10
4	0.05	1.00 = 0.30 + 0.35 + 0.20 + 0.10 + 0.05

TABLE 15.3

Random Number Assignments for Demand in Buy Low Auto Parts Example

Daily Demand	Cumulative Probability *P*(demand ≤ ___)	Random Numbers
0	0.30	01–30
1	0.65	31–65
2	0.85	66–85
3	0.95	86–95
4	1.00	96–00

random numbers ending with the number corresponding to the cumulative probability. Using this approach assign random numbers as shown in Table 15.3. We chose to start with 01 and let the random number 00 represent the number 1.00. These assignments would indicate, for example, that anytime the random number generated is 44, we will associate this with a daily demand of one because 44 is in the interval 31–65 that is assigned to a demand of one unit.

Generate Random Numbers

There are many techniques used to generate random numbers. We could write the numbers on pieces of paper and pull them out of a hat. We could use some mathematical formulas that have been developed to generate random numbers, although the numbers generated using these formulas will eventually start repeating. Therefore, these often are called **pseudorandom numbers**. Mathematical formulas are built into some special computer simulation languages and also in most spreadsheet packages. The user should be aware that using pseudorandom numbers means that if a simulation is run long enough, the exact same sequence of pseudorandom numbers eventually will be used. However, if the pseudorandom numbers do not begin repeating until after the simulation is finished, then this would not be a problem.

Pseudorandom number
A number generated by a mathematical formula that is intended to be random.

Being able to reproduce a specific sequence of pseudorandom numbers sometimes is desirable. This allows different decisions to be evaluated on exactly the same conditions. Differences seen in performance measures in this situation would be due strictly to the impact of the decisions instead of on random fluctuation in the system being simulated.

For our purposes, use a table of random numbers shown in Table 15.4 and simply select numbers from this table. Because these numbers were randomly generated, simply randomly select a starting point and move in any pattern to obtain as many random numbers as needed. To illustrate, the demand for ten days of operation will be generated. Begin by selecting a starting point in the random number table (Table 15.4), such as the top of column 2, which is the number 37. Then move down this column selecting numbers until 10 numbers have been selected. These are shown in Table 15.5.

If a one-digit random number had been needed, you could simply take the first or second digit from each of the two digit numbers. Another option would be to take the number 37 and use the 3 as the first random number and the 7 as the second random number.

Determine the Variable's Value from Random Number

Once the random number is generated, we simply determine which value for the variable is associated with this random number. The first pseudorandom number is 37, which is in the interval 31–65, so the demand on the first day is one. The second pseudorandom number is 71, so demand on the second day is two. This process continues for each of the 10 days in our example as shown in Table 15.5.

TABLE 15.4

Table of Random Numbers

62	37	27	86	64	63	60	45	98	97	82	17	06	14	66	04	10	64
50	71	47	62	67	66	64	30	12	15	74	61	81	31	05	20	25	93
41	11	06	57	17	21	05	54	34	49	39	08	19	38	40	54	11	59
26	73	15	75	51	19	33	81	58	32	81	84	44	56	61	86	72	99
77	85	81	84	33	46	64	14	01	72	65	58	05	57	82	98	51	07
95	98	75	53	28	32	06	53	27	91	21	59	94	37	18	19	82	59
14	93	90	01	44	06	96	14	32	93	19	87	90	32	50	73	27	78
21	34	75	80	55	88	18	04	57	09	03	01	74	81	67	08	60	32
64	95	23	94	37	95	13	40	85	42	48	40	53	23	00	61	89	23
49	75	70	71	01	77	11	66	34	70	07	01	53	74	71	17	52	82
15	45	21	61	19	02	50	49	80	84	27	02	87	31	48	51	14	63
27	83	73	23	09	21	99	28	58	67	20	58	59	41	77	07	41	70
58	65	30	91	18	50	75	39	53	08	90	84	84	55	41	95	61	34
35	57	17	04	23	03	94	14	86	68	31	41	29	02	01	33	12	96
49	70	57	25	56	33	01	34	89	40	70	22	96	17	49	86	78	84
09	83	23	55	77	99	97	03	99	57	91	20	38	29	52	77	99	07
46	64	30	75	04	27	13	10	93	33	13	41	90	27	55	41	90	12
49	62	05	57	13	30	31	64	50	81	55	97	02	38	78	73	40	15
31	36	61	40	43	06	14	34	03	18	06	19	79	78	08	59	26	99
29	62	13	08	70	54	99	03	50	70	31	37	31	08	34	25	55	16
27	41	58	02	11	95	52	29	12	16	43	48	37	19	20	27	47	92
25	50	20	82	77	22	84	64	96	25	97	31	77	88	29	20	93	47
32	61	33	87	37	36	52	33	63	39	63	17	35	15	28	65	28	03
16	51	16	40	29	92	95	05	93	95	66	11	20	38	22	58	48	93
97	73	74	16	99	48	71	29	20	98	50	90	61	83	93	24	34	08
46	91	77	08	70	98	26	77	45	67	01	89	58	03	80	70	68	74
71	36	04	26	56	76	07	53	26	01	21	43	54	06	06	76	31	11
92	40	47	70	94	04	52	78	40	13	30	71	96	19	70	92	97	83
36	37	69	88	07	87	18	39	84	81	34	56	98	15	38	35	49	37
80	56	83	64	26	45	07	59	55	60	44	16	31	26	62	83	17	99
76	59	24	09	39	90	66	02	35	56	89	93	17	49	30	84	14	39
93	14	48	95	50	53	53	96	92	99	35	35	44	34	00	12	01	12
56	77	19	63	60	56	31	30	59	43	91	98	23	70	00	92	08	36
21	46	66	54	25	06	45	53	41	82	33	74	90	73	50	15	18	67
51	05	29	84	58	23	59	46	93	48	37	36	60	46	30	03	46	01
30	35	75	57	59	84	12	30	34	88	27	64	76	15	77	22	21	04
39	98	58	68	45	92	15	68	80	67	49	48	06	88	78	56	37	82
87	92	02	25	57	14	27	26	59	05	23	34	76	35	41	60	24	89
20	35	65	53	99	42	07	05	07	57	96	12	88	04	36	51	09	46
97	81	98	20	14	82	57	90	27	00	21	20	68	95	04	68	37	90
63	29	92	48	93	92	10	88	64	34	79	52	19	31	39	26	45	73
87	83	37	23	84	08	55	75	94	76	37	25	43	19	98	38	41	43

TABLE 15.5

Ten Random Numbers and Corresponding Demand

Random Number	Daily Demand
37	1
71	2
11	0
73	2
85	2
98	4
93	3
34	1
95	3
75	2

Simulating Natural Gas Discoveries

The oil and gas industry looks for natural gas deposits in frontier basins around the world. When such deposits are found, a commercial assessment must be made to decide which discoveries are economically viable. Several global factors influence this decision. These include taxation, royalty, pricing assumptions, and the cost of alternate sources of energy. Depending on these factors, cooperative development efforts among different companies, and different countries, may or may not be feasible.

Consultants to the Canada Oil and Gas Lands Administration (COGLA) and the Nova Scotia Department of Mines and Energy developed a modeling framework combining geological and economic information about natural gas sites. The purpose of the model was to assess the potential of natural gas exploration on Canada's Scotian shelf.

The consultants developed a simulation modeling framework consisting of three submodels. First, a drilling model combined known data to calculate the probability of discovering new natural gas pools. Next, a pool-cost model described the costs associated with exploring for and developing the natural gas pools. Third, a filtration model evaluated whether a given discovery was economically viable. Simulation was necessary to capture the uncertainty inherent in the geologic and economic parameters.

The Canadian and Scotian governments used the model as an exploration and policy-planning tool. As an example, Shell and Mobil were investigating the feasibility of joint development of one of Canada's frontier basins. The 1986 world oil price drop had halted development by eroding the possible savings of a joint development plan. However, the government felt the development would be feasible if an additional trillion cubic feet (TCF) of natural gas was discovered. They used the model to predict the number of exploratory wells required to locate an additional TCF of natural gas. This prediction helped to assess the near-term development prospects of the area. In general, the model helped to put the natural gas potential of the Scotian shelf into a global economic perspective.

SOURCE:
Power, M., and E. Jewkes, March-April 1992. "Simulating Natural Gas Discoveries," *Interfaces* 22 (2): 38-51.

15.5

DEVELOPING THE SIMULATION MODEL—AN EXAMPLE

We will develop a complete simulation for the Buy Low Auto Parts example. Assume management wishes to evaluate the policy of ordering 10 units whenever the inventory level drops to four or less. Management wishes to know how many lost sales will occur with this policy, and what the average daily inventory would be. Assume the inventory on-hand when the simulation begins is six units.

Flowchart
A diagram of the activities and logic used in a simulation.

Begin by preparing a **flowchart** that represents the activities and logic of the simulation. In this example, assume all orders are placed at the end of the day, and all orders arrive at the beginning of the day and are placed into inventory at that time. A flowchart for this situation is given in Figure 15.1. At the beginning of each day, check to see if an order has arrived. If one has arrived, add this amount to the inventory. Then generate the daily demand. If the demand is less than the inventory on-hand, simply adjust the ending inventory and check to see if the reorder point has been reached. If the reorder point has been reached, see if any orders are outstanding before placing another order. If demand is greater than the inventory on-hand, record the lost sales and then check to see if an order is expected to arrive. If there are no units on order, place an order. When an order is placed, use the Monte Carlo process to generate a lead time. At the end of each day, record the information from the simulation and see if enough days have been simulated. If so, stop; otherwise, return to the beginning and start the next day.

Table 15.6 indicates the cumulative probability distributions and random number assignments for both the daily demand and the lead time. Also shown is a simulation of 10 days of operation for Buy Low Auto Parts. The random numbers for daily demand are the same ones used to illustrate the Monte Carlo process. The random numbers used for the lead times are the random numbers starting in the fourth column of Table 15.4 above.

This table shows we started day 1 with an inventory of six units, and demand was one. We begin day 2 with five units and demand is two. This brings the inventory down to three, which is less than the reorder point so an order is placed. A pseudorandom number of 86 (first number in column 4 of random number table) is generated to obtain a lead time of three days. Because this order is placed at the end of the day, it will not arrive until the beginning of day 6. Continue generating demand each day and tabulating the results.

This 10 day simulation shows there were two lost sales, the average ending inventory each day was 3.1, and two orders were placed. To perform an economic analysis of this situation, find the average daily holding cost, average daily stockout cost, and average daily ordering cost. The following costs were given:

$$\text{stockout cost per stockout} = \$25$$
$$\text{holding cost per unit per day} = \$0.05$$
$$\text{ordering cost per order} = \$15$$

FIGURE 15.1

Flowchart for Buy Low Auto Parts Example

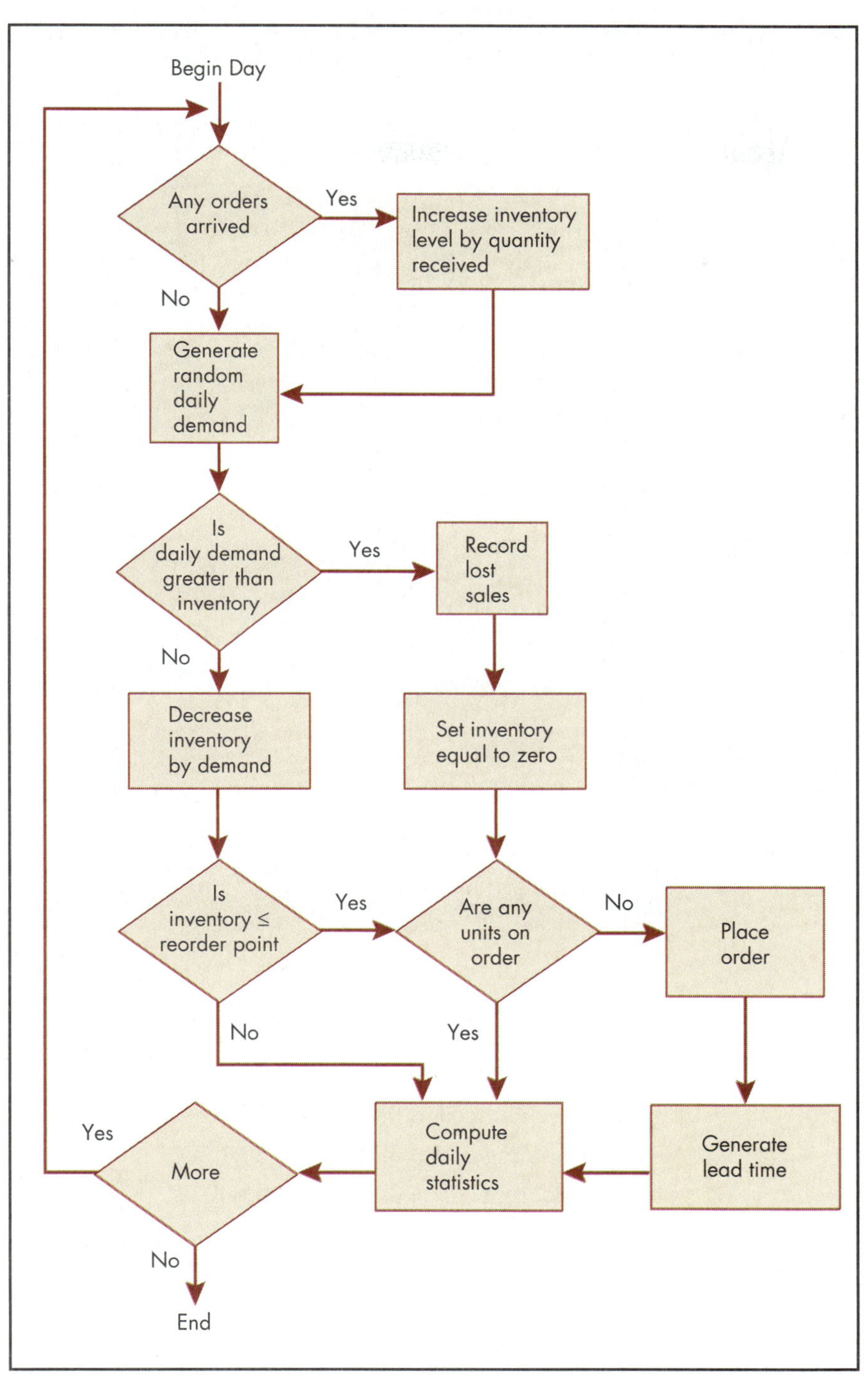

TABLE 15.6

Simulation of 10 Days of Operation for Buy Low Auto Parts Example

Day	Beginning Inventory	Order Received	RN	Daily Demand	Ending Inventory	Lost Sales	Order Placed	RN	Lead Time
1	6		37	1	5	0	No		
2	5		71	2	3	0	Yes	86	3
3	3		11	0	3	0	No		
4	3		73	2	1	0	No		
5	1		85	2	0	1	No		
6	0	10	98	4	6	0	No		
7	6		93	3	3	0	Yes	62	2
8	3		34	1	2	0	No		
9	2		95	3	0	1	No		
10	0	10	75	2	8	0	No		
			Total		31	2			

Daily Demand	Cumulative Probability	Random Numbers
0	0.30	01–30
1	0.65	31–65
2	0.85	66–85
3	0.95	86–95
4	1.00	96–00

Lead Time	Cumulative Probability	Random Numbers
1	0.35	01–35
2	0.80	35–80
3	1.00	81–00

The average number of stockouts per day during this 10 day period is 2/10 = 0.2. The average daily ending inventory is 3.1. The average number of orders per day is 2/10 = 0.2. The costs on a daily basis are:

$$\text{daily stockout cost} = 0.2(25) = \$5.00$$
$$\text{daily holding cost} = 3.1(0.05) = \$0.155$$
$$\text{daily ordering cost} = 0.2(15) = \$3.00$$

In a complete computer simulation, we would certainly use more than 10 days of operation. However, this demonstrates how the simulation would proceed.

After this simulation has been completed, management then may try a different inventory policy, such as ordering 10 units when the level of inventory falls to some value other than four or ordering more than 10 units each time an order is placed. By trying several different possible inventory policies and running the simulation for a large number of days, management would obtain some very helpful information. This may lead to other managerial actions. Perhaps management would decide to try to get a guarantee from the supplier that the delivery would arrive in two days or less. Even if such a guarantee resulted in an additional delivery charge, Buy Low Auto Parts may find this lowers the overall cost of the operation.

15.6 A QUEUING EXAMPLE

Another very common type of problem that often is analyzed using simulation is a queuing problem. While certain types of queuing models may be studied using the analytical models provided in an earlier chapter, there are many queuing problems that do not meet the assumptions necessary for the use of these models. An arrival may decline to enter the system if the queue line is too long, or a customer may decide to leave the system before receiving service if the waiting time in the line is excessive. Simulation may be used to provide the operating characteristics of queuing systems without being limited by the assumptions in the normal queuing models.

In the example to be presented, assume the average time that each arrival waits in line and the idle time for the server are identified as the appropriate measures of performance identified in the problem definition stage. Because a measure of performance (average time in line per unit) is measured on the units being simulated, a variable time increment model must be used.

Garden Grocery Inc.

Garden Grocery Inc. is a corporation which owns and operates small grocery stores throughout west Texas and eastern New Mexico. Several new stores are being planned that will be larger than any of the existing stores. As a result of the growth in the number of stores, a new central supply warehouse is being planned. Trucks will pick up certain types of nonperishable products from this warehouse and deliver these to the individual stores. In the planning process for this new warehouse, a suggestion was made that two loading docks be used instead of just one. With only one loading dock, management is concerned that trucks will be lined up waiting to load and unload, and this may cost an excessive amount of money. To help in this analysis, a study was performed of the arrival rate and the unloading rate of trucks at an existing warehouse. Modifications of these numbers were used to project similar information for the new warehouse. Recognizing this may be modeled as a queuing problem, management considers using analytical techniques for finding the average number of trucks in the queue, the average time in the queue, and so forth. However, management plans to use modifications of this model in the future to evaluate changes in the system, which would violate the assumptions for analytical models. Thus, management has decided to use simulation to analyze this problem.

In this example, we will demonstrate how to determine the average waiting time for trucks if only one loading dock is used. Because both the time between arrivals and the service times are random, we must use the probability distributions for each of these. These distributions along with the cumulative probability distributions and random number assignments are shown in Table 15.7. In planning this simulation, management wants to know the average time each truck spends waiting in line, and it also wants to know how long the loading dock sits idle. Consequently, the data collected during the simulation must include these. Assume the dock opens for business at 7:00 A.M. and there are no trucks waiting at that time. The arrival and loading of 10 trucks will be the limit of this example.

To perform this simulation, select the first 10 numbers in row 4 of the random number table (Table 15.4 above) to simulate the time between arrivals, and select the first 10 numbers in row 1 to simulate the time required at the loading dock for each of these arrivals. Table 15.8 provides the beginning of this simulation. The first arrival occurs six minutes after opening or at 7:06. This truck will require seven minutes at the dock. The second arrival is eight minutes later or at 7:14, and this will require six minutes at the dock.

Because we wish to collect information about the waiting time and idle time for this situation, create another table to help record this information. Use the arrival times and the service times shown in Table 15.8, and create columns to indicate what time service actually begins and what time service ends. Also determine the waiting time for each truck and the idle time at the loading dock.

Table 15.9 shows the first truck arrived at 7:06 and it may begin loading immediately because there are no other trucks at the dock. Thus, the

TABLE 15.7

Probability Distributions and Random Numbers for Garden Grocery Inc. Example

Time between Arrivals	Probability	Cumulative Probability	Random Numbers
6	0.35	0.35	01–35
7	0.25	0.60	36–60
8	0.25	0.85	61–85
9	0.15	1.00	86–00

Service Time	Probability	Cumulative Probability	Random Numbers
5	0.10	0.10	01–10
6	0.35	0.45	11–45
7	0.30	0.75	46–75
8	0.25	1.00	76–00

TABLE 15.8

Monte Carlo Simulation of Time between Arrivals and Service Times for Garden Grocery Inc. Example

Truck	Random Number	Time between Arrivals	Arrival Time	Random Number	Service Time
1	26	6	7:06	62	7
2	73	8	7:14	37	6
3	15	6	7:20	27	6
4	75	8	7:28	86	8
5	51	7	7:35	64	7
6	19	6	7:41	63	7
7	33	6	7:47	60	7
8	81	8	7:55	45	6
9	58	7	8:02	98	8
10	32	6	8:08	97	8

TABLE 15.9

Tabulation of Results for Garden Grocery Inc. Example

Truck	Arrival Time	Service Time	Begin Service	End Service	Waiting Time	Idle Time
1	7:06	7	7:06	7:13	0	6
2	7:14	6	7:14	7:20	0	1
3	7:20	6	7:20	7:26	0	0
4	7:28	8	7:28	7:36	0	2
5	7:35	7	7:36	7:43	1	0
6	7:41	7	7:43	7:50	2	0
7	7:47	7	7:50	7:57	3	0
8	7:55	6	7:57	8:03	2	0
9	8:02	8	8:03	8:11	1	0
10	8:08	8	8:11	8:19	3	0
				Total	12	9

waiting time for this truck is zero. It takes seven minutes to load this truck, so service ends at 7:13. The idle time for the loading dock was six minutes (from 7:00 to 7:06). The second truck arrives at 7:14, but the first truck left at 7:13. Thus, there is one minute of idle time associated with this time period. The second truck will begin loading as soon as it arrives at 7:14. Because it takes six minutes to load this truck, the service ends at 7:20. The third truck arrives at 7:20 and may begin being serviced immediately and is finished at 7:26. The fourth truck arrives at 7:28 so the dock worker is idle for two minutes. The fifth truck arrives at 7:35 but cannot begin service until the previous truck leaves at 7:36. This gives a waiting time of one minute for Truck 5. Similar analysis of the other trucks leaves us with the numbers in Table 15.9 above.

The total waiting time for these 10 trucks was 12 minutes or 1.2 minutes per truck. The idle time for the first hour and eight minutes of operation on this day was nine minutes. While management should certainly not draw any conclusions from this very limited simulation, this does illustrate how the process is used. A computerized version would enable simulation of several thousand days of operation to show how this loading dock may operate. Then the operation could be simulated with two loading docks or one loading dock with additional workers and the results of the simulations could be compared.

15.7

CAUTIONS WHEN USING MONTE CARLO SIMULATION

When a simulation model is used to help managerial decision making, the developer of the model should be aware of some common pitfalls associated with simulation. Some of these are:

1. The initial transient conditions in the simulation may not be indicative of the normal operating conditions of the system to be studied. This may bias the results unless appropriate preventative steps are taken.
2. Pseudorandom numbers repeat themselves eventually and thus, if the number of runs is too high, the results may be misleading.
3. The relationships and structure built into the simulation model may not be valid for all possible values of the input variables. Simulations with extreme values for the input variables may not be valid.

It is very important the model be tested for validity. The results should be recognized as being valid only if the relationships put into the model remain valid for the range of input variables that are tested.

15.8

ADDITIONAL COMMENTS ON SIMULATION

Simulation is a tool that very often is used in business today. Among the reasons that it is so widely used are:

1. Some problems are so complex that analytical tools do not exist or are too difficult to use.
2. Decisions may be tested on the simulation model without disrupting the real-world system. Thus, it is useful for training purposes.

Computer simulation is used to predict ground shaking and potential damage from earthquakes. SOURCE: U.S. Geological Survey Photographic Library, Denver, CO.

A CLOSER LOOK

Knowledge Based Simulation Systems

A relatively new type of computer simulation model is the knowledge based simulation system (KBSS). This type of system combines simulation with knowledge engineering, which is the basis for expert systems. The knowledge and experience of the experts become a part of the simulation system. With this type of system, the manager can use a simulation model without personally possessing expertise in programming, simulation theory, and other areas related to simulation.

While a traditional simulation model only does what the developer of the model plans, a KBSS may suggest possible solutions that should be tried. Thus, the user of the system provides the input describing the particular situation to be modeled and defines the objective or goal of the simulation. The computer then attempts to find good solutions to this.

There are several other features of expert systems that are incorporated into a KBSS. As in an expert system, the user may request the rationale for making specific recommendations, and the KBSS will provide this. Thus, the KBSS may serve as a teaching tool as well as an analytical tool. In the KBSS, external databases may be accessed without having the user explicitly providing them in the simulation. A KBSS often provides the user with the ability to modify models used in the simulation without requiring computer programming.

SOURCE: Merkuryeva, G. G., and Y. A. Merkurev, February 1994. "Knowledge Based Simulation Systems—A Review." *Simulation* 62 (2): 74-89.

3. The basic concept of simulation is easy to understand.
4. Many years of real time may be compressed into a matter of minutes on the computer.

While it may seem that simulation may be used to provide all the answers for a manager, there are limitations:

1. It may be very costly and time consuming to develop a valid simulation model.
2. Simulation does not generate the optimal solution to a problem, it merely tests the decisions specified by the user of the model.
3. Results from the simulation of one situation are unique to that situation and are not often transferable to other situations.

15.9

COMPUTER SIMULATION LANGUAGES

Simulation Language
A computer programming language that is specifically developed for simulation.

We have demonstrated how a Monte Carlo simulation could be performed by hand. This same procedure could be computerized using any number of **simulation languages**. These are computer languages that were specifically developed for simulation. Some of these are specifically designed for particular types of problems. Two of these, GPSS and GASP, are designed for queuing problems. Specifically designed for network problems are SLAM, GERT, and Q-GERT. Other general-purpose simulation languages include SIMSCRIPT and DYNAMO. Many graphical simulation packages for personal computers have been developed for specific purposes, such as factory workflow, product life cycles, airline operations, and traffic systems. These usually require little or no programming as they are designed for end users instead of programmers.

In addition to these special-purpose languages, many popular spreadsheet packages, such as Lotus 1-2-3, Quattro Pro, Excel, and IFPS have random number generators built into the package. Thus, a simulation can be developed using a spreadsheet. There are some special spreadsheet add-in packages, such as @RISK, which perform simulations within a spreadsheet. The use of such a package is very common when performing financial simulations related to capital budgeting, cost analysis, corporate planning, and foreign exchange modeling.

15.10

USING DSS FOR SIMULATION

The DSS software available with this book will perform simulations of specific queuing and inventory problems. However, this does not have the flexibility of a true simulation language. The DSS simulation module only is intended to illustrate some basic simulation systems.

In using DSS, you are asked to supply a seed number for the pseudorandom number generator. By using the same seed number again, you may replicate exactly the event generation of a previous simulation.

DSS Queuing Simulation

In using DSS to perform a queuing simulation, you may select from a variety of probability distributions for the arrival rate. Among these are the normal distribution, uniform distribution, exponential distribution, and a

Prior to setting up construction staging, simulation is used to evaluate strategies before a traffic control system is implemented.
SOURCE: Photo courtesy of Massachusetts Highway Department, Central Artery/Tunnel Project

general discrete distribution where you are asked to input the specific values and probabilities.

Output 15.1 provides you with a sample simulation. The time between arrivals is assumed to be uniformly distributed from three to eight. This

OUTPUT 15.1

DSS Output for Queuing Problem

```
Queuing Simulation

Inputs:

Arrival Distribution         Uniform        3             8

Service Time Distribution    Normal         5             2

Simulation Length         Number            10            20    Time
Initial Number in System     2

Random number generator seed value:  25

Outputs:

Period         Start         Arrivals      Departures    End
 1              2             0             0             2
 2              2             0             0             2
 3              2             0             0             2
 4              2             1             1             2
 5              2             0             0             2
 6              2             0             0             2
 7              2             0             0             2
 8              2             0             1             1
 9              1             0             0             1
 10             1             1             0             2
 11             2             0             0             2
 12             2             0             0             2
 13             2             1             0             3
 14             3             0             1             2
 15             2             0             0             2
 16             2             0             0             2
 17             2             0             0             2
 18             2             0             0             2
 19             2             0             0             2
 20             2             0             1             1
Totals                       --------      --------
                              3             4

Max number in system:  3
Min number in system:  1
Avg number in system:  1.9
```

means the time between arrivals is equally likely to be any value in this interval from the minimum value to the maximum value. The service time is assumed to be normally distributed with a mean of five minutes and a standard deviation of two minutes. The simulation length is specified to be 10 arrivals or 20 minutes whichever occurs first.

OUTPUT 15.2

DSS Output for Inventory Problem

```
Inventory Simulation

Inputs:

Daily Sales Distribution      Normal        50            10

Lead Time Distribution        Normal        12            2

# of Cycles in Simulation     10

Reorder Level (# of units)    650

Random number generator seed value:   25

Outputs:

Cycle #        Lead Time      Sales          QMin (+/-)
 1              10             492            158
 2              12             599            51
 3              16             844           -194
 4              12             613            37
 5              13             620            30
 6              9              468            182
 7              10             519            131
 8              12             588            62
 9              11             606            44
 10             12             569            81

Averages:       11             591            58

Maximum Stockout: -194
Average Stockout:  0
Maximum Surplus:  182
```

The output shows what time each arrival occurs and what time each item leaves the system. The minimum and maximum numbers in the system are shown along with the average number in the system. The average number in the system could be used to determine the waiting time cost of a particular queuing system.

DSS Inventory Simulation

In using DSS for inventory simulations, you may select from a variety of daily sales distributions and lead time distributions. Output 15.2 provides an inventory simulation where the daily sales are assumed to be normally distributed with a mean of 50 and a standard deviation of 10. The lead time is assumed to be normally distributed with a mean of 12 and a standard deviation of two. The number of inventory cycles to be simulated is 10, and the reorder point is 650.

The output shows what the lead time would be in each inventory cycle, and the amount of inventory on-hand when the order arrives. A negative amount indicates a stockout occurred, and the lost sales can be seen from this. A positive amount for this may be used in calculating the holding cost for the safety stock. The simulation could be run again using the same seed to evaluate the impact of changing the reorder point to 600 or 700.

15.11 SUMMARY

In this chapter we studied the steps that are followed when using simulation to help in managerial decision making. These include defining the problem, developing the model, testing and validating the model, designing the experiments, running the simulation, evaluating the results, and implementing the results. A major part of developing most simulation models is the use of the Monte Carlo method where random numbers are assigned to possible values of the variable of interest. A fixed time simulation of an inventory problem was presented. A variable time increment or next event simulation was illustrated in a queuing example. Flowcharts were seen as being very helpful in constructing the simulation model. Most simulation models are developed using some common simulation languages or spreadsheets together with spreadsheet add-ins. Some of the advantages and limitations of using simulation were mentioned.

GLOSSARY

Cumulative probability distribution A probability distribution that gives the probability a variable is less than or equal to a particular value. *p. 640*

Fixed time increment model A simulation model in which the record of occurrences are made at fixed time intervals. *p. 637*

Flowchart A diagram of the activities and logic used in a simulation. *p. 644*

Monte Carlo simulation A simulation in which random numbers are generated and used to represent the occurrence of events. *p. 639*

Next event model A simulation model in which the record of each event is made as it occurs. Also called a variable time increment model. *p. 637*

Pseudorandom number A number generated by a mathematical formula that is intended to be random. *p. 641*

Simulation Language A computer programming language that is specifically developed for simulation. *p. 652*

Simulation The process of developing a representation of a real-world situation and using this to experiment with various decisions. *p. 634*

Variable time increment model A simulation model in which the record of each event is made as it occurs. Also called a next event model. *p. 637*

QUESTIONS

1. Explain the difference between a fixed time increment model and a variable time increment model. Which one should be used if you wish to obtain information about each random event?

2. What are the steps that should be followed when a simulation is being planned to aid a manager in decision making?
3. How are cumulative probability distributions used in Monte Carlo simulation? Explain how you could assign random numbers in a simulation without using the cumulative probability distribution.
4. In an earlier chapter, the economic order quantity model was developed to show how inventory costs could be minimized when certain assumptions, including constant demand rate and constant lead time, are met. Explain why simulation often is used to help make inventory decisions when an analytical technique like the economic order quantity is available.
5. A person has developed a computer simulation model to represent a queuing problem. Based on running 100 days of this model, this person finds the server is idle 23 percent of the day. A manager for this company decides to verify this, and the manager performs a simulation of 100 days using the same input variables that were used in the earlier simulation. However, now the average daily idle time is 27 percent. Does this difference in average idle time mean the model is not valid? Explain.
6. Explain the concept of validity as it relates to simulation models.
7. What is a pseudorandom number?
8. What are some of the limitations and disadvantages of using simulation instead of analytical techniques?
9. A telecommunications company wishes to simulate the operations of a telephone system with links to a satellite orbiting the earth. This system will be capable of handling thousands of calls per minute. A simulation model is developed and six hours of operation are simulated. The initial conditions of the simulation are such that no calls are in the system and statistics on the operation are collected beginning at this time. Discuss the problem that might arise in this situation if special care is not used in setting the initial conditions of the simulation.
10. Explain how the random number table in this chapter could be used to obtain three-digit random numbers.

PROBLEMS

11. The probability distribution for daily demand of a product is given below.

Demand	Probability
13	0.35
14	0.39
15	0.22
16	0.04

a) Develop a cumulative probability distribution for this.
b) Assign random numbers to each of the demand values.
c) Use the first row of the random number table in this chapter to simulate demand for four days.
d) Is this simulation a fixed time increment or a variable time increment simulation?

12. The number of telephone calls arriving at a switchboard range from four to eight per minute as described in the table below.

Number of Calls	Probability
4	0.1
5	0.2
6	0.4
7	0.2
8	0.1

a) Develop a cumulative probability distribution for this.
b) Using one-digit numbers, assign random numbers to each of the number of calls per minute.
c) Simulate five minutes of operation using the second digit of the third column of the random number table in this chapter (i.e., the third column starts with 27, so use the 7 as the first random number).
d) Is this simulation a fixed time increment or a variable time increment simulation?

13. The time in minutes between the arrivals of jobs submitted to a university photocopy center is provided in the following table.

Interarrival Time	Probability
1	0.35
2	0.30
3	0.25
4	0.10

a) Develop a cumulative probability distribution for this.
b) Assign random numbers to each of the interarrival times.
c) Simulate the arrival of 10 jobs using the random number table in this chapter starting in the last row and moving across. Assume the system is empty when the copy center opens at 8:00 A.M. and tabulate the time that each job enters the system.
d) Is this simulation a fixed time increment or a variable time increment simulation?

14. Using the results from Problem 13, suppose the time required to process each job was exactly two minutes. If the copy center only can process one job at a time, tabulate the starting time and finishing time for each job. What is the average time that each job must wait before beginning service?
15. Refer to the situation in Problem 13. Suppose the time required to process each job in the photocopy center varies from one minute to three minutes according to the distribution in the table below.

Processing Time	Probability
1	0.45
2	0.30
3	0.25

a) Develop the cumulative probability distribution for this and assign random numbers.

b) Generate the processing time for each of the 10 jobs used in Problem 14. Start with the first number in the next to last row of the random number table and use the first ten numbers in this row to generate random numbers.
c) What is the average time that each job must wait before beginning service?
d) How much idle time is there from the time the copy center opens until the tenth job is completed?

16. Use column 1 of the random number table to simulate 10 days demand in the Buy Low Auto Parts example. What is the total demand during this 10-day period? Compare this to the total demand during the 10-day period simulated in the example.
17. Eastern State University has sold out every home football game for the last eight years. One way the football program raises money is by selling programs at the football games. The number of programs sold at each game is described by the probability distribution given in the table below.

Number (in Hundreds) of Programs Sold	Probability
23	0.15
24	0.22
25	0.24
26	0.21
27	0.18

Each program costs \$0.80 to produce and sells for \$2.00. Any programs not sold are donated to a recycling center and do not produce any revenue.
a) Simulate the sales of programs at 10 football games. Use the last column in the random number table and begin at the top of the column.
b) If the university decided to print 2,500 programs for each game, what would the average profits be for the 10 games that were simulated?
c) If the university decided to print 2,600 programs for each game, what would the average profits be for the 10 games that were simulated?

18. Referring to Problem 17, suppose the sales of football programs described by the probability distribution in Problem 17 only applies to days when the weather is good. When poor weather occurs on the day of a football game, the crowd is only half of capacity. When this occurs, the sales of programs decreases and the total sales are given in the table below.

Poor Weather Sales

Number (in Hundreds) of Programs Sold	Probability
12	0.25
13	0.24
14	0.19
15	0.17
16	0.15

Programs must be printed two days prior to game day. The university is trying to establish a policy for determining the number of programs to print based on the weather forecast.

a) If the forecast is for a 20 percent chance of bad weather, simulate the weather for 10 games with this forecast.

b) Simulate the demand for programs at 10 games in which the weather is bad. Use column 5 of the random number table and begin with the first number in the column.

c) Beginning with a 20 percent chance of bad weather and an 80 percent chance of good weather, develop a flowchart that would be used to prepare a simulation of the demand for football programs for 10 games.

d) Suppose there is a 20 percent chance of bad weather, and the university has decided to print 2,500 programs. Simulate the total profits that would be achieved for 10 football games.

19. Dumoor Appliance Center sells and services several brands of major appliances. Past sales for a particular model of refrigerators have resulted in the following probability distribution for demand:

Demand per Week:	0	1	2	3	4
Probability:	0.20	0.40	0.20	0.15	0.05

The lead time in weeks is described by the following distribution:

Lead Time (in Weeks):	1	2	3
Probability:	0.15	0.35	0.50

Based on cost considerations as well as storage space, the company has decided to order 10 of these each time an order is placed. The holding cost is $1 for each unit that is left in inventory at the end of the week. The stockout cost has been set at $40 per stockout. The company has decided to place an order whenever there are only two refrigerators left at the end of the week. Simulate 10 weeks of operation for Dumoor Appliance Center assuming there are currently five units in inventory. Determine what the weekly stockout cost and weekly holding cost would be for the problem.

20. Repeat the simulation in Problem 19 assuming the reorder point is four units instead of two. Compare the costs for these two situations.

21. Barges carrying grain from certain grain producing states travel down the Mississippi River and are unloaded at a terminal in Baton Rouge, Louisiana. Only one barge may be unloaded at a time, and if the terminal is busy, the barge must wait. The barges and the terminal operate 24 hours per day, seven days a week. The arrival rate of these barges as well as unloading rates are shown in the tables below.

Time between Arrivals (in Hours):	1	2	3	4
Probability:	0.20	0.35	0.35	0.10

Unloading Time (in Hours):	1	2	3
Probability:	0.30	0.40	0.30

Simulate the arrival and unloading of 20 barges. Determine the average time each barge spends waiting to be unloaded and the idle time for the dock workers at the terminal.

22. Cost data has been collected for Problem 21. It has been determined the cost per hour that a barge spends waiting before it begins being unloaded is $120 per hour. The cost of the unloading crew used in Problem 21 is $80 per hour. Consideration is being given to using a larger crew that would cost $160 per hour and that would cut the unloading time in half for each barge. Using the results of the simulation, would you recommend using the larger crew?
23. Robert Michaels is planning a trip to Las Vegas for a much needed vacation. Before going, Robert plans to study the game of roulette as he hopes to spend many hours at a roulette table. A player has many different types of bets on the table, one of which is simply to be on red or black. If the player bets $1 and wins, the player wins $1. The probabilities of the possible outcomes are shown in the table below.

Outcome	Probability
Red	25/52
Black	25/52
Green	2/52

Simulate 25 games of roulette where the player bets $5 on red each game. What would the average winnings be?
24. Robert Michaels in Problem 23 has decided to use a special betting strategy in playing roulette. He will bet $5 on red in the first game. If he loses, he will double his bet to $10 on the next game. If he loses again, he will again double his bet to $20 on the next hand. He will continue doubling his bet until he wins. When he does win, he will revert to his original bet of $5. Simulate 25 games of roulette using this betting strategy. What would the total winnings be? What is Robert's maximum bet?
25. Kingwood Manufacturing Company produces plastic cases that are used for calculators. There are four different assembly lines used in the production of these cases. On each assembly line is a molding machine that is critical to the production. If a machine breaks down, the cost of the downtime is $180 per hour. A single repair technician working for the company is responsible for all repairs. The salary and benefits for this person is $25 per hour. Each machine has a 15 percent chance of breaking down in any hour. The repair time probability distribution is shown in the table below.

Repair Time (in Hours):	1	2	3	4	5
Probability:	0.1	0.3	0.3	0.2	0.1

Simulate 20 hours of this operation. Determine the total downtime for each of the machines. For this period of time, what is the average hourly downtime cost to the company.
26. In Problem 25, Kingwood Manufacturing is analyzing the possibility of hiring a second and possibly a third service technician. Each technician may be assumed to work at the same rate and would work independently of the other repair technicians. Simulate 20 hours of operation with these changes. What would the average hourly downtime and labor costs be for each of these possibilities?

ANALYSIS IN ACTION

Statewide Development Corporation

Statewide Development Corporation has built a very large apartment complex. As part of the marketing strategy that has been developed, it is stated that if any problems with plumbing or air conditioning are experienced, a maintenance person will begin working on the problem within one hour. If a person must wait more than one hour, a $10 deduction from the monthly rent will be made for each additional hour of time waiting for the maintenance person to arrive. An answering machine will take the calls and record the time of the call if the maintenance person is busy. Past experience at other complexes has shown that during the week when most occupants are at work, there is little difficulty in meeting the one hour guarantee. However, it is observed that weekends have been particularly troublesome.

A study of the number of calls to the office on weekends concerning air conditioning and plumbing problems has resulted in the distribution shown in the table below:

Time between Calls (in Minutes)	Probability
30	0.15
60	0.30
90	0.30
120	0.25

The time required to complete a service call varies according to the difficulty of the problem. Parts needed for most repairs are kept in a storage room at the complex. However, for certain types of unusual problems, a trip to a local supply house is necessary. If a part is available on-site, the maintenance person finishes one job before checking on the next complaint. If the part is not available on-site and any other calls have been received, the maintenance person will stop by the other apartment(s) before going to the supply house. It takes approximately one hour to drive to the supply house, pick up a part, and return to the apartment complex. Past records indicate that on approximately 10 percent of all calls a trip must be made to the supply house.

The time required successfully to resolve a problem if the part is available on-site varies according to the table below.

Time for Repair (in Minutes)	Probability
30	0.45
60	0.30
90	0.20
120	0.05

It takes approximately 30 minutes to diagnose difficult problems for which parts are not on-site. Once the part has been obtained from a supply house, it takes approximately one hour to install the new part.

If any new calls have been recorded while the maintenance person has been away, these will wait until the new part has been installed.

The cost of salary and benefits for a maintenance person is $20 per hour. Management would like to determine whether two maintenance people should be working on weekends instead of just one.

Use simulation to help you prepare a report to management on this problem. State any assumptions you are making about this situation to help clarify the problem.

An Inventory Simulation Spreadsheet Example

Simulate inventory demand for a product. The probability of a sale is given in the table below.

Goods are delivered every 10 days; the quantity delivered is 200.

order quantity	200 per order
carrying cost	$0.50 per day
backorder cost	$6 per day
ordering cost	$300 per order

Probability of selling *x* units per day

Units	Probability
10	0.25
20	0.35
30	0.25
40	0.15

Find the ordering cost, holding cost, backorder cost, maximum number in inventory, and maximum number backordered.

	A	B	C	D	E	F	G	H	I
1	An inventory								
2	simulation								
3									
4	Daily	Probability	Cumulative						
5	demand		probability						
6	10	0.25	0	10					
7	20	0.35	0.25	20			order quantity	200	per order
8	30	0.25	0.6	30			carrying cost	0.5	per day
9	40	0.15	0.85	40			backorder cost	6	per day
10			1				ordering cost	300	per order
11									
12	Random	Day	Daily	Order	Ending	Carrying	Backorder	Ordering	Total daily
13	number		demand	received	inventory	cost	cost	cost	cost
14	0.096	1	10	200	190	95	0	300	395
15	0.757	2	30	0	160	80	0	0	80
16	0.3406	3	20	0	140	70	0	0	70
17	0.252	4	20	0	120	60	0	0	60
18	0.8566	5	40	0	80	40	0	0	40
19	0.9384	6	40	0	40	20	0	0	20
20	0.9603	7	40	0	0	0	0	0	0
21	0.9277	8	40	200	160	80	0	300	380
22	0.3378	9	20	0	140	70	0	0	70
23	0.8351	10	30	0	110	55	0	0	55
24	0.5098	11	20	0	90	45	0	0	45
25	0.8684	12	40	0	50	25	0	0	25
26	0.3447	13	20	0	30	15	0	0	15
27	0.1779	14	10	0	20	10	0	0	10
28	0.3298	15	20	0	0	0	0	0	0
29	0.9511	16	40	200	160	80	0	300	380
30	0.9976	17	40	0	120	60	0	0	60
31	0.8987	18	40	0	80	40	0	0	40
32	0.5319	19	20	0	60	30	0	0	30
33	0.5666	20	20	0	40	20	0	0	20
34	0.1925	21	10	0	30	15	0	0	15
35	0.9047	22	40	0	-10	0	60	0	60
36	0.7409	23	30	200	160	80	0	300	380
37	0.0164	24	10	0	150	75	0	0	75
38	0.0535	25	10	0	140	70	0	0	70
39	0.281	26	20	0	120	60	0	0	60
40	0.1897	27	10	0	110	55	0	0	55
41	0.7126	28	30	0	80	40	0	0	40
42	0.6987	29	30	0	50	25	0	0	25
43	0.408	30	20	0	30	15	0	0	15
44									
45					Totals	1330	60	1200	2590

	A	B	C	D	E	F
1	An Inventory					
2	simulation					
3						
4	Daily	Probability	Cumulative			
5	demand		probability			
6	10	0.25	0	10		
7	20	0.35	=B6	20		
8	30	0.25	=+B7+C7	30		
9	40	0.15	=+B8+C8	40		
10			=+B9+C9			
11						
12	Random	Day	Daily	Order	Ending	Carrying
13	number		demand	received	inventory	cost
14	=RAND()	1	=VLOOKUP(A14,$C$6:$D$9,2)	=+$H$7	=+D14-C14	=IF(E14>0,+E14*$H$8,0)
15	=RAND()	=B14+1	=VLOOKUP(A15,$C$6:$D$9,2)	=IF(E14<=0,$H$7,0)	=+D15+E14-C15	=IF(E15>0,+E15*$H$8,0)
16	=RAND()	=B15+1	=VLOOKUP(A16,$C$6:$D$9,2)	=IF(E15<=0,$H$7,0)	=+D16+E15-C16	=IF(E16>0,+E16*$H$8,0)
17	=RAND()	=B16+1	=VLOOKUP(A17,$C$6:$D$9,2)	=IF(E16<=0,$H$7,0)	=+D17+E16-C17	=IF(E17>0,+E17*$H$8,0)
18	=RAND()	=B17+1	=VLOOKUP(A18,$C$6:$D$9,2)	=IF(E17<=0,$H$7,0)	=+D18+E17-C18	=IF(E18>0,+E18*$H$8,0)
19	=RAND()	=B18+1	=VLOOKUP(A19,$C$6:$D$9,2)	=IF(E18<=0,$H$7,0)	=+D19+E18-C19	=IF(E19>0,+E19*$H$8,0)
20	=RAND()	=B19+1	=VLOOKUP(A20,$C$6:$D$9,2)	=IF(E19<=0,$H$7,0)	=+D20+E19-C20	=IF(E20>0,+E20*$H$8,0)
21	=RAND()	=B20+1	=VLOOKUP(A21,$C$6:$D$9,2)	=IF(E20<=0,$H$7,0)	=+D21+E20-C21	=IF(E21>0,+E21*$H$8,0)
22	=RAND()	=B21+1	=VLOOKUP(A22,$C$6:$D$9,2)	=IF(E21<=0,$H$7,0)	=+D22+E21-C22	=IF(E22>0,+E22*$H$8,0)
23	=RAND()	=B22+1	=VLOOKUP(A23,$C$6:$D$9,2)	=IF(E22<=0,$H$7,0)	=+D23+E22-C23	=IF(E23>0,+E23*$H$8,0)
24	=RAND()	=B23+1	=VLOOKUP(A24,$C$6:$D$9,2)	=IF(E23<=0,$H$7,0)	=+D24+E23-C24	=IF(E24>0,+E24*$H$8,0)
25	=RAND()	=B24+1	=VLOOKUP(A25,$C$6:$D$9,2)	=IF(E24<=0,$H$7,0)	=+D25+E24-C25	=IF(E25>0,+E25*$H$8,0)
26	=RAND()	=B25+1	=VLOOKUP(A26,$C$6:$D$9,2)	=IF(E25<=0,$H$7,0)	=+D26+E25-C26	=IF(E26>0,+E26*$H$8,0)
27	=RAND()	=B26+1	=VLOOKUP(A27,$C$6:$D$9,2)	=IF(E26<=0,$H$7,0)	=+D27+E26-C27	=IF(E27>0,+E27*$H$8,0)
28	=RAND()	=B27+1	=VLOOKUP(A28,$C$6:$D$9,2)	=IF(E27<=0,$H$7,0)	=+D28+E27-C28	=IF(E28>0,+E28*$H$8,0)
29	=RAND()	=B28+1	=VLOOKUP(A29,$C$6:$D$9,2)	=IF(E28<=0,$H$7,0)	=+D29+E28-C29	=IF(E29>0,+E29*$H$8,0)
30	=RAND()	=B29+1	=VLOOKUP(A30,$C$6:$D$9,2)	=IF(E29<=0,$H$7,0)	=+D30+E29-C30	=IF(E30>0,+E30*$H$8,0)
31	=RAND()	=B30+1	=VLOOKUP(A31,$C$6:$D$9,2)	=IF(E30<=0,$H$7,0)	=+D31+E30-C31	=IF(E31>0,+E31*$H$8,0)
32	=RAND()	=B31+1	=VLOOKUP(A32,$C$6:$D$9,2)	=IF(E31<=0,$H$7,0)	=+D32+E31-C32	=IF(E32>0,+E32*$H$8,0)
33	=RAND()	=B32+1	=VLOOKUP(A33,$C$6:$D$9,2)	=IF(E32<=0,$H$7,0)	=+D33+E32-C33	=IF(E33>0,+E33*$H$8,0)
34	=RAND()	=B33+1	=VLOOKUP(A34,$C$6:$D$9,2)	=IF(E33<=0,$H$7,0)	=+D34+E33-C34	=IF(E34>0,+E34*$H$8,0)
35	=RAND()	=B34+1	=VLOOKUP(A35,$C$6:$D$9,2)	=IF(E34<=0,$H$7,0)	=+D35+E34-C35	=IF(E35>0,+E35*$H$8,0)
36	=RAND()	=B35+1	=VLOOKUP(A36,$C$6:$D$9,2)	=IF(E35<=0,$H$7,0)	=+D36+E35-C36	=IF(E36>0,+E36*$H$8,0)
37	=RAND()	=B36+1	=VLOOKUP(A37,$C$6:$D$9,2)	=IF(E36<=0,$H$7,0)	=+D37+E36-C37	=IF(E37>0,+E37*$H$8,0)
38	=RAND()	=B37+1	=VLOOKUP(A38,$C$6:$D$9,2)	=IF(E37<=0,$H$7,0)	=+D38+E37-C38	=IF(E38>0,+E38*$H$8,0)
39	=RAND()	=B38+1	=VLOOKUP(A39,$C$6:$D$9,2)	=IF(E38<=0,$H$7,0)	=+D39+E38-C39	=IF(E39>0,+E39*$H$8,0)
40	=RAND()	=B39+1	=VLOOKUP(A40,$C$6:$D$9,2)	=IF(E39<=0,$H$7,0)	=+D40+E39-C40	=IF(E40>0,+E40*$H$8,0)
41	=RAND()	=B40+1	=VLOOKUP(A41,$C$6:$D$9,2)	=IF(E40<=0,$H$7,0)	=+D41+E40-C41	=IF(E41>0,+E41*$H$8,0)
42	=RAND()	=B41+1	=VLOOKUP(A42,$C$6:$D$9,2)	=IF(E41<=0,$H$7,0)	=+D42+E41-C42	=IF(E42>0,+E42*$H$8,0)
43	=RAND()	=B42+1	=VLOOKUP(A43,$C$6:$D$9,2)	=IF(E42<=0,$H$7,0)	=+D43+E42-C43	=IF(E43>0,+E43*$H$8,0)
44						
45					Totals	=SUM(F14:F43)

	G	H	I
1			
2			
3			
4			
5			
6			
7	order quantity	200	per order
8	carrying cost	0.5	per day
9	backorder cost	6	per day
10	ordering cost	300	per order
11			
12	Backorder	Ordering	Total daily
13	cost	cost	cost
14	=IF(E14<0,+$H$9*(-1)*E14,0)	=IF(D14>0,$H$10,0)	=+F14+G14+H14
15	=IF(E15<0,+$H$9*(-1)*E15,0)	=IF(D15>0,$H$10,0)	=+F15+G15+H15
16	=IF(E16<0,+$H$9*(-1)*E16,0)	=IF(D16>0,$H$10,0)	=+F16+G16+H16
17	=IF(E17<0,+$H$9*(-1)*E17,0)	=IF(D17>0,$H$10,0)	=+F17+G17+H17
18	=IF(E18<0,+$H$9*(-1)*E18,0)	=IF(D18>0,$H$10,0)	=+F18+G18+H18
19	=IF(E19<0,+$H$9*(-1)*E19,0)	=IF(D19>0,$H$10,0)	=+F19+G19+H19
20	=IF(E20<0,+$H$9*(-1)*E20,0)	=IF(D20>0,$H$10,0)	=+F20+G20+H20
21	=IF(E21<0,+$H$9*(-1)*E21,0)	=IF(D21>0,$H$10,0)	=+F21+G21+H21
22	=IF(E22<0,+$H$9*(-1)*E22,0)	=IF(D22>0,$H$10,0)	=+F22+G22+H22
23	=IF(E23<0,+$H$9*(-1)*E23,0)	=IF(D23>0,$H$10,0)	=+F23+G23+H23
24	=IF(E24<0,+$H$9*(-1)*E24,0)	=IF(D24>0,$H$10,0)	=+F24+G24+H24
25	=IF(E25<0,+$H$9*(-1)*E25,0)	=IF(D25>0,$H$10,0)	=+F25+G25+H25
26	=IF(E26<0,+$H$9*(-1)*E26,0)	=IF(D26>0,$H$10,0)	=+F26+G26+H26
27	=IF(E27<0,+$H$9*(-1)*E27,0)	=IF(D27>0,$H$10,0)	=+F27+G27+H27
28	=IF(E28<0,+$H$9*(-1)*E28,0)	=IF(D28>0,$H$10,0)	=+F28+G28+H28
29	=IF(E29<0,+$H$9*(-1)*E29,0)	=IF(D29>0,$H$10,0)	=+F29+G29+H29
30	=IF(E30<0,+$H$9*(-1)*E30,0)	=IF(D30>0,$H$10,0)	=+F30+G30+H30
31	=IF(E31<0,+$H$9*(-1)*E31,0)	=IF(D31>0,$H$10,0)	=+F31+G31+H31
32	=IF(E32<0,+$H$9*(-1)*E32,0)	=IF(D32>0,$H$10,0)	=+F32+G32+H32
33	=IF(E33<0,+$H$9*(-1)*E33,0)	=IF(D33>0,$H$10,0)	=+F33+G33+H33
34	=IF(E34<0,+$H$9*(-1)*E34,0)	=IF(D34>0,$H$10,0)	=+F34+G34+H34
35	=IF(E35<0,+$H$9*(-1)*E35,0)	=IF(D35>0,$H$10,0)	=+F35+G35+H35
36	=IF(E36<0,+$H$9*(-1)*E36,0)	=IF(D36>0,$H$10,0)	=+F36+G36+H36
37	=IF(E37<0,+$H$9*(-1)*E37,0)	=IF(D37>0,$H$10,0)	=+F37+G37+H37
38	=IF(E38<0,+$H$9*(-1)*E38,0)	=IF(D38>0,$H$10,0)	=+F38+G38+H38
39	=IF(E39<0,+$H$9*(-1)*E39,0)	=IF(D39>0,$H$10,0)	=+F39+G39+H39
40	=IF(E40<0,+$H$9*(-1)*E40,0)	=IF(D40>0,$H$10,0)	=+F40+G40+H40
41	=IF(E41<0,+$H$9*(-1)*E41,0)	=IF(D41>0,$H$10,0)	=+F41+G41+H41
42	=IF(E42<0,+$H$9*(-1)*E42,0)	=IF(D42>0,$H$10,0)	=+F42+G42+H42
43	=IF(E43<0,+$H$9*(-1)*E43,0)	=IF(D43>0,$H$10,0)	=+F43+G43+H43
44			
45	=SUM(G14:G43)	=SUM(H14:H43)	=SUM(I14:I43)

CASE FOUR

Simulation at AT&T's Wafer Fabrication Facility

As described in the previous case studies, AT&T uses management science techniques to evaluate factory performance and help make decisions in their Orlando semiconductor wafer fabrication facility (fab). They use queuing models to estimate work-in-process (WIP), cycle times, equipment utilization, and factory throughput. However, there are limitations to the applicability of queuing models. Queuing models predict long-term average system behavior, but do not track actual lots as they pass through the system. Sometimes, AT&T needs to track the impact of individual lots more closely. For these situations, they turn to simulation.

One phenomenon that requires the tracking of individual lots is the existence of "hot lots" in the Orlando wafer fab. Hot lots are lots that have been accorded a higher priority than the other lots in the factory. This prioritization is usually in response to customer demand. The goal is to process the hot lots through the system as quickly as possible. Generally, this means moving hot lots to the front of the queue at every workstation. Sometimes, machines are held idle for hot lots scheduled to arrive shortly. Also, regular lots are sometimes preempted to allow the processing of hot lots. These practices typically reduce the cycle time of the hot lots. However, they can significantly increase the cycle time of the regular lots, and end up reducing the overall throughput of the factory.

Hot lots benefit AT&T by keeping important customers happy. Assessing the cost of hot lots is more difficult. To estimate the impact of individual lot priorities on overall factory throughput, utilization, and cycle time, AT&T uses discrete-event simulation models. The key difference offered by simulation over queuing models is that a simulation tracks the flow of individual entities through the system. Random number generators are used at various points to select among possible alternatives, and each simulation run is a possible history of the factory. Overall performance measures are obtained by averaging across the results observed for the lots leaving the system. The advantage of this is that modelers can simulate any level of detail. For example, AT&T can model sophisticated rules for selecting between lots of different priorities at each machine.

AT&T has observed several drawbacks to using simulation. First, developing a discrete-event simulation model of the Orlando fab required more work than developing the queuing model. Additional data was gathered to develop empirical distributions for failures and processing times. Exercising the simulation model also was labor intensive. When running a simulation model, the computer repeatedly samples from empirical distributions to yield a result. This takes much more time than it takes to solve a set of queuing equations. Also, the output from a single simulation run is a potential result, not the ultimate answer. Several replications are needed of each simulation to become confident of the overall results.

However, the additional information provided by the simulation model outweighs the drawbacks in this application. Using simulation, AT&T's managers can ask questions such as, "What is the impact on factory throughput and cycle times of making 10% of the lots of Product A hot?" They also can look at mitigating the impact of hot lots by applying different

To estimate the impact of individual lot priorities on overall factory throughput, utilization, and cycle time, AT&T uses discrete-event simulation models. CREDIT: AT&T Allentown IC Group

lot selection rules at various workstations. For example, they might find that the negative effect of hot lots on other lots was dramatically reduced if the other lots were never preempted for hot lots (that is, the hot lots merely always went to the front of the queue at each machine). They also could observe how much this change in preemption strategy influenced the cycle time of the hot lots and use this information to decide whether such a change would be worthwhile.

AT&T uses the results of the simulation model to negotiate cost and delivery schedules with customers. For example, an important customer might call up and request just one lot of a special product, processed as quickly as possible. Analysts could simulate the effect of the hot lot on the overall factory capacity and respond to the customer accordingly. The simulation model also would allow the sales force to estimate what the cycle time would be for a particular lot. This type of information could not be obtained using a queuing model, which would only offer long-term, steady-state results.

An example of the use of a simulation model to evaluate the impact of hot lot decisions follows. The example compares the average cycle time of regular lots through a single machine, when there are either 5% or 10% hot lots in the system. Arrivals to the machine are exponentially distributed. Service times are one hour for regular and hot lots, and are deterministic. The machine is down for maintenance 20% of the time. A one-hour set up is incurred whenever the machine changes from processing a regular lot to processing a hot lot, and vice versa. The set-up times also are deterministic. Table 1 shows the average cycle times recorded for the regular lots for simulation runs at different total arrival rates into the system (lots per hour). The cycle times versus start rates are graphed in Figure 1. In all cases, the cycle times from the runs with 10% hot lots are higher than the cycle times for the runs with 5% hot lots. At very high start rates, the impact is most pronounced. AT&T might use a workstation-level simulation model like this to evaluate the impact of hot lots on the bottleneck, instead of running a full factory model.

TABLE 1

Cycle Time Results from Simulation Runs

Observed Start Rate	5% Hot Lots	10% Hot Lots
0.72	21.4	829.0
0.68	9.3	29.4
0.64	6.2	11.3
0.60	4.6	7.1
0.56	3.7	5.1
0.52	3.1	4.0
0.48	2.7	3.4
0.44	2.4	3.0
0.40	2.2	2.6

FIGURE 1

Cycle Time versus Start Rate from Simulation Runs

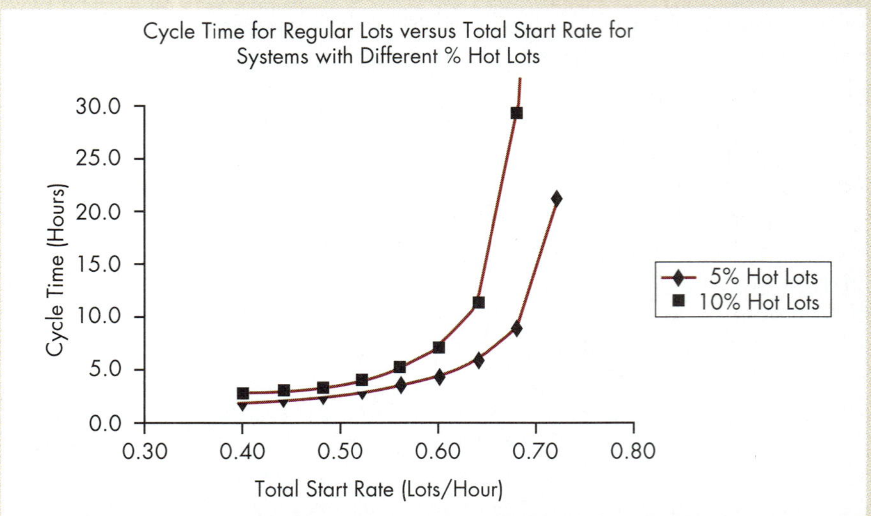

PROBLEM 1

Lots arrive at a production facility at a rate that varies from .4 to .72 lots per hour. Arrivals are exponential. Service time is one hour and deterministic. Five or ten percent of the lots are *hot* lots. The set-up time to switch to a hot lot or regular lot is one hour.

The problem is solved using Monte Carlo simulation.

To develop the simulation, the cumulative probability distribution of both the arrivals and type of service must be calculated. For the interarrival times, the probability that $X \leq x$ is given by $P(X \leq x) = 1–e^{-.4x}$.

Once the cumulative probability distributions are known, use the random number generator in Excel, rand() to generate interarrivals and lot types.

Calculate the time that work starts and ends for a lot. Adjust the starting and ending time to account for regular repair downtime (two hours out of 10), and set-up time for changing lot types.

To find the average time in the system, sum the individual system times for each lot, and divide by the number of lots that were produced during the simulation.

The results follow in the Excel spreadsheet:

Observed Start Rate	5% Hot Lots	10% Hot Lots
.40	2.19	2.33

PROBLEM 2

Solve the problem varying the arrival rate from .44 to .72.

PROBLEM 3

Solve Problem 1 with 7% hot lots.

	A	B	C	D	E	F	G	H	I	J
1	Case 4	Simulation Queuing								
2							5% hot lot			
3	cumulative	interarrival time					cumulative	type of		
4	probability	time					probability	lot		
5	0	0					0	0	hot	
6	0.1	0.25					0.05	1	reg	
7	0.18	0.5								
8	0.26	0.75								
9	0.33	1								
10	0.39	1.25					10% hot lot			
11	0.45	1.5					cumulative	type of		
12	0.5	1.75					probability	lot		
13	0.55	2					0	0	hot	
14	0.59	2.25					0.1	1	reg	
15	0.63	2.5								
16	0.67	2.75								
.	.	.								
.	.	.								
.	.	.								
57	0.99	13								
58	1	13.25								
59										
60		5% hot lot								
61	arrival		lot							
62	random	interarrival	arrival	type of	arrival	service	service	time in	repair	system
63	number	time	number	lot	time	start	end	system	time	available
64	0.449	1.25	0.008	0	1.25	1.25	2.25	1	0	2.25
65	0.583	2	0.289	1	3.25	4.25	5.25	2	0	5.25
66	0.194	0.5	0.504	1	3.75	5.25	6.25	2.5	0	6.25
.	.	.	.	.	.	.	.	.	.	.
.	.	.	.	.	.	.	.	.	.	.
.	.	.	.	.	.	.	.	.	.	.
93	0.745	3.25	0.136	1	80.5	80.5	81.5	1	0	81.5
94	0.857	4.75	0.792	1	85.25	85.25	86.25	1	0	86.25
95										
96					Number of arrival			31		
97					Time in system			67.75		
98					Average time in system			2.19		
99		10% hot lot								
100	arrival		lot							
101	random	interrival	arrival	type of	arrival	service	service	time in	repair	system
102	number	time	number	lot	time	start	end	system	time	available
103	0.887	5.25	0.587	1	5.25	5.25	6.25	1	0	6.25
104	0.406	1.25	0.334	1	6.5	6.5	7.5	1	0	7.5
105	0.717	3	0.937	1	9.5	9.5	10.5	1	0	10.5
.	.	.	.	.	.	.	.	.	.	.
.	.	.	.	.	.	.	.	.	.	.
.	.	.	.	.	.	.	.	.	.	.
132	0.795	3.75	0.995	1	70.5	70.5	71.5	1	0	71.5
133	0.321	0.75	0.903	1	71.25	71.5	72.5	1.25	0	72.5
134										
135					Number of arrival			31		
136					Time in system			72.25		
137					Average time in system			2.33		

	A	B	C	D
1	Case 4	Simulation Queuing		
2				
3	cumulative	interarrival time		
4	probability	time		
5	=ROUND(1-EXP(-0.4*B5),2)	0		
6	=ROUND(1-EXP(-0.4*B6),2)	=+B5+0.25		
7	=ROUND(1-EXP(-0.4*B7),2)	=+B6+0.25		
8	=ROUND(1-EXP(-0.4*B8),2)	=+B7+0.25		
9	=ROUND(1-EXP(-0.4*B9),2)	=+B8+0.25		
10	=ROUND(1-EXP(-0.4*B10),2)	=+B9+0.25		
11	=ROUND(1-EXP(-0.4*B11),2)	=+B10+0.25		
12	=ROUND(1-EXP(-0.4*B12),2)	=+B11+0.25		
13	=ROUND(1-EXP(-0.4*B13),2)	=+B12+0.25		
14	=ROUND(1-EXP(-0.4*B14),2)	=+B13+0.25		
15	=ROUND(1-EXP(-0.4*B15),2)	=+B14+0.25		
16	=ROUND(1-EXP(-0.4*B16),2)	=+B15+0.25		
.	.	.		
.	.	.		
.	.	.		
57	=ROUND(1-EXP(-0.4*B57),2)	=+B56+0.25		
58	=ROUND(1-EXP(-0.4*B58),2)	=+B57+0.25		
59				
60		5% hot lot		
61	arrival		lot	
62	random	interrival	arrival	type of
63	number	time	number	lot
64	=RAND()	=VLOOKUP(A64,$A$5:$B$58,2)	=RAND()	=VLOOKUP(C64,$G$5:$H$6,2)
65	=RAND()	=VLOOKUP(A65,$A$5:$B$58,2)	=RAND()	=VLOOKUP(C65,$G$5:$H$6,2)
66	=RAND()	=VLOOKUP(A66,$A$5:$B$58,2)	=RAND()	=VLOOKUP(C66,$G$5:$H$6,2)
.	.	.	.	.
.	.	.	.	.
.	.	.	.	.
93	=RAND()	=VLOOKUP(A93,$A$5:$B$58,2)	=RAND()	=VLOOKUP(C93,$G$5:$H$6,2)
94	=RAND()	=VLOOKUP(A94,$A$5:$B$58,2)	=RAND()	=VLOOKUP(C94,$G$5:$H$6,2)
95				
96				
97				
98				
99		10% hot lot		
100	arrival		lot	
101	random	interrival	arrival	type of
102	number	time	number	lot
103	=RAND()	=VLOOKUP(A103,$A$5:$B$58,2)	=RAND()	=VLOOKUP(C103,$G$13:$H$14,2)
104	=RAND()	=VLOOKUP(A104,$A$5:$B$58,2)	=RAND()	=VLOOKUP(C104,$G$13:$H$14,2)
105	=RAND()	=VLOOKUP(A105,$A$5:$B$58,2)	=RAND()	=VLOOKUP(C105,$G$13:$H$14,2)
.	.	.	.	.
.	.	.	.	.
.	.	.	.	.
132	=RAND()	=VLOOKUP(A132,$A$5:$B$58,2)	=RAND()	=VLOOKUP(C132,$G$13:$H$14,2)
133	=RAND()	=VLOOKUP(A133,$A$5:$B$58,2)	=RAND()	=VLOOKUP(C133,$G$13:$H$14,2)
134				
135				
136				
137				

	E	F	G	H
1				
2			5% hot lot	
3			cumulative	type of
4			probability	lot
5			0	0
6			0.05	1
7				
8				
9				
10			10% hot lot	
11			cumulative	type of
12			probability	lot
13			0	0
14			0.1	1
15				
16				
.				
.				
.				
57				
58				
59				
60				
61				
62	arrival	service	service	time in
63	time	start	end	system
64	=+B64	=E64	=F64+1	=G64-E64
65	=+E64+B65	=IF(D65<>D64,MAX(J64,E65)+1,MAX(J64,E65))	=F65+1	=G65-E65
66	=+E65+B66	=IF(D66<>D65,MAX(J65,E66)+1,MAX(J65,E66))	=F66+1	=G66-E66
.	.	.	.	.
.	.	.	.	.
.	.	.	.	.
93	=+E92+B93	=IF(D93<>D92,MAX(J92,E93)+1,MAX(J92,E93))	=F93+1	=G93-E93
94	=+E93+B94	=IF(D94<>D93,MAX(J93,E94)+1,MAX(J93,E94))	=F94+1	=G94-E94
95				
96	Number of arrivals			=COUNT(F64:F94)
97	Time in system			=SUM(H64:H94)
98	Average time in system			=H97/H96
99				
100				
101	arrival	service	service	time in
102	time	start	end	system
103	=+B103	=E103	=F103+1	=G103-E103
104	=+E103+B104	=IF(D104<>D103,MAX(J103,E104)+1,MAX(J103,E104))	=F104+1	=G104-E104
105	=+E104+B105	=IF(D105<>D104,MAX(J104,E105)+1,MAX(J104,E105))	=F105+1	=G105-E105
.	.	.	.	.
.	.	.	.	.
.	.	.	.	.
132	=+E131+B132	=IF(D132<>D131,MAX(J131,E132)+1,MAX(J131,E132))	=F132+1	=G132-E132
133	=+E132+B133	=IF(D133<>D132,MAX(J132,E133)+1,MAX(J132,E133))	=F133+1	=G133-E133
134				
135	Number of arrivals			=COUNT(F103:F133)
136	Time in system			=SUM(H103:H133)
137	Average time in system			=H136/H135

	I	J
1		
2		
3		
4		
5	hot	
6	reg	
7		
8		
9		
10		
11		
12		
13	hot	
14	reg	
15		
16		
.		
.		
.		
57		
58		
59		
60		
61		
62	repair	system
63	time	available
64	=IF(MOD(G64,10)>=8,2,0)	=G64+I64
65	=IF(MOD(G65,10)>=8,2,0)	=G65+I65
66	=IF(MOD(G66,10)>=8,2,0)	=G66+I66
.	.	.
.	.	.
.	.	.
93	=IF(MOD(G93,10)>=8,2,0)	=G93+I93
94	=IF(MOD(G94,10)>=8,2,0)	=G94+I94
95		
96		
97		
98		
99		
100		
101	repair	system
102	time	available
103	=IF(MOD(G103,10)>=8,2,0)	=G103+I103
104	=IF(MOD(G104,10)>=8,2,0)	=G104+I104
105	=IF(MOD(G105,10)>=8,2,0)	=G105+I105
.	.	.
.	.	.
.	.	.
132	=IF(MOD(G132,10)>=8,2,0)	=G132+I132
133	=IF(MOD(G133,10)>=8,2,0)	=G133+I133
134		
135		
136		
137		

APPENDIX A

Markov Analysis

Many business situations are stochastic (probabilistic) processes where the state of a system changes from one period to the next. Markov analysis is used to predict which state of the system will occur at each time period in the future. This analysis begins with the identification of the possible states of a system and the transition probabilities that describe the movement from one state to the next. Some common applications of Markov analysis are the study of consumer brand switching, equipment maintenance planning, and accounts receivable analysis.

In using Markov analysis, we will make the following assumptions:

1. There are a finite number of states.
2. The transition probabilities are stable over time.
3. The state in any period depends only on the previous state and the transition probabilities.
4. Changes in the system occur once each time period.

The following notation will be used:

p_{ij} = transitional probability that the system will move from state i in the current period to state j in the next period

For a system which has two states, the matrix of transition probabilities denoted by P would be:

$$P = \begin{bmatrix} p_{11} & p_{12} \\ p_{21} & p_{22} \end{bmatrix}$$

We will illustrate Markov analysis with the following brand-switching example.

Example

Two types of coffee are sold in a small store–Brand X and Brand Y. A careful study of the purchasing habits of the store's clientele reveals that 70 percent of the customers who purchased Brand X on their last purchase will purchase Brand X again on their next purchase, and 30 percent of these people will purchase Brand Y. Of the customers who purchased Brand Y on their last purchase, 80 percent will again purchase Brand Y with the remaining 20 percent switching to Brand X.

We will identify the states as follows:

state 1 = person bought Brand X on last purchase

state 2 = person bought Brand Y on last purchase

p_{11} = probability person who bought X last time buys X again = 0.7

p_{12} = probability person who bought X last time buys Y next = 0.3

p_{21} = probability person who bought Y last time buys X next = 0.2

p_{22} = probability person who bought Y last time buys Y again = 0.8

The matrix of transition probabilities is:

$$P = \begin{bmatrix} 0.7 & 0.3 \\ 0.2 & 0.8 \end{bmatrix}$$

Notice the sum of the probabilities in each row must be 1 because either state 1 or state 2 must be entered in the next time period.

We will use the probabilities just given together with a tree diagram (Figure 1) to illustrate the purchasing pattern for the next two purchases made by a person who last bought Brand X. This means the system currently is in state 1. The probabilities for each brand are shown on the tree. We see the probability that the system goes from state 1 (Brand X) to state 1 (Brand X) in the next period, with probability 0.7, and also to state 1 (Brand X) in the following period, also with probability 0.7, is 0.49. Simply multiply 0.7 by 0.7 to obtain the probability of the intersection of these two events because the two events are independent. They are independent due to the assumption that the state in one period only depends on the previous state and the transition probability.

The system also could be in state 1 two periods in the future if a switch to Brand Y (state 2) is made next period and a switch back to Brand X (state 1) is made in the following period. Thus, the probability the system is in state 1 (Brand X is purchased) two periods in the future is 0.49 + 0.06 = 0.55. This probability also would tell us that if all customers bought Brand X with the last purchase, 55 percent of these people would buy Brand X again two periods in the future.

We could use tree diagrams to determine the probabilities that the system would be in each state several periods into the future, but the tree would get quite large. Matrix multiplication can be used to give us this same information. We will use state probabilities together with the matrix of transition probabilities to determine how the system changes over time.

State Probabilities

The *state probability* $q_i(k)$ is the probability the system will be in state i in time period k. The current time period is denoted with $k = 0$. Thus:

FIGURE 1

Tree Diagram for Brand X Purchaser

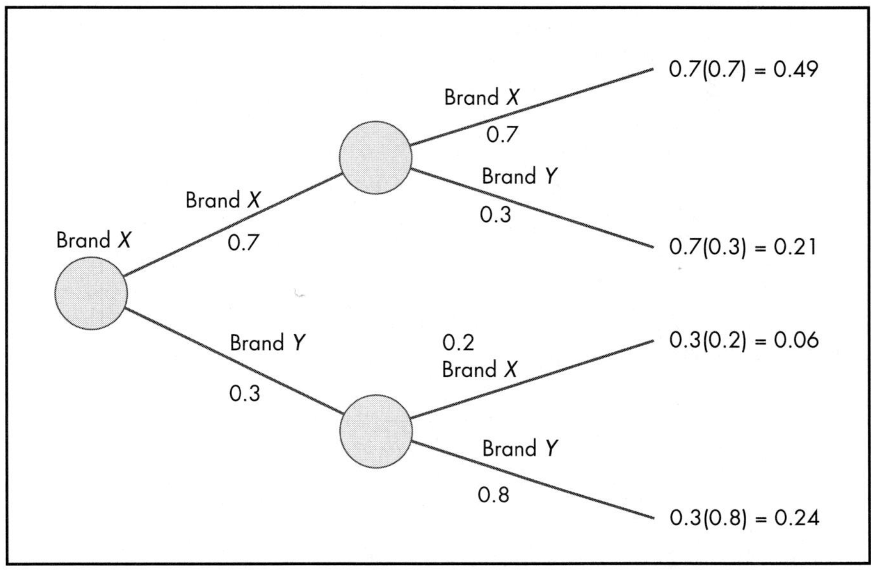

$q_1(0)$ = probability that system is currently in state 1
$q_1(1)$ = probability that system is in state 1 in next period
$q_2(0)$ = probability that system is currently in state 2
$q_2(1)$ = probability that system is in state 2 in next period

A matrix of the state probabilities could be written as a row vector, a matrix with single row, denoted by $Q(k)$. This would be:

$$Q(k) = [q_1(k)\ q_2(k)]$$

For the current period, this would be:

$$Q(0) = [q_1(0)\ q_2(0)]$$

To obtain the state probabilities in the next period, multiply this by the transition matrix.

$$Q(1) = Q(0)\ P$$

$$[q_1(1)\ q_2(1)] = [q_1(0)\ q_2(0)]\begin{bmatrix} p_{11} & p_{12} \\ p_{21} & p_{22} \end{bmatrix}$$

Returning to our previous example, let's suppose all customers bought Brand X with the last purchase. This would mean:

$$q_1(0) = 1$$
$$q_2(0) = 0$$

so

$$Q = [1\ 0]$$

Multiplying this by the matrix of transition probabilities gives:

$$[q_1(1)\ q_2(1)] = [1\ 0]\begin{bmatrix} 0.7 & 0.3 \\ 0.2 & 0.8 \end{bmatrix}$$

In multiplying matrices, multiply each row of the matrix on the left by each column of the matrix on the right. This would be:

$$\begin{aligned} [q_1(1)\ q_2(1)] &= [1(0.7) + 0(0.2) \quad 1(0.3) + 0(0.8)] \\ &= [\ 0.7\ 0.3] \end{aligned}$$

To find the state probabilities for period 2, multiply this result by the transition matrix. This would give:

$$\begin{aligned} Q(2) &= Q(1)P \\ [q_1(2)\ q_2(2)] &= [q_1(1)\ q_2(1)]\begin{bmatrix} p_{11} & p_{12} \\ p_{21} & p_{22} \end{bmatrix} \\ [q_1(2)\ q_2(2)] &= [0.7\ 0.3]\begin{bmatrix} 0.7 & 0.3 \\ 0.2 & 0.8 \end{bmatrix} \\ [q_1(2)\ q_2(2)] &= [0.7(0.7) + 0.3(0.2) \qquad 0.7(0.3) + 0.3(0.8)] \\ &= [\ 0.49 + 0.06 \qquad 0.21 + 0.24] \\ &= [0.55\ 0.45] \end{aligned}$$

These are the same values calculated using the tree diagram earlier. If we were to continue this for more periods into the future, we would find the state probabilities change by smaller and smaller amounts each period. They would approach a steady state condition.

Steady State or Equilibrium Conditions

A *steady state or equilibrium condition* is said to exist if the state probabilities (Q) do not change from one period to the next. This may occur if the transition matrix is stable over time. For ease of exposition, we will define the following:

$$q_1 = \text{steady state probability for state 1}$$
$$q_2 = \text{steady state probability for state 2}$$

To find what the state probabilities would be when a steady state is reached, begin by indicating that the new state probabilities are the same as the old probabilities. This could be expressed as:

$$\begin{aligned} Q &= QP \\ [q_1\ q_2] &= [q_1\ q_2]\begin{bmatrix} p_{11} & p_{12} \\ p_{21} & p_{22} \end{bmatrix} \end{aligned}$$

In the previous example, we would have:

$$[q_1\ q_2] = [q_1\ q_2]\begin{bmatrix} 0.7 & 0.3 \\ 0.2 & 0.8 \end{bmatrix}$$

Multiplying results in:

$$[q_1\ q_2] = [0.7q_1 + 0.2q_2\ \ 0.3q_1 + 0.8q_2]$$

Thus:

$$q_1 = 0.7q_1 + 0.2q_2$$

and

$$q_2 = 0.3q_1 + 0.8q_2$$

Simplifying these equations yields:

$$0.3q_1 - 0.2q_2 = 0$$

and

$$-0.3q_1 + 0.2q_2 = 0$$

These are equivalent equations, so we are left with one equation with two unknowns. However, we also know:

$$q_1 + q_2 = 1$$

We use this and one of the other equations, and solve the two equations simultaneously. This yields:

$$q_1 + q_2 = 1$$
$$0.3q_1 - 0.2q_2 = 0$$

This results in:

$$q_1 = 0.4$$

and

$$q_2 = 0.6$$

This indicates the state probability for state 1 will approach 0.4, and once it is equal to this, it will not change. In this example, this would mean that eventually Brand *X* would have a 40 percent share of the market and Brand *Y* will have a market share of 60 percent. This occurs because the number of people switching from Brand *X* to Brand *Y* is equal to the number switching from Brand *Y* to Brand *X*.

Absorbing States

An *absorbing state* is a state that has a zero probability of moving to any other state. In other words, if an item enters this state, it must remain in this state. This is common in modeling accounts receivables as Markov processes. We will illustrate this in the following example.

A business extends credit to its customers. A bill is sent to the customers, and some customers pay immediately while others wait before paying. Some customers never pay, and the company has some bills that get written off as bad debts. The company classifies each bill as one of the following:

$$S_1 = 0\text{–}30 \text{ day category}$$
$$S_2 = 31\text{–}90 \text{ day category}$$
$$S_3 = \text{paid}$$
$$S_4 = \text{bad debt}$$

Past records are used to obtain the table of transition probabilities below to indicate how these change from one week to the next.

	To			
	S_1	S_2	S_3	S_4
From S_1	0.3	0.2	0.5	0
S_2	0	0.5	0.4	0.1
S_3	0	0	1	0
S_4	0	0	0	1

We would use this to set up the matrix of transition probabilities:

$$P = \begin{bmatrix} 0.3 & 0.2 & 0.5 & 0 \\ 0 & 0.5 & 0.4 & 0.1 \\ 0 & 0 & 1 & 0 \\ 0 & 0 & 0 & 1 \end{bmatrix}$$

This matrix indicates once a bill is paid (state S_3), it cannot enter any other state. Similarly, this indicates if it is written off as a bad debt, it can never leave that category. Thus, both of these are absorbing states.

Additional Topics

When several absorbing states exist, eventually everything in the system will be absorbed by one of these states. To determine what percentage of the bills would enter each of the absorbing states, it is necessary to use what is called the fundamental matrix. References listed at the end of this appendix provide details of this process.

Markov processes also can be used to determine several things that may be of interest to a manager. We could find the average number of periods that must elapse before a system in one state first enters another state and the average number of periods that elapse before the system returns to the present state. It also is possible to find the average time before absorption. Formulas for these may be found in the references.

Managerial Uses of Markov Analysis

Markov processes are used to predict how a system will behave over time if nothing changes. However, managers often make decisions that are aimed at changing the transition probabilities. A new marketing strategy may be designed to prevent as many customers from switching to a competitor's product. Incentives may be given to encourage earlier payments by the customers of a company. A company considering changes of this type would estimate how the transition probabilities would change if these types of decisions are made. Markov analysis is then used to predict how changes in specific transition probabilities would impact the overall system.

References

Hillier, Frederick S., and Gerald J. Lieberman, 1986. *Introduction to Operations Research*. 4th ed. Oakland, California: Holden-Day, Inc.

White, Douglas J., 1985. "Real Applications of Markov Decision Processes." *Interfaces* 15 (6): 73-83.

Winston, Wayne L, 1994. *Operations Research: Applications and Algorithms*. 3rd ed. Belmont, CA: Duxbury Press.

APPENDIX B1

Probabilities for Normal Distribution

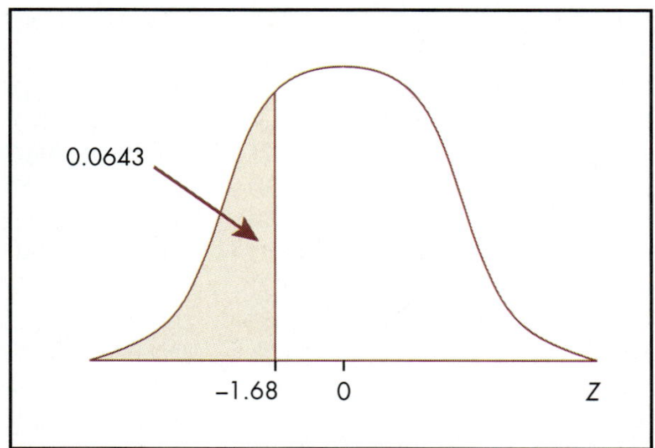

The entries in the table give the probabilities that a standard normal random variable is less than or equal to the Z-value (i.e., $P(Z \leq -1.68 = 0.0643)$.

	Second Decimal Place									
Z	**00**	**01**	**02**	**03**	**04**	**05**	**06**	**07**	**08**	**09**
−3.9	0.0000	0.0001	0.0001	0.0001	0.0001	0.0001	0.0001	0.0001	0.0001	0.0001
−3.8	0.0001	0.0001	0.0001	0.0001	0.0001	0.0001	0.0001	0.0001	0.0001	0.0001
−3.7	0.0001	0.0001	0.0001	0.0001	0.0001	0.0001	0.0001	0.0001	0.0001	0.0002
−3.6	0.0002	0.0002	0.0002	0.0002	0.0002	0.0002	0.0002	0.0002	0.0002	0.0002
−3.5	0.0002	0.0002	0.0003	0.0003	0.0003	0.0003	0.0003	0.0003	0.0003	0.0003
−3.4	0.0003	0.0003	0.0004	0.0004	0.0004	0.0004	0.0004	0.0004	0.0005	0.0005
−3.3	0.0005	0.0005	0.0005	0.0005	0.0006	0.0006	0.0006	0.0006	0.0006	0.0007
−3.2	0.0007	0.0007	0.0007	0.0008	0.0008	0.0008	0.0008	0.0009	0.0009	0.0009
−3.1	0.0010	0.0010	0.0010	0.0011	0.0011	0.0011	0.0012	0.0012	0.0013	0.0013
−3.0	0.0013	0.0014	0.0014	0.0015	0.0015	0.0016	0.0016	0.0017	0.0018	0.0018
−2.9	0.0019	0.0019	0.0020	0.0021	0.0021	0.0022	0.0023	0.0023	0.0024	0.0025
−2.8	0.0026	0.0026	0.0027	0.0028	0.0029	0.0030	0.0031	0.0032	0.0033	0.0034
−2.7	0.0035	0.0036	0.0037	0.0038	0.0039	0.0040	0.0041	0.0043	0.0044	0.0045
−2.6	0.0047	0.0048	0.0049	0.0051	0.0052	0.0054	0.0055	0.0057	0.0059	0.0060
−2.5	0.0062	0.0064	0.0066	0.0068	0.0069	0.0071	0.0073	0.0075	0.0078	0.0080
−2.4	0.0082	0.0084	0.0087	0.0089	0.0091	0.0094	0.0096	0.0099	0.0102	0.0104
−2.3	0.0107	0.0110	0.0113	0.0116	0.0119	0.0122	0.0125	0.0129	0.0132	0.0136
−2.2	0.0139	0.0143	0.0146	0.0150	0.0154	0.0158	0.0162	0.0166	0.0170	0.0174
−2.1	0.0179	0.0183	0.0188	0.0192	0.0197	0.0202	0.0207	0.0212	0.0217	0.0222
−2.0	0.0228	0.0233	0.0239	0.0244	0.0250	0.0256	0.0262	0.0268	0.0274	0.0281
−1.9	0.0287	0.0294	0.0301	0.0307	0.0314	0.0322	0.0329	0.0336	0.0344	0.0351
−1.8	0.0359	0.0367	0.0375	0.0384	0.0392	0.0401	0.0409	0.0418	0.0427	0.0436
−1.7	0.0446	0.0455	0.0465	0.0475	0.0485	0.0495	0.0505	0.0516	0.0526	0.0537
−1.6	0.0548	0.0559	0.0571	0.0582	0.0594	0.0606	0.0618	0.0630	0.0643	0.0655
−1.5	0.0668	0.0681	0.0694	0.0708	0.0721	0.0735	0.0749	0.0764	0.0778	0.0793
−1.4	0.0808	0.0823	0.0838	0.0853	0.0869	0.0885	0.0901	0.0918	0.0934	0.0951
−1.3	0.0968	0.0985	0.1003	0.1020	0.1038	0.1056	0.1075	0.1093	0.1112	0.1131
−1.2	0.1151	0.1170	0.1190	0.1210	0.1230	0.1251	0.1271	0.1292	0.1314	0.1335
−1.1	0.1357	0.1379	0.1401	0.1423	0.1446	0.1469	0.1492	0.1515	0.1539	0.1562
−1.0	0.1587	0.1611	0.1635	0.1660	0.1685	0.1711	0.1736	0.1762	0.1788	0.1814
−0.9	0.1841	0.1867	0.1894	0.1922	0.1949	0.1977	0.2005	0.2033	0.2061	0.2090
−0.8	0.2119	0.2148	0.2177	0.2206	0.2236	0.2266	0.2296	0.2327	0.2358	0.2389
−0.7	0.2420	0.2451	0.2483	0.2514	0.2546	0.2578	0.2611	0.2643	0.2676	0.2709
−0.6	0.2743	0.2776	0.2810	0.2843	0.2877	0.2912	0.2946	0.2981	0.3015	0.3050
−0.5	0.3085	0.3121	0.3156	0.3192	0.3228	0.3264	0.3300	0.3336	0.3372	0.3409
−0.4	0.3446	0.3483	0.3520	0.3557	0.3594	0.3632	0.3669	0.3707	0.3745	0.3783
−0.3	0.3821	0.3859	0.3897	0.3936	0.3974	0.4013	0.4052	0.4090	0.4129	0.4168
−0.2	0.4207	0.4247	0.4286	0.4325	0.4364	0.4404	0.4443	0.4483	0.4522	0.4562
−0.1	0.4602	0.4641	0.4681	0.4721	0.4761	0.4801	0.4840	0.4880	0.4920	0.4960

APPENDIX B1

Probabilities for Normal Distribution (continued)

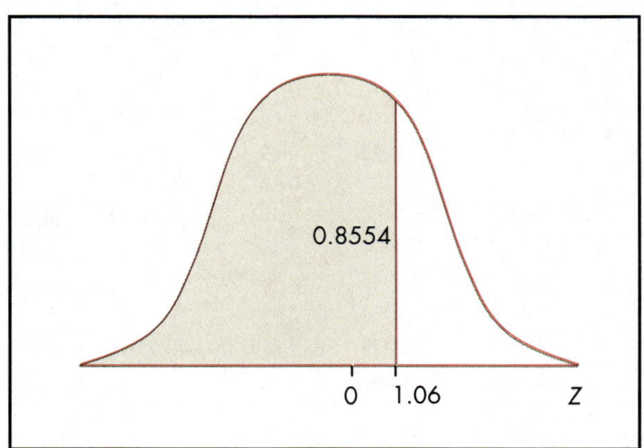

The entries in the table give the probabilities that a standard normal random variable is less than or equal to the Z-value (i.e., $P(Z \leq 1.06) = 0.8554$).

	Second Decimal Place									
Z	00	01	02	03	04	05	06	07	08	09
0.0	0.5000	0.5040	0.5080	0.5120	0.5160	0.5199	0.5239	0.5279	0.5319	0.5359
0.1	0.5398	0.5438	0.5478	0.5517	0.5557	0.5596	0.5636	0.5675	0.5714	0.5753
0.2	0.5793	0.5832	0.5871	0.5910	0.5948	0.5987	0.6026	0.6064	0.6103	0.6141
0.3	0.6179	0.6217	0.6255	0.6293	0.6331	0.6368	0.6406	0.6443	0.6480	0.6517
0.4	0.6554	0.6591	0.6628	0.6664	0.6700	0.6736	0.6772	0.6808	0.6844	0.6879
0.5	0.6915	0.6950	0.6985	0.7019	0.7054	0.7088	0.7123	0.7157	0.7190	0.7224
0.6	0.7257	0.7291	0.7324	0.7357	0.7389	0.7422	0.7454	0.7486	0.7517	0.7549
0.7	0.7580	0.7611	0.7642	0.7673	0.7704	0.7734	0.7764	0.7794	0.7823	0.7852
0.8	0.7881	0.7910	0.7939	0.7967	0.7995	0.8023	0.8051	0.8078	0.8106	0.8133
0.9	0.8159	0.8186	0.8212	0.8238	0.8264	0.8289	0.8315	0.8340	0.8365	0.8389
1.0	0.8413	0.8438	0.8461	0.8485	0.8508	0.8531	0.8554	0.8577	0.8599	0.8621
1.1	0.8643	0.8665	0.8686	0.8708	0.8729	0.8749	0.8770	0.8790	0.8810	0.8830
1.2	0.8849	0.8869	0.8888	0.8907	0.8925	0.8944	0.8962	0.8980	0.8997	0.9015
1.3	0.9032	0.9049	0.9066	0.9082	0.9099	0.9115	0.9131	0.9147	0.9162	0.9177
1.4	0.9192	0.9207	0.9222	0.9236	0.9251	0.9265	0.9279	0.9292	0.9306	0.9319
1.5	0.9332	0.9345	0.9357	0.9370	0.9382	0.9394	0.9406	0.9418	0.9429	0.9441
1.6	0.9452	0.9463	0.9474	0.9484	0.9495	0.9505	0.9515	0.9525	0.9535	0.9545
1.7	0.9554	0.9564	0.9573	0.9582	0.9591	0.9599	0.9608	0.9616	0.9625	0.9633
1.8	0.9641	0.9649	0.9656	0.9664	0.9671	0.9678	0.9686	0.9693	0.9699	0.9706
1.9	0.9713	0.9719	0.9726	0.9732	0.9738	0.9744	0.9750	0.9756	0.9761	0.9767
2.0	0.9772	0.9778	0.9783	0.9788	0.9793	0.9798	0.9803	0.9808	0.9812	0.9817
2.1	0.9821	0.9826	0.9830	0.9834	0.9838	0.9842	0.9846	0.9850	0.9854	0.9857
2.2	0.9861	0.9864	0.9868	0.9871	0.9875	0.9878	0.9881	0.9884	0.9887	0.9890
2.3	0.9893	0.9896	0.9898	0.9901	0.9904	0.9906	0.9909	0.9911	0.9913	0.9916
2.4	0.9918	0.9920	0.9922	0.9925	0.9927	0.9929	0.9931	0.9932	0.9934	0.9936
2.5	0.9938	0.9940	0.9941	0.9943	0.9945	0.9946	0.9948	0.9949	0.9951	0.9952
2.6	0.9953	0.9955	0.9956	0.9957	0.9959	0.9960	0.9961	0.9962	0.9963	0.9964
2.7	0.9965	0.9966	0.9967	0.9968	0.9969	0.9970	0.9971	0.9972	0.9973	0.9974
2.8	0.9974	0.9975	0.9976	0.9977	0.9977	0.9978	0.9979	0.9979	0.9980	0.9981
2.9	0.9981	0.9982	0.9982	0.9983	0.9984	0.9984	0.9985	0.9985	0.9986	0.9986
3.0	0.9987	0.9987	0.9987	0.9988	0.9988	0.9989	0.9989	0.9989	0.9990	0.9990
3.1	0.9990	0.9991	0.9991	0.9991	0.9992	0.9992	0.9992	0.9992	0.9993	0.9993
3.2	0.9993	0.9993	0.9994	0.9994	0.9994	0.9994	0.9994	0.9995	0.9995	0.9995
3.3	0.9995	0.9995	0.9995	0.9996	0.9996	0.9996	0.9996	0.9996	0.9996	0.9997
3.4	0.9997	0.9997	0.9997	0.9997	0.9997	0.9997	0.9997	0.9997	0.9997	0.9998
3.5	0.9998	0.9998	0.9998	0.9998	0.9998	0.9998	0.9998	0.9998	0.9998	0.9998
3.6	0.9998	0.9998	0.9999	0.9999	0.9999	0.9999	0.9999	0.9999	0.9999	0.9999
3.7	0.9999	0.9999	0.9999	0.9999	0.9999	0.9999	0.9999	0.9999	0.9999	0.9999
3.8	0.9999	0.9999	0.9999	0.9999	0.9999	0.9999	0.9999	0.9999	0.9999	0.9999
3.9	1.0000	1.0000	1.0000	1.0000	1.0000	1.0000	1.0000	1.0000	1.0000	1.0000

APPENDIX B2

Values of $e^{-\lambda}$ for Selected Values of λ

λ	$e^{-\lambda}$	λ	$e^{-\lambda}$
0.10	0.9048	4.00	0.0183
0.20	0.8187	4.10	0.0166
0.30	0.7408	4.20	0.0150
0.40	0.6703	4.30	0.0136
0.50	0.6065	4.40	0.0123
0.60	0.5488	4.50	0.0111
0.70	0.4966	4.60	0.0101
0.80	0.4493	4.70	0.0091
0.90	0.4066	4.80	0.0082
1.00	0.3679	4.90	0.0074
1.10	0.3329	5.00	0.0067
1.20	0.3012	5.10	0.0061
1.30	0.2725	5.20	0.0055
1.40	0.2466	5.30	0.0050
1.50	0.2231	5.40	0.0045
1.60	0.2019	5.50	0.0041
1.70	0.1827	5.60	0.0037
1.80	0.1653	5.70	0.0033
1.90	0.1496	5.80	0.0030
2.00	0.1353	5.90	0.0027
2.10	0.1225	6.00	0.0025
2.20	0.1108	7.00	0.0009
2.30	0.1003	8.00	0.0003
2.40	0.0907	9.00	0.0001
2.50	0.0821	10.00	0.0000
2.60	0.0743		
2.70	0.0672		
2.80	0.0608		
2.90	0.0550		
3.00	0.0498		
3.10	0.0450		
3.20	0.0408		
3.30	0.0369		
3.40	0.0334		
3.50	0.0302		
3.60	0.0273		
3.70	0.0247		
3.80	0.0224		
3.90	0.0202		

APPENDIX B3

Table of Random Numbers

62	37	27	86	64	63	60	45	98	97	82	17	06	14	66	04	10	64
50	71	47	62	67	66	64	30	12	15	74	61	81	31	05	20	25	93
41	11	06	57	17	21	05	54	34	49	39	08	19	38	40	54	11	59
26	73	15	75	51	19	33	81	58	32	81	84	44	56	61	86	72	99
77	85	81	84	33	46	64	14	01	72	65	58	05	57	82	98	51	07
95	98	75	53	28	32	06	53	27	91	21	59	94	37	18	19	82	59
14	93	90	01	44	06	96	14	32	93	19	87	90	32	50	73	27	78
21	34	75	80	55	88	18	04	57	09	03	01	74	81	67	08	60	32
64	95	23	94	37	95	13	40	85	42	48	40	53	23	00	61	89	23
49	75	70	71	01	77	11	66	34	70	07	01	53	74	71	17	52	82
15	45	21	61	19	02	50	49	80	84	27	02	87	31	48	51	14	63
27	83	73	23	09	21	99	28	58	67	20	58	59	41	77	07	41	70
58	65	30	91	18	50	75	39	53	08	90	84	84	55	41	95	61	34
35	57	17	04	23	03	94	14	86	68	31	41	29	02	01	33	12	96
49	70	57	25	56	33	01	34	89	40	70	22	96	17	49	86	78	84
09	83	23	55	77	99	97	03	99	57	91	20	38	29	52	77	99	07
46	64	30	75	04	27	13	10	93	33	13	41	90	27	55	41	90	12
49	62	05	57	13	30	31	64	50	81	55	97	02	38	78	73	40	15
31	36	61	40	43	06	14	34	03	18	06	19	79	78	08	59	26	99
29	62	13	08	70	54	99	03	50	70	31	37	31	08	34	25	55	16
27	41	58	02	11	95	52	29	12	16	43	48	37	19	20	27	47	92
25	50	20	82	77	22	84	64	96	25	97	31	77	88	29	20	93	47
32	61	33	87	37	36	52	33	63	39	63	17	35	15	28	65	28	03
16	51	16	40	29	92	95	05	93	95	66	11	20	38	22	58	48	93
97	73	74	16	99	48	71	29	20	98	50	90	61	83	93	24	34	08
46	91	77	08	70	98	26	77	45	67	01	89	58	03	80	70	68	74
71	36	04	26	56	76	07	53	26	01	21	43	54	06	06	76	31	11
92	40	47	70	94	04	52	78	40	13	30	71	96	19	70	92	97	83
36	37	69	88	07	87	18	39	84	81	34	56	98	15	38	35	49	37
80	56	83	64	26	45	07	59	55	60	44	16	31	26	62	83	17	99
76	59	24	09	39	90	66	02	35	56	89	93	17	49	30	84	14	39
93	14	48	95	50	53	53	96	92	99	35	35	44	34	00	12	01	12
56	77	19	63	60	56	31	30	59	43	91	98	23	70	00	92	08	36
21	46	66	54	25	06	45	53	41	82	33	74	90	73	50	15	18	67
51	05	29	84	58	23	59	46	93	48	37	36	60	46	30	03	46	01
30	35	75	57	59	84	12	30	34	88	27	64	76	15	77	22	21	04
39	98	58	68	45	92	15	68	80	67	49	48	06	88	78	56	37	82
87	92	02	25	57	14	27	26	59	05	23	34	76	35	41	60	24	89
20	35	65	53	99	42	07	05	07	57	96	12	88	04	36	51	09	46
97	81	98	20	14	82	57	90	27	00	21	20	68	95	04	68	37	90
63	29	92	48	93	92	10	88	64	34	79	52	19	31	39	26	45	73
87	83	37	23	84	08	55	75	94	76	37	25	43	19	98	38	41	43

APPENDIX C

Answers to Selected Odd-Numbered Problems

Chapter 1

9. (a) \$2,100
   (b) Not necessarily. There may be a salary as well as a commission.
   (c) $I = 500 + 200X$
   (d) It might be as it does combine salary and commission.
   (e) The manager must determine how accurately the model represents the real-world situation.

Chapter 2

13. (a,b) $X_1 = 8$, $X_2 = 0$, profit = \$64
    (c) no, constraint 2
    (d) no, constraint 1
15. (a) The feasible region is a line segment.
    (b) $X_1 = 3$, $X_2 = 2$, profit = \$19
19. (a) $X_1 = 2$, $X_2 = 3$, cost = 65
    (b) surplus = 2 for constraint 1. There is no surplus for the others.
21. (2,6) \$84
23. unbounded
25. unbounded
27. (a) multiple optimal solutions
    (b) \$48
    (c) Yes, \$48
    (d) No. It violates the first constraint.

29. 15 swings, 20 tables, profit = \$1,800, slack for wood = 1,050, slack for labor = 0
31. 100 acres wheat, 300 corn, profit = \$260,000
33. \$25,000 in petrochemical, \$25,000 in utility, risk = 6, return = 9%
35. 25 radio, 10 TV, audience = 145,000
37. cost = \$17, 0.75 barrels WT23, 0.25 barrels AR15, 45% Ingredient A, 41.25% Ingredient B

Chapter 3

15. (a) $X_1 = 8$, $X_2 = 0$, profit = \$64
    (b) No, it violates the second constraint.
    (c) $X_1 = 8$, $X_2 = 0$, profit = \$64
    (d) $X_1 = 8$, $X_2 = 0$, profit = \$64
    (e) it gets smaller
17. (a) $X_1 = 0$, $X_2 = 6$
    (b) 60
    (c) $S_1 = 4$, $S_2 = 0$, $S_3 = 21$
    (d) Feasible region does not change.
19. (a) 80 15" monitors, 20 17" monitors, profit = \$5,600
    (b) 220 assembly hours, 120 inspection hours
    (c) no
    (d) no change in production
    (e) 60 15" monitors, 30 17" monitors, profit = \$5,400
    (f) 59 15" monitors, 31 17" monitors, profit = \$5,430, dual price = 30
21. (a) $X_1 = 50$, $X_2 = 20$, $S_1 = 0$, $S_2 = 0$, profit = 1,650
    (b) 15
    (c) \$15 per unit, $X_1 = 0$, $X_2 = 120$, $S_1 = 0$, $S_2 = 0$, profit = 2,400
    (d) $X_1 = 0$, $X_2 = 120$, $S_1 = 0$, $S_2 = 1$, profit = 2,400
    (e) $X_1 = 60$, $X_2 = 0$, $S_1 = 0$, $S_2 = 0$, profit = 1,500
    (f) $X_1 = 59$, $X_2 = 0$, $S_1 = 0$, $S_2 = 2$, profit = 1,475
23. (a) $X_1 = 1.6$, $X_2 = 4.8$,
    (b) profit = 27.2
    (c) 0
    (d) 22
    (e) $X_1 = 2.4$, $X_2 = 3.2$, profit = 24.8, profit decreased by 2.4, dual price = 0.6
25. (a) 100 acres wheat, 300 acres corn, profit = \$260,000, 900 labor hours
    (b) 140 more hours
    (c) \$200 for each acre and \$200 for each labor hour
27. (a) optimal point (0.5,0.5), cost = \$0.85, other corner point is (1,0)
    (b) feasible region would get smaller, $X_1 = 0.75$, $X_2 = 0.25$, cost = \$0.875
29. (a) 0.4 barrels of WT23, 0.6 barrels of AR15, cost of WT23 must increase by 4
31. Zero \$4, P51 \$0.57, B17 \$9
33. While the percentage change is more than 100%, the optimal basic solution does not change.
35. Slack for lumber increases by 100. Nothing else changes.

Chapter 4

7. $X_1 \geq 0.20(X_1 + X_2 + X_3 + X_4)$
9. (a) Minimize $X_1 + X_2 + X_3$
   Subject to:
   $X_1 \geq 23$
   $X_1 + X_2 \geq 18$
   $X_2 + X_3 \geq 32$
   $X_3 \geq 16$
   $X_1, X_2, X_3 \geq 0$
   (b) add the following constraints
   $X_1 \leq 34.5$
   $X_1 + X_2 \leq 27$
   $X_2 + X_3 \leq 48$
   $X_3 \leq 24$
11. Minimize $4X_{13} + 7X_{14} + 5X_{23} + 7X_{24} + 6X_{27} + 3X_{35} + 2X_{36} + 2X_{37} + X_{45} + 3X_{46} + 4X_{47}$
    Subject to:
    $X_{13} + X_{14} \leq 600$ supply at Toronto
    $X_{23} + X_{24} + X_{27} \leq 500$ supply at Detroit
    $X_{35} + X_{45} = 450$ demand at New York
    $X_{36} + X_{46} = 350$ demand at Philadelphia
    $X_{37} + X_{47} + X_{27} = 300$ demand at St. Louis
    $X_{13} + X_{23} = X_{35} + X_{36} + X_{37}$ shipping through Chicago
    $X_{14} + X_{24} = X_{45} + X_{46} + X_{47}$ shipping through Buffalo
    $X_{13}, X_{14}, X_{23}, X_{24}, X_{35}, X_{36}, X_{37}, X_{45}, X_{46}, X_{47} \geq 0$

13. Maximize audience = $30{,}000X_1 + 22{,}000X_2 + 24{,}000X_3 + 8{,}000X_4$
    Subject to:
    $X_1 \leq 10$ TV ads
    $X_2 \leq 10$ radio ads
    $X_3 \leq 10$ billboards
    $X_4 \leq 10$ newspaper ads
    $800X_1 + 400X_2 + 500X_3 + 100X_4 \leq 15{,}000$ budget
    $X_1 + X_2 \geq 6$ total newspaper and magazine ads
    $500X_3 + 100X_4 \leq 800X_1$
    $X_1, X_2, X_3, X_4 \geq 0$ nonnegativity constraints
17. \$36,666.67 in stocks, \$30,000 in bonds, \$33,333.33 in real estate, return = \$12, 066.67

Chapter 5

17. (b) $S_1 = 120$, $A_2 = 250$, $A_3 = 180$, profit = –430M
19. (b) $S_1 = 230$, $A_2 = 250$, $A_3 = 120$, cost = 370M
23. Minimize $80U_1 + 50U_2$
    Subject to: $4U_1 + 1U_2 \geq 10$
    $2U_1 + 2U_2 \geq 8$
    $U_1, U_2 \geq 0$
25. (a) $S_1 = 12$, $X_1 = 4$, $X_2 = 16$, all other variables = 0, profit = 288
    (b) 0 Department A, 3 Department B, 4.5 Department C

(c) \$0 for hours in Department A, \$3 per hour for hours in Department B, and \$4.50 per hour for hours in Department C
(d) \$1
(e) decrease 4.5, increase 3
(f) 12
(g) 30 – 40
(h) $S_1 = 14$, $X_1 = 3$, $X_2 = 17$, all other variables = 0, profit = 291
(i) No

29. multiple optimal solutions
31. infeasibility

Chapter 6

17. (a) Reno-Phoenix 120, Denver-Phoenix 20, Denver-Cleveland 160, Denver-Chicago 20, Pittsburgh-Chicago 160. Cost = \$5,860.
(b) Reno-Phoenix 120, Denver-Phoenix 20, Denver-Chicago 180, Pittsburgh-Cleveland 160. Cost = \$5,700 (degenerate solution).
(c) Reno-Phoenix 120, Denver-Phoenix 20, Denver-Cleveland 0, Denver-Chicago 180, Pittsburgh-Cleveland 160. Cost = \$5,700.
19. Reno-Phoenix 100, Reno-Chicago 20, Denver-Phoenix 40, Denver-Cleveland 160, Pittsburgh-Chicago 160. Cost = \$6,020.
21. minimum total cost = \$50,900 [\$45,900 + 500(10)]. Total cost has increased \$1 per unit for 500 units.
23. Lubbock-Houston 80, Albuquerque-San Diego 20, Albuquerque-Houston 40, Albuquerque-Mobile 20, Phoenix-San Diego 80, Dummy-Mobile 30. Total profit = \$16,200.
25. (a) 1–Li, 2–Davis, 3–Smith, Dummy–Jones. Total 18.
(b) 1–Davis, 2–Smith, 3–Jones, Dummy–Li. Total 23. Multiple optimal solutions exist.
27. A–3, B–1, C–Dummy, D–2, total time = 17. Machine C is idle.
29. March – 300 units normal time, April – 300 units normal time and 140 units overtime, May – 300 units normal time and 150 units overtime, June – 300 units normal time and 20 units overtime. Total cost = \$201,900. Multiple optimal solutions exist.
31. No change in product is needed. Total cost = \$203,200. Multiple optimal solutions exist.
33. Smith–2, Jones–4, Davis–1, Nguyen–3. Total time = 31 days.

Chapter 7

11. Undertake apartment and shopping center projects. NPV = 33.
15. $X_1 = 8$, $X_2 = 0$, $X_3 = 6$, objective function value = 1,980
17. Sam #1, Gerri #2, Linda #3. Total rating = 14.
19. stock \$150,000, bonds \$75,000, real estate \$25,000, expected return is 11.2 percent
23. (a) Yes
(b) goal 2
(c) idle time
25. Standard 60, Deluxe 60, Chef's Delight 12
27. Standard 60, Deluxe 60, Chef's Delight 60

Chapter 8

11. (a) Week 41
    (b) Nothing would be delayed. The latest start time is 43.
    (c) No
    (d) Yes

13.

Activity	ES	EF	LS	LF	Slack	Critical Path
A	0	7	0	7	0	yes
B	0	4	3	7	3	no
C	7	9	9	11	2	no
D	7	9	7	9	0	yes
E	7	10	10	13	3	no
F	9	13	9	13	0	yes
G	9	13	11	15	2	no
H	13	15	13	15	0	yes
I	15	18	15	18	0	yes

The dummy activity indicates that Activity *A* is a predecessor for Activities *D* and *E*.

15. Critical path B-D-E-G (all have zero slack). Slack for A = 2, C = 2, F = 5.
17. Critical path C-E-G (all have zero slack). Slack for A = 2, B = 2, D = 2, F = 2.
21. due date = 85.2 weeks
23. (a) A 10 and 4/36, B 10 and 4, C 10 and 4/36, D 8 and 1
    (b) The expected completion time for the critical path (A-C) is 20. The expected completion time for B-D is 18.
    (c) variance of A-C = 8/36
    variance for B-D = 5
    (d) almost 1.0000
    (e) 0.95
    (f) The critical path is the path that on the average takes longest. Another path which has a greater variance than the critical path may in certain instances take longer than the critical path.

Chapter 9

11. connect 1–2, 1–3, 3–5, 3–6, 3–7, 6–7. Total distance = 28.
13. connect 1–3, 2–3, 3–5, 4–5, 5–6. Total distance = 40.
15. The flows are 80 on 1–2, 50 on 1–3, 60 on 1–4, 20 on 2–3, 60 on 2–5, 10 on 3–5, 60 on 3–6, 40 on 4–7, 70 on 5–8, 10 on 7–6, 70 on 6–8, 50 on 7–8. Total flow = 190. If 3–6 is closed, the total flow will remain 190 by using other routes.
17. shortest route is 1–3–6–7, total distance is 16
19. best route 1–3–5–6–7–10, total number = 308

Chapter 10

13. (a) 125 units, 40 orders
    (b) decrease 2,250
    (c) ROP = 100

15. (a) $C_h = 1.425$
    (b) 14.25
    (c) 1,000 gallons
17. (a) 213.8
    (b) 1,820 savings
    (c) ROP = 64
19. order 200, total cost = $29,850
21. (a) 200
    (b) 141
    (c) 100
23. 18 units of safety stock, service level = 96%
29. 65,640

Chapter 11

11. (a) 0.1353
    (b) 0.2706
    (c) 0.2706
    (d) 0.1804
    (e) 0.8569
13. (a) 1/3
    (b) 0.6321
    (c) 0.8111
15. (a) $\lambda = 1, \mu = 2$
    (b) *M/M/1*
    (c) $\rho = 0.50$
    (d) $P_0 = 0.50$
    (e) $L_q = 0.50$
    (f) $W_q = 0.50$ minutes
    (g) $W = 1$ minute
17. (a) 4
    (b) 32
    (c) $W = 1$ hour
    (d) 32 hours
    (e) $640
19. $W_q = 0.133$ hours, $L_q = 1.33$, $W = 0.2$ hours, $L = 2$, $P_0 = 0.333$
21. (a) 80
    (b) 10.66 hours
    (c) $266
    (d) 0.66 hours, $16
    (e) 2 tellers
23. $W_q = 0.038$ hours, $L_q = 1.125$, $W = 0.063$ hours, $L = 1.875$ hours

Chapter 12

11. (a) #3
    (b) #2
    (c) #3
    (d) #2

13. (a) 30

(b)

	A	B	C
#1	0	10	60
#2	10	30	50
#3	50	0	0

(c) #2 or #3
(d) #3
(e) 10

15. (a) 40, 50
(b) 120

17. (a) #1
(b) #1
(c) #1
(d) It does not use all information available.

19. (a) #2
(b) #2
(c) #2
(d) It does not use all information available.

21. (a) 1.47, 1.02
(b) Yes
(c) 0.31
(d) 0.93, 1.38, because expected marginal loss is higher, stocking the 26th dozen will lose money on the average

23. Stock papers so that the probability of selling the last paper is at least 0.40.

25. (a) develop the land
(b) No
(c) EVPI = $100,000
(d) $366,666.67

Chapter 13

11. (b) a_2 has expected value of 650

13. –700

15. (b) Alternative a_2 with EV = 240
(c) –40

17. (a) $P(s_1) = 0.5$, $P(s_2) = 0.5$
(b) 0.4
(c) 0.60
(d) 0.875, 0.125, 0.25, 0.75
(e) 0.875
(f) 0.25
(g) 1

19. (b) 2,250
(c) 120

21. University B

23. Normalized matrices

	Cost			
	A	B	C	Average Rating
A	0.111	0.130	0.077	0.106
B	0.556	0.652	0.692	0.633
C	0.333	0.217	0.231	0.260

	Reputation			
	A	B	C	Average Rating
A	0.745	0.636	0.789	0.724
B	0.106	0.091	0.053	0.083
C	0.149	0.273	0.158	0.193

	Quality of Life			
	A	B	C	Average Rating
A	0.455	0.467	0.385	0.435
B	0.455	0.467	0.538	0.487
C	0.091	0.067	0.077	0.078

	Cost	Reputation	Quality	Average Weight
Cost	0.677	0.667	0.700	0.681
Reputation	0.226	0.222	0.200	0.216
Quality	0.097	0.111	0.100	0.103

	Cost	Reputation	Quality	Weighted Average
A	0.106	0.724	0.435	0.2732
B	0.633	0.083	0.487	0.4994
C	0.260	0.193	0.078	0.227
Weights	0.681	0.216	0.103	

Select University B

25. (a)

	Cost		
	A	B	C
A	1	1/5	1/3
B	5	1	3
C	3	1/3	1

	Appearance		
	A	B	C
A	1	9	3
B	1/9	1	4
C	1/3	1/4	1

Quality			
	A	B	C
A	1	5	4
B	1/5	1	1/3
C	1/4	3	1

(b) On appearance, A is extremely strongly preferred to Car B but only moderately preferred to Car C. This would suggest that Car C should be preferred to Car B, instead of B being moderately to strongly preferred to Car C.

27. Normalized matrices

Cost				
	A	B	C	Average Rating
A	0.111	0.130	0.077	0.106
B	0.556	0.652	0.692	0.633
C	0.333	0.217	0.231	0.260

Appearance				
	A	B	C	Average Rating
A	0.692	0.878	0.375	0.648
B	0.077	0.098	0.500	0.225
C	0.231	0.024	0.125	0.127

Quality				
	A	B	C	Average Rating
A	0.690	0.556	0.750	0.665
B	0.138	0.111	0.063	0.104
C	0.172	0.333	0.188	0.231

	Cost	Appearance	Quality	Average Weights
Cost	0.706	0.571	0.800	0.692
Appearance	0.176	0.143	0.067	0.129
Quality	0.118	0.286	0.133	0.179

	Cost	Appearance	Quality	Weighted Average
A	0.106	0.648	0.665	0.2759
B	0.633	0.225	0.104	0.4860
C	0.260	0.127	0.231	0.2380
Weights	0.692	0.129	0.179	

Gina would select Car B.

Chapter 14

11. (a) 17
    (b) 16
    (c) 16.33
    (d) 14.79
13. MSE for naive model = 7.4
    MSE for 2-week moving average = 7.81
    MSE for 2-week weighted moving average = 7.50
    MSE for exponential smoothing = 6.98
15. (a) 24
    (b) 24 for Quarter 1, 25.5 for Quarter 2, 22 for Quarter 3, and 24.5 for Quarter 4
    (c) 1 for Quarter 1, 1.063 for Quarter 2, 0.917 for Quarter 3, and 1.021 for Quarter 4
    (d) 1.020 for Quarter 1, 1.085 for Quarter 2, 0.903 for Quarter 3, and 1.005 for Quarter 4
17. (a) $83,502
    (b) The predicted price is the average price for this type of house. There are other factors influencing the price that are not included in the model.
    (c) Age, size of lot, number of bedrooms.
    (d) 0.3969
19. (a) Yes
    (b) $\hat{Y} = 33.5 + 2.7X$
    (c) 49.7
    (d) 52.4
23. 339 for 1995
    360 for 1996
    443 for 2000
25. MAD = 24.33 for naive model; MAD = 7.93 for trend model
27. MAD = 0.673 for exponential smoothing model; MAD = 0.589 for naive model

Chapter 15

11. (a,b)

Demand	Cumulative Probability	Random Number
13	0.35	01–35
14	0.74	36–74
15	0.96	75–96
16	1.00	97–00

    (c) 14, 14, 13, 15
    (d) fixed time increment
13. (a,b)

Interarrival Time	Cumulative Probability	Random Number
1	0.35	01–35
2	0.65	36–65
3	0.90	66–90
4	1.00	91–00

(c) arrival times: 8:03, 8:06, 8:08, 8:09, 8:12, 8:13, 8:15, 8:18, 8:22, 8:25
(d) variable time increment

15. (a)

Processing Time	Cumulative Probability	Random Number
1	0.45	01–45
2	0.75	46–75
3	1.00	76–00

(b) processing times: 2, 1, 3, 2, 3, 3, 1, 3, 2, 1
(c) average waiting time = 1.3 minutes
(d) idle time = 5 minutes

17. (a) 26, 27, 25, 27, 23, 25, 26, 24, 24, 26
(b) $29,200
(c) $29,400

References and Bibliography

Introduction to Management Science (Chapter 1)

Hesse, Rick, and Gene Woolsey, 1980. *Applied Management Science: A Quick and Dirty Approach*. Chicago: Science Research Associates, Inc.

Higgins, James M., 1991. *The Management Challenge: An Introduction to Management*. 5th ed. New York: MacMillan Publishing Company.

Megginson, Leon C., Donald C. Mosley, and Paul H. Pietri, Jr., 1992. *Management: Concepts and Applications*. 4th ed. New York: Harper Collins.

Robbins, Stephen P., 1991. *Management*. 3rd ed. Englewood Cliffs, N.J.: Prentice Hall.

Rosario, E. A., del, October 1994. "OR Brew Success for San Miguel." *OR/MS Today*: 24–30.

Stair, Ralph M., 1992. *Principles of Information Systems: A Managerial Approach*. Boston: boyd & fraser publishing company.

Stoner, James A. F., and R. Edward Freeman, 1992. *Management*. Englewood Cliffs, N.J.: Prentice Hall.

Swart, William, and Luca Donna, December 1981. "Simulation Modeling Improves Operations, Planning, and Productivity of Fast Food Restaurants." *Interfaces* 11 (6): 35–47.

What's*Best!*, 1995. Chicago: LINDO Systems, Inc.

Linear Programming, Transportation, Transshipment, and Assignment Problems (Chapters 2–6)

Blumenfield, Dennis E., L. D. Burns, C. F. Daganzo, M. C. Frick, and R. W. Hall, 1987. "Reducing Logistics Costs at General Motors." *Interfaces* 17 (1): 26–47.

Bradley, S. P., A. C. Hax, and T. L. Magnanti, 1977. *Applied Mathematical Programming*. Reading, MA.: Addison-Wesley Publishing Company, Inc.

Callen, J., 1991. "Data Envelopment Analysis: Practical Survey and Managerial Accounting Applications." *Journal of Management Accounting Research* (3): 35–57.

Clements, D. W., and R. A. Reid, March-April 1994. "Analytical MS/OR Tools Applied to a Plant Closure." *Interfaces* 24 (2): 1–12.

Dantzig, George B., 1963. *Linear Programming and Extensions*. Princeton, N.Y.: Princeton University Press.

Epstein, Michael K., and John C. Henderson, Winter 1989. "Data Envelopment Analysis for Managerial Control and Diagnosis." *Decision Sciences* 20 (1): 90–119.

Evans, James R, 1986. "Scheduling American League Umpires: A Microcomputer Based DSS." *Proceedings of the Annual Meeting of the Decision Sciences Institute*. Honolulu: 914–916.

Evans, James R., John E. Herbert, and Richard F. Deckro, Spring 1984. "Play Ball! The Scheduling of Sports Officials." *Perspectives in Computing* 4 (1): 18–29.

Gass, Saul, 1975. *Linear Programming*. 4th ed. New York: McGraw-Hill Inc.

Hillier, Frederick S., and Gerald J. Lieberman, 1986. *Introduction to Operations Research*. 4th ed. Oakland, CA.: Holden Day Inc.

Hooker, J. N., 1986. "Karmarkar's Linear Programming Algorithm." *Interfaces* 16 (4): 75–90.

Roy, J., and T. G. Crainic, May-June 1992. "Improving Intercity Freight Routing with a Tactical Planning Model." *Interfaces* 22: 31–44.

Sexton, T. R., S. Sleeper, and R. E. Taggart, Jr., January-February 1994. "Improving Pupil Transportation in North Carolina." *Interfaces* 24 (1): 87–103.

Stroup, J. S., and R. D. Wollmer, 1992. "A Fuel Management Model for the Airline Industry." *Operations Research* 40 (2): 229–237.

Subramanian, Radhika, R. P. Scheff, Jr., J. D. Quillinan, D. S. Wiper, and R. E. Marsten, 1994. "Coldstart: Fleet Assignment at Delta Airlines." *Interfaces* 24 (1): 104–120.

Wagner, Harvey M., 1975. *Principles of Operations Research*. 2nd ed. Englewood Cliffs, N.J.: Prentice Hall.

Winston, Wayne L., 1994. *Operations Research: Applications and Algorithms*. 3rd ed. Belmont, CA.: Duxbury Press.

Yang, D. L., and W. Mou, 1993. "An Integrated Decision Support System in a Chinese Chemical Plant." *Interfaces* 23 (6): 93–100.

Integer Programming and Goal Programming (Chapter 7)

Geoffrion, A. M., and R. E. Marsten, May 1972. "Integer Programming Algorithms: A Framework and State of the Art Survey." *Management Science* 18 (9): 465–491.

Greenberg, H., 1971. *Integer Programming*. New York: Academic Press Inc.

Ignizio, J. P., 1978. "A Review of Goal Programming: A Tool for Multiobjective Analysis." *Journal of the Operational Research Society* 29 (11): 1109–1119.

Ignizio, J. P., 1976. *Goal Programming and Extensions*. Lexington, MA.: D.C. Heath & Co.

Lawler, E. L., and D. E. Wood, 1966. "Branch-and-Bound Methods: A Survey." *Operations Research* 14 (4): 699–719.

Lee, S. M., 1972. *Goal Programming for Decision Analysis*. Philadelphia: Auerbach Publishers.

Nemhauser, G. L., and L. A. Wolsey, 1988. *Integer and Combinatorial Optimization*. New York: John Wiley & Sons Inc.

Plane, D. R., and Claude McMillan, Jr., 1971. *Discrete Optimization: Integer Programming and Network Analysis for Management Decisions*. Englewood Cliffs, N.J.: Prentice Hall.

Salkin, Harvey M., 1975. *Integer Programming*. Reading, MA.: Addison-Wesley Publishing Company, Inc.

Taha, H. A., 1975. *Integer Programming: Theory, Applications, and Computations*. New York: Academic Press Inc.

Zionts, Stanley, 1974. *Linear and Integer Programming*. Englewood Cliffs, N.J.: Prentice Hall.

Project Management: PERT/CPM (Chapter 8)

Chase, Richard B., and Nicholas J. Aquilano, 1995. *Production and Operations Management: Manufacturing and Services*. 7th ed. Chicago: Richard D. Irwin Inc.

Meredith, J. R., and S. J. Mantel, 1989. *Project Management: A Managerial Approach*. 2nd ed. New York: John Wiley & Sons Inc.

Moder, Joseph J., Cecil R. Phillips, and E. Davis, 1983. *Project Management with CPM, PERT, and Precedence Diagramming*. New York: Van Nostrand Reinhold.

Peterson, P., May 1994. "Project Management Software Survey." *PMNETwork* 8 (5): 33–41.

Pritsker, A. A., and W. W. Happ, May 1966. "GERT: Graphical Evaluation and Review Technique, Part I." *Journal of Industrial Engineering* 17 (5).

Pritsker, A. A., and W. W. Happ, June 1966. "GERT: Graphical Evaluation and Review Technique, Part II." *Journal of Industrial Engineering* 17 (6).

Wiest, J., and F. Levy, 1977. *A Management Guide to PERT/CPM*. 2nd ed. Englewood Cliffs, N.J.: Prentice Hall.

Winston, Wayne L., 1994. *Operations Research: Applications and Algorithms*. 3rd ed. Belmont, CA.: Duxbury Press.

Networks (Chapter 9)

Bazaraa, M. S., and J. J. Jarvis, 1977. *Linear Programming and Network Flows*. New York: John Wiley & Sons Inc.

Golden, B., L. Bodin, T. Doyle, and W. Stewart, 1980. "Approximate Traveling Sales Algorithms." *Operations Research* 28: 694–712.

Hu, T. C., 1970. *Integer Programming and Network Flows*. Reading, MA.: Addison-Wesley Publishing Company Inc.

Lawler, E. L., J. K. Lenstra, A. H. G. Rinnooy Kan, and D. B. Shmoys, 1985. *The Traveling Salesman Problem: A Guided Tour of Combinatorial Optimization*. New York: John Wiley & Sons Inc.

Roy, J., and T. G. Crainic, May-June 1992. "Improving Intercity Freight Routing with a Tactical Planning Model." *Interfaces* 22: 31–44.

Vemuganti, R. R., M. Oblak, and A. Aggarwal, Winter 1989. "Network Models for Fleet Management." *Decision Sciences* 20 (1): 182–197.

Inventory (Chapter 10)

Adam, E. E., Jr., and R. J. Ebert, 1992. *Production and Operations Management.* 5th ed. Englewood Cliffs, N.J.: Prentice Hall.

Chase, R. B., and N. J. Aquilano, 1995. *Production and Operations Management: Manufacturing and Services.* 7th ed. Boston: Richard D. Irwin, Inc.

Chopra, V., March 1982. "Productivity Improvement through Closed Loop MRP (Part 1)." *Production and Inventory Management Review and APICS News*: 18–21.

Chopra, V., April 1982. "Productivity Improvement through Closed Loop MRP (Part 2)." *Production and Inventory Management Review and APICS News*: 49–51.

Hadley, G., and T. M. Whitin, 1963. *Analysis of Inventory Systems.* Englewood Cliffs, N.J.: Prentice Hall.

Orlicky, Joseph, 1975. *Material Requirements Planning.* New York: McGraw-Hill Inc.

Perry, William, December 1992. "The Principles of Distribution Resource Planning." *Production and Inventory Management Review and APICS News*: 20–33.

Schonberger, R. J., and E. M. Knod, Jr., 1994. *Operations Management: Continuous Improvement.* 5th ed. Boston: Richard D. Irwin Inc.

Silver, Edward A., and Rein Peterson, 1985. *Decision Systems for Inventory Management.* New York: John Wiley & Sons Inc.

Starr, M. K., and D. W. Miller, 1962. *Inventory Control: Theory and Practice.* Englewood Cliffs, N.J.: Prentice Hall.

Tersine, J. R., 1987. *Principles of Inventory and Materials Management.* 3rd ed. New York: Elsevier North Holland.

Queuing (Chapter 11)

Cooper, R. B., 1972. *Introduction to Queuing Theory.* 2nd ed. New York: MacMillan Publishing Company.

Gross, D., and C. M. Harris, 1974. *Fundamentals of Queuing Theory.* New York: John Wiley & Sons Inc.

Larson, Richard C., November-December 1987. "Perspectives on Queues: Social Justice and the Psychology of Queuing." *Operations Research* 35 (6): 895–905.

Neter, John, William Wasserman, and G. A. Whitmore, 1988. *Applied Statistics.* 3rd ed. Needham Heights, MA.: Allyn & Bacon Inc.

Panico, J. A., 1969. *Queuing Theory: A Study of Waiting Lines for Business, Economics, and Sciences.* Englewood Cliffs, N.J.: Prentice Hall.

Decision Theory (Chapters 12 and 13)

Camm, Jeffrey D., and Timothy H. Burwell, 1991. "Sensitivity Analysis in Linear Programming Models with Common Inputs." *Decision Sciences* 22 (3): 512–518.

Chernoff, H., and L. E. Moses, 1959. *Elementary Decision Theory.* New York: John Wiley & Sons Inc.

Luce, R. D., and H. Raiffa, 1957. *Games and Decisions*. New York: John Wiley & Sons Inc.
Saaty, Thomas L., 1980. *The Analytical Hierarchy Process*. New York: McGraw-Hill Inc.
Schenkerman, Stan, 1983. "Sensitivity of Linear Programs to Related Changes in Multiple Inputs." *Decision Sciences* 24 (4): 879–891.
Shlaiffer, R., 1969. *Analysis of Decision Under Uncertainty*. New York: McGraw-Hill Inc.
Winkler, Robert L., 1972. *An Introduction to Bayesian Inference and Decision*. New York: Holt, Rinehart and Winston Inc.

Forecasting (Chapter 14)

Gaynor, Patricia E., and Rickey C. Kirkpatrick, 1994. *Introduction to Time-Series Modeling and Forecasting in Business and Economics*. New York: McGraw-Hill Inc.
Georgoff, D. M., and R. G. Mardick, 1986. "Manager's Guide to Forecasting." *Harvard Business Review*: 110–120.
Hanke, John E., and Arthur G. Reitsch, 1992. *Business Forecasting*. 4th ed. Needham Heights, MA.: Allyn & Bacon Inc.
Makridakis, Spyros, 1986. "The Art and Science of Forecasting." *International Journal of Forecasting* 2: 15–39.
Wheelright, Steven C., and Spyros Makridakis, 1973. *Forecasting Methods for Management*. New York: John Wiley & Sons Inc.

Simulation (Chapter 15)

@RISK: Risk Analysis for Spreadsheets, 1994. New York: Palisade Corporation.
Emshoff, J. R., and R. L. Sisson, 1970. *Design and Use of Computer Simulation Models*. New York: MacMillan Publishing Company.
Gordon, Geoffrey, 1978. *System Simulation*. Englewood Cliffs, N.J.: Prentice Hall.
Kleijnen, Jack, and Willem van Groenendaal, 1987. *Simulation: A Statistical Perspective*. Chichester, England: John Wiley & Sons Inc.
Law, A. M., and W. Kelton, 1990. *Simulation Modeling and Analysis*. 2nd ed. New York: John Wiley & Sons Inc.
Naylor, Thomas H., Joseph L. Balintfy, Donald S. Burdick, and Kong Chu, 1966. *Computer Simulation Techniques*. New York: John Wiley & Sons Inc.
Pritsker, A. Alan B., and Claude Dennis Pegden, 1979. *Introduction to Simulation and SLAM*. New York: John Wiley & Sons Inc.
Watson, H. J., and J. H. Blackstone, Jr., 1989. *Computer Simulation*. New York: John Wiley & Sons Inc.

Index